Integration and Inclusion of Newcomers and Minorities across Canada

Integration and Inclusion of Newcomers and Minorities across Canada

Edited by John Biles, Meyer Burstein,
James Frideres, Erin Tolley, and Robert Vineberg

Queen's Policy Studies Series
School of Policy Studies, Queen's University
McGill-Queen's University Press
Montreal & Kingston • London • Ithaca

SCHOOL OF
Policy Studies

Publications Unit
Robert Sutherland Hall
138 Union Street
Kingston, ON, Canada
K7L 3N6
www.queensu.ca/sps/

The preferred citation for this book is:
Biles, J., M. Burstein, J. Frideres, E. Tolley, and R. Vineberg, eds. 2011. *Integration and Inclusion of Newcomers and Minorities across Canada*. Montreal and Kingston: Queen's Policy Studies Series, McGill-Queen's University Press.

Library and Archives Canada Cataloguing in Publication

Integration and inclusion of newcomers and minorities across Canada / edited by John Biles ... [et al.].

(Queen's policy studies series)
Includes bibliographical references.
ISBN 978-1-55339-290-3 (pbk.).—ISBN 978-1-55339-291-0 (bound)

1. Canada—Emigration and immigration—History—21st century.
2. Canada—Emigration and immigration—Government policy.
3. Immigrants—Canada—Social conditions—21st century. 4. Canada—Emigration and immigration—Social aspects. 5. Social integration—Canada. I. Biles, John, 1971- II. Queen's University (Kingston, Ont.). School of Policy Studies III. Series: Queen's policy studies series

JV7225.2.I58 2011   325.71'09051   C2011-904818-3

CONTENTS

ACKNOWLEDGEMENTS

Over the past 14 years, the five editors of this volume have all had the good fortune to be involved in the Metropolis Project. Our understanding of immigration, integration, and inclusion has been shaped by interactions with literally thousands of policy-makers from three levels of government, researchers from the full gamut of the Canadian academy, and community and local partners from across the country, all of whom have been part of the Metropolis network. This influence will continue long after Metropolis's sunset at the end of March 2012. We owe this remarkable network a debt of gratitude. We hope that its members have found the journey as rewarding as we have and that they continue to use the knowledge and connections they have developed to make Canadian communities more welcoming. It is not possible to single out all of the individuals who have had an impact on how we have come to view this terrain (many of them graciously agreed to contribute chapters to this volume), although there is no doubt that Bob Annis, Ather Akbari, Fariborz Birjandian, Gerald Clement, James de Finney, Tom Denton, Tracey Derwing, Debbie Douglas, Bridget Foster, Shiva Halli, Tom Jensen, Kevin Lamarque, Claudette Legault, Peter Li, Marie McAndrew, Terry Murphy, Carl Nicholson, Linda Ogilvie, Gérard Pinsonneault, Valerie Pruegger, Stephane Reichold, Jean Renaud, Chris Taylor, Yves Turcotte, Madine VanderPlaat, Lloyd Wong, Deb Zehr, and particularly Baha Abu-Laban have shaped our more comprehensive approach to thinking about how settlement and integration vary across the country. Others who have been especially important in framing how we view integration and inclusion in Canada include Howard Adelman, Rod Beaujot, Annick Germain, Don DeVoretz, Dan Hiebert, David Ley, Krishna and Ravi Pendakur, Brian Ray, and Myer Siemiatycki. Finally, our thinking has been forged in the crucible of debates with colleagues (current and now retired) like Rosalyn Frith, Garnett Picot, and Elizabeth Ruddick. Much of our analysis builds on the evidence base they painstakingly built over the course of their careers.

In particular we would like to thank those who attended the 11th National Metropolis Conference in Calgary in 2009, including the provincial and territorial officials and community partners who read the draft chapters and provided their insights. Similarly, we are indebted to various individuals across the country, including many provincial officials, community partners, and regional staff of Citizenship and Immigration Canada, who have provided invaluable feedback to us on the various chapters in this volume; you have all made the final product stronger and we are grateful.

Arthur Sweetman's encouragement to launch this series and the extra-ordinary work of his colleagues at the Queen's School of Policy Studies have been invaluable in bringing this project to fruition: Keith Banting, Mark Howes, Valerie Jarus, and Maureen Garvie – thank you.

Time we stole away from others to complete this volume must also be recognized – Mary-Lee Mulholland and little Adelaide, Lena Horne, René Ouellette, Marie L'Écuyer, Carol Frideres, and Deborah Tunis. And of course Howard Duncan's support of the project must be recognized.

Finally, and most importantly, we must acknowledge the tremendous work undertaken all the way across the country by the many individuals who work every day to make their communities more welcoming and to assist newcomers as they strive to contribute to this country. Your work is an inspiration to us all, and we hope that this volume may assist you in your important endeavours.

INTRODUCTION: INTEGRATION AND INCLUSION OF NEWCOMERS AND MINORITIES ACROSS CANADA

ERIN TOLLEY, JOHN BILES, ROBERT VINEBERG, MEYER BURSTEIN, AND JAMES FRIDERES

It is now commonplace to call Canada a "country of immigrants," to describe it as "tolerant and multicultural," and to boast about the number of newcomers who choose to make this place their home. Despite the power of these "public ideas" (Reich 1985) and the engagement of researchers and high profile critics (Biles forthcoming; Collacott 2002; Francis 2002; Stoffman 2002), some of the fundamental ideas remain controversial. Moreover, the literature and public discourse seem to have missed some of the more recent policy developments, with research tending to focus on problem identification. Very little attention has been paid to the solution sets that are being attempted by different actors in jurisdictions across the country. This lacuna was picked up by the House of Commons Standing Committee on Citizenship and Immigration (2010) in its recent report on best practices in settlement and by work undertaken by the settlement sector itself (Burstein 2010). We seek to redress this gap here. In particular, while integration and inclusion have now gained traction, the public remains poorly informed on what interventions might be most effective. For this reason, this volume maps out the range of policies and programs being implemented in various communities across Canada. We have sought to lay the groundwork for future work and to equip all communities to attract, welcome, include, and retain the citizens and workers they need to guarantee long-term prosperity.

A central premise of our work is that the challenges involved in integration, belonging, and inclusion cannot be shouldered by newcomers alone.

Integration and Inclusion of Newcomers and Minorities across Canada, ed. J. Biles, M. Burstein, J. Frideres, E. Tolley, and R. Vineberg. Montreal and Kingston: Queen's Policy Studies Series, McGill-Queen's University Press.

This is clearly reflected in the *Immigration and Refugee Protection Act* (2001), which states that successful integration "involves mutual obligations for new immigrants and Canadian society." This position has come to be known as the "two-way street" model of integration, and it recognizes the vital role that established Canadians have in facilitating newcomer immigration, integration, and inclusion (Biles 2008; Frideres 2008; Tolley 2011b; Winnemore and Biles 2006). The same concept is also enshrined in the 1988 *Canadian Multiculturalism Act* and has even older historic roots. In the 1959 *Canada Year Book*, the article "Postwar Integration of Immigrants" observed, "The ultimate responsibility for integration rests with the Canadian people for, without their acceptance of the newcomers into community life, there can be no integration" (Dominion Bureau of Statistics 1959, 183).

The role Canadians play in the integration process includes an openness to immigration in general, hiring newcomers and recognizing their credentials, working with them as colleagues and classmates, acknowledging immigrants on the streets and in supermarkets, and encountering immigrants as doctors, caregivers, neighbours, and friends. While this role does not imply abandoning "Canadianness," it does require flexibility to adapt our social, economic, and cultural practices to accommodate newcomers, as well as a willingness to accept difference and to appreciate the benefits of immigration and diversity. Critically, it also entails recognizing that newcomers have a legitimate voice in our civic and democratic life, even if paying attention to this voice sometimes results in decisions we do not like.

The benefits of immigration have, in some senses, been magnified by specific economic and demographic trends. As Canada's population ages and its fertility rate continues to drop, immigration has become increasingly important as a potential mechanism to facilitate economic development and adjustment. In addition, immigration has been positioned as a way of responding to labour market gaps and out-migration from Canada's regions, smaller centres, and official language minority communities. The benefits to the country's economic and social prosperity can only be reaped, however, if immigrants choose to remain in Canada and are able to find housing, employment, and a promising future.

As a result, immigration and settlement issues have risen in prominence on the policy agenda, and there is a growing awareness that integration does not happen spontaneously but requires government action and community cooperation. The shifting composition of the immigrant population and its increased diversity have played a role in the increased attention to integration, as has research suggesting that some immigrants have not fared very well in the labour market (Sweetman and Warman 2008), fears that newcomers' attachment to Canada is weaker than in the past (Reitz and Banerjee 2007), and reports that immigrants and minorities are living "parallel lives" in so-called ethnic enclaves (Chianello 2009).

The launch of the Centre for Immigration Policy Reform in the fall of 2010 was emblematic of these concerns. The centre supports continued immigration, but insists that newcomers have an unequivocal commitment to basic Canadian values and a strong loyalty to Canada. Moreover, the centre suggests that "greater effort should be made to ensure that immigrants to Canada are willing and able to integrate fully into the Canadian economy and society within a reasonable timeframe" and argues that the "increasingly numerous and large ethnic districts in our larger cities ... [slow] down the process of integration into Canadian society" (Centre for Immigration Policy Reform 2011). The centre points to immigrants' declining labour market performance and the higher numbers of refugees and sponsored family class members who are "often limited in their official language skills" as the source of newcomers' integration challenges (Centre for Immigration Policy Reform 2011). While these arguments partially explain declining economic outcomes, they are far from the only explanations. Nonetheless, they have a powerful effect on the narrow framing of immigration debates, on our understanding of integration outcomes, and on the policies and programs that have been adopted.

Given this increasing public and political interest, it is not surprising that immigration has been highlighted in successive speeches from the Throne. In addition, issues related to immigration, integration, and inclusion are regularly linked to other policy agendas, including regional economic development, national security, the labour market, public safety, and foreign affairs, with immigration issues increasingly overlaid on policy frameworks related to health, education, housing, and even the environment. For policy-makers this means grappling not just with the complexities of immigration, integration, and inclusion but also with the ways that they intersect with other spheres of governance. Immigration and integration are not stand-alone issues, and addressing them requires a whole-of-government approach as well as the collaboration of communities, non-governmental organizations, the education sector, and other key stakeholders.

This horizontality is in some ways a legacy of Canada's historical approach to immigration which, along with agriculture, was identified in the *Constitution Act, 1867*, as a matter of concurrent federal-provincial jurisdiction. Although the colonial provinces had, prior to that time, actively recruited immigrants and provided them with a few basic services upon arrival, by acknowledging the overlapping division of labour between the two levels of government, the Constitution signalled the importance of immigration to the new federation as a policy domain so central that it would not be entrusted to just one level of government. At the same time, it formalized the centrality of Canada's provinces and regions to the success of the immigration program. Even so, following the First World War, the provinces (and later, the territories) largely left the field to the federal government, at least until the mid-1970s when provincial interest accelerated (Knowles 2007; Tolley 2011b; Vineberg, this volume). In the past 15 years the provinces and territories have become particularly active, which has dramatically changed the immigration landscape not only in terms of the policy agenda but also in terms of the available resources, program delivery models, and community involvement. This shift has come about because, within certain parameters, the provinces and territories are able to exercise considerable latitude when it comes to addressing issues related to immigration and, in particular, those related to integration and inclusion. A number of different models have developed, with Quebec, British Columbia and Manitoba, for example, having been transferred exclusive responsibility for settlement (albeit through different mechanisms[1]), while the federal government retains a much more active role in the other provinces. Quebec also has the power to select its own immigrants, and a number of provinces have developed more active recruitment programs (Citizenship and Immigration Canada 2011). Municipalities have taken on some responsibilities related to integration and inclusion, often unwillingly as a result of fiscal downloading from the provinces, although a number of federal-provincial and federal-territorial agreements explicitly identify them as important partners (Citizenship and Immigration Canada 2010a). These arrangements provide us with a laboratory to examine the elements of each model and to determine whether some lessons can be transferred across provinces, territories, and regions.

There has also been an enormous increase in the resources directed toward the settlement of newcomers, with Citizenship and Immigration Canada (CIC) more than tripling its expenditures since 2006. Provincial governments have also increased their contributions (Biles 2008). In addition, a burgeoning number of agencies, think tanks, and institutes are taking an active interest in immigration, including the Institute for Research on Public Policy, Public Policy Forum, the Maytree Foundation, the Mowat Institute, the Metropolis Project, the Canada West Foundation, and the Fraser Institute. A number of innovative practices are being explored and adopted, including the Local Immigration Partnerships Program, ministerial advisory councils, and the creation of several immigrant employment councils. Broader government initiatives, among them the Provincial Nominee Program, the introduction of the Canadian Experience Class, improvements in the foreign credential recognition process like the Foreign Qualifications Recognition Framework, a pilot voucher system for language acquisition, and revisions to the test that newcomers must pass prior to becoming Canadian citizens, all testify that the additional resources invested in settlement have sparked innovation and experimentation.

Given the increased number of players and programs, as well as the injection of new funds, it is an appropriate time to take stock. In what follows, we provide the first comprehensive, nation-wide overview of immigration, integration, and inclusion in Canada and offer a description and assessment of what the provinces and territories are doing in these areas. The authors discuss the approaches that have been undertaken, which organizations and institutions are most and least active, and what impact these factors have had on immigration, integration, and inclusion. In this respect, the chapters catalogue the current state of play and suggest modes of practice and models of governance that would more effectively involve all three levels of government as well as other key stakeholders. While we do touch upon municipal level engagement, readers interested in this particular subject are also encouraged to consult the companion volume, *Immigration, Integration, and Inclusion in Ontario Cities* (Andrew et al. forthcoming), which provides a more detailed overview of approaches taken by local governments.

In adopting a provincial and territorial lens to examine immigrants' integration and inclusion across the country, this study differs from others that have been more national or historical in scope (Beach, Green, and Reitz 2003; Biles, Burstein, and Frideres 2008; Kelley and Trebilcock 2010; Knowles 2007), have examined governance arrangements (Leo and August 2009; Seidle 2010; Tolley and Young 2011), or focused on specific cities (Good 2009; Poirier 2004) or particular facets of integration, including civic and political (Andrew et al. 2008; Bloemraad 2006), economic (McDonald et al. 2010) and social (Banting, Courchene, and Seidle 2007) dimensions. Given that the provinces and territories are more interested, involved, and implicated in the integration and inclusion of newcomers and minorities, our focus seems not only appropriate but long overdue.

It should be noted, however, that this volume is not simply a series of disparate provincial case studies. Indeed, each of the authors has approached the subject using a similar framework, set of guiding questions, and objectives. This unity of focus allows readers to easily chart parallels and variations across each of the provinces. In this way, it becomes clear that the "national approach" to immigration, integration, or inclusion is intertwined with the many different provincial and territorial strategies. The reader will come to see that a number of models and strategies are being pursued in each jurisdiction. This volume thus provides a single source for readers to explore the funding and organization of the country's immigration, integration, and inclusion programs, as well as the institutional arrangements that underlie these policies. We tell an often ignored story about policy evolution and the solutions that have emerged in response to shifting goals, new incentives, and changing service needs across jurisdictions.

Although the volume offers a compendium of immigration, integration, and inclusion initiatives, it also provides broader, but important, insights into intergovernmental relations, multi-level governance arrangements, and the role of communities and NGOs in policy formation and service delivery – what Leo and August (2009) describe as "deep federalism." The chapters that follow may therefore inform work in other policy fields, particularly those in which new governance models or collaborative policy-making are being pursued. These insights are relevant even where policy responsibility technically lies with one level of government, given that a number of fields, such as transportation, health care, the labour market, and education, have become de facto areas of concurrent jurisdiction with federal, provincial, territorial, and even municipal governments playing some role in authoring and delivering policy and programs. This volume focuses specifically on Canada, a country that others often look to for advice on policies related to immigration and multiculturalism (Kymlicka 2008), as well as for insights into federalism and multi-level governance arrangements (Papillon 2008; Sykes 2008). On these counts Canada is often viewed as a model. While we would argue that it is an imperfect model, it is nonetheless one that has seen considerable success, particularly when viewed comparatively (see, for example, Banting et al. 2006; Migration Policy Group 2011; Tolley 2011a), and there is much in this volume that can inform the work that other countries are doing to craft and improve their own immigration, integration, and inclusion policies. This study is particularly timely in a period in which multiculturalism has apparently fallen somewhat out of favour, especially in Europe, with integration budgets contracting, and fears about national security and illegal migration creating suspicions and increasing tensions (Migration Policy Institute 2010). In what follows, we elaborate on the context in which this volume has emerged, discuss the main themes that run through it, and highlight some of its principal contributions.

CONTEXT AND CONSIDERATIONS

Canada's recent and increased focus on immigration, integration, and inclusion is related in part to the size of migration flows; more specifically, however, it is generated by the diversification of those flows. Each year Canada welcomes roughly 250,000 immigrants (Citizenship and Immigration Canada 2010b). Of these, the largest single source country is now China, which provided 11.5 percent of all permanent residents to Canada in 2009, followed closely by the Philippines (10.8 percent) and India (10.4 percent). Only 3.8 percent of permanent residents came from the next largest source country, the United States (Citizenship and Immigration Canada 2010b). The bulk of Canada's permanent residents – 60.9 percent – are economic immigrants and their accompanying dependents, although this percentage varies across the provinces and territories, as is noted in the chapters that follow, with some provinces, such as Manitoba and Saskatchewan, seeing upwards of 80 percent of their permanent residents arriving in the economic class (Citizenship and Immigration Canada 2010b). Across the country, immigrants comprise 19.8 percent of the population, and although immigration is a long-standing phenomenon, more than half (55 percent) of the immigrants now resident in Canada arrived in the past 15 years (Statistics Canada 2007a).

The composition of Canada's newcomer population has shifted, which has had an impact on the country's racial, ethnic, religious, and linguistic makeup. In many ways, it is this diversity that brings immigration to life for Canadians; it is a visual indicator of the scale and reach of migration, and of the need to achieve integration and inclusion (Edmonston and Fong 2011). As newcomers settle and raise families, diversity is no longer simply an outgrowth of immigration; rather, it is increasingly made-in-Canada (Chui, Tran, and Maheux 2008; Statistics Canada 2006). This fact is important because while it is expected that immigrants will struggle when they first arrive, it is generally assumed that settlement and integration programs will ease the transition and newcomers will eventually become full and valued contributors to society. Unfortunately, this is not always the case; children of immigrants – especially visible minorities – report incidences of discrimination and feelings of exclusion even when they were born in Canada and are educated and highly qualified (Cheung 2006; Reitz and Banerjee 2007).

The persistence of these negative experiences is a challenge to inclusion and all the more worrying given that the number of people identifying as members of a racial, ethnic, linguistic, or religious minority is increasing. According to the 2006 Census, 16.2 percent of Canadians belong to a visible minority group, meaning that they identify as non-white or non-Caucasian in race or colour (Statistics Canada 2008). Canadians report more than 200 ethnic origins, and 19.7 percent list a non-official language as their mother tongue (Statistics Canada 2007b, 2008). Moreover, in 2001, when data on religion were last collected, although 70 percent of Canadians identified as Roman Catholic or Protestant, nearly 5 percent identified as Muslim, Buddhist, Hindu, or Sikh (Statistics Canada 2003). The percentage of Canadians identifying with non-Christian religions is expected to increase substantially by 2031, given that this population tends to be younger and have higher birthrates. As a result, within two decades, approximately 14 percent of the Canadian population will identify with a non-Christian religion, and about half of these people will be Muslim (Statistics Canada 2010). This projection has given rise to questions about religious accommodation and about the balancing of rights and responsibilities. Based on the assumption that religious pluralism leads to a clash of values, *Discover Canada*, the revised study guide developed to help immigrants prepare for the citizenship exam, makes reference to these concerns, noting explicitly that men and women are equal in Canada and that "barbaric cultural practices" such as spousal abuse, "honour killings," and female genital mutilation are not permitted (Citizenship and Immigration Canada 2009, 9).

These issues are only some of the more high profile concerns that predominate around the world and find echoes in Canadian public discourse whenever a case involving a newcomer comes to light. For example, media debates remain preoccupied with so-called honour-based violence, the propensity of immigrant youth to become radicalized, and what could be termed "resistance to integration" (Belkhodja 2008; Henry and Tator 2002; Mahtani 2008). This popular discourse covers a range of behaviours from benign residential concentration to a rejection of society, laws, and norms that results in criminality and terrorist violence. Ryan does a good job of exploring the range of debates surrounding what he terms "multicultiphobia" in his book of the same name (2010). These concerns, regardless of their often shaky evidentiary foundations, have a disproportionate and constraining influence on policy discussions as they shape public opinion, with immigration and its effects increasingly highlighted in public opinion polling (Adams 2007; Jedwab 2008). To ensure that this discourse becomes better informed, there is renewed emphasis on establishing benchmark information on settlement and integration outcomes, including the measures that appear in *Immigration and Integration in Canada in the Twenty-First Century* (Biles et al. 2008) and, more recently, in an agreed upon federal-provincial-territorial set of indicators on settlement and integration.

In addition to these domestic developments, Canada's immigration policies operate in a much changed international environment, with an increasing number of countries joining the race to attract newcomers. More than ever, Canada needs to differentiate itself if it is to have a competitive edge in attracting the highly skilled. Facilitating immigrants' integration and inclusion into Canadian society is one means of leveraging our advantage. Although in time the vast majority of immigrants integrate successfully, stories abound about doctors driving taxis, devaluation of foreign credentials, and the potential for discrimination. Immigrants' transnational networks and, in particular, the Internet allow for information exchange and sharing. Within this context, Canada is taking steps to remain an attractive destination, and we see, as a result, a number of innovative strategies are being developed.

Not only are a greater number of countries competing for the most highly skilled immigrants (Gates 2008; Naik, Koehler, and Laczko 2008) but even within our own borders, we see provinces, territories, and municipalities, particularly in smaller and mid-sized centres, competing to recruit and retain newcomers. In many regions in-migration is viewed as central to long-term economic and demographic prosperity. Following the Quiet Revolution, Quebec determined that control of immigration could serve to improve its demographic "weight" within Canada and the proportion of francophones within the province. But Quebec was not alone in identifying immigration as both a challenge to, and a solution for, demographic imbalance; as early as the 1980s, Manitoba brought similar concerns to the notice of the federal government and in the 1990s led the provincial lobbying that resulted in the creation of the Provincial Nominee Program (Vineberg, this volume). For Manitoba and the other Prairie provinces, this approach has reaped major benefits. Immigration to the Prairies increased from about 9.5 percent in 1999 to 17.6 percent in 2009, almost exactly their proportion of Canada's overall population. In absolute terms this represents an increase from about 17,000 immigrants in 1999 to over 44,000 in 2009. By contrast, the share of immigration to the Atlantic provinces, while doubling from 1.3 percent to 2.6 percent over the same decade, remains well below the region's 6.7 percent share of Canada's total population (Citizenship and Immigration Canada 2010b). This trend has not escaped the attention of the region's governments, and several have developed population strategies in which immigration features prominently.

Provinces are also becoming more active players in the selection of immigrants generally, not only through Provincial Nominee Programs but also through employer-driven temporary foreign worker programs and strategies to attract foreign students. As well as attractive forces, this across-the-board growth in provincial involvement reflects a change in "admissions technology." The general relaxation in the long-standing prohibition against landing immigrants from within Canada or adjusting the status of temporary workers to give them permanent residency has sharply lowered the cost of processing for provinces. While provinces have been reluctant to make the sort of investment Quebec has done in overseas processing capacity, the change in federal philosophy toward in-Canada processing has obviated the need for such onerous investments. Increasing student and temporary worker numbers and rising in-Canada landings confirm this shift, with these newcomers viewed as particularly attractive because they are thought to be "easier" to integrate and less in need of settlement services. Provinces, particularly the smaller ones, have concluded that a multi-faceted attraction and recruitment strategy can serve their interests and make them more competitive in the global marketplace. This said, provinces have also begun to realize that to retain the newcomers they recruit, they must become more welcoming, in part by adapting many of their programs and services available to mainstream populations.

This volume spans a period of not only increasing government concern with immigration, integration, and inclusion but also growing academic interest in the subject. One of the first large-scale research projects was the Metropolis Project, supported by the Social Sciences and Humanities Research Council (SSHRC), CIC, several other federal departments, universities, and key players in the settlement sector. A number of provinces and municipalities also came onside. SSHRC went on to fund other immigration-related projects. The most recent is the Welcoming Communities Initiative, which looks primarily at immigration, integration, and diversity in Ontario's second and third tier cities, a focus that is indicative of how policy interest has evolved. SSHRC also provided resources to two Major Collaborative Research Initiatives, one on public policy and municipalities and the other on ethnicity and democratic governance. In both studies, immigration and multiculturalism have been among the priorities. These initiatives have promoted the importance of research and vastly increased the number of empirical and theoretical publications on the subject.

Our volume is situated within this broad field of literature, bringing together insights from the work on immigration, integration, and inclusion but also drawing on research on multi-level governance, intergovernmental relations, and collaborative policy-making (see, for example, Cameron and Simeon 2000, 2002; Seidle 2002; Young and Leuprecht 2004). We are informed in particular by the literature on place-based policies, which views communities as important loci of public policy-making (Bradford 2005). The emphasis on place-based policies is driven partly by socio-demographic factors and also by concerns over economic development; on both fronts, cities are becoming increasingly important policy actors. In employing a perspective that places the activities of key – often local – stakeholders at the forefront, this volume advances the perspective that responses to immigration, integration, and inclusion cannot be developed only from above. Rather, good governance requires an awareness of local conditions, on-the-ground experiences, and interactions with the organizations and individuals who are witness to the effects of immigration and the consequences of policy action and inaction.

HIGHLIGHTS AND THEMES: VOLUME OVERVIEW

This volume is organized into 13 chapters and a conclusion. The first two chapters provide a history of federal provincial relations regarding immigration and an exploration of broader multiculturalism/interculturalism policies in the provinces. Each of the following chapters focuses on one province, addressing policies and programs designed to aid integration and inclusion; chapter 13 considers the same question across the three territories. The conclusion summarizes key findings of the volume and identifies potentially critical future trends and issues. A number of themes emerge. First, immigration is clearly a key component of the Canadian landscape, but work is needed to ensure that we capitalize on this resource by facilitating newcomer integration and ensuring that all Canadians – regardless of origin, race, ethnicity, language, or religion – feel welcomed and included. If newcomers are unable to integrate successfully, immigration will not achieve the goals that we, as a society, have established.

Second, there is evidence that federal, provincial, and territorial interest in immigration, integration, and inclusion is evolving. Following World War II, provincial interest in immigration met with federal resistance, and federal responses largely focused on containing this interest. Nonetheless, over time, the provinces have become important players. This change has led to the involvement of regional development agencies as well as economic development ministries. The reasons for – and nature of – provincial interest in immigration show significant variations. While Ontario and British Columbia, the major beneficiaries of federal immigration selection policies in the postwar period, tended to limit their interest in immigration to increased funding for social services, others sought first to influence federal policy to increase immigration to their province and, then, in the face of limited results, opted to seek authority to select and to settle immigrants within their jurisdiction. The federal government, not wanting to replicate the Canada-Quebec arrangement that ceded control of immigration to that province, developed the Provincial Nominee Program, originally conceived of as a "niche" program to fill specific regional needs not met by federal programs. Led by Manitoba, the provinces adapted the program to their own policy priorities and developed it into a major element of Canada's overall immigration program (Vineberg, this volume). As a result, the policy landscape is variegated and fluid.

Third, there is the matter of the changing demographics of the newcomer population, the locales where they choose to settle, and their status. Immigrants now come from a wider range of source countries, and there is increased ethnocultural diversity. The introduction of the Canadian Experience Class and the emphasis on international students and temporary workers have also altered the demographic composition of the newcomer population. Accompanying these changes is a slow but notable shift in the range of communities where newcomers are choosing to settle. Although the vast majority of newcomers at one time chose to settle in Montreal, Toronto, and Vancouver (the so-called MTV phenomena), this pattern has changed, with Calgary added to the mix and several other cities becoming increasingly important destinations. Moreover, efforts to attract and retain newcomers to a wider range of communities have proved successful. These changes are reflected in different institutional responses and shifting federal/provincial/municipal arrangements.

Fourth, it is clear that immigration, integration, and inclusion must be examined using a sub-national lens. The assumption that we can effectively develop integration and inclusion policies and programs by looking only at what happens in Montreal, Toronto, and Vancouver is now seen as outdated. The strategies that function successfully in cities where the majority of the population is foreign-born are fundamentally different from those that will work in smaller urban settings or even rural areas, where the newcomer population tends to be smaller. For this reason, policies and programs must be sensitive to the context into which immigrants are integrating and address issues related to receptivity and the warmth of the welcome.

Fifth, while provincial and territorial governments have reawakened to the need for active engagement in attracting and retaining newcomers and minorities, many of the critical elements of successful integration and inclusion strategies are controlled by municipalities and other local actors. This is particularly true in Ontario where previous provincial governments have downloaded significant responsibilities to municipalities, but it is also important in other jurisdictions. This recognition has led to a greater emphasis on place-based analyses and strategies. Given the number of new actors and the deeper involvement of long-standing players, there is a need to examine and share new and innovative policies and practices across jurisdictions. Our analysis shows that no one level has a monopoly on innovation and best practice. Cooperation and collaboration are necessary, and we must find ways to do this better, particularly as it relates to the involvement of municipalities.

Finally, although an exhaustive analysis was stymied by data limitations in some jurisdictions, this volume is to date one of the most complete accounts of the immigration, integration, and inclusion initiatives being pursued in the Canadian provinces and territories. In documenting these approaches, we illustrate a number of best and promising practices and provide evidence and ideas for future policy-making, program design, research, and evaluation.

NOTE

1.   Through the Canada-Quebec Accord, responsibility for the settlement of newcomers has been devolved to Quebec. In the cases of British Columbia and Manitoba, Citizenship and Immigration Canada has signed realignment agreements whereby the provincial governments manage settlement programming on behalf of CIC. This arrangement is subject to renewal and carries accountability provisions not shared with the Canada-Quebec Accord, which continues indefinitely.

REFERENCES

Adams, M. 2007. *Unlikely Utopia: The Surprising Triumph of Canadian Multicultural-ism*. Toronto: Penguin.
Andrew, C., J. Biles, M. Siemiatycki, and E. Tolley. 2008. *Electing a Diverse Canada: The Representation of Immigrants, Minorities, and Women*. Vancouver: UBC Press.
Andrew, C., J. Biles, M. Burstein, V. Esses, and E. Tolley, eds. Forthcoming. *Immigration, Integration, and Inclusion in Ontario Cities*. Montreal and Kingston: McGill-Queen's University Press.
Banting, K., R. Johnston, W. Kymlicka, and S. Soroka. 2006. "Do Multiculturalism Policies Erode the Welfare State? An Empirical Analysis." In *Multiculturalism and the Welfare State*, ed. K. Banting and W. Kymlicka, 49-91. Toronto: Oxford University Press.

Banting, K., T.J. Courchene, and F.L. Seidle, eds. 2007. *Belonging? Diversity, Recognition, and Shared Citizenship in Canada.* Montreal: Institute for Research on Public Policy.

Beach, C.M., A.G. Green, and J.G. Reitz. 2003. *Canadian Immigration Policy for the Twenty-First Century.* Montreal and Kingston: McGill-Queen's University Press.

Belkhodja, C. 2008. "The Discourse of New Individual Responsibility: The Controversy over Reasonable Accommodation in Some French-Language Newspapers in Quebec and Canada." In *Immigration and Integration in Canada in the Twenty-First Century,* ed. J. Biles, M. Burstein, and J. Frideres, 253-67. Montreal and Kingston: McGill-Queen's University Press.

Biles, J. 2008. "Integration Policies in English-Speaking Canada." In *Immigration and Integration in Canada in the Twenty-first Century,* ed. J. Biles, M. Burstein, and J. Frideres, 139-186. Montreal and Kingston: McGill-Queen's University Press.

—Forthcoming. "The Metropolis Project: A Model Worth Emulating?" In *Managing Immigration and Diversity in Canada: A Transatlantic Dialogue with Spain and Europe in the New Age of Migration,* ed. D. Rodríguez-García. Montreal and Kingston: McGill-Queen's University Press.

Biles, J., M. Burstein, and J. Frideres. 2008. *Immigration and Integration in Canada in the Twenty-First Century.* Montreal and Kingston: McGill-Queen's University Press.

Bloemraad, I. 2006. *Becoming a Citizen: Incorporating Immigrants and Refugees in the United States and Canada.* Berkeley: University of California Press.

Bradford, N. 2005. "Place-Based Public Policy: Towards a New Urban and Community Agenda for Canada." CPRN Discussion Paper F-51. Ottawa: Canadian Policy Research Networks.

Burstein, M. 2010. "Reconfiguring Settlement and Integration: A Service Provider Strategy for Innovation and Results." Paper commissioned by Canadian Immigrant Settlement Sector Alliance. At http://integration-net.ca:81/infocentre/2010/007_1e.pdf (accessed 20 January 2011).

Cameron, D. and R. Simeon. 2000. "Intergovernmental Relations and Democratic Citizenship." In *Governance in the Twenty-First Century: Revitalizing the Public Service,* ed. B.G. Peters and D.J. Savoie, 58-119. Montreal and Kingston: McGill-Queen's University Press.

—2002. "Intergovernmental Relations in Canada: The Emergence of Collaborative Federalism." *Publius* 32(2):49-71.

Centre for Immigration Policy Reform. 2011. "Aims and Objectives." At http://www.immigrationreform.ca/aims-objectives-centre-policy-immigration-reform-canada.shtml (accessed 23 May 2011).

Cheung, L. 2006. *Racial Status and Employment Outcomes.* Ottawa: Canadian Labour Congress. At http://www.canadianlabour.ca/sites/default/files/pdfs/034-Racial-Status-and-Employment-Outcomes-EN.pdf (accessed 13 December 2010).

Chianello, J. 2009. "Jason Kenney Fires up the Melting Pot." *Ottawa Citizen,* 18 April. At http://www2.canada.com/ottawacitizen/news/observer/story.html?id=b0356c16-110d-4134-961e-b7e5c4a8bbed (accessed 20 January 2011).

Chui, T., K. Tran, and H. Maheux. 2008. "Canada's Ethnocultural Mosaic, 2006 Census." Catalogue No. 97-562-XIE2006001. Ottawa: Minister of Industry.

Citizenship and Immigration Canada (CIC). 2009. *Discover Canada: The Rights and Responsibilities of Citizenship.* Ottawa: Minister of Public Works and Government Services. At http://www.cic.gc.ca/english/pdf/pub/discover.pdf (accessed 13 December 2010).

—2010a. "Federal-Provincial/Territorial Agreements." At http://www.cic.gc.ca/ english/department/laws-policy/agreements/index.asp (accessed 13 December 2010).

—2010b. *Facts and Figures 2009 – Immigrant Overview: Permanent and Temporary Residents.* Ottawa: Her Majesty the Queen in Right of Canada. At http://www. cic.gc.ca/english/pdf/research-stats/facts2009.pdf (accessed 13 December 2010).

—2011. "Provincial Nominees: Who Can Apply?" At http://www.cic.gc.ca/ english/immigrate/provincial/apply-who.asp (accessed 20 January 2011).

2009. *Discover Canada: The Rights and Responsibilities of Citizenship.* Ottawa: Minister of Public Works and Government Services. At http://www.cic.gc.ca/english/ pdf/pub/discover.pdf (accessed 13 December 2010).

Collacott, M. 2002. "Canada's Immigration Policy: The Need for Major Reform." Fraser Institute Paper, 23 September. At http://www.fraserinstitute.org/ research-news/display.aspx?id=12866 (accessed 21 January 2011).

Dominion Bureau of Statistics. 1959. *Canada Year Book 1959.* Ottawa: Queen's Printer.

Edmonston, B. and E. Fong. 2011. *The Changing Canadian Population.* Montreal and Kingston: McGill-Queen's University Press.

Francis, D. 2002. *Immigration: The Economic Case.* Toronto: Key Porter.

Frideres, J. 2008. "Creating an Inclusive Society: Promoting Social Integration in Canada." In *Immigration and Integration in Canada in the Twenty-First Century,* ed. J. Biles, M. Burstein, and J. Frideres, 77-101. Montreal and Kingston: McGill-Queen's University Press.

Gates, S. 2008. *Strategic Human Capital Measures.* New York: Conference Board.

Good, K.R. 2009. *Municipalities and Multiculturalism: The Politics of Immigration in Toronto and Vancouver.* Toronto: University of Toronto Press.

Henry, F. and C. Tator. 2002. *Discourses of Domination: Racial Bias in the Canadian English-Language Press.* Toronto: University of Toronto Press.

House of Commons Standing Committee on Citizenship and Immigration. 2010. "Best Practices in Settlement Services." March. At http://www2.parl.gc.ca/ HousePublications/Publication.aspx?DocId=4388396&Language=E&Mode= 1&Parl=40&Ses=3 (accessed 20 January 2011).

Jedwab, J. 2008. "Receiving and Giving: How Does the Canadian Public Feel about Immigration and Integration?" In *Immigration and Integration in Canada in the Twenty-First Century,* ed. J. Biles, M. Burstein, and J. Frideres, 187-210. Montreal and Kingston: McGill-Queen's University Press.

Kelley, N. and M. Trebilcock. 2010. *The Making of the Mosaic: A History of Canadian Immigration Policy.* 2nd ed. Toronto: University of Toronto Press.

Kymlicka, W. 2008. "Marketing Canadian Pluralism in the International Arena." In *The Comparative Turn in Canadian Political Science,* ed. L.A. White, R. Simeon, R. Vipond, and J. Wallner, 99-120. Vancouver: UBC Press.

Knowles, V. 2007. *Strangers at Our Gates: Canadian Immigration and Immigration Policy, 1540–2006.* Rev. ed. Toronto: Dundurn Press.

Leo, C. and M. August. 2009. "The Multilevel Governance of Immigration and Settlement: Making Deep Federalism Work." *Canadian Journal of Political Science* 42(2):491-510.

Mahtani, M. 2008. "How Are Immigrants Seen – And What Do They Want to See? Contemporary Research on the Representation of Immigrants in the Canadian English-Language Media." In *Immigration and Integration in Canada in the Twenty-*

First Century, ed. J. Biles, M. Burstein, and J. Frideres, 231-51. Montreal and Kingston: McGill-Queen's University Press.

McDonald, T., E. Ruddick, A. Sweetman, and C. Worswick. 2010. *Canadian Immigration: Economic Evidence for a Dynamic Policy Environment.* Montreal and Kingston: McGill-Queen's University Press.

Migration Policy Group. 2011. *Migrant Integration Policy Index.* At http://www.mipex.eu (accessed March 2011).

Migration Policy Institute. 2010. "Top Ten Immigration Stories of 2010." *Migration Info Source.* December. At http://www.migrationinformation.org/ (accessed 13 December 2010).

Naik, A., J. Koehler, and F. Laczko. 2008. *Migration and Development: Achieving Policy Coherence.* Geneva: International Organization for Migration.

Papillon, M. 2008. "Is the Secret to Have a Good Dentist? Canadian Contributions to the Study of Federalism in Divided Societies." In *The Comparative Turn in Canadian Political Science,* ed. L.A. White, R. Simeon, R. Vipond, and J. Wallner, 123-39. Vancouver: UBC Press.

Poirier, C. 2004. "Ethnocultural Diversity, Democracy, and Intergovernmental Relations in Canadian Cities." In *Canada: The State of the Federation 2004 – Municipal-Federal-Provincial Relations in Canada,* ed. R. Young and C. Leuprecht, 201-20. Montreal and Kingston: McGill-Queen's University Press.

Reich, R.B. 1988. *The Power of Public Ideas.* Cambridge: Ballinger Publishing.

Reitz, J.G. and R. Banerjee. 2007. "Racial Inequality, Social Cohesion, and Policy Issues in Canada." In *Belonging? Diversity, Recognition and Shared Citizenship in Canada,* ed. K. Banting, T.J. Courchene, and F.L. Seidle, 489-545. Montreal: Institute for Research on Public Policy.

Ryan, P. 2010. *Multicultiphobia.* Montreal and Kingston: McGill-Queen's University Press.

Seidle, F.L. 2010. *The Canada-Ontario Immigration Agreement: Assessment and Options for Renewal.* Toronto: Mowat Centre, University of Toronto. At http://www.mowatcentre.ca/research-topic-mowat.php?mowatResearchID=12 (accessed March 2011).

—2002. "The Federal Role in Canada's Cities: Overview of Issues and Proposed Actions." CPRN Discussion Paper F-27. Ottawa: Canadian Policy Research Networks.

Statistics Canada. 2003. "Religions in Canada: 2001 Census Analysis Series." Catalogue No. 96F0030XIE2001015. Ottawa: Minister of Industry. At http://www12.statcan.ca/english/census01/Products/Analytic/companion/rel/pdf/96F0030XIE2001015.pdf (accessed December 13, 2010).

—2006. "Study: Fertility among Visible Minority Women." *The Daily.* June 30. Ottawa: Minister of Industry. At http://www.statcan.gc.ca/daily-quotidien/060630/dq060630b-eng.htm (accessed 13 December 2010).

—2007a. "Immigration and Citizenship Highlight Tables." *2006 Census.* Catalogue No. 97-557-XWE2006002. Ottawa: Minister of Industry. At http://www12.statcan.gc.ca/census-recensement/2006/dp-pd/hlt/97-557/Index-eng.cfm (accessed 13 December 2010).

—2007b. "Language Highlight Tables." *2006 Census.* Catalogue No. 97-555-XWE2006002. Ottawa: Minister of Industry. At http://www12.statcan.ca/census-recensement/2006/dp-pd/hlt/97-555/Index-eng.cfm (accessed 13 December 2010).

—2008. "Ethnocultural Portrait of Canada Highlight Tables." *2006 Census.* Catalogue No. 97-562-XWE2006002. Ottawa: Minister of Industry. At http://www12.
statcan.ca/census-recensement/2006/dp-pd/hlt/97-562/index.cfm?Lang=E
(accessed 13 December 2010).

—2010. "Study: Projections of the Diversity of the Canadian Population." *The
Daily.* 9 March. Ottawa: Minister of Industry. At http://www.statcan.gc.ca/
daily-quotidien/100309/dq100309a-eng.htm (accessed 13 December 2010).

Stoffman, D. 2002. *Who Gets In? What's Wrong with Canada's Immigration Program
and How to Fix It.* Toronto: Macfarlane, Walter, and Ross.

Sweetman, A. and C. Warman. 2008. "Integration, Impact, and Responsibility: An
Economic Perspective on Canadian Immigration Policy." In *Immigration and
Integration in Canada in the Twenty-First Century*, ed. J. Biles, M. Burstein, and
J. Frideres, 19-44. Montreal and Kingston: McGill-Queen's University Press.

Sykes, S. 2008. *A Survey of the World's Oceans: International Approaches to Managing
Diversity and Implications for Second Generation Acculturation.* Ottawa: Policy
Research Initiative.

Tolley, E. 2011a. *Multiculturalism Policy Index: Immigrant Minority Policies.* Kingston:
Queen's School of Policy Studies. At http://www.queensu.ca/mcp/immigrant/
evidence/ImmigrantMinorities.pdf (accessed 1 July 2011).

—2011b. "Who Invited Them to the Party? Federal-Municipal Relations in Immigrant Settlement Policy." In *Immigrant Settlement Policy in Canadian Municipalities*, ed. E. Tolley and R. Young, 3-48. Montreal and Kingston: McGill-Queen's
University Press.

Tolley, E. and R. Young. 2011. *Immigrant Settlement Policy in Canadian Municipalities.* Montreal and Kingston: McGill-Queen's University Press.

Winnemore, L. and J. Biles. 2006. "Canada's Two-Way Street Integration Model:
Not without Its Stains, Strains and Growing Pains." *Canadian Diversity* 5(1):
23-30.

Young, R. and C. Leuprecht, eds. 2004. *Canada: The State of the Federation 2004 –
Municipal-Federal-Provincial Relations in Canada.* Montreal and Kingston: McGill-
Queen's University Press.

CHAPTER 1

HISTORY OF FEDERAL-PROVINCIAL RELATIONS IN CANADIAN IMMIGRATION AND INTEGRATION

ROBERT VINEBERG

The complex relationships between federal and provincial governments in Canada are often reflected in what appear to be isolated incidents. This chapter offers a survey of the legislative and working relationships that have existed between the two levels of government from Confederation to the present day for the purpose of promoting and controlling immigration to Canada. While the provincial interest in immigration is often perceived to be a recent phenomenon, this is in fact not the case. In many ways, the pattern described here in terms of immigration reflects the larger picture of federal-provincial relations since Confederation.

PRELUDE

> In each Province the Legislature may make Laws in relation to Agriculture in the Province, and to Immigration into the Province; and it is hereby declared that the Parliament of Canada may from Time to Time make Laws in relation to Agriculture in all or any of the Provinces, and to Immigration into all or any of the Provinces; and any Law of the Legislature of a Province relative to Agriculture or to Immigration shall have effect in and for the Province as long and as far only as it is not repugnant to any Act of the Parliament of Canada. (Section 95, Constitution Act, 1867)

This chapter is based on a paper published in *Canadian Public Administration*, vol. 30, No. 2 (Summer,1987).

Integration and Inclusion of Newcomers and Minorities across Canada, ed. J. Biles, M. Burstein, J. Frideres, E. Tolley, and R. Vineberg. Montreal and Kingston: Queen's Policy Studies Series, McGill-Queen's University Press.

When the Fathers of Confederation included the above section in the draft of the British North America Act, they were doing nothing revolutionary. Though they may not have spoken of the concept of concurrent jurisdiction, as we do, it only made sense that all levels of government of an under-populated agrarian country would be actively interested in both immigration and agriculture.

Settlement of immigrants had been a preoccupation of the colonial governments for over a century. Nova Scotia had appointed an agent in London as early as 1761, and other provinces followed suit at later dates. After the American Revolution, Lower Canada passed the *Act Respecting Aliens* in 1794 and Nova Scotia passed the *Aliens Act* in 1798. Both acts authorized a "political" examination of American immigrants. There was no legislation applying specifically to overseas migrants at the time.

Following an influx of often unhealthy immigrants in the late 1820s, Nova Scotia, New Brunswick, and Lower Canada all passed legislation imposing a head tax on every immigrant, with the funds "to be used for the care of the sick and destitute coming off the ships and for forwarding them to their destinations" (C&I 1958, 165). In 1831 a quarantine station was established by Lower Canada at Grosse Isle near Quebec City. (It would be taken over by the federal government in 1867 and remained in operation until about the turn of the century.) Quarantine stations were also set up at Halifax and Saint John. The quarantine facilities and the head tax remained Canada's main protective measures until 1862.

CONFEDERATION

By the time of Confederation, the three provinces – the United Canadas, New Brunswick, and Nova Scotia – had all developed considerable experience in immigration and were actively seeking settlers to open up their lands. Until 1892 the minister of agriculture was also made responsible for immigration, due to the obvious connection between the two areas, and to the tradition established earlier in the United Canadas. The grant of concurrent powers in the field of immigration created the problem (which still exists today) of defining the sphere of action of the two levels of government: "As it was absolutely necessary to come to some understanding between the general and the local Governments on the concurrent subject of Immigration, it was determined to hold a conference of delegates appointed to represent their respective Governments" (Minister of Agriculture 1870, 6).

The first federal-provincial conference on immigration took place in Ottawa in October 1868 and was regarded as an important affair. The Dominion of Canada was represented by Sir John A. Macdonald, the prime minister, and J.C. Chapais, the minister of agriculture. The provinces of Ontario, Quebec, and New Brunswick sent representatives at the same level. Nova Scotia, the separatist province of the day, was not represented!

Prior to the conference, the government of Quebec, eerily foreshadowing the view of another Quebec government a century later, observed that "as each province must be held to know best its own want and the comparative advantages which it can offer to immigrants from other countries, it is highly important that each should have its own agent for this service; accredited certainly by the federal government; perhaps subject to its confirmation, and to instructions approved by it" (Skilling 1945, 12).

The Dominion in its response agreed that it would be desirable "to define the powers and the duties of the general and local governments severally interested in the subject of immigration." The result of the conference of 30 October 1868 was Canada's first federal-provincial immigration agreement. Among its key provisions was the decision that the Dominion government would establish an immigration office in London and an agency on the continent of Europe, together with other offices as deemed appropriate. It would also assume the costs of operating the quarantine stations at Grosse Isle, Halifax, and Saint John, as well as the nine inland immigration offices. The provinces, for their part, were free to appoint agents of their own abroad as they saw fit (LAC 2006, PC1868-0981, 18 December 1868). The agreement of 1868 also provided that legislation required to implement it should be enacted as soon as possible. The agreement led directly to Canada's first *Immigration Act* in 1869. It also specified that conferences on immigration should be held annually, and until 1874 such conferences frequently did occur. In 1869, there was an agreement on the form of provincial publicity, and at the conference of 1870 it was agreed that the provinces would advise the federal government of the number of labourers needed. This provision was not enshrined in legislation, however, until the *Immigration Act* of 1976!

The conference of September 1871 was attended by delegates from all the founding provinces as well as the new provinces of Manitoba and British Columbia. The 1868 agreement was updated, principally to oblige the Dominion government to "maintain a liberal policy for the settlement and colonization of Crown lands in Manitoba and the Northwest Territories" and to require the provinces not to alter "the terms of its system as communicated, without reasonable notice" so as not to disappoint intending immigrants (LAC 2006, PC1871-1397, 25 September 1871). The provinces did not immediately send their own resident agents abroad but for a while availed themselves of the services of the federal agents. In the early 1870s, however, the provinces began to establish offices abroad or send agents abroad during the emigration (i.e., shipping) season. Apparently there was a feeling that the federal agents were inadequate to meet the demand of the provinces for settlers.

The result was an unfortunate rivalry between the provinces and the Dominion government. A federal-provincial conference in November

1874 addressed the issue: "It was generally admitted in the discussions which took place, that separate and individual action of the Provinces in promoting immigration, by means of agents in the United Kingdom and the European Continent, led not only to waste of strength and expense and divided counsels, but in some cases to actual conflicts, which had an injuriously prejudicial effect on the minds of intending emigrants. It was, therefore, thought advisable to vest in the Minister of Agriculture, for a term of years, the duty of promoting immigration to the Provinces from abroad, which had hitherto been exercised by them individually, under the provisions of the Act of Confederation" (Minister of Agriculture 1875, x).

The conference also agreed that "independent agencies for any of the Provinces shall be discontinued," but that "each province shall be authorized to appoint a Sub-Agent to obtain office accommodation for him in the Canadian Government offices in London" and that salaries of the sub-agents would be paid by the provinces and the four contracting provinces – Ontario, Quebec, New Brunswick, and Nova Scotia – would "contribute towards the increased office expenses in London." Similarly, it was provided that, should other provinces wish to avail themselves of space, they would also defray any federal costs. The agreement was to have been in place for five years and renewable for another five years unless notice was given.

It was not until 1892, shortly after the Immigration Branch had been transferred to the Department of the Interior, that it was discovered that the rent for offices in London agreed to in 1874 had never been paid by the provinces. It transpired that the federal government had never requested any rent in 18 years, and no province had volunteered it! Subsequently, the minister of the interior recommended to cabinet that the immigration agencies in Ontario, Quebec, and British Columbia should be closed, as the dominion government was only encouraging and promoting immigration to Manitoba and the Northwest Territories; the other provinces could look after the settlement of immigrants themselves (LAC 2006, PC1892-1507, 28 May 1892). In one area, however, cooperation was more evident. After an intensive lobbying effort, British Columbia succeeded in 1885 in convincing the federal government to impose a head tax of $50 on Chinese immigrants in order "to restrict and regulate Chinese immigration." This tax was subsequently increased to $100 in 1900 and to $500 in 1903 (Dept. of M&I 1974b, 5, 7).

By 1912 the Dominion government returned to the idea of coordinating the efforts of the two levels of government. It proposed that the Dominion appoint and pay two salaried agents designated by each province and that such agents be accommodated in a general Canadian building in London, if a sufficiently large building were obtained. However, this consolidation proposal was never acted upon, as the First World War intervened before a more commodious building could be found. Elsewhere, Quebec had sometime earlier appointed an agent general in Paris. In 1892, with the creation of the Department of Trade and Commerce, this agent was also appointed as Canadian "commissaire general," and his new trade and commerce duties began to take on more importance than immigration (Hill 1977, 11, 42).

The First World War marked the end of the so-called open period of immigration, during which the emphasis was on attracting farmers with capital, farm labourers and female domestic servants. The *Immigration Act* of 1869 (Canada 1869) did restrict the admission of those likely to be a health risk or a public charge and imposed a "capitation" duty of $1.00 or $1.50 on all immigrants aged one year and over. The first major overhaul of the *Immigration Act* came in 1906 and added prohibitions on a range of health and criminal grounds (Canada 1906). Apart from these provisions and the Chinese head tax, the restrictions were minimal. The war interrupted large-scale immigration, which peaked with the admission of over 400,000 immigrants in 1913. From 1914 to 1918 no means of transport was available to emigrants, and the European nations needed their manpower for their armies.

INTERVAL

During the First World War, immigration did continue from the United States, but this represented only a fraction of that experienced in the decade prior to the war. While the continental offices were closed, the offices in Britain remained opened, if only to be ready to resume immigration with the war's end. Even after the armistice, European immigration could not resume immediately as emigration officers in Britain were preoccupied with aiding the efforts to repatriate Canadian servicemen. The need for passenger shipping for servicemen also precluded any opportunity for a large-scale civilian movement until the spring of 1920. Similarly, though a dominion-provincial conference on immigration publicity was held in 1920, provincial governments were, for the most part, more concerned with reintegration of returning servicemen and dealing with attendant postwar disruptions. Any significant volume of immigrants would be seen to simply aggravate an already bad unemployment situation. The prewar immigrant flood was never to be seen again.

The first major postwar review of immigration was undertaken by the select Standing Committee on Agriculture and Colonization in 1928. The committee recommended that special efforts be made "to extend the field of action of the provincial authorities particularly in the matter of placement, settlement and supervision of immigrants, and that, with this in view, the Federal Government consider contributing to defray the cost of provincial cooperation for that purpose." The committee also observed that "the responsibility and control of the selection of immigrants no matter by whom recruited must rest solely and exclusively with the

Government of Canada" (Dept. of Immigration and Colonization 1930, 5, 7). Little came of the committee report, as it was issued on the eve of the Great Depression, and on 21 March 1931 an order-in-council was passed restricting immigration to British subjects from Great Britain and the "old Dominions" and to Americans. The only exceptions were wives and children under eighteen years of age of Canadian residents and "agriculturalists" from other countries. In all cases immigrants had to have sufficient means to maintain themselves, or their sponsors had to have the means to receive them (LAC 1906, PC1931-695, 21 March 1931).

As a result of the restrictions, immigration dropped steadily from 104,806 in 1930 to 14,382 in 1933 and did not return to significant numbers until 1946. Understandably, the provinces, preoccupied with other problems and desperately under-financed, virtually withdrew from the field of immigration. Indeed, in its submission to the Royal Commission on Dominion-Provincial Relations in May 1938, the Department of Mines and Resources, which now housed the Immigration Branch, declared baldly that "no provincial organizations exist for any of this work" (LAC 1938). Some provinces were, however, very interested in *preventing* immigration. In the West, opposition to "Slavic" races and certain religious sects was not uncommon. The role of several provinces, and Quebec in particular, in pressing a rather willing federal government to restrict the immigration of Jewish refugees from 1938 onward is one of the saddest and most reprehensible episodes in federal-provincial relations, especially because the federal government was willing to acquiesce (Abella and Troper 1986). Agreement does not always produce positive results.

POSTWAR

The relative unimportance of the immigration program in the pre-war and war years was epitomized by its place as a small branch of the Department of Mines and Resources. But with the end of the Second World War, change was inevitable. The Canadian government had to deal with the resumption of normal immigration as well as a flood of refugees and displaced persons, and the Immigration Branch of the Department of Mines and Resources was inadequate to meet the demand. Accordingly, on 19 January 1950, the government created a new Department of Citizenship and Immigration and gave it a mandate to expand the immigration service. While immigration that year actually fell to 73,912 from 95,217 the previous year, the newly invigorated immigration service quickly increased immigration almost threefold to 194,391 in 1951. A return to high levels of immigration resulted in a certain revival of provincial interest in immigration. Several of the provinces reopened European offices, and all devoted attention to the settlement and adaptation of immigrants. All, that is, except Quebec: the Duplessis government was not only isolationist but xenophobic. It had no interest in receiving immigrants, let alone in promoting immigration and services for immigrants.

Despite the reawakening of interest in immigration, the federal government created the new Department of Citizenship and Immigration and established its mandate without any obvious regard for the legitimate constitutional interests of the provinces in immigration. The postwar federal government was one that was used to acting as it saw fit in the national interest. It perceived immigration as a national program, and therefore it assumed full responsibility for recruitment, selection, and admission of immigrants. Cabinet did, however, direct the new department to develop consultative arrangements with the provinces and with national organizations (Hawkins 1972, 177). The Department of Citizenship and Immigration chose to interpret the cabinet direction as applying solely to the field of settlement, in which provincial cooperation was essential. A Settlement Service had been established by the Department of Mines and Resources in 1948, and it already dealt extensively with provincial authorities. A language training agreement was signed by all provinces but Quebec in 1953.

The second important aspect of settlement was that of welfare assistance and hospitalization. In the era before universal health insurance, paying for medical and hospital expenses was a major concern for immigrants, and the Immigration Branch set out to come to joint-sharing arrangements with the provinces. Ontario, receiving the largest share of immigrants, was the first target, and in 1952 that province and the federal government agreed to "an equal sharing, by the federal and provincial government of welfare assistance and hospitalization, for immigrants who, through accident or illness, became indigent during the twelve months immediately following their arrival in Canada" (Dept. of C&I 1952, 21). Negotiations followed with other provinces, and by 1954 similar agreements were concluded with British Columbia, Alberta, Saskatchewan, Manitoba, Nova Scotia, and Newfoundland (Dept. of C&I 1954, 26). These agreements remained in effect into the mid-1960s, but with the advent of the Canada Assistance Plan and federal-provincial hospitalization agreements, they became for the most part inoperative.

The mandate of the new department included a review of the *Immigration Act*, part of which dated from the 1910 legislation. The Immigration Branch, together with the Department of Justice, prepared the new legislation, apparently without any serious consultation with the provinces. Once the new act and regulations came into effect on 1 June 1953, the Immigration Branch did arrange a series of meetings with provincial governments during the month (Quebec and British Columbia did not attend). The 1953–54 Annual Report of the department states that "the exchange of views on the immigration policy and program proved useful to both federal and provincial representatives ... the meetings resulted in the development of close liaison in all matters respecting immigration" (ibid., 24, 25). These words, however, did not change the reality that immigration in the 1950s was a federal program in which the federal government orchestrated provincial involvement solely when it felt it was necessary to do so.

Only Ontario seemed to have taken a real interest in immigration in the 1950s. Certainly, numbers had something to do with this: between 1946 and 1971, Ontario received 53 percent of the over 3.5 million immigrants to Canada. In 1951 the province established an Industrial Placement Plan, and from its office in London began to recruit skilled immigrants in the United Kingdom and Europe for Ontario's expanding industries. Ontario marketed immigration widely and attracted increasingly large proportions of immigrants destined to Canada. Alberta and British Columbia also began to promote immigration through their London offices.

The Hungarian uprising in 1956 created one of those situations in which the help of the provinces was needed. The large influx of Hungarian refugees that followed the Soviet invasion required the federal government to solicit the provinces' cooperation, and in order to encourage them to take large numbers, the federal government concluded special agreements with Ontario, Saskatchewan, and British Columbia. Under these agreements, "The federal government assumed full responsibility for the maintenance and care of Hungarian refugees during their first year in Canada regardless of their status in this country. After that period the provincial authorities ... accept responsibility for all welfare and hospitalization expenses" (Dept. of C&I 1959, 27).

In 1957, the Hungarian uprising and the exodus from Britain following the Suez crisis contributed to a total of 282,000 immigrants choosing Canada, the highest number since 1913. However, a year later the figure was more than halved, as the economy was gripped by recession. As unemployment climbed, immigration dropped by 1961 to a postwar low of barely 71,000. Once again, what provincial interest there was in immigration seemed to decline with the declining numbers.

Reawakening

When the Canadian economy began to recover, immigration figures jumped once again so that in 1966 almost 200,000 immigrants arrived. In an effort to strengthen policy links between economic needs and immigration, the government merged the National Employment Service with the Immigration Branch and reconstituted them in 1966 as the Department of Manpower and Immigration. The Immigration White Paper of that year also explicitly acknowledged the link between the labour market and immigration (Minister of Manpower and Immigration 1966, 7). The provinces too were awakening to the relationship between immigration and their economies. The three Prairie provinces established small immigration bureaus, as did Quebec. Thus, including Ontario, five provincial governments had distinct units dealing with immigration by 1966.

It would be in Quebec, however, that a full blossoming of these several immigration bureaus would occur. The political, economic, social and intellectual ferment in Quebec in the early 1960s, *la révolution tranquille*, transformed the provincial society. The government of Jean Lesage realized that skilled immigrants could contribute to the development of the Quebec's economy and that it might be easier to integrate non-North American migrants into the francophone majority. In 1965 a Quebec Immigration Service was established within the provincial Ministry of Cultural Affairs (Quebec 1981, 90). It is significant that the Immigration Service in Quebec was first attached to its Ministry of Cultural Affairs since Quebec's preoccupation with immigration had traditionally been cultural. In the past, immigration had been perceived as a cultural invasion, destroying the linguistic balance of the province. From 1965, however, increasingly immigration came to be perceived as a tool to strengthen the francophone nature of Quebec society.

The small Quebec Immigration Service grew quickly, and by 1967 it was planning its transformation into a full-fledged department of government. Legislation was introduced in early1968 and became law in November of that year. The federal government agreed in principle to allow the Quebec Immigration Department to place agents abroad to counsel prospective immigrants. In some ways, the Quebec model was that of the Ontario Selective Placement Service, but in time its scope would grow beyond that of Ontario's operation. The Quebec Immigration Department operated on two fronts. First, it placed agents in Canadian embassies in Rome, Athens, and Beirut and at the Délégation générale du Québec in Paris. Second, it established a facility to offer language training and adaptation services to immigrants. As the initial steps towards this second goal, Quebec acceded to the federal-provincial language training agreement in 1969, 16 years after all other provinces had agreed to it. The following year the Centres d'orientation et de formation des immigrants (COFI), established by the Quebec Department of Education, were taken over by the Quebec Immigration Department. The COFI offered language training and an optional orientation program to the Quebec and Canadian way of life.

The federal Department of Manpower and Immigration, within its own organization, encouraged federal-provincial dialogue. Due to its vast size on the manpower side, it was organized into five regions (Atlantic, Quebec, Ontario, Prairies/NWT and British Columbia/Yukon), and this regional structure was also adopted by the Canada Immigration Division, as the Immigration Branch was now known. A decade later, the regional structure would be revised and expanded to ten regions, paralleling each province. As a result, senior-level federal immigration officials were located in each province. The proximity of the federal officials facilitated operational consultation and cooperation and provided the federal government with a network for the exchange of information and policy input with the provinces.

On 17 September 1973 Robert Andras, then minister of manpower and immigration, announced a full-scale review of Canadian immigration policy. A small task force was established within the department to carry out the review and was charged with preparing a Green Paper to be known as the Canadian Immigration and Population Study (CIPS). The CIPS was the first stage of a process that would culminate with the proclamation of a new *Immigration Act* almost five years later. Times had changed in the 1970s, and the government was determined to consult widely in developing the Green Paper and to encourage the provinces to participate in the process. In the preface to the Green Paper, the government noted: "Because the provinces share a constitutional responsibility with the Federal Government in the immigration field, they were notified of the review, and their views were requested. Over the course of the past year contacts between the two levels of government have been developed, and information exchanged, as work on the review progressed" (Dept. of M&I 1974a, ix).

The authors of the study expressed the usual caveat that a "Green Paper neither makes recommendations nor announces courses of action the Government believes should be pursued" (ibid., xi). Nevertheless, it was clear from the language used in the subsequent discussion on federal-provincial relations that the federal government had already decided to involve the provinces in immigration to a greater degree than ever before since Confederation:

> Clearly, there is no constitutional bar to more active and widened collaboration between the central government and the provinces, the purpose being to make immigration policy more sensitive to the provinces' and territories' requirements. As already noted, numerous fields of provincial and territorial responsibility are immediately and directly affected by immigration decisions, and by the measure of success the individual immigrant enjoys on settling in Canada ...

> The selection of those immigrants who respond most effectively to the genuine requirements of the Canadian economy depends heavily on detailed and continuously updated information about the state of job markets in all parts of the country ...

> Another field where the Federal Government is now endeavouring to work in closer co-operation with the provinces relates to the provision of those services that immigrants may require to help them solve problems they encounter in adjusting to life in Canada ...

> Immigration policy development must take place within a framework that embraces longer term demographic, economic, cultural and social objectives. It follows that the value of regular exchanges between Ottawa and provincial

governments is not limited simply to matters that immediately concern effective program management. In the future, national policy formation could be enriched through consultation between the two levels of government which approaches immigration in the wider context of all those Canadian goals to which immigration's contribution is relevant. (Ibid., 57, 58)

Following the tabling of the Green Paper, a special joint committee of the Senate and House of Commons was created. For four months in the spring of 1975, it held hearings across Canada to gauge the public's response to the Green Paper. The committee reported to Parliament in November 1975 and, apart from its general recommendations, which included a recommendation that the minister of immigration announce annual immigration targets after consultation with the provinces, it made several specific observations with respect to federal-provincial cooperation:

Vigorous efforts are needed to involve the provinces more closely in order to ensure that immigration policy reflects varied regional requirements. The Committee is aware that the federal government would welcome ... collaboration ... along the following lines:

- a permanent joint federal-provincial committee to coordinate the development and implementation of immigration policy ... ;
- a provincial presence in immigrant selection; this could involve sending officers abroad for counselling and promotional duties ... ;
- collaboration on scrutinizing teaching institutions receiving foreign students and on fixing the numbers of foreign students accepted by each institution;
- cooperation on immigrant services beginning with a joint evaluation of needs. (Canada 1975, 18)

The committee also noted Quebec's special interest in immigration from a cultural viewpoint and made the following recommendation:

The French fact is an essential element in the political and cultural life of Canada. Therefore, the Committee agrees that to the economic, social, and other considerations which normally enter into the formulation and application of immigration policy must be added a concern for the maintenance of the French-Canadian presence in a healthy and thriving condition. The Committee realizes that this goal cannot be achieved primarily through immigration policy. But it considers that the Government of Canada should not refrain from any reasonable effort within the limits of its jurisdiction which could contribute to the realization of this objective. (Ibid., 62, 63)

A year later, on 24 November 1976, the government tabled its new immigration bill (C-24), incorporating most of the committee's recommendations. The bill received second reading in March 1977, and the

Standing Committee on Labour, Manpower and Immigration spent over 70 hours on clause-by-clause study. The bill was passed by the House on 25 July 1977 and received royal assent on 5 August 1977. Due to the need to prepare new immigration regulations and entirely revise instructions to immigration officers, the *Immigration Act, 1976* was not proclaimed until 10 April 1978 (Canada 1977). On this date a new era in federal-provincial relations in immigration began.

THE ERA OF CONSULTATION

The 1976 *Immigration Act* was unique among the legislation that has governed the admission of aliens to Canada. For the first time the objectives of Canadian immigration policy were enunciated. The second of these objectives was "to enrich and strengthen the cultural and social fabric of Canada, taking into account the federal and bilingual character of Canada" (section 3(b)). In order to fulfill the objectives, section 7 specified:

> The Minister, after consultation with the provinces concerning regional demographic needs and labour market considerations and after consultation with such other persons, organizations and institutions as he deems appropriate, shall lay before Parliament ... a report specifying
>
> (a) the number of immigrants that the Government of Canada deems it appropriate to admit during any specified period of time; and
> (b) the manner in which demographic considerations have been taken into account in determining that number.

This section provided the authority for the annual consultations that have taken place with the provinces since 1978 and non-governmental organizations since 1980 and for the preparation of the annual report to Parliament on immigration levels. Cooperation with the provinces was intended to be an ongoing process, and section 109 expressed the government's intentions in that respect:

> (1) The Minister shall consult with the provinces respecting the measures to be undertaken to facilitate the adaptation of permanent residents to Canadian society and the pattern of immigrant settlement in Canada in relation to regional demographic requirements.
> (2) The Minister, with the approval of the Governor in Council, may enter into an agreement with any province or group of provinces for the purpose of facilitating the formulation, coordination and implementation of immigration policies and programs.

Pursuant to the new act, the first round of consultations on immigration levels took place during the spring and summer of 1978. Launched by the minister, they were followed up by meetings between regional federal officials and provincial officials. The annual report, tabled in November 1978, summarized the responses of the provinces, which were of a preliminary and tentative nature (Dept. of E&I 1978, 24–8). The Atlantic provinces were, for the most part, satisfied with the levels of immigration and were inclined to leave their determination to the federal government. Nova Scotia recommended, as had the special committee, that levels should cover a three-year period. Quebec noted that it was in the midst of studies to determine appropriate levels of immigration, given its own priorities and objectives, for a minimum of five years. Ontario, on the other hand, refused to express an opinion, stating that, in its view, levels determination was a federal prerogative. This remained Ontario's position for another three decades. Of the western provinces, only Saskatchewan expressed a desired range for immigration levels to that province while the other provinces responded in general terms. Nevertheless this first renewed effort of consultative planning seemed to be well received. The level for immigration in 1979 was fixed at 100,000.

That same year saw a spectacular demonstration of the limitations to planning. During the consultations, the government sought provincial support for setting immigration levels over a period of three to five years, with an annual revision. The consultations exercise was cut short by the Southeast Asian refugee crisis. On 18 July 1979 the government, having informed the provinces in advance, announced that it would accept 50,000 Southeast Asian refugees during the remainder of 1979 and in 1980. When the annual report was tabled that November, the government noted that it was "not bound to base its determination of future immigration levels solely on an aggregation of provincial preferences" (Dept. of E&I 1979, 29, 30). While the government remained committed to consultation, it reserved its prerogative to determine the total levels in the national interest. The fact that Ontario, which received over 45 percent of immigrants to Canada, did not express desired levels meant that the federal government could set levels without aggravating those provinces that did express desired levels.

The three-year planning cycle was not introduced until November 1981 when levels for the years 1982–84 were announced. This cycle met general approval from the provinces, as it permitted improved coordination of immigration flows and planning for infrastructure needs for new immigrants (Dept. of E&I 1981, 10, 23, 49). Unfortunately, the Employment and Immigration department found it impractical to follow a long-term plan, and planning returned to an annual basis shortly afterwards.

The following year, 1982, the levels consultation exercise was expanded to include the Yukon and Northwest Territories. Once again the consultations were pre-empted to a certain extent by events. A recession took hold in the winter of 1981–82, and it was soon clear to the government that labour market immigration from other countries experiencing similar difficulties would increase far beyond projected levels unless controls were imposed. These restrictions were put in place on 1 May 1982 and provided that independent immigrants (i.e., those not sponsored by relatives or not refugees) would require pre-arranged job offers approved by a Canada Employment Centre. The restriction kept the levels of selected workers within the range announced following the 1981 consultations. An aspect of the 1982 consultations was to solicit continuing approval from the provinces for this action. In the circumstances, this was forthcoming. The recession continued until late 1984, with unemployment remaining high into 1985. The provinces continued to support measures to keep immigration for the labour market restrictive, and provincial feedback in the consultative process focused on family immigration and refugees, together with immigration settlement. The provinces also took advantage of the consultation process to express increasingly sophisticated views on immigration – clear evidence that the federal government had succeeded in raising the general level of awareness of immigration policy issues with most provincial governments.

The other aspect of federal-provincial cooperation that was born of the reviews of the 1970s is the phenomenon of federal-provincial agreements. Following the series of comprehensive multilateral federal-provincial agreements on immigration in the decade after Confederation, almost a century passed before further general agreements were entered into. Those that were concluded related to issues of immigrant settlement rather than general policy. As noted above, section 109 of the *Immigration Act* highlighted the federal conviction that formal bilateral agreements with the provinces on matters relating to broad issues of immigration policy would be beneficial.

The first such agreement actually predated the new *Immigration Act*. Ottawa and Quebec had cooperated closely during the early development of the Quebec Immigration Department, and the joint decision to allow Quebec immigration counsellors to work abroad was confirmed by a formal agreement to delineate the role of these officers. On 18 May 1971, Otto Lang, federal minister of manpower and immigration, and François Cloutier, Quebec minister of immigration, signed the first federal-provincial immigration agreement of the modern era. Known as the Lang-Cloutier Agreement,[1] it was designed to encourage an increase in the francophone content of the immigration movement; encourage francophone applicants to choose to settle in Quebec; and authorize Quebec to attach "orientation officers" to Canadian missions abroad (section 2).

The operative section of the agreement concerned the promotion of the province as a destination: "The regular and normal role of an officer of the Quebec Department of Immigration is to provide further information beyond that supplied by the Federal party on living and working conditions in Quebec to applicants destined to that province" (section 10a).

The Lang-Cloutier Agreement remained in effect for four years, during which the Quebec Immigration Service (QIS) established itself abroad and developed an expertise not available to other provinces. The new service also found that many francophone officers of the federal Immigration Foreign Service were interested in working for the QIS, thus allowing it to staff itself with experienced professionals. This cadre of officers felt themselves to be capable of far more than an informational role, and it was also the desire of the QIS to play a real role in immigration to Quebec. Through a series of negotiations with the federal government, Quebec was progressively able to obtain real authority in immigrant selection.

In 1975 the Quebec government indicated that it wished to renegotiate the Lang-Cloutier Agreement. After four years' experience, it wished to take part in the selection process itself. A new agreement was signed in October 1975 by Robert Andras, federal minister of manpower and immigration, and Jean Bienvenue, Quebec minister of immigration. Section 6 of the agreement provided that (1) all immigrants destined to Quebec would be interviewed by a Quebec Immigration Service (QIS) officer; (2) formal consultations would be held with the QIS officer before the federal officer took the decision in the case; and (3) a joint federal-provincial committee would be established for exchange of information, consultation on immigrant settlement, and interpretation and implementation of the agreement. The Andras-Bienvenue Agreement provided Quebec with substantial input into final selection decisions without ceding to it the ultimate authority to select immigrants.

In 1976 the Parti Québecois came to power in Quebec. After a review of the Andras-Bienvenue Agreement, it requested the negotiation of a new agreement that would give more authority to the province. In 1977 Parliament passed the new *Immigration Act* that authorized the federal minister of immigration to enter into immigration agreements with the provinces (section 109). The federal government, therefore, wished to be seen to be entering into federal-provincial immigration agreements and so agreed to commence negotiations. The agreement signed by Bud Cullen, the federal minister of employment and immigration, and Jacques Couture, the Quebec minister of immigration, on 20 February 1978 was much more detailed than either of the earlier agreements and covered most aspects of selection abroad and settlement in Quebec. It involved a clear devolution of power from the federal to the provincial government. This devolution seems to have been the intention of the federal negotiators, and it would have been in keeping with the attitude of the Trudeau government prior to the first Quebec referendum on separation. The federal government wanted to demonstrate that, in the realm of immigration, federalism could work, and this meant giving Quebec a substantial say in immigration. The Quebec government, for its part, sought greater authority in all spheres related to cultural and social endeavour and especially in the area of external affairs. As a result, the goals of the two parties were compatible, though for contradictory reasons.

The Cullen-Couture agreement was in fact in negotiation while the new *Immigration Act* was proceeding through Parliament. There were some sharp exchanges at committee stage, since some Progressive Conservative MPs were not at all convinced by the minister's assurances that he was not going to sign away federal supremacy. In the outcome, the agreement did go beyond what even the legislation drafters anticipated, with the result that there was considerable heartburn over statutory authority for some of the implementing regulations.

In section I(1) of the Cullen-Couture Agreement, Canada and Quebec agreed to (1) cooperate in all areas relating to migration movements and demography, and (2) participate jointly in the selection of persons wishing to settle permanently or temporarily in Quebec.

The heart of the agreement was section III, which dealt with selection. While it stipulated the general principle that selection would be "on a joint and equal basis, according to separate sets of criteria for Canada and for Quebec," it went on to limit the generality of this statement in Quebec's favour in the case of independent immigrants. In fact, Quebec was given an effective veto in the selection of independent immigrants by stipulating that "the landing of an independent immigrant in Quebec requires Quebec's prior agreement."

The agreement conferred no authority on Quebec for the determination of eligibility of Family Class immigrants, that is, close family members, sponsored by relatives in Canada. However, section V did allow the province to determine the financial capability of sponsors to live up to their sponsorship obligations. Refugees continued to be determined to be refugees by the federal government pursuant to its responsibilities under the United Nations Convention on the Status of Refugees, but their selection as immigrants was jointly carried out by Canada and Quebec. The final decision to issue a visa to all classes of immigrants was taken by the federal government following statutory procedures such as medical examinations and security and criminal checks. The agreement also had provisions relating to foreign students, persons coming into Quebec for medical treatment, and temporary foreign workers. Employment and Immigration Canada and the Quebec Immigration Department agreed to common operational directives for implementing the agreement. As a result, Quebec became the only province to become involved directly in immigration selection. It would be two decades before similar powers would be extended to other provinces.

Quebec today has immigration agents in seven locations around the world and processes North American and North African applications from its headquarters in Montreal. Nevertheless, this is still a very small service in comparison to the Immigration Service of Citizenship and Immigration Canada, which has immigration facilities at about 90 of Canada's missions abroad.

While Quebec was the first province in the modern era to conclude a federal-provincial immigration agreement, it is no longer alone in this area. The federal government wanted to promote the image of cooperative federalism across the country; it also did not want it to appear that Quebec was the only province with an immigration agreement. In the spirit of the new *Immigration Act*, the federal government had invited all provinces to enter into agreements even prior to proclamation of the act, and it persuaded two other provinces to sign on along with Quebec. On 20 February 1978, Cullen, the minister of employment and immigration, and Marc Lalonde, the minister of state for federal-provincial relations, signed both the Quebec agreement and the Canada-Nova Scotia Immigration Agreement, and three days later they signed the Canada-Saskatchewan Immigration Agreement.

Over the next year, other provinces saw that the agreements did meet growing needs, and immigration agreements were also concluded with Newfoundland, New Brunswick, and Prince Edward Island. Each agreement was different and was negotiated to meet both federal and provincial needs while establishing mechanisms for ongoing consultation and cooperation. The agreements spawned different procedures, directives, and sub-agreements in each province, but in every case they brought about improved communications and understanding on the part of both levels of government. All the other provincial agreements of this period were brief in comparison to the Quebec agreement. They did not require the detail necessary to establish a joint selection system, but they did bind each party to extensive policy consultation and exchange of information as well as specifying certain categories of immigrant, such as entrepreneurs, teachers, and invalids, about which provincial input would be mandatory. Similarly, the existence of a system in six provinces encouraged a certain degree of emulation in the federal-provincial relations of the remaining four provinces and the two territories. The variety of methods of working within a single framework of the constitution and the *Immigration Act* was described as "asymmetric federalism" (McRoberts 1985, 90, 91). A single goal can be attained in many ways, and this is proved daily within the Canadian immigration program.

After observing the experiences of those provinces with immigration agreements, Alberta entered into negotiations in 1981. These were suspended the following year but revived in 1984 following the election of a federal Conservative government, and an agreement with Alberta was signed in 1985. In 1983 British Columbia indicated its desire to commence negotiations, but no agreement was concluded at that time. In 1984 Saskatchewan advised the minister of employment and immigration that it wished to renegotiate certain aspects of the Canada-Saskatchewan Immigration Agreement, demonstrating a belief in the long-term viability of federal-provincial immigration agreements.

While Ontario and Manitoba continued to prefer not to obtain formal agreements, both adopted many of the same procedures developed subsequent to the other agreements. Each regional immigration office was, and still is, in almost daily contact with provincial authorities obtaining provincial input concerning either individual cases or policy issues.

THE ERA OF DEVOLUTION AND REGIONALIZATION

In 1984, Brian Mulroney's Progressive Conservatives defeated the Liberals and formed a government committed to "bringing Quebec into the Constitution." To that end, Mulroney commenced constitutional discussions that led to the Meech Lake Agreement. An element of Quebec's constitutional propositions, presented to the federal government on 15 May 1985, included the proposal that "the Constitution should enlarge upon the Cullen-Couture Agreement of 1978 by confirming the paramountcy of Québec's powers in the matter of selection, and by extending that paramountcy to the integration and settlement of immigrants" (Quebec 1985, 29).

The constitutional negotiations ultimately resulted in the Meech Lake Accord on 3 June 1987. The accord included the "constitutionalization" of federal-provincial immigration agreements, in particular the Cullen-Couture Accord. Sections 2 and 3 of the accord provided that:

2. The Government of Canada will, as soon as possible, conclude an agreement with the Government of Quebec that would

(a) incorporate the principles of the Cullen-Couture agreement on the selection abroad and in Canada of independent immigrants, visitors for medical treatment, students and temporary workers, and on the selection of refugees abroad and economic criteria for family reunification and assisted relatives,

(b) guarantee that Quebec will receive a number of immigrants, including refugees, within the annual total established by the federal government for all of Canada proportionate to its share of the population of Canada, with the right to exceed that figure by five per cent for demographic reasons, and

(c) provide an undertaking by Canada to withdraw services (except citizenship services) for the reception and integration (including linguistic and cultural) of all foreign nationals wishing to settle in Quebec where services are to be provided by Quebec, with such withdrawal to be accompanied by reasonable compensation, and the Government of Canada and the Government of Quebec will take the necessary steps to give the agreement the force of law under the proposed amendment relating to such agreements

3. Nothing in the Accord should be construed as preventing the negotiation of similar agreements with other provinces relating to immigration and the temporary admission of aliens. (Canada 1987)

The accord required the approval of the Parliament of Canada and the legislatures of all provinces by 23 June 1990. As the Manitoba and Newfoundland legislatures did not approve it by the deadline, the accord failed (Gall 2011).

A second round of constitutional negotiations began immediately and resulted in the Charlottetown Accord. Section 27 of that accord provided that:

A new provision should be added to the constitution committing the Government of Canada to negotiate agreements with the provinces relating to immigration.

The Constitution should oblige the federal government to negotiate and conclude within a reasonable time an immigration agreement at the request of any province. A government negotiating an agreement should be accorded equality of treatment in relation to any government which has already concluded an agreement, taking into account different needs and circumstances. (Canada 1992)

The Charlottetown Accord also failed, this time in a national referendum on 26 October 1992 in which it was rejected by six provinces and Yukon (McConnell and Gall 2011).

In the wake of the failure of Meech Lake, the federal government did not await the outcome of further constitutional negotiations to move on the Meech commitment to conclude a new immigration agreement with Quebec, incorporating the principles of the Cullen-Couture agreement. The result is the current Canada-Quebec accord, signed on 5 February 1991 by the federal minister of employment and immigration, Barbara McDougall, and the Quebec minister of cultural communities and immigration, Monique Gagnon-Tremblay. It came into force on 1 April 1991.

The 1991 Canada-Quebec Accord is very similar to the Cullen-Couture Accord but includes a number of important changes. Section 2 contains an important new objective: "An objective of this Accord, is among other things, the preservation of Québec's demographic importance within Canada and the integration of immigrants to that province in a manner that respects the distinct identity of Québec."

The accord also incorporates the Meech Lake commitments that:

6. Canada undertakes to pursue a policy with respect to immigration levels that will allow Québec to receive, out of the annual total established for the country as a whole, the percentage of immigrants referred to in Section 7,

with Québec having the right to exceed this figure by five per cent of the Canadian total for demographic reasons.

7. Québec undertakes to pursue an immigration policy that has as an object-ive the reception by Québec of a percentage of the total number of immigrants received in Canada equal to the percentage of Québec's population compared with the population of Canada. (Canada and Quebec 1991)

Section 6 deviates from the Meech text in one important aspect. The potentially trouble-causing word "guarantee" is omitted, and in place, both parties have undertaken to pursue policies consistent with that goal (Becklumb 2008, 3).

Finally, Quebec's wish to assume responsibility for settlement was confirmed in sections 24 and 25:

24. Canada undertakes to withdraw from the services to be provided by Québec for the reception and the linguistic and cultural integration of permanent residents in Québec.

25. Canada undertakes to withdraw from specialized economic integration services to be provided by Québec to permanent residents in Québec.

Annex B of the accord sets out the compensation to be paid to Quebec for the provision of settlement services to immigrants in Quebec. The formula is controversial because it provides for a continual increase in payments to Quebec according to a complicated formula based both on government spending generally and on increases (but not decreases) to the number immigrants destined to Quebec. Therefore, the compensation under the accord will increase even if immigration to Quebec does not (Becklumb 2008, 6). The effect has been that transfers to Quebec under the accord have been increased from $75 million in 1991–92 (ibid., 5) to $258.4 million in 2011–12 (CIC 2010b). This rapid increase in transfers to Quebec in comparison to spending in the rest of Canada has led to complaints from other provinces (but more about this in due course).

As Canada eased out of the economic slowdown of the early 1990s, es-pecially in the West, the three Prairie provinces were concerned that they were not receiving their proportional share of immigration to Canada. The Atlantic provinces joined in the push for better "regionalization" of immigration. Manitoba, in particular, argued that application of the na-tional selection criteria did not select immigrants for Manitoba's needs, especially in the skilled and semi-skilled trades. The federal government did not want ten Canada-Quebec accords, as that would put it out of the business of selecting immigrants for the labour market, but it knew that something was required to appease the provinces. Therefore, in 1995 the "Provincial/Territorial Nominee" category was developed to allow provinces and territories to "meet specific local and regional economic immigration objectives … The category [would] allow each province or territory to identify a limited number of economic immigrants to meet specific regional needs and/or to receive priority attention for immigration processing each year" (CIC 1995, 9, 10). The intention was that the Provincial Nominee Program (PNP) would be small. The initial target set in the 1996 levels plan was 1,000.

The offer of PNPs was the impetus for a new round of negotiations with the provinces, both to develop new comprehensive or "framework" agreements and also to conclude Provincial Nominee Agreements. It was not surprising, given its intense lobby for selection tools, that Manitoba was first out of the blocks. It signed the first new framework agreement on 22 October 1996. This agreement provided for Annexes for Provincial Nominees and for "settlement realignment," and negotiations to those ends started soon after.

Settlement realignment was an idea that came out of the federal government's Program Review exercise in 1995–96 designed to address the large federal deficit. In Program Review, "Ministers were asked to review their own portfolios and provide their view on the federal government's future roles and responsibilities. Government programs and activities were reviewed using six tests: serving the public interest; necessity of government involvement; appropriate federal role; scope for public sector/private sector partnerships; scope for increased efficiency; and affordability" (Dept. of Finance 1995)

Citizenship and Immigration at that time had to absorb some $62 million in budget cuts and so proposed turning over administration of the Settlement Program to provinces that wished to take it on, the rationale being that settlement program efficiencies could be gained as provinces deliver social services and education.

CIC held nationwide consultations on "settlement renewal" in 1996 with the hope of convincing as many provinces as possible to take on delivery of settlement programs – the federal government, of course, transferring their budget. However, the provinces, while welcoming the proposal, were not happy with the level of settlement funding which, except in Quebec, had remained the same for several years. This resulted in the federal government offering to increase spending outside Quebec from its base of $118.4 million by $62.3 million. The new funds, ironically almost exactly the same amount that CIC was expected to save from its operating budget in Program Review, were made available in 1997–98 (CIC 1997, 18; CIC 1998, 28).

The new funding persuaded Manitoba and British Columbia to conclude settlement realignment agreements in 1998. Therefore, the following year, both provinces began delivering settlement services (CIC 1999, 26).

At the same time, the regulatory process to create the Provincial Nominee Category finally was concluded and the first agreements were signed with Saskatchewan, British Columbia, and Manitoba in 1998 (ibid.,

52). New Brunswick and Newfoundland followed in 1999, Prince Edward Island and Yukon in 2001, and Alberta and Nova Scotia in 2002 (CIC 2003a, 14). A Provincial Nominee Annex was included in the immigration agreement that Ontario ultimately concluded in 2005 (see below), and the Northwest Territories concluded a Provincial Nominee Agreement in 2009. This left only Nunavut without an agreement giving it authority to select economic immigrants. While the agreements were all originally pilot projects for fixed periods and with low numerical limits, all have been renewed indefinitely and without numerical limits.

Manitoba, which had pushed so hard for a program to allow provinces to meet their own labour market needs, was the first province to make large-scale use of the PNP. In 2002, 1,527 Provincial Nominees (PNs) were admitted to Manitoba. This amounted to 70 percent of the 2,172 PNs admitted nationally that year. It also represented fully one-third of all immigrants to Manitoba in 2002. The growth of Manitoba's PNP has driven the increase in immigrants to that province from a low of fewer than 3,000 in 1998 to 13,520 in 2009. Other provinces have been ramping up their own PNPs, but in 2009 Manitoba still accounted for one-third of the over 30,000 PNs Canada admitted in that year (CIC 2010a). Thus, the Provincial and Territorial Nominee programs are serving as the main instruments of regionalization by drawing immigrants to destinations other than Montreal, Toronto, and Vancouver.

As noted earlier, many provincial governments watched with dismay as settlement funding to Quebec increased annually and, after 1997, the funding in other provinces remained the same. Ontario, which received the most immigrants, led the chorus of complaint. Ontario Premier Dalton McGuinty fiercely denounced "the unfairness that had seen our province receive 57 per cent of new immigrants but only 34 per cent of national funding." Ontario officials calculated that Ontario was receiving $819 per immigrant for settlement services whereas Quebec received $3,806 per immigrant (McGuinty 2005). In 2005, with a federal general election approaching, the government of Paul Martin authorized CIC to put sufficient funding on the table to conclude the first-ever immigration agreement with Ontario on 21 November 2005 (Canada and Ontario 2005). The crucial funding arrangements are found in section 8 of the agreement:

> 8.1 Beyond the annual settlement funding currently allocated in Ontario, in the order of $109.6 M in 2004-05, Canada agrees to invest additional resources for settlement services and language training for prospective immigrants to, and immigrants residing in Ontario. Canada commits to providing incremental funding that will grow over a five-year period to reach a cumulative total of $920 M in new investments by 2009-10. For planning purposes, this incremental funding is projected to be disbursed in accordance with the following profile: 2005–06 – $50 M; 2006–07 – $115 M; 2007–08 – $185 M; 2008–09 – $250 M; 2009–10 – $320 M.

The enormous increase in settlement funding was welcomed in Ontario, but as it was restricted only to Ontario, the deal angered other provinces, British Columbia and Alberta in particular. When the Conservative government was elected in January 2006, with Prime Minister Harper being from Alberta, Ed Stelmach, then Alberta's minister of international and intergovernmental affairs, was quick to state that Alberta wanted the new federal government to address immigration programs and deal with issues about the per capita funding of immigrant settlement programs (CTV.ca 2006). Wally Oppal, the BC minister responsible for immigration, also indicated that his province wanted to negotiate a similar funding deal to that of Ontario (AMSSA 2005). The lobbying for equal funding resulted in the 2006 federal budget allocating a $77 million increase in settlement funding outside Ontario and Quebec in order to redress the funding disparity (CIC 2006). However, this amount only partly addressed the disparity, and in 2008-09, a further $121.6 million was directed to the other provinces to create a rough parity among all provinces (CIC 2007). The major beneficiaries, of course, have been new immigrants who now have far greater access to immigrant settlement programs, especially language training, across the country.

A recent phenomenon in federal-provincial relations is an increasing openness in some provinces to recognizing the role of major cities in the integration of immigrants and the impact of immigration on civic infrastructure and services. The first agreement to include a city as signatory was the Canada-Manitoba-Winnipeg Memorandum of Understanding on Private Refugee Sponsorship Assistance, signed on 13 November 2002 (Canada, Manitoba and Winnipeg 2002). Through this agreement, the City of Winnipeg supports private refugee sponsoring groups who might not otherwise feel able to take on the financial commitment involved in such sponsorships. Annex F of the Canada-Ontario Immigration Agreement explicitly provides for immigration agreements with Ontario municipalities. On 29 September 2006 the City of Toronto was the first Ontario municipality to conclude an agreement under these provisions. It provides for tripartite consultation and cooperation on immigration and immigrant settlement in Toronto (Canada, Ontario and Toronto 2006). Section 7.3 of the Canada-Alberta agreement also recognizes the importance of involving municipalities, but Alberta was not willing to go as far as Ontario. The agreement indicates only that "Canada and Alberta agree to maintain and advance a dialogue on the appropriate role of municipalities in program and policy development in accordance with their respective authorities" (Canada and Alberta 2007, 7.3.3).

Finally, in recognition of the growing importance of immigration to the provinces and territories, on 16 October 2002 the federal minister of citizenship and immigration, Denis Coderre, convened the first modern-era meeting of federal-provincial-territorial ministers responsible for immigration (CIC 2003b). Since then, ministers have met more or less annually in order to ensure that immigration policy and operations are coordinated at both the levels of officials and politicians.

Ends and Means

As long as Canada remains an immigrant-receiving country, federal-provincial cooperation will remain an issue in the field of immigration policy. In the early years of Confederation, the provinces actively participated in the field. However, as the Dominion government gained more experience than the provinces in immigration and in the years of the great migration at the turn of the twentieth century concentrated on peopling the federal territories of the West rather than the established provinces, the interests and activities of the provinces diminished and almost disappeared; they did not revive until after the Second World War. The revival was led by the recruitment efforts of Ontario, but in the late 1960s the initiative among the provinces was assumed by Quebec. Today, along with Quebec, all provinces and territories have given an immigration mandate to one of their departments, and many have large and sophisticated immigration operations.

In the late 1970s and early '80s, a foundation was laid for innovative and mostly harmonious cooperation in the field of immigration policy. To this foundation was added, in the late 1990s and the first years of this century, a far more comprehensive superstructure of provincial and territorial involvement in immigration. The new generation of federal-provincial and federal-territorial agreements no longer carries a termination date. The agreements are recognized as a permanent element of managing immigration in Canada. Furthermore, they all acknowledge the bilingual character of Canada and provide for a review of the agreements on a regular basis. Thus, both levels of government accept the concept that their partnership pursuant to section 95 of the *Constitution Act* is fluid and must, through negotiation, evolve to meet the changing priorities of Canadians and their governments.

The variety within the immigration program, the variety of approaches of the several provincial governments, and, the fact that immigration deals with millions of unique individuals adds difficulty and challenge to policy management. Consultation and cooperation take time and effort, but it seems clear that the result is a better, more informed and more nuanced immigration program that better meets the needs of Canada and its provinces, territories, and regions.

NOTE

1. Due to the large number of agreements with Quebec, the previous Canada-Quebec immigration agreements are referred to here by the names of the ministers who signed the agreements. This practice is used in this paper for agreements with the province of Quebec only.

REFERENCES

Abella, I. and H. Troper. 1986. *None Is Too Many: Canada and the Jews of Europe, 1933–1948*. Toronto: Lester & Orpen Dennys.

Affiliation of Multicultural Societies and Services Agencies of BC (AMSSA). 2005. "Federal Immigrant Funding Increases." *AMSSA Insider*, December 2005. At http://www.amssa.org (accessed 8 October 2008; document no longer available).

Becklumb, P. 2008. *Immigration: The Canada-Quebec Accord, BP-252E*, Law and Government Division, Parliamentary Research Branch. Ottawa: Library of Parliament. At http://www2.parl.gc.ca/content/lop/researchpublications/bp252-e.pdf (accessed 4 April 2011).

Canada. 1869. *An Act Respecting Immigration and Immigrants, 32-33 Victoria c. 10*. Ottawa: Malcolm Cameron.

—1906. *An Act Respecting Immigration and Immigrants, 6 Edward VII, c. 19*. Ottawa: King's Printer.

—1975. Special Joint Committee of the Senate and of the House of Commons on Immigration Policy. *Report to Parliament*. Ottawa: Parliament of Canada.

—1977. *Revised Statutes of Canada, 1976-77 c. 52: An Act Respecting Immigration to Canada*. Ottawa: Information Canada.

—1987. *The 1987 Constitutional Accord* (Meech Lake Accord). Canadian Encyclopedia online. At http://www.thecanadianencyclopedia.com/index.cfm?PgNm=TCE&Params=A1ARTA0010100 (accessed 1 October 2008).

—1992. *Consensus Report on the Constitution*, August 28, 1992, Final Text (Charlottetown Accord). Canadian Encyclopedia online. At http://www.thecanadianencyclopedia.com/index.cfm?PgNm=TCE&Params=A1ARTA0010099 (accessed 1 October 2008).

Canada and Alberta. 2007. *Agreement for Canada-Alberta Cooperation on Immigration*. Citizenship and Immigration Canada – About Us – Laws and Policies – Agreements. At http://www.cic.gc.ca/english/department/laws-policy/agreements/alberta/can-alberta-agree-2007.asp (accessed 8 October 2008).

Canada, Manitoba, and Winnipeg. 2002. *Canada-Manitoba-Winnipeg Memorandum of Understanding on Private Refugee Sponsorship Assistance*. Citizenship and Immigration Canada – About Us – Laws and Policies – Agreements. At http://www.cic.gc.ca/english/department/laws-policy/agreements/manitoba/can-man-mou.asp (accessed 8 October 2008).

Canada and Ontario. 2005. *Canada-Ontario Immigration Agreement*. Citizenship and Immigration Canada – About Us – Laws and Policies – Agreements. At http://www.cic.gc.ca/english/department/laws-policy/agreements/ontario/ont-2005-agree.asp (accessed 7 October 2008).

Canada, Ontario, and Toronto. 2006. *Canada-Ontario-Toronto Memorandum of Understanding on Immigration and Settlement.* Citizenship and Immigration Canada – About Us – Laws and Policies – Agreements. At http://www.cic.gc.ca/english/department/laws-policy/agreements/ontario/can-ont-toronto-mou.asp (accessed 7 October 2008).

Canada and Quebec. 1991. *Canada-Québec Accord Relating to Immigration and Temporary Admission of Aliens* (Canada-Quebec Accord). Citizenship and Immigration Canada – About Us – Laws and Policies – Agreements. At http://www.cic.gc.ca/english/department/laws-policy/agreements/quebec/can-que.asp (accessed 1 October 2008).

Citizenship and Immigration Canada (CIC). 1995. *A Broader Vision: Immigration Plan – 1996 Annual Report to Parliament.* Hull: Supply and Services Canada.

—1997. *Performance Report for the Period Ending March 31, 1997.* Ottawa: Supply and Services Canada.

—1998. *Report on Plans and Priorities, 1998–99.* Ottawa: Supply and Services Canada, 1998.

—1999. *Performance Report for the Period Ending March 31, 1999.* Ottawa: Supply and Services Canada.

—2003a. *Annual Report to Parliament on Immigration, 2003.* Ottawa: Public Works and Government Services.

—2003b. *Performance Report for the Period Ending March 31, 2003, Minister's Message.* At http://www.collectionscanada.gc.ca/webarchives/20060116232310/www.tbs-sct.gc.ca/rma/dpr/02-03/0203dpr-rmr_e.asp (accessed 4 April 2011).

—2006. *Settlement Funding Allocations.* At http://www.cic.gc.ca/English/department/media/backgrounders/2006/2006-11-10.asp (accessed 8 October 2008).

—2007. *Settlement Funding Allocations for 2008-09.* At http://www.cic.gc.ca/english/department/media/backgrounders/2007/2007-12-17.asp (accessed 8 October 2008).

—2010a. *Digital Library – Facts and Figures 2009.* Ottawa: Public Works and Government Services Canada). CD available from distributionservices-services-desdistributions@cic.gc.ca

—2010b. *Government of Canada 2011–12 Settlement Funding Allocations.* CIC – Media Centre – Backgrounders-2010. At http://www.cic.gc.ca/english/department/media/backgrounders/2010/2010-12-07.asp (accessed 4 April 2011).

CTV.ca. 2006. *Albertans Claim Victory after Conservative Win.* 24 January 2006. At http://www.ctv.ca/servlet/ArticleNews/story/CTVNews/20060124/west_reaction_060124/20060124?hub=Canada (accessed 8 October 2008).

Department of Citizenship and Immigration (C&I). 1952. *Annual Report, 1951–52.* Ottawa: Queen's Printer.

—1954. *Annual Report, 1953–54.* Ottawa: Queen's Printer.

—1958. "Developments in Canadian Immigration." In *Canada Year Book 1957–58.* Ottawa: Queen's Printer.

—1959. *Annual Report, 1958–59.* Ottawa: Queen's Printer.

Department of Employment and Immigration (E&I). 1978. *Annual Report to Parliament on Immigration Levels.* Ottawa: Information Canada.

—1979. *Annual Report to Parliament on Immigration Levels.* Ottawa: Information Canada.

—1981. *Annual Report to Parliament on Immigration Levels.* Ottawa: Information Canada.

Department of Finance. 1995. *Getting Government Right – Program Review Overview.* Budget 1995 Fact Sheet 6. At http://www.fin.gc.ca/budget95/fact/FACT_6e. html (accessed 2 October 2008).

Department of Immigration and Colonization. 1930. *Annual Report 1928–29.* Ottawa: King's Printer.

Department of Manpower and Immigration (M&I). 1974a, *Immigration Policy Perspectives.* Vol. 1, *Report of the Canadian Immigration and Population Study.* Ottawa, Information Canada.

—1974b. *The Immigration Program.* Vol. 2, *Report of the Canadian Immigration and Population Study.* Ottawa: Information Canada.

Gall, G.L. 2011. "Meech Lake Accord." In the *Canadian Encyclopedia* online. At http://www.thecanadianencyclopedia.com/index.cfm?PgNm=TCE& Params=A1SEC824207 (accessed 4 April 2011).

Hawkins, F. 1972. *Canada and Immigration, Public Policy and Public Concern.* Montreal and London: McGill-Queen's University Press.

Hill, M. 1977. *Canada's Salesmen to the World.* Montreal: McGill-Queen's University Press.

Library and Archives Canada (LAC). 1938. *Immigration Files.* RG76, vol. 626, File 951760 Ft. 4, Reel C-10442.

Library and Archives Canada (LAC). 2006. *Orders-in Council,* RG2, Privy Council Office, Series A-1-a. At http://www.collectionscanada.gc.ca/databases/orders/ index-e.html (last modified 15 November 2006 (accessed 2 April 2011).

McConnell, W.H. and G.L. Gall. 2011. *Constitutional History.* Canadian Encyclopedia online. At http://www.thecanadianencyclopedia.com/index. cfm?PgNm=TCE&Params=A1SEC818742 (accessed 4 April 2011).

McGuinty, D. 2005. "Remarks by Dalton McGuinty, Premier of Ontario on Narrowing the $23 Billion Gap Statement to the Legislative Assembly, May 9, 2005." Ontario.ca – Newsroom. At http://news.ontario.ca/opo/en/2005/05/ remarks-by-dalton-mcguinty-premier-of-ontario-on-narrowing-the-23-billion-gap-statement-to-the-legis.html (accessed 19 December 2010).

McRoberts, K. 1985. "Unilateralism, Bilateralism and Multilateralism: Approaches to Canadian Federalism." In *Intergovernmental Relations* ed. R. Simeon. Vol. 63 of the Research Studies of the Royal Commission on the Economic Union and Development Prospects for Canada. Toronto: University of Toronto Press.

Minister of Agriculture. 1870. *Report for the Half Year of 1867 and for 1868.* Ottawa: Queen's Printer.

—1875. *Annual Report 1874.* Ottawa: Queen's Printer.

Minister of Manpower and Immigration. 1966. *Canadian Immigration Policy: White Paper on Immigration.* Ottawa: Information Canada.

Quebec. 1981. *Ministère de l'immigration, rapport annual, 1980–1981.* Québec: Gouvernement du Québec.

—1985. *Draft Agreement on the Constitution: Proposals by the Government of Québec.* Quebec: Government of Quebec.

Skilling, H.G. 1945. *Canadian Representation Abroad.* Toronto: Ryerson.

Chapter 2

Policy Frameworks for Managing Diversity in Canada: Taking Stock for Taking Action

Joseph Garcea and Neil Hibbert

This chapter provides an overview of a particular set of policy frameworks that have been developed and implemented by the federal, provincial, and territorial governments for facilitating the integration and inclusion of immigrants and members of racial, cultural, and religious minorities. The focus is on four policy frameworks: multiculturalism, human rights, anti-racism, and employment and pay equity. Immigrant settlement policies per se are beyond the scope of this chapter; they are covered in subsequent chapters devoted to the immigration, settlement, and integration policies of the federal, provincial, and territorial governments. In examining the aforementioned policy frameworks, the two central objectives are, first, to describe their similarities and differences across the provinces and territories, and second, to ascertain the ways and extent to which individually and collectively contribute to the integration and inclusion of immigrants and members of racial, cultural, and religious minorities. The chapter reveals that the four policy frameworks are remarkably similar across provinces and territories, albeit with some notable differences in the case of the articulation and implementation of multiculturalism policies in some provinces and especially the territories; employment and pay equity; and anti-racism policies, plans, and programs. It also reveals that, despite the differences in the precise scope of the various policy frameworks, individually and collectively they provide a relatively progressive, broad, robust, and arguably well-resourced policy and program web (Johnson and Joshee 2007; Joshee 2007) to facilitate the integration

Integration and Inclusion of Newcomers and Minorities across Canada, ed. J. Biles, M. Burstein, J. Frideres, E. Tolley, and R. Vineberg. Montreal and Kingston: Queen's Policy Studies Series, McGill-Queen's University Press.
© 2011 The School of Policy Studies, Queen's University at Kingston. All rights reserved.

and inclusion of immigrants and minorities. The chapter concludes that despite the progress that has been made, challenges of integration and inclusion still persist and must be addressed.

Before delving into the overview and analysis of the four policy frameworks for facilitating the integration and inclusion of immigrants, a caveat is in order in relation to Aboriginals. First, many of the policies that impinge on them were not developed exclusively in relation to immigrants; many were developed, at least in part, in relation to Aboriginals and to members of other groups whose demographic profiles fall within the scope of intersectionalities of diversity (e.g., women, persons with disabilities, etc.). This is particularly true of anti-racism policies in various jurisdictions. However, in some jurisdictions, and particularly in the three northern territories where Aboriginals constitute the majority of the population, the existence and the precise focus and scope of those frameworks have been heavily influenced by policy goals and objectives related to Aboriginals.

MULTICULTURALISM POLICY FRAMEWORK

During the past 40 years, multiculturalism policies have been enacted by the federal and provincial governments (Garcea 2006). Today the federal government and six of the provincial governments (i.e., British Columbia, Saskatchewan, and the four Atlantic provinces) have adopted what they have explicitly labelled as multiculturalism policies. Whereas the federal government and three provinces (British Columbia, Saskatchewan, and Nova Scotia) have enacted multiculturalism statutes, three provinces (New Brunswick, Newfoundland, and PEI) have adopted multiculturalism policies that are not embedded in statutes. Moreover, Quebec has adopted what, for symbolic and to a lesser extent substantive purposes, it has labelled its interculturalism policy. At the core of this policy has been its *Council on Intercultural Relations Act* of 1984, which is still in force today. Over time this statute has been supplemented by a series of policy statements and statutes related to immigration and integration (noted below, this chapter).

The jurisdictions without a separate or singular multiculturalism or interculturalism policy are two provinces, Alberta and Ontario, and the three territories (Yukon, Northwest Territories, and Nunavut). Alberta and Ontario have included provisions related to multiculturalism in statutes that deal with matters other than multiculturalism. At one point in recent decades both of those provinces adopted separate and singular multiculturalism policies (i.e., Ontario 1977–82; Alberta 1990–96), but eventually they opted to supplant them with policies that dealt more with other policy matters, rather than multiculturalism per se. In Alberta, the only policy provision related to multiculturalism today is found in the

Human Rights Act (Alberta 2009), which superseded with only some very minor amendments the *Human Rights, Citizenship and Multiculturalism Act* (Alberta 2000). The preamble to both of Alberta's statutes merely states that "multiculturalism describes the diverse racial and cultural composition of Alberta society and its importance is recognized in Alberta as a fundamental principle and a matter of public policy" (Alberta 2010). Similarly, the only provisions contained in Ontario's *Ministry of Citizenship and Culture Act* (1990) are in the section regarding the function of that agency, which does not even explicitly mention multiculturalism. Instead, it refers to the "pluralistic nature of Ontario society" and the need for the ministry to:

(a) encourage full, equal and responsible citizenship among the residents of Ontario;

(b) stress the full participation of all Ontarians as equal members of the community, encouraging the sharing of cultural heritage while affirming those elements held in common by all residents;

(c) ensure the creative and participatory nature of cultural life in Ontario by assisting in the stimulation of cultural expression and cultural preservation; and

(d) foster the development of individual and community excellence, enabling Ontarians to better define the richness of their diversity and the shared vision of their community.

TABLE 1
Statutes and Policies Related to Multiculturalism or Interculturalism in Force in 2009

Jurisdiction	Title of Statute or Policy
Canada	*Canadian Multiculturalism Act* (1988)
British Columbia	*British Columbia Multiculturalism Act* (1996)
Alberta	*Human Rights Act* (2009)
Saskatchewan	*Saskatchewan Multiculturalism Act* (1997)
Manitoba	*Manitoba Multiculturalism Act* (1992) *Manitoba Ethnocultural Advisory and Advocacy Council Act* (2001)
Ontario	*Ministry of Citizenship and Culture Act* (1990)
Quebec	*Council of Intercultural Relations Act* (1984)
Nova Scotia	*Nova Scotia Multiculturalism Act* (1989)
New Brunswick	*New Brunswick's Policy on Multiculturalism* (1986)
Prince Edward Island	*Provincial Multiculturalism Policy* (1983)
Newfoundland and Labrador	*Policy on Multiculturalism* (2008)

Source: Authors' compilations.

The policies of the three northern territories are also relatively silent on multiculturalism. Nevertheless, they also value and respect the multiculturalism ethos, as is evident in the Yukon's *Human Rights Act,* which stipulates that it should be "interpreted in ways that is consonant with the preservation and enhancement of the multicultural heritage of the residents of the territory" (Yukon 2002). Other policies of the three territories that are the subject of analysis in this chapter tend to deal more extensively and explicitly with the promotion and preservation of the Indigenous cultures and the rights of Indigenous peoples than with multiculturalism per se.

KEY PROVISIONS IN MULTICULTURALISM POLICIES

The content of the multiculturalism policies across jurisdictions is remarkably similar, especially the content regarding the policy goals, responsibility for advancing those goals, allocation of resources for advancing those goals, and rights of cultural groups and their members.

Policy Goals. Invariably all multiculturalism policies are intended to contribute to two broad overarching goals: firstly, creating warm, welcoming, and inclusive communities; and secondly, maximizing the economic, social, cultural, and political integration of immigrants and members of minority groups. In keeping with those two overarching goals are several sets of policy objectives, including fostering each of the following (Garcea 2006):

- Awareness and appreciation of cultural diversity and the value of such diversity
- Cross-cultural understanding
- Social cohesion and harmony
- Participation by members of ethno-cultural groups in the economic, social, cultural and political spheres
- Preservation, promotion, and sharing of cultural heritages.

Responsibility for Advancing Policy Goals. Responsibility for advancing goals is generally assigned either to a cabinet minister or, as is the case in Nova Scotia, a cabinet committee. Generally, ministers are assisted by departmental officials working in a multiculturalism branch, office, secretariat, or commission. In performing their functions, ministers and their officials are assisted by advisory committees at both the federal level and the provincial level (i.e., British Columbia, Manitoba, Ontario, Quebec, Nova Scotia, New Brunswick, and PEI). In recent years, the function of these advisory bodies has broadened from providing advice on multiculturalism per se to devoting more attention to the actual integration and inclusion of new immigrants.

Resources for Advancing Multiculturalism Policy Goals. The multiculturalism policies generally contain provisions regarding who is responsible for the allocation of resources for multiculturalism programs and projects, the types of initiatives that should be supported, and the types of organizations that will qualify to apply for funding for various types of initiatives designed to advance the policy goals. However, the policies are silent on the amount of financial resources and the precise types of programs or projects that should be funded. Those particular matters are subject to governmental decisions and discretion. All jurisdictions have established some funding programs devoted to supporting multiculturalism initiatives in governmental and non-governmental sectors. In the case of the federal government, it provides funding directly to community based organizations and to provincial governments pursuant to provisions in bilateral agreements. In British Columbia, for example, federal funds are transferred to the provincial government pursuant to Annex B of the Agreement for Canada-British Columbia Co-operation on Immigration. Such agreements with provinces related to funding multiculturalism programs are sanctioned by provisions in the *Canadian Multiculturalism Act* that explicitly authorize ministers of the federal Crown to negotiate and sign them.

An example of a federal program designed to deliver funds directly to community based organizations is Inter-Action. This program has been established by Citizenship and Immigration Canada (CIC) for the purpose of providing funds to community based organizations and to private sector organizations (though not for profit) for initiatives that will facilitate "the socio-economic integration of individuals and communities and their contributions to building an integrated and socially cohesive society" (Canada 2010a). Toward that end, the program funds initiatives that enhance positive interaction among cultural and faith communities. It has two funding streams, for projects and for events. Whereas the former provides funding for long-term, multi-year community engagement and development projects to promote integration, the latter provides funding for projects that foster intercultural/interfaith understanding, civic memory and pride, or respect for core democratic values.

The level of funding and types of funding programs vary across jurisdictions. Precise calculations and comparisons are very difficult not only because of the multifaceted nature of the actual multiculturalism programs and projects but also due to the wide array of funding programs. Whether the level of funding is adequate and the distribution of funds is appropriate has been and remains a matter of considerable debate in the public realm.

PROVISIONS ON THE PROTECTION OF RIGHTS FOR CULTURAL GROUPS
AND THEIR MEMBERS

None of the policies provides any cultural group or organization or any
of their members with special or unique rights. Instead, the policies state
that the rights of such groups and their members should be recognized
and respected to the fullest extent possible, subject only to the norms and
principles of a liberal democratic society, the Canadian Charter of Rights
and Freedoms, human rights acts, and any other official government
policies that do not contravene either the constitution, the human rights
acts, or any other constitutionally valid statutes. As discussed elsewhere
in this chapter, the recognition and protection of their rights is provided
in the federal and provincial human rights acts and two sections of the
Charter, namely, section 15(1), which deals with equality rights, and section 27, which states that the "Charter shall be interpreted in a manner
consistent with the preservation and enhancement of the multiculturalism
heritage of Canadians."

PROVISIONS ON MATERIAL BENEFITS FOR CULTURAL GROUPS AND
ORGANIZATIONS PROMOTING MULTICULTURALISM

None of the policies provides any cultural group or organization or their
members with special or unique financial or non-financial benefits or supports. Many of the policies are completely silent on this matter, but some
state that the provision of any benefits to which the groups are entitled
should not be adversely affected by discriminatory policies or practices. It
is generally understood, however, that cultural organizations are entitled
to apply for program and project funding. Their success in being funded
is contingent on two key criteria: first, that the proposed programs or projects are consonant with the goals and objectives of the funding program;
and second, that they are incorporated as not-for-profit organizations.
The second criterion is articulated explicitly in British Columbia's multiculturalism policy, which states that only "a not for profit organization
may apply to the minister for a grant" (British Columbia 1996). Whether
the multiculturalism policy framework has contributed to or hinders the
integration and inclusion of immigrants and members of racial, ethnic,
and religious minorities in Canada is a highly debated issue (Garcea
2009). We side with those who believe that multiculturalism policies
have been and continue to be valuable for the integration and inclusion
of immigrants and minorities both at the symbolic and practical levels.
At the symbolic level, they serve as a reminder that cultural diversity is
generally valued and respected in Canada. At the practical level, they
provide a legitimate statutory or non-statutory basis for governments to

develop policies, program, and projects that contribute to the two over-arching goals of creating warm, welcoming, and inclusive communities and of promoting the economic, social, cultural, and political integration of immigrants and minorities.

HUMAN RIGHTS POLICY FRAMEWORK

Another set of policies designed to facilitate the integration and inclusion of immigrants and minorities is embodied in the Canadian Charter of Rights and Freedoms as well as human rights acts and codes of the federal, provincial, and territorial governments. The Charter, as well as all of those acts and codes, echoes the key principles articulated in what is referred to as the International Bill of Human Rights, which consists of the Universal Declaration on Human Rights (UDHR) signed by Canada in 1948 as well as the two international covenants on human rights (i.e., International Covenants on Economic, Social and Cultural Rights and the International Covenant on Civil and Political Rights) that were drafted in 1966 and came into force in 1976 (UNAC 2010). Those United Nations documents impose a moral obligation on member states to protect and preserve a wide range of rights and freedoms of citizens and various categories of permanent and temporary residents (e.g., immigrants and refugees).

CANADIAN CHARTER OF RIGHTS AND FREEDOMS

The Canadian Charter of Rights and Freedoms affords all immigrants with permanent resident status the same rights and freedoms, except for the political rights to vote or stand for elected office within the political system, as are afforded to citizens in relation to the policies and actions of the federal, provincial, and territorial governments. Section 2 guarantees them fundamental freedoms (i.e., conscience and religion, thought, belief, opinion, and expression, peaceful assembly, and association). Section 6 guarantees them mobility rights to enter and exit Canada and to move within Canada based on citizenship standing. Citizens have the right to enter, remain in, or leave the country, and citizens and permanent residents have the right not only to move and take up residence in any province but also to gain a livelihood in any province. The only limitation to the internal mobility rights is that they are subject to any laws in a province that do not discriminate on the basis of present or previous residence, or that provide reasonable residency requirements as qualification for receiving publicly provided services. Sections 7 to 14 safeguard their legal rights, including the right to life, liberty, and security of the person, as well as protection from unreasonable search or seizure, the right to be informed of the reason for the arrest or detention, and the right to an interpreter if they do not understand the language in legal proceedings.

Section 15 provides immigrants and minorities with equality rights and the benefits that might accrue to them through equity programs. Section 15.(1) states that "Every individual is equal before and under the law and has the right to the equal protection and equal benefit of the law without discrimination and, in particular, without discrimination based on race, national or ethnic origin, colour, religion, sex, age or mental or physical disability." Section 15.(2) sanctions equity as follows: "Subsection (1) does not preclude any law, program or activity that has as its object the amelioration of conditions of disadvantaged individuals or groups including those that are disadvantaged because of race, national or ethnic origin, colour, religion, sex, age or mental or physical disability."

Section 20 provides immigrants and minorities with the right to communicate and receive services from the federal parliament and government in either official language where either the number of persons who speak those languages or the nature of the service warrants it. It also provides them with that right in relation to the New Brunswick legislature and government.

Section 27 provides additional rights and protections for immigrants and minorities insofar as it states that the "Charter shall be interpreted in a manner consistent with the preservation and enhancement of the multicultural heritage of Canadians."

Although the Charter guarantees all members, including immigrants and members of minority groups, many rights and freedoms, those rights and freedoms are not absolute. They can be limited or circumscribed either by Section 1, which states that they are subject to "such reasonable limits prescribed by law as can be demonstrably justified in a free and democratic society," and the notwithstanding clause articulated in Section 33, which authorizes the national parliament or a provincial legislature to expressly declare in legislation that all or part of any statute shall be valid notwithstanding a provision in section 2 or sections 7 to 15 of the Charter. In effect, therefore, the fundamental freedoms, legal rights, and equality rights are not absolute.

NATIONAL, PROVINCIAL AND TERRITORIAL HUMAN RIGHTS ACTS/CODES

Policies articulated in human rights acts and codes also perform an important role in the integration and inclusion of immigrants and minorities. Indeed, this has been the major purpose of such statutes and policies since their inception in the 1940s. Their genesis can be traced to 1944 when Ontario enacted the *Racial Discrimination Act* and to 1947 when Saskatchewan enacted the *Bill of Rights Act* (Howe and Johnson 2000). Between 1951 and 1961 several provinces and the federal government enacted either employment practices acts (i.e., Ontario in 1951, Manitoba, Nova Scotia, and Canada in 1953), or fair accommodations acts (i.e., Ontario in 1954, Saskatchewan in 1956, Manitoba, Nova Scotia, and New Brunswick in 1959, and British Columbia in 1961). In 1960, of course, the federal government also enacted the Canadian Bill of Rights that, despite the fact that most if not all of its contents are now embodied in the Charter and the federal government's *Human Rights Act*, still remains on the books as a notable piece of human rights legislation that applies only to the federal government within the context of the Canadian federal system. Its core provisions are designed to guarantee fundamental legal rights and the fundamental freedoms of religion, speech, assembly and association, and the press, without discrimination on the basis of race, national origin, colour, religion, or sex (Canada 1960). Since 1962 each province and the federal government has enacted human rights acts.

PRINCIPAL PURPOSES OF HUMAN RIGHTS ACTS / CODES

The principal purposes of the various human rights acts in force today are: (a) to ensure that everyone recognizes and respects the human rights of all citizens and permanent residents; (b) to eliminate or at least reduce the adoption of policies or practices that are discriminatory; (c) to provide avenues for filing complaints for those who feel that their human rights have been transgressed; and (d) to require compensatory action and/or corrective action from anyone who has transgressed either a person's rights or a particular provision of the human rights act or code.

The general areas in which discrimination is prohibited tend to be wide ranging. In British Columbia, for example, this includes discrimination or harmful behaviour in the following areas: publications; accommodation for members of any designated groups; access to a particular service or facility; purchase of property; renting property; employment advertisements; wages; employment; and membership in or representation by trade union, employers' organization, or occupational association (British Columbia 1996). Other statutes are generally not as specific or clear regarding the precise areas in which discrimination is not allowed. Instead, they tend to list the prohibited grounds of discrimination without specifying the areas in which it is prohibited; consequently, they are deemed to apply to all areas of the lives of citizens, permanent residents, and other people who are lawfully residing in Canada, other than those areas that may be specifically excluded.

Prohibited Grounds of Discrimination in Human Rights Acts/Codes. All human rights statutes contain provisions related to the prohibited grounds of discrimination. The lists of prohibited grounds of differential treatment in provincial, territorial, and federal statutes and policies are quite extensive. They include race, colour, nationality, ancestry, place of origin, language, physical or mental disability, association, social condition, social origin, dependence on alcohol or drugs, gender, pregnancy or childbirth, sexual orientation, family status, marital status, age, receipt of public assistance, record of criminal conviction, and pardoned conviction. Although the lists of prohibited grounds of discrimination in most Canadian jurisdictions are very similar, they are not completely identical. Nevertheless, all contain key provisions that provide immigrants and minorities some protection from discrimination in most, if not all, areas or dimensions of their daily lives based not only on race, nationality, ethnicity, ancestry, and place of origin but also on other prohibited grounds of discrimination.

In addition to the provisions regarding prohibited grounds of discrimination, the human rights statutes also contain provisions related to what might be termed prohibited grounds or modes of conduct or actions in relation to any particular group or individual. This includes, for example, harassing and hateful conduct or actions directed either at a particular group or the members of a particular group by virtue of their race or religion and the distribution of hate literature.

Special Exemptions for Religious Groups and Not for Profit Organizations in Human Rights Acts/Codes. Generally, the human rights statutes also contain provisions that provide exemption for religious institutions and not-for-profit organizations from having to adhere to all the grounds of discrimination if doing so would not only contravene their legitimate fundamental purpose for existence (or, if you will, their raison d'être) but could possibly also compromise their ability to exist. In other words, these types of institutions and organizations can adopt what otherwise would be seen as discriminatory exclusionary policies or practices if they have valid or legitimate reasons for doing so. In some of the statutes, there is no explicit reference to religious institutions and not-for-profit organizations. Instead, what one finds is a more general provision, such as the one contained in section 11 of Alberta's statute regarding reasonable and justifiable contravention to the effect that "a contravention of this Act shall be deemed not to have occurred if the person who is alleged to have contravened the Act shows that the alleged contravention was reasonable and justifiable in the circumstances."

Provisions Related to Special Equity Programs in Human Rights Acts/Codes. Another set of provisions within human rights acts that have important implications for immigrants and members of minority groups are those that permit or even compel institutions, organizations, or companies to create special programs for designated groups that have been the victims of systemic discrimination or other inequities. Such provisions are intended to facilitate efforts to eliminate systemic discrimination and provide some redress for historical inequities. The predominant forms of such programs are employment equity policies. All human rights statutes, except Alberta's, contain explicit provisions regarding this particular matter. Alberta's statute neither prohibits nor sanctions such efforts but is simply silent on the matter. These provisions reveal a broadening of the scope of human rights statutes over time from preventing and penalizing discriminatory actions on a very limited number of prohibited sites of discrimination and for a very limited number of designated groups, to a larger number of prohibited sites and a larger number of designated groups, and ultimately a broadening of the notion of discrimination to include systemic equity concerns.

Provisions Related to Public Education in Human Rights Acts/Codes. Another set of provisions in human rights statutes that have been beneficial for the integration and inclusion of immigrants and members of minority groups are those that mandate or at least permit human rights commissions to undertake public education initiatives so as to increase awareness of the social value of diversity as well as the harmful social effects of discrimination and other negative behaviours such as harassment of individuals and hate campaigns aimed at groups. Such provisions are included to facilitate efforts of commissions to take either a lead or supportive role in the creation of warm, welcoming, and inclusive communities into which immigrants and members of minorities will be able to integrate with greater ease, respect, and dignity.

Provisions Related to Human Rights Commissions and Tribunals in Human Rights Acts/Codes. The human rights statutes also contain provisions related to the creation, mandates, and powers of human rights commissions and human rights tribunals (Hucker 1997). Such commissions have similar structures and functions across jurisdictions. They receive and initiate complaints of human rights violations, and they attempt mediated settlements. When mediated settlements cannot be achieved, commissions establish an independent tribunal to hear and make a judgment on the complaint. Whereas at least two jurisdictions (i.e., Ontario and Canada) have established permanent tribunals, in all other jurisdictions they are established as the need arises. Since 2008 Ontario has been unique in Canada by virtue of its Human Rights Commission no longer having a direct role in hearing and mediating complaints of discrimination (OHRC 2008). Complaints of rights violations are now heard and mediated by the permanent Human Rights Tribunal of Ontario, supported by the newly created Human Rights Legal Support Centre, which offers advice and resources to prospective complainants. The Ontario Human Rights

Commission's new mandate includes human rights promotion, proactive and preventative measures, conducting public inquiries, assisting with reviews of legislation, and reporting annually to the provincial legislature on the state of human rights.

Anti-Racism Policy Framework

In addition to the anti-racism policies, plans, and programs developed and implemented within the scope of the human rights acts and codes discussed in the previous section, the integration and inclusion of immigrants and minorities have been pursued by what are commonly and broadly referred to as anti-racism action plans or programs. Anti-racism plans and programs exist at the federal, provincial, and local levels.

Federal Anti-Racism Action Plan

The primary federal anti-racism policy initiative, released in 2005, is A Canada for All: Canada's Action Plan Against Racism (CAPAR), a relatively comprehensive strategy designed to provide policy coherence across 20 federal departments and agencies. Coordinated by the Department of Citizenship and Immigration (CIC 2010a), CAPAR represents "the federal government's approach to addressing broad social policy issues such as social cohesion and systemic barriers to inclusion" (ibid.). In achieving CAPAR's goals, the federal government promotes anti-racism initiatives both within and beyond its departments and agencies. It provides special allocations to its own departments and agencies, which use some of those allocations for their own anti-racism programming while distributing the rest to provinces pursuant to bilateral immigration agreements as well as providing grants to special agencies and community groups for programs and projects aimed at eliminating racism and race based barriers to inclusion and participation. CAPAR also promotes the values of multiculturalism, and makes grants to university-based researchers to build the knowledge base regarding various aspects of racism and anti-racism (Canada 2005).

In assessing CAPAR's contribution to anti-racism, the 2010 Annual Report on the Operation of the Canadian Multiculturalism Act states that its activities "continued to achieve results in key areas such as law enforcement, workplace discrimination, youth and newcomer integration, race-based issues in the justice system, and hate-crime reporting" (CIC 2010b). The report outlines new and ongoing initiatives to promote CAPAR's policy goals across federal departments. Through the Department of Citizenship and Immigration, CAPAR-funded activities include the Welcoming Communities Initiative (WCI), which "supports locally based approaches that foster settlement and integration by breaking down barriers and building welcoming and inclusive communities" (ibid.). Approaches in this regard include working with and supporting societal organizations to "meet newcomers' needs," such as settlement workers and partnerships in schools, libraries, and community health centres as well as mentoring, networking, and outreach programs. In 2009–10, more than $4 million was allocated through the WCI to 35 projects as part of the "Modernized Settlement Program." The other major CAPAR initiative through the Department of Citizenship and Immigration is the development of the nationally standardized data collection on hate-motivated crime, in partnership with the Canadian Centre for Justice Statistics (part of Statistics Canada). The 2008 report reveals the ongoing and heightened need for initiatives of this sort, as hate-motivated crime increased by 35 percent from 2007 to 2008 (ibid.).

Other notable CAPAR initiatives across federal departments include those developed by the Department of Justice and the Department of Human Resources and Skills Development. Under CAPAR the Department of Justice pursues "equality before the law" through the Justice Partnership and Innovation Fund which supports projects that explore racialized issues in the justice system such as "overrepresentation of certain racialized groups, both as victims and perpetrators" and develops approaches of "intervention" and "public legal education information" (ibid.). The Department of Human Resources and Skills Development's major contribution under CAPAR is the Racism-Free Workplace Strategy, which "aims to help employers address racism through removing discriminatory barriers to recruitment, retention and advancement of visible minorities and Aboriginal peoples in the workplace" (ibid.). As an example of policy supplementation in Canada's diversity management framework, it constitutes "an important part of the Government of Canada's broader commitment to enhancing social inclusion through employment equity and multiculturalism." The strategy functions primarily to raise "awareness among employers and employees in workplaces covered under the *Employment Equity Act* and the Federal Contractors Program about the benefits of fair and inclusive workplaces" (ibid.). In 2009–10, 76 sessions were delivered to federally regulated employers on themes including "Building Inclusive Workplaces," the "Business Case for Racial Diversity," and "Mastering Aboriginal Inclusion."

PROVINCIAL ANTI-RACISM POLICIES, ACTION PLANS, AND PROGRAMS

Provincial and territorial governments have also established some special anti-racism policies, action plans, or programs that can be grouped into two categories. The first category consists of narrowly oriented, single-sector initiatives, and the second consists of broadly oriented multi-sector initiatives, comparable in form and scope to the federal government's CAPAR. All provinces and territories have several narrow-based single-sector policies, action plans, or programs. For example, in most provinces, anti-racism action plans or programs have been developed for the education sector to achieve at least two key objectives (SafeHealthySchools Org. 2010). The first is to enlighten students on the existence of racism and the need to eliminate it by infusing the curriculum with anti-racism instructional modules. The second objective is to eliminate structural inequalities in educational experiences and outcomes faced by minority racial groups within the educational system. Two notable examples of policies that address both of those objectives are Manitoba's Kindergarten to Grade 12 Action Plan for Ethnocultural Equity (Manitoba 2006) and British Columbia's Diversity BC Schools (British Columbia 2004), established in 2001 and updated in 2008 (SafeHealthySchools.Org 2010). Only Quebec and British Columbia have established broad-based multi-sector action plans. Each of these is discussed in turn below.

Quebec's Anti-Racism Action Plan

Quebec's anti-racism action plan has been articulated in three successive policy statements and one statute. The first policy statement was the Declaration of Intercultural and Interracial Relations adopted by the National Assembly in 1986 (Quebec 1986). The declaration condemns racism and commits the provincial government to encourage the full participation of every person in the economic, social, and cultural development of Quebec, regardless of colour, religion, or ethnic or national origin. The key principles of this policy were echoed in the 1990 policy, Au Québec pour bâtir ensemble: Énoncé de politique en matière d'immigration et d'intégration (Quebec 1990), which articulated the goals and objectives of integrating newcomers into the Quebecois milieu in a way that contributed to full integration and respect for their rights, and minimized racism and other barriers to the full development of the Quebec society and economy. In 2004 Quebec adopted the three year immigration and integration action plan. Its key goals related to anti-racism include lending greater support to employers and institutions in building a more inclusive Quebec, and emphasizing the value of immigration to Quebec's development and its fight against discrimination (Quebec 2004).

The Quebec government's commitment to anti-racism is also articulated in the three policy brochures issued in 2008 in the wake of the Bouchard-Taylor Commission on reasonable accommodations for racial, ethnic, and religious minorities. One brochure focuses on measures to facilitate the linguistic economic, social, and political integration of immigrants, and another focuses on articulating common values that should be adhered to both by immigrants and citizens. The latter policy brochure even contains a declaration of Quebec's common values that would be made available to newcomers to sign. The brochures and the declaration articulated the common values that Quebec is a liberal, democratic, and pluralist society in which political and religious authority are separate; Quebec society is founded on the primacy of the rule of law in which discrimination on the grounds enumerated in Quebec's Charter of Rights and Freedom, including race, is not permitted; and rights and freedoms in Quebec must be exercised in ways that do not adversely affect either the rights of others or the common good (Quebec 2008).

In recent years Quebec has established the Diversity Action Program, designed to provide financial support for organizations devoted to advancing the objectives of the Ministry of Immigration and Cultural Communities to achieve the full participation of persons of all origins in the development of Quebec society. The stated goals and objectives are to support members of cultural communities to integrate into the labour market, foster intercultural understanding, prevent and combat discrimination, prevent immigrant youth from joining street gangs, support persons who experience exclusion due to discrimination, and orient and train persons from cultural communities to participate in civic affairs by, among other things, occupying key positions in advisory and governing bodies (Quebec 2010).

During the past two years the Quebec government has been shepherding Bill 16 through the legislature. That bill, titled *An Act to Promote Action by the Administration with Respect to Cultural Diversity*, is designed to empower the minister responsible for immigration and integration to direct the administration to undertake initiatives related to cultural diversity, and to combat discrimination based on race, colour, religion, or ethnic or national origin (Quebec 2009). These initiatives include developing and implementing a policy and action plan to foster society's openness to cultural diversity and the full participation of members of cultural communities in Quebec society. The bill also requires administrative agencies, including the National Assembly, to adopt a cultural diversity management policy that is separate and distinct from their policies related to equal access to employment. The new policies are to outline policy goals and the means by which to achieve them and to report on the success of their implementation. It also stipulates that the Council of Intercultural Relations is responsible for advising the minister on the full participation of members of ethnocultural communities, and that a system of annual progress reports must be established.

British Columbia's Anti-Racism Action Plan

As part of its ongoing commitment to strengthen multiculturalism and eliminate racism in British Columbia, the provincial government commissioned a scoping review that identified eight emerging and promising practices in multiculturalism and anti-racism programming from several jurisdictions including Canada, Australia, New Zealand, and the United Kingdom. Governmental and non-governmental organizations were encouraged to review this programming as part of their efforts to improve their own practices (British Columbia 2008a). Over the past five years British Columbia has implemented a diversity management and anti-racism action plan consisting of two key complementary components: WelcomeBC and EmbraceBC. WelcomeBC, launched in 2007 by the provincial Immigration and Integration Branch, has a "twofold purpose: to assist immigrants in accessing a wide variety of settlement and integration services, and to ensure that B.C. communities have the capacity to be welcoming and inclusive" (British Columbia 2010a). This component is co-funded by the provincial and federal governments pursuant to the bilateral Canada-British Columbia immigration agreement through the British Columbia Settlement and Adaptation Program (BCSAP) for which the primary goal is to "support the successful settlement and adaptation of immigrants and refugees to British Columbia" (British Columbia 2010a). Funding for special community projects under the WelcomeBC initiative is disbursed through the following four facets of the Welcoming and Inclusive Communities Program (WICWP): community partnership development, knowledge development and exchange, public education, and demonstration projects. The WICWP is a three-year project launched in June 2008 (to be evaluated in June 2011) with the aim of strengthening "community capacity to support immigrant settlement and integration, to eliminate racism, to value and respect multiculturalism, and foster welcoming and inclusive communities" (British Columbia 2008b). The WICWP was developed by the Multiculturalism and Inclusive Communities Office (MICO) of the Ministry of the Attorney General, which is responsible for funding and managing anti-racism and multiculturalism initiatives through the British Columbia Anti-racism and Multiculturalism Program (BCAMP).

EmbraceBC contributes to achieving the goals and objectives of WelcomeBC's Settlement and Inclusive Communities priority of increasing understanding and appreciation of cultural diversity, multiculturalism, and the elimination of racism (British Columbia 2010c). It does so by supporting projects that create an inclusive multicultural society in which both newcomers and communities play a role in successful integration. The stated priorities of EmbraceBC are to achieve the following:

- Encourage full participation in all aspects of the economic, social, cultural, and political life of British Columbia.
- Engage a broad and diverse group of partners and participants.
- Build trust and relationships between Aboriginal and non-Aboriginal peoples.
- Address racist behaviour and practices which impede the full participation of individuals and groups in civil society.

- Develop responsibility and ownership on an individual and communal level to eliminate racism.
- Promote and support a leadership model that reflects the diversity of stakeholders involved in a project.
- Demonstrate an understanding and analysis of complex intersectional identities and the relationship of gender, sexual orientation, religion, and class with race and ethnicity (British Columbia 2010d and 2010e).

EmbraceBC derives its mandate from the provincial Multiculturalism Act, is administered by MICO, and allocates funds received from the federal government pursuant to the bilateral immigration agreement between the federal and provincial governments to cultural groups committed to fostering multiculturalism and combating racism. In advancing the objectives of the two interrelated programs' action plans, the provincial government has developed tools that can be used by communities and employers, and provides funding for initiatives undertaken by what are referred to as "communities of interest."

EmbraceBC provides funding to support multiculturalism and anti-racism projects in the areas of arts engagement, community engagement and dialogue, inclusive leadership and mentorship, interfaith bridging, organizing against racism and hate, and public education (British Columbia 2010e). Several notable resources and campaigns have been developed. A notable example is the Safe Harbour: Respect for All project, which aims to equip businesses and organizations to be welcoming and inclusive of diverse customers and employees. Other examples include three anti-racism programs for youths. One of these, Multiculturalism in Communities: A Guide to Developing and Sustaining Dialogue Change Agent Handbook, is designed to provide youth aged 15–20 with useful information regarding myths and facts about racism and questions to consider. It can be used by youth to develop personal pride and accountability in creating positive change in their communities and to understand that as individuals, they have the ability to prevent racism. The second project is Make a Case Against Racism, which encourages students in grades 4–7 to take personal responsibility for preventing racism, while celebrating the province's cultural diversity through music and art. Designed to complement provincial school curriculum, the initiative uses a proactive approach to examining discrimination. The third project is a video contest titled Racism Stop It! (British Columbia 2010e).

MUNICIPAL ANTI-RACISM POLICY INITIATIVES

Today, municipalities are central actors in anti-racism initiatives and, by reflecting specific contextual challenges, contribute to the diversity and diffusion of anti-racism policy. Increasingly municipalities have autonomous policy-setting roles in the area of anti-racism, beneath the overarching, and frequently supportive, roles of provincial and federal governments (Icart, Labelle, and Antonius 2005). In response to particular and localized diversity-related policy challenges, many Canadian municipalities have created relatively robust anti-racism initiatives. Notable examples include Toronto's "Plan of Action for the Elimination of Racism and Discrimination" adopted in 2001, the "Montreal Declaration against Racial Discrimination" adopted in 1989, replaced in 2002 with the "Montreal Declaration on Cultural Diversity and Inclusion" (ibid.), and Saskatoon's successive cultural diversity and race relations policies, action plans, and committees established since 1989, for which it received the Federation of Canadian Municipalities (FCM) anti-racism award (Garcea and Garg 2009).

Municipal anti-racism initiatives have been fostered not only by more progressive and proactive officials at the municipal level but also by special initiatives established by the federal and provincial governments. An example of such an important initiative by the federal government is the Welcoming Communities funding program established pursuant to the its anti-racism action plan (i.e., CAPAR), which provides funding for local communities to develop various initiatives designed to eliminate racism and to foster a positive environment that will facilitate the integration of immigrants. An example of an important initiative by a provincial government is found in Ontario where the OHRC has developed the manual "Anti-Racism and Anti-Discrimination for Municipalities," designed to help municipalities initiate and improve their anti-racism and anti-discrimination programs. In addition to outlining issues, options, and approaches, it includes best practices in various jurisdictions for dealing with racism and discrimination (OHRC 2010).

The anti-racism programs of municipalities have also been fostered by progressive special initiatives established by national and international organizations. At the national level, the Federation of Canadian Municipalities (FCM), composed of municipalities and provincial and territorial municipal associations, adopted the declaration on "Improving Interracial Relations in Canadian Municipalities" (FCM 1986) and the "Policy Statement on Interracial Relations" (FCM 1993). As part of its efforts to profile and promote best practices of managing diversity and eliminating racism, the FCM instituted an award given annually to a municipality that has established a significant anti-racism or diversity management policy or program. In 2003 the FCM, in partnership with the Laidlaw Foundation, also commissioned the report "Building Inclusive Communities: Cross-Canada Perspectives and Challenges" (Clutterbuck and Novick 2003) to provide municipalities with a comprehensive conceptualization of social inclusion that would be useful in their efforts to build inclusive and supportive communities. Collectively, these initiatives by FCM encourage and assist municipalities in developing and implementing anti-racism programs (Icart, Labelle and Antonius 2005). In recent years the initiatives of both the FCM and its members have been stimulated by UNESCO's ten-point action plan titled International Coalition of Cities against Racism, launched in 2004 to assist the development of municipal anti-racism policies and programs (CCFU 2006). Under this initiative the Canadian Commission for UNESCO (CCU) developed the Canadian Coalition of Municipalities against Racism and Discrimination (CCMARD). The CCMARD was officially launched 2007 in Calgary to implement the ten-point action plan and to develop further directions of anti-racism and discrimination initiatives. Currently there are 40 Canadian signatory municipalities to the CCMARD.

EMPLOYMENT EQUITY, PAY EQUALITY, AND PAY EQUITY FRAMEWORK

The employment equity policy framework together with the pay equality and pay equity frameworks have had and continue to have important implications for the economic integration and inclusion of immigrants and members of minority groups. The employment equity framework in Canada has international, national, provincial, and municipal (local) components. Some of these components are linked with each other in a complementary and supplementary manner to provide an employment equity framework that is relatively broad, comprehensive, and robust (Canada 2001). The purpose of the various components of this framework is to advance one or both of the following objectives: to protect the human rights of all citizens and non-citizens (i.e., permanent residents, and persons on special visas) in the workplace (Ventura 1995), and to provide a legal basis to establish employment equity policies programs for designated groups. Toward these ends, the various components of the employment equity policy framework contain provisions that (1) outline prohibited grounds of discrimination in the workplace against citizens, permanent residents, and persons on special visas; (2) outline the principles and parameters of any employment policies or programs for designated groups; and (3) identify the designated groups.

The employment equity, pay equality, and pay equity policies of the national, provincial, and territorial governments are underpinned by the International Labour Standards, which were promulgated by the International Labour Organization (ILO), a United Nations agency mandated to facilitate negotiation of and adherence to the standards by signatory countries (Gravel and Delpech 2008). The ILO's Elimination of Discrimination in Respect of Employment and Occupation Convention (No. 111) promulgated in 1958 was ratified by Canada in November 1964. This convention supplemented the Equal Remuneration Convention (No. 100) promulgated in 1951, which was eventually ratified by Canada in November 1972. Whereas Convention 100 is based on the core principle of equal pay for equal work, Convention 111 is based on the principle that employees should not be subject to direct or indirect (i.e., systemic) discrimination that limits equality of opportunity on the basis of race, colour, sex, religion, political opinion, nationality, social origin, and other criteria as may be determined the federal government after consultation with representative employers' and workers' organizations. As a signatory of those two conventions, the federal government, and by extension also the provincial and territorial governments, are compelled to adhere to their core principles and provisions, especially given that they are affirmed in the constitution and in statutes (Eid 2001).

NATIONAL EMPLOYMENT EQUITY POLICIES AND PROGRAMS

At the national level, employment equity policies and programs designed to improve conditions of members of disadvantaged groups are sanctioned by the equity provisions in section 15 (2) of the Canadian Charter of Rights and Freedoms. Section 25(2) states that the previous section on equality rights "does not preclude any law, program or activity that has as its object the amelioration of conditions of disadvantaged individuals or groups including those that are disadvantaged because of race, national or ethnic origin, colour, religion, sex, age or mental or physical disability." This includes any law, program, or activity established by the federal, provincial, and territorial governments as well by regional and local governments and public authorities. It does not include private sector organizations, which are subject to federal, provincial, and territorial statutes or policies for purposes of employment equity (Canadian Bar Association 2010).

The federal government has enacted three statutes that have implications for employment equity within the scope of its jurisdictional authority – the *Canadian Human Rights Act*, the *Public Service Act*, and the *Employment Equity Act*. Collectively, these three statutes deal with employment equity in relation to the federal public service per se, other components of the federal government's administrative system, and federally regulated employers.

EMPLOYMENT EQUITY PROVISIONS IN THE *CANADIAN HUMAN RIGHTS ACT*

The *Canadian Human Rights Act* contains two sets of provisions related to the establishment of employment equity plans by employers. Whereas section 16 (1) sanctions the creation of employment equity policies, plans, or programs on a voluntary basis with or without the assistance of the Human Rights Commission, section 53 (2) authorizes commission officials to issue an order to any organization against whom a claim of discriminatory practice has been substantiated to adopt a special program, plan, or arrangement, including an employment equity plan.

EMPLOYMENT EQUITY PROVISIONS IN THE *PUBLIC SERVICE EMPLOYMENT ACT*

The *Public Service Employment Act* (PSEA) also sanctions the establishment of employment equity programs in the federal public service. More specifically, section 22(2) of the PSEA authorizes the Public Service Commission (PSC) to make regulations to facilitate the implementation of employment equity programs for members of the four designated groups (women, visible minorities, persons with disabilities, and Aboriginal people) listed in section 3 of the *Employment Equity Act*. Section 3 of the PSEA regulations stipulates that a member of a designated group may be appointed, in accordance with the employment equity program, without regard to any priority afforded to any other person who is not a member of a designated group. The responsibility for advancing the goals and objectives of employment equity within the public service rests with the Treasury Board, the Public Service Commission, and departmental deputy ministers.

EMPLOYMENT EQUITY PROVISIONS IN THE *EMPLOYMENT EQUITY ACT*

The *Employment Equity Act* (EEA) establishes the grounds for the development and implementation of employment equity policies, plans, or programs for the above four designated groups working in the federal public service, federally regulated employers, and federal contractors (Canada 2010b). This is by far the most ambitious employment equity legislation in the country in terms of the number of governmental and non-governmental employers to which it applies, the number of employees covered, and the strict mandatory requirement for employers falling within the scope of the act to develop an equity plan and submit annual reports on their respective plans.

The *Employment Equity Act* applies only to some organizations in the public and private sectors (Canada 2010c). In the public sector it applies to the following three portions of federal public administration: (a) those set out in Schedule I or IV to the *Financial Administration Act*; (b) those set out in Schedule V to the *Financial Administration Act* that employ at least one hundred employees; and (c) those not specified in any schedule of the *Financial Administration Act* that employ at least 100 employees, including the Canadian Forces and the Royal Canadian Mounted Police, as may be specified by order of the Governor in Council on the recommendation of the Treasury Board in consultation with the minister responsible for the specified portion. However, it does not apply to a departmental corporation as defined in section 2 of the *Financial Administration Act* (section 3).

In the private sector, the EEA applies to firms that employ at least one hundred employees on or in connection with a federal work, undertaking, or business as defined in section 2 of the Canada Labour Code. This includes an array of federally regulated employers such as banking companies, broadcasting companies, telecommunication companies, transportation companies (air, land, and maritime) that operate interprovincially, corporations controlled by two or more provincial governments, and corporations that deal with uranium or grains. It also includes corporations established to perform any function or duty on behalf of the Government of Canada either on a contractual or partnership basis.

Section 5 of the EEA stipulates that all public and private sectors employers that fall within the scope of that statute must submit an employment equity plan and an annual report demonstrating that their efforts and results are in compliance with the principles of employment equity in managing their human resources. However, section 6 of the act states that employers are not obligated to implement employment equity programs or a particular employment equity initiative if this will cause undue hardship, the hiring of unfit or unqualified persons, promotion not based on merit, or the creation of new positions.

FEDERAL CONTRACTORS PROGRAM

In addition to the employment equity frameworks established in the three statutes discussed above, the federal government also established the Federal Contractors Program (FCP) to advance the goals and objectives of the EEA in relation to contracts worth at least $200,000 signed by the federal government with companies that employee at least 100 employees. The FCP requires companies to establish employment equity plans or programs that are consonant with the federal guidelines (2010d). Four agencies are involved in regulating employment equity at the federal level. The Canadian Human Rights Commission deals with plans and complaints related to both private and public sector employers that are federally regulated; the Public Service Commission is responsible for employment equity within the context of human resource management in the federal public service; the Treasury Board Secretariat oversees the actual administration of employment equity in the context of all federal departments and agencies; Human Resources and Skills Development Canada (HRSDC) is responsible for compliance reviews related to the FCP and also for conducting research related to the EEA and collecting data related to employers regulated by the federal government.

Provincial and Territorial Employment Equity Programs

In all provinces and territories, except for Alberta, employment equity policies and practices for either or both the public and private sectors are explicitly sanctioned by human rights statutes or other special statutes (Canada 2001). While Alberta's *Human Rights Act* is essentially silent on employment equity, its section 11 provides protection for any organization or firm in the public or private sector wishing to establish an employment equity policy, plan, or program. Section 11 states that a "contravention of this Act shall be deemed not to have occurred if the person who is alleged to have contravened the Act shows that the alleged contravention was reasonable and justifiable in the circumstances" (Alberta 2009). An information sheet articulates the commission's commitment to supporting "the development and creation of employment equity policies and programs" by providing consulting and education services as required (Alberta 2010).

Whereas human rights statutes with provisions related to employment equity generally cover both public and private sector employers, the special statutes or policies apply more narrowly. Moreover, most, if not all, of those that apply to the public sector tend to apply only to the provincial or territorial public services per se, rather than other governmental organizations at the provincial, territorial, or local government levels. The notable exception is Quebec's *Act Respecting Access to Employment in Public Bodies* (that employ at least 100 employees), which applies not only to the provincial government but also to regional and local municipal governments and special purpose authorities (e.g., education, health, and social services). Insofar as any of those other governmental organizations have established employment equity policies, plans, or programs, they have done so on either a voluntary or mandatory basis pursuant to the human rights legislation rather than another special statute or policy. Alberta and Ontario remain the only provinces or territories that do not have an employment equity policy, plan, or program for the public service or the broader provincial public sector.

Generally the human rights statutes contain at least two sets of provisions related to the establishment of employment equity (and in some instances also pay equity) policies, plans, or programs. One set of provisions sanctions and provides guidelines for establishing such policies, plans, or programs on a voluntary basis by any employer in the public or private sectors. The other set empowers the provincial human rights commission to issue an order to any employer in either of those sectors to develop and implement such policies, plans, or programs if a judgment of a complaint concludes that the employer has transgressed the principles of non-discrimination and equity in relation to one or more of its employees.

Ontario is the only province or territory that shifted from a mandatory to a voluntary employment equity framework. In 1995, just two years after the *Employment Equity Act* was promulgated, Premier Mike Harris's Progressive Conservative government repealed and replaced it with the voluntary Equal Opportunity Plan. Nevertheless, section 14(1) of the *Human Rights Act* still sanctions employment equity, broadly affirming the goals of equal opportunity and non-discrimination in the workplace. More specifically, the section states that an equality right in that act "is not infringed by the implementation of a special program designed to relieve hardship or economic disadvantage or to assist disadvantaged persons or groups to achieve or attempt to achieve equal opportunity or that is likely to contribute to the elimination of the infringement of rights under Part I."

The policies of various provinces and territories exempt some organizations not only from adhering to provisions for establishing employment equity programs but also from transgressing some prohibited grounds of discrimination. Most exemptions are for benevolent, not-for-profit agencies or organizations, including religious and ethno-cultural organizations. More specifically, they exempt organizations trying to advance some particular public or group good for which some flexibility in hiring practices is deemed essential and justifiable. Exemptions of this nature are generally not included for governmental organizations. An example of such an exemption, however, exists in Quebec where, pursuant to the *Act Respecting Access to Employment in Public Bodies*, two Aboriginal governance bodies are exempt: the Cree Regional Authority and the Kativik Regional Government.

The provincial and territorial statutes and policies that explicitly sanction employment equity generally list one or more of the following as designated groups: women, Aboriginals, visible minorities, persons with disabilities, and persons with language limitations (see Table 2). In most provinces and territories the focus is on the four designated groups listed in the federal employment equity framework (i.e., Aboriginals, visible minorities, persons with disabilities, and women). However, there are at least four notable exceptions: both New Brunswick and Manitoba include military veterans; Quebec includes persons who speak neither French nor English and are not members of any other designated groups; New Brunswick does not include women; and Nunavut has only one designated group, the Nunavummiut, who are officially recognized as "beneficiaries" pursuant to Article 23 of the Nunavut Land Claims Agreement) for all job competitions with the departments and public agencies listed in Schedules A and B of the *Financial Administration Act*. For these "beneficiaries," Nunavut has established a general preferential hiring policy, and supplementary hiring program for students from land claims' "beneficiaries" groups. (i.e., the Nunavut Summer Student Employment Equity Program). No designated groups are identified in

Alberta's *Human Rights Act,* Ontario's *Human Rights Act,* or Ontario's Employment Opportunities Plan. Instead, they permit employers to establish employment equity initiatives on a voluntary basis for selected designated groups subject to the approval of the respective Human Rights Commissions.

TABLE 2
Comparative Table of Employment Equity Regimes

Jurisdiction	Statutory Articulation of EE Principle	Private Sector EE Compliance (Voluntary, Mandated,* or Required**)	Civil/Public Service EE Policies	Existence of EE Guidelines and Support for Employers
BC	X	Mandated	X	X
Alberta	X***	Voluntary	No Policies	X
Saskatchewan	X	Mandated	X	X
Manitoba	X	Mandated	X	X
Ontario	X	Mandated	X	X
Quebec	X	Required	X****	X
Nova Scotia	X	Mandated	X	X
New Brunswick	X	Mandated	X	X
Newfoundland and Labrador	X	Mandated	X	X
PEI	X	Mandated	X	X
Yukon	X	Mandated	X	X
NWT	X	Mandated	X	X
Nunavut	X	Mandated	X	
Canada	X	Required	X****	X

* Mandated refers to employment equity plans that can be ordered by tribunals.
** Required refers to employment equity plans that are required by statute.
*** The employment equity principle is inferred in section 11 of the Alberta Human Rights Act
**** Quebec has a separate statute for its entire public sector, and Canada has a separate statute for employment equity in the public sector.

Source: Authors' compilations.

FEDERAL, PROVINCIAL, AND TERRITORIAL PAY EQUALITY AND PAY EQUITY POLICIES

During the past 25 years, pay equality and pay equity policies have also contributed to facilitating fair economic integration of immigrants and members of minority groups with respect to the level of compensation they receive in the labour market. Whereas pay equality policies provide them equal compensation for "the same or substantially similar work" (subject to some variance for seniority and merit), pay equity policies provide them with equal pay for "work of equal or comparable value."

The principle and practice of pay equality has been established in all jurisdictions except Nunavut. In most jurisdictions, the pay equality provisions are included in human rights statutes. However, in four provinces (Saskatchewan, Manitoba, Nova Scotia, and New Brunswick) and one territory (Yukon), they are contained in labour and employment statutes. Generally the statutes apply to employers in the public and private sectors. Equal pay policies are complaint driven, in that they require employees to file a complaint to trigger corrective action (Canada, HRDCC 2006).

Pay equity policies exist at the federal and provincial levels but not at the territorial level (Equal Pay Coalition 2010). At the federal level, the pay equity provisions are contained in the *Canadian Human Rights Act.* Policies at the provincial level started to emerge in the mid-1980s. Between 1986 and 1996, six provinces enacted pay equity statutes: Manitoba in 1986, Ontario in 1987, Prince Edward Island in 1988, New Brunswick and Nova Scotia in 1989, and Quebec in 1996. Four provinces – Alberta, Saskatchewan, British Columbia, and Newfoundland and Labrador – and the three territories have not enacted pay equity legislation. Of the four provinces, all except Alberta have developed policy frameworks for negotiating pay equity with their public service employees, Newfoundland and Labrador in 1988, British Columbia in 1995, and Saskatchewan in 1997. Thus, Alberta and the three territories are the only jurisdictions with neither pay equity legislation or a framework for negotiating pay equity with unions representing public sector employees.

Despite many similarities in the equity policies of the provinces, some notable differences exist in terms of their coverage of the public and private sectors. Whereas the pay equity policies of Ontario and Quebec apply both to the public and private sectors, those of the rest of the provinces apply only to either the public service per se or to the public sector more broadly defined. In New Brunswick the policy applies only to public service employees, while in British Columbia, Manitoba, and Newfoundland, it applies to the entire provincial public sectors. In Saskatchewan, Nova Scotia, and Prince Edward Island, it applies to the broader public sector. In Saskatchewan, for example, it includes not only provincial agencies such as Crown corporations, Treasury Board agencies, boards and commissions, but also educational and health authorities (i.e., the Saskatchewan Institute of Applied Sciences and Technology, the regional colleges, and the health sector). Similarly, in Nova Scotia it includes universities, health care facilities, and municipalities, and in Prince Edward Island it includes Crown corporations as well as universities and colleges, nursing homes, and other public agencies identified in the regulations.

TABLE 3
Comparative Table of Designated Groups in Employment Equity Statutes and Policies

Jurisdiction	Women	Aboriginals (Inuit)	Visible Minorities	Persons with Disabilities	Military Veterans*	Persons with Official Languages Deficiencies
BC	Policy	Policy	Policy	Policy		
Alberta	Alberta's *Human Rights Act* does not specify designated groups					
Saskatchewan	Policy	Policy	Policy	Policy		
Manitoba	Policy	Policy	Policy	Policy	Statute	
Ontario	Neither of the following specify designated groups: • Ontario's *Human Rights Act* • Ontario's Equal Opportunity and Diversity Policy					
Quebec	Statute	Statute	Statute	Statute		Statute***
Nova Scotia	Policy	Policy	Policy**	Policy		
New Brunswick		Policy	Policy	Policy	Statute	
Newfoundland and Labrador	Policy	Policy		Policy		
PEI	Policy	Policy	Policy	Policy	Statute	
Yukon	Policy	Policy		Policy		
NWT	Policy	Policy	Policy	Policy		
Nunavut		Policy				
CANADA	Statute	Statute	Statute	Statute	Statute	

* Military veterans are not specified as a designated group in employment policies but receive hiring preference in some civil/public service acts and regulations.
** Nova Scotia explicitly lists "African Nova Scotians" as a special visible minority group.
*** Quebec identifies as a designated group the persons of non-English and non-French mother tongues and who are neither Aboriginal nor visible minorities.

Source: Authors' compilations.

In summary, individually and collectively the employment equity, pay equality, and pay equity policy frameworks contribute to the fair economic integration of immigrants and members of minorities as well as others, by supplementing anti-discriminatory provisions in other policy frameworks and also by providing a basis for progressive policies and practices that attempt to maximize equality and fairness in the labour market.

CONCLUSION

The central objective of this chapter has been, first, to provide an overview of the four policy frameworks – multiculturalism, human rights,
anti-racism, and employment equity, equal pay, and pay equity – that
have been developed and implemented by the federal, provincial, and
territorial governments to manage cultural and ethnic diversity, and
second, to explain their role in facilitating the integration and inclusion
of immigrants and members of racial, cultural, and religious minorities
into mainstream social and economic institutions.

Collectively, the four policy frameworks contribute to the integration
and inclusion of minorities and immigrants in a range of complementary
ways. These include facilitating the creation of warm, welcoming, and
inclusive communities, recognizing and safeguarding their fundamental
human rights and protecting them from various forms of discrimination, and establishing special programs they can access as members of
designated groups.

The analysis also reveals that the four policy frameworks are remarkably similar across provinces and territories, albeit with some
notable differences in the cases of the articulation and implementation
of multiculturalism policies in some provinces and especially the territories; employment and pay equity; and anti-racism policies, plans,
and programs. It also reveals that, despite the differences in the precise
scope of the various policy frameworks, individually and collectively
they provide a relatively progressive, comprehensive, robust policy
framework or policy web to facilitate the integration and inclusion of
immigrants and minorities.

This chapter further suggests that in their respective efforts to create warm, welcoming, and inclusive communities, these frameworks
not only foster effective integration and inclusion of various categories
of immigrants and ethnocultural minorities for their own benefit and
opportunities but they also function toward broader societal benefits
by creating and fostering social cohesion and harmony. The diversity
management project in Canada, including that aspect of it that deals
with the integration and inclusion of immigrants and minorities, continues to evolve due to what can generally be described as a collective
commitment to and iteration of its basic values of fairness, opportunity,
and inclusion. Despite existing and emerging challenges (or more likely,
because of them), that commitment will have to continue with a clear
focus on the policy frameworks described in this chapter. In addition to
improving the design, implementation, and resourcing of various aspects
of those policy frameworks per se, special attention must also be devoted
to improving the design, implementation, and resourcing of the related
programs and projects.

REFERENCES

Alberta. 2009. *Human Rights Act*. At http://www.qp.alberta.ca/574.cfm?page=A25P5.cfm&leg_type=Acts&isbncln=9780779744060

—2010. "Employment Equity Information Sheet. Alberta Human Rights Commission." At http://www.albertahumanrights.ab.ca/EmployEquity.pdf

British Columbia. 1993. *Multiculturalism Act*. 1996. At http://www.bclaws.ca/EPLibraries/bclaws_new/document/ID/freeside/00_96321_01

—1996. *Human Rights Code*. At http://www.bclaws.ca/EPLibraries/bclaws_new/document/ID/freeside/00_96210_01#section11

—2004. "Diversity in BC Schools: A Framework" (updated 2008). At http://www.bced.gov.bc.ca/diversity/diversity_framework.pdf

—2008a. "Promising Practices and New Directions in Multiculturalism and Anti-Racism Programming: A Scoping Review." At http://www.embracebc.ca/local/embracebc/pdf/promising_practices_new_directions.pdf

—2008b. "Welcoming and Inclusive Communities and Workplaces Program." At http://www.welcomebc.ca/wbc/service_providers/programs/welcome_program/index.page

—2010a. WelcomeBC. "Ministry of Advanced Education and Labour Market Development." At http://www.welcomebc.ca/local/wbc/docs/wicwp_program_guidelines.pdf

—2010b. "EmbraceBC." At http://www.embracebc.ca/programs/org.html

—2010c. "EmbraceBC: Promoting Multiculturalism and Eliminating Racism in British Columbia." At http://www.embracebc.ca/embracebc/resources/index.page?WT.svl=Centre

—2010d. "EmbraceBC: Resources and Campaigns: Promoting Multiculturalism and Eliminating Racism in British Columbia." At http://www.embracebc.ca/embracebc/resources/index.page?WT.svl=LeftNav

—2010e. "EmbraceBC Program Guidelines." At http://www.embracebc.ca/local/embracebc/pdf/embracebc_guidelines.pdf

Canada. 1960. *Canadian Bill of Rights*. At http://laws.justice.gc.ca/PDF/Statute/C/C-12.3.pdf

—1988. *Canadian Multiculturalism Act*. At http://lois.justice.gc.ca/eng/C-18.7/page-1.html

—2001. *Employment Equity Act Review: A Report to the Standing Committee on Human Resources Development and the Status of Persons with Disabilities*. At http://www.hrsdc.gc.ca/eng/lp/lo/lswe/we/review/report/main.shtml

—2005. *A Canada for All: Canada's Action Plan Against Racism*. Ottawa: Department of Canadian Heritage.

—2010a. "Inter-Action: Canada's New Multiculturalism Grants and Contributions Program." At http://www.cic.gc.ca/english/multiculturalism/funding/index.asp#projects

—2010b. *Canadian Employment Equity Act*. At http://laws.justice.gc.ca/en/E-5.401/index.html

Canada. Human Resources and Skill Development Canada. 2006. Equal Pay Legislation in Canada. At http://www.rhdcc-hrsdc.gc.ca/eng/labour/labour_law/esl/equal_pay.shtml#_edn2

Canadian Bar Association. 2010. "Charter of Rights and Freedoms: Equality Rights." At http://www.cba.org/bc/public_media/rights/232.aspx

Citizenship and Immigration Canada (CIC). 2010a. "Racism StopIt." At http://www.cic.gc.ca/english/multiculturalism/march21/contest.asp

—2010b. *Annual Report on the Operation of the Canadian Multiculturalism Act, 2009–2010*. Ottawa: Citizenship and Immigration Canada.

CCFU. 2006. *Coalition of Municipalities Against Racism and Discrimination: 10 Point Action Plan*. Ottawa: Canadian Communities for UNESCO.

Clutterbuck, P. and M. Novick. 2003. "Building Inclusive Communities: Cross-Canada Perspectives and Challenges." Prepared for the Federation of Canadian Municipalities and the Laidlaw Foundation. At http://www.ohcc-ccso.ca/en/webfm_send/228

Eid, E. 2001." Interaction between International and Document Human Rights Law: A Canadian Perspective." Presented to the Sino Canadian International Conference on the Ratification and implementation of Human Rights Covenants: Beijing, China. At http://www.icclr.law.ubc.ca/Publications/Reports/E-Eid.PDF

Equal Pay Coalition. 2010. "Provincial Pay Equity Legislation." At http://www.equalpaycoalition.org/other_prov.php

FCM. 1986. *Improving Interracial Relations in Canadian Municipalities*. Ottawa: Federation of Canadian Municipalities.

—1993. *Policy Statement on Interracial Relations*. Ottawa: Federation of Canadian Municipalities.

Garcea, J. 2006. "Provincial Multiculturalism Policies in Canada, 1974–2004: A Content Analysis." Special issue, "Multicultural Futures: Challenges and Solutions," *Canadian Ethnic Studies*:1-20.

—2009. "Postulations on the Fragmentary Effects of Multiculturalism in Canada." Special issue, "Multiculturalism Discourses in Canada," *Canadian Ethnic Studies*:141–60.

Garcea, J., and S. Garg. 2009. "Cultural Diversity, Race Relations, Immigration and Integration in Saskatoon." *Our Diverse Cities* 6(9):150-5.

Gravel, E., and Q. Delpech. 2008. "International Labour Standards: Recent Developments in Complementarity between the International and National Supervisory Systems." *International Labour Review* 147(4). At http://www.ilo.org/public/english/revue/download/pdf/s5_note_gravel_delpech.pdf

Howe, R.B. and D. Johnson. 2000. *Restraining Equality: Human Rights Commissions in Canada*. Toronto: University of Toronto Press.

—2002. "A (New) Human Rights Commission for Canada?" Human Rights Research and Education Centre Bulletin 44, University of Ottawa.

Icart, J.C., M. Labelle, and R. Antonius. 2005. *International Coalition Against Racism: Indicators for Evaluating Municipal Policies Aimed at Fighting Racism and Discrimination*. Montreal: Center for Research on Immigration, Ethnicity, and Citizenship (CRIEC).

Johnson, L. and R. Joshee. 2007. "Introduction: Cross-Border Dialogue and Multicultural Policy Webs." In *Multicultural Education Policies in Canada and the United States*, ed. R. Joshee and L. Johnson. Vancouver: UBC Press.

Joshee, R. 2007. "Opportunities for Social Justice Work: The Ontario Diversity Policy Web." *EAF Journal* 18.

Manitoba. 2006. "Kindergarten to Grade 12 Action Plan for Ethnocultural Equity (2006–2008)." At http://www.edu.gov.mb.ca/k12/docs/reports/equity/action_plan.pdf

OHRC. 2008. *Annual Report 2007–2008*. Toronto: Ontario Human Rights Commission.

—2010. Anti-racism, Anti-discrimination for Municipalities. At http://www.ohrc.on.ca/en/resources/news/cmard

Quebec. 1986. *Declaration of Intercultural and Interracial Relations*. Quebec National Assembly. At http://www.quebecinterculturel.gouv.qc.ca/fr/lutte-discrimination/declaration-relations.html

—2004. "Shared Values, Common Interests to Ensure the Full Participation of Quebecers from All Cultural Communities in the Development of Quebec: Action Plan 2004–2007." At http://www.micc.gouv.qc.ca/publications/fr/planification/PlanAction20042007-summary.pdf

—2008. "Affirmer les valeurs communes de la société québécoise: Mesures pour renforcer l'action du Québec en matière d'intégrations immigrants." At http://www.micc.gouv.qc.ca/publications/fr/mesures/Mesures-ValeursCommunes-Brochure2008.pdf

—2009. "Bill 16: *An Act to Promote Action by the Administration with Respect to Cultural Diversity*." At http://www.assnat.qc.ca/en/travaux-parlementaires/projets-loi/projet-loi-16-39-1.html

—2010. "Programme Action Diversity (PAD)." At http://www.immigration-quebec.gouv.qc.ca/publications/fr/action-diversite/DOC_PAD_20092010.pdf

Quebec. MCCI. 1990. "Au Québec pour bâtir ensemble: Énoncé de politique en matière d'immigration et d'intégration." Montreal: Ministère des Communautés culturelles et de l'immigration.

SafeHealthySchools Org. 2010. Canadian Education Trend Report: Anti-racism and Multicultural Education: Description of Some Current Activities in Canada--Coordinated Approaches. At http://www.safehealthyschools.org/whatsnew/racism.htm

Sen, A.2009. *The Idea of Justice*. Cambridge: Belknap Press.

Ventura, C. 1995. *From Outlawing Discrimination to Promoting Equality: Canada's Experience with Anti-Discrimination Legislation*. Geneva: International Labour Office, Employment Department.

Yukon. 2002. *Human Rights Act*. At http://www.gov.yk.ca/legislation/acts/huri.pdf

Chapter 3

The Integration and Inclusion of Newcomers in British Columbia

Daniel Hiebert and Kathy Sherrell

We adopt two conceptual starting points in this chapter that have helped us understand the evolution of the province of British Columbia's contribution to immigrant settlement and integration. First, initiatives on settlement and integration have been shaped by an ideology of neo-liberalism that has been pervasive in the province since the 2001 election, when the Liberal Party came to power after ten years of government by the New Democratic Party. Shortly after assuming office, the Liberals introduced a major reduction in personal income tax and then began a determined effort to trim expenditures. The implications for managing integration have been widespread. Programs have been evaluated for their efficiency and outcomes and, where possible, funding streams have been reorganized around an ethos of competition and, when possible, cost-recovery. These changes have significantly affected the framework of settlement service delivery in the province.

Second, we believe it helpful to contextualize our discussion of settlement policy by outlining four different configurations that such policy could take:

1. Newcomers could be entirely responsible for their own settlement and integration, with no services provided for them. That is, there could be no government involvement on this issue. Newcomers would be expected to make all of the adjustments required of living in a new society, while there would be no expectation for society to change as a result of immigration.

Integration and Inclusion of Newcomers and Minorities across Canada, ed. J. Biles, M. Burstein, J. Frideres, E. Tolley, and R. Vineberg. Montreal and Kingston: Queen's Policy Studies Series, McGill-Queen's University Press.

2. A single branch or department of government could be given the task of providing settlement and integration services. The services could be delivered by government itself or through other agencies, such as non-governmental organizations (NGOs). But the attention and activity of government would be limited, with immigrant integration operating in a kind of "silo," isolated from the rest of the state.

3. The goal of integration could become so important as to be adopted throughout government (often called a "whole of government" approach), with many departments coordinating their efforts across the fields of social and economic policy. Fully developed, such a system would include all three orders of government working to common purpose.

4. An additional element could be added to coordinated activities across government by diffusing the expectation for integration to society more broadly. This diffusion could take the form of partnerships between government, the private sector, and various community organizations including NGOs, and would attempt to enhance the ability for society to welcome and accept newcomers. That is, society as a whole would adjust itself to receive and accommodate newcomers, with government assuming a leadership role but nevertheless working in unison with other actors and institutions.

We believe this schematic way of thinking of government involvement in the settlement and integration process helps to focus our assessment of BC's role. Responsibility for the integration and inclusion of newcomers and minorities in the province is jurisdictionally complex. In broad terms the BC government has always been in charge of areas such as social services, health, and education which immigrants use just like everyone else. Until recently, the federal government was in charge of providing some specific settlement services for immigrants in BC. This changed beginning in 1991 with the signing of the Cullen-Couture Agreement. The chapter explains the nature of the shifting responsibilities and discusses how these changes intersected with larger developments in governance of the province, namely the neo-liberal turn described above.

In general, the scale of settlement services, particularly language training, was rather poor in British Columbia relative to the rest of Canada, but new investments in the settlement system since 2006 have meant rapid changes in the situation. While much of the investment is based on additional money from Ottawa, the province has also allocated funds to several of its own priorities. Later in the chapter, we offer an explanation for this unexpected trend of program growth in an age of fiscal austerity.

At the present time, British Columbia is establishing a number of innovative programs, well beyond what would have been imagined five or so years ago. The Welcoming and Inclusive Communities and Workplaces Program (WICWP) is one such example. Moreover, the emphasis by the Ministry of Advanced Education and Labour Market Development (ALMD) – the ministry primarily responsible for immigration policy and programs in the province[1] – on expanded engagement strategies within and between government ministries, and different levels of government, as well as with non-governmental organizations and academics, speaks to a new approach to governance. Jurisdictions are learning from each other to design innovative approaches and develop best practices.

After a brief historical and demographic summary of immigration and settlement in British Columbia, this chapter will provide an overview of key actors in the provision of settlement services provincially. While that landscape has been evolving rapidly over the past few years, we conclude by outlining several concerns about program gaps, as well as the difficulty of evaluating the impact of programs.

A HISTORICAL AND DEMOGRAPHIC PORTRAIT OF IMMIGRATION AND SETTLEMENT IN BRITISH COLUMBIA

In 2006, BC's population was 4.1 million, a 5.3 percent increase from that recorded in the 2001 Census (Statistics Canada 2008).[2] The province is home to 13 percent of Canada's population and receives an average of 16 percent of the immigrants arriving in the country every year. British Columbia has four CMAs, which together account for 67 percent of its population. Vancouver, the third largest city in Canada, has a population of 2.1 million, slightly more than half of the provincial total. The other CMAs in the province are Victoria, home to 330,088 people; Kelowna, with 162,276; and Abbotsford, with 159,020. Recent immigrants disproportionately settle within the Lower Mainland region: 80 percent of all immigrants and 90 percent of recent immigrants live in the Metro Vancouver and adjacent Abbotsford metropolitan areas, compared with 59 percent of BC's total population (MIB 2008a).

The size and profile of BC's foreign-born population has undergone a significant transformation in the last 20 years. Over one-quarter (27.5 percent) of British Columbians are foreign born (up from 21.9 percent in 1986). As might be expected, given its location, the province receives a much higher proportion of its newcomers from Asia and the Pacific and a much lower proportion of immigrants from South and Central America than do other provinces. Mainland China, India, and the Philippines remained the top three source countries for immigrants to British Columbia in 2007, though the list of important source countries also includes Iran, South Korea, and the United Kingdom (IPI 2008). Increased migration from Asian countries has significantly altered the ethno-cultural composition of the province over the last two decades. Unlike residents of British or European descent, the majority of whom are Canadian born or have lived in Canada for a number of decades, over 70 percent of those reporting Chinese and East Indian origins were born outside the country (Statistics Canada 2008; MIB 2008b).

British Columbians identified over 200 ethnic origins in the 2006 Census, reflecting a mixture of current and historical immigration trends (MIB 2008b; Statistics Canada 2008). The rise in migration from non-European countries has resulted in a considerable increase in the proportion of BC's population identifying as members of a visible minority group, from 21.6 percent in 2001 to 24.8 in 2006 (Statistics Canada 2008). British Columbia's visible minority population exceeded 1 million in the 2006 Census, an increase from 836,400 in 2001. The vast majority of this group (86.8 percent in 2006) lives in Metro Vancouver (Statistics Canada 2008; MIB 2008b). The top three visible minority groups in the province – Chinese, South Asian, and Filipino – are predominantly foreign born, with many having arrived since 2001.

In 2007, almost 70 percent of adult immigrants to British Columbia (aged 15 and over) arrived with official language proficiency (MIB 2008b). Conversely, however, approximately 15 percent of recent immigrants reported no English language ability upon arrival (BC Stats 2008). While the language ability of newcomers remains high overall, it varies significantly between immigration admission classes. Official language proficiency is highest among those entering as Live-In Caregivers and Skilled Workers (89 and 82 percent, respectively), and lowest among refugees (under 33 percent) (IPI 2008).

The profile of recent immigrants continues to be younger than the total BC population, with over half of those arriving between 2001 and 2006 in the 25–54 age group (IPI 2008; BC Stats 2008). New immigrants are typically better educated than the native-born population; over 70 percent possess some form of university degree or other post-secondary training.[3] Yet lagging immigrant incomes and higher unemployment rates (compared with the Canadian-born population) are among the challenges facing immigrants in the province today (IPI 2008). Immigrants in British Columbia continue to earn less than their Canadian-born counterparts regardless of gender or level of education, and this situation is especially troubling for those with university degrees.

Labour force participation and employment rates for immigrants in British Columbia are lower than those for the total population. In 2006, recent immigrants had an unemployment rate of 11 percent, compared to 7 percent for those arriving prior to 2001 and 5 percent for the non-immigrant population (Vancouver Foundation 2008). The combination of lower labour force participation and employment rates and lower earnings means that immigrants in British Columbia have a higher prevalence of low income than the total population: 23.4 and 17.8 percent for before-tax and after-tax measures, respectively, as compared with 17.3 and 13.1 percent for the provincial population as a whole (BC Stats, n.d.).

Settlement Patterns

As noted, BC's foreign-born population is overwhelmingly concentrated in the Vancouver and Abbotsford metropolitan areas. While the dominance of Vancouver as the primary destination of newcomers to the province remains strong, the 2004–07 period witnessed an increase in recent immigrants bypassing Vancouver to settle in Abbotsford. Approximately four in ten residents of Vancouver and Abbotsford are foreign born, compared with 27.5 percent of British Columbians and 19.8 percent of the population of Canada as a whole (MIB 2008b). Moreover, recent immigrants represent 7.0 percent of the population of Vancouver and Abbotsford, compared with 4.4 percent of the population of British Columbia and 3.6 percent of the population of Canada. As is the case for the province as a whole, just over half of all immigrants in the Lower Mainland arrived between 1991 and 2006 (Vancouver Foundation 2008; MIB 2008a). China, India, the Philippines, and South Korea are the top four source countries for recent immigrants to Vancouver.

In 2006, nearly three-quarters of recent immigrants in Metro Vancouver lived in four municipalities: the City of Vancouver, Richmond, Burnaby, and Surrey. In contrast to the historical dominance of Vancouver as the primary point of reception, by 2006 only 28.7 percent of newcomers lived in the municipality, while 46 percent were located in the other three aforementioned municipalities. Over the past five years Surrey has reported the most rapid growth in foreign-born persons of all Canadian cities (BC Stats 2008). Between 2001 and 2006, for example, the foreign-born population in Surrey increased by over 30 percent.

The social geography of visible minority groups within Vancouver and Abbotsford has become increasingly complex in the past two decades. Members of visible minority groups account for 41.7 percent of Metro Vancouver's population (or 40.9 percent of the Vancouver-Abbotsford population, combined). Actually, more than half of the residents of three municipalities identify as visible minorities: Richmond (65.1 percent), Burnaby (55.4 percent) and the City of Vancouver (51.0 percent) (MIB 2008b). In Abbotsford, this is the case for 22.8 percent of the population, with nearly three-quarters of this group tracing their ancestry to South Asia.

Although the Kelowna and Victoria metropolitan areas both have sizeable immigrant populations (15 and 19 percent, respectively), they are more likely to report having arrived prior to 1991 (75 percent) and less likely to identify as a member of a visible minority group (5 and 10 percent, respectively). Immigrants in Victoria and Kelowna fare better economically, on average, than their counterparts in Vancouver and Abbotsford as well as in British Columbia as a whole. In Vancouver, immigrants earned approximately two-thirds that of the Canadian-born population, regardless of whether or not they had a university degree (Hiebert 2009). While immigrants have settled across British Columbia, the continued concentration of foreign-born and visible minority populations within Metro Vancouver and Abbotsford means that we have limited the remainder of our analysis to the Lower Mainland region.

WHO'S WHO IN SETTLEMENT AND INTEGRATION IN BRITISH COLUMBIA

This section focuses upon the key actors in immigrant integration and settlement in British Columbia. These include federal, provincial, and municipal governments as well as organizations such as the United Way and the Vancouver Foundation. The provision of settlement services is frequently done through Immigrant Serving Agencies (ISAs), multicultural or ethno-specific organizations, or education institutions.

Federal, Provincial, and Municipal Governments

Jurisdiction over immigration in Canada has always been complicated. The *British North America Act* that established the legal foundations of the nation state specified that immigration would be regulated by the federal and provincial governments jointly. In practice, for most of Canadian history the federal government has taken the lead and has set admission levels (in consultation with provinces and territories), defined admission procedures, managed the admission system, and administered integration programs. Provincial governments have always been involved in the provision of "regular" services for immigrants, just as they are for the population as a whole. Immigrants are therefore eligible for provincial health care programs, can send their children to public schools (a municipal service supported by funds from the provincial government), and so on.[4] In effect, the federal government has played the active role in immigration while provincial governments have played passive roles.

This jurisdictional configuration has been redefined over the past generation. Beginning with the Cullen-Couture Agreement (also known as the Canada-Quebec Accord) of 1991, some of the federal responsibilities for immigration have been devolved to provinces. The particular instrument relevant for this chapter is the Agreement for Canada-British Columbia Co-operation on Immigration (CBCCI), first signed in 1998 and renewed in 2004 and 2010 (CIC 2004a, 2004b). Among other things, the CBCCI enables British Columbia to intervene in the immigrant selection process through a Provincial Nominee Program initiated in 2001. In this case the provincial government can fast-track immigrants it considers particularly desirable (i.e., important to the economic development of the province) by nominating them for immediate processing by the federal government, under admission rules defined by British Columbia.

The CBCCI also devolves responsibility for most integration services to the provincial government, based upon a transfer of funding from Ottawa to Victoria.[5] This significant departure from previous practice gives the province a much more active role in the immigration process. The provincial government, guided by its responsibilities as outlined in the CBCCI, defines the package of services to be provided for newcomers. These services are coordinated by WelcomeBC, an umbrella initiative that includes oversight for multiculturalism, anti-racism programming, the Welcoming and Inclusive Workplaces Program (WICWP), and the provision of settlement services.

Before outlining these services, an important qualification must be noted. The federal government retains its responsibility to facilitate the settlement and integration of Government Assisted Refugees (GARs). More precisely, this means that the federal government continues to administer the Resettlement Assistance Program (RAP), which helps GARs in several ways, most notably through the provision of a basic income for the first year in Canada, which is expected to approximate the amount of money received by a recipient of the provincial social assistance system. Beyond the RAP, refugees are expected to use the services offered to all immigrants, such as language training or general orientation services. Also, once the period of RAP funding has been completed, responsibility for the well-being of refugees shifts to the province.

The BC government administers three key programs with respect to immigrant settlement and multiculturalism programs: the BC Settlement and Adaptation Program (BCSAP); the BC Anti-Racism and Multiculturalism Program (BCAMP); and the Welcoming and Inclusive Communities and Workplaces Program (WICWP). Each is addressed in turn below.

The BC Settlement and Adaptation Program (BCSAP)

The provincial government makes arrangements with non-government organizations and educational institutions to provide direct services to newcomers during their first three years in Canada. Under the auspices of the British Columbia Settlement and Adaptation Program (BCSAP), the Ministry of Advanced Education and Labour Market Development (ALMD) contracts non-governmental organizations and educational institutions to deliver direct services to newcomers.[6] The full range of services provided by NGOs (Immigrant Serving Agencies, or ISAs) supported through BCSAP funds is very extensive and beyond the scope of this chapter. Rather than itemizing them in detail, it is more relevant to understand the general nature of these services.

BCSAP supports four streams of services:

1. ISAs and school boards provide Information and Support Services, either in the offices of ISAs or in schools. These services include orientation information, referral to mainstream services when appropriate, and a variety of other types of support. In essence, ISAs or school boards help individual immigrants, mainly through counsellors.
2. ISAs coordinate Community Bridging Services. These mainly revolve around the Host Program, which seeks to match people with experience living in Canada (which could mean people born in Canada or immigrants who arrived some time ago) with newcomers. The aim of this service is to help newcomers indirectly through people who "know the ropes." From a sociological perspective, it can be thought of as a way to widen the network of acquaintances of newcomers and thereby enhance their social capital.
3. Language training is offered through the English Language Services for Adults (ELSA) program. This training is provided by a variety of educational institutions, some of which have been established and are managed by ISAs. In order to reduce barriers to access, many of the third-party organizations also provide free on-site child minding for dependent preschool-aged children of ELSA learners. Note that children are expected to receive language training in the school system, either in regular or special ESL classes. Also note that ELSA programs combine language education with a broader introduction to Canada that includes information on how the labour market operates. Funding increases have enabled the provision of additional classes and ensured timely access to ELSA classes.[7]
4. Finally, BCSAP allocates some of its funds for Sectoral Support and Delivery Assistance. This last category includes support for special initiatives that could enhance service delivery in one or more of the other streams, plus financial aid for coordination among ISAs. Sectoral support for settlement and multiculturalism agencies and English Language services is provided by the Affiliation of Multicultural Societies and Services Agencies of BC (AMSSA) and the English Language Services for Adults Network (ELSA Net) respectively, while the British Columbia Immigrant Employment Council (BCIEC) will provide sectoral support on labour market initiatives.

In 2005, in the midst of a period of profound fiscal restraint, $22 million was dedicated to BCSAP, at a time when British Columbia received a little over 40,000 immigrants. This suggests a per capita funding base at that time of about $550 per person. That is, while the list of programs is impressive and their intent is certainly laudable, the actual resource base of BCSAP has been quite modest considering the scale of issues faced by immigrants who have come from all over the world, with many languages, educational backgrounds, and cultural sensibilities. However, the level of funding for BCSAP has increased sharply in the last few years, to $70 million in 2008–09.[8] In light of this added funding, a number of new programs are being introduced. For example, settlement workers have been placed in schools to assist immigrant families in adjusting to school culture and to facilitate integration to the broader community. The Settlement Workers in Schools (SWIS) program, launched in 2007 and expanded in 2008, encompasses 20 school districts across British Columbia. Total funding for the 2008–09 school year was $8.6 million. A similar program has been introduced for public libraries. English language programs are being augmented; targeted programs are also in pilot stages for refugee children, francophone immigrants, and special services for immigrant seniors. The Step Ahead: Settlement Enhancement Project, for example, is a two-year pilot program that provides in-home services to newcomers facing multiple barriers to settlement. It is too soon, of course, to evaluate the impact of these enhancements and new initiatives.

In keeping with the neo-liberal ideology discussed at the outset of the chapter, BCSAP funds are allocated through a competitive process in which the government issues Requests for Proposals and ranks applications submitted by ISAs for quality and economic efficiency. Two parts of the BC government are involved in immigration directly, and almost every branch is involved indirectly (e.g., health, education, justice). The CBCCI is negotiated by the Ministry of Advanced Education and Labour Market Development (AELMD), which also administers BCSAP funds and the Provincial Nominee Program.[9] The Ministry of the Attorney General (MAG) is responsible for multiculturalism and plays a leading role in anti-racism initiatives.

It is important to understand that immigrants are not required to use the services available to them. All of the programs described here are optional rather than mandatory.[10]

The BC Anti-Racism and Multiculturalism Program (BCAMP)

The primary goal of the BC Anti-Racism and Multiculturalism Program is the prevention and elimination of racism through enhanced community understanding of cultural diversity and multiculturalism. Funding is available through (1) grants to organizations for projects to promote anti-racism and multiculturalism (e.g., cross-cultural dialogues, education programs); (2) community funding to respond to racism and hate activities (e.g. the Critical Incident Response Model); and (3) grants for supporting anti-racism and multiculturalism initiatives.

In 2007–08, over $475,000 of WelcomeBC funding was awarded to 20 projects across the province (e.g., Terrace, Kelowna, Duncan, Campbell River, and the Lower Mainland) to promote multiculturalism and anti-racism initiatives through enhancing community understanding. Of these awards, over $270,000 went to support youth initiatives (MAG 2008). The November 2006 provision of increased federal funding enabled the province to provide approximately $1 million to organizations to support anti-racism and multiculturalism programs (MAG 2006). Arguably, however, the resources dedicated to BCAMP remain limited, given the scale of the issues involved and, more recently, the capacity of the host society to welcome immigrants.

The Welcoming and Inclusive Communities and Workplaces Program (WICWP)

Successful integration is an important prerequisite for social cohesion and requires the establishment of welcoming and inclusive communities and workplaces. The government can only do so much to help immigrants integrate, and the process is limited by the degree of accommodation offered by society at large. Community capacity to support and include immigrants varies significantly across the province. More resources exist within places like Vancouver and Surrey; however, the settlement of immigrants outside these areas suggests that a broader approach to community engagement is advisable.

The Welcoming and Inclusive Communities and Workplaces Program (WICWP) represents the keystone of BC's evolving approach to settlement (IIB 2009). It comprises four community-level program components, as well as a number of ministry-led initiatives:

1. Community Partnership Development aids communities in identifying and coordinating collaborative relationships and sustainable partnerships with key stakeholders and diverse groups to promote welcoming and inclusive communities.
2. Knowledge Development and Exchange facilitates the ability of communities to promote knowledge development and sharing among stakeholders, diverse groups, and community members more broadly.
3. Public Education: Assistance on this front is provided to enable communities to facilitate cross-cultural understanding and increase public awareness (e.g., through the distribution of materials, toolkits, resources, etc).
4. Finally, through the WICWP program communities, stakeholders, and other groups may gain support in designing, implementing, delivering, and evaluating Demonstration Projects to promote

innovative approaches to fostering a more welcoming environment for newcomers.

Additional, ministry-led initiatives under the WICWP program include a research component that seeks to identify gaps in literature and policy; sectoral partnerships to promote workplace diversity and create culturally competent workplaces; and an Inter-Governmental Engagement Initiative that enables government staff from all levels of government to exchange ideas on welcoming and inclusive communities.

Non-BCSAP Progams

Although most programs and services for newcomers are supported through BCSAP, additional funding is provided through federal (e.g., Service Canada; Canadian Heritage, HRSDC, Western Economic Diversification Canada) and provincial (e.g., Ministry of Children and Family Development; Ministry of Economic Development) government ministries. According to an estimate made by a source from the settlement sector, 37 percent of non-BCSAP services for newcomers are funded by the provincial government, 29 percent from charity and community foundations, 23 percent from the federal government, 8 percent from private donations, and 3 percent from municipal governments (Charles et al. 2008). The wide range of programs funded includes community and business development, employment and skills training, and health promotion. Municipal governments play a more indirect role; they offer services that immigrants consume just like other residents, such as parks, libraries, public transportation, and education. Dedicated programs for newcomers are predominantly found in Metro Vancouver and include initiatives aimed at women, refugee claimants, youth, and families, as well as more general community development. Each of the municipalities that comprise Metro Vancouver, especially the larger ones, also have appointed social planners who specialize in working with diverse groups, and who attempt to ensure that there is good communication between these communities and municipal government. Some municipalities have been more proactive, including the City of Vancouver and the City of Surrey, which we highlight here. However, it is important to remember that the scope of initiatives targeting integration is increasing in many municipalities, in part led by funds becoming available through the WICWP program.

Vancouver, for example, has established special task forces on diversity and immigration. The latter body, the Mayor's Task Force on Immigration, in 2007 released a report that included recommendations for improving the connection between immigrants and the civic government. Accordingly, in late 2008 the city hosted a summit on immigration and employment in an effort to encourage local employers to better value the skills and pre-migration labour market experience of immigrants.

In addition, Vancouver provides financial support to non-profit organizations in the city through its Community Services Grant Program. While not all grants are specific to newcomers – the total amount of support was nearly $2.9 million (Vernooy 2008) – those awarded in 2008 included Inland Refugee Society of B.C. ($51,764); MOSAIC (Community Development, $70,000); MOSAIC/Strathcona (Vietnamese Family Counselling Project, $53,000); PIRS Outreach Workers ($53,128); SUCCESS (Bridging the Gap Family Services Advocacy, $45,900); and SUCCESS (Youth at Risk Program, $60,000).

The adoption of Surrey's Social Plan in 2006, which identified diversity as one of the five areas requiring consideration, and a multicultural advisory committee in 2007 speak to the active efforts of that city in responding to changing population needs. The introduction of the WICWP initiative has prompted Surrey's politicians to bring together stakeholders to consider how to make the city more welcoming for newcomers. As with Vancouver, funding for non-profit groups or organizations is also available through the City of Surrey Community Grants Program.

Universal Service Providers

Charity and community foundations represent the second and third largest sources of funding for newcomers after the provincial government. In Metro Vancouver, programs and services supported by these institutions include drop-in programs (e.g., for preschoolers, children, youth, seniors, and women), family support, and community outreach programs. While some, including the United Way of the Lower Mainland and various community foundations, award grants to those providing services and programs, others, including the Red Cross of the Lower Mainland, deliver immigrant and refugee-specific programs more directly.

United Way of the Lower Mainland (UWLM)

The UWLM is the largest organization supporting community programs and services in British Columbia. Recognizing that communities undergoing rapid growth through migration may lack sufficient resources and programs to facilitate integration, the UWLM has designated Immigrant and Newcomer Integration as a targeted priority area. The UWLM supports the delivery of culturally competent programs that promote accessibility to mainstream services, facilitates capacity building among service providers and other stakeholders, and funds research on newcomer populations.

To this end, in 2007 the UWLM awarded 22 grants worth a total of $787,976, including Strong Beginnings: Building an Integrated and Inclusive Learning community (Frog Hollow Neighbourhood House, $70,000) and Community Capacity Building for Newcomers, Multi-purpose Agencies and Public Institutions in the Tri-Cities (MOSAIC, $70,000). Two other projects of note, the Burnaby Newcomer Planning Table (Burnaby Family Life Institute, $35,000) and the North Shore Newcomer Service Planning Table (North Shore Multicultural Society, $35,000) seek to develop concrete plans among multiple stakeholders to work together in establishing more inclusive communities.

The Vancouver Foundation[11]

The Vancouver Foundation is another organization that contributes grants to youth and community development programs throughout Metro Vancouver, including youth training and peer support and early childhood-focused settlement programs. As with UWLM grants, those provided by the Vancouver Foundation are frequently geared towards assisting newcomers, including those who have been in Vancouver for a number of years, to transition to mainstream services. Awards to programs in 2007 included one for bus passes for immigrants and refugees as well as at-risk and homeless youth (given to five organizations in the Lower Mainland, including ISSofBC, $83,000); the First Contact Program (Canadian Red Cross, $40,000); the Enhanced Parenting and Family Literacy Program for ESL Families (Pacific Immigrant Resources Society, $69,000); the Multicultural Youth Circle Program (MY Circle) (ISSofBC, $90,000 over three years); the llustrated Journey Youth Project (La Boussole, $50,000); the First Steps ECD Refugee Settlement Project (School District #36 Surrey, $45,000); and Grade 8 Immigrant Youth At Risk (School District #41 Burnaby, $35,000).

The Surrey Foundation

Successful integration of immigrants into Surrey is one of four priority areas for the Surrey Foundation (Surrey Foundation 2009). Grants awarded by the Surrey Foundation in 2008 that directly benefit immigrants and refugees included Women Without Permanent Status In Canada (YWCA of Vancouver, $75,000), and the First Contact Project (Canadian Red Cross Society Lower Mainland Region, $130,000).

Red Cross of the Lower Mainland (RCLM)

The RCLM oversees a number of programs and services to facilitate integration and increase community understanding.

The First Contact Refugee Claimant Reception Program is headed by the Canadian Red Cross in partnership with Settlement Orientation Services (SOS) and the Inland Refugee Society (IRS). Drawing upon a multi-agency partnership of federal and provincial government ministries, NGOs, churches, and housing providers, First Contact provides basic information (in first languages) about food, shelter, and medical care to newly arrived refugee claimants. Funding for First Contact has been obtained from a variety of sources, including the Vancouver Foundation, the Law Foundation of BC, VanCity Community Foundation, the United Way of the Lower Mainland, the Government of BC, and the Canadian Red Cross.

"A Story to Tell and a Place for the Telling," a dialogue series organized by the RCLM, features refugee stories and panel discussions on refugee issues. These dialogues, held in Vancouver and open to the public at no charge, seek to promote community understanding of the challenges faced by refugees.

Smart Start programs offer first-aid classes to vulnerable communities to build capacity to deal with emergency situations. The programs are delivered in 18 languages and are available at no charge.

VanCity Community Foundation

On a smaller scale, the VanCity Community Foundation, in partnership with MOSAIC, supports a micro-loans program that facilitates access to capital to enable low-income earners and newly arrived immigrants to start their own home-based business or to acquire certification and skills training.

Immigrant Serving Agencies (ISAs)

Among dozens of non-profit immigrant serving agencies (ISAs) in metropolitan Vancouver, four are particularly comprehensive and significant: DIVERSEcity, ISSofBC, MOSAIC, and SUCCESS. Each provides a wide range of programs that are based on BCSAP funding as well as funds from other sources. Each has a cadre of settlement counsellors who, collectively, are capable of interacting with clients in many languages. These ISAs are also able to draw upon an extensive network of volunteers to provide services beyond those funded by BCSAP. All four agencies have multiple service sites in the Vancouver region and in other parts of British Columbia. All are members of AMSSA, the umbrella organization of multicultural and immigrant serving agencies.

DIVERSEcity Community Resources Society

Offering employment services programs, settlement services, English language training, and family services, DIVERSEcity is also home to the New Canadian Clinic, which seeks to meet the health care needs of government assisted refugees. DIVERSEcity operates with funding from the Federal and Provincial Governments, BC Gaming Commission, the UWLM, and other foundations, and from fundraising as well as fee-for-service programs.[12]

Immigrant Services Society of British Columbia (ISSofBC)

In addition to settlement services and employment and language training programs for immigrants and refugees, ISSofBC provides orientation services and temporary accommodation for government assisted refugees. ISSofBC is the lead agency in the Refugee Trauma Program launched in 2008, which provides mental health assistance to refugees. ISSofBC operates with funding from all levels of government, the UWLM, and other miscellaneous contributors. In 2008, ISSofBC received nearly $10 million for its programs, a figure that accounted for over 80 percent of its total revenues. In 2007–08, 93 percent of its program funding came from the provincial and federal governments.[13]

MOSAIC

MOSAIC offers employment and English language training services, as well as programs geared towards family and settlement services. MOSAIC is the lead agency on the Step Ahead project and organizes job fairs for immigrants and refugees in Vancouver. Funding revenues are obtained from a wide variety of sources, including all three levels of government (79 percent), fee for service programs (14 percent), and other donations and foundations.[14]

SUCCESS

SUCCESS has expanded its original mandate both geographically and beyond the Chinese-Canadian community. In addition to offices throughout Metro Vancouver, the Northern B.C. Newcomer Integration Service Centre has been opened in Fort St John to help newcomers to access services. Beginning in 2009, prospective immigrants to Canada were able to access pre-landing settlement and employment services at SUCCESS offices in Seoul and Taipei. Total revenues for SUCCESS in 2007–08 were

$26,108,775, of which almost 70 percent was obtained from the three levels of government.[15]

Beyond these large ISAs, there are many smaller ones that tend to focus on particular groups, such as refugee claimants or immigrants from Africa. In other words, metropolitan Vancouver has a rich field of ISAs dedicated to assisting immigrants in a wide variety of ways.

Issue-Based NGOs

A number of issue-based NGOs are working towards improved living and working conditions for immigrants and refugees in Vancouver and Abbotsford. Among them is the Tenants' Resource and Advisory Centre (TRAC), which seeks to promote affordable housing and tenants' rights in British Columbia. While not specific to immigrants and refugees, TRAC has been active in facilitating first-language access to their *Tenant Survival Guide* (2006) and *Tenants' Guide* (a condensed version of the *Tenant Survival Guide*) in 14 non-official languages.

The Law Foundation of BC (LFBC), the Law Students' Legal Advice Program (with funding from the LFBC), and Access Justice (a non-profit society) partner with local ISAs, including ISSofBC, MOSAIC, and SUCCESS to provide legal assistance programs to immigrants throughout Metro Vancouver and the Fraser Valley.

Finally, Justicia for Migrant Workers (J4MW) BC promotes the rights of migrant farm workers through the Low Skilled Workers Program (LSWP) and the Canadian Seasonal Agricultural Workers Program (CSAW), as well as the rights of farm workers without status. In addition to lobbying government for policy changes, J4MW provides opportunities through research and political organizing for migrant workers to speak without fear of repercussions.

Universities

While colleges have played a vital role in offering ESL programs to newcomers, BC universities have acted in much more limited ways. Of course, they have long hosted international students who are in Canada on temporary visas. They also admit as regular students newcomers trying to upgrade their skills or credentials. But none of the universities has adopted a more active role in the integration process. Moreover, other than supporting the Metropolis project, none has seen fit to establish significant teaching or research programs dealing with immigrant integration. The University of British Columbia is currently engaged in a review of its approach to diversity, but this is largely disconnected from a concern with immigration per se.

MAJOR ISSUES / CHALLENGES FOR INTEGRATION AND SETTLEMENT IN BRITISH COLUMBIA

The past five years have witnessed substantial improvements in the services and programs provided to immigrants and refugees in the province. An array of new pilot programs have been introduced, services in general have expanded, and there has been an overarching shift in the orientation of programs towards a more targeted, as opposed to universal, client base. In spite of these initiatives, challenges remain with respect to specific groups and to issues of housing and income security, as well as with the ability to assess the impact of changes made to integration and settlement services. In light of the current economic climate, these challenges may become acute.

Temporary Foreign Workers (TFWs)

Thus far, we have discussed settlement and integration in British Columbia with a focus on permanent migrants. Yet one of the largest challenges facing the province today is associated with temporary migrants. While the number of permanent immigrants arriving in British Columbia, and Canada more broadly, declined in 2006 and again in 2007, the opposite is true for temporary residents (Ilves 2008). In 2006, the total of 42,084 new immigrants settling in the province was far surpassed by the arrival of 62,535 temporary migrants. More than one in five temporary foreign workers who arrived in Canada in 2006 settled in British Columbia.

Temporary workers (and temporary work visas) represent an effective way for employers to meet short-term or regional skill and labour shortages. Unlike with the immigration program, however, the government does not impose numerical limits or targets on the Temporary Foreign Worker Program (TFWP). Rather, employers can hire foreign workers as needed to fill vacancies for jobs deemed "occupations under pressure." The close connection between this program and the labour market is evident when considering settlement patterns. TFWs are more geographically dispersed than are immigrants to British Columbia, with 40 percent living outside Metro Vancouver, compared with 15 percent of new immigrants (Ilves 2008). The number of TFWs in BC more than doubled between 1997 and 2006. The latest figures indicate the flows of TFWs have continued to climb, reaching over 44,000 in 2009, nearly triple the number received in 2001. Those entering represent a diverse group of high and low skilled occupations, including live-in caregivers, seasonal agricultural workers, and high-tech workers.

Previous research demonstrates that "lower" skilled workers are vulnerable to exploitation and discrimination (cf. Pratt 2008). Programmatic restrictions that require live-in caregivers and seasonal agricultural workers to live and work on the employers' property, for example, increase their vulnerability. Those in the skilled and professional classes face other challenges. Unlike lower skilled workers, skilled and professional migrants are permitted to bring their spouses and children to Canada. While these spouses and children are afforded access to health care and the K-12 school system, neither they nor the worker can access settlement services, including even the most basic of free English language classes.

The 2008 implementation of the Temporary Foreign Workers Outreach Project (TFWOP), which enabled 25 Immigrant Integration Coordinating Committee (IICC) member agencies to provide outreach and training workshops to TFWs and their employers throughout BC, is promising in this regard. Funded by the BC Ministry of Labour and Citizen's Services, Employment Standards Branch, the program targets the diverse needs of TFWs and attempts to inform both TFWs and employers on their respective rights and responsibilities. While such programs represent a promising new practice, we believe it is insufficient in light of the continued exclusion of TFWs from BCSAP services and programs, particularly given recent changes to the broader immigration program.

Until very recently, a strict delineation of permanent and temporary migration streams was a cornerstone of Canada's immigration program. Permanent migrants, as opposed to those on temporary visas, are provided with access to services to facilitate their integration into Canadian communities. Yet the expansion of the Temporary Foreign Workers Program in 2006 and the 2008 introduction of the Canadian Experience class (CEC) effectively establish temporary migration as a pathway to permanent residency. Given the rapid expansion in TFW programs and the blurring of the permanent and temporary migration programs, the exclusion of TFWs and their families from settlement services should be reconsidered.

Underemployment and Rising Poverty among Immigrants and Refugees

It is well known that the skills of newcomers in British Columbia are underutilized. Some of the more significant challenges for meaningful labour market integration, in the province as elsewhere in Canada, are language barriers, non-recognition of credentials obtained prior to landing in Canada, lack of familiarity with job-seeking practices in Canada, and a lack of Canadian work experience (e.g., Sherrell, Hyndman, and Preniqi 2005; Krahn et al. 2000). In spite of higher skill levels among immigrants arriving in British Columbia, there is increasing poverty among newcomers. Underemployment is actually greatest among those with the highest levels of education, regardless of the sector in which they are seeking employment. The BC Immigrant Employment Council (BCIEC), convened in the fall of 2008, is dedicated to improving the match between the skills brought by immigrants and the labour market (cf. www.iecbc. ca). It remains to be seen, however, whether this initiative will succeed.

Housing and Newcomers

The majority of BC's foreign-born population, particularly recent immigrants, have settled within Metro Vancouver's unforgiving housing market. Housing prices that are amongst the most expensive in Canada are accompanied within the rental market by high rents, low vacancies, and a lack of purpose-built rental units. Although some immigrants arrive in Vancouver with substantial savings and move quickly into homeownership (cf. Hiebert and Mendez 2008, Hiebert, Mendez, and Wyly 2008), others face significant challenges in obtaining adequate and affordable housing (cf. Sherrell and ISSofBC 2009; Francis 2009; Sherrell 2008; Hiebert et al. 2005). In Vancouver, homeownership rates among newcomers are higher than might be expected by their low incomes, something Hiebert, Mendez, and Wyly (2008) attribute to the decision to allocate to housing a significant proportion of the household income and/or wealth transferred from abroad. Ley's (1999) analysis reveals that homeownership may be accomplished by combining the incomes of a number of adult income earners, in effect substituting bodies for capital.

Research shows that today's newcomers are more likely to experience low incomes and high levels of poverty (Picot 2004). The Canada Mortgage and Housing Corporation defines housing affordability in relative terms, when a household allocates 30 percent or less of its gross income to shelter. Immigrants and refugees frequently allocate a far higher ratio, in many cases well over 50 percent (Hiebert and Mendez 2008; Murdie 2008, 2004; Hiebert et al. 2005; Zine 2003).

Yet housing is not one of the core services provided to immigrants under the BCSAP funding envelope. We believe this decision should be re-evaluated. Newcomers with low incomes and precarious legal status face an especially high risk of exploitation.

Refugee Issues

The 2002 implementation of the Immigration and Refugee Protection Act (IRPA) led to sweeping change in the profile of Government Assisted Refugees arriving in Canada. Since then, greater priority has been given to those in need of immediate protection rather than the earlier emphasis on "ability to establish." Beginning in 2003, when the first post-IRPA GARs landed in Canada, the profile of GARs has included more multi-barriered individuals, including those with low literacy levels in their original languages and significant physical and mental health issues, as well as increased numbers of single-headed households and large households, and a much higher number of children and youth who were born and raised in refugee camps with limited exposure to formal education.

Given these emerging needs, changes have been made in the provision services for GARs in the province. Beginning in April 2007, ISSofBC introduced extended orientation programming that includes ongoing monitoring and follow-up of clients throughout the first year. A number of pilot projects have also been introduced, including the Step Ahead Settlement Enhancement Project, which provides outreach to multi-barriered refugee households; Trauma Information and Support Services, which assists GARs and refugee claimants in Vancouver and Burnaby; and targeted Early Childhood Development (ECD) programs, including the First Steps ECD Refugee Settlement Projects in Surrey and Burnaby, which involve integrated, multi-agency service delivery to refugee children and their caregivers to provide settlement and developmental supports.

But these new initiatives take place against the backdrop of major funding challenges. Significantly, funds for the Resettlement Adaptation Program (RAP) have been frozen since 1998, despite the much greater need associated with the new GAR population. Also, it remains to be seen whether the pilot programs will receive continuing funding. The conclusions of several recent research projects undertaken in Metro Vancouver all point to the difficulties faced by refugee newcomers (Sherrell and ISSofBC 2009; Francis 2009; Sherrell, D'Addario, and Hiebert 2007; McLean, Friesen, and Hyndman 2006; Cubie 2006). In other words, even with all this effort, the configuration of refugee resettlement programs has many gaps.

Tracking Changes, Measuring Outcomes

As we have seen, there has been considerable development in the type and extent of services available to newcomers in the province. Enhanced programming, new pilot projects, and heightened concern about settlement and integration are promising. Yet there are major data lags and gaps, and the scale of research within government agencies remains limited, especially considering the injection of new funding. Unfortunately, vital administrative data is held by a variety of ministries (e.g., health, housing, education, immigration), and linking these files is very difficult in an age of privacy concerns. The assessment of new programs is also anything but straightforward. Can WICWP actually improve community readiness for newcomers across the province, for example? Can improved attitudes be engineered? How would we measure attitudinal shifts? What is the impact of settlement workers in schools? Will settlement workers

in libraries help? These potentially important initiatives are being undertaken in an atmosphere of austerity intensified by the current recession
and the inevitable budget cuts ahead. These programs will face intense
scrutiny, and it is unclear whether there are sufficient data to provide a
strong business case to maintain them.

CONCLUSION

We conclude by returning to the conceptual issues raised at the outset
of the chapter: the nature of social policy – in this case, on newcomer
integration – in a neo-liberal climate, and the role of government and
society in the integration process. The imposition nearly a decade ago of
neo-liberal values on the settlement and integration sector led to a situation best described by a senior provincial bureaucrat (name withheld)
as "managing down." That is, in the early to mid 2000s, the envelope of
funding available for these services fell in per capita terms. The dramatic
shift to a more competitive bidding process for NGOs, arguably, exacerbated an already charged situation.

How can we reconcile this gloomy perspective with the larger story of
this chapter, which has been about the effervescence of new programs in
the past five years? The answer lies in a curious and awkward convergence
of two "layers" of neo-liberalism. Since 2005, transfers from the federal
to the provincial government, as part of the CBCCI, have expanded substantially as the per capita funding base for settlement has been made
more uniform across Canada. (In other words, British Columbia was not
receiving a fair share of this funding until recently, particularly when
compared with Quebec.) Under its own ideology of neo-liberalism, the
federal government made accountability a key ingredient in the expansion
of these transfer payments. To receive more money, the province has been
required to spend the extra amount on settlement services and to show
that it has done so. Despite the austerity of the day, therefore, spending
in the area of settlement effectively tripled. The provincial ministry responsible for immigrant integration knew there were needs and received
more money to address them, money that was protected from one layer
of neo-liberalism (the provincial) by another (the federal). In partnership
with NGOs, the ministry targeted efforts to areas of particular need.

But this positive situation may not have a happy ending. We have yet
to see the response of the federal government to the mounting deficit
that has arisen in the recent recession. Cuts in integration funding are
certainly within the realm of possibility. In that case, the BC government
will almost certainly follow suit and reduce its own commitment to this
area. Given the large number of pilot programs, there is much flexibility
in spending regimes that will, unfortunately, enable the imposition of

reduced funding. As noted, the nature of data on settlement means that it will be difficult to build an effective case to protect settlement programs if such a scenario emerges.

Secondly, how have these recent developments changed the overall configuration of integration policy? We introduced four types of policy earlier in this chapter: no support for integration; limited and specific support; a whole-of-government approach; and a whole-of-society approach. Clearly, the age of "no support" ended long ago in British Columbia as elsewhere in Canada. For the most part, since the 1970s we have seen the evolution of our second type of policy regime in the province: with a limited part of the provincial government responsible for newcomer integration. Over the years the location of the relevant department(s) within government has changed, of course, but the scope of interest within government as a whole has been limited. In fact, we would argue that a fully coordinated approach to integration, with program and data sharing across all of the ministries dealing with social policy, remains an elusive goal.

But at least some of the "restless" policy initiatives of the past half-decade have incorporated elements of what we have called the third and fourth policy regimes. For example, on the issue of refugees, the need for coordination across the fields of immigrant services, health, and social welfare is increasingly understood (as is the need for greater communication and collaboration between the three orders of government and the NGO community). So the contours of a whole-of-government approach are becoming discernable in that area, though much remains to be done.

Within this broader context, the WICWP program is perhaps the most interesting of all, since it is the first attempt of policy experimentation in the fourth type of regime. WICWP is based on the belief that society must prepare itself for newcomers, which involves engagement with a much wider array of partners than ever before. WICWP seeks to reach out to institutions once considered far removed from the issue of newcomer integration, such as Rotary Clubs, Girl Guides, and the private sector more generally, to name just a few examples. Further, WICWP has the goal of educating the public about the importance of immigration and thereby improving attitudes to newcomers across society. As such, it is a far-reaching and bold initiative.

We are not arguing that there has been a secular shift in the nature of integration policy in British Columbia, but that recent developments indicate that such a shift may be possible. In the current economic climate, however, the likelihood of such a positive outcome is highly questionable. The more important question in the foreseeable future will probably become how to justify already existing programs rather than to imagine even better ones.

NOTES

1. This chapter was written in 2009 and revised in 2010. Since then, the responsibilities for settlement and integration policy have been reconfigured, again. At the time this footnote is being written early in 2011, nearly all policy and service provision related to immigration in British Columbia has been allocated to the Ministry of Regional Economic and Skills Development (RESD). Multicultural programs (e.g., anti-racism initiatives) have also been shifted to RESD. However, there is much political uncertainty in the province following the abrupt resignation of Premier Gordon Campbell in the face of widespread criticism of the party. Given public scepticism over the Liberal government, the new premier may seek to shake up the bureaucracy and, if so, there may be yet another reconfiguration of responsibilities for immigration by the time this chapter is published.
2. Unless otherwise indicated, demographic information draws upon 2006 Census data.
3. Education levels are highest among those arriving in the Skilled Worker and Provincial Nominee Programs and lowest among refugees to British Columbia (IPI 2008).
4. All provincial services are available to permanent residents, but temporary residents can only gain access to a selected number.
5. There is controversy over the allocation of these funds. The government of British Columbia allocates some to its general revenue, under the assumption that newcomers use general services such as health and education. It dedicates approximately half of the funds transferred from Ottawa to ISAP. Advocates argue that this ratio should be higher. A good introduction to this debate can be found in statements made to the Standing Committee on Citizenship and Immigration, Evidence Number 46, Vancouver, 19 February 2003.
6. Temporary residents are not eligible to access BCSAP programs and services.
7. Multi-barriered individuals who require additional assistance may access blended services offering "Information, Support and English Language Services."
8. This figure was provided by Bill Walters, at that time the executive director of the Immigrant Integration Branch (IIB), Ministry of Advanced Education and Labour Market Development, Government of British Columbia, in a personal conversation held in November 2008.
9. The 2008 reorganization of the Immigration Initiatives Branch (IPI) and the Immigration Policy and Initiatives Branch (IPI) into AELMD brought immigration, concern with employment and labour market, and international recruitment (e.g., the Provincial Nominee Program) under the mandate of one ministry.
10. This is in contrast to a number of European countries that have made participation in settlement programs mandatory for immigrants who wish to renew their visas.
11. In light of global financial uncertainty, both the Vancouver and Surrey Foundations suspended their 2009 calls for proposals.
12. Data obtained from DIVERSEcity's 2007–08 annual report. Unfortunately the report did not specify the breakdown of individual funding sources.

13. Data obtained from ISSofBC's 2007–08 annual report.
14. Data obtained from the MOSAIC 2007–08 annual report.
15. Data obtained from the SUCCESS 2007–08 annual report.

REFERENCES

BC Stats. 2008. *2006 Census Fast Facts: Immigrant Population of British Columbia.* Victoria: BC Stats.
—n.d. *Profile of Immigrants: British Columbia.* Produced for the Multiculturalism and Immigration Branch. Victoria: BC Stats.
Charles, G., E. Tocol, T. Welsh, and J. Bassu. 2008. *Inventory and Analysis of Community Services for Immigrants and Refugees in British Columbia.* Vancouver: AMSSA.
Citizenship and Immigration Canada (CIC). 2004a. *Backgrounder: Agreement for Canada-British Columbia Co-Operation on Immigration.* At http://www.cic.gc.ca/english/department/media/backgrounders/2004/2004-04-05.asp (accessed 28 January 2009).
—2004b. *Agreement for Canada-British Columbia Co-Operation on Immigration – 2004.* At http://www.cic.gc.ca/english/department/laws-policy/agreements/bc/bc-2004-agree.asp
Cubie, D. 2006. *New Beginnings: Insights of Government-Assisted Refugees in British Columbia into Their Settlement Outcomes.* Vancouver: Immigrant Services Society of British Columbia.
Francis, J. 2009. "You Can Not Settle Like This": The Housing Situation of African Refugees in Metro Vancouver. MBC Working Paper Series 09-02. Simon Fraser University, Burnaby, BC.
Hiebert, D. 2009. "The Economic Integration of Immigrants in Metropolitan Vancouver." *Choices* 15(7):2-42.
Hiebert, D. and P. Mendez. 2008. "Settling In: Newcomers in the Canadian Housing Market, 2001–2005." MBC Working Paper Series, WP 08-04. Simon Fraser University, Burnaby, BC.
Hiebert, D., S. D'Addario, and K. Sherrell. 2005. *The Profile of Absolute and Relative Homelessness among Immigrants, Refugees, and Refugee Claimants in the GVRD: Final Report.* Vancouver: MOSAIC.
Hiebert , D., P. Mendez, and W. Wyly. 2008. "The Housing Situation and Needs of Recent Immigrants in the Vancouver Metropolitan Area." MBC Working Paper Series 09-01. Simon Fraser University, Burnaby, BC. At http://mbc.metropolis.net
Ilves, E. 2008. "Temporary Foreign Worker Trends in B.C." Special issue, "Our Invisible Workforce: Temporary Foreign Workers in B.C.," *CULTURESWest* 26(2):10-11.
Immigrant Integration Branch (IIB). 2009. *Welcoming and Inclusive Communities and Workplaces Program.* Information sheet. Victoria: Ministry of Advanced Education and Labour Market Development (AELMD).
Immigration Partnerships and Initiatives Branch (IPI). 2008. *Immigration Trends Highlights 2007.* Victoria: Ministry of Advanced Education and Labour Market Development (AELMD).
Krahn, H., T. Derwing, M. Mulder, and L. Wilkinson. 2000. "Educated and Underemployed: Refugee Integration into the Canadian Labour Market." *Journal of*

International Migration and Integration / *Revue de l'intégration et de la migration internationale* 1(1):59-84.

Ley, D. 1999. "Myths and Meanings of Immigration and the Metropolis." *Canadian Geographer* 43(1):2-19.

McLean, J., C. Friesen, and J. Hyndman. 2006. "The First 365 Days: Acehnese Refugees in Vancouver, British Columbia." RIIM Working Paper, 06-07. Simon Fraser University, Burnaby.

Ministry of Attorney General (MAG). 2006. "Increased Funding Promotes Racial Understanding." News Release 2006AG0036-001442. Victoria, BC.

—2008. "Funding Supports Anti-Racism and Multiculturalism." News Release 2008AG0031-000998. Victoria: Ministry of the Attorney General.

Multiculturalism and Immigration Branch (MIB). 2008a. *Census 2006: Regional Settlement of Immigrants in British Columbia.* Victoria: Ministry of the Attorney General.

—2008b. *The Ethnic Diversity of Visible Minorities and Ethnic Origins in B.C.* Victoria: Welcome BC.

Murdie, R. 2004. "Housing Affordability: Immigrant and Refugee Experiences." In *Finding Room: Policy Options for a Canadian Rental Housing Strategy*, ed. J.D. Hulchanski and M. Shapcott, 147-58. Toronto: CUCS Press.

—2008. "Pathways to Housing: The Experiences of Sponsored Refugees and Refugee Claimants in Accessing Permanent Housing in Toronto." *Journal of International Migration and Integration* 9(1):81-101.

Picot, G. 2004. "The Deteriorating Economic Welfare of Canadian Immigrants" *Canadian Journal of Urban Research* 13(1):25-45.

Pratt, G. 2008. "Thinking about the Ethics of Temporary Foreign Worker Programs." *CULTURESWest* 26(2):8-9.

Sherrell, K. 2008. *A Comparative Analysis of Housing Trajectories of Government-Assisted Refugees and Refugee Claimants in Two Canadian CMAs.* Report prepared for the Homelessness Partnering Secretariat.

Sherrell, K. and ISSofBC. 2009. *At Home in Surrey? The Housing Experiences of Refugees in Surrey, B.C.* At http://www.issbc.org

Sherrell, K, S. D'Addario, and D. Hiebert. 2007. "On the Outside Looking In: The Precarious Housing Situations of Successful Refugee Claimants in the GVRD." *Refuge* 24(2):64-75.

Sherrell, K., J. Hyndman, and F. Preniqi. 2005. "Sharing Wealth, Spreading the 'Burden'? The Settlement of Kosovar Refugees in Smaller British Columbia Cities." *Canadian Ethnic Studies* 37(3):76-93.

Statistics Canada. 2008. *Census 2006.* Ottawa: Statistics Canada.

Vancouver Foundation. 2008. "Vancouver Foundation's Vital Signs for Metro Vancouver (2008)." At http://www.vancouverfoundationvitalsigns.ca/admin-panel/files/pdfs/VFVS_2008.pdf

Vernooy, M. 2008. *Administrative Report on 2008 Community Services Grants and Rent Subsidy Allocations.* City of Vancouver.

Zine, J. 2003. *Living on the Ragged Edges: Absolute and Hidden Homelessness among Latin Americans and Muslims in West Central Toronto.* Toronto: Informal Housing Network Project.

CHAPTER 4

FOUR STRONG WINDS: IMMIGRATION WITHOUT DIRECTION IN ALBERTA

JAMES FRIDERES

SETTLEMENT PATTERNS

In 1905 the province of Alberta was carved out of what was then the Northwest Territories. The growth of population in the province occurred in four separate waves. The first wave of immigrants (pre-1910) was largely of British background but included others from central and eastern Europe and resulted from the "opening of the West." However, the attraction to the Canadian West during the 1800s was minimal, given that more fertile lands were still available in the great plains of the United States and the district of Alberta had a population of less than 20,000 by 1885. After 1896, greater numbers of immigrants were settling in Albert because of the overall improvement of the Canadian economy and the actions of the then federal minister of the interior, Clifford Sifton, who was responsible for immigration. Sifton's active promotion, coinciding with the end of readily available land south of the 49th parallel and the booming economy, saw Alberta's population increase to nearly 400,000 by 1911. Nearly half of the newcomers were immigrants, both from Europe and the United States, once free land was no longer available south of the border. The other half came from central and eastern Canada.

The second wave arrived immediately after World War I when the Canadian government initially allowed entry only to British and American immigrants. However, it now began to expand its list of "acceptable" ethnic/cultural groups. During the 1920s, nearly 100,000 new immigrants came to Alberta. Then in 1925 the federal government approved the Railways Agreement that allowed the railway companies to promote immigration to Canada internationally. Under this plan, close to 200,000

Integration and Inclusion of Newcomers and Minorities across Canada, ed. J. Biles, M. Burstein, J. Frideres, E. Tolley, and R. Vineberg. Montreal and Kingston: Queen's Policy Studies Series, McGill-Queen's University Press.

central and eastern Europeans were brought to Canada, most settling in the Prairie Provinces. With the advent of the Great Depression, Canada laregly closed its doors to immigration until the end of World War II. The third wave began after the war and lasted until the 1970s. At this time, immigrants' interest in settling in Alberta and the province's interest in attracting immigrants were not great; Alberta had ample labour supply as it focused its economic activities on agricultural and oil/gas extraction activities.

The most recent wave (1980–present) has brought increased numbers and a new type of immigrant to Alberta (Lamba, Mulder, and Wilkinson 2000). As Alberta began to diversify its economy and engage in the knowledge-based economy, new perspectives on immigrants as a labour force began to emerge. In turn, as technology became an important component of the province's economic and industrial development, interest in migrating to Alberta increased. During this same time, Alberta became an important global player because of the abundance of coal, oil and gas that it was willing to export. In the early 1980s the annual number of international immigrants landing in the province approached 20,000, although as the 1980s' recession developed, the numbers decreased, reaching a low of 9,000 in 1985. By the early 1990s, immigration had rebounded to over 18,000, only to drop again to 11,000 by 1998. Since then, however, there has been a steady increase to over 27,000 in 2009, representing 9 percent of national immigration, but still less that Alberta's 10 percent share of the national population.

Early residential settlement patterns focused on rural areas throughout the province, and newcomers from specific ethno-cultural groups tended to establish residence near other members of their group. As a result, blacks, Ukrainians, Jews, Poles, Germans, and other ethno-cultural groups created rural enclaves throughout the province (Derwing et al. 2005). After World War II, immigrants were less interested in agrarian pursuits and found jobs in the large urban centres. As ethnic enclaves began to emerge in the urban centres, they acted as magnets for immigrants who followed. By the 1950s, urban centres in Alberta had residential concentrations of a variety of ethnic groups including Chinatowns and Little Italys. Only in the late twentieth century did these communities begin to disperse, so that today the ethnic concentrations in urban centres reflect class rather than ethnicity. To be sure, there are major concentrations of ethnic groups in urban centres, but generally these are voluntary associations and are based on financial criteria. For example, in certain areas housing is cheaper, and ethno-cultural institutions are in place to accommodate various ethnic groups. Many immigrants who have achieved middle class status have moved out of their initial settlement area into newer suburban communities. On the other hand, other immigrants have chosen to remain in their initial residence because they have developed networks and social linkages there, or they are saving their money for other activities (e.g., remittances, return to homeland). Today there is some ethnic concentration in the two major urban areas of Calgary and Edmonton, but nothing approaching the level seen in many other Canadian urban centres. Indeed, within the province there is little ethnic concentration; although in urban centres Chinatowns can still be found, these are more commercial than residential. There are some exceptions to this and the town of Brooks is one example; the establishment of large slaughtering plants near the town and the concomitant need of a large unskilled but well paid labour force has drawn many recent immigrants.

This chapter now goes on to present demographic information on the current status of immigration in the province, the relationship between the province and the federal government, and the role of the provincial government with regard to immigration. It also assesses how other constituents such as municipalities and immigrant service providers address the needs of immigrants entering the province, and the section that follows focuses on various programs provided for immigrants and the financing and philosophy behind such programs. The chapter concludes by identifying challenges that confront both immigrants and the province as newcomers become a permanent component of the population dynamics.

IMMIGRATION TO ALBERTA

The issue of immigration has not received much attention from political leaders in Alberta over the past century. One might argue that the province focused much more attention on immigration shortly after its creation in 1905 than it has done until recently. Indeed, up to the late twentieth century, the provincial government appeared largely to ignore immigration and the challenges it brought. Government policies or programs did not place a high priority on issues relating to immigrant integration, including human rights. Only after labour shortages were identified by the private sector did the province actively engage in trying to increase the number of immigrants coming to Alberta and attempt to develop strategies to retain them and provide integrative services.

Much of the policy developed in Alberta with regard to immigration and immigrant integration has focused on economic dimensions. Little attention has been paid to the social and cultural aspects of immigrants and immigrant integration. The underlying assumption of most of Alberta's immigration policies is that the province needs a larger labour force in order to deal with the actual and anticipated development projects projected for the next decades. In short, it wants to ensure that Alberta has the necessary numbers, knowledge, and skills in its labour force to meet anticipated demands. It wants to control the entry of individuals so that they match the labour force needs of the province at a particular point in time. Long-term investments in the local population, for example, in Aboriginal people, is not viewed as an alternative. Moreover, the strategy of bringing in immigrants to deal with labour shortages at a particular time (e.g., professors, nurses, and doctors), worked well in the past (McDonald et al. 2010). As a result of this philosophy and history, much of the provincial effort is focused on bringing in temporary workers who can be converted to permanent residents through the Provincial Nominee Program.

DEMOGRAPHIC PROFILE OF ALBERTA

Table 1 provides an overview of where immigrants coming to Alberta have originated over the past half-century. It reveals changing patterns, with European and North/Central American immigrants decreasing in numbers, and immigrants from Africa and Asia showing commensurate increases. The result of the arrival of visible minorities in large numbers has been a change in the "colour" of Alberta.

TABLE 1
Source of Immigrants to Alberta by Year, 1966–2006, Percentage

	1966	1971	1981	1988	1996	2001–06[a]	2009
Europe	62	33	43	18	22	15	18
Africa	2	2	4	5	5	12	18
Asia	8	13	36	60	64	59	51
Australia	2	3	1	1	1	1	1
N/Cent.Am.	19	30	9	13	5	7	4
Carrib.	2	4	2	2	2	1	1
South Am.	2	6	4	2	1	5	9
Other	2	9	1	1	1	1	1
Total No.	10,946	8,653	19,277	14,025	13,892	103,685	27,107

[a] The 2001–06 period represents a five-year average of 17,280 immigrants per year, considerably higher than proceeding time periods except for the early 1980s.
Source: Government of Alberta (2004a, 2010a, 2011).

Until the 1970s a majority of the immigrants were from Britain, the United States, and Western Europe. Since then, major changes in the ethnic demography of Alberta have occurred. Today more than half the immigrants entering Alberta are Asian, with substantial numbers from Africa, Central and South America, and the South Pacific. Of those emigrating from Asia in the past three decades, we find that three countries (India, China, Philippines) each make up nearly 10 percent of the total immigrant population, increasing to more than 35 percent of immigrants coming to Alberta since 2001. As a result of this shift, Alberta's visible minority population has grown much faster than the population as a whole – by nearly 34 percent between 1996 and 2006, while the total Alberta population grew by 7 percent. Today 14 percent of the province's population is "visible minority," a figure projected to increase to over 20 percent by 2017. The top five source countries sending immigrants to Alberta are the Philippines, India, China, the United Kingdom, and the United States, in that order.

Table 2 identifies the number of immigrants entering Alberta over the past decade. It reveals a steady increase in the numbers and also reveals that Alberta's share of immigrants coming to Canada has risen from 6.4 percent in 1998 to 9 percent by 2009. It also reveals the composition of immigrants in Alberta has, over the past two decades, become more focused on economic immigrants and a major decrease in refugees. At the same time the percentage of family immigrants has remained constant.

TABLE 2
Permanent Residents in Alberta by Year and Class, 1988–2008 (percent)

Category	1988	1998	2001	2004	2008	2009
Family	30.8	33.8	30.3	31.5	32.6	30.4
Economic	52.3[a]	54.6	58.3	53.1	54.0	62.5
Refugees	7.5	11.4	11.5	13.4	10.6	3.9
Other	8.8[b]	0.2	0.0	2.1	2.8	3.1
Total	14,025	11,187	16,408	16,474	24,185	27,017

[a] This includes the category of "independent" and "designated."
[b] This is the category identified as "assisted."
Source: Government of Alberta (2004a, 2010a, 2011).

Accompanying the shift in immigrants' countries of origin has been a dramatic change in the languages used and religions practices by immigrants. For example, before 1961, 95.5 percent of the population spoke English in the home with 4.6 percent speaking a non-official language at home (Frideres 1998). By 2009 English speakers in the home declined to just fewer than 70 percent while the number of non-official language speakers increased to nearly one-quarter of the permanent residents (Edmonston and Fong 2011). Religious affiliation also dramatically changed. Before 1961, 85 percent of Albertans were Christian, with 13 percent declaring no religious affiliation. The remainder was equally divided among Muslim, Jewish and Other. As of 2006, only 52 percent were Christian, 12 percent Muslim, 1 percent Jewish, and 15 percent Other, with 21 percent declaring no formal religious affiliation. Overall, it is projected that there will be substantial growth of the Muslim, Hindu, and Sikh populations in Alberta, and most of this will take place in the two largest urban centres (Cardozo and Pendakur 2008). Data show that 63 percent of immigrants arrive at the working age (20–59), although one-fifth of the immigrants to Alberta in the past decade were under the age of 12. An additional 10 percent were between 13 and 19. Along with this we find that nearly half of permanent residents have a post-secondary credential (Alberta 2010).

During the past two decades, Alberta has led the country in population growth (1.6 percent per year), double the national rate. However, half of that growth has been from inter-provincial migration, and only 14 percent was a result of direct immigration. By the year 2000, Alberta was accepting well over 15,000 immigrants a year. Of these, 89 percent were settling in Calgary and Edmonton. In 2011 the Conference Board of Canada estimates that Alberta is expected to have more than 165,000 new interprovincial (40,000) and international migrants (125,000) over the 2011–15 period (Bernard 2011).

In addition to the permanent residents entering Alberta, the province has supported a major increase in temporary foreign workers and business people. The argument made by the Alberta government is that these temporary residents contribute to Alberta's economic development by filling gaps in the labour market, enhancing trade, and purchasing goods and services. In 2000, Alberta brought in nearly 11,000 temporary foreign workers, less than 10 percent of all temporary foreign workers in the country. The largest number went to the city of Calgary. However, by 2009, Alberta had increased the number to nearly 30,000 and this made up nearly 16 percent of all temporary foreign workers in Canada. In addition, over one-third of the workers were not situated in Calgary or Edmonton. As of 2009, Alberta had nearly 66,000 temporary foreign workers, making up nearly one-fourth of all of Canada's temporary foreign work force. Of these workers, 40 percent are situated in "other Alberta" (e.g., northern Alberta), followed by Calgary (31 percent) and then Edmonton (24 percent).

There are historical differences between Calgary and Edmonton, with early migrants coming to Calgary from the United States and/or the United Kingdom, while those coming to Edmonton were predominantly from Germany and/or Ukraine. These early differences have influenced the policies and programs implemented by the two urban centres to this day (Krahn, Derwing, and Abu-Laban 2003). The national-origin distribution of immigrants in Alberta has remained largely stable over the past decade. Today the overall immigrant population in Alberta is just over a half a million. Of these, 56 percent came before 1991, 24 percent between 1991, and 2000 and the remainder (29 percent) since 2001. In each of the two large urban centres, 15 percent of the population is foreign born. In smaller centres such as Red Deer, Brooks, and Lethbridge that foreign-born population is below 9 percent. Other towns such as Grand Prairie, Camrose, and Lloydminster have much smaller immigrant populations.

The number and distribution of the immigrant population in Alberta shows that Calgary was and continues to be the dominant urban centre drawing immigrants to Alberta (see Table 3). With one-third of the provincial population, the city consistently draws more immigrants than the rest of the province. Between 1993 and 2003, it took in nearly 100,000 immigrants, and Edmonton received just over 50,000.

TABLE 3
Number of Permanent Immigrants Residents in Alberta by Urban Area, 1998–2008

Urban Area	Numbers by Year				
	1998	2001	2004	2008	2009
Medicine Hat	104	165	151	181	161
Lethbridge	168	174	177	300	483
Calgary	6,006	8,499	9,448	13,025	13,708
Red Deer	169	213	254	674	537
Edmonton	3,796	4,582	5,056	7,512	8,508
Other AB	1,048	1,237	1,539	2,674	3,612
Total	11,187	14,705	16,474	24,185	27,017

Source: Government of Alberta (2004a, 2010a, 2011).

We find that just over three-quarters of migrants to Alberta are Canadian citizens. Of those, nearly 10 percent are also citizens of at least one other country. If we look only at the immigrants coming to Alberta in the 1991–2002 period, just over 71 percent have taken out Canadian citizenship and nearly 12 percent of those also hold citizenship of at least one other country.

Projections of immigrants living in Alberta indicate that by 2017 over 23 percent of the population in Calgary will be immigrants, 18 percent in Edmonton, with the rest of the province having only an 8 percent immigrant population. Alberta's visible minority population is projected to grow substantially in the future. For example, in 2006, 22 percent of the population in Calgary, 17 percent in Edmonton, was categorized as visible minority. However, Statistics Canada estimates those figures will increase by 2017 to 27 percent in Calgary and 18 percent for Edmonton. Specifically, it is estimated that well over a quarter-million Chinese and South Asians will reside in Alberta by 2017, in addition, to over 60 thousand Blacks and Filipinos (each). Smaller numbers (ranging from 11,000 Japanese to 35,000 Arabs) for other visible minority groups will bring the total number of visible minorities living in Alberta to nearly 600,000 by 2017.

The Players

As noted earlier, the Government of Alberta had little interest in immigration or immigrant settlement until the 1980s. Immigration was considered a federal issue and funding to deal with immigrants came from the federal government. Only Citizenship and Immigration Canada provided funds to settlement service agencies to facilitate social and economic integration of immigrants. The few provincial programs that existed were oriented toward the assimilation of newcomers. From an historical perspective, then, the Government of Alberta has been a recent player in the recruitment, retention, and provider of programs for immigrants.

Most of the organizations established in Alberta to deal with immigrants and immigrant integration in the 1970s were created by local community and religious organizations that determined that immigrants needed help in settling into Canada. These early organizations usually provided translation and housing services for recent immigrants and some were linked to various religious institutions. By the early 1980s these service agencies were obtaining funds from a variety of sources, including the United Way, churches, post-secondary educational institutions, the federal government and, indirectly, other levels of government (e.g., Alberta Advanced Education and the City-Preventative Social Services). By the mid-1980s, while the demand for services was high, Alberta was experiencing a recession, and few provincial departments were prepared to support immigrant serving agencies. However, the province did provide some funding for the Settlement Program and subsequently created the Immigrant Vocational Language Referral Centre (now the Immigrant Language Vocational Assessment-Referral Centre). Moreover, in 1985, the province signed one of the first immigration agreements with the federal government but let it expire in 1990. It was only in the late 1980s and early '90s that these agencies began to expand because of increased funding from federal sources, professionalization of the staff, and increased demand for their services. The increased staff and funding led to the creation of formal bureaucratic structures to ensure that immigrants would be served and accountability would be achieved as required by their funders.

Today, nearly all immigrant services are provided by independent third-party organizations (NGOs) and public and separate school boards, yet are funded by government. As these agencies have grown, they have developed multiple sources of funding, most notably from the federal government and specifically from Citizenship and Immigration Canada. Other more modest funding comes from a variety of sources, for example, the province (Alberta Employment and Immigration), lottery funds, municipalities, private foundations, other federal departments, the private sector, and the United Way. These agencies can now support a range of programs including settlement/integration services, language and vocational assessments, community based children and parent programs, youth programs, career programs, citizenship classes, and language programs (Alberta 2008).

Alberta's Relationship with the Federal Government

For many years, Alberta was content to leave immigration and immigrant integration as mainly the responsibility of the federal government. Existing federal programs along with current "mainstream" provincial programs in the province were seen as providing the necessary support for immigrant integration. Even though the province was not interested in becoming involved with immigration issues, it was an early leader in linking some of its activities in the area of immigration with federal agencies. For example, the province worked with federal authorities so that organizations applying for funds could use a single "combined" application form. This form represents a sense of collaboration with the federal government that few other provinces have undertaken. Today other forms of collaboration such as the Forum of Labour Market Ministers, the Council of Ministers of Education, Ministers of Health, Canadian Heritage, and Human Resources and Skills Development are all part of the pan-Canadian network that the Alberta government has supported to better coordinate its activities with regard to immigration and immigrant integration (Alberta 2007). Overall, the federal government has been active in supporting immigrants and immigrant integration in Alberta. During the past two decades, over $67 million has been allocated to the province for settlement, language training, and other immigrant integration programs. At the same time, provincial settlement budgets have been reduced, as the 2008–10 recession brought fiscal restraints to programs.

More recently Alberta accepted responsibility with the federal government for the settlement and integration of immigrants after they arrive in Alberta. As the twentieth century came to a close, it became clear that Alberta's labour needs far exceeded the capacity in the province. The provincial government began to focus on immigration as well as the retention of immigrants. In 2002, Alberta signed an agreement with the federal government to co-fund settlement adaptation services for immigrants under the Integrated Services Program (Alberta 2004). This agreement simply "codified" what had been ongoing practice since 1985 at the time of the first Canada-Alberta Immigration Agreement. Then in 2007, Alberta signed the Agreement for Canada-Alberta Cooperation on Immigration. This framework agreement provides Alberta with a mechanism to increase the economic benefits of immigration to the province, based on economic priorities and labour market conditions, by permitting Alberta to continue to nominate provincial candidates by incorporating an updated Provincial Nominees annex replacing the original 2002 Provincial Nominee Agreement. This new agreement authorizes the processing and admission to Canada of candidates nominated by Alberta. In 2010, Alberta was given permission to increase the number of provincial nominees well above the limit set previously by the federal government.

ROLE OF PROVINCIAL GOVERNMENT IN INTEGRATION / SETTLEMENT / INCLUSION OF NEWCOMERS AND MINORITIES

Until late in the twentieth century, Alberta, like other provinces, had not assumed responsibility for the provision of immigrant integration services. For example, in 1992, the Alberta government released *Bridging the Gap: A Report of the Task Force on the Recognition of Foreign Qualifications.* However, this report simply encouraged Ottawa to establish a central agency to assess foreign education and work credentials. As Biles, Burstein, and Frideres (2008) point out, at the same time provincial participation in integration has come about as many sectors integral to the integration process, such as education and housing, are the responsibility of provincial governments. The booming economy, the small numbers of immigrants coming to the province, and their ability to integrate into Alberta's social and economic fabric made them relatively invisible. Those who were not absorbed by mainstream culture were quickly integrated into the ethno-cultural communities. Moreover, until recently, the provincial government insisted that funding for immigrant and ethnic service agencies could only be funded on a 50–50 basis; that is, the province would match (up to 50 percent) funding obtained from other sources (Alberta 2005). However, in recent times, the new arrangements are 80–20, with the bulk of the funding coming from Citizenship and Immigration Canada. In addition, the province has long taken the stance that ethnic "specific" organizations will not be funded unless they provided services to "all Albertans."

The booming economy in the last decade of the twentieth century and early in the twentieth-first, along with projections of even more development in the province, forced the Alberta government to look at immigration as one way to meet the demands of the labour market. For the first time, politicians also began to acknowledge an aging labour force and a declining birth rate in the province. More importantly, employers pointed out that labour shortages were constraining the development activities of the private sector as well as increasing labour costs. The government of Alberta thus began to focus on labour force replacement as well as on increasing the size of the labour force. Government officials also began to note that professional designations, employer biases, and immigration procedural requirements combined to disrupt the fit between real market needs and the type of available labour (Azmier 2005). They found that the barriers to immigration success included discriminatory hiring practices by employers, professional associations with self-interested motivations, and negative attitudes toward immigrants among some of the Canadian-born population (and vice versa) as important factors in immigration and immigrant integration that could only be dealt with by the provincial government. As a result the Alberta government created the International Qualifications Assessment Service, which evaluates the education of individuals who obtained their education abroad. The service is a collaborative effort on the part of immigrant-serving agencies, post-secondary institutions, employers, and various federal and provincial government agencies. In 1995 Alberta collaborated with Saskatchewan to provide the full range of educational assessment for immigrants.

While international immigration was the mainstay for the population of Alberta in the early twentieth century, the province noted that today its impact is in decline. For example, in the past quarter-century, the Prairie provinces' share of immigrants had been cut in half (from 21 percent in the early 1980s to less than 10 percent by 1995 before climbing back to over 16 percent in 2008). The declining immigration levels throughout the 1990s posed a major problem for the Alberta government in terms of its desire to grow the economy, meet future population needs, and raise the value of cultural diversity. Population experts also pointed out that nearly one-third of the immigrants left the province within a five year period. As such, the provincial government developed an interest in both recruiting and retaining immigrants.

In 2004, the government of Alberta consulted with the province's business and economic leaders on how to recruit new international immigrants to the province. Six guiding principles were articulated: the process should be community-based, collaborative, fair and inclusive, holistic, sustainable, and accountable. One year later the Alberta government outlined its strategic framework that would lead to a more coordinated policy and program approach to immigrants and immigration. In 2005, the provincial government published its first major policy on immigrant integration, Supporting Immigrants and Immigration to Alberta.

This immigration policy was based on four strategic directions:

1. supporting communities as they work to become welcoming and being inclusive of immigrants and their families;
2. increasing the number of immigrants who will live in Alberta;
3. expanding programs and services that integrate immigrants and their families into daily life; and
4. helping immigrants access labour market opportunities.

However, to integrate the policy, a number of other provincial departments, municipalities, and community organizations were charged with providing services for immigrants to achieve the above goals. At that time, four provincial departments were placed in charge of fulfilling the policy: Human Resources and Employment, Economic Development, Advanced Education and International and Intergovernmental Relations. Other departments such as Community Development, Innovation and Science, and Health and Wellness were identified as having a role to play in supporting immigrants and immigration to Alberta.

More recently, with a change in premiers, old departments were phased out or changed and new departments created. The Alberta Provincial Nominee program became the Alberta Immigrant Nominee program in 2008. Originally located in the Economic Development Ministry, this program is now operated on behalf of the government of Alberta by the Ministry of Employment and Immigration in conjunction with Citizenship and Immigration Canada (CIC) in order to expedite the processing of an application for permanent residence. It has been designed to support Alberta's economic growth. Individuals nominated by Alberta (along with spouses and dependent children) are allowed to apply for permanent resident status, although CIC makes a final decision about the permanent resident application. Thus far, few immigrants have come to Alberta under this plan although projections for 2009–12 are that as many as 8,000 a year come through this program. However, in 2010, Alberta cancelled two components of the Alberta Immigrant Nominee program. Specifically, it no longer accepts applications under the US Visa Holder Category and the Family Stream program. This means that no Canadian visas will be granted to those having temporary US work permits and wishing to immigrate to Canada and work here. Also, those wanting to immigrate to Alberta under the category of Family Stream (family members of residents of Alberta) will not be granted Canadian visas although those who qualify under other streams will still be able to apply. Out of the total 4,200 visas granted to migrants wanting to move to Canada in 2010, about 1,400 Canadian visas were granted for the above two categories of provincial nominee programs.

Today, the Alberta Employment and Immigration Department is responsible for immigration policy for the province, primarily through settlement programs, language training programs, and federal/provincial relations and agreements related to immigration. It is also responsible for the coordination of Government of Alberta immigration initiatives and programs. In addition, the province engages in activities related to immigrant integration that are supported by CIC. These include general settlement assistance involving information, orientation, interpretation/translation, or referral services for recent immigrants through contracts with a network of immigrant serving agencies. Language assessment and referral services also are co-funded with CIC. Employment readiness programs (counselling and workshops to assist immigrants in understanding the Canadian workplace and how to find a job) are co-funded as well. Finally, enhanced language training programs to assist skilled immigrants in acquiring the technical and workplace language skills to practice their profession in Alberta are supported by both the federal and provincial governments.

The Alberta Employment and Immigration Department directly funds English as a second language (ESL) programs in both Calgary and Edmonton. They provide funding for ESL services/classes for immigrants who are not eligible for federal language instruction under the LINC programming; they develop and fund "bridge to work" programs that are designed to assist immigrants in gaining Canadian work experience and upgrading their skills to fully use their knowledge and expertise in the Alberta labour market. This department also has provided funds to urban centres to develop and publish a "newcomer guide" for use by immigrants wanting to use various services (e.g., social, religious, education).

The Alberta Employment and Immigration Department provides programs and services related to jobs through funds it obtained from the federal Department of Human Resources and Skills Development Canada under the Labour Market Agreement. It helps businesses and industries match skilled foreign workers with specific job opportunities, helps employers meet their needs for skilled workers, and provides a job order bank service, assistance for Albertans with disabilities, and funding to develop and support projects with industry, business, community, and employer groups with common labour market needs. The job bank provides a listing of jobs available across the province, with detailed information about job openings, qualifications, and descriptions of the jobs for all Albertans, not just immigrants.

As noted earlier, the provincial government's emphasis is on providing services for all Albertans, although these services may also support newcomers. For example, the Alberta Child Support Services and the Alberta Adult Health Benefit program provide services for all of Albertans but also include support for permanent resident immigrants.

Role of Municipalities

Until recently, almost none of the urban centres in Alberta (with the exception of Edmonton) had exhibited any desire to develop policies or programs focused on immigrant recruitment, retention, or integration. For example, while Calgary in 2000 established the Calgary Cultural and Racial Diversity Task Force made up of community groups, city councillors, city staff, and provincial and federal government representatives, business leaders were conspicuously absent; five years later the effort was abandoned due to differences in vision, lack of funding, and a disconnect between community supporters and decision-makers, as well as a unclear infrastructure. The city argued that its Fair Calgary Policy was sufficient to ensure integration of immigrants. By 2007, the Calgary Foundation graded the immigrant experience in Calgary as C– (Fortney 2007). In early 2011, Calgary City Council approved a new Welcoming Community Policy. This policy aligns with the previous Fair Calgary, and is consistent with the city's diversity and inclusion framework currently under development. The new policy creates a welcoming community for all residents while at the same time continues to provide appropriate, acceptable and responsive services and employment opportunities for immigrants to Calgary.

Municipalities' argument is that services to immigrants are not part of their mandate and that the issue is a federal/provincial concern. They argue that they receive no specific funding for this area and thus at an official level have not become involved in it. As a result, municipalities allow the NGO immigrant serving agencies, provincial bodies, and various ethno-cultural organizations to deal with immigrants and their needs. Indirectly and on a pilot basis, municipalities sometimes provide funding to ethno-cultural organizations to deal with generic needs of immigrants. More recently municipalities began to address the immigrant and immigrant integration issue at an informal level. For example, both Calgary and Edmonton have participated and support the Canadian Coalition of Municipalities against Racism and Discrimination.

Urban centres differ in terms of their action with regard to immigrants. Calgary has invested minimally in immigration and/or immigrant integration in the city, and its primary involvement is through the Family and Community Support Services. For example, in 2006 it committed and administered $1 million for programs serving immigrants in Calgary. Yet the city argues that with limited authority and resources available, as a corporate entity it is not able to provide an inclusive and effective set of services for immigrants. Some minor pilot projects, for example, "Guide for Cultural Understanding" brochures for six ethic visible minority senior groups and the hiring of one intern in the pilot Immigrant Internship Project, have been funded by the city. However, no substantive policies or programs have been established to support immigrant recruitment, retention, or integration. However, at an informal level, the city has become involved through providing support for NGOs, supporting research, and helping different agencies in the city deal with immigrant integration.

On the other hand, Edmonton adopted a policy on immigration and settlement in mid-2007. The policy focuses on seven areas: economic integration, intergovernmental relations, service access and equity, planning and coordination, communication, public awareness and education, community building and inclusion, and immigrant women. Through these policies, the city is committed to a municipal environment that attracts and retains immigrants and their families. The establishment of this policy gave rise to the Emerging Immigrant and Refugee Communities Grant program. The grants range from $5,000 to $20,000 and are directed toward supporting and strengthening emerging immigrant and refugee communities, enhancing the integration of immigrants into the "multicultural mosaic," and encouraging immigrants to remain in the city. Specific grants can be obtained for such things as space/rental subsidy, organizational development, and establishment of community based programs.

Edmonton has also created an immigrant internship program and established an Office of Diversity and Inclusion, and works with the Edmonton

Region Immigrant Employment Council (funded by Citizenship and Immigration Canada) to attract immigrant labour and to enhance integration. The Office of Intergovernmental Affairs ensures that the City of Edmonton has representation on the Alberta Tri-Lateral Table on the Community Sustainability working group. In addition, the community services department has hired a "multicultural community recreation coordinator" to provide strategic outreach to immigrants and refugee communities and assist in their access to city services and programs. In early 2009 the city introduced the Citizen and New Arrival Information Centre at City Hall to help new arrivals get settled. The program, funded by Alberta Employment and Immigration, has also published a newcomer's guide in six different languages to enhance access to information about the city.

UNIVERSAL SERVICE PROVIDERS

A number of organizations such as the Wild Rose Foundation, Muttart Foundation, and Kahanoff Foundation provide funding for programs that are not specifically linked to immigrant integration but may benefit newcomers. A major "universal" organization in Alberta that supports immigrant integration (directly and indirectly) is the United Way. For example, the United Way of Edmonton has budgeted over $8 million for its Network of Core Services to help those in financial need or requiring social support. The United Way has also targeted "homelessness" as a core issue and provided funding for agencies in Edmonton with similar interests. At the same time the United Way provides funding for specific NGOs whose mandate is for immigrant integration, but it does not support "settlement services" which it sees as the responsibility of Citizenship and Immigration Canada. For example, in Calgary, the Immigrant Services Calgary, Calgary Catholic Immigrant Services, and Calgary Immigrant Women's Association all receive strong financial support from the United Way as long as the programs focus on themes that are in line with its philosophy. However, the United Way changes its "themes" periodically, and thus organizations must continually craft their programs to meet current themes. In Edmonton, the United Way provides similar financial support to agencies such as the Mennonite Centre for Newcomers and the Centre for Immigrant Women.

The Edmonton Board of Education has recognized the multicultural character of students and put in place policies, professional development, and resources to assist staff in responding to a range of student needs. Focus is on strategies that promote success for students who are English language learners: provision of cultural and language interpretation, liaison with both the home and the cultural communities, and conflict mediation; implementation of policy on anti-discrimination and on "value, respect diversity"; and promotion of a school environment that responds to linguistic and cultural needs of students. In Calgary, the Calgary Board of Education and the Calgary Catholic School Board have established welcome centres for immigrant students. Their activities range from the intake of newcomer students to supporting immigrant parents in a new educational environment. A discontinued elementary school has been converted to a community outreach centre, where immigrants wanting to register their children in the Calgary Board of Education can receive support. In addition, the Calgary Bridge Foundation works with the Calgary Board of Education to provide in-school settlement activities and youth services. The city has established some pilot projects and is currently evaluating the efficacy of the programs.

Provincially funded organizations such as Vibrant Communities (Edmonton and Calgary), Momentum (Calgary) and the Immigrant Access Fund (for all of Alberta) provide initiatives to increase stability for employers and employees; as well, they provide small, low-cost loans to individuals who might otherwise not be eligible. The Centre of Newcomers (Calgary) supports newcomer settlement and immigrant settlement programs; its goal is to help integrate newcomers in the community by providing them with services and initiatives that promote diversity, participation, and citizenship. The centre receives the bulk of its funding from CIC and Alberta Human Resources and Employment.

The Alberta Learning Information Service, the provincial gateway to helping individuals plan and achieve their educational and career success, is also available to immigrants. The service provides them with information for career planning, post-secondary education and training, and educational funding. The advisory committee is made up of representatives from the universities, colleges, Alberta Education, Alberta Advanced Education, and other organizations that work in the learning environment (e.g., Alberta Teachers' Association, Universities Coordinating Council.)

Immigrant Service Provider Organizations

Each of the major urban areas in Alberta has established immigrant service-provider organizations. Table 4 identifies the major current organizations. These organizations have multi-million dollar budgets (some exceeding $7 million), a large number of employees (both paid and volunteers), and complex organizational structures to deal with the multitude of programs offered; they are major employers in their communities. These organizations are in direct contact with the immigrant population, as they provide services and they are aware of the changing needs of immigrants (Burstein 2010). However, they remain marginal to the decision-making process within all levels of governments. At the same time their reach is considerable, with estimates that 15,000 to 20,000 immigrants utilize these services every year. Moreover, they remain marginal within the larger community, and few CEOs of these service-providing organizations are recognized as community leaders or as contributing value-added activities that require their voice in local politics or policy decisions regarding immigration and immigrant integration. It should be noted that many of the programs offered to immigrants come through "mainstream" organizations, and thus it is difficult to tease out the immigrant component of these programs. For example, the Calgary After School Partner program is supported by the City of Calgary as well as by 20 other organizations. However, it is not limited to immigrant youth even though a large proportion of its clientele is in fact immigrant youth. In relation to this, there is currently a move by service providing organizations to develop satellite centres within larger urban centres as well as providing centres in the surrounding smaller communities. Moreover, several pan-Canadian partnerships have been created among service providing agencies across Canada.

TABLE 4
Major Immigrant-Serving Agencies in Alberta, 2010

Calgary	Calgary Bridge Foundation for Youth
	Calgary Catholic Immigration Society
	Immigrant Services Calgary (formerly Calgary Immigrant Aid Society)
	Calgary Immigrant Women's Association
	Calgary Multicultural Centre
	Centre for Newcomers
	Calgary Immigrant Education Society
	Calgary Immigrant Educational Society
	Jewish Family Service Calgary
	Francophone Newcomers Centre
Edmonton	ASSIST Community Services Centre
	Change Together: A Centre for Immigrant Women
	Acces Emploi
	Catholic Social Services
	Changing Together – A Centre for Immigrant Women
	Edmonton Immigrant Services Association
	Edmonton Mennonite Centre for Newcomers
	Edmonton Regional Immigrant Employment Council
Other Cities	Global Friendship Immigration Center, Brooks
	Immigrant Settlement Services, Grand Prairie
	Lethbridge Family Services–Immigrant Services, Lethbridge
	YMCA of Wood Buffalo, Immigrant Settlement Services, Fort McMurray
	Saamis Immigration Services Association, Medicine Hat
	Catholic Social Services: Immigration and Settlement, Red Deer
	Central Alberta Refugee Effort – CARE Committee, Red Deer
	Brooks and County Immigration Services, Brooks

These agencies provide information and guidance for immigrants once they arrive in Alberta. Major activities of each include the provision of services such as health care (e.g., Public Health Agency of Canada), language training, and family and interpretive services. However, they also provide other services to deal with emerging immigrant needs such as jobs counselling. Because funders do not wish to fund services that other organizations provide, these immigrant serving agencies are always careful to coordinate their programs with other agencies in the same city. Moreover, funders are reluctant to continue funding to programs over time, and thus NGOs are required to be creative in developing "new" programs. Nevertheless, there is some overlap simply because some immigrant needs such as language training cannot be met by just one organization, or one organization cannot provide services in a variety of geographical locations. However, it is important to note that many of the immigrant service agencies are now expanding their geographical scope and establishing "branch" offices in smaller towns to provide selected services to communities outside the major urban centres. While Table 4 identifies the major immigrant service agencies, smaller organizations throughout the province are also involved in providing services to newcomers.

Several umbrella associations have also been created in order to coordinate the activities of the increasing number of NGOs providing services to immigrants. The first, the Alberta Association of Immigrant Serving Agencies, has been in existence for the past quarter century. It includes 20 member organizations from eight communities across Alberta serving more than 14,000 immigrants annually. It works closely with all levels of government, ethno-cultural organizations, and business communities across the province. Its major goal is to serve as a provincial forum to identify and recognize the needs of immigrants and to influence political actions. It also provides a network sharing work information and lobbies on behalf of immigrants. Its major funders are the Family and Community Support Services, United Way, the Government of Alberta and Citizenship and Immigration Canada. A second umbrella association, the Ethno-Cultural Council of Calgary (now called the Immigrant Sector Council of Calgary), has been created to facilitate the collective voice of Calgary's visible minority communities to bring about social, economic, and political change. A third, smaller organization called the Alberta Network of Immigrant Women is a provincially based network of immigrant women's organizations that provides a forum for member organizations to discuss relevant issues and to facilitate the development of solutions for issues that challenge immigrant women and their families.

ISSUE/ETHNO CULTURAL GROUP BASED NGOS

In Edmonton, the Mennonite Centre for Newcomers (established in 1984) and the Catholic Social Services have been the mainstay organizations assisting immigrant settlement and integration. These organizations, like the Calgary Immigrant Aid Society (now called Immigrant Services Calgary) and Calgary Catholic Immigrant Services, emerged as a "charitable" model in helping newcomers. However, over the years they, and others like them, have become professional, business enterprises with multi-million dollar budgets and a complex organizational structure reflecting the multiplicity of programs they offer to immigrants. Originally, ethno-cultural organizations in Alberta (including those seeking federal funds) were only eligible for receiving provincial funds if they agreed to provide services to any Albertan. Since then, many of these organizations were able to obtain funding from the federal government for language programs and began to offer services to specific ethno-cultural groups. The result today is that a number of immigrant service agencies provide programs for similar activities (e.g., ESL programs).

First started in the 1970s with financial help from what is now Canadian Heritage, many of these organizations have continued to serve their respective ethno-cultural communities. New immigrant groups have found sufficient funding to provide minimal services for their community, although they continually find themselves as the "second tier" of service providers. For example, the Chinese Community Service Association has been in operation since the mid-1970s, and its mandate and vision are broad and have changed over time. Today, they are focused on such programs as "anti-bullying," youth employment, and reducing criminal activities. Moreover, their programs are collaborations with other government agencies (e.g., Solicitor General, Calgary Health Region) and other community organizations (e.g., Calgary Immigrant Women's Association). Like other such organizations, their funding comes from numerous federal departments, provincial departments, and the private sector.

UNIVERSITIES AND COLLEGES

Universities and colleges have played marginal roles in the integration of immigrants. In the early 1970s, post-secondary educational institutions found the supply of trained scholars and researchers in Canada insufficient to meet their expanding activities. They thus embarked upon an international recruitment program to bring professors and teachers from around the world. As post-secondary institutions developed Canadian expertise, the need for foreign professors diminished, although specific areas in the post-secondary system (e.g., medicine, engineering) continue to recruit new faculty.

As institutions, they have focused their efforts on providing various language programs that allow foreign students to enrol into academic and technical programs within their own institution. However, their initial entry into these language training programs was based on financial considerations, and today these programs are based on "cost recovery," with the overall motivation of increasing foreign student recruitment, in turn enhancing revenues for the institution. (Successful graduates of these programs may then enrol in the institution, and the institution thus receives foreign tuition, in some cases four times that of the regular tuition.) In short, many of these programs are geared not to permanent immigrants but rather to temporary immigrants wishing to attend post-secondary educational institutions. While the colleges (e.g., NAIT, SAIT, Bow Valley) have developed specific credentialling and skill programs by which to increase their foreign student population, universities have resisted this strategy.

Teacher programs in post-secondary educational institutions across the province have only recently taken an interest in pedagogy and classroom issues related to culturally diverse classrooms in the primary and secondary school system. However, education faculties across the province have not created programs to help train teachers to deal with multicultural classrooms.

PROGRAMS

As most of the programs for immigrants and immigrant integration are provided to immigrants through NGO service agencies, below is a brief profile of these programs, their focus, and their goals.

Language Training

In Calgary and Edmonton alone, over 40 different organizations provide language training to immigrants (e.g., ILVARC, LINC). In order to obtain funding, each organization has developed an idiosyncratic program for the provision of language services. Each program has unique entrance requirements, different levels of language proficiency, different length of time for program completion, different age groups and sex of participants, and variations in whether the student has to be referred by another agency or not, whether the program is conversational or written or for professionals or general public, and whether or not students are Canadian citizens. In addition, both Calgary and Edmonton have created centres that assess language proficiency. Funding for these organizations comes from Alberta Employment and Immigration in partnership with CIC. These two centres also have linkages with various immigrant serving agencies and Community Adult Learning Councils that may provide language training in smaller communities across the province.

Major post-secondary educational institutions (e.g., University of Alberta, Mount Royal University) as well as numerous NGOs and other institutions provide language (e.g., ESL) programs for immigrants. Alberta Employment and Immigration, in partnership with CIC, supports two centres, the Immigrant Language and Vocational Assessment Referral Centre, Calgary, and Language Assessment, Referral and Counseling Centre, Edmonton, that assess language proficiency and provide up-to-date information on ESL programs running in those cities. However, ESL services or classes available in smaller centres across Alberta are also available from Volunteer Tutor Adult Literacy programs and Community Adult Learning Councils. Currently there are more than 80 Community Adult Learning Councils across the province (e.g., Bashaw Adult Learning Council, Fox Creek Adult Learning Board).

Employment, Training, and Career Services

Alberta has now identified immigrants as an essential strategy to address their current and future labour market shortages. It is estimated that within five years immigration will account for all of the net labour market growth in Alberta. The province has also recognized that many immigrant skilled workers are under-employed (45 percent) or over-qualified for their current job (49 percent) and that their home country education and/or work experience is not recognized (64 percent) (Azmier, Huynh, and Molin 2004). To ensure immigrant employment support (where new immigrants to Alberta can learn about finding a job and what employers want), Alberta Employment and Immigration and CIC fund a number of organizations to provide specifically designed employment readiness programs. These services include counselling and workshops. Centres providing employment services have been established in Edmonton (Personal Support and Development Network, Bredin Institute, Edmonton Mennonite Centre for Newcomers), and Calgary (Bow Valley College, Calgary Catholic Immigration Society, Calgary Immigrant Women's Association, Centre for Newcomers).

The International Qualifications Assessment Service program was not widely used and was shelved by 2005. Three years later the province introduced a new plan to improve recognition of foreign-earned qualifications, training, and experience. The Foreign Qualifications Recognition Plan for Alberta (operated by Advanced Education and Technology) is an attempt to expand the labour market and strengthen the economy of the province. This plan supports and enhances two other key government strategies:

Building and Educating Tomorrow's Workforce, and Supporting Immigrants and Immigration to Alberta. The plan recognizes the importance of the role of several stakeholders – including employers, educational institutions, professional regulatory organizations, and immigrant servicing agencies – in bringing newcomers into the labour market. The plan's goal is to facilitate the labour market integration of skilled immigrants, ensuring that immigrants receive timely and equitable recognition of their credentials, and promoting a collaborative and supportive environment and continuous improvement in the qualification recognition process.

The Edmonton Region Immigrant Employment Council is unique in Alberta and is a multi-stakeholder (industry, three levels of governments, settlement serving agencies and ethno-cultural communities), industry-led council working to identify and foster solutions leading to more successful integration of local immigrants into the Edmonton region labour market. The council's goals are to act as a knowledge broker and referring agency, to develop pilot services and programs for immigrant employment, and to function as a catalyst in addressing systemic barriers in public policy and procedure. Today, Calgary Region Immigrant Employment Council has focused on assisting local employers in implementing appropriate strategies designed to enable skilled immigrants to secure and retain employment. Recently it has embarked upon a pilot "mentoring" project that links skilled immigrants with employers. Its goal is to build inclusive workplaces that bring together skilled immigrants and established professionals.

Education

Academic upgrading programs (including computer access) are available in a number of colleges, boards of education and institutes and libraries. In addition, other community organizations (e.g., Mustard Seed, Careers in Transition, and NGOs) provide programs for both immigrant and native-born Albertans.

The Calgary Board of Education has established the Pathways to Partnership program that creates effective partnerships between Calgary Board of Education schools and immigrant serving agencies. The relationships between these agencies and schools are dynamic and change with the situation. Overall their relationships tend to be school-linked programs offered by agencies at the school or for school students in community locations such as libraries. For example, Immigrant Services Calgary has a preschool and family literacy program, while the Calgary Immigrant Women's Association is linked to the Calgary Board of Education through two programs, Culture Clubs and Community Volunteer Services, as well as providing cross-cultural parenting classes.

Health

The federal government recently signed a memorandum of understanding with the province on Alberta-destined health care professionals. The two levels of government agreed to a pilot project to improve and facilitate the selection and processing of applications of individuals in the health care sector (e.g., physicians, pharmacists, registered nurses, and physiotherapists). This agreement was based on the provincial projection of having a shortage of over 16,000 health care workers by 2017. Alberta also has developed a series of Health Career Centres for internationally educated health professionals. Two centres, Bredin Institute Centre (Edmonton) and Bow Valley College (Calgary), have been created to help immigrants, at no cost, obtain career coaching, through engagement in study groups and referrals as they work toward meeting the requirements for professional practice in Alberta. They serve many health professionals (e.g., physicians, dietitians, health care aides, social workers, occupational therapists). This program has a three-year budget of $1.4 million. In addition, the province has established a program that allows foreign-trained physicians who do not meet the Alberta standards to obtain the necessary education and training so as to be able to practice. Major immigrant service providers ensure that immigrants have access to these programs. However, other organizations (e.g., YWCA, Simon House Recovery Centre, Families Matter) also provide services for both immigrant and non-immigrant individuals.

The three-year pilot program Seeds of Empathy is offered in 15 Alberta daycare centres to teach preschoolers respect for and acceptance of others through guided interactions with a baby and parent. The goal is to have 65 centres run the program by 2011. The program grew out of the Roots of Empathy program offered in nearly 400 Alberta classrooms to over 9,000 children in kindergarten and Grade 1.

Youth Programs

The YMCA, Youth Employment Centre, and other organizations (e.g., Ability Society, Centre for Newcomers) provide a variety of programs for youth, both immigrant and non-immigrant. For example, the Ability Society provides young people with a series of workshops with an emphasis on life skills and basic business skills to make them employment ready. They also gain practical work experience directed toward their intended employment plans. On the other hand, the Calgary Immigrant Women's Association youth program addresses the needs and concerns of culturally diverse women between the ages of 12 and 19 and provides leadership opportunities and training. The Calgary Achievement Centre for Youth has two programs that focus on immigrant youth, one related to supporting occupational choices, the other focusing on language training. In 2010, the Genesis Centre was developed to provide immigrant services beyond the downtown core. This outreach centre will involve other service-providing agencies in Calgary and be supported by the city and other philanthropic organizations.

Finance

The Provincial Immigrant Access Fund, established in 2005, recently approved $1 million in micro-loans to help immigrants to Alberta get the accreditation and training they need to work in their field. Nearly 200 applicants have been provided with funds, ranging for such training/education as physicians, engineers, accountants, nurse medical technologists, electricians, and jewellers, through their loan delivery partners, Momentum and the Edmonton Mennonite Centre for Newcomers. Funding for the program comes from the Alberta government and from the Western Economic Diversification Canada, along with nearly $1 million in donations from the private sector (e.g., HSBC Bank Canada). Thus far, 32 of 183 loan recipients have completed their accreditation or training. This organization provides loans of up to $5,000 to help Alberta's immigrants obtain the accreditation, upgrading, or training they need to work in their profession or trade. Loans may be used for tuition, exam fees, qualification assessments, books and course materials, a living allowance during study time, or other related expenses. Thus far the default rate is less than 1 percent.

MAJOR ISSUES / CHALLENGES

To meet current labour demands, Alberta has embarked upon an aggressive temporary foreign worker program in order to accommodate the booming economy. The province chose this path in spite of projections by economists and policy analysts that net labour force growth, as well as net population growth, would occur solely through permanent migration by 2011 and 2031, respectively (Gluszyski and Dhawan-Biswal 2008). Between 2003 and 2007 there was a 225 percent increase in temporary foreign workers in Alberta. By 2011 nearly 70,000 temporary foreign workers were living in the province. As a proportion of population, Alberta has 12.5 times more temporary workers than the United States. Moreover, 13.5 percent of Canada's workers on restrictive, temporary visas are currently working in Alberta. Out of the total immigrants in Canada, Alberta attracted the largest number of immigrants in the period 2005–10.

The plan allows temporary resident immigrants to sidestep the federal point system. In short, even if "temporary" immigrants do not have the requisite points to qualify for permanent residency, they can come to Alberta to work for two years and then apply for an extension, as long as it is processed before the initial work permit expires. Alternatively, they could switch employers at the end of the two years and, working with a second employer, remain in Canada for an additional two years.

Under this program, temporary foreign workers would be allowed to apply for permanent resident status while in Canada as long as their work visa was still in effect. The implications are staggering. First of all, the number of temporary foreign workers in Alberta in 2008 was higher than that of permanent immigrant residents who arrived in that year. In addition, few of those on temporary work visas have been provided with services to help them integrate (Sheldon Chumir Foundation 2009). Nevertheless, there have been some piloted settlement programs for temporary foreign workers supported by Immigrant Settlement Services. For example, a program in Lloydminster focuses on the needs of both immigrants and temporary foreign workers living in the area. It also provides a range of supports to community organizations and businesses that relate to temporary foreign workers. The specific program (delivered through Catholic Social Services) offers professional educational workshops for newcomers, the community, and employers. In Red Deer and Edmonton, Catholic Social Services provides information and referrals, supportive counselling, interpretation and translation services, and advocacy for temporary foreign workers and their families. There also is concern that much of the wages earned in Alberta by these temporary workers will be sent home as remittances to help support their families. Thus the wages earned will not be spent in Alberta or in Canada, and the economic impact of temporary foreign workers will be of primary use to employers.

Since 2001 the *Immigration and Refugee Protection Act* has allowed employers different ways in which they can recruit temporary foreign workers through an array of different mechanisms. For example, the new act allows employers to recruit workers beyond "skilled," such that they include unskilled workers such as waitresses and hotel workers. In addition, temporary workers can extend their two year work permits, and they can apply for permanent status while holding a temporary foreign worker certificate (Saloojee 2003). According to the act, temporary foreign workers are bound to particular employers and hence particular geographic locations. Given that the legal status of temporary migrant workers is tied to employers, those employers hold yet more power in the relationship and as such, these temporary workers are more vulnerable to coercion and/or abuse in the workplace.

Immigrant serving agencies carry out most of the programs supporting immigrants and immigrant integration. Moreover, their major funding comes from federal departments. However, even though they are on the ground providing the services and interacting with immigrant clients and so have an intimate understanding of the issues and needs confronting immigrants, their voice is not solicited nor given priority consideration in the development of policy (Burstein 2010). In addition, the ethno-cultural organizations that also provide second-tier services to members of their community have an even lower profile in policy development than the settlement agencies.

Between 15 percent and 19 percent of the total budgets of immigrant-serving organizations goes towards administrative matters in dealing with funders and so is not allocated for immigrant integration. Because different rules and reporting activities are required by each of the funders, the agencies spend considerable time and money addressing the unique and idiosyncratic requirements.

There is growing pressure from municipal governments for a "new deal" in their relationship with federal and provincial governments. Their requests include increased resources for immigrant settlement and a greater political voice in immigration policy. In recent years, major urban centres have not only enlarged their role in providing support services to newcomers, but have also been obliged to deal with the multiple aspects of an increasingly ethno-racially diverse population with respect to municipal programs and policies. Extra pressures have been placed on municipalities by downloading of responsibilities to municipalities by higher levels of government, severe cutbacks in public spending, and the lack of an integrated and effective pan-Canadian policy for newcomer settlement (Omidvar and Richmond 2003). Local governments could make essential contributions to the development of long-term planning for immigrant settlement and play a key role as brokers in bringing to the table other partners such as NGOs and immigrant community organizations.

The drive for urban reform provides an important impetus for the active political involvement of immigrant communities in urban politics, just as the mobilization of these communities is essential in ensuring that urban reform results in improved immigrant settlement. Linking urban reform to immigrant settlement thus has real potential for the policy application of a social inclusion framework.

CONCLUSION

Alberta's provincial government has focused on increasing the number of immigrants strictly as an economic venture. From its limited analysis of the labour force and economic projections, it understands that a shortage of skilled labour is looming. Nevertheless, before taking on the immigration issue, it identified a number of solutions to alleviate this labour shortage: increased engagement with Aboriginal people, the recruitment of more women into the labour force, reforms to mandatory retirement-age laws, and increased training for youth. This analysis revealed that even if all of the alternative scenarios were put into effect, the numbers would still not meet the short-term future labour demand without increased immigration. Similarly, from an economic perspective, the province recognizes that immigration is the cheapest and quickest way of meeting current labour demands, since immigrants arrive with skills and education.

This perspective was based on traditional assumptions about immigration, without taking into account that the province is now competing in a global environment and competition from other nation states is high. In the end, Alberta opted for a program of increased temporary and permanent international immigration. It was felt that immigrants coming to Alberta would be highly educated and / or trained, with vocational skills, and would be within the labour force working age. As such, it was felt that they could easily integrate into the current labour market. However, to allow them to enter this market, the province would work with the federal government to streamline the immigration process and deal with the issue of foreign credentials. It thus found itself working with the federal government and developing a strategy for recruiting immigrants for the labour force.

Alberta's changes in policy with regard to immigration and immigrant integration are reactive to the province's changing demographic profile. Until the 1960s the focus was on assimilation of white European / American immigrants. By the 1970s, with the influx of the "boat people," a new ethos of "sharing" culture and "being tolerant" emerged. By the 1980s further diversity of the population was evident and new "anti-racist" programs were introduced. However, in the 1990s the province became concerned with the rising deficit and embarked on a decade of budget reductions. A majority of the "people programs" were cut and many disappeared completely. Not until well into the twentieth-first century would a new interest in immigrant integration and inclusion emerge.

In the past two decades, there has been increased competition among global forces such as the United States, Australia, and Germany to recruit highly skilled immigrants. Even if a skilled immigrant chooses Canada, over 30 percent leave via new exit doors (Reitz 2004). Thus, Canada and Alberta are not managing skilled immigration flows as well as they would like to think. The combined costs of human capital loss (including recruitment, "churning costs" – training, settlement, leaving) and loss of productivity are projected to exceed $3 billion annually by 2015. In short, current provincial actions have not fully supported immigrant integration. The insistence by the province on micro-managing the entry of immigrants into Canada is based on the old nineteenth-century model, which continued to work during the twentieth century. However, global conditions and the context of immigration in the twentieth-first century require new strategies to attract and retain immigrants in Canada. In 2008 Canada created the Canadian Experience Class, which offers permanent residency to international students and internationally trained workers of various skilled categories following the completion of 12–24 months of work in Canada – on the basis of a temporary work authorization. However, these temporary workers can only be retained permanently if the employer approves. This program resulted in a shift of primary decision-making power around permanent residency from the state to employers (Valiani 2009).

The insistence that labour needs are independent of criteria for entry into Canada has led to substantial problems in Alberta. The current policy of the federal skilled workers program uses one set of criteria to admit immigrants and "hopes" that it will somehow address the labour short-ages in various parts of the country. Certainly immigrants who meet the necessary points are allowed into Canada, but when they attempt to enter the labour market, they face major barriers for which provincial govern-ments are unprepared and only now trying to deal with. For example, medical doctors, trained and experienced, have the "points" to enter Canada, but when they attempt to practice are assessed by the provincial professional medical association and rejected. In 2010, the federal govern-ment took the initiative and signed a Pan-Canadian Framework for the Assessment and Recognition of Foreign Qualifications with all provincial governments. The federal government took this leadership in the absence of action by provincial governments who were in control of recognizing foreign credentials specifically in licensed professions but who did not establish a process of assessing immigrants easily and in a transparent manner. The Foreign Credential Recognition Program and the Foreign Credentials Referral Office (established in 2007) are now the key federal initiatives in place to support the implementation of the framework. Under this framework, the federal government will develop the principles that guide the process of foreign credential recognition, establish standards for the timely handling of requests, and identify key occupations that will be the priority for developing recognition standards.

In addition, Citizenship and Immigration Canada has been consulting with Canadians during 2010–11 with regard to the Federal Skilled Worker Program introduced in 2002. CIC has has met with key stakeholders in five cities across the country and has encouraged the public to provide input to the department. The goal of these consultations is to determine what changes, if any, are needed to help select immigrants most suited to integrating into Canadian life. For example, it is consulting on whether skilled trade workers should be required to have a level of language pro-ficiency equivalent for professionals, how the program might be made more accessible to skilled tradespeople that better contribute to success in the Canadian work force, whether or not placing greater emphasis on younger immigrants is a preferred strategy, and whether or not points might be redirected from work experience to other factors that better contribute to success in the Canadian labour market.

Because of Alberta's refusal for so long to develop an immigration policy, immigrant serving agencies have found it difficult to make a case for funding new services that the communities and the immigrant serving agencies identified as being necessary. It is true that recently the province has provided significant support for ESL programs and for some employment support services, although many of the immigrant community's needs have not received support. The lack of policy and programs by municipalities has also led to a lack of support for immigrant integration. Recent commitments by the provincial agency Community Support Services have been one significant change.

The elaboration of a new vision of integration involves the identification of mutual obligations and benefits for both immigrants and the host society with respect to all the social, economic, and political institutions of Canadian society. As Omidvar and Richmond (2003) note, all levels and departments of government must be held accountable for the results of immigrant integration, not only with respect to the provision of adequate resources for immigrant settlement but also in terms of the necessity for broad public policy discussion on the nature and goals of the newcomer settlement journey and its impact on our social, cultural, and political institutions. There must be adequate resources for immigrant integration, the protection of the community-based agencies and the development of mechanisms to directly include the voices of leaders from the immigrant and refugee communities.

References

Alberta. 2004. *Integrating Skilled Immigrants into the Alberta Economy*. Edmonton.
Alberta. 2004a. *An Overview of Immigration to Alberta*. Edmonton: Alberta Learning.
—2005. *Supporting Immigrants and Immigration to Alberta*. Edmonton.
—2007. *A Profile of Alberta Seniors*, Edmonton: Seniors and Community Supports.
—2008. *The Spirit of Alberta: Alberta's Cultural Policy*. Edmonton: Ministry of Culture and Community Spirit.
—2010. *A Foreign Qualification Recognition Plan for Alberta, Progress Report, 2009-2010*. Edmonton.
—2010a. *Alberta Labour Force Profiles*. Edmonton: Employment and Immigration.
—2011. *Alberta Immigration Progress Report*. Edmonton: Employment and Immigration.
Azmier, J. 2005. "Improving Immigration: A Policy Approach for Western Canada." *Building the New West*, no. 42 (March). Calgary: Canada West Foundation.
Azmier, J., V. Huynh, and K. Molin. 2004. "Increasing Western Canadian Immigration." *Building the New West*, no. 31 (May). Calgary: Canada West Foundation.
Bernard, M.-C. 2011. *Provincial Outlook: Economic Forecast*, Ottawa: Conference Board of Canada.
Biles, J., M. Burstein, and J. Frideres. 2008. *Immigration and Integration in Canada in the Twentieth-First Century*. Montreal and Kingston: McGill-Queen's University Press.

Burstein, M. 2010. *Reconfiguring Settlement and Integration: A Service Provider Strategy for Innovation and Results.* Ottawa: Canadian Immigrant Settlement Sector Alliance.

Cardozo, A. and R. Pendakur. 2008. *Canada's Visible Minority Population, 1967–2017.* Metropolis British Columbia, Working Paper Series No. 08-05.

Derwing, T., H. Krahn, J. Foote, and L. Diepenbroek. 2005. *The Attraction and Retention of Immigrants to Edmonton.* Edmonton: University of Alberta, Prairie Centre of Excellence for Research on Immigration and Integration.

Edmonston, B. and E. Fong. 2011. *The Changing Canadian Population.* Montreal and Kingston: McGill-Queen's University Press.

Fortney, V. 2007. "Immigrants Struggle to Find Equal Footing in City." *Calgary Herald,* 12 October, A1.

Frideres, J. 1998. "Language in Alberta: Unilingualism in Practice." In *Language in Canada,* ed. J. Edwards, 443-60. New York: Cambridge University Press.

Gluszyski, T. and U. Dhawan-Biswal. 2008. *Reading Skills of Young Immigrants in Canada: The Effects of Duration of Residency, Home Language Exposure and Schools.* Ottawa: Strategic Policy and Research, Human Resources and Social Development Canada.

Krahn, H., T. Derwing, and B. Abu-Laban. 2003. *The Retention of Newcomers in Second and Third Tier Cities in Canada.* Edmonton: Prairie Centre of Excellence for Research on Immigration and Integration and the University of Alberta.

Lamba, N., M. Mulder, and L. Wilkinson. 2000. *Immigrants and Ethnic Minorities on the Prairies: A Statistical Compendium.* Edmonton, Prairie Centre of Excellence.

McDonald, T. E. Ruddick, A. Sweetman, and C. Worswick, eds. 2010. *Canadian Immigration.* Montreal and Kingston: McGill-Queen's University Press.

Omidvar, R. and T. Richmond. 2003. *Towards the Social Inclusion of New Canadians.* Toronto: Laidlaw Foundation.

Reitz, J. 2004. Canada: Immigration and Nation-Building in the Transition to a Knowledge Economy." In *Controlling Immigration: A Global Perspective,* ed. W. Cornelius, T. Tsuda, P. Martin, and J. Hollifield, 97-133. Stanford, CA: Stanford University Press.

Saloojee, A. 2003. *Social Inclusion, Anti-Racism and Democratic Citizenship.* Toronto: Laidlaw Foundation.

Sheldon Chumir Foundation. 2009. *Toward Equal Opportunity for all Albertans.* Calgary: Sheldon Chumir Foundation.

Valiani, S. 2009. *The Shift in Canadian Immigration Policy and Unheeded Lessons of the Live-In Caregiver Program.* At http://ccrweb.ca/temporaryworkers.htm

CHAPTER 5

SETTLEMENT AND INTEGRATION IN SASKATCHEWAN: EVOLUTION OF ORGANIZATIONAL ROLES, COMPLETENESS, AND CAPACITY

JOSEPH GARCEA

INTRODUCTION

This chapter provides an overview and analysis of some key developments in Saskatchewan's settlement and integration system. The central objective is fourfold: first, to outline the evolution of the alignment of roles performed by governmental and non-governmental organizations within the settlement and integration systems during the past decade; second, to examine the effects that the alignment of roles has had on organizational completeness and organizational capacity within the system; third, to identify the persistent challenges in the settlement and integration system; and fourth, to discuss what is being done and what should be done to address those challenges. For purposes of this chapter, "organizational completeness" (or "institutional completeness") of that system (Breton 1964; Rosenberg and Jedwab 1992) refers to the extent to which existing organizations are deemed adequate and appropriate for providing settlement and integration programs and services for newcomers, and "organizational capacity" refers to the extent that, collectively, the various governmental and non-governmental organizations have the means and resources to develop and deliver settlement and integration programs and services.

The major findings are that several important initiatives undertaken during the past decade have resulted in a substantial realignment of roles,

Integration and Inclusion of Newcomers and Minorities across Canada, ed. J. Biles, M. Burstein, J. Frideres, E. Tolley, and R. Vineberg. Montreal and Kingston: Queen's Policy Studies Series, McGill-Queen's University Press.

improving both organizational completeness and organizational capacity within the settlement and integration system. Nevertheless, significant challenges persist in the alignment of roles, organizational completeness, and organizational capacity that compromise the amount and quality of services for immigrants and refugees. To address those challenges, even more extensive and effective coordination and collaboration is required among governmental and non-governmental agencies on a more systematic and sustained basis.

OVERVIEW OF IMMIGRATION FLOWS TO SASKATCHEWAN

A full appreciation of contemporary initiatives related to the settlement and integration of newcomers and minorities in Saskatchewan requires an understanding of the number and destinations of immigrants arriving in the province, as well as their countries of origin and their racial, ethno-cultural, and linguistic composition.

After the initial massive wave of 500,000 immigrants from 1880 to 1910, Saskatchewan did not receive many immigrants during much of the next century. Even in recent decades when the larger provinces were receiving substantial immigration flows, flows to Saskatchewan were small. This is evident in successive censuses from 1991 to 2006, which reveal that immigrants constituted only 5 percent of the province's population (Statistics Canada 2006a). During the past decade, however, the immigration flows to Saskatchewan have been increasing steadily each year. This is particularly true of the period 2005–10. The total number of immigrants arriving in Saskatchewan through both the national and provincial programs has increased from approximately 1,564 in 1998 to 6,890 in 2009 (Table 1).

TABLE 1
Immigration to Saskatchewan, 1999–2009

	1999	2000	2001	2002	2003	2004	2005	2006*	2007*	2008*	2009*	Total
Regina	538	672	542	556	562	656	630	821	910	1,406	2,058	9,351
	31%	35.7%	31.8%	33.2%	33.7%	33.8%	29.7%	30.1%	25.9%	29.1%	29.9%	30.5%
Saskatoon	806	791	769	721	631	802	843	1,164	1,618	2,061	2,562	12,768
	47%	42%	45.2%	43.3%	37.8%	41.2%	39.8%	42.7%	46%	42.6%	37.2%	41.6%
Other	385	419	393	390	475	485	646	739	988	1,368	2,271	8,559
	22%	22.3%	23%	23.4%	28.5%	25%	30.5%	27.1%	28%	28.3%	33%	27.9%
Sask.	1,728	1,882	1,704	1,667	1,668	1,943	2,119	2,724	3,516	4,835	6,891	30,678

Source: CIC (2008).
*CIC (2009d).

The increased flows resulted largely from the provincial government's special efforts to establish and expand the Saskatchewan Immigration Nominee Program (SINP). Whereas in 1998 all immigrants arrived through the national program, by 2009 only 37 percent arrived through that program and the remaining 67 percent arrived through the provincial program (Table 2). The SINP flows consisted of approximately 36 percent principal applicants and approximately 64 percent dependants (Table 3). The provincial government's immigration strategy released in June 2009 projected that by 2010 approximately 3,400 principal applicants would be admitted, which, when combined with their spouses and children, would result in more than 10,000 immigrants arriving in Saskatchewan for that year through the SINP (Saskatchewan 2009a, 2009b).

TABLE 2
Total Immigrant Landings by Immigrant Category

Immigration Category	1998	1999	2000	2001	2002	2003	2004	2005	2006	2007	2008	2009	Grand Total
Provincial nominees													
Total		18	37	41	73	173	323	468	960	1,837	3,037	5,031	11,998
Federal immigrants													
Economic immigrants	647	749	786	673	580	502	560	550	622	509	628	507	7,313
Refugees	524	509	648	588	601	501	560	614	626	617	552	646	6,986
Family class	393	452	411	402	363	412	456	456	477	514	549	628	5,513
Other immigrants					50	80	44	31	39	39	69	78	430
Total	1,564	1,710	1,845	1,663	1,594	1,495	1,620	1,651	1,764	1,679	1,798	1,859	20,242
Grand total	**1,564**	**1,728**	**1,882**	**1,704**	**1,667**	**1,668**	**1,943**	**2,119**	**2,724**	**3,516**	**4,835**	**6,890**	**32,240**

Source: CIC Micro Data (2009).

TABLE 3
Landings of Provincial Nominees, by Applicant and Dependent

Immigration Category	1999	2000	2001	2002	2003	2004	2005	2006	2007	2008	2009	Grand Total
Provincial nominees												
Principal applicant	6	12	12	21	53	109	162	352	674	1,109	1,858	4,368
Dependant	12	25	29	52	120	214	306	608	1,163	1,928	3,173	7,630
Grand total	**18**	**37**	**41**	**73**	**173**	**323**	**468**	**960**	**1,837**	**3,037**	**5,031**	**11,998**

Source: CIC Micro Data (2009).

Approximately 72 percent of immigrants arriving in Saskatchewan during the past decade were destined for the two largest cities (Saskatoon 41.6 percent, and Regina 30.57 percent), with 27.9 percent destined for the rest of the province (Table 1). Both the number and percentage of immigrants destined for the rest of the province increased from a low of 22 percent (385) at the start of the decade to a high of 33 percent (2,271) by the end. Of those destined for the rest of the province, the vast majority continued to be destined for other cities, particularly Moose Jaw, Prince Albert, North Battleford, Swift Current, and Humboldt (Anderson 2006; Garcea 2006a, 2007).

In addition to experiencing a substantial increase in the volume of immigration, during the past decade Saskatchewan also experienced a substantial increase in its immigrant retention rate. Whereas at the start of the decade the overall retention rate was approximately 50–60 percent for the entire province and slightly higher for the two largest cities (Anderson 2006; Garcea 2006a, 2007), by the middle and latter part of the decade it had climbed to approximately 80–85 percent (Pruegger and Cook 2009). The retention rate was 37.5 percent for 1990–95, 58.6 percent for 1995–2000, and 79.9 percent for 2000–05 (CIC 2006b, 2010).The improved retention rate was largely due to the economic boom that Saskatchewan started experiencing in 2007, and the fact that the majority of immigrants arriving during the second half of the decade were provincial nominees who had prearranged employment.

The recent increase in the volume of immigration has resulted in Saskatchewan receiving substantially more immigrants from a wider range of countries in the Asian, Pacific, African, Middle Eastern, and European regions than in previous decades (CIC 2008, 32-3). This trend is consistent with immigration flows to the other two Prairie provinces as well as most, if not all, other provinces. The top ten source countries for immigration to Saskatchewan during the past decade include the Philippines, China, India, South Africa, Iraq, and Afghanistan, which collectively constitute 42 percent of newcomers (Table 4). A substantial proportion of those in the "Other Countries" category are also from non-European countries, many of which provide immigrants who are likely to be considered visible minorities. Two notable demographic characteristics of those flows are that they reflect a broader racial and ethnocultural heterogeneity than was evident in previous decades, and many of them are members of visible minorities. These characteristics of the immigration flows are much more evident in the larger cities that are receiving the largest number of immigrants. Nevertheless, these recent flows have not transformed substantially the cities' racial or ethnocultural profile. When compared to the largest cities in Canada, Saskatchewan's two largest cities have less visible racial and ethnocultural diversity, especially when the Aboriginal population is not included. In 2006 the visible minority population was 33,895 (3.5 percent) for Saskatchewan, 14,870 (6.5 percent) for the Saskatoon CMA, 12,605 (6.5 percent) for the Regina CMA, and 6,420 (1.2 percent) for the rest of the province outside those two cities (Statistics Canada 2006a, 2006b). The racial and ethnocultural profile of Saskatchewan and its largest communities still primarily reflects the descendants of approximately 500,000 immigrants largely from Western and Eastern Europe who settled in the province from 1890 to 1910, and the Aboriginal population.

TABLE 4
Total Immigrant Landings, Top Source Countries (Country of Birth)

Country of Birth	1998–2009	
	#	%
Philippines	5,604	17
China	3,279	10
England	1,716	5
India	1,377	4
United States	1,306	4
Ukraine	1,169	4
South Africa	1,128	3
Iraq	1,073	3
Afghanistan	943	3
Sudan	778	2
Other	13,867	43
Grand total	**32,240**	**100**

Source: CIC Micro Data (2009).

Over the past decade, the percentage of immigrants to the province who speak neither official language has been 41.9 percent, ranging from approximately 32 percent to almost 50 percent. The percentage who speak English has been 54.6 percent, ranging from approximately 47 percent to 60 percent, and the percentage who speak both English and French has been 3.5 percent, ranging from approximately 1.6 percent to 8.2 percent (CIC 2008, 30-1).

To date, neither the racial and ethnocultural heterogeneity of the immigration flows nor the linguistic characteristics have created any major controversies. Indeed, even the increase in immigration flows has not created controversies of any notable scope. At most they have contributed to ruminations regarding whether Saskatchewan really needs immigrants or whether resources should be devoted to training and employing Aboriginal and non-Aboriginal people in the province who are either unemployed or underemployed.

EVOLUTION IN ROLES PERFORMED BY KEY ORGANIZATIONS

In Saskatchewan as in other provinces, two major interrelated trends have been evident in the evolution of roles performed by governmental and non-governmental organizations during the past decade. One trend is the expansion in the constellation of governmental and non-governmental agencies involved in performing key roles within that system. This trend has entailed a shift from involvement only by the federal government and a few settlement service agencies to involvement by a multiplicity of governmental and non-governmental agencies. The other trend is the gradual but significant expansion in the types and number of roles performed within the settlement and integration system by governmental and non-governmental agencies. Both of those trends are closely linked to an increase over the most recent decade in the types and number of settlement and integration programs and services provided. All three trends have been evident primarily in the four largest cities, and to a lesser extent also in many of the other nine smaller cities. In smaller urban and rural areas, these trends have been either very limited in scope or not evident at all.

Roles of the Federal and Provincial Governments

During the past decade the general alignment of roles between the Canadian and Saskatchewan governments for the settlement and integration of immigrants and refugees has been articulated in two bilateral framework agreements. The first was initially signed in 1998 (CIC 1998). This agreement was amended slightly in 2003 (CIC 2003) and supplemented with a memorandum on post-graduation employment for international students in 2004, which was subsequently expanded in scope in 2006 and 2008 (CIC 2004, 2006a, 2009a).

The second agreement, which replaced the first, was signed in 2005 and is still in force (Saskatchewan 2005a, CIC 2009b). The 2005 agreement contained most of the provisions of the 1998 agreement regarding settlement and integration, including those regarding the shared responsibility of the the federal and provincial governments to do the following:

- Consult and collaborate with each other in fostering economic, social, and political integration of newcomers;
- Participate in provincial and local mechanisms established to foster cooperation in developing and delivering settlement and integration services; and
- Recognize, foster, and support the involvement in settlement of integration of municipal governments, local and regional authorities (e.g., health and school boards), and non-governmental organizations (e.g., religious, ethno-cultural, labour, and business).

Both agreements also contained provisions to the effect that in developing and implementing settlement and integration programs and services, the two governments would be mindful of the bilingual and multicultural character of Canada. The only difference between the two agreements in this respect was that whereas the 1998 agreement explicitly noted the federal government's interest in programming that was consonant with the bilingual and multicultural characteristics of the country, the 2005 agreement also noted the provincial government's interest in these matters (CIC 2005). Thus, the 2005 agreement stated that the provincial government shared the federal government's interest enhancing the vitality of French language communities in the province and that, pursuant to the provincial *Multiculturalism Act*, it was committed not only to promoting awareness and appreciation of the social, cultural and economic benefits of immigration but also to facilitating the settlement and integration of immigrants into the multicultural provincial society. The agreements also stated that the federal and provincial governments recognized the benefits of citizenship and that, although the federal government would continue to be responsible for establishing the regulations for acquiring citizenship, both orders of government would work together to promote good and active citizenship.

Those provisions were consonant with three important provincial policies related to settlement, integration, and inclusion of newcomers. The first of these is the *Act to Promote and Preserve Multiculturalism* (1997), which reflects the spirit of the provincial motto "From many peoples, strength" (Garcea 2006b). As part of the long list of noble policy goals and objectives related to multiculturalism in the province, it explicitly states the government will "promote awareness and understanding of the social, cultural and economic benefits of continuing immigration to Saskatchewan; and ... facilitate the settlement of immigrants in Saskatchewan and their adaptation to and integration into Saskatchewan society" (Saskatchewan 1997). The second important policy is the French-Language Service policy, which states that the provincial government recognizes that "linguistic duality is a fundamental characteristic of Canada and that Saskatchewan's Francophone community is an important component of that linguistic duality," and that it is "committed to enhancing the services offered to Saskatchewan's Francophone community in support of the development and vitality of this community" (Saskatchewan 2009d). The policy applies to the provincial government, its departments, crown corporations, and other agencies. The policy highlights two categories of service goals; one is related to communication from the provincial government to members of the francophone community in French, and another is related to actual service delivery in French. The policy also states that the Joint Provincial Government/Francophone Community French-Language Services Liaison Committee will serve as an advisory committee for the implementation of this policy. The third important policy is the Saskatchewan Human Rights Code. The code exists to ensure that everyone's human rights, including those of newcomers and members of minority groups, are not abrogated. The code also provides the statutory basis for the existence, operation and funding of the Human Rights Commission, which is responsible both for providing public education to preclude abrogation of those rights and also for investigating and remedying any abrogation of those rights (Saskatchewan 2007).

The agreements also contained two important sets of provisions regarding the roles and responsibilities of the federal and provincial governments in funding settlement and integration services for newcomers. The first set dealt with their roles and responsibilities related to two particular categories of newcomers: refugees and provincial nominees. More specifically, the provisions stated that whereas the federal government would be responsible for providing immediate essential services for any refugees that it sponsored who landed and resided in Saskatchewan, the provincial government was to be responsible for any special settlement support needs of provincial nominees selected under SINP. This included reimbursing other provincial governments for any social programs that Saskatchewan's provincial nominees accessed in their respective provinces for up to three years after their arrival in Canada.

The second set of provisions dealt with the roles and responsibilities of the two orders of government in funding other newcomer settlement and integration programs in the province. Although both orders of government contribute financial resources to such programs, the agreements obliged only the federal government to provide any funding. They did not oblige the provincial government to contribute either on its own or through any cost-sharing arrangements. In keeping with the provisions of those agreements, Saskatchewan is one of the provinces in which the federal and provincial governments have been using the parallel funding model rather than the devolved model used by Quebec, British Columbia, and Manitoba, for directing funds to agencies delivering settlement and integration programs. This model was used even in the case of cost-sharing in 2005 when the federal and provincial government each contributed $200,000 to launch the Enhanced Language Training (ELT) program (Saskatchewan 2005b).

Federal and provincial funding for settlement and integration services has increased substantially over the past decade. Pursuant to the provisions in the 1998 agreement, the federal government was committed to provide $2.938 million for the fiscal years 1997–98, 1998–99, and 1999–2000. Over the subsequent four years, federal funding dropped slightly but generally remained within that same range. After 2005–06, it started to increase substantially. Thus, whereas the basic funding (i.e., not including funding for enhanced language training, anti-racism, and the immigration portal) was $2,577,750 for 2005–06, in the subsequent two years it increased to $3,247,595 for 2006–07 and $3,985,192 for 2007–08. Both basic and total funding (i.e., basic funding plus funding for enhanced language training, anti-racism, and the immigration portal) continued to increase in the fiscal years 2008–09 to 2010–11. Total funding was $6,025,004 for 2008–09, $8,030,275 for 2009–10, and $10,127,313 for 2010–11 (Table 5).The data indicate a fourfold increase in the level of federal funding from 2005–06 to 2010–11. The increase was due to a combination of an increase in the level of federal funding and an increase in the volume of immigration to the province. The increase coincided with the utilization of the new funding formula initially implemented in 2006–07 to calculate only the special increase in federal funding for that fiscal year, and then to calculate all federal settlement and integration funding starting the following fiscal year (CIC 2007). Since the funding formula was established, federal funds have been allocated through four major funding categories: basic funding, enhanced language training, anti-racism, and the immigration portal. Thus, for example, the total allocation to Saskatchewan for the fiscal year 2010–11was $10,621,884, including $9,891,429 for basic funding, $377,847 for Enhanced Language Training, $82,078 for anti-racism, and $270,530 for the immigration portal. For 2010–11, Saskatchewan received 4.36 percent of total federal funding (i.e., $651,621,168) allocated to all provinces and territories except Quebec and Ontario (CIC 2009b).

TABLE 5
Federal Settlement Funding Allocations

2005–06	2006–07	2007–08	2008–09*†	2009–10*†	2010–11*°
$2,577,750	$3,247,595	$3,985,192	$6,025,004	$8,030,275	$10,127,313

Source: CIC (2007), *Basic Settlement Funding Allocation*, at http://www.cic.gc.ca/english//department/media/backgrounders/2007/2007-12-17.asp#tphp%20idtphp
*2008/2009–2010/2011 have ELT, anti-racism, and portal funding included in basic funding.
†Source: CIC (2008). *Backgrounder, Settlement Funding Allocations*, at http://www.cic.gc.ca/english//department/media/backgrounders/2008/2008-12-22.asp#tphp%20idtphp
°Source: CIC (2009), *Letter to Provinces on Settlement Funding Allocation*.

Whereas the bulk of federal settlement funding to Saskatchewan is transferred directly to community based agencies, some of it is also transferred to the provincial government. Both sets of transfers have increased substantially during the past five years. The federal transfers to the provincial government for cost-shared initiatives have increased from $200,000 in 2006–07 to $955,000 in 2007–08, $2,166,000 in 2008–09, and $2,134,000 in 2010–11.

Provincial funding during the past decade has also increased substantially, particularly for the second part of the decade. The provincial government ventured into funding settlement agencies with only $100,000 annually from 2000–01 to 2004–05 and then $150,000 in 2005–06, rising to $7,791,000 in 2010–11 (Table 6). The recommendation made in two provincially commissioned reports of 2002 and 2003 for a major increase in such funding was not heeded until after the 2005 agreement was signed (Saskatchewan 2002, 2003). In subsequent fiscal years the amount of provincial funding budgeted for settlement and integration increased steadily and substantially to the point where it has constituted the largest portion of the provincial immigration budget, which increased from $450,000 in 2000–01 to almost $13 million in 2009–10 (Table 7), to pay both for increased allocations for settlement and integration programs and for the expanding administrative costs: staffing numbers increased from less than five at the start of the decade to approximately 70 by the end of the decade (Saskatchewan 2009c). Three important points must be noted regarding the funding data. First, in some of the past few years the budgeted amount exceeded actual expenditures by a few hundred thousand dollars because, given the scope and pace of program development, it was not always possible to implement all the planned initiatives. Second, although most of those funds went to settlement service providers, some may have been used for other purposes related to the settlement and integration programming in the province. Third, a small proportion of annual provincial allocations for settlement and integration may have been supported by federal funding from some other federal funding programs such as labour market training. Although the bulk of federal and provincial funding for settlement and integration has been provided by the lead ministries responsible for immigration at federal and provincial levels, some of it has also been provided by other federal and provincial agencies (e.g., Canadian Heritage and SaskCulture) responsible for funding cultural and multicultural programming delivered largely through project funding for community based organizations.

TABLE 6
Provincial Settlement Funding Allocations, 2001–02 to 2010–11

	2001–02	2002–03	2003–04	2004–05	2005–06	2006–07	2007–08	2008–09	2009–10	2010–11
Salaries	$700	$635	$644	$796	$873	$2,457	$3,260	$3,422	$3,965	$3,852
Goods and services	$150	$150	$200	$248	$712	$3,202	$1,682	$1,053	$1,193	$1,193
Transfers for public services	$100	$100	$100	$100	$150	$400	$3,548	$5,439	$7,856	$7,791
Total expenditure (in $000s)	$950	$885	$944	$1,144	$1,735	$6,059	$8,490	$9,914	$13,014	$12,836

Source: Saskatchewan Ministry of Finance, Provincial Budget (Estimates) at http://www.finance.gov.sk.ca/budget/

TABLE 7
Provincial Immigration Expenditures, 2000–01 to 2009–10

	2000–01	2001–02	2002–03	2003–04	2004–05	2005–06	2006–07	2007–08	2008–09	2009–10
Expenditures in $000s	$450	$950	$885	$944	$1,144	$1,735	$6,059	$8,490	$9,914	$13,014

Source: Saskatchewan Ministry of Finance, Provincial Budget (Estimates) at http://www.finance.gov.sk.ca/budget/

Roles of Municipalities

Generally, most municipal governments in Saskatchewan have not performed substantial roles in the actual provision of settlement and integration services on a regular and continuing basis. They have tended to leave that function to community based agencies and funding responsibility for it primarily to the federal and provincial governments. For their part municipalities have focused on the development and implementation of policies and programs designed to create warm and welcoming communities.

To that end, a few of the largest municipalities, but particularly the cities, have developed either one or both of two major types of interrelated policies. The first type focuses on cultural diversity and race relations policies per se, and the second focuses on diversity and equity in the workplace. The notable example in this respect is the City of Saskatoon, which adopted the Cultural Diversity and Race Relations Policy that articulates the following four major policy outcomes:

- The workforce [in Saskatoon and in City Hall] will be representative of the population of Saskatoon;
- There will be zero tolerance for racism or discrimination in Saskatoon;
- Community decision-making bodies will be representative of the whole community of Saskatoon; and
- There will be awareness and understanding in the community regarding the issues, and acceptance of the various cultures that make up Saskatoon. (City of Saskatoon 2004)

Saskatoon's policy has been influential not only for the settlement and integration of newcomers but also in that city's community planning (Garcea 2009). Unlike Saskatoon, most other municipalities have not articulated such policy outcomes in writing, though in some cases their civic officials have articulated them orally. Similarly, unlike Saskatoon, most municipalities have not established a Cultural Diversity and Race Relations Committee. Two other cities with comparable committees are

Moose Jaw and Prince Albert (City of Moose Jaw 2009; City of Prince Albert 2009a). Those committees, like their counterpart in Saskatoon, have encouraged their respective city councils to join the Coalition of Municipalities against Racism and Discrimination, which is supported by the Canadian Commission for United Nations Educational, Scientific and Cultural Organization (UNESCO) as well as the Saskatchewan Human Rights Commission (City of Prince Albert 2009a, 2009b).

In recent years some of the largest municipalities have started to consider whether to become more directly and actively involved in the settlement and integration of newcomers and how they should do so. The most notable example of this in the recent years has been the City of Saskatoon. At the behest of its Cultural Diversity and Race Relations Committee, the city entered into a partnership with the federal and provincial government for two interrelated initiatives. The first was to produce a report outlining not only the needs of Saskatoon for immigrants and the needs of immigrants in Saskatoon, but also issues and options related to building organizational capacity within and beyond City Hall to deal with immigration and integration. That report, which dealt with a wide array of issues and options regarding immigration, integration, and inclusion, was co-funded by the federal, provincial, and city governments (Pontikes and Garcea 2006).

The second initiative, which was spawned by the first, was the establishment of the City of Saskatoon Immigration Project (SIP). Its purpose was to act on recommendations contained in the aforementioned report so as "to foster effective and efficient planning and coordination of services among government agencies, employers and community groups providing settlement and integration services in Saskatoon" (Saskatchewan 2008a, 2008b). In the background document for this initiative, the three governments stated that the project was designed to "promote and coordinate early settlement and integration support for immigrants and refugees moving to Saskatoon ... by fostering a welcoming environment for newcomers, developing a governance model for the immigration plan, developing sector specific strategies, and increasing residents' awareness of the positive contributions of immigrants to Saskatoon" (Saskatchewan 2008b). Funding for the initial two years of the project from 2007 to 2009 totalled $167,450 based on the following contributions from the three governments:

- Citizenship and Immigration Canada, $74,250 (August 2007–31 March 2009);
- Saskatchewan Advanced Education, Employment and Labour $49,600 (August 2007–August 2008 (with the possibility for some additional funding to 31 March 2009 thereafter);
- City of Saskatoon, $43,600 (August 2007–31 March 2009) (ibid.).

In 2009 the three levels of government agreed to continue to fund the project for at least one additional year. The federal government's funding for those initiatives in Saskatoon is comparable to the type of funding that it was also providing to Ontario city regions to establish Local Immigration Partnership initiatives headed by local councils mandated to develop models, strategies, and projects to assist new immigrants with their settlement needs (CIC 2009c). The purpose of the funding in Saskatoon was to hire an immigration resource coordinator (IRC) whose principal role was to explore options for implementing some of the recommendations of the report *Building Saskatoon to Become a Global City* (Pontikes and Garcea 2006). In particular, the IRC was to facilitate capacity building and coordination within the immigration and integration sector and to provide advice to the city administration and council on next steps in developing and implementing an immigration action plan for the city. In the subsequent three years, the IRC has been very instrumental in coordinating a series of forums focused on six sub-sectors (i.e., health, education, settlement, employment, housing, and policing).The forums were constructive in creating awareness regarding a wide range of immigration, settlement, integration, and inclusion issues and options, fostering linkages and partnerships among key stakeholders and service providers, and helping policy-makers of the three levels of government and various local authorities to consider what further improvements are needed (Garcea and Garg 2009).

Roles of Community and Economic Development Agencies

Some community and economic development agencies in cities and larger towns also perform valuable roles in supporting initiatives related to settlement, integration, and inclusion of newcomers and minorities. One category of such organizations consists of those that contribute funding to immigrant services provider agencies. Notable examples are the United Way agencies in Regina and Saskatoon, both of which fund some immigrant services provider agencies. Another example is the Saskatoon Community Foundation. In recent years the foundation partnered with the United Way and several organizations in the immigration sector (e.g., Saskatoon Open Door Society (SODS), Global Gathering Place (GGP), Saskatchewan Intercultural Association (SIA), International Women of Saskatoon (IWS)) and other community based organizations to apply for a start-up grant from the Maytree Foundation's special initiative titled Assisting Local Leaders with Immigrant Employment Strategies (ALLIES) (Maytree Foundation 2009). The purpose of the grant is to create an immigrant employment council comparable to that of TRIEC in Toronto, which would develop local programs to meet the needs of employers and skilled immigrants living in the Saskatoon city-region.

Regional economic development authorities and chambers of commerce in cities and larger towns may support local initiatives for the attraction, integration, and inclusion of newcomers and minorities. They do so largely by supporting the programming initiatives of settlement service agencies and encouraging their members to do the same, and by participating in creation and operation of local committees that deal with immigration, integration, and inclusion issues. In at least a couple of instances, however, they have also established their own programs for newcomers. Two notable examples are the Saskatoon Regional Economic Development Authority (SREDA 2009), which during the past decade has contracted or hired persons to facilitate the recruitment and settlement of business, investor, and skilled immigrants, and the Battlefords Chamber of Commerce, which was instrumental in establishing and operating the Battlefords Immigration Centre (Battlefords Chamber of Commerce 2009).

Roles of Local Immigrant Services Provider Agencies

In Saskatchewan, settlement and integration services are delivered primarily by locally or regionally based non-governmental immigrant services provider agencies. Such agencies tend to exist primarily in most of the 13 cities, which range in population size from 5,000 to over 200,000, and one or two of the largest towns. In the remaining 850 municipalities, the vast majority of which have populations of less than 300 and receive few, if any, immigrants, do not have a local immigrant services provider agency. The number of immigrant services provider agencies in the various communities tends to range from one to four. The variance is correlated largely with the population size; however, variance also exists among communities of comparable size, as is evident in the case of the two largest cities, both with populations close to the 200,000 range. Whereas Regina has only two such agencies, namely Regina Open Door Society (RODS) and Regina Immigrant Women Centre (RIWC), Saskatoon has four, namely Saskatoon Open Door Society (SODS), Saskatchewan Intercultural Association (SIA), International Women of Saskatoon (IWS), and Global Gathering Place (GGP).

The next two largest cities, Moose Jaw and Prince Albert, both with populations of over 30,000, have two immigrant service provider agencies apiece. In Moose Jaw the two agencies are the Moose Jaw Multiculturalism Council (MJMC) and the Immigrant Women of Moose Jaw (IWMJ); in Prince Albert they are the Prince Albert Multicultural Council (PAMA) and the YWCA. The other cities and large towns with immigrant services provider agencies tend to have only one, almost all of them established during this decade largely as a result of increased opportunities to access federal and provincial funding. Generally, all of the aforementioned agencies in large and small centres provide a wide range of settlement and integration programs and services. These include initial reception orientation programs; interpretation/translation programs; ESL instruction; employment training; career mentorship programs; social and recreational programming; special health education programs; medical and educational referral programs; and counselling and support programs. However, the precise number and types of programs and services that each of those agencies provides tend to vary based on their mission, the number of immigrants and refugees they serve, and the resources available to them.

Roles of Local Coordinating Committees and Provincial Umbrella Organizations

In recent years, in an effort to achieve a higher degree of coordination and collaboration in programming in the two largest cities, settlement and integration coordinating committees have been established. The membership consists of the major agencies that received government funding for the delivery of settlement services in those communities as well as representatives of the provincial and federal governments. Their membership continues to be a point of debate among members and non-members, revolving around the issue of whether other stakeholder agencies actively involved in this sector (e.g., ethnocultural associations, refugee advocacy and support groups) should be included as members.

At the provincial level the Saskatchewan Association of Immigrant Settlement and Integration Agencies (SAISIA) has served as an umbrella provincial organization in the settlement and integration sector. In recent years SAISIA has consisted of six full members (i.e., Global Gathering Place–Saskatoon, International Women of Saskatoon, Regina Open Door Society, Saskatoon Open Door Society, Moose Jaw Multicultural Council, and Prince Albert Multicultural Council), and two associated members (i.e., Battlefords Immigration Resource Centre, Ukrainian Canadian Congress–Saskatchewan Provincial Council Inc.). SAISIA is affiliated to the Canadian Immigrant Settlement Sector Alliance (CISSA–ACSEI), which is the national umbrella organization of immigrant and refugee services and advocacy agencies. The limited number of members is reflective of the number of agencies that were involved in providing settlement and integration services for most of the past quarter century. It remains to be seen whether the assortment of additional agencies that have become involved in providing services during the past five years in several major centres will become SAISIA members in the near future. The key functions of SAISIA are to identify issues and options of importance related to the agencies and the newcomers they serve and to articulate those issues to the various orders of government and other public service agencies. As well, SAISIA participates collaboratively in key policy and program development initiatives (e.g., Enhanced Language Training (ELT) and Prior Learning Assessment and Recognition (PLAR)) (SAISIA 2009).

In 2003, in an effort to expand the scope of the advice received on reviewing and reforming the immigration, settlement and integration system in Saskatchewan, the provincial government established the Saskatchewan Settlement and Integration Planning Council (SSIPC). The SSIPC consisted of all SAISIA members, but also members of other community based organizations involved in that policy sector. Although it met several times during and after that particular policy review, the SSIPC fell into desuetude. This created a void that the provincial government tried to fill in various ways through the use of existing and emerging consultative and coordinative mechanisms.

Roles of Saskatchewan Regional Newcomer Gateways

A major innovation in providing settlement and integration services in Saskatchewan has been the creation of the Regional Newcomer Gateway Connection Program (RNGCP). Its role is to provide settlement and integration services to newcomers destined to smaller communities that generally do not receive many immigrants and do not have settlement service agencies. Toward that end, the provincial government is establishing a system of 11 regional service districts, each made up of approximately 40 to 100 communities within a radius of about 150 kilometres from the community designated as the service hub for the region. Within each regional gateway, one agency is assigned the lead role in assisting immigrants to access services that will facilitate their adaptation and integration into the labour market and community (Table 8). Services include access to settlement advisors, English language assessments, language training, orientation sessions, and career and employment services. The stated desired outcomes are:

- Early identification of immigrants' needs;
- Timely and relevant referral to available services that meet their specific needs;
- Increased awareness of services available in Saskatchewan among immigrants;
- Increased participation of immigrants in mainstream services and programs suitable to their needs;
- Enhanced participation of immigrants in the labour force; immigrants obtain meaningful work;
- Immigrants taking a proactive role in the development of their own integration plan;
- Immigrants being aware of their own needs in order to adapt, settle and integrate to the community and their work place;
- Immigrants' involvement in the development of their own settlement plan (Saskatchewan 2010a, 2010b).

MAP 1
Saskatchewan Regional Newcomer Gateways

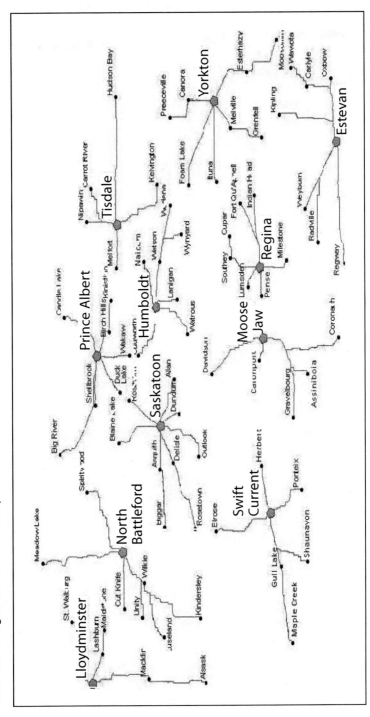

Source: Government of Saskatchewan (2010), "Regional Newcomer Gateways," at http://www.saskimmigrationcanada.ca/immigration-gateway-map/

TABLE 8
Saskatchewan Regional Gateway System

Regional Gateway	Regional Service Agency
Lloydminster Regional Gateway	Catholic Social Services
North Battleford Regional Gateway	Battlefords Immigration Resource Centre
Prince Albert Regional Gateway	YWCA Prince Albert
Tisdale Regional Gateway	Town of Tisdale
Humboldt Regional Gateway	Prairie Innovation Enterprise Region
Saskatoon Regional Gateway	Saskatoon Newcomer Information Centre
Swift Current Regional Gateway	Newcomer Welcome Centre
Moose Jaw Regional Gateway	Moose Jaw Multicultural Council
Regina Regional Gateway	Regina Newcomer Welcome Centre
Yorkton Regional Gateway	Saskatchewan Abilities Council
Estevan Regional Gateway	Sunrise Community Futures

Source: Saskatchewan (2010); Saskatchewan Regional Gateways at
http://www.saskimmigrationcanada.ca/immigration-gateway-map/

To support the work of the regional service agencies, settlement advisors / coordinators are contracted to help newcomers who have been in Canada for less than two years to access both general community services and specialized newcomer services. As well, over time 13 language assessors will be contracted to administer within the respective gateway service areas the Canadian Language Benchmark Placement Test (CLBPT) to all newcomers who have been in Canada for less than eight years. Both the advisors and assessors will have flexible hours to meet with newcomers within seven days following the service request. The gateway-based service strategy also includes the delivery of both community focused and employment focused English language classes to newcomers who have been in Canada for less than five years. Whereas the community focused language classes would be open to all recent newcomers, the employment focused classes would be open to unemployed newcomers who have been in Canada for less than five years and need the training to assist them in finding and retaining entry-level employment. The objective in both types of language classes is to ensure that newcomers have access to the services without waiting for more than one month where they are available, and to supplement these services with formal and informal training and tutoring. Starting in January 2010, the provincial government funding became available for short-term projects (i.e., six months or less) designed to facilitate interaction between newcomers and long-term residents as well as the active involvement of newcomers in community activities. All of the aforementioned programs are funded by the provincial government but delivered by several immigrant serving agencies and ethnocultural organizations (Saskatchewan 2010a, 2010b). Clearly, Saskatchewan's provincial government has been willing to use both types of organizations to increase organizational capacity for developing and delivering services.

Roles of Multicultural NGOs

Saskatchewan also has a network of nine regional and local multicultural councils (i.e., Regina, Saskatoon, Battlefords, Moose Jaw, Prince Albert, Yorkton and District, Weyburn and District, Southwest, and Potashville) that perform important roles in the integration and inclusion of newcomers. Whereas some of these councils provide only multiculturalism and interculturalism programming (e.g., cultural festivals, promoting the values and goals of multiculturalism and interculturalism, and facilitating cross-cultural training sessions), others (e.g., Moose Jaw and Prince Albert) also provide settlement and integration programming.

The regional and local multicultural councils are members of the Multicultural Council of Saskatchewan (MCoS), a non-profit umbrella organization established in 1975, just four years after the provincial Multiculturalism Act was enacted. The mission of MCoS and its members is to preserve and enhance the multicultural character of Saskatchewan; to foster cross-cultural understanding, an anti-racism movement, and an appreciation of the benefits of cultural diversity; and to promote equality in the social, economic, cultural, and political spheres. MCoS is funded by the provincial ministry responsible for culture, as well as by two of its agencies, SaskCulture and Saskatchewan Lotteries, and the federal Canadian Heritage department. MCoS also serves as the Secretariat for SaskCulture's Multicultural Community of Interest Committee (MCOI) (SaskCulture 2007; Weeseen and Olfert 2008). MCOI consists of representatives of SaskCulture, MCoS, Le Conseil Culturel, Saskatchewan Organization of Heritage Languages (SOHL), Saskatchewan German Congress, and Ukrainian-Canadian Congress–Saskatchewan Provincial Council (UCC–SPC), as well as five committee members who are not direct (first-line) members of the preceding organizations. These five committee members are drawn from a list of individual candidates nominated by the broad multicultural community. MCOI is mandated to provide SaskCulture Inc. with reviews and advice on a range of matters regarding multiculturalism, including multicultural policies and issues at the local, provincial, and national level, and to foster public understanding and support for multicultural initiatives. It is also mandated to facilitate meetings and training of the multicultural community annually and to provide an assessment of the effectiveness and efficiency in its performance of the secretariat role.

Roles of Ethnocultural Organizations

Several ethnnocultural organizations also perform key roles in settlement and integration of newcomers. Most tend to be concentrated in the two largest cities, and the bulk of the rest are located in the other 11 cities and a handful of the larger towns. The degree of involvement by these organizations tends to vary substantially. The most active ones tend to be those located in the largest cities and towns that have been receiving the largest proportion of newcomers from their respective ethnocultural background (e.g., Ukrainian, German, Chinese, Filipino, etc.), and the least active ones are those based both in larger and smaller municipalities that receive few immigrants from their respective ethnocultural backgrounds.

Among the most highly institutionalized and proactive ethnocultural organizations that engage in the settlement, integration, and inclusion of newcomers are the provincial and local chapters of the Ukrainian Canadian Congress (UCC). The UCC–Saskatchewan Provincial Council (UCC–SPC) is the provincial umbrella organization headquartered in Saskatoon. The UCC–SPC has seven local chapters in cities and towns with substantial Ukrainian communities (i.e., Saskatoon, Regina, Prince Albert, the Battlefords, Yorkton, Weyburn, and Canora). In the fall of 2007, the Saskatoon and Regina affiliates of the UCC–SPC, with some financial support from the provincial government, hired immigration settlement councillors. Their principal function was to assist newcomers with their needs. The coordinator in Regina was hired to provide services three days per week in that city, with an additional 30 days devoted to outreach for immigrants living in other communities in Southern Saskatchewan (UCC–SPC 2007). As well, through a grant provided by that same provincial ministry, the UCC–SPC is attempting to implement a program for expanded ESL training; for example, the UCC-Regina Branch offered ESL classes to Ukrainian immigrants in the evenings and on Saturdays from March to June of 2009 (UCC–SPC 2009). The UCC–SPC also produced and distributed manuals in English and Ukrainian, developed a bilingual website, and organized workshops to orient newcomers to various aspects of the province and the services, published *VISNYK*, the UCC–SPC news magazine, and provided "for-fee" services such as oral language interpretation and translation of documents.

The Saskatchewan German Council (SGC) is another highly institutionalized ethnocultural organization. It represents over 32 German organizations including 12 local clubs in the cities of Saskatoon, Regina, Prince Albert, North Battleford, Humboldt, Yorkton, Estevan, Swift Current, Melville, Lloydminster, and the towns of St Walburg and Fox Valley. The SGC performs an advocacy role on a range of immigration and multiculturalism issues in Saskatchewan. In the 1990s it was at the forefront of the push for increased German immigration to various communities with the aforementioned member clubs. In Humboldt, for example, it supported the efforts of civic officials to attract and settle more German immigrants to the community. Its intiatives included Partnerschaft Saskatchewan, formed in 2001–02 with the Saskatoon Regional Economic Development Authority (SREDA) and Carleton Trail Regional Economic Development Authority (Humboldt and District), to attract immigration and investment from Germany (Saskatchewan German Council 2009).

Another notable ethnocultural organization that is actively involved in immigration and integration is L'Assemblé communitaire fransaskoise, which is interested in the integration and inclusion of newcomers into Saskatchewan's francophone community. It has established a website for francophone immigrants and migrants, produced several booklets to assist them, and hired three staff members to deal with immigration and integration issues. One of the three, located in Regina, is responsible for the overall immigration and integration program; the other two, one in Saskatoon and another in Regina, assist newcomers with settlement and employment (Assemblée communautaire fransaskoise 2009).

Roles of Religious and Issue-Based Organizations

Religious and issue-based organizations are also involved in supporting newcomers, sponsoring refugees, and providing support services for many refugees and immigrants. The major religious organizations involved in this area include regional and local units of various Christian religions (e.g., Catholic, Anglican, United, Mennonite), Christian-based benevolent organizations (e.g., Mennonite Central Committee, Salvation Army), and non-Christian religious institutions.

Among non-religious, issue-based NGOs, the ones most significantly involved in facilitating the integration and inclusion of refugees include the Saskatoon Refugee Coalition and the Regina Refugee Coalition. These organizations are not only strong advocates for prospective refugees and refugee claimants but also provide support for their settlement, integration, and inclusion. Another such issue-based NGO is the Saskatoon Housing Initiatives Partnership (SHIP), formed in 1999 by a coalition of citizens and organizations. SHIP's mission is to provide affordable housing ownership options for people who need them, including newcomers and minorities. SHIP tries to help organizations that are providing emergency shelters, transition housing, affordable rental accommodation, co-housing, cooperative housing, and affordable homes.

Roles of Educational Institutions

Educational institutions perform important roles in the economic, social, cultural, and political integration of newcomers through their curricular and extra-curricular programming. Elementary and high schools within the public, private, Catholic and Fransaskois school systems perform several key roles in the social and cultural integration of newcomer students, including those on student visas, and to some extent even their families. Schools provide regular and specialized programs for orienting all newcomer students – and in some schools, other members of their families – to various aspects of living in Canada. One innovative program launched in 2005 by the Greystone Elementary School in Saskatoon has consisted of a series of afterschool orientation sessions for parents of newcomer children (Pontikes and Garcea 2006).

Post-secondary institutions also contribute to the integration of international students and their families. They provide a mix of assessment, support, and orientation services. Whereas some services are offered to all students, others are designed specifically to meet the needs of international students. For example, the University of Saskatchewan and the University of Regina both have specialized offices that provide services to international students, including airport pickup for first-time students; assistance to register for a provincial health card; registration and orientation to the university and the community; assistance with immigration regulations and documents; advocacy within the university and referrals to professionals or organizations that can help with anything they may need for their health or integration into the community; and social and cultural activities (University of Regina 2009; USISSO 2009a, 2009b). Both universities provide financial support for some international students in the form of entrance scholarships and emergency loans.

During the past decade some post-secondary institutions have also developed targeted programs for training newcomers with specialized skills that have been in short supply within the province. The first of these programs was the Long-Haul Truck Driver Project at the Saskatchewan Institute of Applied Sciences and Technology (SIAST), designed in 2003. The program permitted trucking firms to recruit prospective long-haul truck drivers as temporary foreign workers for six months who, upon successful completion of their training, would be hired as permanent employees and become permanent residents through the SINP (Saskatchewan 2005c).

In subsequent years, special training programs for health professionals were also developed by both SIAST and the University of Saskatchewan. In 2006, the University of Saskatchewan's College of Medicine established a program to prepare approximately 25 physicians trained outside Canada to meet the provincial requirements. The province contributed an initial $115,000 for a program coordinator and the development and delivery of a new exam preparation course, and made a commitment to continue funding the program in subsequent years (University of Saskatchewan 2006). Shortly thereafter, SIAST developed the Orientation to Nursing in Canada for Internationally Educated Nurses (ONCIEN) certificate program. The basic admission requirement is a letter from the Saskatchewan Registered Nurses' Association (SRNA) recommending the candidate for the program based on the English language proficiency test score (SIAST 2009a).

In recent years, SIAST has partnered with the provincial and federal governments to develop an overseas occupational and language skills assessment and development project for potential SINP candidates (SIAST 2007a). The $3 million project has been co-funded by the provincial and federal governments from 2008 to 2012 (SIAST 2008a). The purpose of this project, the first of its kind in Canada, is to assess whether prospective immigrants have adequate English language skills and technical skills at a standard comparable to those of SIAST's certificate and diploma programs (SIAST 2009b). SIAST has established a network of partner institutions overseas mandated to provide not only assessment and certification services but also "gap training" to allow applicants to meet the labour market standards prior to their arrival in Canada. The project focuses on three countries (Ukraine, Philippines, and Vietnam) and approximately three to five occupations in critical demand in Saskatchewan (e.g., welding, millwork and machinery, and carpentry). A key role in this project is performed by the Saskatchewan Apprenticeship and Trade Certification Commission (SATCC), which is responsible for credentialing in these vocations. The skills demonstrated by the prospective immigrants are certified officially in a Skills Passport, which is guaranteed to their prospective employers. Some of the careers for which prospective immigrants may be certified fall within HRSDC's national "Red Seal" certification program for tradespeople, which allows their credentials to be recognized throughout Canada without their having to write additional examinations in each province (SIAST 2007b and 2008b). To date, the Skills Passport project has been established in the Philippines and Ukraine. In the future it will be offered in more countries and will focus on technical skills for more careers.

SIAST's initiatives in the Philippines and Vietnam have been facilitated partly by the provincial government's decision to negotiate and sign the MOU on Cooperation in Labour, Employment and Human Resource Development with the Philippines in 2006 (Saskatchewan 2006a, 2006b) and Vietnam in 2010 (Saskatchewan 2010c, 2010d). The MOUs outline the roles and responsibilities of the governments as well as the "employer agencies" from Saskatchewan and the "sending agencies" from the Philippines and Vietnam that are approved by the national governments of those countries. Key provisions regarding the alignment of roles and responsibilities of the governments and the employers and sending agencies include those related to the identification of eligible employer and sending agencies; the recruitment, assessment, and training of workers; the selection of workers; and the protection of workers. The agreements state that a key role of both employer and sending agencies is to communicate with each other on various matters including the identification of prospective workers; the precise nature of the job offer; skill assessment of prospective workers; skill development of workers; and other arrangements for workers to travel to and work in Saskatchewan. The sending agencies are also responsible for providing prospective workers with a clarification of job offers, any training they may need for the job for which they are being considered, and an orientation to working and living in Saskatchewan. To increase the likelihood that prospective immigrants from the Philippines and Vietnam would be successful both in economic and social integration when they arrived in Saskatchewan, the agreements state that the governments would collaborate in providing them with employment and English language training, as well as an orientation to various aspects of Saskatchewan's geography, climate, economy, and culture before leaving their home countries. It is too early to provide a definitive assessment of the value of these agreements, but preliminary indications are that they have been useful in improving the efficiency and effectiveness of the immigration programs and processes from each of those countries. By helping to make the immigration system much more predictable, professional, and productive, these intiatives have benefited governments, the agencies involved, and immigrants.

In 2010, pursuant to the recommendations of participants in an immigration consultation process, the provincial government established the Saskatchewan International Education Council (SIEC). Membership includes the assistant deputy ministers responsible for immigration and post-secondary education; representatives of the major post-secondary institutions (i.e., universities, regional colleges, and SIAST); Luther College, a small private college; and representatives of the public and Catholic school boards in Saskatoon and Regina. The council provides a forum where institutions involved in international education can collaborate in advising the government on best policies and practices related to, among other things, the attraction, settlement, and integration of international students (Saskatchewan 2010e).

ASSESSMENT OF THE EFFECTS OF THE ALIGNMENT OF ROLES AND PERSISTENT CHALLENGES

The previous section has revealed three interrelated trends during the past decade within the settlement and integration system: an expansion in the constellation of governmental and non-governmental agencies involved in performing key roles; a gradual but significant expansion in the roles of those agencies; and an increase in the types and number of settlement and integration programs and services provided by the agencies. The objective in this section is to assess the effects of those trends for organizational completeness and organizational capacity within the settlement and integration system, and to identify and discuss the persistent challenges.

The general consensus is that those trends have had a positive effect both on organizational completeness and on organizational capacity within the settlement and integration system. Positive effects on organizational completeness are evident in the increasing number and types of organizations performing key roles within that system during the past decade as compared to the number and types involved in previous decades. This is equally true of governmental and non-governmental organizations. Positive effects on organizational capacity are evident in the increased degree of institutionalization, the increased amount of resources, and increased number and scope of programs and services that are developed and delivered by the increased number and types of organizations. The consensus is that the positive effects have been most substantial and significant in the two largest cities and to some, albeit much lesser extent, also in smaller cities and numerous other urban and rural communities.

Notwithstanding those positive effects, the consensus is also that many of the challenges identified in reviews of the system during the past decade persist (Saskatchewan 2002, 2003; Pontikes and Garcea 2006; Insightrix 2008a, 2008b). These include challenges related to the alignment of organizational roles, organizational completeness, and organizational capacity. In the case of the alignment of organizational roles, the persistent challenge is that neither full clarity nor agreement has been achieved regarding which governmental or non-governmental organizations are, and should be, responsible for performing some key roles in providing settlement and integration services. Indeed, in some instances, tensions and minor disputes have emerged among organizations regarding their respective roles and responsibilities. The sources of such conflict are the various types of organizational imperatives related to, among other things, the designing, implementing, or funding policies, programs and projects; the precise configuration of partnerships; and the apportionment of credit for positive outputs and outcomes and blame for negative ones.

In the case of organizational completeness, the persistent challenge is that many communities do not have a full panoply of organizations need-ed to provide settlement and integration services. Even communities that have one or more settlement service agencies to provide some programs and services either do not have other types of agencies that could provide additional programs and services, or those agencies are either unaware of what they could do or unwilling to do it. These include, for example, a wide range of social, health, and educational agencies, neighbourhood level organizations in the largest cities (e.g., community associations in Saskatoon and Regina), and professional and trades certification bodies.

In the case of organizational capacity, the persistent challenge is that to date neither the key settlement services organizations nor other types of service organizations in various sectors (e.g., health, social, and justice) have all of the requisite human and financial resources to provide the pro-grams and services needed by newcomers. This situation persists despite the extensive increase in additional resources provided by the federal and provincial governments as well as some of the major community-based funding agencies to various service provider organizations. The result is what might be termed a "capacity gap" that governmental and non-governmental agencies within various policy sectors continue to struggle to eliminate or at least to narrow.

Governmental and non-governmental stakeholders continue to explore the potential means for addressing those challenges. In 2009 the provincial government developed a new immigration strategy based on consultations with more than 300 representatives of business and industry, community-based organizations, municipal governments, educational institutions, and professional associations. The new strategy, which boldly states that the goal is to develop the provincial immigration program "to be the best in Canada," articulated two strategic directions related to settlement and integration. The first was to develop and implement a new settlement and integration service delivery model based on the observations of participants in the consultations regarding the need for "strong community-based settlement supports, coordinated and comprehensive language assessment and training services, and better recognition of international credentials." Moreover, the new service delivery model was designed to "emphasize shared responsibility for settlement outcomes" and "empower immigrants to make their own decisions" (Saskatchewan 2009a). The three key components of the new model are pre-arrival information, orientation, and planning services; connections to appropriate community services; and specialized language and employment services. In keeping with this strategic direction, the provincial government tripled the number of trained language assessors, produced fact sheets on licensing process for 43 regulated occupations, and announced that in the future it would:

- Implement a new service delivery model, settlement programs, and language programs in collaboration with community partners;
- Launch a comprehensive Competency Recognition Strategy, consistent with the pan-Canadian framework for qualification recognition, as announced by the first ministers in January 2009; and
- Enhance financial supports for immigrants engaged in licensing assessments and skill upgrading programs, including a new micro-loan program (ibid.).

The second strategic direction is to enhance partnerships and cooperation between and among the governmental and stakeholder agencies. Pursuant to this strategic direction, the provincial immigration ministry, in partnership with its federal counterpart, established Newcomer Information Centres in several Saskatchewan communities. The provincial ministry also made a commitment to:

- Lead the development and implementation of a government-wide forum and strategy on immigration in Saskatchewan, to ensure that

there are adequate public services to respond to the needs of a growing and diverse population;

- Increase capacity to support employers looking to recruit workers
  using the provincial nominee program and to work with employers, business associations, and other stakeholders to identify labour
  market needs;
- Engage stakeholders and fund research, program development and
  delivery to improve existing systems and supports for immigrants
  seeking to work in key regulated professions and trades; and
- Partner with stakeholders to develop anti-racism campaigns (ibid.).

The hope is that the directions articulated in the provincial government's
immigration strategy will help to address the persisting challenges noted
above that impede efforts to meet the settlement and integration needs
of newcomers destined to various types of communities in the province.

CONCLUSION

During the past decade, governmental and non-governmental agencies
have become increasingly proactive in developing and implementing policies, programs, and projects in Saskatchewan's settlement and integration
system. Moreover, there has been an increase not only in the number and
types of agencies involved in performing key roles within that system
but also in the number and types of roles that they perform. Despite the
improvements that have been achieved in the alignment of roles among
governmental and non-governmental agencies, organizational completeness, and organizational capacity, challenges persist in each of these areas.

Dealing with those challenges is imperative because it has important
implications not only for optimizing the settlement and integration of
many immigrants and refugees but also for optimizing their contribution to communities in the province. There are many approaches and
initiatives that governmental and non-governmental agencies and agents
can and should undertake either individually or jointly to deal with the
issues discussed above, as well as others. One of the most important approaches is engaging in constructive collaboration and coordination for
two interrelated purposes: first, establishing appropriate and adequate
governance frameworks; and second, developing, implementing and
evaluating policies, programs, and projects.

Establishing adequate and appropriate bipartite and multipartite governance and management frameworks and mechanisms is imperative
because they are operating what can be described as an insufficiently
coordinated polycentric settlement and integration system within a
multifaceted multi-level governance context. The success in establishing
appropriate and adequate governance and management frameworks

and mechanisms will depend on the extent to which the stakeholders are guided by their shared vision to optimize the settlement and integration experiences of newcomers. Governmental and non-governmental agencies and their agents must guard against allowing their respective competing organizational and personal interests and imperatives to interfere with the efficient development and implementation of effective policies, programs, and projects. There is a shared understanding among them and informed observers that during the past decade those interests and imperatives have hindered their efforts to achieve even more improvements in the settlement and integration system. Thus, many of the same agencies and agents that share credit for improvements must also share some responsibility for the fact that even more improvements were not achieved. More importantly, they now share responsibility for ensuring that in the future existing and emerging challenges are efficiently and effectively addressed.

Note

The author would like to thank governmental officials, representatives of community based organizations, and the research assistants for their contributions to the production of this chapter.

References

Anderson, A. 2006. "Population Trends." *Encyclopedia of Saskatchewan*. Canadian Plains Research Centre. At http://esask.uregina.ca/entry/population_trends.html

Assemblée communautaire fransaskoise. 2009. *Destination Saskatchewan*. At http://www.immigrationsaskatchewan.org/#

Battlefords Chamber of Commerce. 2009. *Programs – Battlefords Immigration Resource Centre*. At http://www.battlefordschamber.com/programs.php

Breton, R. 1964. "Institutional Completeness of Ethnic Communities and the Personal Relations of Immigrants." *American Journal of Sociology* 70(2):193-205.

Citizenship and Immigration Canada (CIC). 1998. *Canada-Saskatchewan Immigration Agreement*.

— 2003. "Canada and Saskatchewan Agree to Amend and Extend Immigration Agreement." News release, 23 November. At http://news.gc.ca/web/article-eng.do;jsessionid=ac1b105430d70a4849dce2e9436cb1c290cc4fabf627.e34Rc3iMbx8Oai0Tbx0SaxiLahr0?crtr.sj1D=&mthd=advSrch&crtr.mnthndVl=&nid=32099&crtr.dpt1D=&crtr.tp1D=&crtr.lc1D=&crtr.yrStrtVl=&crtr.kw=citizenship&crtr.dyStrtVl=&crtr.aud1D=&crtr.mnthStrtVl=&crtr.yrndVl=&crtr.dyndVl=

— 2004. *Canada-Saskatchewan Memorandum of Understanding on Post-Graduation Employment for Foreign Students*. 6 May.

— 2005. *Canada-Saskatchewan Immigration Agreement, 2005*. At http://www.cic.gc.ca/ENGLISH/department/laws-policy/agreements/sask/sask-agree-2005.asp

—2006a. *Canada-Saskatchewan Memorandum of Understanding on the Off-Campus Work Permit Program for International Students.* 10 April. At http://www.cic.gc.ca/english/DEPARTMENT/laws-policy/agreements/sask/can-sask-mou.asp

—2006b. *The Interprovincial Mobility of Immigrants in Canada – Immigrants Landed from 2000 to 2006.* At http://www.cic.gc.ca/english/resources/research/interprov-mobility/section3.asp

—2007. *Settlement Funding Allocations for 2008–09.* At http://www.cic.gc.ca/english/department/media/backgrounders/2007/2007-12-17.asp

—2008. *Facts and Figures 2008.* At http://www.cic.gc.ca/english/pdf/research-stats/facts2008.pdf

—2009a. *Federal-Provincial/Territorial Agreements.* At http://www.cic.gc.ca/english/department/laws-policy/agreements/index.asp

—2009b. *Letter to Provinces-Settlement Allocations 2009–10 and 2010–11.*

—2009c. "Canadian Government Announces Local Immigration Partnerships for Two More Ontario Regions." *CIC News: Canada Immigration Newsletter.* At http://www.cicnews.com/2009/11/advantage-wealth-settlement-services-immigrants-canada-11749.html

—2009d. *Facts and Figures 2009.* At http://www.cic.gc.ca/english/resources/statistics/facts2009/permanent/02.asp

—2010. *Interprovincial Mobility of Immigrants in Canada.* Produced by Ima Okynny-Myers. At http://www.cic.gc.ca/English/pdf/research-stats/interprov-mobility.pdf

City of Moose Jaw. 2009. *Boards, Committees, and Commissions: Race Relations Committee.* At http://www.moosejaw.ca/cityhall/clerks/committees.shtml

City of Prince Albert. 2009a. *Minutes of Meeting of Race Relations and Social Issues Committee.* 7 January. At http://www.citypa.ca/Portals/0/PDF2/Committee/Race_Relations_and_Social_Issues/minutes/2009%2001%2007%20Race%20Relations%20and%20Social%20Issues%20Committee%20Minutes.pdf

City of Prince Albert. 2009b. *Executive Committee Agenda.* 19 January. At http://www.citypa.ca/Portals/0/PDF2/Committee/Executive/agenda/2009%2001%2019%20-%20Order%20of%20Business.pdf

City of Saskatoon. 2004. *Cultural Diversity and Race Relations Policy,* 9 February. At http://www.saskatoon.ca/org/clerks_office/policies/C10-023.pdf

Garcea, J. 2006a. "Attraction and Retention of Immigrants by Saskatchewan's Major Cities." *Our Diverse Cities* 2:14-19.

—2006b "Provincial Multiculturalism Policies in Canada, 1974-2004: A Content Analysis." *Canadian Ethnic Studies* 38(3):1-20.

—2007. "Immigration to Smaller Communities in Saskatchewan." *Our Diverse Cities* 3:134-9. At http://canada.metropolis.net/pdfs/ODC_Summer07_3_en.pdf

—2009. "Diversity Planning in Saskatoon." *Plan Canada.* Special edition, *Welcoming Communities: Planning for Diverse Populations* (Spring):38-42.

Garcea, J. and S. Garg. 2009. "Cultural Diversity, Race Relations, Immigration, and Integration in Saskatoon: The Processes of Developing Institutional Arrangements." *Our Diverse Cities* 6 (Spring):150-5. At http://dsp-psd.pwgsc.gc.ca/collections/collection_2010/cic/Ci2-1-6-2009-eng.pdf#page=46

Insightrix. 2008a. *Immigration Action Plan Gap Analysis.* Report prepared for the City of Saskatoon, 22 May. At http://www.saskatoon.ca/DEPARTMENTS/

Community%20Services/Communitydevelopment/Documents/gap_
analysis_report.pdf

—2008b. *Checklist for Immigration Action Plan*. May. Document prepared for the City of Saskatoon. At http://www.saskatoon.ca/DEPARTMENTS/Community%20 Services/Communitydevelopmenet/Documents/checklist.pdf

Maytree Foundation. 2009. *Integration Programs*. At http://maytree.com/integration/allies/grants

Pontikes, K. and J. Garcea. 2006. *Building Saskatoon to Become a Global City: A Framework for an Immigration Action Plan*. Report prepared for the City of Saskatoon. At http://www.saskatoon.ca/DEPARTMENTS/Community%20Services/Communitydevelopment/Documents/immigration_study_executive_summary.pdf

Pruegger, V. and D. Cook. 2009. "An Analysis of Immigrant Attraction and Retention Patterns among Western Canadian CMAs." *Our Diverse Cities* 6, 44-6.

Rosenberg, M. and J. Jedwab. 1992. "Institutional Completeness, Ethnic Organizational Style and the Role of the State: The Jewish, Italian and Greek Communities of Montreal." *Canadian Review of Sociology and Anthropology* 29:266-77.

Saskatchewan. 1997. *Multiculturalism Act*. 28 April. At http://www.qp.gov.sk.ca/documents/English/Statutes/Statutes/M23-01.pdf

—2002. *Meeting Needs and Making Connections: A Report on the Saskatchewan Immigrant and Refugee Settlement Needs and Making Connections*. At http://www.saskatoon.ca/DEPARTMENTS/Community%20Services/Communitydevelopment/Documents/needs_retention_study.pdf

—2003. *Open Up Saskatchewan: A Report on International Immigration and Inter-Provincial In-Migration Initiatives to Increase the Population of the Province of Saskatchewan*. At http://www.saskatoon.ca/DEPARTMENTS/Community%20Services/Communitydevelopment/Documents/open_up_sk.pdf

—2005a. *Backgrounder: Canada-Saskatchewan Immigration Agreement*. At http://www.gov.sk.ca/news-archive/2005/6/01-491-attachment.pdf

—2005b "New Funding for Recent Immigrants." News release, 6 June. At http://www.gov.sk.ca/news?newsId=ec9771c7-c89d-42f4-9076-f3f9bfa5d553

—2005c. "Saskatchewan's Immigration Program Helps Fill Trucker Shortages." News release, 19 December. At http://www.gov.sk.ca/news?newsId=4573551a-3d28-4d66-8395-2e8ff5c6ed96

—2006a. *Memorandum of Understanding Between Saskatchewan and Philippines on Immigration*. At http://www.aeel.gov.sk.ca/memorandum-understanding-sk-philippines

—2006b. "Government Signs Immigration Agreement with the Philippines to Bring More Skilled Workers to Saskatchewan." News release, 18 December. At http://www.aee.gov.sk.ca/immigration/sinp/whats_new.shtml#12

—2007. *Saskatchewan Human Rights Code*. At http://www.qp.gov.sk.ca/documents/English/Statutes/Statutes/S24-1.pdf

—2008a. "Saskatoon Announces Immigration Project Designed to Support Settlement and Retention of Newcomers." News release, 28 March. At http://www.gov.sk.ca/news?newsId=e9a32bc3-9db1-40ee-b111-f284cf4bec98

—2008b. "Backgrounder: Saskatoon Immigration Project." 28 March. At http://www.gov.sk.ca/adx/aspx/adxGetMedia.aspx?mediaId–454&PN=Shared

—2009a. "Saskatchewan Immigration Strategy: Strengthening our Communities and Economy." At http://aeel.gov.sk.ca/adx/aspx/adxGetMedia.aspx?

DocID=2198,2194,104,81,1,Documents&MediaID=2388&Filename=sk-immigration-strategy-brochure.pdf

—2009b. "Province Unveils New Immigration Policy." News release, 19 June. At http://www.gov.sk.ca/news?newsId=cff28780-f5c1-4fd5-ab91-c848d027efa8

—2009c. *Annual Report, 2008–09.* At http://www.aeel.gov.sk.ca/2008-09-annual-report

—2009d. *French Language Services Policy.* At http://www.ops.gov.sk.ca/fab-daf/

—2010a. *Regional Newcomer Gateways.* At http://www.saskimmigrationcanada.ca/immigration-gateways

—2010b. *Regional Newcomer Gateway Connections: Supporting Immigrant Integration in Saskatchewan's Communities (Estevan and SE Regional Hub Service Area).* At http://www.aeel.gov.sk.ca/regional-newcomer-gateway-connections-call-for-proposals

—2010c. "Agreement Signed between Saskatchewan and Vietnam." News release, 14 January. At http://www.gov.sk.ca/news?newsId=573c9df3-ef95-46dd-8440-1cf3676f7985

—2010d. *Memorandum of Understanding between Saskatchewan and Vietnam on Immigration.* At http://www.aeel.gov.sk.ca/memorandum-understanding-sk-vietnam-english

—2010e. "Provincial International Education Council Education." News release, 29 April. At http://www.gov.sk.ca/news?newsId=b8f98493-34dd-4295-916f-8f8455c82c8a

Saskatchewan Association of Immigrant Settlement and Integration Agencies (SAISIA). 2009. "SAISIA Inc.–About Us." At http://www.saisia.ca/index.php

Saskatchewan Institute of Applied Science and Technology (SIAST). 2007a. *Saskatchewan Urban Training Needs Assessment 2007.* Prepared by the Institutional Research and Analysis (IR&A). September 2007. At http://www.siast.sk.ca/about/reports_statistics/documents/0703_sutnareport.pdf

—2007b. "*SIAST Develops Program to Assess Foreign Credentials of Skilled Workers.*" News release. At http://www.siast.sk.ca/marketing/documents/fcr2007release.pdf

—2008a. *Enhancing Foreign Credential Recognition Support for Labour Market Needs in Saskatchewan.* At http://www.siast.sk.ca/employers/pdf/enhancingforeign-credential.pdf

—2008b. *Project Summary: Enhancing Foreign Credential Recognition to Support Labour Market Needs in Saskatchewan.* At http://www.siast.sk.ca/employers/pdf/enhancingforeigncredential.pdf

—2009a. *Orientation to Nursing in Canada for Internationally Educated Nurses.* At http://www.siast.sk.ca/programs_courses_descriptions/IENAPCERT.shtml

—2009b. "SIAST's Skills Passport Program Opens Doors for Immigrants: Technical, Language Skills Assessment Offered in Ukraine, Philippines." News release, 5 October. At http://www.siast.sk.ca/marketing/documents/skills passport2009release.pdf

SaskCulture. 2007. *Terms of Reference: Multicultural Committee.* July 2007. At http://www.mcoi.ca/index.php?id=13

Saskatoon German Council. 2009. "History." At http://www.saskgermancouncil.org/about-2/history/

Saskatoon Regional and Economic Development Authority (SREDA). 2009. "SREDA Initiatives." At http://www.sreda.com/en/pages/13/sreda_initiatives.html

Statistics Canada. 2006a. "Proportion of Foreign-Born Population, by Province and Territory (1911–2006 Censuses)." At http://www12.statcan.gc.ca/census-recensement/2006/as-sa/97-557/vignettes/NatHistImmig_ec.swf

—2006b. "Visible Minority Population, by census Metropolitan Areas (2006 Census)." At http://www40.statcan.ca/l01/cst01/demo53f-eng.htm

Ukrainian Canadian Congress-Saskatchewan Provincial Council (UCC-SPC). 2007. "Immigration Settlement Coordinator for Regina and South Saskatchewan." At http://www.ucc.sk.ca/branches/reginaBr/20070907EmplOpp RegImmigSettl.htm

—2009. "Notice of Expanded English Second Language (ESL) Training." At http://www.ucc.sk.ca/branches/reginaBr/200903095ESLNotice.htm

University of Regina. 2009. "ISSO–UR International Student Group." At http://www.facebook.com/group.php?gid=26419214114

University of Saskatchewan. 2006. "New Government Program to Aid Foreign-Trained MDs." *On Campus News* 14(8): 3.

University of Saskatchewan International Student Office (USISSO). 2009a. "International Student Spouses' Program." At http://www.students.usask.ca/international/during/resources/

—2009b. "International Friendship Program." At http://www.students.usask.ca/askus/results.jsp

Weeseen, S. and M.R. Olfert. 2008. *Cultural Policy in Saskatchewan.* Regina: Saskatchewan Institute of Public Policy. At http://www.uregina.ca/sipp/documents/pdf/PPP54_online_FINAL.pdf

CHAPTER 6

MANITOBA: THE STRUGGLE TO ATTRACT AND RETAIN IMMIGRANTS

TOM CARTER AND BENJAMIN AMOYAW

Immigration has shaped the current demographic, social, cultural, and economic landscape of Manitoba. This chapter discusses immigration to the province, highlighting the policies and programs that have been used to facilitate the attraction and integration of newcomers to the province. A brief history of immigration in Manitoba describes the various waves of immigrants, source countries, push-pull factors, major policy initiatives, and settlement patterns. The past can provide "lessons learned" and also helps explain the mosaic of cultures that exists today. The focus of the chapter then moves to the past decade, as the introduction of the Manitoba Provincial Nominee Program (PNP) in 1998 marked a significant shift in immigration policy. It has been the major influence in immigration in the province over the past ten years.

The next section of the chapter focuses on the actors involved in the attraction, retention, and integration of newcomers: the role the actors play, the programs they deliver, and the services they provide. This discussion builds on the circumstances of the last decade as this is the time frame within which much of the current immigration infrastructure has been developed.

We develop a demographic profile of the province, focusing on the proportion of immigrants, the ethnic mix, the presence of visible minorities, and the various language groups and religions to illustrate the role that immigration has played in shaping cultural diversity in the province. We discuss the Aboriginal population in the profile as well, as this sector of the population faces many challenges not unlike those facing immigrants.

The chapter ends with commentary on the challenges the province faces in attracting and retaining immigrants and achieving broader provincial

Integration and Inclusion of Newcomers and Minorities across Canada, ed. J. Biles, M. Burstein, J. Frideres, E. Tolley, and R. Vineberg. Montreal and Kingston: Queen's Policy Studies Series, McGill-Queen's University Press.

policy objectives through immigration. We highlight potential policy changes required to improve integration and inclusion.

THE EARLY HISTORY OF IMMIGRATION TO MANITOBA

Early History to 1870

Prior to the arrival of the first European settlers, what is now the Province of Manitoba was home to a number of Aboriginal tribes. With a hunting and gathering economy, their lifestyle was relatively nomadic, although considerable trade between the groups was common. Agricultural pursuits were less so, although a primitive form of settled agriculture was practised along the Red River and at the junction of the Red and the Assiniboine Rivers, an early meeting place for trade and interaction between the many different tribes that moved through the area (Coates and McGuiness 1987).

With the arrival of British and French fur traders, many Aboriginals became guides, trappers, and hunters and were very involved in the fur trade. Many of the early fur traders took Aboriginal wives, and the resulting mixed race came to be known as Métis. In 1812, a hundred years after the arrival of the fur traders, the first agricultural settlers arrived in the Winnipeg area from Scotland, sponsored by Lord Selkirk. After a shaky start, agriculture became established, and waves of European settlers flowed in. Aboriginals became more marginalized, fell victim to disease, and were pushed out of the more favourable agricultural areas. Eventually through a series of treaties they were placed on reserves (Friesen 1984). Immigration did not get off to a good start in Manitoba; the transition from Aboriginal to European settlement was not a good example of integration and inclusion. However, it was the "host" population that suffered most, not the newcomers.

1870–1929

Manitoba became a province in 1870. At the time of Confederation, the provincial population was 25,228 (Table 1), up from 2,417 in 1831 and 6,523 in 1856 (Coates and McGuiness 1987). Population growth after 1871 reflects the significant role that immigration has played in the province. Between 1871 and 1881, the population increased 147 percent and then grew another 145 percent over the next decade. Although interprovincial migration from Ontario (Vineberg 2010) accounted for a significant number of arrivals in this period, international immigration was a major driver of population growth.

TABLE 1
Manitoba, Population

Year	Population	Ten Year Change (%)	Absolute Change
1871	25,228		
1881	62,260	147	37,032
1891	152,506	145	90,246
1901	255,211	67	102,705
1911	461,394	81	206,183
1921	610,118	32	148,724
1931	700,139	15	90,021
1941	729,744	4	29,605
1951	776,541	6	46,797
1956	850,040	—	73,499
1961	921,686	19	71,646
1966	963,066	13	41,380
1971	988,245	7	25,179
1976	1,021,505	6	33,260
1981	1,026,241	4	4,736
1986	1,063,015	4	36,774
1991	1,091,942	6	28,927
1996	1,113,898	5	21,956
2001	1,119,583	3	5,685
2006	1,148,401	6	28,818

Source: Statistics Canada (various years).

The flow of immigrants was temporarily slowed by the deep depression of the 1890s but resumed again toward the turn of the century: over the decade the population increased 67 percent to reach 255,211 in 2001. Through the following decade, the population almost doubled to 461,000. Immigration slowed to a trickle during World War I but resumed after the war. The population increased by a third to over 600,000 by 1921 and reached 700,000 by the end of the next decade. During the 1870 to 1929 period, the population increased by 675,000 people or about 2,700 percent. Natural increase and interprovincial migration accounted for some of this growth, but the principal driver was immigration (Raspovich 1984).

The forces behind immigration to the province during this period included both push and pull factors. The poor and unemployed of Europe and the British Isles were looking to escape the conditions of the slums. People were being displaced by agricultural consolidation and events like the potato famine in Ireland. Europe needed an escape destination for surplus and marginalized people, while the Canadian government needed people to develop a staples economy (agriculture) and help turn the prairies into the "grain basket" of the world. Exports were needed to feed a hungry Europe as well as markets in eastern Canada and the United States. Within this context Canada pursued a proactive immigration policy (Friesen 1984).

The principal program introduced to make a proactive policy work was the passing of the *Federal Dominion Lands Act* in 1872. This act created what is now known as *The Homestead Act*. Under this legislation, for a fee of $10, a person was entitled to claim one quarter-section (160 acres), providing certain criteria were met. The claimant had to live on the land for at least six months of each year, break 40 acres over the first three years, and establish a permanent residence on the land. A second quarter could be obtained for about $2.50 an acre. Land, basically free, was the drawing card to attract immigrants (Coates and McGuiness 1987).

Although the policy was proactive, there was a lack of infrastructure to get people to Manitoba, at least in significant numbers. Sailing into Hudson Bay, then taking York boats down the river system to Winnipeg, was time consuming, not to say dangerous. Overland by Red River cart, although used extensively, was also slow. Neither approach could get exports out in the volume and with the speed required. The answer was the railway, which reached Winnipeg and Brandon in 1881. This facilitated the flow of people in and the export of goods out. The policy, the program, and the infrastructure were now in place to facilitate the flow of immigrants.

While most of the earliest settlers were of British origin, arrivals from other parts of the world soon increased the population's ethnic and cultural diversity. The first Mennonites (65 people) arrived from Russia in 1874, followed by another 6,000 during the next five years (Loewen 2006). In 1875 francophone settlers arrived from Massachusetts and Quebec. The first group of Icelanders came in 1875, with more following in 1876 and 1878. Between 1879 and 1882 over 58,000 immigrants arrived in the province (Smith 1984), and by 1882 large parts of southern Manitoba were settled. The first immigrants from Ukraine arrived in the late 1890s, with over 30,000 Ukrainians settling in the province by 1914. Immigrants from Poland arrived during the same period. Most Ukrainian and Polish people settled in the park belt and woodlands south and east of the Riding Mountains, as by this time much of the good agricultural land had been claimed (Coates and McGuiness 1987).

The 1870 to 1929 period clearly illustrates that the foundations of what is now Manitoba was built on immigration. The province's economy, culture, and early society developed around the various immigrant groups arriving during this period; immigrants were the early provincial builders.

1929–1946

The Great Depression following the 1929 stock market crash, and then World War II slowed immigration to a trickle. Unemployment rates were very high during the Depression, demand for agricultural products dropped, and there were few opportunities to attract newcomers. The population during the 1921 to 1931 period grew by only 90,000 people, then by only 29,000 in the following decade (Table 1). In the period 1939 to 1946 the focus on the war effort and the international conflict prevented most movements over international borders. Surviving the Depression and winning the war were the focuses of the time.

1946–1976

Between 1946 and 1976 immigration to Manitoba resumed, but not on the scale prior to 1929. Annual immigrant arrivals averaged 6,234 between 1946 and 1955 for a ten-year total of 62,000. Approximately 45,000 arrived during the next decade for an annual average of 4,477 (Table 2). This figure would have been even lower had it not been for a substantial number of refugees from Hungary following the 1956 revolution.

TABLE 2
Manitoba, Immigrant Arrivals, 1946–2009

Years	Total Arrivals	Annual Average
1946–1955	62,343	6,234
1956–1965	44,772	4,477
1966–1975	67,479	6,748
1976–1985	48,313	4,831
1986–1995	49,666	4,966
1996–2005	50,293	5,029
2006–2009	45,747	11,437

Source: Citizenship and Immigration Canada: Historical Archives (various years).

Why the lower numbers? Unlike Alberta, and to some extent Saskatchewan, Manitoba did not benefit from the growth of an increasingly diversified economy, remaining instead rooted in agriculture and mining ventures. The largest share of immigrants during this period arrived between 1946 and 1955 when some agricultural workers were still needed and agriculture was considered a vocation, but the process of rural depopulation was already underway. Between 1936 and 1946 the farm population decreased by 35,000, then declined from 225,000 to 162,000 from 1946 to 1966. The rural-to-urban shift fed the job requirements of growing urban centres, so there was less need for international immigrants (Smith 1984). Workers were still required in communities such as the mining centres of Flin Flon and Thompson, and Manitoba developed an immigrant recruitment program in the mid-1960s. Numbers increased, but poor working conditions and low salaries in mining centres attracted few immigrants, although average annual arrivals increased to 6,700 in the 1966–1975 period.

The economy was stronger throughout much of the late 1960s and early 1970s, but most immigrants opted to go to cities, mainly those outside Manitoba, where there were better job opportunities and larger numbers of people from their home countries to provide social support networks (Friesen and Loewen 2009). In 1966, Manitoba immigration officials travelled to London to promote immigration to the province with the director of Canada's Immigration Services in the United Kingdom. While numbers subsequently did increase, the most significant problem the province faced during this period was low retention. Immigrants came, but secondary migration quickly saw them leave the province for large cities like Toronto, Vancouver, and Calgary, and other locations in Ontario, Alberta, and British Columbia. Manitoba struggled with this problem from the 1960s right through to the 1990s. "Bring them in, then lose them," was a constant theme for at least four decades. Manitoba was not able to compete. Out-migration of the non-immigrant population was also characteristic of this period, and population growth was modest.

As the outset of this period, source areas of immigration were still focused on Europe and the British Isles. Following World War II, more people began to arrive from the Netherlands, Italy, Germany, and Greece. Immigrants from Asian countries, particularly from the Philippines, also started to arrive toward the end of the 1960s, following the elimination of discrimination based on nationality and race in the 1962 Immigration Regulations and the introduction of the points system in the 1967 Immigration Regulations.

1976–1998

The period 1976–1998 saw little that was spectacular or noteworthy about immigration to the province. Annual average arrivals remained below 5,000, at times falling well below 4,000 (Table 2). The province's economy was not weak, but it was not as strong as elsewhere and immigrants moved on to greener fields. Secondary migration continued and Manitoba became a destination along the way. Diversity among arrivals, however, continued to grow. Countries of origin changed significantly, shifting from Europe to East Asia, South East Asia, and South Asia: to China, Philippines, India, Hong Kong, and Pakistan, for example. Later in this period African and Latin American countries also became sources of new immigrants.

Taking Stock in the Late 1990s

After 1929 immigration to Manitoba ran out of steam. Why? Agricultural lands were basically occupied, and a rural to urban shift was occurring.

People were not needed to settle and work the land. The rural-to-urban shift helped fill jobs opening up in growing urban centres, principally Winnipeg, again reducing the need for immigration. Manitoba's economy, although reasonably strong, was less so than economies in Ontario, British Columbia, or Alberta. Manitoba was battling a problem it has had since it joined Confederation: trying to attract immigrants away from Canada's major centres. Toronto, Canada's largest city, accounted for 16.4 percent of the overall population; it has attracted 40.3 percent of recent immigrants (those arriving between 2001 and 2006). The three largest Census Metropolitan Areas (CMAs) of Montreal, Toronto, and Vancouver together contain 34.7 percent of the country's population and 68.9 percent of recent immigrants (Carter, Pandey, and Townsend 2010). Recent immigrants are less likely to live in the smaller, "second tier" cities like Winnipeg than the population as a whole.

In addition, with growing numbers of ethnic groups and nationalities arriving in Canada, they looked for support and social needs where their ethno-cultural numbers were higher. This was not in Manitoba. The ethno-cultural threshold for most groups was not high enough to be an attraction. Provincial population growth during the period 1961–2006 averaged less than 1 percent annually (Statistics Canada 2008a). Manitoba was in "snooze mode." If immigration in Manitoba were a baseball game, the grand slam home run was hit in the late 1800s and early 1900s. After 1961 there were little more than a few base hits. If people stole a base, it generally meant stealing away to Toronto, Calgary, or Vancouver. The game was less than spectacular. Few runs were scored.

By the early 1990s the situation was such that the Government of Manitoba, with the support (one might say urging) of some municipalities and the business community, started to rework provincial immigration policy. Certain factors cried out for a more proactive immigration policy. One was the aging population; the median age of the Manitoba population climbed by more than ten years from the late 1960s to reach 38 in 2006 (ibid.). This demographic, combined with slow growth and net negative interprovincial migration and the resulting loss of younger people to provinces like Alberta and British Columbia, was leading to labour force shortages in various sectors of the economy. In addition, many centres throughout the province were declining. Even Winnipeg experienced very slow growth. More people were required to address labour force shortages, stimulate the economy, and slow population aging and centre decline. As the next section illustrates, 1998 marked a turning point in immigration policy in the province.

MANITOBA IMMIGRATION AND THE PROVINCIAL NOMINEE PROGRAM

That turning point was the introduction of the Provincial Nominee Program (PNP). The first federal-provincial agreements creating nominee programs were signed in 1998 by British Columbia, Manitoba, and Saskatchewan; they represent a departure from federally administered immigration programs, as provinces play a direct role in determining the goals and criteria for immigration. Potential immigrants apply for permanent resident status directly through the province, and applications are vetted by provincial officials to determine if they meet the criteria of the program. Acceptable applicants are then nominated by the province for permanent resident status. Citizenship and Immigration Canada (CIC) determines whether each nominee fulfills federal admissibility requirements related to health, criminality, and security (Canada 2003).

Manitoba sees the PNP as a way to deal with existing and impending skill shortages and as a vehicle to increase population growth – in both Winnipeg and rural areas. In order to meet these economic and demographic goals, applicants must be well suited to Manitoba's labour market needs and also be good candidates for successful settlement and integration. Like other provinces, Manitoba has created streams within the Nominee Program that facilitate the entry of people needed to meet specific labour force requirements. There are two broad streams: the Skilled Worker PNP and the Business PNP. The Skilled Worker PNP has to accommodate workers with levels of education and skills different from those who meet the eligibility criteria of the Federal Skilled Workers Program (FSW) – truck drivers and welders, for example. Programs under the Business PNP are aimed at attracting business immigrants who will establish new or joint ventures to create jobs and other benefits. To facilitate the many objectives, the different streams of the Skilled Worker PNP have included Employer Direct, International Student, Family Support, Community Support, Strategic Recruitment Initiatives, and a General Stream (Manitoba Labour and Immigration 2006a). Under the Business PNP there are two streams: the Program for Business Investors and the Young Farmer Nominee Program.

The various streams are designed to be integrated and complementary in nature (Clement 2005). Wide-ranging criteria and flexible guidelines allow applicants to be directed to the best route on a case-by-case basis. For example, if a person does not have a job offer but has a family member in the province, that application can be shifted to the Family Support Stream. Foreign students, who now have the approval of the federal government to remain for up to three years after their studies are complete, can apply under the International Student Stream if they have a job offer. Temporary Foreign Workers are eligible to apply for permanent residence after they have been in Manitoba for six months, and many are sponsored by their employer under the Employer Direct Program. In May 2004 major revisions to the PNP were undertaken that increased the emphasis on applicants' employability, ability to adapt to changing labour market conditions, and pre-existing community connections. These changes were made after it became apparent that the "high demand occupation list" on which selection had been primarily based could not keep up with changes in the labour market (Leo and August 2009).

The province also hopes to use the PNP to strengthen francophone immigration. The goal is to reach a point where 7 percent of all arrivals under the PNP are francophone – from the Caribbean, North Africa, Europe, or other regions where French is the language of choice.

The nominee programs do not restrict a successful nominee's ability to move between provinces, as this would violate the mobility rights of new immigrants provided under the Charter of Rights and Freedoms. Consequently, provincial officials work to develop categories and selection criteria that maximize the likelihood that immigrants will stay in the province. Obtaining acceptable employment soon after arriving has been identified as the most compelling reason for new immigrants to remain in the community where they initially settle (Canada 2003; Derwing and Krahn 2008), and this makes the Employer Direct Stream very important. Family and community connections are also an important determinant of settlement, explaining the presence of the Family and Community Support Streams. Specific criteria for each stream are provided on the Manitoba Labour and Immigration website.[1] Points are awarded for education and training (particularly in areas of labour shortages), work experience, knowledge of English or French, a connection in Manitoba (family, friends, or employer), and settlement supports (family, community, and money to maintain the family).

The PNP provides an incentive for immigrants to come to smaller provinces or centres by establishing criteria that can be more easily met than the federal selection criteria and by offering expedited processing times. By easing and speeding the process, the program influences the regional distribution of immigrants and enhances the ability of smaller centres to attract immigrants to slow or halt population decline, while simultaneously bringing in younger members to offset the effects of an aging population. Developing immigration policy at a local level also allows communities to identify and recruit potential immigrants who are better suited to integrating into the community and/or have skills that meet local labour market conditions. Better matches improve retention and increase the economic benefits of immigration.

The PNP has become the primary tool for increasing immigration to Manitoba, and the effects have been significant. In 1999, the year the first applicants arrived, the PNP provided 11 percent of all arrivals; the federal Skilled Workers Program and business class contributed 38 percent, family class 28 percent, and refugees 21 percent. By 2009 the PNP's proportion of total new arrivals had increased to 75 percent; skilled workers and business class immigrants had fallen to approximately 5 percent, family class to 11 percent, and refugees to 8 percent (Manitoba Labour and

Immigration 2010a). While there has been no appreciable decline in the actual number of people arriving under the other categories, the number arriving through the PNP has risen, increasing the overall number of new arrivals in the province. The total number of people moving to the province under the PNP increased from 418 in 1999, the year after the program was introduced, to 10,518 in 2009 (ibid.).

In 1999, the immigration rate to the province was 3.3 immigrants per thousand residents, well below the national rate of 6.3 per thousand. In 2009, Manitoba's rate was 11.3 per thousand, well above the national rate of eight per thousand. Manitoba's share of immigration to Canada has increased from 1.9 percent in 1998 to 5.4 percent in 2009 (CIC 2010). In addition, the PNP has improved the regional distribution of immigration, with a greater proportion of immigrants settling in centres outside of Winnipeg. Prior to the introduction of the PNP, approximately 90 percent of new arrivals settled in Winnipeg. In 2008 almost 35 percent of provincial nominees were destined for communities outside Winnipeg (Manitoba Labour and Immigration 2010a). Since 2000, close to 16,000 immigrants chose to settle outside of Winnipeg. This increasing flow to centres outside Winnipeg can be attributed to a number of factors: better match with labour demands under the program, proactive involvement of communities in settlement planning, more involvement by employers throughout the province, and the greater control that the province has over nomination and selection of immigrants (Carter, Morrish, and Amoyaw 2008). Based on these successes, the province has announced the ambitious target of expanding immigration to the province to 20,000 per annum by 2016 (Manitoba Labour and Immigration 2006b). The program is also helping to increase cultural diversity in the province. Based on country of birth, immigrants from the Philippines continue making up more than a quarter of arrivals. Another quarter comes from countries of the former Soviet Bloc (Mennonites), usually by way of Germany. Other regions or countries well represented include Africa, China, India, Ukraine, Latin America, Israel and the Middle East, and Asia (Manitoba Labour and Immigration 2010a).

Studies by Carter, Pandey, and Townsend (2010), Pandey and Townsend (2010), Carter et al. (2009), and Carter, Morrish, and Amoyaw (2008) suggest the program has led to better integration and retention. Using data from the Longitudinal Immigrant Database (IMDB) and personal interviews with key informants and with principal applicants and their spouses arriving under the program, these studies have evaluated the program on the basis of a number of outcomes including difficulties with labour market integration, satisfaction with program administration, integration services, trajectories in incomes and poverty levels, housing experiences, satisfaction with communities and schools, and other indicators important in the settlement integration and retention process. Key findings include:

Labour force trajectories are positive. Almost everyone who wanted to work was working, with 84 percent entering the labour force in the first three months after arrival. Close to 90 percent of those working had permanent jobs. Although initially many nominees were not working in their field of expertise, trajectories toward desired career objectives were positive. By the third year, principal applicants were much more likely to be working in occupations in which they had training or experience (83 percent) compared to 57 percent in year 1.

Income and poverty trajectories are positive. As provincial nominees live here longer, they are less likely to be low income. In the first two years, 60 percent were below Low Income Cut-Offs (LICOs), but this proportion dropped to 25 percent after three years, though they remained higher than for native born Manitoban households (17 percent before tax) in 2006 (Statistics Canada 2008b). Average household incomes of nearly $50,000 are only $10,000 less than the provincial average; 85 percent of gross income came from employment, a higher proportion than for the population as a whole. The trend of increasing financial well-being is also reflected in the responses to the question "How would you describe your household's present financial situation?" Of those living here over three years, 94 percent said they had enough money to meet or exceed their basic needs, compared to 67 percent for the most recent arrivals.

Home ownership increases. As provincial nominees live in the province longer, they are more likely to become homeowners. Of the longer term residents, 76 percent own compared to only 39 percent of the most recently arrived (66 percent of provincial households are homeowners).

Language skills improve. The longer provincial nominees live in Manitoba, the better their language skills: 91 percent of those here for three years or more said they could easily communicate in English, compared to 78 percent of the most recent newcomers.

Most newcomers plan to remain in the province. Retention rates one year after arrival have consistently been above 80 percent. The longer that provincial nominees live in Manitoba, the more likely it is that they will support other family members to move here as well. Only 15 percent of the most recent arrivals have supported family to come here, compared to 46 percent of respondents living here longer than three years.

Cultural and community ties and activities expand. Approximately 40 percent of those living in Manitoba longer than three years said they take part in wider community activities, compared to 28 percent of recent arrivals. The proportion of respondents who participate in activities with people from the same ethnic or cultural group falls from 73 to 58 percent over the period; maintaining ties to others of the same cultural group also appeared to lose some importance over time. The percentage of those saying that such ties are very important to them decreased from two-thirds for recent arrivals to 39 percent for those living in Manitoba over three years. The social network of participants expands with time; they are involved in a wider range of activities and have developed friendships beyond their own ethnic and cultural group. They are becoming more active members of the broader community. Nominees expressed relatively high levels of satisfaction with their communities as places to live, and these high satisfaction levels were common throughout the province and for both visible minority and non-visible minority groups, suggesting integration is working well. Further, a high proportion of the interviewees stated that their experience in Manitoba had been better than expected and they had encouraged and supported other family and friends to apply under the program or they planned to do so. They have "taken root" and feel generally positive about their decision to immigrate to and make their home in Manitoba. The successes of the program to date can be expected to perpetuate future immigration to the province.

During the key informant interviews, a number of additional benefits of the nominee program were mentioned. Among them were that investor immigrants have helped expand the pool of capital for business start-ups and expansions; the new arrivals contribute to the global connectivity of the province through communications and knowledge transfer operating between immigrants and co-ethnics abroad; new arrivals increase the province's competitive advantage in various sectors of the economy; and they have contributed to increasing cultural diversity. However, key informants also noted that waves of immigrants from different source countries arriving in recent years and the growing proportion of visible minorities amongst them are increasing the "social distance" between immigrants and the host population. They noted that this may require policy and program changes in many areas other than immigration policy to ensure that discriminatory practices do not become a problem and communities remain welcoming places that encourage new arrivals to stay.

Despite the positive assessment of their resettlement and integration experience, nominees also raised concerns that deserve attention. Survey participants identified recognition of their credentials as the one major obstacle in obtaining jobs. A significant proportion of both principal applicants and spouses were disappointed because they could not get jobs in their field of expertise. In addition, several new arrivals encountered barriers in efforts to upgrade their skills, and many struggled with a lack of language skills. More work remains to be done on developing community acceptance of diversity, building community awareness of immigrant needs, and strengthening community capacity to accommodate these needs. This undertaking may require the province to invest more in settlement and support services for immigrants and on developing welcoming communities.

SETTLEMENT SERVICES: THE PLAYERS AND THEIR ROLES

Settlement services play an important role in the resettlement and integration process. Provision of settlement and integration services follows three different models in Canada. In the most commonly used model, the services are administered by local CIC offices and delivered by non-governmental organizations. Alberta has opted for a co-management role in settlement services, with provincial officials and the CIC jointly determining settlement priorities and programming. In Manitoba, British Columbia, and Quebec, agreements have been reached with the CIC that transfer administration of these services directly to the provinces (Seidel 2010).

In 1990 Manitoba consolidated immigration, settlement, and language services within a single provincial department (Leo and August 2009). A 1996 agreement with the federal government provided for some settlement realignment, giving the provinces the right to be consulted on immigration policy. Provincial nominee and settlement annexes were signed again in 1998, and the province assumed full responsibility for the administration and delivery of settlement services. The settlement realignment agreements also transferred the federal funding to the provinces. This agreement was renewed in 2003 and the province is currently in negotiations with the federal government on a renewal and extension of another agreement (Carter, Pandey, and Townsend 2010).

Immigration and settlement programming is currently handled in Manitoba by the Immigration Division of the Provincial Department of Labour and Immigration. While much of the funding for these services is provided by the CIC, the province also contributes. The department has 70 full time equivalent staff and an annual budget of $31,433,000, including a federal contribution of $25,355,000 for settlement services (Manitoba Labour and Immigration 2010b). A number of representatives within the settlement provider community have indicated that services improved immediately upon the provincial government assuming management of services (Leo and August 2009, Carter, Pandey, and Townsend 2010). The province has worked in consultation with Manitoba communities, businesses, and educational and professional organizations to develop attraction, settlement, and retention strategies and deliver the necessary services.

Figure 1 provides the settlement strategy framework illustrating the comprehensive nature of settlement services. Basic components include pre-arrival information, language training, settlement and community supports, employment supports, qualification and recognition supports, special programs, and delivery and field development supports (Manitoba Labour and Immigration 2010c). This model is currently being revised and new programs are being introduced. The province is developing a new settlement continuum that starts the settlement and integration process

FIGURE 1. Manitoba Settlement Strategy

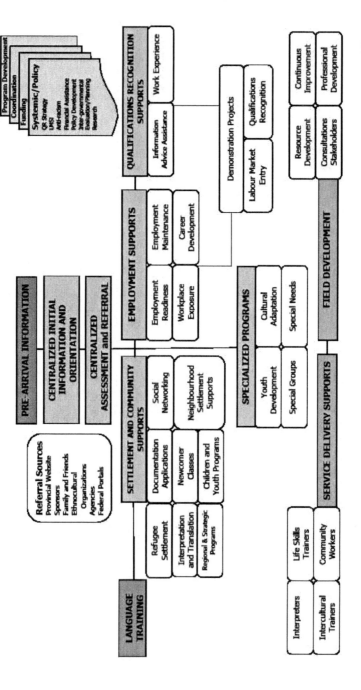

Settlement and Labour Market Services Branch   Manitoba Labour and Immigration   June 26, 2007

Source: Reprinted with permission from Manitoba Labour and Immigration (2010c).

for newcomers in their home countries. Pre-arrival services include help with developing a career plan based on Manitoba-specific labour market information and guidance on qualification recognition procedures the applicant may have to follow if credential upgrading is required. The pre-arrival services also include access to Manitoba's English Online language program. These pre-arrival services (still in the pilot project stage) should help address the concerns some arrivals expressed about lack of knowledge of labour market circumstances and unanticipated credential recognition problems (Carter et al. 2009).

Once immigrants arrive, a new program called Manitoba Start provides a centralized intake centre that assesses the immediate needs of newcomers and refers them to appropriate services. The program and the centre reduce confusion about where to go for post-arrival services and address a criticism expressed in the recent evaluation of the program (ibid.). The province has also expanded employment services with more emphasis on career coaching, development of client-focused career plans and referrals to "gap training," and matching of client skills with job market requirements (Manitoba Immigration Services Branch 2010). The province is working to provide a strong and comprehensive service continuum. The nature of the broad range of services and the roles and responsibilities of the various organizations are highlighted in the three case studies profiled below.

Case Study 1: Manitoba Interfaith Immigration Council Inc.

This registered charitable organization operating for over 50 years out of Welcome Place in Winnipeg is open to all faith communities. With an annual budget $2.8 million (2010 Annual Report), its major funders are CIC ($1.2 million) and the Province of Manitoba ($1.3 million); other funds come from the United Way, City of Winnipeg, Winnipeg School Division, Winnipeg Foundation, and fundraising activities. The staff of 60 plus volunteers who work with refugees and refugee claimants include multilingual settlement counsellors.

Services

- *Arrival services*: meet refugee claimants at the US border and refugees at the airport, establish settlement plans;
- *Orientation services*: introduce newcomers to Canadian life, culture, norms, customs, transportation system, health care system, financial services, legal system, etc.;
- *Referral services*: provide access to a range of services such as health care, education, recreation, child support, income assistance, etc.;

- *Interpretation services*: offer translation and interpretation;
- *Life skills and training*: assist newly arrived refugees to learn basic life skills, practical activities to foster independence, shopping skills, job search, etc.;
- *Housing services*: provide transitional housing (self-contained furnished suites), assistance with finding permanent housing, moving to a permanent residence, obtaining household furnishings, education on tenant/landlord rights and responsibilities;
- *Sponsorship services*: act as a sponsorship agreement holder, help with visas, sponsorship applications, work with community/faith and family sponsorship groups;
- *Protection services*: provide help for refugee claimants, facilitating access to lawyers, legal aid, obtaining work permits, permanent residence status, etc.;
- *Volunteer services*: offer tours and orientation, friendship and support, providing conversational English, training youth to be a support network.

Challenges

- An increasing workload but not always appropriate increases in budget;
- Refugees are becoming a higher needs group, but budget is not increasing accordingly
- Staff have limited expertise in some areas;
- Caseload is too high to allow for sufficient follow-up;
- Finding adequate and affordable housing is difficult – can only help families find their first independent home (Manitoba Interfaith Immigration Council 2010, key informant interviews).

Case Study 2: New Journey Housing

This non-profit organization, funded by a local philanthropic entrepreneur, was established to assist and train newcomers as they search for decent and affordable housing. Their clientele include those who are low income as well as those ready and able to move towards options such as home ownership.

Basic Goals

- assist newcomers (immigrants and refugees) seeking housing;
- educate newcomers, landlords, caretakers, and the public on issues related to newcomer housing;

- link landlords and tenants;
- guide newcomers and landlords in the rental process;
- partner with other housing initiatives and supportive agencies in assisting newcomers to settle in Manitoba and work toward their housing goals;
- advocate on behalf of newcomers;
- provide a one stop destination for all housing help and information;
- give newcomers the tools to find and retain housing;
- provide rental and homeownership counselling (New Journey Housing 2010).

Case Study 3: Eastman Immigrant Services (EIS)

EIS is part of Manitoba Labour and Immigration's regional network of immigrant services funded by Manitoba Labour and Immigration, CIC, and the Steinbach Chamber of Commerce. It services the southeast area of Manitoba with headquarters in Steinbach. Steinbach City Council, the Steinbach Chamber of Commerce, and local employers have been actively involved in its organization and development. In the past decade more than 5,000 immigrants have settled in the area

EIS is characteristic of the strong partnership approach to immigrant services that exists in Manitoba, with school divisions, health care, recreation, housing organizations, faith based groups, local employers, and surrounding rural municipalities taking an active role in attraction, integration, and retention activities for newcomers. It works largely with immigrants arriving under the PNP, but also provides services to refugees. While EIS provides some services directly, its main function is as a facilitator to bring together newcomers and the services they need.

Services

- *Orientation services*: organizes pre-visits to the area, helps with school registration, registering for child tax benefits, Manitoba Health Care, etc. Facilitates access to orientation programs on Canadian culture and customs, the health care system, financial services, the legal system, rights and responsibilities, and information on Steinbach and area;
- *Language referrals*: facilitates newcomers' access to language training programs;
- *Translation and interpretation services*: works with schools, employers, doctors, hospitals, immigration offices, and others;
- *Employment services*: Provides counselling, e.g., career coaching, resumé writing, job search support, on-the-job language training, occupational and safety training, and training programs for immigrant truck drivers;

- *Housing services*: provides education on housing characteristics, home operation, renting and buying a home and also helps with the housing search process. Other services include arranging accommodation when people first arrive; distributing information on different housing options; encouraging people to rent out basement suites and provide room and board; providing information on landlord/tenant regulations and responsibilities.
- *Volunteer services*: organizes volunteers to work with new arrivals.
- *Special events and social networking programming*: provides regular programming and special events (picnics, Christmas parties, etc.) to get newcomers and the community together to build community awareness and acceptance;
- *Resource centre*: offers a centre containing information on a wide range of topics – how to access various services and other information to help newcomers settle into the area. Also provides computer access for job searches (Eastman Immigrant Services 2010, key informant interviews).

Other prominent service organizations include the Société Franco-manitobaine. Through l'Accueil francophone, the organization has developed settlement capacity and support services for francophone immigrants. The Immigrant Centre (formerly the International Centre) also has a long history of serving immigrants in Manitoba.

In addition to the activities profiled in the case studies, other service initiatives of importance include provincial recruitment activity. Recent activity includes renewal of an agreement with the Philippines to streamline immigration processes and build stronger connections, and an agreement with Iceland to assist Manitoba employers in recruiting skilled workers. Promotion of the program abroad is extensive and has included recent visits to China, Germany, France, and Latin American countries. The province has been particularly active in efforts to increase the number of French-speaking immigrants.

Website information[2] has been expanded and upgraded. In a recent evaluation of the PNP (Carter et al. 2009), 95 percent of the participants who used the website rated it as a useful or very useful source of pre- and post-arrival information. Many participants suggested that it should contain expanded and more recent information on labour market conditions and credential recognition issues and be available in languages other than French and English. This matter is being addressed through the pre-arrival pilot project previously discussed.

Special programming for children and youth includes after-school care, tutoring, homework clubs, computer access, workplace internships, summer activities, and extracurricular classes such as theatre and art. There is also support for social networking activities that assist newcomers to develop social networks through programs such as host and volunteer programs, conversation circles, social clubs, and special community events.

Through the Entry Program, newcomer classes cover topics such as citizenship preparation, where to look for jobs, employment standards, the education system, location of services, banking, transportation services, the legal system, renting apartments, and information on culture and lifestyle characteristics.[3] In the program evaluation conducted by Carter et al. (2009), participants in the program found it very useful and felt it should be expanded and made more readily and conveniently available throughout the province.

The province also seeks to improve integration through labour market services and employer engagement. In 2002 it developed the Framework for a Manitoba Strategy on Qualifications Recognition, which established principles to ensure skilled immigrants have access to the information and resources necessary to prepare for qualifications recognition. Initiatives that have built on this strategy include assessments of job experience and qualifications, career development planning, employment counselling and placement, and assistance with assessment of qualifications and examinations, fees, courses, and class material. The province has also been working with professional organizations such as those of the engineering and nursing professions to improve procedures in licensing and establishment of credentials and training requirements. Specific to qualifications recognition, the province has developed increased information about recognition pathways and enhanced supports and programs with relevant partners to speed up the recognition and retraining process. Enhanced information guides such as *The Employers Guide to Hiring, TIPs for Hiring Newcomers,* and *Internship Programs* have also been prepared.[4]

On the regulatory side, the province has passed the *Fair Registration Practices in Regulated Professions Act* (2009), to ensure that regulated professions and people applying for registration in those professions are governed by practices that are transparent, objective, impartial, and fair. This act helps to ensure immigrants are treated fairly when they apply to enter certain professions and their credentials are fairly assessed. It has established the office of the Manitoba Fairness Commission that works with the professions to ensure immigrants receive fair and equitable treatment. The province also passed the *Worker Recruitment and Protection Act* (2009) to strengthen and improve protection for foreign workers. The act requires persons (employers and consultants) who assist foreign workers in finding employment in Manitoba to register in the province, apply for and hold a licence, and abide by a range of enforcement provisions; it prohibits them from collecting a fee from prospective workers. Work with the Manitoba Registered Nurses Association focuses on ensuring safe and ethical recruitment of nurses from abroad.

Under the broad umbrella of the Manitoba Immigration Integration Program, more than $9.7 million was provided to 72 service providers to deliver many of these services (Manitoba Labour and Immigration 2010b).

Spending on Adult English as an Alternate Language totalled $13.6 million in the 2008–09 budget year, with over 14,000 immigrants and refugees taking classes. Programs are offered through schools, colleges, and community based organizations and being expanded regionally as more newcomers settle outside the City of Winnipeg. In 2008–09 regional programs were expanded from 12 to 18 locations (ibid.).

The province also carries out extensive consultations with its partners on an annual basis through a series of workshops, presentations, and meetings with employers, municipalities, service providers, and other government departments. These consultations have been strengthened by the formation of the Manitoba Immigration Council. The 12 members of the council, ranging from private sector employers to academics, represent key stakeholders in the attraction, retention, and settlement of immigrants. The council is responsible for providing the minister with information and advice on attracting and retaining immigrants and the settlement services they require. The Manitoba Ethnocultural Advisory and Advocacy Council plays a similar role, advising the minister on multiculturalism issues in Manitoba.

Other active partners in the settlement and integration process include local municipalities. Although they have no constitutional responsibilities for immigration, many have taken an active role in settlement services. Brandon, Steinbach, Winkler, Morden, Altona, Portage la Prairie, and Winnipeg have all been active partners with other levels of government and community organizations. Both the universities of Manitoba and Winnipeg have introduced programs targeted at the immigrant and refugee communities. The objectives of these programs are to improve access to educational programs and to facilitate integration in the community. What this discussion clearly highlights is that delivery of services in the province is based on a broad partnership between governments, institutions, community based organizations, and the private sector.

Provincial Demographics and Growing Diversity at the Turn of the Twenty-First Century

Immigration is changing population growth, distribution, and diversity in the province. Manitoba has experienced relatively slow growth in recent decades. The 2006 population of 1,148,401 represented an increase of just 16 percent since 1971; Canada's population has increased 47 percent since 1971. Despite its prominence in Manitoba, the Winnipeg CMA had the lowest rate of growth of the ten largest metropolitan areas in Canada between 1976 and 2001: 5.2 percent compared to an average 22 percent for the top ten CMAs. Even with Winnipeg's slow growth, 96 percent of the growth in the province since 1971 occurred there (Carter 2009). Immigration had been reinforcing the uneven growth in the province since over 80 percent of new arrivals settled in the city.

As previously noted, growth became an imperative for the province if it was to maintain a viable economy. With higher levels of international immigration, the province has now ceased to be an exporter and become an importer of people. Most recent population figures indicate the provincial population reached 1,232,700 as of 1 April 2010, up 7.3 percent since 2006. Manitoba recorded its most rapid rate of growth since 1972 in the first quarter of 2010 (Manitoba Bureau of Statistics 2010).

Lower levels of net interprovincial migration and a strong economy have also strengthened population growth. The recent recession was mild in Manitoba; job losses were less significant in the province than in other parts of Canada. Job creation continued throughout most of the recessionary period. In the first seven months of 2010, Manitoba's employment increased by 10,600, or 1.7 percent, above the national average of 1.3 percent. The unemployment rate has stayed well below the national average. In the first seven months of 2010, Manitoba's unemployment rate averaged 5.4 percent, the second lowest in Canada behind Saskatchewan. Historically, Manitoba's unemployment rate averaged 2.0 to 2.5 percentage points below the national rate. In 2009, this spread increased to 3.1 points. Manitoba used to have a low unemployment rate because people left the province for jobs elsewhere (ibid.). However, recently people have been coming back and there are more international immigrants than at any point in the last 60 years. In the year ending 1 April 2010, 11,080 more people moved to Manitoba than left. During the same period, net international migration for the province totalled 12,508, more than its net interprovincial out-migration of 1,428 – the smallest out-migration since 1985 (ibid.).

The recent wave of immigrants is changing the demographic profile of the province. Manitoba's immigrant population totalled 168,354 persons in 1951, 22 percent of its total population (Table 3). In 2006 the immigrant population numbered 151,230 persons, 13 percent of the population. This percentage reflected lower levels of immigration after 1975 (Table 2). In 1951, 14 percent of the immigrant population had moved to Manitoba within the ten years preceding the 1951 Census; the remainder (86 percent) who had had been in Manitoba at least ten years largely reflected the rapid settlement in the late 1800s and early 1900s followed by the 1930s Depression and the war years when there was very little immigration. In 2006 the proportion of recent immigrants (previous ten years) had risen to 31 percent, and the proportion of established immigrants was correspondingly lower at 70 percent.

TABLE 3
Manitoba, Ethno-Cultural Groups, 1951–2006

	1951	1996	2001	2006	1951–2006		1996–2006	
	#	#	#	#	#	% change	#	% change
Total population	**776,541**	**1,113,898**	**1,119,583**	**1,148,401**	**371,860**	**48**	**34,503**	**3**
Immigrants	168,354	135,945	113,660	151,230	–17,124	–10	15,285	11
% of total population	22	12	10	13				
Recent immigrants[a]	23,401	31,190	32,345	46,276	22,875	98	—	—
% of total immigrants	14	23	28	31				
Visible minorities	N/A	77,355	87,115	109,095	—	—	31,740	41
% of total population	—	7	8	10				
Aboriginal	32,000	128,910	150,045	175,395	143,395	448	46,485	36
% of total population	4	12	13	15				

[a] Figures for 1996 are based on immigrants who arrived in the previous five years. For 1951, 2001, and 2006, figures are based on immigrants who arrived in the previous ten years.

Source: Manitoba Bureau of Statistics (2008a).

In 1951 the top five countries of birth for Manitoba's resident immigrant population were the United Kingdom, Russia, Poland, the United States, and Austria. In 2006 the top five had changed only slightly, to the Philippines, the United Kingdom, Germany, Poland, and the United States. The diversity of recent arrivals is not reflected in this distribution, as the higher movements of people to Manitoba have occurred since the 2006 Census. Manitoba's recent pattern of immigration, changing source countries, and ethnic groups to a large extent mirrors that of the nation as a whole, with significant immigrant flows from East and South East Asia and growing numbers from Africa, Latin America, and the Middle East. There are a several exceptions, however. The province has been the destination of a much larger proportion of German Mennonites and people from the Philippines than other regions or cities of Canada. In this, chain migration has certainly played a role. People from the Philippines began arriving in Winnipeg in 1959, and families have continued to support the arrival of other family members through the family reunification program and more recently through the PNP. German Mennonites arrived first in the late 1800s seeking greater religious freedom. They settled first in rural areas of the province (Winkler, Morden, and Steinbach) where they pursued an agricultural lifestyle. Although in recent years many have moved to Winnipeg and become very successful business entrepreneurs, the initial settlement has been a magnet for recent arrivals (Loewen 2006). Many of these are ethnic Germans who returned to Germany after the break-up of the former Soviet Union but have since moved to Canada. The rural agricultural life style is still an attraction, but religious and family ties play a role. The province has also marketed the PNP to the Mennonite group.

Filipinos Thrive and Put Down Roots

from the *Winnipeg Free Press*, 18 August 2010

- Now number more than 38,000 at last census count;
- First arrived in 1959 (nurses);
- One of the fastest growing minority groups in the city and the largest Filipino group per capita in Canada;
- First large group to come to Winnipeg included hundreds of garment workers from the late 1960s into the 1980s;
- Grew through the federal family-reunification program (family sponsorship) and federal domestic workers program;
- Second big wave started in 1999 under PNP – drew more skilled immigrants;
- Many left political strife at home;
- Able to integrate into mainstream yet remain distinct;
- Leaving Winnipeg for other major centres uncommon among Filipinos.

Between 1991 and 2006 Manitoba's foreign born population increased from 12 to 14 percent. Diversity, however, is reflected in the fact that 58 percent of the foreign born came from more than 150 countries in addition to the top five source regions. Geographically, the percentage of foreign born increased in most Manitoba regions, although Winnipeg has the highest proportion at 20 percent, with the highest proportions of foreign born in the downtown and inner city area. The eastern and central parts of the province that include centres such as Winkler, Morden, Altona, and Steinbach have also been major destination points for immigrants in recent years. The greatest increases in foreign born have also occurred in these two regions (Manitoba Bureau of Statistics 2008c).

The changes in source countries has meant a growing proportion of visible minorities amongst new arrivals. In 1996 just over 77,000 people, or 7 percent of the population, were considered visible minority. By 2006 the number had risen to over 109,000 and nearly 10 percent of the population (Table 4). This rise is changing the ethnic mix in many communities, even outside the City of Winnipeg, although 94 percent of the total people considered visible minority live in Winnipeg. The top five groups include Filipino, South Asian, black, Chinese, and Latin American, with the Filipino group containing more than double the number of the next most common group, South Asian. Visible minorities add diversity

TABLE 4
Manitoba, Visible Minorities, 1996–2006

	1996	2006	1996–2006	
	#	#	#	% change
Total visible minorities	**77,355**	**109,095**	**31,740**	**41**
Top six groups	69,755	101,660	31,905	46
% Total	90	93		
Filipino	25,910	37,790	11,880	46
% Total	33	35		
South Asian	12,110	16,565	4,455	37
% Total	16	15		
Chinese	12,340	13,705	1,365	11
% Total	16	18		
Black	10,775	15,655	4,880	45
% Total	14	14		
South East Asian	4,520	5,670	1,150	25
% Total	6	5		
Latin American	4,100	6,275	2,175	53
% Total	5	6		
Others	7,600	7,435	−165	−2
% Total	10	7		

Source: Statistics Canada (2008b).

to many aspects of everyday life in the province: markets, restaurants, community based organizations, schools and universities, neighbourhood characteristics, politics, and the arts. The many spinoffs, investment being one of them, are positive, but the visible minority presence also raises challenges, including discrimination.

Although not international immigrants, the province's Aboriginal population must be mentioned in the context of increasing diversity. Aboriginal numbers have grown rapidly in the province in recent years. From an estimated 32,000 in 1951, the provincial Aboriginal population reached 175,000 in 2006 (Manitoba Bureau of Statistics 2008b). Since 1996 the Aboriginal population has increased about 36 percent, compared to a 3 percent increase for the total population, 11 percent for immigrants, and 41 percent for visible minorities (Table 3). Aboriginal people are moving to Winnipeg and other larger urban centres in Manitoba in significant numbers. The approximately 68,000 Aboriginal people in the Winnipeg CMA represent approximately 10 percent of the population and one-third of the provincial Aboriginal population (Statistics Canada 2008b). Their numbers in the Winnipeg CMA are double those of the Filipinos, the largest visible minority group.

Though they are internal migrants, Aboriginal people face many of the same challenges as some of the international arrivals, particularly the refugee population (Carter et al. 2008). Low skill levels, deep poverty, large young families, difficulty adapting to an urban culture, discrimination in the job and housing markets, and housing affordability represent just a few of the problems shared with newcomers. With such similar characteristics, Aboriginal people and refugees are competing for the same low cost, often poor quality housing, for social housing, and for jobs in the unskilled service sector. In Winnipeg in particular, both groups tend to be concentrated in Winnipeg's inner city (ibid.) where one finds low cost housing and many of the service agencies that work with these groups. Juxtaposition and competition often lead to hostility and growing dislike, leading to incidents of personal threats and occasionally personal violence and competing youth gangs. The competition is most evident in the housing market. Because of the very low vacancy rates, the property management sector is able to be selective in its renting and eviction processes. It is no secret in Winnipeg (and in larger centres like Brandon) that Aboriginals are on the bottom rung of the property ladder from the property management perspective (ibid.). A perception (although little solid research to support it) that Aboriginals are not good tenants, at least not as good as refugees and immigrants, only serves to exacerbate the tension between the groups.

The increasing ethno-cultural diversity brings other changes as well. The proportion of people speaking one of the two official languages changed little between 1996 and 2006, but more than 40 languages are spoken at home in the province, more than double the variety of languages spoken in 1951. The French language in the province is also being strengthened by the arrival of francophone immigrants and refugees. This diversity also extends to religion with more than 40 faiths recognized in the 2006 Census, again more than double the number listed in 1951. New churches dot the landscape.

Challenges and Concluding Comments

Ethno-cultural diversity is increasing in Manitoba, and the dynamics at work include chain migration, family reunification, attraction of ethnic and religious ties, marketing for particular skills under the PNP, attraction and potential of a rural, agricultural lifestyle, and of course, availability of jobs.

Several lessons emerge from the Manitoba experience. Programs should build on local strengths and history. In Manitoba's immigrant history, two groups, the German Mennonites and the Philippine population, have had a long-standing relationship with the province. The PNP has capitalized on these ethnic and cultural connections by marketing the program in the source regions of these groups. Family and friends already in the province act as magnets and provide built-in support mechanisms for new immigrants. Provincial authority to design and deliver immigrant services also makes a positive difference. Services designed and delivered at the local level are likely to be more effective in meeting the needs of arrivals. Building partnerships with local communities and community based organizations to develop attraction and retention strategies results in better integration and retention possibilities and has been a strong aspect of immigration policy in the province. Making resources available to build capacity in immigrant serving agencies that provide many of the services and deal with immigrants on a day-to-day basis has also strengthened settlement and integration services. Finally, a good working relationship between the province and employers has assisted in identifying existing and emerging labour force shortages and helped develop approaches to resolving credential recognition problems.

Although Manitoba can be proud of the strength of its efforts in providing settlement and integration services, it has been less successful in integrating immigration policy with other policies that are also important in the settlement and integration process. For example, the province has never developed an adequate housing policy to support immigrant arrivals, particularly in the rental housing sector. Key informants suggest there is also a need for better liaison with the education, health, economic development, and labour sectors to ensure services are available to meet the demand generated by the increasing number of immigrants. Portable school classrooms, long waiting lists for family doctors, and economic development initiatives that bring in temporary foreign workers without the required housing in place are cause for concern. Such criticisms are being addressed through the newly established Growth Strategy Committee. This committee brings together all provincial departments with a role in immigration to coordinate initiatives to facilitate settlement and integration. The committee is in the early stages of its work.

The problems of credential recognition and credit for foreign work experience have also not been resolved to the satisfaction of many immigrants. Some immigrants feel they have been victims of false, or at least poor, information. Although this problem may not rest solely with program operation, it does stress the need for current, accurate pre-arrival information as well as local programs that can assess the need for and provide credential upgrading. Another key area of concern to be addressed is the interface between the immigrant and Aboriginal communities. Reducing competition and conflict requires a range of services, from more affordable housing to community based programming that provides social networking, awareness building, and opportunities to share and understand each others' culture and common problems and issues.

The introduction of the PNP has been a turning point in immigration policy in the province. Despite some problems and unresolved issues, indicators of integration, inclusion, and retention are positive since the program's introduction. While the service infrastructure established to serve the needs of nominee arrivals also serves other classes of arriving immigrants, nominees dominate the provincial immigration picture. Their material and social well-being improves with time as they expand their social networks and a large proportion achieve their dream of homeownership. Language skills are improving, as is their labour force experience. They are moving toward their career objectives and most feel established enough to support other family members who want to immigrate to the province. They generally feel positive about their decision to immigrate to Manitoba and make their home here.

NOTES

1. See http://www2.immigratemanitoba.com.
2. See http://www.immigratemanitoba.com.
3. See http://www.entryprogram.ca.
4. *The Employers Guide to Hiring Newcomers* is available online at http://www2.immigratemanitoba.com/asset_library/en/work/pdf/emp_hireguide2009-05.pdf; *Tips for Hiring Newcomers* is at http://www2.immigratemanitoba.com/asset_library/en/work/pdf/emp_hiretips2009-05.pdf; *Internship Programs* is at http://employmentsolutionsforimmigrantyouth.mb.ca/ett-internship-program/index.html.

REFERENCES

Canada. 2003. *Report of the Standing Committee on Citizenship and Immigration: The Provincial Nominee Program: A Partnership to Attract Immigrants to All Parts of Canada.* Ottawa: Communications Canada.

Carter, T. 2009. "Manitoba." In *Foundations of Governance: Municipal Government in Canada's Province,* ed. A. Sancton and R. Young. Toronto: University of Toronto Press.

Carter, T., M. Morrish, and B. Amoyaw. 2008. "Attracting Immigrants to Smaller Urban and Rural Communities: Lessons Learned from the Manitoba Provincial Nominee Program." *Journal of International Migration and Integration* 9(2):161-83.

Carter, T., M. Pandey, and J. Townsend. 2010. *The Manitoba Provincial Nominee Program: Attraction, Integration and Retention of Immigrants.* Ottawa: Institute for Research on Public Policy.

Carter, T., C. Polevychok, A. Friesen, and J. Osborne. 2008. *The Housing Circumstances of Recently Arrived Refugees: The Winnipeg Experience.* Winnipeg: Manitoba Labour and Immigration.

Carter, T., C. Polevychok, J. Osborne, M. Adler, and A. Friesen. 2009. *An Evaluation of the Manitoba Provincial Nominee Program.* Winnipeg: Manitoba Labour and Immigration: Immigration Division.

Citizenship and Immigration Canada (CIC). 2010. *Facts and Figures 2009: Immigration Overview.* Ottawa: Citizenship and Immigration Canada.

Clement, G. 2005. *Growing through Immigration: An Overview of Immigration and Settlement in Manitoba.* Winnipeg: Manitoba Labour and Immigration, Immigration Division.

Coates, K. and F. McGuiness. 1987. *Manitoba: The Province and the People.* Edmonton: Hurtig Publishers.

Derwing, T.M. and H. Krahn. 2008. "Attracting and Retaining Immigrants outside the Metropolis: Is the Pie Too Small for Everyone to Have a Piece?" *Journal of International Migration and Immigration* 9(2):185-202.

Eastman Immigrant Services. 2010. At http://www.eastmanimmigrantservices.com

Friesen, G. 1984. *The Canadian Prairies: A History.* Toronto: University of Toronto Press.

Friesen, G. and R. Loewen. 2009. *Immigrants in Prairie Cities: Ethnic Diversity in Twentieth Century Canada.* Toronto: University of Toronto Press.

Leo, C. and M. August. 2009. "The Multilevel Governance of Immigration and Settlement: Making Deep Federalism Work." *Canadian Journal of Political Science* 42(2):491-510.

Loewen, R. 2006. *Diaspora in the Countryside: Two Mennonite Communities in Mid-Twentieth Century North America.* Toronto: University of Toronto Press.

Manitoba Bureau of Statistics. 2008a. *Ethnicity Series: A Demographic Profile of Manitoba.* Vol. 1, *Manitoba's Foreign Born Population.* Winnipeg: Manitoba Bureau of Statistics.

—2008b. *Manitoba's Aboriginal Community: A 2001 to 2026 Population and Demographic Profile.* Winnipeg: Manitoba Bureau of Statistics.

—2008c. *Immigration: The Census in Manitoba, 1951 to 2006.* Winnipeg: Manitoba Bureau of Statistics.

—2010. *Manitoba Economic Highlights.* Winnipeg: Manitoba Bureau of Statistics.

Manitoba Immigration Services Branch. 2010. *Manitoba Immigration Service Continuum*. Winnipeg: Manitoba Labour and Immigration, Immigration Division.

Manitoba Interfaith Immigration Council Inc. 2010. *Annual Report*. At http://www.miic.ca/reception.aspx

Manitoba Labour and Immigration. 2006a. *Manitoba Provincial Nominee Program Guidelines*. Winnipeg: Labour and Immigration.

—2006b. *Manitoba Immigration Facts: 2006 Statistical Report*. At http://www2.immigrate manitoba.com/asset_library/en/resources/pdf/mb_immigrat_reprt_06.pdf

—2010a. *Manitoba Immigration Facts: 2009 Statistical Report*. Winnipeg: Labour and Immigration.

—2010b. Annual Report for 2009/2009. Winnipeg: Manitoba Labour and Immigration: Immigration Division.

—2010c. *Manitoba Settlement Strategy*. Winnipeg: Labour and Immigration: Immigration Branch.

New Journey Housing. 2010. At http://www.newjourneyhousing.com/about.php

Pandey, M. and J. Townsend. 2010. "Provincial Nominee Programs: An Evaluation of the Earnings and Retention Rates of Nominees." Department of Economics Working Paper No. 2010-01. Winnipeg: University of Winnipeg.

Raspovich, A.W., ed. 1984. *The Making of the Modern West: Western Canada since 1945*. Calgary: University of Calgary Press.

Seidel, F.L. 2010. *The Canada-Ontario Immigration Agreement: Assessment and Options for Renewal*. Toronto: Mowat Centre for Policy Innovation Paper.

Smith, P.J. 1984. "Urban Development Trends in the Prairie Provinces." In *The Making of the Modern West: Western Canada since 1945*, ed. A.W. Raspovich. Calgary: University of Calgary Press.

Statistics Canada. 2008a. *Canadian Demographics at a Glance*. Cat. No. 91-003-XWE (25 January). Ottawa: Statistics Canada

—2008b. *Community Profiles: Winnipeg CMA, Brandon, Steinbach, and Manitoba*. Ottawa: Statistics Canada.

Vineberg, R. 2010. *Immigration and Demographic Change in Canada and Manitoba*. Brandon: Rural Development Institute, Brandon University.

CHAPTER 7

INTEGRATION AND INCLUSION IN ONTARIO: THE SLEEPING GIANT STIRS

JOHN BILES, ERIN TOLLEY, CAROLINE ANDREW, VICTORIA ESSES, AND MEYER BURSTEIN [1]

As in the rest of Canada, the last century in Ontario has been marked by immigration and the desire to build an inclusive society. In fact, because this province has for decades received the majority of newcomers to the country, its history of immigration and diversity is more longstanding than elsewhere. Notwithstanding this, the province's record, as we shall illustrate, has been mixed. Indeed, in past decades the provincial government has been far less active than many of its counterparts both in terms of pursuing a strategy and fostering an inclusive and equitable society. Immigration, in other words, appeared to be something that "happened" rather than something that was sought or which the provincial government wished to actively steer.

In this chapter, we provide an overview of Ontario's immigration, integration, and inclusion landscape, charting the evolution of the province's policy framework, highlighting the key players, and illustrating some of the principal features and challenges. While Ontario has had a long history of immigration, it is large-scale refugee flows that have shaped much of the integration infrastructure over the past 60 years, a fact that is often lost in the provincial narrative. In particular, the arrivals of Hungarians in the 1950s, Czechs in the 1960s, Ugandans and Southeast Asian "boat people" in the 1970s, Somalis in the 1980s, and Sudanese in the 1990s, amongst others, have had a profound effect on Ontario's approach to integration and inclusion, a theme throughout this chapter. More recently, a new change factor has emerged, although its import is not yet clear. The engagement of municipalities, particularly the City of

Integration and Inclusion of Newcomers and Minorities across Canada, ed. J. Biles, M. Burstein, J. Frideres, E. Tolley, and R. Vineberg. Montreal and Kingston: Queen's Policy Studies Series, McGill-Queen's University Press.

Toronto as well as other cities and local community organizations, in immigration planning and management has been much more pronounced in Ontario than in other jurisdictions in Canada. In the integration and inclusion field, this engagement has generated many best practices that have emerged in the province and spread to other jurisdictions. We are arguably at a point where Ontario communities are being so altered by immigration and diversity that a fundamental rethink of integration and inclusion strategies is needed. We conclude this chapter with several recommendations. While the provincial government still has much to learn, it appears that the sleeping giant has begun to stir.

History of Integration and Inclusion in Ontario

The responses to continuous immigration and the diversification of Ontario's population can be divided into four broad periods: from early beginnings to the postwar era when there was little in the way of settlement programming but much of the province's human rights infrastructure was developed; from the late 1960s through to the 1980s when the arrival of increasingly diverse newcomers became more pronounced; the yo-yo era of the 1990s when a left-leaning government sought to create a wider provincial infrastructure focused on integration and inclusion, which was successively pared back by more conservative regimes; and, finally, the current era, which emerged with the signing of the Canada-Ontario Immigration Agreement in 2005.

Getting Started: From Early Beginnings to the Postwar Period

Although many of the integration challenges that exist in Ontario today were apparent prior to the postwar period, there were nonetheless very few settlement services or initiatives designed to encourage the inclusion of minorities. Those that did exist were mostly provided by charitable or religious organizations – in many cases organizations still central to integration and inclusion initiatives today (Biles and Ibrahim 2005; Kelley and Trebilcock 1998). In Ontario, two of the larger organizations to first take an interest in settlement were the Imperial Order of the Daughters of the Empire (IODE), now gone from the field, and the YMCA/YWCA, which remains actively involved in settlement and integration. Since the end of the nineteenth century, the YMCA/YWCA has facilitated social interaction between newcomers and the host society through English classes, housing, and complimentary club memberships (Amin 1987).

A contemporary organization, the United Way, entered the settlement field in Toronto. Initially it was called the United Community Fund and, along with religious organizations, volunteers, and private donations, it funded three settlement houses: University Settlement in 1910, Central Neighbourhood in 1911, and St Christopher's in 1912, all three still in existence (O'Connor 1986; Central Neighbourhood 2009; University Settlement 2009). These houses offered cultural and educational programs, public lectures, health programs, activities for children, and courses for employment and language. At first, workers lived at the houses, but space constraints eventually ended this practice, and the houses evolved into neighbourhood serving agencies and community centres (Amin 1987).

The postwar period saw the advent of what we today refer to as immigrant service provider organizations. These included the International Institute of Metropolitan Toronto in 1957, the Italian Immigrant Aid Society (IIAS) in 1956, and COSTI (the abbreviated form of the Italian equivalent of Centre for Organizing Technical Training for Italians) in 1962. The latter two merged in 1981 and continue their work today; we discuss COSTI in greater detail below. Other established minority communities were also creating organizations that provided a range of services to their co-ethnic communities. From their inception, ethno-specific organizations provided services in a culturally competent fashion in the language of the new arrivals. Nonetheless, co-ethnic exploitation was a serious concern, in that not all helping hands offered to newcomers were without ulterior motives (ibid.). Even today the tug of war between ethno-specific and "mainstream" service providers remains, as do debates about the need for professional standards in the settlement sector.

This period also saw the federal government offering some settlement services to newcomers, although the range of recipients was limited. It included the foreign-born family members of Canadian-born soldiers and refugees who arrived in Canada following the Second World War. The federal Department of Citizenship and Immigration, created in 1950, signed language training agreements with all provinces except Quebec and also provided basic settlement supports to immigrants (see Vineberg, this volume). Some funds were also allocated to non-governmental organizations to provide settlement services to newcomers on the government's behalf (Tolley 2011). Until it was disbanded in 1966, the department's Settlement Service also worked to place immigrants in jobs and to establish them in small businesses or on farming operations across the country (Vineberg 2010). Apart from this, the period saw little active engagement by either the federal or provincial governments. When asked about government funding for settlement services during this time, Edith Ferguson, one of the most widely respected figures in Ontario settlement history, noted "I don't think they realized the necessity for it … I don't think they thought they had much duty towards immigrants. They were here and it was a wonderful country and they all got along … Immigrants always got along … you didn't worry about them" (in Amin 1987). In spite of this relative absence of engagement in immigrant settlement, it was during this time that Ontario developed a legislative framework to address formal equality. Four new pieces of legislation were introduced: *Fair Employment Practices* (1951), *Fair Accommodation Practices* (1954), the *Ontario Anti-Discrimination Commission Act*[2] (1958), and the *Ontario Human Rights Code* (1962) (Bagnall 1984). Together, this legislation provided minorities with some protection against discrimination and also signalled that racism would no longer be tolerated in Ontario, at least not officially.

Racial Diversity Provides a Wake-Up Call

Immigration reforms in the 1960s saw the removal of explicit race-based selection criteria from the country's immigration policy and dramatically altered the range of source countries from which Canada's immigrants originated. While racism had always existed in Ontario as elsewhere, the consequent increase in visible minority newcomers elevated concerns about prejudice and discrimination and shone a light on the need for policy responses. To this end, Ontario issued a policy statement on multiculturalism in 1977 and followed up with the *Ministry of Culture and Citizenship Act* (1977) which outlined a number of principles to guide provincial policies and programming in this area (Garcea 2006). The Ontario Human Rights Commission also established its Community, Race and Ethnic Relations Unit in 1976 (Young 1994).

In the late 1960s, the federal government began to provide reception services at Toronto International Airport. In 1971, these services were replaced by a provincial program that morphed in 1973 into Ontario Welcome House in response to the arrival of Ugandan refugees. Ontario Welcome House assisted with the reception of newcomers and, in particular, facilitated access to government services. Multilingual staff steered newcomers through the formalities of immigration and customs and provided guidance on accessing housing and counselling, securing employment, and applying for health cards, social insurance numbers, and schools. The Welcome House also offered free morning and evening English classes for working mothers, as well as childcare for full-time language students. In January 1978 it was providing service to 837 clients per month, but with the arrival of Southeast Asian refugees, the services were expanded considerably and by the fall of 1979, more than 2,000 clients were being served (Fine-Meyer 2002). In 1983, three more Toronto branches were added to the original House, and throughout the 1980s these continued to serve approximately 2,000 clients each month. An additional branch was created in Hamilton in 1985 (Amin 1987). In the late 1990s, however, the provincial government eliminated the Ontario Welcome Houses, and reception services once again become the sole responsibility of Citizenship and Immigration Canada (CIC).

Beginning in the early 1970s, the provincial and federal governments also began to provide a wider range of settlement services. These included information and referral services, employment and assessment counselling, interpretation and translation, basic needs support, and health programs targeting newcomers. The federal government played an important fiscal role. The federal Secretary of State was already providing some funding to support various immigrant programs, and in 1982 the federal Department of Manpower and Immigration introduced the Immigrant Settlement and Adaptation Program (ISAP), which expanded on several similar programs that had been offered on a smaller scale in Toronto, Montreal, and Vancouver by the former Department of Citizenship and Immigration (Akotia 1992; Vineberg 2010). The provincial government was not absent, however; it introduced the Multicultural Service Program Grants in 1985 to help stabilize community-based organizations (Amin 1987). Although the program no longer exists under this guise, the provincial government continues to provide some support to the settlement sector.

Various language programs were also offered during this period, including cost-shared English-as-a-Second-Language (ESL) courses developed by the federal and provincial governments for delivery by secondary organizations. In addition, four language training pilot projects launched for parents and pre-school children in 1967 were formalized as a program in 1970. By 1978, they were known as the Newcomer Language/ Orientation Classes. This program included approximately 350 programs and involved 120 pre-schools; eventually, boards of education began to co-sponsor these programs. The federal department of Employment and Immigration also began to purchase student spaces in schools and community colleges; these were intended to provide newcomers with an opportunity to develop language skills for the workplace. This initiative was the precursor to the Language Instruction for Newcomers to Canada (LINC) program (Amin 1987). Although provision of English and French language instruction remained the focus, the Ministry of Education did approve a heritage language program in 1997, which helped newcomers maintain their mother tongues (Young 1994).

The post-1960s era also saw the advent and enhancement of settlement and integration services in a wider array of Ontario municipalities. Examples include London's Cross Cultural Learner Centre, founded in 1969, Ottawa's Catholic Immigration Centre, which opened in 1970, and the Ottawa Carleton Immigrant Services Organization (OCISO), which opened in 1977. While gaps remained, the provision of settlement services was becoming increasingly evident across the province. Organizations began to cooperate, and the Ontario Council of Agencies Serving Immigrants (OCASI) emerged as an umbrella organization representing the provinces' various service-providing agencies; it was funded by the federal and provincial governments, and we discuss it in greater detail below.

The early 1980s was a time of tremendous growth in the immigrant population, with more than 80,000 refugees arriving in Canada between

1979 and 1981, most of them so-called "boat people" from Southeast Asia. This movement changed the integration and inclusion landscape forever. A citizen-organized strategy to promote private sponsorship of refugees resulted in more than 40 Ontario communities establishing local committees to sponsor refugees (Fine-Meyer 2002). These often set the stage for greater community engagement with immigrant and refugee issues. For example, Project 4000, led by Ottawa mayor Marion Dewar, brought 4,000 refugees to Ottawa, and this project remains one of the touchstones of the city's civic identity.

This period was also a high water mark for provincial government engagement in immigrant settlement. While the federal departments of Manpower and Immigration and the Secretary of State continued to deliver the bulk of services including labour market preparation, vocational services, and adult language training, the provincial government also became increasingly active. In addition to reception services and the Ontario Welcome House, mentioned above, the province's Indochinese Refugee Unit provided translation, language training, job placement, information kits, and employment referral services along with access to the provincial health care system. The province also funded service provider organizations, including the University Settlement House, the YMCA, the Toronto Chinese Town Services, and others. In terms of scale, the Ministry of Culture and Recreation's Newcomer Language/Orientation Classes grants program had a budget of $670,000 in 1980–81, with close to $100,000 more allocated to refugees. This funded 232 programs across the province. The Newcomers Services branch had 50 full-time and 20 part-time staff in 1980 (ibid.). By 2010 this complement had grown only modestly to 75 full-time equivalent employees.

In addition, the Ministry of Education established a regionally organized Indochinese Unit that assisted the entry of Vietnamese children into the Ontario school system. This was just one initiative undertaken by the ministry, which remains one of the most important players in the integration and inclusion field. Of the more than 200,000 immigrant children who arrived in Canada in the 1980s, more than 55 percent had no facility in either official language. In response, the federal government provided funding to the provinces to deliver school-based services, including the hiring of psychologists, translators, social workers, ESL instructors, administrators, and support staff, as well as developing curricular materials and establishing welcome teams in many schools. Concrete examples include the "survival kits" the Ministry provided to teachers, which contained culturally sensitive materials to ease the transition of refugee children into the school system, and booklets like *Vietnamese Children's Stories* and *Cambodian Legends*, which helped introduce the culture and history of these countries. In 1980–81 the provincial government allocated more than $24 million for refugee resettlement, with $20 million going to the Ministry of Education (ibid.).

It was not just the Education Ministry that was active. The Health Ministry coordinated the distribution of refugee medical information and acted as a liaison with municipal health officers. Moreover, the Ministry of Community and Social Services provided income support for refugees once the year of sponsorship had ended. The Ontario Multicultural Development Branch of the Human Rights Commission also contributed. Importantly, these initiatives were co-funded by the federal and provincial governments, with the federal government matching provincial funds (ibid.). Collectively these initiatives and programs marked an important financial departure in the history of settlement and integration in Ontario. For the first time, governments – not religious, charitable, or community organizations – were the largest single funder of agencies providing services to newcomers in the province (Amin 1987). This period also saw high levels of coordination – perhaps the highest ever – both across and within governments.

Nonetheless, while provincial ministries were becoming increasingly active in immigrant settlement, business immigration and federal funding remained the primary preoccupations. The province tended to have minimal involvement in planning and managing immigration and entered into no formal federal-provincial agreements on immigration or settlement. Ontario was not involved in annual discussions to help set immigration levels, nor did it participate actively in immigrant recruitment campaigns (Garcea 1994). At the same time, racial tensions were escalating and were particularly apparent in Toronto. After several so-called "subway beatings" targeting South Asian youth, a report entitled "Now Is Not Too Late" was submitted to the Metropolitan Toronto Council in November 1977. It asked the municipal government to take action and was followed a year later by anti-racism stalwart Frances Henry's report, "The Dynamics of Racism in Toronto" (Young 1994). This report established a trend indicative of the increased scrutiny given to matters of integration and inclusion in the province, whereby various academics have denounced in a very public fashion the city's record of inclusion. The most recent example is Michael Ornstein's 2006 report on ethno-racial groups in Toronto.

The Integration and Inclusion Yo-Yo

The election of a New Democratic government in 1990 ushered in a 15-year period of integration and inclusion yo-yoing in Ontario. On the campaign trail, the NDP promised to create an anti-racism strategy for Ontario and, once elected, renamed the 1987 *Ontario Policy on Race Relations* the *Ontario Anti-Racism Policy*. It mandated anti-racism training in the Ontario Public Service, established an Ontario Anti-Racism Advisory Working Group, and undertook consultations on changes needed to bring policies, programs, and legislation in line with the new anti-racism policy (Harney 2002). In 1991 the government established an Ontario Anti-Racism Secretariat within the Citizenship Ministry (Young 1994). In addition, the Minister of Education introduced amendments to the *Education Act*, which while initially unsuccessful, came to pass in 1992 when a directive was issued requiring all Ontario school boards to adopt employment equity and ethno-cultural policies by 1995 (ibid.).

Race riots in Toronto in 1992 focused attention on issues related to discrimination and led the government to appoint Stephen Lewis as special advisor on race relations. Lewis lost little time and by June 1992 had issued his report. Its recommendations targeted the criminal justice system, the Ministry of Education, the Ontario Training and Adjustment Board, and the Citizenship Ministry, including the Ontario Anti-Racism Secretariat and the Access to Trades and Professions branch. The report also made passing reference to the importance of housing, culture, health and social services, funding, and opportunities for young people, and it reflected the frustration felt by the individuals and groups Lewis met with in Toronto, Ottawa, and Windsor. As Lewis concludes near the end of the report, "The crux of the matter is the abiding sense, in so many of the visible minority communities, that the society has irreversibly changed and the government has yet to acknowledge it" (1992, 33).

While the provincial New Democratic government was widely viewed as a champion of inclusion – and racial inclusion, in particular – its record was not entirely unambiguous and it was often motivated by fiscal considerations. For example, it drastically reduced the social assistance available to sponsored immigrants through the new *General Welfare Act* and *Family Benefits Act* in 1993 (Sinclair-Jones 1995). It also actively pursued an agreement with the federal government to help defray the cost of reception and settlement services. At the time, the Ontario minister responsible for immigration stated, "It's a great strain on our budget, [and] a great difficulty for community based agencies who are trying to provide and meet those basic needs ... We should have some form of arrangement to get the support systems that are needed ... I don't think it's fair to go out and encourage people to come to this country and there are not enough services in place or the dollar value is not there to provide assistance to help them to settle in Ontario" (in Garcea 1994, 471-2).

In June 1995, the provincial New Democrats were defeated by the Conservatives. Consistent with its promise of implementing a "Common Sense Revolution," the new government rapidly set about scaling back many of the inclusion initiatives introduced by the NDP, with the first speech from the throne repealing the *Ontario Employment Equity Act*. The Anti-Racism Secretariat was eliminated, and multi-lingual access to social assistance programs provided by the Ministry of Social Services was discontinued. Funding for Access to Trades and Professions and training funds provided by the Ontario Training and Adjustment Board were also significantly reduced (Sinclair-Jones 1995). One survey in Toronto found that 61 percent of settlement services experienced a funding decrease, 18 settlement programs were eliminated, and five settlement agencies were shut down, just in the government's first year in office (Social Planning Council of Metropolitan Toronto et al. 1997). In addition, forcible municipal amalgamations and the downloading of services profoundly changed the Ontario landscape. Municipal governments became increasingly responsible for settlement-related services, although often not with corresponding fiscal support. This downloading created pressures not just on governments but in the integration and inclusion field in general.

These cuts and unilateral changes, in part, explain why municipalities and non-governmental partners remain sceptical of the provincial government, even today as it seeks to play a more active role in settlement and integration. This history has also caused resistance to the province's call for the devolution of responsibility for settlement and integration from the federal to the provincial government. For instance, in a June 2009 discussion paper, the Ontario Council of Agencies Serving Immigrants (OCASI) notes that the council "has opposed devolution since 1995 and reaffirmed this position in 2005." This attitude is not solely ideological and was reinforced when the Liberal government came to power in 2003. While the new government did give greater attention to issues related to integration and inclusion, it opted not to restore provincial investments in these areas. Nonetheless, it expanded the infrastructure, creating the Ministry of Citizenship and Immigration and moving the labour market unit from the Ministry of Training, Colleges and Universities to the new department (OCASI 2009). The reorganization signalled a new interest in the labour market integration of newcomers, a focus that would continue with the twinning of the Canada-Ontario Immigration Agreement with the Canada-Ontario Labour Market Development Agreement and the tabling of the *Fair Access to Regulated Professions Act* in 2006. At the same time, anti-racism and inclusion re-emerged on the agenda, particularly in the face of a report by Roy McMurtry and Alvin Curling (2008), which would note that there had been little action taken on many of the recommendations made by Stephen Lewis (1992) more than a decade earlier.

Other aspects of integration and inclusion also received attention in this period, most notably in two debates related to religion. The first grew out of public outcry over the use of *sharia* tribunals to arbitrate matters of family law, while the second related to the public funding of non-Catholic religious schools. Although both cases ostensibly dealt with freedom of religion and questions of equality, the government responded differently to each. In the *sharia* case, former Attorney-General Marion Boyd was tasked with examining the issue and in a 2004 report proposed that the 1991 *Arbitration Act* be left in place and that religious tribunals be permitted to arbitrate matters of family law. In spite of her report, the government concluded that all religiously affiliated tribunals should be abolished in

Ontario, and the *Arbitration Act* was amended accordingly. In contrast, on the issue of public funding for non-Catholic religious schools, the government took a different tack, opting not to provide funding to religious schools other than what was already provided to Catholic institutions. Premier Dalton McGuinty argued that any expansion in funding to other religious schools would "risk unravelling the 'social cohesion' [that is a result of] children of many religious, ethnic and economic backgrounds growing up together in public schools … It's about the kind of Ontario that you want … [The government doesn't] think that Ontarians believe that improvement or progress is defined as inviting children of different faiths to leave the publicly funded system as we know it and go to their own schools … that takes us backwards" (Ferguson 2007).

Finally, although Ontario's settlement programs underwent significant shifts in commitment throughout this period, the province continued to operate an active and effective business immigration program focused on attracting entrepreneurs and investors. This area constituted a significant source of expertise and intelligence on immigration matters within the Ontario government. It also accounted for important and generally positive federal-provincial relations, though some signs of tension were becoming evident in provincial concerns around the cost of health, education, and, laterally, social assistance. With the 1995 election of the Conservative government in Ontario and the political realization that immigration had entered a new period of sustained, high level intake, these concerns were reframed as fair-share arguments. This reframing was, in effect, code for Ontario seeking a level of federal assistance equivalent to that received by Quebec on an immigrant per capita basis. At this time, the volume of federal-provincial exchanges rose considerably, and we entered a new period in Ontario's approach to immigration and settlement.

A Whole New World: The Canada-Ontario Immigration Agreement

Up until 2005, Ontario's relationship with the federal government in immigration and settlement matters ranged from cooperative to conflictual, with little in the way of formal agreements. In other provinces, arrangements varied, with the federal department of Citizenship and Immigration Canada signing realignment agreements with Manitoba in 1996 and British Columbia in 1998; these agreements were in response to fiscal pressures and saw funds transferred to the provinces, which then delivered settlement services on behalf of the federal government. Meanwhile, the 1978 Cullen-Couture Agreement gave Quebec jurisdiction over the recruitment and selection of immigrants to the province, while the 1991 Canada-Quebec Accord gave the province responsibility for the design and delivery of its settlement services. In all other jurisdictions, the federal government continued to be solely responsible for immigrant selection and settlement services. Under the Conservatives, the Ontario government had indicated a willingness to negotiate with Citizenship and Immigration Canada, but only if the department dramatically increased its funding to the province. Such an increase was not forthcoming until 2005, when immigrant settlement was flagged by the provincial government in its campaign to address the so-called "fiscal imbalance"; in essence, the province argued that Ontario's share of the tax burden was not proportionate to the federal services it received. Fortuitously, in the run-up to the 2004 federal election, the federal government was eager for support in seat-rich Ontario,[3] which likely helped the two sides reach an agreement.

In November 2005 the Canada Ontario Immigration Agreement (COIA) was signed, committing an additional $920 million in new federal funding for settlement services and language training programs in Ontario over the next five years. Its primary objectives were to improve outcomes for newcomers, build partnerships with municipalities, and increase the economic benefits of immigration. For the first time, in other words, the Government of Ontario would become an active player and was given increased responsibility for the integration of newcomers to the province. Following the signing of the agreement, the first major step was the initiation of a joint federal-provincial consultation to develop a strategic plan for COIA. This process took place in spring 2006 and involved a broad range of stakeholders. It concluded that newcomers' main areas of need were employment, language, housing, education, health care, education, childcare, financial stability, initial orientation, information and guidance, cultural integration, and social and emotional support (Interquest Consulting 2006). Subsequently, a joint federal-provincial strategic plan was launched, comprised of four strategies:

- Develop a flexible, coordinated system of settlement services with strong linkages and clear pathways to services that newcomers need, such as language-training, labour-market integration, and social services;
- Build on existing services to develop and implement a comprehensive language assessment, referral, and training system that assists newcomers to become competent in English or French as quickly as possible;
- Work with municipalities and federal-provincial government departments to build partnerships that will integrate newcomers into the economic and social life of Ontario communities; and
- Design, fund, and administer settlement and language training programs based on how well they support desired outcomes (Ontario Ministry of Citizenship and Immigration n.d.).

Importantly, the implementation of the strategic plan is guided by a range of Settlement and Language Training Working Groups established under the COIA's governance structure with representatives from the three levels of government. These working groups provide municipalities with a level of influence largely unheard of in other jurisdictions. Indeed, the COIA is the only federal-provincial agreement that thus far includes an appendix to guide the development of partnerships with municipalities. The engagement of the three levels of government and the development of an institutionalized governance structure unquestionably marks a departure for Ontario and provides one example of collaborative policy development.

The original COIA expired in April 2010, although the agreement was extended for an additional year (Citizenship and Immigration Canada 2010a). The province made it clear that following this extension, there is a desire to pursue, at a minimum, a realignment agreement similar to those that CIC has with Manitoba and British Columbia, but at best a devolution agreement, which would be an arrangement similar to that which exists with Quebec (Council of the Federation 2010; Government of Ontario 2010, 129). Nonetheless, the federal minister responsible for immigration has been considerably less sanguine, noting, "We weren't prepared to rush into that kind of an arrangement because we want to look at the long-term implications of what that would mean for settlement services. It's a shared jurisdiction. We put up most of the money at the federal level and I really do believe there's an important nation-building element in immigration and in settlement" (Media Q 2010a, online). The minister's observation suggests that while Ontario may be on the cusp of a new era in integration and inclusion, its exact form is still somewhat unclear. Meanwhile, however, immigration continues apace. As we shall see in the sections that follow, while the legislative and policy framework remains a work in progress, the province, its people, and the institutions that serve them continue to change and diversify.

A PORTRAIT OF ONTARIO TODAY[4]

Ontario's population in 2006 stood at 12,160,282, representing 38.5 percent of Canada's total population. As Table 1 indicates, 15 of Canada's 33 Census Metropolitan Areas (CMAs), including four of the country's ten most populous CMAs, are in Ontario. The province is largely urbanized, with 81.2 percent of its total population residing in CMAs. Most of the province's immigrants (97.1 percent) live in urban areas, with a full 58.2 percent living in the 15 CMAs. Toronto, Hamilton, Windsor, Kitchener, Ottawa, and London are the CMAs with the highest proportion of immigrants in the province and, as Table 1 shows, very recent immigrants have tended to settle predominantly in Toronto, Windsor, Ottawa, Kitchener, and Guelph, contributing to growing visible minority populations in these centres. Urban concentration has a centralizing effect that can facilitate the delivery of settlement services, but service provision may be strained in areas with a large immigrant population or where small immigrant populations result in limited or inefficient program delivery.

TABLE 1
Ontario's Census Metropolitan Areas, 2006

Census Metropolitan Area	Population	Percent Change, 2001–06	Rank among All 33 CMAs in Canada	Immigrant Population (%)	Very Recent Immigrants[a] as a Proportion of All Immigrants (%)	Visible Minority Population (%)
Ontario	12,160,282	6.6	–	28.3	17.1	22.8
Toronto	5,113,149	9.2	1	45.7	19.3	42.9
Ottawa–Gatineau	1,130,761	5.9	4	18.1	17.3	16.0
Ontario portion	*846, 802*	*5.0*	*–*	*21.5*	*16.5*	*19.4*
Hamilton	692,911	4.6	9	24.4	12.5	12.3
London	457,720	5.1	10	20.5	14.9	11.1
Kitchener	451,235	8.9	11	23.1	16.4	13.8
St Catharines – Niagara	390,317	3.5	12	18.3	10.8	6.6
Oshawa	330,594	11.6	14	16.4	7.7	10.3
Windsor	323,342	5.0	16	23.3	18.5	16.0
Barrie	177,061	19.2	21	12.8	9.4	5.8
Greater Sudbury	158,258	1.7	24	6.7	6.3	2.1
Kingston	152,358	3.8	25	12.5	11.7	5.8
Guelph	127,009	8.2	28	20.4	15.2	12.7
Brantford	124,607	5.5	30	13.0	7.5	5.5
Thunder Bay	122,907	0.8	31	10.4	5.4	2.7
Peterborough	116,570	5.1	33	9.4	8.3	2.7

[a] Very recent immigrants are those who arrived in Canada between 2001 and 2006.
Sources: Statistics Canada (2006b, 2006d).

In Ontario, which is home to 54.9 percent of Canada's total immigrant population, the effects of immigration are especially noticeable, with more than one-quarter (28.3 percent) of the province's total population having been born in another country; this amount is the highest in the country. Nonetheless, the proportion of new arrivals who choose Ontario as their initial destination is declining, with 42.4 percent of Canada's newcomers opting to settle in Ontario in 2009 compared to 58.7 percent nine years earlier (Citizenship and Immigration Canada 2010b). The drop in part reflects the increased competition for immigrants, with most other provinces now actively involved in recruiting newcomers to settle within their borders.

A more even distribution of newcomers could have positive implications for communities struggling to meet the needs of large immigrant populations. Yet there may also be political implications, given that settlement funding provided through the COIA was partly a response to the province's disproportionate share of the country's newcomer population. If that population declines, the impending renegotiation of COIA could see arguments for a claw-back or redistribution of resources.

It is worth noting, however, that while the proportion of newcomers who choose to initially settle in Ontario is declining, the province still boasts a high retention rate, with a large majority of its immigrants choosing to remain rather than moving elsewhere. One study of immigrant tax-filers who landed in Canada between 1991 and 2006 found that Ontario retained 91.5 percent of the newcomers who initially settled in the province (Okonny-Myers 2010). As well, Ontario, along with Alberta and British Columbia, remains an important site of secondary migration for immigrants choosing to leave other provinces (ibid.). Thus even as its share of newcomers declines, the province is likely to remain home for a large proportion of Canada's immigrants.

According to Citizenship and Immigration Canada's landings data, just over 106,000 immigrants settled in Ontario in 2009 (Citizenship and Immigration Canada 2010b). Of these, 51.3 percent entered in the economic class, which includes skilled workers, business immigrants, and investors, as well as spouses and dependents, while 31 percent came to the province as part of the family class. Refugees comprised 11.8 percent of newcomers to Ontario in 2009. Compared to the rest of Canada, Ontario receives a lower proportion of economic immigrants (60.9 percent across Canada), a higher proportion of family class immigrants (25.9 percent across Canada), and a slightly higher proportion of refugees (9.1 percent across Canada). Moreover, very recent immigrants – those who arrived in Canada in the previous five years – account for 17.1 percent of the province's immigrants. This is noteworthy because very recent immigrants tend to be those most reliant on settlement services.

Ontario's immigrants come from more than 200 countries, the most common countries of origin in 2006 being India (15.0 percent), China (13.3 percent), Pakistan (7.5 percent), Philippines (6.5 percent), Sri Lanka (3.2 percent), and the United States (3.2 percent). The diverse origins have contributed to a visible minority population that now comprises 22.8 percent of the province's total population. In addition, in 2006, 26.1 percent of Ontario's population recorded a mother tongue other than English or French. While most Ontarians (82.1 percent) speak English in the home, 46.0 percent of the province's immigrants speak a non-official language most often in the home, a proportion that falls to 3.2 percent among non-immigrants. The most common non-official languages spoken in Ontario's homes are Chinese, Punjabi, and Italian, suggesting that the maintenance of heritage languages is not solely the purview of recent immigrants.

Ontarians report diverse ethnic origins, with more than 200 ethnicities recorded in the 2006 Census. As Table 2 indicates, more than half of the province's population (57.0 percent) reports a single ethnic origin, while 43.0 percent report multiple ethnic origins. Among those reporting a single ethnic origin, the most common are Canadian, English, Chinese, Italian, and East Indian, while among those reporting multiple ethnic origins, the most common responses include English, Scottish, Irish, Canadian, French, and German.

TABLE 2
Most Common Ethnic Origins in Ontario, 2006

Ethnic Origins	Total Responses[a]	Single Responses	Multiple Responses
Total population	*12,028,895*	*6,854,340*	*5,174,555*
English	2,971,360	639,830	2,331,530
Canadian	2,768,870	1,201,125	1,567,740
Scottish	2,101,100	257,535	1,843,565
Irish	1,988,940	215,115	1,773,825
French	1,351,600	182,510	1,169,090
German	1,144,560	216,630	927,930
Italian	867,980	485,685	382,295
Chinese	644,465	543,320	101,145
East Indian	573,250	454,365	118,885
Dutch	490,995	161,710	329,285
Polish	465,560	169,225	296,335
Ukrainian	336,355	85,615	250,740
North American Indian	317,890	87,895	229,990
Portuguese	282,870	189,405	93,460
Filipino	215,750	159,155	56,600

[a] Respondents who reported multiple ethnic origins are counted more than once in this table, as they are included in the multiple responses for each of the origins they reported. As such, the sum of the ethnic groups in this table is greater than the total population count.

Source: Statistics Canada (2006c).

Data on religion were last collected in the 2001 Census, when 8.8 percent of the population reported a non-Christian religious affiliation. Of these, 3.1 percent said they were Muslim, 1.9 percent said they were Hindu, 1.7 percent said they were Jewish, 1.1 percent said they were Buddhist, and 0.9 percent said they were Sikh. Roman Catholics account for 34.3 percent of the population, while 16.0 percent of Ontarians report no religious affiliation. The remainder (40.9 percent) report various Christian affiliations, including United, Anglican, Baptist, Presbyterian, Protestant, Orthodox, and Pentecostal. The Muslim population increased by 142.2

percent between 1991 and 2001 and, with a median age of 27.5 years, it is expected to continue to grow.

TABLE 3
Selected Demographics in Ontario, 2006

Total population	12,160,282
As a proportion of national population	*38.5%*
Immigrant population	3,398,725
As a proportion of province's total population	*28.0%*
Very recent immigrants (immigrated between 2001 and 2006)	580,740
As a proportion of total immigrant population	*17.1%*
Recent immigrants (immigrated between 1996 and 2000)	471,470
As a proportion of total immigrant population	*13.9%*
Immigrated before 1991	1,884,440
As a proportion of total immigrant population	*55.5%*
Visible minority population	2,745,205
As a proportion of total population	*22.8%*
Aboriginal population	242,495
As a proportion of total population	*2.0%*
Non-Christian religious affiliation[a]	993,995
As a proportion of total population	*8.8%*
Mother tongue neither English or French	3,134,045
As a proportion of total population	*26.1%*

[a] Includes Muslim, Hindu, Jewish, Sikh, and Buddhist religious affiliations.
Sources: Statistics Canada (2001, 2006a).

While 94.0 percent of the Canadian population 18 years and older holds Canadian citizenship, this percentage is slightly lower in Ontario where 91.9 percent holds Canadian citizenship. Among immigrants in Ontario, 79.2 percent are citizens, a figure that is somewhat misleading given that the 20.8 percent who are not citizens includes very recent immigrants who may not yet be eligible for Canadian citizenship. Indeed, when we look at Ontario immigrants who arrived in the country prior to 1991, 90.4 percent have acquired Canadian citizenship, a figure that suggests a high rate of integration among those who are eligible to naturalize. Some Ontarians (4.2 percent), most of them immigrants, hold more than one citizenship.

With greater urbanization, a declining birth rate, and an aging population, immigration is expected to become increasingly important to Ontario. Ontario's working age population – those between 15 and 64 years of age – comprises 68.3 percent of the total population and, as in the rest of Canada, is aging rapidly, Indeed, between 2001 and 2006, the proportion of Ontario's population who were 80 years of age and over increased by 29.9 percent, one of the highest percentage increases in the country and higher than the national average of 25.5 percent. The median age in the province is now 39.0 years, an increase of 1.8 years since 2001 but slightly below the median Canadian age of 39.5 years.

As this brief profile illustrates, Ontario is a growing and increasingly diverse province. Projections compiled by Statistics Canada suggest this trend is likely to continue well into the future, not just in Ontario but across the country. For example, by 2031, approximately one-third of the Canadian population will identify as visible minority, and one-quarter will be foreign-born (Malenfant et al. 2010). In addition, the number with a non-Christian religious affiliation is likely to double to 14 percent, while the proportion with a mother tongue that is neither French nor English is projected to rise to approximately 30 percent (ibid.). This growth in diversity is likely to occur almost exclusively in Canada's 33 CMAs, 15 of them in Ontario. In Toronto the changes are expected to be particularly marked, with projections suggesting that about half of the city's population will be foreign born by 2031, although Ottawa, Windsor, Kitchener, and Hamilton are also all expected to have foreign-born populations above the projected national average of 26.5 percent (ibid.). By 2031, approximately 60 percent of Torontonians are likely to identify as visible minorities, and about 30 percent will have non-Christian religious affiliations. While this change is of course indicative of the enormous impact immigration has had on the province, it is also suggestive of what is required of the province's policy and program framework: flexibility, adaptation, and an ability to respond to the changes – and challenges – of the future. In the sections that follow, we evaluate the existing landscape and provide some suggestions for the road ahead.

THE INTEGRATION AND INCLUSION "PLAYERS"

Federal-Provincial Relationship

As Vineberg indicates in his chapter on federal-provincial relations (this volume), provincial interest in immigration has varied over the years. Nonetheless, Ontario has in general displayed little interest in active immigration management. The only exception is perhaps the province's long-standing activity on the business immigration file. While interest has risen since the Canada-Ontario Immigration Agreement was signed, Citizenship and Immigration Canada continues to deliver federal settlement programs in Ontario, and these comprise the lion's share of settlement funding in the province. In 2009–10, CIC's expenditures under the

Canada-Ontario Immigration Agreement totalled $392,324,134, with nearly 300 settlement organizations holding contribution agreements with the department (Government of Canada 2011). The provincial government, by comparison, provides modest funds through its own settlement program, as well as additional resources that flow through a number of departments whose work touches on integration and inclusion. While settlement funds are largely managed by CIC, both governments have nonetheless worked closely to implement COIA, and the extensive consultation process has improved settlement services in Ontario. Meanwhile, efforts are being made to ensure that the services offered by the federal and provincial governments are complementary. Unfortunately, with COIA set to expire, tensions have arisen at the political level with the province eager to see settlement funds and responsibility devolved to it, but the federal government not necessarily appearing keen to oblige.

Provincial Government

As is the case federally (see Biles 2008), Ontario has a lead immigration ministry in addition to several other departments that provide services to immigrants and minorities. The number of players and the limited public access to detailed information on provincial expenditures make it somewhat difficult to disentangle who does what on these files. Further complicating the issue, federal funding is distributed to the province through a variety of vehicles. For example, Human Resources and Skills Development Canada transfers funds directly to Ontario to support the immigration portal and labour market programming. Consequently, some of the "provincial" expenditures in fact originate from federal coffers. Despite this complexity, we have attempted to chart the landscape as comprehensively as possible, relying on public documents, enquiries to provincial officials, and existing research in the field, including a companion volume on integration and inclusion in Ontario cities (Andrew et al. forthcoming).

Ministry of Citizenship and Immigration

The lead provincial department is the Ministry of Citizenship and Immigration, which has an overall responsibility for matters related to newcomers, volunteerism, and women's issues. In 2008–09, the ministry had 336 employees and a total budget of $148 million, of which $104 million was expended on programs related to citizenship and immigration (Ontario Ministry of Citizenship and Immigration 2009). This amount was projected to increase to $133 million in 2010–11 (Ontario Ministry of Citizenship and Immigration 2010b). Here, the ministry has the lead on developing provincial policies and programs to support the successful integration of newcomers into Ontario in five priority areas: attracting newcomers, coordinating settlement services, language training, labour market integration, and community and employer engagement. Fairly modest programming supports each of these priority areas. For example, in 2009–10 the ministry spent $65.8 million on language training, $38.4 million on labour market programming, $10 million on settlement and integration grants, and $1 million on volunteer initiatives, for a total of $115.4 million (Shatilla 2010). The ministry also oversees a number of immigration initiatives, including the Provincial Nominee Program, an Ontario web portal to complement the federally funded Going to Canada portal project, and collaboration with other ministries – notably Economic Development and Trade and Training, Colleges and Universities – to attract skilled workers and international students to the province.

In the area of multilingual services and language training, the federal and provincial governments have sought, particularly under the COIA, to ensure program complementarity. This is important as it is an area of significant provincial expenditure. For example, in 2007, $5.3 million was allocated to 80 community settlement agencies for the provincial ministry's Newcomer Settlement Program, with an additional $2.1 million spent on the Language Interpreter Services Program to aid non-English speaking victims of domestic violence (Ontario Ministry of Citizenship and Immigration 2007). The ministry spent an additional $52 million for non-credit adult ESL and French-as-a-Second-Language (FSL) programs, delivered through the continuing education departments of Ontario school boards (ibid.). Finally, in 2009–10, Newcomer Settlement Program services were accessed by 120,000 newcomers, while 100,000 learners enrolled in ESL and FSL programs, and Language Interpreter Services were accessed by 4,500 victims of domestic violence (Ontario Ministry of Citizenship and Immigration 2009).

Some of the most interesting initiatives have been pursued with respect to labour market training. This is, in some ways, not surprising given that the COIA was twinned with the Canada-Ontario Labour Market Development Agreement and thus highlighted the natural connections between immigration and the labour market. As the provincial lead on the national Foreign Qualifications Framework, the Ontario Ministry of Citizenship and Immigration has played an active role in Global Experience Ontario. This project provides bridge training programs to internationally trained workers to facilitate their entry into most registered professions, although those related to health care fall under the Ministry of Health (Ontario Ministry of Citizenship and Immigration 2011). The Ministry of Citizenship and Immigration has also provided assistance to the Ontario Public Service Internship Program, which helps newcomers obtain assignments in provincial ministries and crown agencies.

On the citizenship front, the ministry promotes community and citizen engagement and works to strengthen partnerships and the voluntary sector, in general. In 2009-10, the province trained 1,555 non-profit representatives on risk management and liability in voluntary sector organizations and offered a series of 73 workshops in 34 communities across Ontario. In addition, ten community dialogues were held to support culturally diverse volunteers. The ministry also created and distributed an inventory of resources that focused on engaging new Canadians as volunteers; this was distributed to volunteer centres in over 170 communities across the province (Ontario Ministry of Citizenship and Immigration 2009).

Prompted by the COIA, the ministry has worked actively to engage municipalities in issues related to integration and inclusion. In addition to simply encouraging partnerships, the COIA provides the framework for the Municipal Immigration Committee, which brings together the three levels of government. This committee was one the earliest proponents of the Local Immigration Partnerships program, which has since been funded by Citizenship and Immigration Canada and provides communities with resources to address immigration and integration issues collaboratively. The COIA also earmarked $10 million in funding for the development of municipal web pages targeting newcomers. Links to these pages are included in the provincial immigration portal, and by 2009–10, 13 municipalities had active immigration web pages (ibid.). In addition, the provincial ministry continues to fund Ontario's Community Builders Program, which provides grants of up to $30,000 to organizations that promote diversity, build community capacity, or enhance community engagement. In 2010, eligible projects had to demonstrate that they contributed to strengthening social inclusion through innovative ideas, models, or practices, improved accessibility to community services through cross-sectoral partnerships, or made better use of existing resources (Ontario Ministry of Citizenship and Immigration 2010a). All of these initiatives provide municipalities with resources and infrastructure to engage in and address issues related to immigration, settlement, integration, and inclusion.

The Ministry of Citizenship and Immigration is also responsible for the *Fair Access to Regulated Professions Act* (2006), which applied to 35 regulated professions in the province and was amended in 2009 to also include 26 trades. This act ensures that credentialing and licensure processes are transparent, objective, and impartial. Regulatory bodies are required to undergo compliance audits and must submit annual reports on their practices. This oversight is the responsibility of the Office of the Fairness Commissioner, which was created as part of the act. The office had an annual budget of $1.6 million in 2008–09 and reports annually to the ministry. In 2007, similar legislation was passed in Manitoba, and that province now has a fairness commissioner; meanwhile, legislation passed in Nova Scotia in 2008 called for the appointment of a review officer (Office of the Fairness Commissioner 2010).

Finally, the Ontario Women's Directorate, a companion division of the Ministry of Citizenship and Immigration, funds immigrant women's groups both directly and indirectly. In the latter case, funding is provided to programs designed to prevent violence against women and increase women's economic security, as well as through the coordination of a cross-ministry Domestic Violence Action Plan (Ontario Ministry of Citizenship and Immigration 2004, 2009). The plan seeks to encourage mainstream, universal programs and services to adopt a targeted approach to women from diverse and at-risk communities, including Aboriginals, ethno-cultural and racial minorities, francophones, persons with disabilities, seniors, and those living in more isolated areas. Diversity was a central component of the original plan, which included promises to develop training initiatives, foster attitudinal change, and improve the accessibility of domestic violence courts (Ontario Ministry of Citizenship and Immigration 2004). Nonetheless, the most recent ministry update of the plan (2007) focuses more on meeting the needs of francophone women than those of immigrant and minority women. Still, there has been much activity in this area, with OCASI initiating ten related pilot projects, as well as training 30 minority women on violence prevention and 190 settlement service providers on domestic violence issues (ibid.).

Outside the Ministry of Citizenship and Immigration, a number of other provincial ministries touch upon issues of import to newcomers and minorities. These can be loosely organized into social ministries (Children and Youth Services; Community and Social Services; Culture; Health and Long-Term Care; and Education), economic ministries (Training, Colleges and Universities; Agriculture, Food and Rural Affairs; Economic Development and Trade; and Labour), and justice ministries (Attorney General; and Community Safety and Correctional Services). Before examining each of these, we will look briefly at the Ministry of Municipal Affairs and Housing, the funnel through which much federal funding flows to the other ministries and directly to municipalities.

Ministry of Municipal Affairs and Housing

This ministry works with municipalities and other stakeholders to build strong communities. Its priorities are the strengthening of local economies, the improvement of green spaces, and the promotion of a housing market that is able to meet a range of housing needs. The ministry also works with other provincial departments and with the federal government to harmonize policy directions and outcomes, streamline resources, reduce regulatory burdens, and facilitate cooperation in areas related to municipalities and housing. Given that newcomers and minorities are more likely to live in poverty than many other groups, the ministry's work on social housing issues is particularly relevant. One of the core principles of the Long-Term Affordable Housing Strategy (Ontario Ministry of Municipal Affairs and Housing 2010c) is inclusion, whereby "All persons have the right to equal treatment and protection from discriminatory practices that limit their housing opportunities." The ministry has done important work on diversity issues and is one of the few provincial departments that has implemented a diversity framework, manager training, and information sessions aimed at encouraging a culture of inclusion among its employees (ibid. 2009). Moreover, the Landlord and Tenant Board, which reports to the ministry, publishes its *Guide to the Residential Tenancies Act* in 12 languages as one means of advising newcomers of their rights and responsibilities as tenants.

Ministry of Children and Youth Services

The Ministry of Children and Youth Services was created in 2003 to bring together children and youth programs from the Ministries of Community and Social Services, Health and Long-Term Care, and Community Safety and Correctional Services. Most of the ministry's funding is allocated to agencies that provide services on its behalf. In addition, it directly operates eight youth justice facilities and two mental health facilities. It is also responsible for the province's probation offices; the licensing of childcare; income support through the Ontario Child Benefit; early identification and intervention services for young children and their families; behavioural intervention, respite, and rehabilitative supports for children with special needs; outreach to at-risk youth; child protective services; and community and custodial programs for youth aged 12 to 18 at risk or in conflict with the law.

In 2008–09, the ministry's priorities included early learning and child development, the reduction of child poverty, assistance to children with special needs, improved outcomes for youth at risk, and addressing the roots of youth violence (Ontario Ministry of Children and Youth Services 2008a). Nonetheless, in large measure, its announcements, strategic framework and annual results-based plan focus on programming for Aboriginal, francophone, and disabled children and youth. There is no mention of immigrants and little of minority children and youth. Indeed, apart from an often-used speaking point that "this highly diverse and talented group of young people is the key to Ontario's future success," newcomer and minority youth are almost invisible in this ministry's work (Ontario Ministry of Children and Youth Services 2008b, 2009). Although its programs no doubt benefit newcomer and minority children, their absence from the explicit policy agenda is notable.

Nonetheless, we see significant activity in a number of the ministry's other programs. These include the Youth Challenge Fund, which provides $21 million in grants to youth-led projects in 13 priority Toronto neighbourhoods; these funds are allocated by the United Way. Further, the Youth Opportunities Strategy receives $10.9 million annually; it was expanded in 2007–08 to include not just Toronto and the Durham Region but also Windsor, Thunder Bay, Ottawa, Hamilton, London and communities policed by the Nishnawbe-Aski Police Service. The strategy includes training, summer job opportunities, and programs aimed at encouraging youth to stay in school and avoid future conflict with the law. A third program is the Youth in Policing Initiative, which provides youth with an opportunity to undertake summer employment with local police forces; this is a means of developing skills and supporting police-community relations. In 2007, the program was completed by 159 youth. Also notable is the African Canadian Youth Justice Program, which provides $700,000 per year to the African Canadian Legal Clinic to assist African-Canadian youth who are in conflict with the law (McMurtry and Curling 2008). Finally, the Northern Ontario Grant Assistance Program offers incentive grants to attract social service and rehabilitation professionals to positions in provincial ministries that have offices in Northern Ontario. Although not specifically targeting immigrants, this program could be used to recruit foreign-trained professionals to northern communities.

Ministry of Community and Social Services

Even in the early 1990s, when considerably less emphasis was placed on inclusive consultations, the Ministry of Community and Social Services included immigrants and refugees in its study of social assistance recipients. In focus groups these participants identified as particularly problematic the lack of access to training programs, interpreters, and culturally sensitive information on how the social assistance system worked. As one outcome, the Multi-lingual Access to Social Assistance Program was established in 1992, although it was eliminated three years later when the government changed (Sinclair-Jones 1995).

Today the ministry's mandate is to build thriving and inclusive communities by strengthening the economic and civic contributions that Ontarians can make. It focuses on building resilience and removing obstacles that impede participation in community life. Programming focuses on social and community services, income and employment supports, services for adults with developmental disabilities, and improved access for persons with disabilities. Perhaps the most widely known program is Ontario Works, which is Ontario's welfare and social assistance program. Services are delivered either by the ministry itself or through third-party service deliverers, which include municipalities, First

Nations, or community organizations (Ontario Ministry of Community and Social Services 2009).

Although the Ministry of Community and Social Services funds many organizations that serve newcomers and minorities (see Andrew et al. forthcoming), these groups are largely absent from its core documents, suggesting that while they are among the ministry's clients, they are not an explicit target group. Emphasis is instead placed mostly on Aboriginals, francophones, the homeless, and persons with disabilities. In 2009–10 the only reference to immigration was a commitment to work with the Ministry of Citizenship and Immigration and several other organizations to modernize Ontario Works, the Ontario Disability Support Program, and Employment Ontario – all programs that can be accessed by newcomers and minorities, although they do not specifically target these populations (Ontario Ministry of Community and Social Services 2009).

Ministry of Culture

The Ministry of Culture works to build a strong and stable cultural sector that contributes to a prosperous, creative economy and vibrant, liveable communities. It offers a wide range of programs, but we focus here on public libraries, the Ontario Trillium Foundation, the Ontario Seniors Secretariat, and Municipal Cultural Planning. Although the ministry's reports are silent on the extent to which public libraries and the Trillium Foundation advance integration and inclusion in Ontario, existing research suggests that both are important players (Andrew et al. forthcoming). Libraries are community hubs that advance literacy, promote lifelong learning, and are a vital source of information for newcomers (Quirke 2007). Through the COIA, Citizenship and Immigration Canada provides funding to support the placement of settlement workers in libraries in several cities, including London, Ottawa, Toronto, and Windsor. For its part, the Ontario Trillium Foundation provides grants for arts, culture, sports, recreation, human and social services, and environmental programs, many of which support immigrants and minorities. The foundation receives its funding from Ontario's charitable casinos, and in 2009 its $120 million budget resulted in approximately 1,500 grants.

Meanwhile, the ministry's Seniors Secretariat has two main roles. First, it leads horizontal policy initiatives and, second, it engages in education campaigns that not only target seniors but also inform the broader public about the contributions that seniors make to Ontario. This work includes the maintenance of a network of seniors groups and service organizations, as well as the publication of the *Guide to Programs and Services for Seniors in Ontario*, available in seven languages. In addition, Multicultural Seniors Outreach focuses on the barriers faced by minority seniors and on developing information modules and materials to improve their access to programs and services. Concrete activities to improve access have included a conference, Services for Multicultural Seniors, and the publication *Diversity in Action: A Toolkit for Residential Settings for Seniors*, which encourages facilities to develop more welcoming environments for clients from diverse backgrounds (Ontario Ministry of Culture 2009).

Finally, Municipal Cultural Planning enables communities in transition, most notably those in northern and rural Ontario, to develop strategies to retain populations, attract new workers, and make investments to diversify local economies. Although the program is not explicitly an immigration initiative, some communities have used its resources to make themselves more welcoming to newcomers and minorities. On a range of other more symbolic fronts, the Ministry of Culture has also sought to better reflect diversity in Ontario. These efforts include increases in funding to the Ontario Arts Council, which is intended to support Aboriginal, francophone, and culturally diverse artists and arts organizations, as well as programs celebrating the province's multicultural heritage. These include the *Asian Heritage Act* (2005), *Celebration of Portuguese Heritage Act* (2001), *German Pioneers Day Act* (2000), *Irish Heritage Day Act* (2004), *South Asian Heritage Act* (2001), and *United Empire Loyalists' Day Act* (1997).

Ministry of Health and Long-Term Care

The Ministry of Health and Long-Term Care works to build a sustainable and publicly funded health care system. Although at one time it focused on the delivery of health care services, its mandate increasingly emphasizes stewardship through, for example, establishing overall strategic directions, developing legislation and regulations, and planning and establishing funding models to support the health care system. The ministry's programming includes children's health, seniors care, mental health services, emergency health services, emergency management, disease-based public health risk management, regulation of health care professionals, the Ontario Health Insurance Plan, Telehealth Ontario, and the provision of French-language health services.

The ministry's program that most directly assists foreign-trained health professionals in gaining access to their professions in Ontario is Healthforce Ontario, a government information portal that helps connect qualified newcomers to bridge-training programs and residency placements (Ontario Ministry of Health and Long-Term Care 2011a). Related programming includes the Centre for the Evaluation of Health Professionals Educated Abroad, which helps foreign-trained medical graduates with the recognition of their credentials (ibid. 2011b). Several of the ministry's programs also directly affect newcomers and minorities. These include the African and Caribbean Council on HIV / AIDS in Ontario (formerly the HIV Endemic Task Force), which is a coalition of service providers, researchers, policy-makers, and community members working to prevent the spread of HIV and AIDS. In addition to funding these targeted programs, the ministry reaches out through the publication of resources in multiple languages; fact sheets on SARS were produced in English and Chinese, while information on West Nile virus is available in 25 languages (ibid. 2010). With respect to infrastructure, the ministry spends roughly $200 million per year on 54 community health centres across the province. Many of these centres are located in disadvantaged neighbourhoods with high proportions of minorities and newcomers. They provide services that could be considered from "cradle to grave," in that programs range from pre- and post-natal support to outreach to seniors and everything in between (Andrew et al. forthcoming; McMurtry and Curling 2008). At present, Citizenship and Immigration Canada is considering a pilot project that would see settlement workers placed in health centres, similar to the program that already exists in a number of public libraries. This initiative is indicative of federal and provincial efforts to increase points of access and to target facilities that immigrants and minorities tend to use most.

Ministry of Education

The Ministry of Education administers the system of publicly funded elementary and secondary school education in Ontario. It issues curricula, sets requirements for student diplomas and certificates, and provides funding to school boards for academic instruction and the building and maintenance of schools. It also sets policy for student assessment, which is carried out by the Education Quality and Accountability Office. Ontario's schools are administered by 72 district school boards and 33 school authorities. There are four kinds of school boards – English Public, English Catholic, French Public, and French Catholic. These boards encompass more than 4,000 elementary schools and nearly 900 secondary schools in Ontario; in 2008–09 the government's total investment in education was $19.06 billion.

Schools are key sites of integration and inclusion where many of the debates about immigration, diversity, and multiculturalism take place (Haynes 1999; Young 1994). Many reports and studies have argued for the need for more inclusive practices within the Ontario school system (Community Health Systems Resource Group 2005; McMurtry and Curling 2008). Somewhat surprisingly, however, ethno-cultural and religious diversity is not prominent in the Ministry of Education's structure. For example, while there is a "French Language, Aboriginal Learning and Research Division" in the ministry's organizational chart, there is no equivalent division for newcomers or minorities, even though second language learning also falls under the department's purview (Ontario Ministry of Education 2009).

That said, as is the case in several other ministries, while mention of newcomers and minorities is scarce in high-level official documents, there are numerous programs that target newcomers and minorities, most often at the local school board level (Andrew et al. forthcoming). A particularly good example is Parents Reaching Out, which provides grants to school councils, parent organizations, non-profit organizations, and post-secondary institutions to increase parents' involvement in education. Information about the program is available from the ministry in more than 27 languages. Since 2006 the government has provided more than 5,500 grants and supported over 200 regional projects, which together represent a total investment of more than $10 million. Examples of initiatives include the organization of a series of parenting workshops by the Floradale Public School in Mississauga as well as workshops organized by the Association for Women of India in Canada, which focused on increasing the participation of South Asian parents in the education of their children (Ontario Ministry of Education 2010). Other examples of the ministry's programming include the Learning Opportunities Grants, the Ontario Focused Intervention Partnership, and the Ontario Youth Apprenticeship Program; all three provide opportunities for students who are at elevated risk of experiencing poor academic achievement (McMurtry and Curling 2008).

Ministry of Training, Colleges and Universities

The Ministry of Training, Colleges and Universities (OMTCU) is responsible for post-secondary education, employment, and training in Ontario. From an integration and inclusion perspective, the ministry's work on employment and training is particularly important. In this area, the ministry develops policy directions for adult education and labour market training, sets standards for occupational training, and manages programs on adult literacy and basic skills. The most central component for our purposes is Employment Ontario, which works with job seekers, young people, and newcomers to facilitate their entry into the labour market, as well as providing opportunities for training and education. It also provides support to employers looking to hire. In 2009, the Canada-Ontario Labour Market Agreement provided additional support to Employment Ontario to allow it to assist an extra 15,000 job seekers per year. Funding was also provided to make post-secondary education more accessible to Aboriginals, immigrants, francophones, and persons with disabilities.

Nonetheless, while newcomers are mentioned in departmental reports, the ministry's organizational structure does not include any units specifically focused on immigrants or minorities, although it does have a stand-alone branch focused on French language and Aboriginals. More promisingly, this is the ministry with lead responsibility for foreign credential recognition (OMTCU 2009) and, given that international student enrolments are likely to increase as a result of municipal interest and universities' own proactive strategies, the ministry will no doubt need to accord greater attention to newcomers and their eventual transition into the Ontario labour market. In addition, OMTCU manages a loan program that provides individuals with up to $5,000 to cover assessment, training, and exam costs related to the recognition of foreign qualifications.

Ministry of Agriculture, Food and Rural Affairs

Importantly, we see the immigrant labour market spreading geographically as Ontario's rural communities become increasingly interested in attracting and retaining newcomers. Indeed, many centres have concluded that their demographic survival depends upon their ability to augment their populations with immigrants both from within Canada and from overseas. These include permanent residents and citizens but also temporary foreign workers and seasonal agricultural workers who are becoming increasingly important to the continued success of the Ontario farm sector. Here the Ontario Ministry of Agriculture, Food and Rural Affairs is taking a leading role, although the bulk of its work vis-à-vis integration and inclusion has thus far focused on research, analysis, and coordination. In late 2002 the Ontario Rural Research and Services Committee set several priorities for rural research and services, among them labour force development, community capacity, and immigration/migration. More recently, immigration and migration were noted as priorities for the 2008–12 partnership with the University of Guelph, although the precise direction was initially undefined. As the partnership's planning document notes, "There is increasing importance given to immigration attraction and retention in rural areas, but it is not clear what policy tools or approaches would best promote the objective" (Ontario Ministry of Agriculture, Food and Rural Affairs 2008).

Nonetheless, the ministry has established the "Community Immigrant Retention in Rural Ontario" program, a two-year pilot project that includes the Ministry of Citizenship and Immigration, the Ministry of Training Colleges and Universities, and the Ministry of Northern Development, Mines and Forestry (Ontario Ministry of Agriculture, Food and Rural Affairs 2009, n.d.). The project uses a collaborative research model to undertake case studies of three rural communities. A key output will be the creation of a toolbox that communities can use to attract and retain skilled immigrants. The initiative also offers assistance to communities applying for federal and provincial funding, including a series of planned workshops for municipal officials, local organizations, businesses, and immigrant service providers.

Ministry of Economic Development and Trade

The mandate of the Ministry of Economic Development and Trade is to provide leadership to sustain and enhance the economic competitiveness and growth of Ontario businesses and to promote Ontario as an investment location. This mandate is carried out through the creation of cross-government connections that support trade promotion, foreign direct investment, and business immigration. Most relevant here is the ministry's management of the Ontario Immigrant Investor Program (Ontario Ministry of Economic Development and Trade 2009). Although economic considerations such as the cost of labour, availability of skills, tax concessions, and tax rates are all factors that potential investors consider, Ontario's multiculturalism is also an important selling point. The availability of culturally sensitive health care, language training, and school programs for immigrant and minority children are attractive to prospective business immigrants and CEOs contemplating a move to Ontario. Thus, while the ministry does not itself contribute directly to settlement and integration, it has an important stake in the success of the process and in using it to brand Ontario internationally.

Ministry of Labour

The Ministry of Labour is mandated to ensure workplaces are safe, fair, and healthy and that relationships between employers are productive and mutually beneficial. The ministry contributes to the labour market integration of newcomers and temporary foreign workers by overseeing compliance with the *Employment Standards Act*. In this regard, the ministry's Occupational Health and Safety Program manages the *Occupational Health and Safety Act* and the Safe at Work Ontario strategy. In December 2009 the provincial government announced changes to the *Employment Standards Act* to protect live-in caregivers in Ontario from unscrupulous employers (Ontario Ministry of Labour 2009a). The ministry also oversees the Pay Equity Office and the Pay Equity Hearings Tribunal (Ontario Ministry of Labour 2009b). Many of its publications and outreach activities are provided in multiple languages.

Ministry of the Attorney General

Among its responsibilities, the Ministry of the Attorney General is responsible for the Ontario Human Rights Tribunal, Ontario Legal Aid, the Ontario Municipal Board, and family arbitration. These quasi-judicial bodies are called upon to resolve disputes among citizens. Although the ministry was an early adopter of inclusion, having enacted in 1962 the first Human Rights Code in Canada, various reports (Lewis 1992; McMurtry and Curling 2008) have recommended that it pay greater attention to justice and policing issues involving newcomers and minorities. At present, despite having the provincial lead on anti-racism, the ministry has no programs directed specifically at newcomers and minorities, but there are some related policies.

Notable among these is the province's human rights legislation, which was amended in 2008 to transfer responsibility for processing complaints under the Human Rights Code from the Ontario Human Rights Commission to the Human Rights Tribunal of Ontario. The tribunal includes a Human Rights Legal Support Centre, which offers legal services to individuals who believe they have been the victims of discrimination. These services include legal advice, assistance with completing applications to the tribunal, and legal representation. Meanwhile, the Ontario Human Rights Commission has been tasked with promoting a culture of human rights in the province. This includes conducting public inquiries, initiating its own applications on perceived matters of discrimination, intervening in proceedings of the Human Rights Tribunal, and engaging in proactive measures to prevent discrimination through public education, policy development, and research and analysis. The commission has also been given increased independence from the attorney general.

The ministry oversaw the 2006 *Family Statute Law Amendment Act*, which provides that "family arbitrations based on non-Canadian laws and principles – including religious principles – will have no legal effect and will not be enforceable by the courts." While the act did not explicitly target newcomers and minorities, its introduction was fuelled by the public outcry over the use of *sharia* family law. Similarly, while land use decisions are often framed as being taken in the broader public interest, many of these have particular effects on newcomers and minorities. The Ontario Municipal Board is an independent organization that reports to the attorney general and hears applications and appeals related to land use, development, and expropriation. Decisions may include those involved with the placement of sites of worship as well as matters related to multicultural planning, which are outlined in the *Planning Act* (McLellan and White 2005).

Ministry of Community Safety and Correctional Services

Finally, the Ministry of Community Safety and Correctional Services has five major clusters of activity related to public safety. These are policing, correctional services, public safety, emergency management, and inter-ministerial liaison. Interestingly, this ministry's public reporting is more focused on diversity than that any of the other departments we examined, with the obvious exception of the Ministry of Citizenship and Immigration. Indeed, all five of its key priorities and results for 2009–10 address issues related to diversity (Ontario Ministry of Community Safety and Correctional Services 2009). This proactive stance may be partly a response to the McMurtry and Curling (2008) report but may be also an effort to comply with the Ontario Human Rights Tribunal's requirement that the ministry address issues related to discrimination, racism, and sexism in correctional services workplaces. In response to this requirement, the ministry established a 45-person Organizational Effectiveness division that reports to the deputy minister of Correctional Services. The division is tasked with leading the organizational and cultural changes required to improve and diversify the workplaces under the ministry's aegis (Ontario Ministry of Community Safety and Correctional Services 2009).

There are of course other ministries in the Ontario government that provide services to newcomers and minorities. While our examination has not been exhaustive, it has been comprehensive and covers the bulk of the programming related to integration and inclusion. We thus now shift our attention away from the federal and provincial governments and toward municipalities and civil society organizations. Here we examine local and community-based initiatives through a province-wide lens, although a companion volume (Andrew et al. forthcoming) provides extensive case studies of 12 Ontario municipalities. These case studies, by their very nature, illustrate the richness and diversity of programming across Ontario communities in a way that our overview simply cannot.

Municipalities

We begin with the municipal level. With respect to their role in integration and inclusion, Ontario's municipalities stand out in two ways. First, in comparison to municipalities in other provinces, those in Ontario have far more significant responsibilities in the areas of public health and social services. These responsibilities, combined with highly diverse populations, have a marked impact on municipal activities. Second, the Canada-Ontario Immigration Agreement provides a much more explicit role for municipalities than what is detailed in the federal-provincial agreements in most other provinces. In fact, it is the only agreement to include an annex specifically on partnerships, as well as a memorandum of understanding that outlines the relationship between the federal and provincial governments and the City of Toronto.

More recently, the City of Toronto Newcomer Initiative was launched by Citizenship and Immigration Canada. It was developed in collaboration with the provincial and municipal governments and will assist newcomers wishing to access municipal services by placing settlement workers in public health offices, childcare facilities, shelters, and community recreation centres. This initiative is specific to Toronto (Citizenship and Immigration Canada 2010c). In other words, Toronto is, in many ways, a special case that we will not delve into fully here.

Turning toward municipal activities, a good starting point is the Association of Municipalities of Ontario (AMO), which represents nearly all of the province's 444 municipalities. The association is involved in the governance structure for the COIA; it co-chairs the Municipal Immigration Committee and contributes to the settlement working groups. A recent Association brief advocates for an enhanced municipal role in immigration and makes the argument that this is appropriate given that municipalities are the level of government "closest" to the people; nonetheless, the AMO's main thrust appears to be the securing of increased funding from the senior levels of government (AMO 2008). Apart from this, an examination of the association's website suggests that immigration is not among the organization's major priorities, although it is listed as an area of interest to cities. Meanwhile, the Association française des municipalités de l'Ontario, which primarily represents smaller municipalities as well as Toronto, Ottawa, and Sudbury, had at one point engaged in various studies on the representation of visible minorities in local government. Recently, however, it has focused on other areas.

Despite the seeming low priority the municipal umbrella organizations accord to immigration, individual municipalities continue to pursue some targeted initiatives to attract and retain newcomers in their communities. One of the most interesting initiatives is the introduction of the Local Immigration Partnerships (LIPs), which are an experiment in multi-level, collaborative governance. Within the Greater Toronto Area, these partnerships are organized at a neighbourhood level, while outside of the GTA they are organized at a municipal level. The LIPs are funded by federal government contribution agreements that provide incentives to communities to work together to develop strategies and action plans that will better integrate newcomers. Funding supports the creation of a council – akin to a board of directors – as well as stakeholder consultations, research and information gathering, and the development of a strategic action plan. At the time of this writing, there were over 35 active LIPs in the province.

A preliminary study conducted in spring 2010 noted several ways in which the LIPs were adding value to the integration and settlement landscape. These included the combination of local expertise and experimentation with provincial and national programs, the intersection of economic development and social inclusion measures, the investment in community and public policy leadership, and the elevated profile that has been accorded to immigrant settlement and integration in the LIPs

(Andrew and Bradford 2010). The study concludes that both the process and outcomes are important and likely mutually reinforcing. The LIP strategies and action plans are scheduled for completion in 2011; at that time, a more thorough analysis of the initiative's impact can be conducted.

There are, however, numerous ways in which municipalities can affect the integration and inclusion of immigrants and minorities. For example, Ottawa's Our Diverse Cities initiative looked at 12 municipal policy fields, charting the impact of municipal planning, the provision of adequate public transit in areas where newcomers are settling, and the development of appropriate consultation processes, particularly where zoning issues or policy proposals may overlap with issues of culture or identity (*Our Diverse Cities* 2007). Planning is a critical process as it can affect the public's reaction to decisions over the placement of sites of worship, large ethnic businesses, or funeral parlours. Finding ways to respond to public concerns – whether from majority or minority populations – is a key feature of welcoming communities.

Police services may also be critical to the integration and inclusion of immigrants and minorities; police can serve as arbiters of conflict and protectors of citizens' safety and security. Even disagreements between the police and diverse communities can serve as a catalyst for change, with various municipal police forces having shown a willingness to adapt to the populations they serve. There have been campaigns to recruit new and more diverse officers and to scrutinize recruitment processes to ensure they are fair and equitable. Other initiatives have included the creation of advisory committees, intercultural training, addressing staff retention, and establishing informal crisis management networks that can be vital when tensions erupt.

Municipal recreation services can also affect integration in ways related to accessibility, fees, the availability of affordable equipment, and the cost of transportation (Heisz and Schellenberg 2004). Relevant as well is the process for determining recreational needs, the range of activities that are offered, and the appeal of programs to newcomers and minorities. Some municipalities offer women-only swim times in municipal pools in an effort to provide culturally sensitive programming to minority communities (Poirier, Germain, and Billette 2006); others have adapted playing fields to accommodate soccer and cricket teams. Some cities waive registration fees, while others target swimming classes at immigrant children. All of these are examples of initiatives that attempt to respond to the changing needs of the population.

Municipalities play a key role in the provision of public health services, and a number of initiatives have been undertaken with newcomers and minorities in mind. The City of Ottawa, for example, has a dedicated staff position for overseeing multicultural health issues in the municipal Health Department. This position has led to more targeted public information campaigns, culturally sensitive services, and support for linguistic and cultural interpretation services. Community networks have also been established around refugee health in several municipalities, with various stakeholders working to coordinate services.

Cultural activities are a further area where municipal policy has had a significant impact on integration and inclusion. In London, for example, considerable attention has been devoted to cultural policy as an avenue that can promote integration and inclusion. In their programming, municipalities may choose to highlight the various contributions that are made by newcomer communities. They may support festivals or art events that showcase the richness and diversity of Ontario's culture or use culture as a way of linking communities. This is often evident in a city's arts programming, which may include courses on Japanese flower arranging, Indian cooking, belly dancing, or reiki.

In the area of employment and economic development, municipalities are also key. They may provide referral services, training in resumé and interview preparation, or support for internships or direct placement employment services. In many municipalities, we also see efforts to link economic development plans with the employment placement services offered by settlement agencies; this is a means of matching new businesses and development initiatives with a skilled and prospective workforce. In addition, cities are working to capitalize on the entrepreneurialism of many newcomers, with some municipalities facilitating the development of immigrant-run businesses through training, awareness, and collaboration with lending institutions.

We look lastly at school boards, which although separate from the municipal governance structure, merit mention because of the role they play in the integration of newcomer children and their families. Although activities vary by board both in degree and type, programs include after-school activities, homework clubs, curriculum development and adaptation, and intercultural training. Many schools have hired multicultural liaison officers who serve as an important link between schools, students, and newcomer and minority families; the Multicultural Liaison Program was engineered by the Ottawa Community Immigrant Services Organization and is now available across the province. Finally, in 2008, Citizenship and Immigration Canada signed agreements with school boards in Belleville, Burlington, Cornwall, Guelph, Hamilton, Kitchener, London, Mississauga, Oshawa, Ottawa, Toronto, Windsor, and York, which now see schools in these districts delivering adult language programs.

In short, what emerges from this list of policy areas is that municipalities have considerable scope for creating and shaping policies to better integrate and include newcomers and minorities. Almost every area of municipal policy has an impact on the integration of newcomers, and while good practices are far from the norm, good examples can be found across the province. Moreover, while municipal policy is the primary instrument through which communities affect integration and inclusion, it is not the only tool in the toolbox. Municipalities can, as large employers, encourage integration and inclusion through positive workplace practices as well as through the provision of grants to community groups and the purchase of goods and services from a wide range of providers. They can create positive spaces for civil society, and collaborate with the many other organizations that work to integrate and include newcomers and minorities in Ontario. We turn next to these groups.

Civil Society

An enormous number of civil society organizations are at work on integration and inclusion issues in Ontario. In the calendar year of 2008, Citizenship and Immigration Canada alone signed more than 500 contribution agreements with agencies that provide settlement and integration services to newcomers.[5] Given that most agreements run for a three-year period, we can estimate that those signed in a single year represent about one-third of all existing agreements; in other words, perhaps as many as 1,500 separate projects or organizations are tackling various integration and inclusion issues in Ontario. While we cannot provide exhaustive coverage of this terrain, we use these contribution agreements as indicative of the range of organizations active in this field in Ontario. We divide civil society into five groups and look at each in turn. These include "universal" service providers, immigrant service provider organizations, multicultural NGOs, issue-based organizations, and universities and colleges.

"Universal" Service Providers

A number of so-called "universal" service providers have long been active in the settlement and integration field. Two of the largest are the YMCA/YWCA and the United Way. Both have Christian roots but have long since secularized. In 2008, YMCA/YWCA organizations were funded by Citizenship and Immigration Canada to deliver services in Barrie, Brantford, Cambridge, Hamilton/Burlington, Kitchener/Waterloo, London, Mississauga, Ottawa, St Catharine's, Toronto, and Windsor. Citizenship and Immigration Canada also provided funding to the local United Way in Peel and to the national umbrella organization of the United Way. Unlike the YMCA/YWCA, the United Ways are more often funders than recipients of resources or direct providers of services. Other organizations that fall into this category include the Maytree Foundation and the Learning Enrichment Foundation; each received $10 million and $2 million, respectively, from Citizenship and Immigration Canada in 2008.

Maytree is particularly noteworthy as it pioneered three pilot initiatives that have had an important impact on integration and inclusion in Ontario. These initiatives are DiverseCity Counts, ALLIES, and the Toronto Region Immigrant Employment Council. DiverseCity Counts is a three-year research project spearheaded by Maytree and conducted by the Diversity Institute at Ryerson University. It focuses on the presence (or absence) of racial diversity in leadership positions in the Greater Toronto Region with a focus on the public, corporate, voluntary, and education sectors, as well as the media, elected bodies, and government-appointed boards (Cukier et al. 2010). ALLIES, which stands for Assisting Local Leaders with Immigrant Employment Strategies, another Maytree project, supports local initiatives to increase immigrant employment. One of its most visible undertakings is to act as a clearinghouse for local immigrant employment councils. The first of these councils, the Toronto Region Immigrant Employment Council (TRIEC), was spearheaded by Maytree in 2003 and works with companies to recruit and retain skilled immigrants. TRIEC has supported internships and mentoring for newcomers as well as various initiatives to engage employers. In a 2008 evaluation, it was found that of those immigrants who had completed a four-month internship through TRIEC, 80 percent had found work; of those who found work, 85 percent did so in their field of expertise (TRIEC 2008). TRIEC has been so successful that the model has been employed in other cities. Ontario's immigrant employment councils now include the Waterloo Region Immigrant Employment Network, Hire Immigrants Ottawa, the London-Middlesex Immigrant Employment Council, and the Niagara Immigrant Employment Council (Adey and Gagnon 2007; ALLIES 2010; McFadden and Jantzen 2007; Alboim and McIsaac 2004).

Immigrant Service Provider Organizations

Service provider organizations are those that provide direct services to immigrants. Here, we distinguish umbrella organizations, generic service providers, ethno-specific organizations, and faith-based organizations. The categories are not mutually exclusive or exhaustive but provide a rubric for thinking about the type, form, structure, and focus of the organizations that service immigrants in Ontario.

Bringing the service provider community together is the Ontario Council of Agencies Serving Immigrants (OCASI). This is an umbrella organization that was founded in 1978 after a federally funded workshop drew attention to the need for sectoral coordination. Initially, OCASI consisted of 11 Toronto-based agencies, but today it spans the province and includes over 100 organizations (Wayland 1995). Broadly speaking, OCASI advocates on behalf of the settlement sector, provides networking opportunities for settlement workers, and organizes professional development opportunities (Amin 1987; Wayland 1995). The evolution of OCASI and its funding base is indicative of the important role that government support plays. At its genesis, OCASI was funded through a federal grant, with provincial resources being added in 1982; later, additional funding was provided by the federal Multiculturalism Program (Wayland 1995). Today, OCASI is still heavily funded by Citizenship and Immigration Canada; in 2008, it signed eight contribution agreements with the department, which were spread over three years and were worth more than $10 million. The Ontario Ministry of Citizenship and Immigration, by contrast, provides roughly $172,000 in annual funding to OCASI. Recently, it also contributed $500,000 to a training project and $250,000 for a province-wide survey of immigrants (Shatilla 2010). OCASI's annual report suggests that approximately 84 percent of its budget comes from the federal government, 6.8 percent from the provincial government, and 5.5 percent from foundations; 3.2 percent is self-generated, and 1 percent is sourced municipally (OCASI 2010).

Some service provider organizations are more "generic" in focus, with no ties – whether existing or historic – to any particular ethno-racial, religious, or linguistic community. The bulk of service provider organizations fall into this category, which includes the Ottawa Community Immigrant Services Organization (OCISO), Belleville's Quinte United Immigrant Services, Cornwall and District Immigrant Services Agency, Hamilton's Settlement and Integration Services Organization, London's Cross-Cultural Learner Centre, and Windsor's New Canadians' Centre of Excellence. The Italian technical training centre, COSTI, meanwhile, is an interesting hybrid. Although it began as an ethno-specific organization serving only Italian-origin immigrants in Toronto, it has since expanded into a generic service provider that serves a range of clients in Toronto, Hamilton, and North York (COSTI 2009).

Generic service provider organizations can be contrasted with those that have a more ethno-specific orientation, targeting populations from particular ethno-racial communities or specific source countries and regions. To receive public funds, they must be prepared to provide services to any client in need, but ethno-specific organizations tend to specialize in service provision to specific populations or those with unique needs. These organizations thus play a vital role as a cross-cultural bridge and a link between newcomer communities and the host society. Most of the ethno-specific agencies that receive funding from Citizenship and Immigration Canada are based in Toronto and Mississauga. In 2008, recipients included the Afghan Association of Ontario, the Chinese Association of Mississauga, the Palestine House Educational and Cultural Centre, the Vietnamese Community Centre of Mississauga, Asian Community AIDS Services, the Canadian Arab Federation, Canadian Ukrainian Immigrant Aid Society, Eritrean Canadian Community Centre of Metropolitan Toronto, the Ethiopian Association in the GTA and Surrounding Regions, the South Asian Women's Centre, the Tamil Eelam Society of Canada, and the YMCA Korean Community Services. Other recipients outside the GTA included African Community Services of Peel and the Ottawa Chinese Community Service Centre.

Service provider organizations may also have a linguistic focus, an emphasis reinforced in the wake of Citizenship and Immigration Canada's commitment to enhance the capacity of francophone minority communities across the country and to attract and retain francophone immigrants. In Ontario, CIC funds three full-time networks to support francophone immigration, which have been set up in the province's eastern, northern, and southwestern regions. Contribution agreements have been signed with several francophone service provider organizations. In 2009-10, CIC estimates suggest that it contributed $11 million to settlement services for French-speaking immigrants in Ontario (Andzama 2011).

Yet other service provider organizations have their roots in a faith community; those with Judeo-Christian origins are most common. In Ontario, the three largest faith-based service providers are those connected to the Mennonite, Catholic, and Jewish faiths. These include the Mennonite New Life Centre of Toronto, the Catholic Immigration Centre in Ottawa, and the Catholic Cross-Cultural Services in Scarborough. Citizenship and Immigration Canada has signed contribution agreements with several Jewish organizations in Toronto, including Jewish Family and Child Services, Jewish Vocational School Toronto, and Jewish Vocational Services of Metropolitan Toronto, as well as with Ottawa's Jewish Family Services. Catholic school boards in Belleville, Hamilton, Kitchener, London, Ottawa, and Toronto also received funds.

Multicultural NGOs

Turning from the immigrant service providers to the multicultural NGOs, we find a number of organizations that while ostensibly focused on diversity issues writ large, nonetheless also receive funding to deliver settlement services. These include the Brampton Multicultural Centre, Fort Erie Multicultural Centre, Guelph and District Multicultural Centre, Halton Multicultural Council, Sudbury Multicultural and Folk Arts Association, Thunder Bay Multicultural Association, Welland Heritage Council and Multicultural Centre, and Multicultural Council of Windsor and Essex County. Often these organizations' service provider role evolved as growing numbers of immigrants made their way to smaller centres; in many cases, multicultural NGOs were the only agencies available to provide settlement services and thus were able to carve out a niche role. Although multicultural organizations exist in many larger centres, their dual role as immigrant service providers is most evident in smaller communities.

Issue-Based Organizations

In addition to those organizations that largely provide services – whether universal, immigrant, or multicultural – we find a number that organize themselves according to thematic or priority issues; most prominent in the immigration field are those that focus on women, health, and employment. We discuss each of these in turn.

Looking first at those organizations that focus on women, we find considerable work highlighting the intersection between gender, immigration, and diversity, particularly around contentious issues such as family violence. There has also been a movement since the 1980s to promote access to language training for immigrant women, and a wide assortment of organizations provide services in this area. They include Hamilton's St Joseph's Immigrant Women's Centre, Ottawa's Immigrant Women Services, Toronto's Mothercraft, Newcomer Women's Services, the Rexdale Women's Centre, the Riverdale Immigrant Women's Centre, the Working Women Community Centre, Windsor Women Working with Immigrant Women, and Women's Enterprise Skills and Training of Windsor. Some organizations, such as Toronto's South Asian Women's Centre, target women originating from particular regions; others, such as Afghan Women's Counselling and Integration Community Support Organizations, focus on various ethno-specific groups.

From our research, it is clear that while there is a need for culturally sensitive and appropriate health services for immigrants and issue-based organizations that make this their focus, this is an area where there are potentially some gaps in settlement funding. For example, in 2008, Citizenship and Immigration Canada signed agreements with just three health organizations in Ontario. These were the Kingston Community Health Centre, Toronto's Access Alliance Multicultural Community Health Centre, and the Canadian Centre for Victims of Torture. Of course, there are other ways in which immigrants' health needs are served – whether through the Community Health Centres described earlier or through the provision of federally funded health care to government-sponsored refugees in their first year in Canada – but the absence of explicit funding for organizations that focus specifically on immigrant health is notable, particularly when one compares this to the level of funding allocated to employment-focused organizations.

Indeed, there are numerous groups devoted to immigrant employment in Ontario. Most focus on imparting basic skills and providing newcomers with information about job opportunities, although these groups also include the immigrant employment councils described above. In addition, a number of interesting projects have been funded in this area by Citizenship and Immigration Canada. These include the Global Experience@Work Project, which is led by the Ontario Chamber of Commerce and seeks to develop – in partnership with the province's 160 local chambers – strategies to improve the integration of internationally trained workers. Meanwhile, the Colleges of Ontario Network for Education and Training (CON*NECT) aims to increase the capacity of small and medium-sized enterprises to hire and retain immigrants.

Universities and Colleges

Finally, we look at universities and colleges. The Canadian Experience Class offers a pathway to permanent residence for international students who are fast becoming a central part of regional economic development strategies in many provinces. Ontario has also added streams for international students with masters degrees and doctorates to its Provincial Nominee Program (Government of Ontario 2011). Given that Citizenship and Immigration Canada has committed to doubling the number of foreign students by 2014, universities and colleges will continue to be key sites for attracting and integrating newcomers to Canada (Media Q 2010b).

Colleges also play an important role in providing language and bridge-to-work training to newcomers, including generic language as well as career-specific enhanced language training. In 2008, Citizenship and Immigration Canada signed contribution agreements for language training with colleges in Hamilton, Kitchener, London, Ottawa, Toronto, and Welland. Post-secondary institutions are undertaking various credentialing initiatives, including the Veterinary Skills Training and Enhancement Program at the University of Guelph and the School of Optometry at the University of Waterloo; both were supported through contribution agreements with Citizenship and Immigration Canada in 2008. Several universities also offer training to students who want to work in the settlement sector. These programs include Ryerson's Master of Arts in Immigration and Settlement Studies and Western's Collaborative Graduate Program in Migration and Ethnic Relations.

In addition to these more tangible programs, universities and colleges can take on important leadership roles in their communities. Sometimes they are able to do this as a result of research or analysis that can reveal gaps in services or emerging problems, but the role may also stem from their capacity to bring together stakeholders and access external funding. Certainly, the Social Science and Humanities Research Council has encouraged this leadership through its support for programs that engage non-academic stakeholders in university research. One recent beneficiary is the Welcoming Communities Initiative, a collaborative, cross-sectoral. and province-wide network of stakeholders interested in immigration, integration, and inclusion. Established in March 2009, it draws its 200-plus membership from a consortium of 17 Ontario universities, settlement organizations, and other NGOs from across the province, and from the municipal, provincial, and federal governments. The Welcoming Communities Initiative undertakes action research and knowledge transfer that aims to develop, test, and implement strategies to promote the settlement of immigrants and minorities in cities across Ontario, with a particular focus on small and medium-sized cities. The initiative emphasizes strong local partnerships and deep community involvement as a means of ensuring applicability and uptake. A comparative approach allows for cooperation and assessment of best practices across cities. In this way the initiative is working to determine what in fact makes a community welcoming.

Major Challenges

As this inventory suggests, there is no shortage of effort or activity. In some ways, this should come as no surprise, given the number of immigrants who settle in Ontario, their increasingly diverse profile, and the resources made available through the Canada-Ontario Immigration Agreement. What is surprising, however, is that there is little interdepartmental collaboration on the integration and inclusion files and, moreover, that issues related to racism, discrimination, and equity tend not to have received much high-level attention, even while governments sign agreements and transfer dollars to support integration and settlement initiatives. We thus argue that challenges remain, and we take up just a few of these here.

Profile and Horizontality

Most notably, our research suggests that, in comparison to other provinces, Ontario has taken a relatively low-key approach with newcomers and minorities. Not only does there not appear to be a robust senior level infrastructure in place to coordinate efforts across government but issues related to racial, religious, and ethno-cultural diversity are accorded a low profile even by ministries that deliver relevant services. Indeed, most of the ministries we examined pay particular attention to francophone, Aboriginal, and disabled Ontarians, and clear horizontal efforts are made with respect to seniors and women, but there is in general silence with regard to newcomers and minorities. The problem is long-standing, and the lack of focus on racial, religious, and ethno-cultural diversity has been described elsewhere (Lewis 1992; McMurtry and Curling 2008). In the absence of any comprehensive or sustained cross-government strategy to include newcomers and minorities, one may question the province's desire for increased responsibility over settlement services. In particular, the lack of coordinating mechanisms and absence of a strong provincial focus on immigrants and minorities undercut the argument that settlement services would be better coordinated if responsibility were to be devolved to the province (see Mowat Centre 2010).

Reporting and Accountability

The low visibility accorded to diversity is reinforced by the paucity of information pertaining to provincial activities and expenditures. Unlike the federal government, which publicly releases information on all contribution agreements over $25,000, no such information is available provincially. Similarly, while annual reports published at the federal level, such as those on multiculturalism and employment equity, provide a wealth of information on initiatives – and shortfalls – in these areas, this level of reporting is not replicated at the provincial level. The disparity was reinforced by the rescinding of the provincial *Employment Equity Act*, which historically required the publication of employment equity targets and achievements in Ontario. As new legislation has not been introduced, the gap persists. The absence of extensive and transparent reporting on settlement activities, employment equity, and inclusion initiatives leaves the impression that the province does not yet take these issues as seriously as its federal counterparts. It also stymies efforts to evaluate the province's record and, if necessary, to demand better.

Need for an Immigration Strategy

Although many of Ontario's small and medium-sized communities are working to attract newcomers, retain them, and develop programs that ensure a warm welcome, the bulk of the province's efforts have thus far focused on Toronto. While this pattern is in part simply a reflection of the scope of immigration and diversity in that centre, as second and third tier cities grow and change, the province will require a more comprehensive and far-reaching strategy that takes into account shifts already beginning to occur. Although it is in these smaller centres that a "made in Ontario" approach is likely to emerge, there is a need to look at other provinces that have found innovative ways to address the challenges associated with integration and settlement in less populous or more remote and rural communities. In particular, the province must give attention to forging a connection between strategies that focus on local economic development, on the one hand, and immigration, diversity, and inclusion, on the other. Although the Ontario government appears to desire a revamped framework that would see responsibility for all settlement programming devolved to the province, it may want to consider a more targeted approach that would devolve only those programs and services that support regional economic development needs and related diversity and settlement needs in cities outside of Toronto. This kind of strategy would acknowledge – and harness – the important link between immigration and regional economic development and could provide a small-scale laboratory where the province could manageably experiment with devolution.

Balancing the Needs of the Metropolis with Those of the Rest of Ontario

Of course, one reason that the province has yet to develop such a regional immigration strategy is the dominance of the Greater Toronto Area and its status as the primary recipient of newcomers to the province. Nonetheless, other municipalities are increasingly demanding a more active strategy to help them to attract and retain newcomers and minorities. Recent immigration data show that the proportion of newcomers who settle in Toronto each year has declined in the past decade and that other Ontario cities are increasingly receiving a larger share (Citizenship and Immigration Canada 2010b). The challenge facing the provincial government is the need to balance the priorities of the Greater Toronto Area with those of communities in the rest of the province. While additional resources provided under the Canada-Ontario Immigration Agreement have allowed for expansion and strengthening of settlement services to a wider range of Ontario communities, balancing the needs of the metropolis and those of other communities will not be easy. This situation is complicated by economies of scale, in that the delivery of services in more densely populated areas is simply more cost effective than in rural or smaller centres. It is hoped that the Local Immigration Partnerships initiative will offer some solutions, but this is unarguably an area where politics, long-standing grievances, and economic and demographic realities are likely to complicate matters.

Moving beyond the Usual Suspects

While the Canada-Ontario Immigration Agreement saw a dramatic increase in resources expended on settlement and integration in Ontario, the lion's share of these funds was absorbed by the immigrant service provider organizations and other agencies that have been dominant players in the field for decades. On the one hand, this funnelling capitalizes on the institutional memory and best practices that these organizations have developed over time and, by improving remuneration for specialized staff, has enabled agencies to retain them. On the other hand, however, it may provide disincentives for engagement with so-called "mainstream" institutions, contributing to the ghettoization of immigration and integration policy and preventing the building of horizontal alliances. Within the sector, there is some resistance to any shift, with many agencies sceptical of cooperation and fearful that it will lead to a reduction of resources, influence, or autonomy. Outside the sector we see the results, with a number of the institutions that deal regularly with immigrants and minorities – including school boards, hospitals, and police services – not explicitly incorporating these populations in any way into their programming or strategic plans. In directing resources for integration and inclusion primarily to immigrant service provider organizations and settlement agencies, the government is, unintentionally or not, giving other institutions a means of avoiding these issues and ignoring the need for real change. Importantly, we should look to the Local Immigration Partnerships initiative, which is based on the notion of cross-sectoral collaboration and thus offers a new way to do business. Given that immigration and diversity are now intertwined in nearly every policy area, such a change is long overdue (Burstein 2010).

Municipal Engagement

Without question, the principal success of the Canada-Ontario Immigration Agreement has been the active engagement of municipalities (Seidle 2010), and the last five years have been marked by considerable progress in this regard. That being said, municipal involvement in immigration poses interesting questions about subsidiarity and the level of government that should be responsible for settlement services. One way out of the federal-provincial quandary may be to place more reliance not on municipalities in general but on structures such as the Local Immigration Partnerships, which engage a broader range of stakeholders and institutions. The House of Commons Standing Committee on Citizenship and Immigration (2010) highlighted the potential of the Local Immigration Partnerships and instructed Citizenship and Immigration Canada to develop them further. Indeed, Ontario's Local Immigration Partnerships are engaged in the development of strategic plans to address local settlement and inclusion needs, and these involve a number of players from the community sector, in addition to the federal, provincial, and municipal governments. These plans could form the basis for collaboration and coordination through which the two senior levels of government could finance local strategies in accordance with the priorities of implicated ministries. Management of the strategies and control of the purse strings could be retained by federal and provincial authorities or could be delegated, in whole or in part, to municipalities and their civil society partners.

Trust

Ironically, municipalities in Ontario are more actively engaged than those in most other provinces, and yet the sometimes tense history of inclusion and integration policy, the forced amalgamations, and the unilateral downloading of social services to municipalities have resulted in a deep level of distrust of the provincial government on the part of municipalities and other local actors. Experience with realignment agreements in Manitoba and British Columbia suggests that a provincial government that has developed effective, trusting relationships with local communities and civil society organizations will fare far better in the delivery of settlement programming. The province thus must focus on forging such links with municipalities and other stakeholders and engaging with them in an honest, frank, and fair manner.

CONCLUSIONS

Although the profile of immigration to Ontario has changed over the years, and integration and inclusion have evolved, many of the challenges in this policy area are long-standing. For example, when assessing the principal hurdles facing the settlement sector more than two decades ago, Amin (1987) pointed to coordination, the reduction of service duplication, improved assessment, and finding a balance among ethno-specific and more universal service providers. There are echoes of these challenges in our own depiction of the current state. The thread that extends throughout our entire narrative is the lack of a comprehensive, long-term and horizontal approach to immigration, integration, and inclusion in Ontario. This is notable, given that investments have been made to coordinate government action on family violence, persons with disabilities, Aboriginals, and francophones and French-language service provision. We have also argued, however, that a single-minded focus on immigration and integration is insufficient; issues related to inclusion and equity must also be taken seriously. Reports dating back at least three decades have emphasized the importance of addressing racism and discrimination, noting the need to develop appropriate infrastructure and secure leadership at the top.

   As we have pointed out, none of this can be done in isolation. Rather, federal, provincial, and municipal governments must work together with other stakeholders to build welcoming and inclusive communities. Achieving this end may require a shift in attitude, a change in focus, and efforts to build new and more trusting relationships. Contrary to some views, devolution or simply increasing resources are not the only available policy tools. The Local Immigration Partnerships initiative offers one innovative approach, and Ontario should look as well at strategies adopted in other provinces.

Emerging from our analysis is the sense that while there has been much activity related to immigration, integration, and inclusion in Ontario, it is difficult to identify a clear, over-arching approach. The strategy instead seems piecemeal, perhaps happenstance, and without clear account-abilities or defined outcomes. Although there have been successes, there are also gaps and failings. What is clear, however, is a desire to do better, not just for immigrants and minorities but for all Ontarians. The sleeping giant has stirred and, we are hopeful, may soon fully awaken.

NOTES

1. The opinions expressed in this chapter are those of the authors and not ne-cessarily those of Integration Branch, Citizenship and Immigration Canada, nor the Government of Canada.
2. The Anti-Discrimination Commission was renamed the Ontario Human Rights Commission in 1961.
3. Political motivations have had a marked influence on federal-provincial immigration agreements. The 1991 Canada-Quebec Accord, for example, was partly a response to the failure of the Meech Lake Accord, while COIA's signing was an attempt by the federal Liberal government to address dis-satisfaction in Ontario. When the Conservatives came to power federally in 2006, they responded to a different set of political pressures and subsequently increased settlement funding to the other provinces to bring funding in line with Ontario's allocation.
4. Unless otherwise noted, all data in this section are drawn from Statistics Canada's Census data for 2001 and 2006 (Statistics Canada 2001, 2006a, 2006b, 2006c, 2006d).
5. Under the 2006 *Federal Accountability Act*, all contribution agreements over $25,000 must be posted on federal departmental websites. The result has been a wealth of information not otherwise available. Similar information is unavailable for the other orders of government, although the $20 million in grants awarded by the Ontario Ministry of Citizenship and Immigration in 2006 can be found online.

REFERENCES

Adey, G. and C. Gagnon. 2007. "Engaging Employers: Strategies for the Integra-tion of Internationally Trained Workers in Ottawa." *Our Diverse Cities* 4:54-8.

Akotia, C.S. 1992. "Kitchener-Waterloo Immigrant Settlement and Adaptation Program (ISAP): A Process and Outcome Evaluation." Master's thesis, Wilfrid Laurier University.

Alboim, N. and E. McIsaac. 2004. "TRIEC: A Research Proposal in Action." *Our Diverse Cities* 1:146-7.

ALLIES. 2010. "Immigrant Employment Councils across Canada." At http://www.alliescanada.ca (accessed 19 September 2010).

Amin, N. 1987. "A Preliminary History of Settlement Work in Ontario: 1900–Present." Paper prepared for the Ministry of Citizenship, Citizenship Development Branch. At http://ceris.metropolis.net/virtual%20library/other/amim1.html (accessed 13 March 2009).

Andrew, C. and N. Bradford. 2010. "Local Immigration Partnership Councils: A Promising Canadian Social Innovation." Paper prepared for Citizenship and Immigration Canada.

Andrew, C., J. Biles, M. Burstein, V. Esses, and E. Tolley, eds. Forthcoming. *Integration and Inclusion in Ontario Cities*. Montreal and Kingston: McGill-Queen's University Press.

Andzama, F. 2011. Personal correspondence with authors. 6 January.

Association of Municipalities of Ontario. 2008. *Putting out the Welcome Mat: Why Immigration Matters to Ontario's Municipalities*. Toronto: AMO. At http://www.amo.on.ca/AM/Template.cfm?Section=Home&TEMPLATE=/CM/ContentDisplay.cfm&CONTENTID=151503 (accessed 13 June 2010).

Bagnall, J.C. 1984. "The Ontario Conservatives and the Development of Anti-Discrimination Policy, 1944–1962." Ph.D. diss., Queen's University.

Biles, J. 2008. "Integration Policies in English-Speaking Canada." In *Immigration and Integration in Canada in the Twenty-First Century*, ed. J. Biles, M. Burstein, and J. Frideres, 139-86. Montreal and Kingston: McGill-Queen's University Press.

Biles, J. and H. Ibrahim. 2005. "Religion and Public Policy: Immigration, Citizenship and Multiculturalism – Guess Who's Coming to Dinner?" In *Religion and Ethnicity in Canada*, ed. P. Bramadat and D. Seljak, 154-77. Toronto: Pearson Education.

Burstein, M. 2010. "Reconfiguring Settlement and Integration: A Service Provider Strategy for Innovation and Results." Paper prepared for the Canadian Immigrant Settlement Sector Alliance.

Central Neighbourhood. 2009. "About Us." At http://www.cnh.on.ca/index.html (accessed 14 March 2009).

Citizenship and Immigration Canada (CIC). 2010a. "Canada and Ontario to Extend the Canada-Ontario Immigration Agreement." News release, 5 May. At http://www.cic.gc.ca/english/department/media/releases/2010/2010-05-05.asp (accessed 6 May 2010).

—2010b. "Facts and Figures 2009: Immigration Overview – Temporary and Permanent Residents." Ottawa: Citizenship and Immigration Canada. At http://www.cic.gc.ca/english/resources/statistics/facts2009/index.asp (accessed 5 November 2010).

—2010c. "Government of Canada Invests in Toronto, in Program Developed with the Province of Ontario and the City of Toronto." News release, 3 December. At http://www.cic.gc.ca/english/department/media/releases/2010/2010-12-03.asp (accessed 24 January 2011).

Community Health Systems Resource Group, Toronto Hospital for Sick Children. 2005. "Early School Leavers: Understanding the Lived Reality of Student Disengagement from Secondary School." Report prepared for the Ontario Ministry of Education and Training. At http://www.edu.gov.on.ca/eng/parents/schoolleavers.pdf (accessed 10 June 2010).

COSTI. 2009. "History." At http://www.costi.org/whoweare/history.php (accessed 14 March 2009).

Council of the Federation. 2010. "Premiers Working to Sustain Economic Recovery." Press release, 5 August. At http://www.councilofthefederation.ca/pdfs/Prem_Working_to_Sustain_Economic_Recovery.pdf (accessed 24 January 2011).

Cukier, W., M. Yap, J. Miller, and P. Bindhani. 2010. *DiverseCity Counts 2.* Toronto: Diversity Institute. At http://www.diversecitytoronto.ca/wp-content/uploads/DC-counts2-lowres.pdf (accessed 18 September 2010).

Ferguson, R. 2007. "School Funding a Key Issue: McGuinty." *Toronto Star,* 23 August. At http://www.thestar.com/news/article/249086 (accessed 28 May 2010).

Fine-Meyer, R. 2002. "Unique Refugees: The Sponsorship and Resettlement of Vietnamese 'Boat People' in Ontario, 1978–1980." Master's thesis, University of Toronto.

Garcea, J. 1994. "Federal-Provincial Relations in Immigration, 1971–1991: A Case Study of Asymmetrical Federalism." Ph.D. diss., Carleton University.

—2006. "Provincial Multiculturalism Policies in Canada, 1974–2004: A Content Analysis." *Canadian Ethnic Studies* 38(3):1-20.

Government of Ontario. 2010. *Budget 2010: Open Ontario: Ontario's Plan for Jobs and Growth. 2010 Ontario Budget Papers.* Toronto: Queen's Printer for Ontario. At http://www.fin.gov.on.ca/en/budget/ontariobudgets/2010/papers_all.pdf (accessed 24 January 2011).

—2011. "Opportunities Ontario: International Student Category." At http://www.ontarioimmigration.ca/en/pnp/OI_PNPSTUDENTS.html (accessed 24 January 2011).

Harney, S. 2002. *State Work: Public Administration and Mass Intellectuality.* London: Duke University Press.

Haynes, J.M. 1999. "The Streaming of Black Socio-Economically Disadvantaged Youths in Ottawa's Educational System." Master's thesis, McGill University.

Heisz, A. and G. Schellenberg. 2004. "Public Transit Use among Immigrants." *Canadian Journal of Urban Research* 13(1):170-92.

House of Commons Standing Committee on Citizenship and Immigration. 2010. "Best Practices in Settlement Services." Committee Report. Ottawa: Parliament of Canada. At http://www2.parl.gc.ca/content/hoc/Committee/403/CIMM/Reports/RP4388396/cimmrp02/cimmrp02-e.pdf (accessed 13 June 2010).

Interquest Consulting. 2006. "Newcomers to Ontario: Hearing Their Needs and the Solutions." Consultation report prepared for Citizenship and Immigration Canada on the development of settlement and language training strategies in support of the new Canada-Ontario Immigration Agreement. At http://www.cic.gc.ca/english/resources/publications/settlement/coia-summary.asp (accessed 20 September 2010).

Kelley, N. and M. Trebilcock. 1998. *Making the Canadian Mosaic.* Toronto: University of Toronto Press.

Lewis, S. 1992. *Report on Race Relations in Ontario.* Report prepared for the Government of Ontario.

McFadden, P. and R. Janzen. 2007. "The Importance of Immigrants to Waterloo Region's Prosperity: A Dynamic Collaborative Community Response." *Our Diverse Cities* 4:104-7.

McLellan, J. and M. White. 2005. "Social Capital and Identity Politics among Asian Buddhists in Toronto." *Journal of International Migration and Integration* 6(2):235-54.

McMurtry, R. and A. Curling. 2008. *The Review of the Roots of Youth Violence.* Vol. 1: *Findings, Analysis and Conclusions.* Report prepared for the Government of Ontario. At http://www.opsba.org/index.php?q=advocacy_and_action/critical_media_literacy/review_of_roots_of_youth_violence_report (accessed 9 June 2010).

Media Q. 2010a. "After-Caucus Media Scrum with Minister Jason Kenney." Transcript prepared for Citizenship and Immigration Canada. May 5.

—2010b. "Minister Addresses the Economic Club of Canada." Transcript prepared for Citizenship and Immigration Canada. 9 June.

Malenfant, É.C., A. Lebel, and L. Martel. 2010. "Projections of the Diversity of the Canadian Population." Catalogue no. 91-551-X. Ottawa: Minister of Industry. At http://www.statcan.gc.ca/pub/91-551-x/91-551-x2010001-eng.pdf (accessed 19 September 2010).

Mowat Centre. 2010. *Executive Summary: The Canada-Ontario Immigration Agreement* and *International Perspectives on Immigrant Service Provision.* Toronto: Mowat Centre. At http://www.mowatcentre.ca/general/Executive_Summary_27052010.pdf (accessed 11 June 2010).

OCASI. 2009. "Canada-Ontario Immigration Agreement (COIA): Crafting the Vision for the Sector." www.ocasi.org (accessed 19 September 2010).

—2010. *Annual Report 2010.* Toronto: OCASI.

O'Connor, P. 1986. "The Story of St Christopher House, 1912–1986." At http://www.stchrishouse.org/st-chris/history/TheStoryOfStChristop.php (accessed 14 March 2008).

Office of the Fairness Commissioner. 2010. "Frequently Asked Questions." At http://www.fairnesscommissioner.ca/en/about/faq.php (accessed 19 September 2010).

Okonny-Myers, I. 2010. *The Interprovincial Mobility of Immigrants in Canada.* Ottawa: Citizenship and Immigration Canada. At http://www.cic.gc.ca/english/pdf/research-stats/interprov-mobility.pdf (accessed 5 November 2010).

Ontario Ministry of Agriculture, Food and Rural Affairs. n.d. "CIRRO: Community Immigrant Retention in Rural Ontario." At http://www.is-gw.ca/downloads/intersections09/ElDakikyPDF.pdf (accessed 13 June 2010).

—2008. "Agricultural and Rural Policy." At http://www.omafra.gov.on.ca/english/research/priorities/ruralpolicy.htm (accessed 15 March 2009).

—2009. "Community Immigrant Retention in Rural Ontario." At http://www.reddi.gov.on.ca/pdf/cirronewsletter.pdf (accessed 13 June 2010).

Ontario Ministry of Children and Youth Services. 2008a. *Results-Based Plan Briefing Book, 2008-09.* Toronto: Ministry of Children and Youth Services. At http://www.gov.on.ca/children/graphics/247796.pdf (accessed 15 March 2010).

—2008b. *Realizing Potential: Our Children, Our Youth, Our Future.* Ontario Ministry of Children and Youth Services Strategic Framework, 2008–12. Toronto: Ontario Ministry of Children and Youth Services. At http://www.children.gov.on.ca/htdocs/English/about/strategicframework.aspx (accessed 10 June 2010).

—2009. *Results-Based Plan Briefing Book, 2009–10.* Ministry of Children and Youth Services. At http://www.children.gov.on.ca/htdocs/English/about/Results_2009-2010.aspx (accessed 10 June 2010).

Ontario Ministry of Citizenship and Immigration. n.d. *Strategic Plan for Settlement and Language Training: Canada-Ontario Immigration Agreement.* At http://www.citizenship.gov.on.ca/english/publications/strategicplan/ (accessed 19 January 2008).

—2004. *Domestic Violence Action Plan for Ontario*. At http://www.citizenship.gov.
on.ca/owd/english/resources/publications/dvap/dvap.pdf (accessed 10 June
2010).

—2007. *Domestic Violence Action Plan – Update*. At http://www.citizenship.gov.
on.ca/owd/english/resources/publications/dvap/dvap.update.pdf (accessed
10 June 2010).

—2009. *Results-Based Plan Briefing Book, 2009–10*. Toronto: Ministry of Citizenship
and Immigration. At http://www.citizenship.gov.on.ca/english/publications/
rbp2009-2010.shtml (accessed 8 June 2010).

—2010a. "Grants and Funding." At http://www.citizenship.gov.on.ca/english/
grantsandfunding/ocb.shtml (accessed 8 June 2010).

—2010b. *Results-Based Plan Briefing Book, 2010–11*. Toronto: Ministry of Citizenship
and Immigration. At http://www.citizenship.gov.on.ca/english/publications/
rbp2010-2011.shtml#4 (accessed 24 January 2011).

—2011. "Global Experience Ontario." At http://www.citizenship.gov.on.ca/
english/keyinitiatives/geo.shtml (accessed 24 January 2011).

Ontario Ministry of Community and Social Services. 2009. *Results-Based Plan
Briefing Book, 2009–10*. Toronto: Ministry of Community and Social Services.
At http://www.mcss.gov.on.ca/documents/en/mcss/publications/about/
MCSS_Published_Resultsbased_Plans_200910_en.pdf (accessed 10 June 2010).

Ontario Ministry of Community Safety and Correctional Services. 2009. *Results-
Based Plan Briefing Book, 2009–10*. Toronto: Ministry of Community Safety and Cor-
rectional Services. At http://www.mcscs.jus.gov.on.ca/english/publications/
RbP0910/RbP200910.html (accessed 12 June 2010).

Ontario Ministry of Culture. 2009. *Results-Based Plan Briefing Book, 2009–10*. Toronto: Ministry of Culture. At http://www.culture.gov.on.ca/english/about/
MCL_Briefing_Book_2009_10.doc.pdf (accessed 11 June 2010).

Ontario Ministry of Economic Development and Trade. 2009. *Results-Based
Plan Briefing Book, 2009–10*. Toronto: Ministry of Economic Development. At
http://www.ontariocanada.com/ontcan/1medt/downloads/results_based_
plan2009_10.pdf (accessed 11 June 2010).

Ontario Ministry of Education. 2009. *Results-Based Plan Briefing Book, 2009–10*.
Toronto: Ministry of Education. At http://www.edu.gov.on.ca/eng/about/
annualreport/ (accessed 10 June 2010).

—2010. "Parents Reaching Out Grants."At http://www.edu.gov.on.ca/eng/
parents/reaching.html (accessed 10 June 2010).

Ontario Ministry of Health and Long-Term Care. 2010. "About Us." At http://
www.health.gov.on.ca/en/ (accessed 10 June 2010).

—2011a. "Healthforce Ontario." At http://www.healthforceontario.ca/ (accessed
24 January 2011).

—2011b. "International Medical Graduates." At http://www.health.gov.on.ca/
english/providers/project/img/img_mn.html (accessed 24 January 2011).

Ontario Ministry of Labour 2009a. "Helping Live-In Caregivers." At http://www.
news.ontario.ca/mol/en/2009/12/helping-live-in-caregivers.html (accessed
24 January 2011).

—2009b. *Results-Based Plan Briefing Book, 2009–10*. Toronto: Ministry of Labour.
At http://www.labour.gov.on.ca/english/about/pdf/rbp_09-10.pdf (accessed
12 June 2010).

Ontario Ministry of Municipal Affairs and Housing. 2009. *Results-Based Plan Briefing Book, 2009–10.* Toronto: Ministry of Municipal Affairs and Housing. At http://www.mah.gov.on.ca/Page6512.aspx (accessed 12 June 2010).

—2010."Building Foundations: Building Futures. Ontario's Long-Term Affordable Housing Strategy." At http://www.mah.gov.on.ca/AssetFactory.aspx?did=8590 (accessed 15 June 2011).

Ontario Ministry of Training, Colleges and Universities. 2009. *Results-Based Plan Briefing Book, 2009–10.* Toronto: Ministry of Training, Colleges and Universities. At http://www.edu.gov.on.ca/eng/tcu/about/annualreport/0910/200910RbP_En.pdf (accessed 10 June 2010.

Ornstein, M. 2006. *Ethno-Racial Groups in Toronto, 1971–2001: A Demographic and Socio-Economic Profile.* Toronto: York University Institute for Social Research. At http://www.yorku.ca/isr/download/Ornstein--Ethno-Racial_Groups_in_Toronto_1971-2001.pdf (accessed 13 May 2010).

Our Diverse Cities. 2007. Ontario edition (fall).

Packard, R. 1997. "Celebrating Our Heritage." At http://www.jias.org/JIAS/jiasweb.htm (accessed 15 March 2009).

Poirier, C., A. Germain, and A. Billette. 2006. "Diversity in Sports and Recreation: A Challenge or an Asset for the Municipalities of Greater Montréal?" *Canadian Journal of Urban Research* 15(2):38-49.

Quirke, L. 2007. "More than Books: Examining the Settlement Services of the Toronto and Windsor Public Libraries." *Our Diverse Cities* 4:156-60.

Seidle, L. 2010. *The Canada-Ontario Immigration Agreement: Assessment and Options for Renewal.* Toronto: Mowat Centre. At http://www.mowatcentre.ca/pdfs/mowatResearch/12.pdf (accessed 13 June 2010).

Shatilla, S. 2010. Personal correspondence with John Biles. 15 January, 24 January.

Sinclair-Jones, H. 1995. *"Backlash": A Study on Discrimination against Immigrants and Refugees in Access to Social Services in Ontario.* Report prepared for Metropolitan Toronto Chinese and Southeast Asian Legal Clinic.

Social Planning Council of Metropolitan Toronto, City of Toronto, and Metro Toronto Community Services. 1997. *Profile of a Changing World: 1996 Community Agency Survey.* Toronto: Municipality of Metropolitan Toronto.

Statistics Canada. 2001. *Census of Population: Highlight Tables.* Ottawa: Minister of Industry. At http://www12.statcan.ca/english/census01/products/highlight/Religion/Index.cfm?Lang=E (accessed 28 December 2008).

—2006a. *Census of Population: Highlight Tables.* Ottawa: Minister of Industry. At http://www12.statcan.ca/english/census06/data/highlights/index.cfm (accessed 28 December 2008).

—2006b. *Community Profiles.* Ottawa: Minister of Industry. At http://www12.statcan.ca/english/census06/data/profiles/community/Index.cfm?Lang=E (accessed 28 December 2008).

—2006c. *Ethnic Origins, 2006 Counts, for Canada, Provinces and Territories: 20 Percent Sample Data.* Ottawa: Minister of Industry. At http://www12.statcan.ca/english/census06/data/highlights/ethnic/index.cfm?Lang=E (accessed 28 December 2008).

—2006d. *Population and Dwelling Counts, for Census Metropolitan Areas, 2006 and 2001 Censuses: 100 Percent Data.* Ottawa: Ministry of Industry. At http://www12.statcan.ca/english/census06/data/popdwell/Table.cfm?T=101 (accessed 28 December 2008).

Tolley, E. 2011. "Introduction: Who Invited Them to the Party? Federal-Municipal Relations in Immigrant Settlement Policy." In *Immigrant Settlement Policy in Canadian Municipalities*, ed. E. Tolley and R. Young, 3-48. Montreal and Kingston: McGill-Queen's University Press.

Toronto Region Immigrant Employment Council. 2008. *Annual Report 2008: Our First Five Years*. Toronto: TRIEC. At http://www.triec.ca/system/files/325/original/2008_TRIECAnnualReview_FINAL.pdf (accessed 8 June 2010).

University Settlement. 2009. "History." At http://www.usrc.ca/history.html (accessed 14 March 2008).

Vineberg, R. 2010. "A History of Immigration Settlement Services in Canada." Unpublished paper commissioned by Integration Branch, Citizenship and Immigration Canada.

Wayland, S. 1995. "Immigrants into Citizens: Political Mobilization in France and Canada." Ph.D. diss., University of Maryland. At http://ceris.metropolis.net/Virtual%20Library/other/wayland1/wayland1h.html (accessed 14 March 2009).

Young, T.L. 1994. "Anti-Racism and Ethnocultural Equity Policies in Ontario Schools: An Historical Examination." Master's thesis, University of Toronto.

CHAPTER 8

IMMIGRATION IN QUEBEC: PROFILE AND PLAYERS

ANNICK GERMAIN AND TUYET TRINH

Integration of "newcomers" and inclusion of minorities today is a highly complex reality for which it is difficult to identify the parameters and the players involved. It is also a constantly changing reality where new players arrive on the scene, others change names, and some disappear. The same is true of programs and action plans. Over the past few years, we have witnessed major government decentralization in Quebec in order to better respond to the needs of immigrants; at the same time, there have been efforts to recentralize in response to a tightening of government purse strings. This dual movement also affects the para-public sector and numerous civil society organizations. The links between the various players are being redefined as well, creating new forms of governance that are unstable, to say the least.

For want of space, our focus here is on immigration more than inclusion. We therefore do not discuss the issue of Aboriginal Canadians, who number over 100,000 in Quebec. Nor do we discuss foreigners who come to work or study temporarily, although they made up nearly 40 percent of the new arrivals to Quebec in 2006 and represent a client groups that Quebec would like to retain (Dumas and Bélair-Bonnet 2010).[1]

This chapter provides a brief profile of immigration to Quebec, particularly recent immigration, and then goes on to look at the main players involved *specifically* in the reception and integration of immigrants. This overview is, of course, highly incomplete.[2] Our main goal has been to identify trends in the current restructuring of the playing field for those involved specifically in managing immigration matters. In our conclusion we identify some challenges that seem to be arising in the evolving landscape of immigration management in Quebec.

Integration and Inclusion of Newcomers and Minorities across Canada, ed. J. Biles, M. Burstein, J. Frideres, E. Tolley, and R. Vineberg. Montreal and Kingston: Queen's Policy Studies Series, McGill-Queen's University Press.

HISTORICAL OVERVIEW

If we equate immigration with immigration policies, the history of immigration in Quebec is relatively recent,[3] although the history of ethnic diversity dates back to the early days of New France, when the first settlers arrived in these "few acres of snow" in the early seventeenth century. After that time, Quebec's population was made up of Aboriginal peoples, white colonists, and a few black slaves. The British conquest in 1760 would result in diversifying the population through the arrival of Scots, English, and, later, Irish newcomers from the British Isles, followed by Loyalists who fled the American Revolution.

One million British immigrants sailed into Quebec City, Montreal, and the Atlantic colonies between 1816 and 1851 (Harvey et al. 1987, 8). In fact, from 1831 to 1866, the majority of Montreal's population was anglophone. Throughout the nineteenth century, Quebec attracted fewer migrants than the other Canadian provinces and retained still fewer. The province also lost many rural French Canadians who went to the United States to find work; from the second half of the nineteenth century, Quebec held a peculiar position in the North American economic landscape as a source of migrant workers for New England. Quebec also began to recruit foreign workers, including Chinese, Italians, and blacks. The case of workers of Italian origin has been well documented by Ramirez (1991). According to the author, villages in southern Italy became well integrated into the North American economy in a system of labour recruitment that started out to be temporary but increasingly became permanent (Ramirez 1991, 67). Although Quebec was often a stepping stone in a longer trajectory that finished with a return to one's native village, temporary migrant workers made a significant contribution to the development of the urban and industrial economy of the metropolitan centre. They also helped trigger a change in its ethnic composition (Ramirez 1991). This brief profile highlights how immigration and emigration were woven together from the outset.

Observers will note that for a long time "French Canada did not engage in immigration, but simply practised a form of social assistance for immigrants" (Camille L'Heureux, 1954, quoted in Harvey et al. 1987, our translation). Newcomers were forced to seek support from members of their communities or mutual aid societies. In fact, the massive arrival of immigrants from Ireland referred to above would give rise to a broad mobilization of civil society, including churches, to receive the newcomers at the end of a voyage undertaken in extremely perilous conditions. Many transited through Grosse Île near Quebec City to be quarantined, and surviving orphans were adopted by Quebec families.

The twentieth century saw significant acceleration and diversification of international, non-British immigration, but it was largely an urban, even a metropolitan, phenomenon. The province had few cities; most of its population congregated along the St Lawrence River. The territory could even be qualified as "macrocephalous," given the size of the metropolis: Montreal accounted for nearly half the province's population and gross domestic product.

The city would therefore play an important role in the social geography of immigration. However, at the start of the twentieth century, Montreal was not yet as cosmopolitan a metropolis as other major North American cities: in 1901, 60.9 percent of the inhabitants were of French origin and 33.7 percent stated that they were from the British Isles, leaving just 5 percent for other origins (Linteau 1992). But the situation would change rapidly. According to Statistics Canada, Montreal now has the third highest number of foreign-born residents in Canada (740,400), just after Vancouver (831,300) although trailing far behind Toronto (2,320,200). In 2006 Montreal edged out Vancouver in terms of recent immigrants welcomed, receiving 14.9 percent of all immigrants to Canada against 13.7 percent for Vancouver and 40.4 percent for Toronto.

DEMOGRAPHICS

Quebec, Ontario, and British Columbia are the three provinces that are home to the majority of Canada's population born abroad. However, unlike the other two provinces, Quebec's share of immigrants (13.8 percent) is lower than its demographic weight (23.8 percent). Nevertheless, it has recorded the highest increase in immigrants over the past five years. Quebec's share of recent immigrants (those arriving within the last five years) who have settled in the province is 17.5 percent, a significant increase compared to just 13.7 percent in 2001 (Chui, Tran, and Maheux 2007, 16). According to Statistics Canada, from 2001 to 2006, net international migration clearly outstripped natural increase. In 2006, immigrants accounted for 11 percent (851,555) of Quebec's 7,546,130 inhabitants.

Immigrant retention rates are generally agreed to have improved in recent years. These rates vary depending on immigrants' knowledge of French and on immigration class. While 80.2 percent of the 381,000 immigrants admitted to Quebec between 1998 and 2007 were still in the province at the beginning of 2009, that figure was only 35.2 percent for business people (MICC 2009).

As shown in Map 1, the immigrant presence[4] continues to be largely concentrated in the Montreal metropolitan area, with 87 percent of Quebec's immigrants living there (about 20 percent of the city's overall population), while 3 percent live in the CMA of Quebec City (4.6 percent of the overall population), 1 percent in Sherbrooke (6.3 percent of the overall population), and 3 percent living on the Quebec side of the Ottawa-Gatineau

CMA (8.7 percent of the overall population). Fewer than 3,000 immigrants live in the other CMAs – notably Trois-Rivières, where they comprise 2.2 percent of the overall population, and Saguenay, where they comprise 2 percent of the overall population.

MAP 1
Immigrant Population Concentrations and CMAs in Quebec, 2006

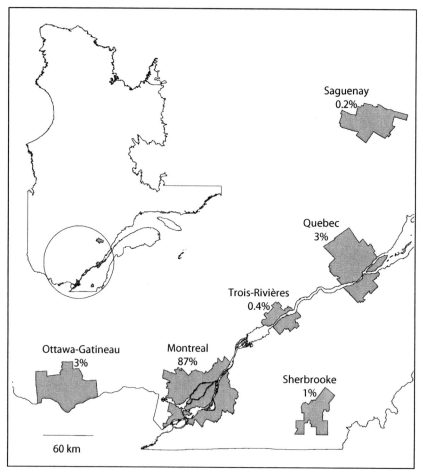

Source: Statistics Canada (2006).

The immigrant population in Quebec can be divided into three categories, according to when they arrived in Canada: those arriving prior to the 1970s (21 percent of all immigrants included in the 2006 Census), the waves of immigration from 1970 to 2000 (56 percent), and recent immigrants arriving since 2001 (23 percent). Placed in the context of these migratory waves, these three periods illustrate the significant changes in immigrant origins – changes not unrelated to the evolution of immigration policies and international fluctuations. The first period, early immigration, corresponded to the arrival of a significant contingent of Ashkenazi Jews from Lithuania and Eastern Europe at the start of the twentieth century, followed by Italians and other Europeans. Italian immigration increased spectacularly after the two world wars and the Depression of the 1930s. Even today, Italians form the largest group of current immigrants by country of birth (Figure 1).

FIGURE 1
Number of Immigrants and Recent Immigrants from Top Ten Birthplaces, Quebec, 2001–06

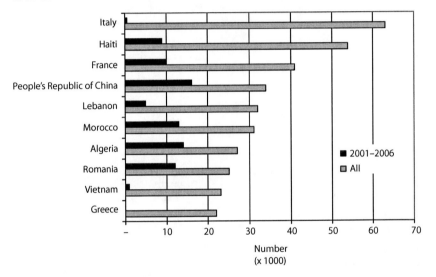

Source: Statistics Canada (2001, 2006).

In the period following the Second World War, the regions of origin for immigrants who chose Quebec as their destination become more diversified. The decade of the 1960s was a benchmark in Quebec's political, social, and economic history and a major turning point in immigration history for both the province and Canada (Linteau 2009, 34). Concurrent with the administration of international law, as well as the appearance of new demographic and economic issues, Canada adopted new immigration legislation that paved the way for new classes of migrants: family reunification, refugees, and economic immigrants. In addition, the legislation required the federal government henceforth to consult the provinces on immigration matters (Pâquet 2005, 202). From that point on, Quebec became a significant player in immigration.

This "new immigration" was characterized by a preponderance of nationals coming from developing countries, resulting in a significant increase in the proportion of visible minorities. Today, 9 percent of Quebec's population and 16 percent of that of Montreal claim to be visible minorities, although this includes people born in Canada. Blacks form the largest group (29 percent) of those who state that they are members of a visible minority.

Today, Quebec stands out from other Canadian provinces by virtue of the wide diversity of countries of birth of its immigrants, as shown in the index of ethnic diversity developed by Apparicio, Leloup, and Rivet (2007).

In Quebec as in other parts of Canada, from 2001 to 2006 Asia became the primary source of immigrants (28.7 percent), followed by Africa (26 percent), Europe (23.3 percent), and the Americas and the Caribbean (21.6 percent). However, Quebec's immigration policy, particularly the weight given to knowledge of French, will play an increasingly important role in determining the provenance of the province's immigrants. In the past ten years, North Africa has been the province's primary source of immigrants, with 61,521 people (MICC 2008e, 24) while France and Romania are still among the main source nations. Some authors thus refer to a re-concentration of immigration (Pinsonneault 2005). Of particular note is the increase in the number of immigrants from the People's Republic of China.

The diversity of source nations for immigration also prompted a religious diversity that has taken root since the 1980s, but whose absolute numbers in relation to the population as a whole remains modest. Roman Catholics continue to make up the vast majority (5,930,380, or 83 percent) of Quebecers, followed by 400,325 people who in the 2001 Census declared that they had no religious affiliation; 108,620 identified as Muslim, 89,920 as Jewish, 85,475 as Anglican, 52,950 as United Church, 50,015 as Greek Orthodox, and 41,380 as Buddhist. When we look at religious diversity within the immigrant population, Catholics dominate, with 324,795 people, followed by 75,280 Muslims, 73,995 Protestants, 59,600 Orthodox, 29,600 Buddhists, and 29,045 Jews. In addition, 74,615 immigrants stated that they had no religious affiliation (Statistics Canada, 2001, Table 97F0022XCB01004; see also Castel 2008).

The linguistic profile is also more diversified if we consider mother tongues. For Quebec as a whole, 5,877,660 people list French as their mother tongue, while 575,555 list English.

In recent years Quebec has had no trouble attracting mainly French speaking immigrants, as was the case in 2007, when they accounted for 60.4 percent of those admitted – a notable increase over 1991, when 37 percent stated that they spoke French.

As in the rest of Canada, recent immigrants in Quebec (2002–06) are generally highly skilled, particularly those in the economic class, where 43.3 percent of immigrants have at least 17 years of education (MICC 2008e, 31).

FIGURE 2
Breakdown of Mother Tongues Other than English and French, Quebec, 1996 and 2006

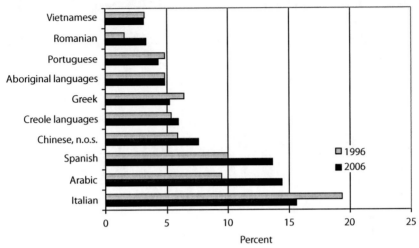

Source: Statistics Canada (1996, 2006).

FIGURE 3
Level of Education, Quebec, 2006

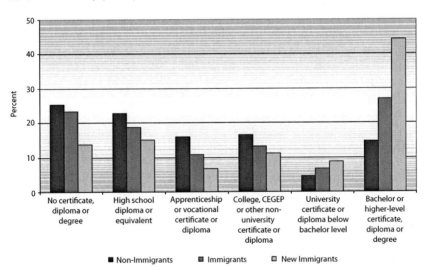

Source: Statistics Canada (2006).

Immigrants to Montreal also tend to be young adults, and more come as small households compared to immigrants to the other two major metropolitan centres in Canada, Toronto and Vancouver (Rose, Germain, and Ferreira 2006). The data in Table 1 also show that newcomers who settled in Montreal in the last ten years are much less likely to be part of multi-family households than their counterparts in Toronto or Vancouver. A number of factors may explain this phenomenon, including a more open real estate market in Montreal and the makeup of Montreal's immigrant population.

FIGURE 4
Age Groups, Quebec, 2006

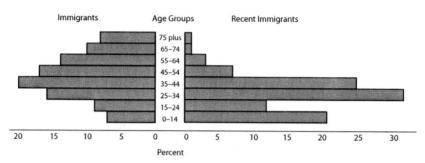

Source: Statistics Canada (2006).

TABLE 1
Composition of Households Supported by Immigrants Arriving in Canada Less than Ten Years Ago, 2001

	Number of Households	Non-Family Households (%)	Single-Family Households			Multi-Family Households (%)
			Couples without Children (%)	Couples with Children (%)	Single Parent Families (%)	
Montreal	74,780 (100%)	26.6	13.2	44.9	12.7	2.6
Toronto	235,205 (100%)	15.4	12.9	52.2	11.3	8.2
Vancouver	95,085 (100%)	15.2	13.2	54.1	9.3	8.3

Source: Statistics Canada, 2001 Census, special compilations prepared for the Metropolis Project Centres of Excellence, in Hiebert et al. (2007).

Settlement Models

The geography of immigration in Quebec and, more broadly, of cultural communities in the province, is unique. Not only is immigration outside the Montreal CMA extremely modest in absolute numbers but its composition changes according to immigration status: skilled workers, business people, and other economic immigrants are highly concentrated in

Montreal (over 85 percent), whereas immigrants who are members of the family class or refugees are mostly found elsewhere (20 percent and over).

For many years immigration within the CMA did not spread beyond the Island of Montreal, apart from a few directly adjacent municipalities, as shown in Map 2. In this regard, Montreal differs from Toronto and Vancouver, where large numbers of immigrants live both in the suburbs and in the city centre. However, when we look at the settlement of recent immigrants, we can see that significant developments have occurred since 2001.

MAP 2
Concentration of Immigrants in the Montreal CMA, 2006

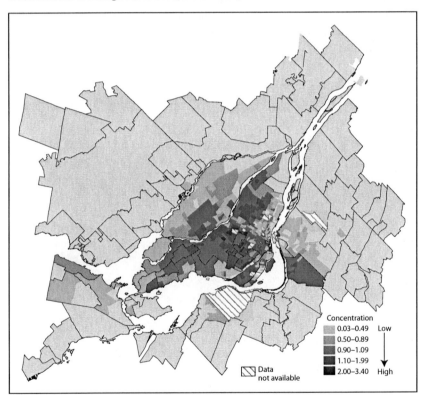

Source: Statistics Canada (2006).

Recent immigrants remain highly concentrated in the centre of the Island; in 2006, 76.3 percent of newcomers to Quebec were settled in metropolitan Montreal, down from 2001, when the proportion of new-comers reached 81.9 percent. Neighbouring municipalities drew in 15 percent: Laval, 5.4 percent; Longueuil, 4.7 percent; Brossard, 2.3 percent;

Dollard-des-Ormeaux, 1.2 percent; and Côte-Saint-Luc, 1.4 percent (Chui, Tran, and Maheux 2007, 23).

Immigration to the regions is progressing, albeit at a slow pace. In 2000 the number of immigrants who settled outside metropolitan Montreal in the first year after landing was 4,169, but numbers rose to 5,968 in 2006 (MICC 2008d, 41) due to an increase in individuals selected under the economic class.

Settlement models for immigrants (and for descendants of immigrants) vary widely. However, most neighbourhoods, ranging from middle-class suburbs to low-income enclaves in and around core districts, can be considered multi-ethnic. These neighbourhoods vary in terms of proportion of immigrants (up to 60 percent in some enclaves, and from 10 percent to 20 percent in certain suburbs or older core neighbourhoods) and degree of wealth, both of which are generally not linked, except in areas with a concentration of recent immigrants. Certain areas are characterized by

MAP 3
Concentration of Recent Immigrants in the Montreal CMA, 2006

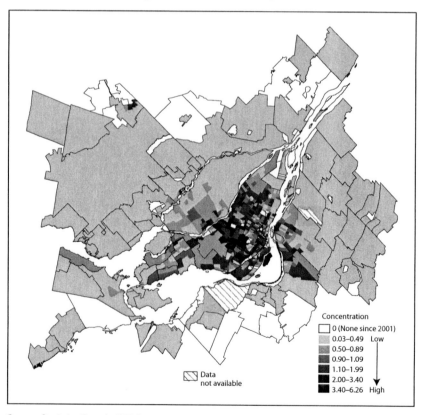

Source: Statistics Canada (2006).

an ethno-cultural dominance (e.g., Italians in Saint-Léonard), but change occurs rapidly. This leads to transitions – for example, from a Greek community to a South Asian community in Parc-Extension – but such transitions always take place against a backdrop of ethnic diversity. Overall, the immigration landscape in the province is becoming increasingly fluid and complex (Germain and Poirier 2007).

THE MAIN PLAYERS

A good overview of the major stakeholders, particularly the Ministère de l'Immigration et des Communautés culturelles (MICC, Department of immigration and cultural communities) and the Ministère de l'Éducation, du Loisir et du Sport (MELS, Department of education, recreation and sport), was given in a previous volume (Biles et al. 2008) by Patricia Rimok and Ralph Rouzier from the Conseil des relations interculturelles (CRI, Intercultural relations council) (CRI 2008, 187-209). We have tried to update this overview and to give complementary information while introducing more players to give the reader a sense of this complex governance system.

Federal-Provincial Relations

In his chapter on the history of federal-provincial relations in the area of immigration and integration at the beginning of the present volume, Robert Vineberg deals primarily with the origin of Canada-Quebec agreements, Quebec having played a pioneering role in the devolution of powers in immigration. Suffice it to say here that, under section 95 of the *Constitution Act, 1867,* and according to the Canada-Quebec Accord Relating to Immigration and Temporary Admission of Aliens[5] (the Gagnon-Tremblay/McDougall Accord), signed in 1991, jurisdiction over immigration is shared with the Canadian government, with the latter prevailing in the event of a conflict, and with Quebec having exclusive control over reception and integration. It should be noted that Quebec has played an important role in selecting economic candidates and refugees abroad since the signing of a 1978 agreement.

The federal government provides Quebec with over $200 million in financial compensation for the province's provision of reception and integration services and French language instruction for immigrants. More specifically, the purpose is to:

- Ensure the reception of all permanent residents and provide them with a referral service in order to refer them to the government services most appropriate to their needs;

- Counsel permanent residents in order to facilitate and accelerate their adaptation and integration into Quebec society;
- Assist permanent residents in determining their initial place of settlement in Quebec;
- Assist permanent residents in integrating into the Quebec labour market;
- Provide permanent residents with the means to learn the French language and to become familiar with the principal characteristics of Quebec society; and
- Provide permanent residents in need with temporary financial assistance.

Since 2008 the MICC has had sole responsibility for managing the federal government's financial compensation and for distributing that compensation to other departments for newcomer integration activities further to interdepartmental agreements. Previously these contributions passed through the province's consolidated revenue fund, which hindered transparency and attracted criticism from a number of pressure groups. Today the MICC exercises clear leadership to ensure consistency in the actions of the Government of Quebec and the partners with which it associates so that it can fulfil its mandate.

At the Provincial Level

The pages that follow demonstrate that these partners – other Quebec departments, regions, and municipalities, and civil society organizations, particularly community organizations – have increased in recent years. Without conducting an exhaustive review, we nevertheless identify the main players, but not without first taking a look at the role of the MICC.

Ministère de l'immigration et des communautés culturelles

The MICC is celebrating its fortieth anniversary, and over the course of those years it has changed names a number of times, mainly because of political philosophy concerns in relation to the concept of *cultural communities*, a term originally used to refer to all persons who were not of French-Canadian origin (Juteau 1986).

It is important to bear in mind the four objectives that have formed the basis of the Government of Quebec's immigration policy since the 1991 policy statement:

1. The demographic recovery of Quebec;
2. Economic prosperity;

3. The perennial reality of the French fact; and
4. Openness to the world.

However, no overview of the MICC's main activities would be complete without first putting it into context in relation to the events surrounding the reasonable accommodation crisis, a crisis that, in February 2007, led to the establishment of the Consultation Commission on Accommodation Practices Related to Cultural Differences, co-chaired by Gérard Bouchard and Charles Taylor (2008). This debate, which began with concerns about religious diversity considerations in certain public institutions and which in the end came to include a number of immigration issues, roused the interest of a good number of stakeholders all over the province of Quebec and, particularly, the main players in integration policy. While it may seem as though a page was turned with the publication of the Bouchard-Taylor report, this debate has had a profound impact on all stakeholders in all matters regarding, among other things, ideas about integration and the manner with which immigration issues are handled in the face of public opinion (Potvin 2010).

In response to the Bouchard-Taylor Commission and as a preventive action, the MICC introduced two sets of measures in March 2008. One set focused on francization, while the other focused on integration, in particular of Maghrebian (or North African) immigrants. These measures were developed under a policy entitled To Enrich Quebec, Better Integration (MICC 2008f). From that policy came a document entitled *Measures pour renforcer l'action du Québec en matière d'intégration en emploi des immigrants, une réponse spécifique aux besoins des Québécois originaires du Maghreb* (Measures to strengthen Quebec's action with respect to the employment integration of immigrants, a response specific to the needs of Quebecers from the Maghreb) (MICC 2008a), as a direct result of the many complaints voiced at the hearings of the Bouchard-Taylor Commission on the serious employment integration difficulties faced by Maghrebi communities.

This was followed in October 2008 by the simultaneous announcement of a number of policy tools in a document entitled *Diversity, An Added Value – Government Policy to Promote Participation of All in Quebec's Development 20082013* (MICC 2008c), and in measures such as the *Declaration on the Common Values of Quebec Society* (MICC 2008g). The latter contains a highly controversial proposition that was clearly dictated by earlier events. It was proposed that candidates sign a declaration on the Quebec Selection, application, agreeing to respect the common values of Quebec, the values being French as the common language, freedom and democracy, secularism of the state, pluralism, the rule of law, gender equality, and respect for the rights of others and for the general well-being. In fact, the document contains the long-awaited policy on preventing racial discrimination, without actually presenting it as such.

The government also launched its *Plan stratégique, 2008–2012* (MICC 2008d), which focuses mainly on four issues:

1. *Mutual commitment from the immigrant and Quebec society.* This first issue caused the most debate because, while it was meant to be a discrimination prevention measure, it was also a way "to reinforce the message sent to immigrants about the common values of Quebec society and to ensure that immigrants understand and agree to respect these values" (MICC 2008d, 11, our translation).
2. *Immigration as a means of supporting the economic and demographic development of Quebec and its regions.* Supporting employers in diversity management and accelerating the recognition of foreign credentials are two important aspects of government action. The MICC has, in particular, increased the number of measures to help candidates deal with professional bodies. In recent years the MICC has largely refocused its attention on the contributions that immigrants can make to Quebec's prosperity (Turcotte, 2010).
3. *The successful francization and integration of immigrants.* This includes earlier and better francization of a larger number of candidates, in particular by diversifying the training offered in order to better reach immigrants in the Family Class and by beginning francization before candidates arrive in Quebec (Cantin 2010). The *Learning about Quebec* guide, which is available online, was put together to provide general information about Quebec, what to do before leaving for Quebec, and how to begin the settlement process, as well as information on social integration, employment, places to settle, and so on. It should be noted that the MICC considers francization and integration to be closely linked, and this is reflected in the structure of the French courses, which focus on both learning the language and interpreting the common values and the social and cultural codes of Quebec.

    The MICC also emphasizes economic integration, given that the unemployment rate for immigrants, and particularly members of visible minorities, continues to be much higher than that for the rest of the general population. This third issue directly concerns the topic of immigration regionalization. Since 2004, the MICC has increased the number of agreements with regional partners, as will be discussed later on.
4. *A more effective and better-focused organization that is supported by many partnerships.* Below, we touch on some of the partnerships that help ensure that the MICC's interventions reflect local conditions. Moreover, the MICC intends to "monitor the evolution, within the various components of the Quebec population, of the three main factors that contribute to social cohesion: 1) adherence to common values; 2) knowledge of French; and 3) employment rate" (MICC 2008d, 17, our translation).

The MICC relies mainly on four programs to facilitate the reception and integration of immigrants. Through these programs, the MICC establishes various partnership agreements.

1. Through the Programme d'accueil des nouveaux arrivants (PANA, Reception program for newcomers), 67 community organizations receive funding to offer support services for settlement and labour market adaptation. These three-year agreements have funding totalling $7.7 million per year ($8.9 million in 2008–09).

2. The Programme regional d'intégration (PRI, Regional integration program) is based on both regionalization agreements with regional and municipal partners, which will be discussed shortly ($3,051,000 in 2007–08), and on a partnership with 18 community organizations (amounting to $1,018,051; see MICC 2008e). The number of immigrants admitted since 2000 who remain established outside the census metropolitan area of Montreal the year following their admission fluctuates at around 6,000 people. This proportion is slowly but steadily increasing.

3. The Programme d'appui aux relations civiques et interculturelles (PARCI, Civic and intercultural relations support program) was regionalized and consists of 64 projects.

4. The Programme d'intégration linguistique pour les immigrants (PILI, Linguistic integration program for immigrants) funds French as a second language training in colleges, universities, and community organizations. A number of options are available (full or part time, general or specialized courses, in varying locations: community organizations, universities, CÉGEPs, school board offices, workplaces). In addition, the Programme d'aide financière pour l'intégration linguistique des immigrants (PAFILI, Financial aid program for the linguistic integration of immigrants) provides allowances to full-time participants. The MICC is now trying to promote online French language courses in Quebec and abroad. These courses are at the intermediate level and are designed for individuals who have previous knowledge of French (Cantin 2010, 158). The purpose of the online courses is to meet the needs of diverse clienteles and increase flexibility in course offerings, particularly with regard to certain targeted occupational groups. Every year the site receives 250,000 visits and has more than 81,000 users (ibid.). The recent cuts in MICC and Emploi-Québec French language learning programs, announced in the 2010 budget, are in line with the focus on this web-based self-training for immigrants.

We now present the MICC's main government partners, to whom it distributes $150 million.

Ministère de l'éducation, du loisir et du sport (MELS)

This department plays an extremely important role in immigrant integration, one of the few departments with immigration action plans and an integration policy, as is well documented by Rimok and Rouzier (CRI 2008, 190). In accordance with an agreement with the MICC, the MELS received $66.8 million in 2008–09 to fund immigrant integration and francization support services "in adult education centres or in vocational training centres that offer services to adult immigrants, as well as services for French language learning and professional and technical training for immigrants" (translation). Moreover, the MELS is pursuing the implementation of its educational integration and intercultural education policy (1997) entitled A School for the Future. The Direction des services aux communautés culturelles (Cultural communities services branch) offers financial support ($6.6 million) at the early childhood, elementary, and secondary school levels for school board projects in two programs – reception and support for immigrant students, and intercultural rapprochement in schools – and offers support for school staff by providing them with intercultural training sessions and teaching aids for newly arrived immigrant students who are severely behind in their schooling. The MELS also supports the development of local diversity management policies in school boards (Fortin 2008, 37).

Ministère de la santé et des services sociaux (MSSS)

As part of an agreement with the MICC, the Ministère de la Santé et des Services sociaux (Department of health and social services) received $12.2 million for 2008–09. Under the Programme régional d'accueil et d'intégration des demandeurs d'asile (PRAIDA, Regional program for the reception and integration of refugee protection claimants), the MSSS offers health and social services to clients involved in complex status regularization process in cases of unplanned immigration. This program includes a psychosocial component (social workers helping refugee protection claimants) and a health component (preventive and primary care for refugee protection claimants, as well as treatment of infectious diseases from other countries). The program also includes a last resort assistance fund to ensure minimum necessary income for refugee protection claimants who are not eligible for social assistance programs. Moreover, the MSSS funds community organizations in Montreal that offer integration, assistance, and support services for immigrant families and immigrant women. Since Quebec's health and social services network was reorganized in 2004, the 95 Centres de santé et de services sociaux (CSSS) (Health and social services centres) have been playing an increasingly important role, particularly the Montagne CSSS, which manages the program in Montreal.

It should be noted that there is no one organization in Montreal that brings together all stakeholders involved in integration issues.

Finally, one particular intiative deserving some mention is the Banque interrégionale d'interprètes (International pool of interpreters), which has been serving Montreal and its surrounding areas (Montérégie, Laval, and when necessary, Lanaudière, Estrie, and Laurentides) since 1993. Managed by the Agence de la santé et des services sociaux de Montréal (Montreal health and social services agency), this service supports the work of organizations and public and semi-public agencies, and facilitates access to services for immigrants.

Ministère de l'emploi et de la solidarité sociale (MESS)

The interdepartmental agreement promoting the labour market integration of immigrants and members of visible minorities establishes the respective responsibilities of the MICC and the Ministère de l'emploi et de la solidarité sociale (Department of labour and social solidarity) on a budget of $66.3 million.

Our colleagues Marie-Thérèse Chicha and Éric Charest (2008) have elsewhere described the details of these programs. They indicated from the outset that "sharing the responsibilities for the labour market integration of new immigrants between the department in charge of immigration and Emploi-Québec is not easy. In principle, the MICC's mission is to offer labour market adaptation services, while Emploi-Québec's mandate is to offer pre-employability and employability services. The distinction between these services seems clear in theory, but in practice it is impossible to distinguish between the individual interventions according to whether they relate to adaptation or employability" (Chicha and Charest 2008, 18, translation).

Individuals born outside Canada constitute part of Emploi-Québec's priority clientele because they are considered at risk of prolonged unemployment. In 2007–08, 16 percent of all new participants in Emploi-Québec's measures and services were immigrants. On the Island of Montreal, this percentage stands at 41 percent. The most important program managed by Emploi-Québec is the Programme d'aide à l'intégration des immigrants et des minorités visibles en emploi (PRIIME, Employment integration assistance program for immigrants and members of visible minorities). This program, which has a budget of approximately $5 million, is funded by Investissement Québec, a government agency responsible for managing the Immigrant Investor Programs. (Immigrant investors have invested $4 billion between 2000 and 2008, according to Turcotte (2010).)

Emploi-Québec estimates that 76 percent of participants who completed this program in 2007–08 found employment (MICC 2008e, 153-4). Since its creation in the spring of 2005, 3,270 people have benefited from this program. The Pacte pour l'emploi (Pact for employment) is expected to increase the number of PRIIME participants. Immigrants who are not eligible (persons who immigrated more than two years ago) could benefit from similar support, via wage subsidies, in the job entry component. Tax credits would compensate employers for on-site French language programs for immigrants.

In 2006–07, Emploi-Québec entered into 78 service agreements in 11 regions, totalling $7.6 million; approximately 50 of those agreements are in the area served by the Montreal branch of Emploi-Québec. This reflects the important role in terms of support services for labour market integration that the network of employability community organizations plays. That said, the funded measures are universal, meaning that they do not specifically target immigrants, even though the demographics are such that the majority of those who benefit are in fact immigrants.

Finally, an important public player under Emploi-Québec that merits mention is the Comité d'adaptation de la main-d'œuvre – personnes immigrantes (CAMO-PI) (Labour market adaptation committee – immigrants). This committee's mandate is essentially to study the labour market situation of immigrants and offer solutions.

Ministère du développement économique, de l'innovation et de l'exportation

The MICC recently reached an agreement with the Ministère du développement économique de l'innovation et de l'exportation (Department of economic development, innovation and exports) that focuses on renewing the entrepreneurial base, supporting businesses, sharing information, and jointly conducting studies and research. In particular, the agreement will target the integrated service offering in diversity management, the immigration and diversity training needs of business advisors, and diversity considerations within businesses.

Regions and Municipalities

Regional Plans and Municipal Agreements

The MICC has increased the number of agreements with local partners since 1999, when the Action Plan for welcoming and integrating immigrants in French was launched in Montreal neighbourhoods, coordinated by the City of Montreal's Bureau des affaires interculturelles. Two projects launched at the time and still in operation provide an overview of continuing initiatives in this area. The first is Habiter la mixité, a series of projects carried out in cooperation with Montreal's Office municipal d'habitation among immigrant HLM (social public housing) households; there is a report on these projects in Bernèche, Dansereau, and Germain (2005). The second project is Contact: Le plaisir des livres, put on in the public libraries of Montreal and aimed at very young children and their immigrant parents.

The number of agreements with local partners has increased since 2004, with authorities at the municipal and regional levels covering a broad diversity of projects and areas of involvement relating to immigrants. Between 2004 and 2007 annual or three-year agreements were signed with various Quebec municipalities, and regional plans were drawn up in conjunction with some of the Conférences régionales des élus (CREs) involving a series of local partners. In fact, the immigration regionalization strategy is essentially handled through the agreements that the MICC has with local authorities to solicit the buy-in of these stakeholders. There are 11 regional action plans in effect, and some 15 agreements have been signed with CREs (MICC 2008e).

Five agreements were signed with municipalities in recent years (MICC 2008e):

1. A three-year agreement worth $4,500,000 was signed in 2006 with the City of Montreal, equivalent to the MICC contribution (see below);
2. A three-year agreement worth $1,575,000 was signed in 2005 with the City of Quebec (MICC contribution was $900,000);
3. A three-year agreement worth $330,000 was signed in 2005 with the City of Sherbrooke;
4. A three-year agreement worth $180,000 (to which the city added $120,000) was signed in 2007 with the City of Shawinigan; and
5. An eight-month agreement worth $65,000 was signed in 2007 with the City of Gatineau.

In all cases these agreements support services to facilitate the reception and settlement of newcomers. Amounts committed vary by region and do not appear proportional to the percentages of immigrants in each region. In the case of the Montreal Region, the amounts may seem paltry when compared with the volume of clients, but in this specific instance the numerous delays seem to have resulted from the complexity of the network of partners in putting the action plan together. A broad consultation was carried out in 2006 on an action plan for the Montreal Region (actually Montreal Island, because it is an administrative region) covering immigration, integration, and cultural relations, which did not come together as an effective action plan until March 2009 (CRE 2006). The MICC and the CRE signed an interim agreement for $375,000 for

2007–08 in order to kick-start certain projects and finalize preparations for a partnership that is still in the planning stages (Dumas and Bélair-Bonnet 2010). Nevertheless, the Montreal CRE included in its 2008–09 action plan, under the heading of "Social Development," a number of projects dealing with the retention of international students, with the recognition of acquired skills and knowledge, and with female immigrants and youth. Two projects deserve special mention because they involve groundbreaking areas or stakeholders: Vivacité Montréal supports young creative artists (immigrants and minorities) and ALLIÉS (launched by the CRE and the McConnell Foundation in 2007 based on the project initiated in Toronto in 2003 by the Maytree Foundation) is designed to mobilize business leaders. These projects involve numerous partners. The proposed amounts are still extremely modest at this point. We return below to the role of the McConnell Foundation.

In closing, we could also mention a recent initiative, Défi Montréal, launched by the Quebec government to integrate immigrants into the labour force (with funding of $6 million over three years). This broad project is coordinated by the new Conseil régional des partenaires du marché du travail de Montréal and mobilizes the Montreal CRE, the City of Montreal and the Chambre de commerce du Montréal métropolitain.

City of Montreal

Montreal municipal reform led to the merger in 2000 and then partial demerger in 2006 of Montreal Island municipalities and resulted in a new level in the already complex municipal structure for managing diversity. Cross-cultural issues have now been essentially taken over by the boroughs of the City of Montreal, but the results of this devolution of responsibilities (along with city planning, snow removal, etc.) are quite puzzling. For instance, in a borough as densely populated with immigrants as Côte des Neiges/Notre Dame de Grâce (76,500 immigrants, or 47 percent of the borough's total population), cross-cultural issues or settlement issues do not appear as an item in the 2009 budget. This invisibility does not necessarily mean inaction, but one can doubt the importance of immigration in the municipal agenda.

At the city level, Montreal supports 37 projects under its agreement with the MICC ($4.5 million). Some of these projects are managed by the city, while others are managed in cooperation with certain partners, such as the Office municipal d'habitation de Montréal (OMHM), which primarily manages the social (public) housing stock. Most of the projects are delivered by community organizations (Wexler and La Ferrière 2010).

The city also has two diversity-support programs, with total funding of $500,000. One deals with community activities, and the other is dedicated to festivals and amateur cultural events.

Other programs do not specifically target issues involving the integration of immigrants and minorities although such issues often concern them quite closely, such as the agreement to fight poverty and social exclusion ($24 million agreement with MESS) or the MICC-Montréal International economic partnership and the Montréal Conférence régionale des élus (CRE). This agreement covers the period of 2009 to 2011 and is supported by $1.4 million from Montréal International, $1.2 million from the MICC and $200,000 from the Montreal CRE, intended to encourage permanent residence among skilled temporary workers in the greater Montreal area.

Educational Institutions: Universities and Colleges

Educational institutions are encouraged to play an increasing role in integrating immigrants. This aspect was referred to above in conjunction with MELS, but there are other initiatives as well.

As stated earlier, the MICC has numerous agreements with various partners in the field of education with a view to diversifying its francization programs. So, in the case of full-time courses, 66.9 percent were taken in colleges, 17.1 percent in universities, and 6.1 percent in the public schools system (MICC 2008e, 30). Collège Rosemont received a mandate from MICC to administer the francization distance learning course entitled Francization en ligne (FEL), referred to previously. The CÉGEP du Vieux Montréal, working with the MICC, designed a French-as-a-second-language course for nurses, and the course at CÉGEP Édouard-Montpetit is intended for health professionals, while the Université de Montréal is piloting a course for engineers.

UQAM's community services support occasional research in partnership with community organizations that work with immigrants, such as the Table de concertation des organismes au service des personnes réfugiées et immigrantes (TCRI) (see below). Université de Sherbrooke has just launched a training course on intercultural mediation; the program is interdisciplinary and is overseen by five faculties. McGill University, in conjunction with the Jewish General Hospital, has launched a Cultural Consultation Service on mental health to take into account the cultural diversity of Montreal's population.

Finally, the colleges have become more and more essential because they offer vocational courses pegged to the workplace, and these have become increasingly popular with immigrants. As a result, various colleges (CEGEPs) have submitted plans to MELS for technology transfer centres in innovative social practices, specifically on integrating immigrants into the labour market (Gulian 2010).

Civil Society Institutions

There are numerous agencies involved in facilitating the reception and integration of immigrants, and on a broader basis these include cultural communities within civil society, whether these are community associations or organizations. One could no doubt theorize that an increasing share of the intervention will fall to them in Quebec, similar to what happens in other provinces but under a distinctive partnership model with the state. However, unlike what is seen in the other provinces, the major portion of the reception and integration services is being handled by public institutions. Before dealing with community organizations, we must first describe the increasing role of foundations.

Charitable Foundations

Until recently, Quebec had very few charitable foundations because for a long time the church was dominant in this area. Today, charitable foundations are flourishing.

Centraide of Greater Montreal. For many years, Centraide of Greater Montreal has been a key player in issues of immigrant integration. Centraide supports 14 organizations that serve refugees and/or immigrants out of a total annual budget of $1.8 million. More importantly, in recent years, Centraide has supported some initiatives to build collaborative communities, some of which focus specifically on the integration of immigrants and on the challenge of a more harmonious existence (Centraide du Grand Montréal, 2000). The Accessibilité initiatives ($248,000) in particular are designed to raise awareness among social and community stakeholders of the realities of immigration and of the cultural communities in a given area, generally a neighbourhood. Centraide supports community work in neighbourhoods inhabited by disadvantaged and immigrant populations in order to improve accessibility to services and resources. The projects explore various ways of reaching out to stakeholders, facilitating cooperation, renewing intervention tools, and fostering participation among immigrants.

J.W. McConnell Foundation. Established in 1937 in Montreal, the McConnell Foundation was the second family foundation created in Canada, following the Massey Foundation. In its early years it mainly supported certain health and university institutions, but the increased state funding in these areas, starting in the 1960s to 1970s, led it to refocus its grants beginning in the 1980s. The foundation was then given a broader national focus and addressed special needs and innovative projects developed by organizations dedicated to community action (McConnell Foundation website). Its action focused especially on bridging the gap between four large groups of actors: social, private, government, and university. As mentioned above, the foundation, in collaboration with the Toronto-based Maytree Foundation, launched the Assisting Local Leaders with Immigrant Employment Strategies (ALLIES) program in 2007; ALLIES "creates more inclusive communities by helping skilled immigrants find jobs matching their skills" (ibid.). The total funding for this program is $3 million, in addition to $1 million from the Maytree Foundation, $800,000 from Citizenship and Immigration Canada, and additional contributions from private-sector and government partners.

A Rich and Diverse Web of Community-Based Organizations

While the advent of foundations is still recent in Quebec, community-based organizations have been around for a long time. Organizations working with immigrants have long remained separate from the so-called autonomous community-based organizations. Several factors explain this distance, which has actually diminished a great deal in recent years. First, the organizations serving immigrants, often created and run by immigrants, have long hesitated to adopt a militant approach. As well, the traditional community was hesitant to include representatives of cultural communities, to avoid fragmenting the concept of social development serving specific clienteles. Finally, in 1996 the Government of Quebec encouraged a shift from a cultural to a civic perspective by supporting community actions that were not ethno-specific but instead had a citizens' vision (Helly, Lavallée, and McAndrew 2000). The world of community-based organizations and associations working to serve immigrants remains nonetheless extremely heterogeneous. This vast conglomeration includes well-established community-based organizations that administer various programs funded through agreements with departments; small-scale organizations run by a handful of volunteers; and as many ethno-specific organizations as multi-ethnic or sectorial ones. As part of research conducted in 2002 on the participation of organizations serving immigrants and / or cultural communities to the neighbourhood round tables in Montreal, we compiled and compared the lists of mono-ethnic and multi-ethnic organizations used by the Bureau des affaires interculturelles (Intercultural affairs bureau) of the City of Montreal (913 organizations), by Quebec's Ministère des relations avec les citoyens et de l'Immigration (Department of citizen relations and immigration, presently MICC) (62 organizations), and by the TCRI (95 organizations) (Germain et al. 2002). This research showed the significant involvement of the various types of organizations in the neighbourhood round tables, which in Montreal play a significant role in community dynamics.

Furthermore, since 2004, the Government of Quebec has reintroduced collaboration with cultural communities by appointing liaison officers and by organizing round tables concerning, more specifically, Maghrebian, Latin American, and South Asian communities; recently, however, all reference to cultural communities was removed during the department's reorganization.

To conclude, we can try to assess the growing but modest part played by community intervention in immigrant integration. Reichhold (2010, 39) estimates that 6.3 percent of the funding is earmarked for immigrant integration, knowing that the government allocates some $16 million to community-based organizations. Both in terms of francization services (10 percent of full-time francization courses are provided by community-based organizations) and regional settlement assistance (under PRI – the regional integration program – 18 organizations receive funding from MICC for regional settlement programs for immigrants), intervention by community-based organizations, which are much smaller than their counterparts in the other provinces, remains limited. In 2007–08, MICC provided over $2,014,680 to 185 projects organized by community partners, with special attention paid to female immigrants or women from cultural communities. Eight projects focused on reaching out to isolated immigrants. But employment integration remains a key vehicle of community action, in collaboration with MICC or with Emploi-Québec. How tasks should be shared among the different types of stakeholders is, however, not always clear. A few major decentralization operations still to come include reception at the airport and front-line training to assist with settlement; these could be taken on by community-based organizations.

Table de concertation des organismes au service des personnes réfugiées et immigrantes. Among the community-based organizations, some are defined less as service organizations than as advocacy organizations. These two missions are sometimes difficult to carry out simultaneously, and given the growth of the community sector mobilized by immigration issues and the complexity of the files handled, an umbrella organization was required to represent the community. The Table de concertation des organismes au service des personnes réfugiées et immigrantes (TCRI, Round table of organizations serving refugees and immigrants), created in 1979, groups together 127 community-based organizations that are devoted to defending and protecting refugees, immigrants, and individuals without status in Quebec and that are involved in the settlement and integration of all classes of newcomers in the areas of services, assistance, support, sponsorship, reflection or solidarity (TCRI 2008). In recent years the TCRI has been particularly active on several fronts involving immigration policy. In its questioning of governments and political parties, it often made itself heard publicly, defending immigrants' rights but also defending budget adjustments for community-based organizations, given the increase in immigration levels (Reichhold 2010). The budgets seem to have evolved at a very different speed than the immigration levels.

However, the TCRI is also active in round tables and handles training, information, and occasionally research.

Fédération des chambres de commerce du Québec. The Fédération des chambres de commerce du Québec (FCCQ, Quebec's federation of chambers of commerce) is piloting, among other things, a special project on best practices called Miser sur une main d'oeuvre diversifiée: Un avantage competitif pour les PME (Relying on a diversified labour force: A competitive edge for SMEs) in cooperation with MICC, Emploi-Québec, and Quebec's Ministère du développement économique, de l'innovation et de l'exportation (Department of economic development, innovation and exportation). It is also piloting about 20 training courses across Quebec.

Conclusion: A Few Challenges

Quebec's immigrant population has increased significantly, in absolute numbers and in proportion to the total population, especially since 2001. This trend will likely continue, as the department in 2010 increased its targets in terms of annual immigration volume to attract between 52,400 and 55,000 immigrants, in addition to foreign students and temporary workers. A few unknowns threaten these tendencies, including the recent economic crisis and the competition of other Canadian provinces or other countries more accessible to certain immigrants. In addition, it is unknown whether the labour force needs based on demographic previsions will remain high (650,000 jobs must be filled by 2013, according to Emploi-Québec) if there are increases in productivity or changes in technology.

In the short term, the increase is expected to continue. It is less clear whether this increase will be as advantageous for immigrants as for the host society. The perception of the speed of the changes risks being a critical factor: it could be the difference between a disruptive evolution and a harmonious adaptation.

Community groups are feeling unconfortable with the gap between increasing clientele and slow-growing budgets, We also do not know how the dynamics evolve within the communities: generational effects or cultural changes could affect recruitment and the particular organizational culture of the community partners. Perhaps it is time to conduct a sound investigation into the work conditions of NGO or community groups (see the work of Matthieu Hély in France in 2008).

Temporary workers, who are more and more numerous, bring many private enterprises into this complex system of actors involved in immigration management, raising questions about governance. The dynamic that governs the partnerships between government departments and community-based organizations often appears more like competition than collaboration. These ambiguities refer to a fundamental question related to the right balance between community intervention, which is close to the clientele, and state intervention, which is based both on logic of socialization to citizenship and logic of rationalization of public services – two logics that are sometimes inconsistent.

The relative decentralization of programs to local partners (regions and municipalities) might not move at the same speed as the awareness and mobilization of elected officials. In addition, it is not only in the domain of immigration that there is a reconfiguration of missions granted to various levels of government. And at the local level, immigration is not necessarily a priority: when intercultural issues go head to head with snow removal, it is clear which priority will win! Furthermore, while in some regions the local actors and their elected officials seem to mobilize around issues of immigration, in others it is instead a matter of demobilization. That is the case in the Montreal region, which has serious governance issues anyway.

While MICC's circle of partners has already grown considerably, it must make room for still more new players. Some institutions have just begun to size up the intercultural challenges caused by the change in their clientele; this is the case in cultural milieus. Others, such as business environments, try too often to ignore them.

The first agents of immigrant integration are Quebecers themselves, whether native born or immigrants. How will attitudes change in the face of minorities being less and less a numerical minority? Perhaps the reasonable accommodation saga was just a taste of what is to come. In that respect, the extremely polarized distribution of immigration across Quebec could slow down the speed of adjustment. Moreover, the debates and tensions occurring in certain countries such as France, Switzerland, and Belgium concerning philosophies of "living together" should be examined and discussed carefully because they are part of the context in which our public opinion evolves through the media.

NOTES

1. See "Temporary Foreign Workers," special number of *Canadian Issues* (spring 2010), published by the Association for Canadian Studies.
2. The bulk of this chapter was drafted in early 2009. We then went on to prepare for the 12th National Metropolis Conference in Montreal in March 2010 and, in preparation for that event, edited a special issue of *Our Diverse Cities* focused on Quebec. While this chapter does not attempt to provide an update of the material presented at the 2009 conference held in Calgary in March 2009, we occasionally refer the reader to supplementary information found in articles in the special issue of *Our Diverse Cities* no. 7 (2010). Our thanks go to Nathalie Vachon of the INRS-UCS, who prepared the maps and tables for this chapter, and to Myriam Richard, a student in the Master of Urban Studies program.

3. For a history of immigration in Quebec, please refer to Linteau (2009), and for background on immigration classes and policies, Pâquet (2005).
4. Nearly 50,000 (48,910) non-permanent residents should be added.
5. According to Robert's *Dictionnaire historique de la langue française* (2000), "alien" (*aubain*) in the feudal period referred to a protected foreigner who was subject to duties and taxation.

REFERENCES

Apparicio, P., X. Leloup, and P. Rivet. 2007. "La diversité montréalaise à l'épreuve de la ségrégation: Pluralisme et insertion résidentielle des immigrants." *Revue de l'intégration et de la migration internationale / Journal of International Migration and Integration* 8(1):63-87.

Bernèche, F., F. Dansereau, and A. Germain. 2005. *L'accueil et l'accompagnement des immigrants récemment installés en HLM dans des quartiers montréalais: L'expérience du projet Habiter la mixité.* Montreal: INRS Urbanisation, Culture et Société.

Biles, J., M. Burstein, and J. Frideres, eds. 2008. *Immigration and Integration in Canada in the Twenty-First Century.* Montreal and Kingston: McGill-Queen's University Press.

Bouchard, G. and C. Taylor. 2008. *Fonder l'avenir, le temps de la conciliation.* Commission de consultation sur les pratiques d'accommodement reliées aux différences culturelles. Rapport. Gouvernement du Québec.

Cantin, L. 2010. "Franciser plus tôt, franciser plus, franciser mieux les personnes immigrantes." *Nos diverses cités* 7:156-60.

Castel, Frédéric. 2008. "Envahissement des minorités religieuses au Québec?" In *L'Annuaire du Québec 2008*, ed. M. Venne, 133-40. Montreal: Fides.

Centraide du Grand Montréal. 2000. *Bâtir des communautés d'entraide et soutenir leur capacité d'agir.* Chantier sur les enjeux sociaux.

Chicha, M.-T. and É. Charest. 2008. "L'intégration des immigrés sur le marché du travail à Montréal: Politiques et enjeux." Institut de recherche en politiques publiques (IRPP). *Choix* 14 (2).

Chui, T., K. Tran, and H. Maheux. 2007. *Immigration au Canada: Un portrait de la population née à l'étranger, Recensement de 2006.* Ottawa: Statistics Canada.

Conférence régionale des élus de Montréal. 2006. *Plan d'action de la région de Montréal en matière d'immigration, d'intégration et de relations interculturelles.*

Conseil des relations interculturelles, P. Rimok, and R. Rouzier. 2008. "Integration Policies in Quebec: A Need to Expand the Structures?" In *Immigration and Integration in Canada in the Twenty-First Century*, ed. J. Biles, M. Burstein, and J. Frideres, 187-209. Montreal and Kingston: McGill-Queen's University Press.

Dumas, M.-C. and F. Bélair-Bonnet. 2010. "Capter la mobilité internationale. Une réflexion sur l'immigration à Montréal au 21e siècle." *Nos diverses cités* 7:18-24.

Fondation McConnell. At http://www.mcconnellfoundation.ca/fr/ (accessed 3 June 2010).

Fortin, L. 2008. "La prise en compte de la diversité à l'école: Bilan des actions gouvernementales." In *L'accommodement raisonnable et la diversité religieuse à l'école publique: Normes et pratiques*, ed. M. McAndrew, M. Milot, J.-S. Imbeault, and P. Eid, 27-41. Montreal: Fides.

Germain, A. and C. Poirier. 2007. "Les territoires fluides de l'immigration à Montréal ou le quartier dans tous ses états." *Revue GLOBE* 20(1):107-20.

Germain, A., M. Sweeney, J. Archambault, J. Mongeau, and J.E. Gagnon. 2002. *La participation des organismes s'occupant d'immigrants et/ou de communautés culturelles aux instances de concertation de quartier.* Montreal: INRS – Urbanisation, Culture et Société.

Gulian, T. 2010. "L'intégration professionnelle des immigrants: Des défis persistants aux solutions novatrices." *Nos diverses cités* 7:151-5.

Harvey, F., J. Kurtness, B. Ramirez, N. Henchey, D. Latouche, S. Constantinides, and A. Laperrière. 1987. *Le Québec français et l'école à clientèle pluriethnique: Contributions à une réflexion.* Conseil de la langue française, Québec: Les publications du Québec.

Helly, D., M. Lavallée, and M. McAndrew. 2000. "Citoyenneté en redéfinition des politiques publiques de gestion de la diversité: La position des organismes non gouvernementaux québécois." *Recherches sociographiques* 41(2):271-98.

Hély, M. 2008. "À travail égal, salaire inégal: Ce que travailler dans le secteur associatif veut dire." *Sociétés contemporaine* 69:125-48.

Hiebert, D., A. Germain, B. Murdie, V. Preston, J. Renaud, D. Rose, E. Wyly, V. Ferreira, P. Mendez, and A. Murnaghan. 2007. *The Housing Situation and Needs of Recent Immigrants in the Montreal, Toronto, Vancouver CMAs.* N.p.:Canada Mortgage and Housing Corporation.

Juteau, D. 1986. "De l'État et les immigrés: De l'immigration aux communautés culturelles." In *Minorités et État*, ed. P. Guillaume. Talence et Québec: Presses universitaires de Bordeaux, Presses de l'Université Laval.

Linteau, P.-A. 1992. *Histoire de Montréal depuis la Confédération.* Montreal: Boréal.

—2009. "Les grandes tendances de l'immigration au Québec (1945–2005)." In "L'histoire de l'immigration au Québec depuis 1945: Nouvelles approches, nouveaux enjeux," ed. Y. Gastaut. Special issue, *Migrance* 34 (2):30-41.

Ministère de l'éducation, du loisir et du sport. 2008a. Comité consultatif sur l'intégration et l'accommodement raisonnable en milieu scolaire (2007). *Une école québécoise inclusive: Dialogue, valeurs et repères communs.* Gouvernement du Québec.

—2008b. *Étude exploratoire du cheminement scolaire des élèves issus de l'immigration: Cohorte de 1994–1995 des élèves du secondaire.* Bulletin Statistique de l'éducation 34, Gouvernement du Québec.

Ministère de l'immigration et des communautés culturelles (MICC). 2008a. "Pour enrichir le Québec. Intégrer mieux. Une réponse spécifique aux besoins des Québécois originaires du Maghreb. Mesures pour renforcer l'action du Québec en matière d'intégration en emploi des immigrants." Gouvernement du Québec.

—2008b. "Pour enrichir le Québec. Affirmer les valeurs communes de la société québécoise. Mesures pour renforcer l'action du Québec en matière d'intégration des immigrants." Gouvernement du Québec.

—2008c. "La diversité: Une valeur ajoutée. Plan d'action pour favoriser la participation de tous à l'essor du Québec." Gouvernement du Québec.

—2008d. "Plan stratégique 2008–2012." Gouvernement du Québec.

—2008e. "Rapport annuel de gestion 2007–2008." Gouvernement du Québec.

—2008f. "Pour enrichir le Québec: Intégrer mieux." Gouvernement du Québec.

—2008g. "Pour enrichir le Québec: Affirmer les valeurs communes de la société québécoise." At http://www.immigration-quebec.gouv.qc.ca/fr/avantages/valeurs-communes/index.html

—2009. "Présence en 2009 des immigrants admis au Québec de 1998 à 2007." Gouvernement du Québec.

Pâquet, M. 2005. *Tracer les marges de la cité: Étranger, immigrant et État au Québec 1627–1981*. Montreal: Boréal.

Pinsonneault, G. 2005. "L'évolution de la composition du mouvement d'immigration au Québec au cours des dernières décennies." *Santé, Société et Solidarité* 1:49-65.

Potvin, M. 2010. "Discours sociaux et médiatiques dans le débat sur les accommodements raisonnables." *Nos diverses cités* 7:83-9.

Ramirez, B. 1991. *Par monts et par vaux: Migrants canadiens-français et italiens dans l'économie nord-atlantique, 1860–1914*. Montreal: Boréal.

Reichhold, S. 2010. "L'action communautaire au service de la population ou de l'État." *Nos diverses cités* 7:39-44.

Rose, D., A. Germain, and V. Ferreira. 2006. "La situation résidentielle et les besoins en matière de logements des immigrants récents dans la région métropolitaine de Montréal." Rapport de recherche. Montreal: Société canadienne d'hypothèques et de logement.

Statistics Canada. 1996. *1996 Census*. Ottawa: Statistics Canada.

—2001. *2001 Census*. Ottawa: Statistics Canada.

—2006. *2006 Census*. Ottawa: Statistics Canada.

Statistique Canada. 2009. *Recensement de 2006, Montréal*. January.

Table de concertation des organismes au service des personnes réfugiées et immigrantes (TCRI). 2008. Rapport d'activités, 2007–08.

"Temporary Foreign Workers." 2010. Special issue, *Canadian Issues* (spring).

Turcotte, Y. 2010. "L'immigration au Québec: Un apport direct à sa prospérité." *Nos diverses cités* 7:13-17.

Wexler, M. and S. La Ferrière. 2010. "Montréal: Programmes d'habitation et réponses aux besoins des ménages immigrés." *Nos diverses cités* 7:199-204.

CHAPTER 9

IMMIGRATION AND DIVERSITY IN NEW BRUNSWICK

CHEDLY BELKHODJA AND CHRISTOPHE TRAISNEL

In the last census, held in 2006, some 26,400 people out of the total population of 729,995 in New Brunswick reported being immigrants. This represents about 3.7 percent of the population, a fairly low rate when compared to other provinces but consistent with the rates in the other Atlantic provinces. In recent years, the issue of immigration has become more prominent in New Brunswick. Although immigration was often brought up under Bernard Lord's Conservative government (1999–2005), it was not until the Liberals came into power in 2005 that a government policy and a specific structure were developed to address it. In *Our Action Plan to Be Self-Sufficient in New Brunswick*, released 23 November 2007, Shawn Graham's government stated that immigration was needed to fuel the province's demographic growth, which was being seriously threatened by an aging population, a low birth rate, and the exodus of young people.

Immigration has accordingly become a priority for New Brunswick, which is committed to attracting skilled immigrants and to more effectively integrating them by providing support to settlement organizations, to ensure that more immigrants stay in the province. When it created the Population Growth Secretariat, the province set itself ambitious targets: to increase immigration to the province by 5,000 people per year by 2015 and to increase immigrant retention from 60 percent to 80 percent (New Brunswick 2008). Those targets were bolstered by the federal government's declared intent to help build capacity for receiving French-speaking immigrants in francophone minority communities in Canada, particularly in New Brunswick. Indeed, in its *Roadmap for Canadas's Linguistic Duality, 2008–2013*, the federal government announced $10

Integration and Inclusion of Newcomers and Minorities across Canada, ed. J. Biles, M. Burstein, J. Frideres, E. Tolley, and R. Vineberg. Montreal and Kingston: Queen's Policy Studies Series, McGill-Queen's University Press.

million in assistance for francophone immigration to New Brunswick for the next four years. The funding was for promoting New Brunswick to immigrants in francophone markets and the integration and settlement of newcomers in francophone communities across New Brunswick. In addition, the funding was to be used to strengthen the settlement and integration infrastructure in the province's francophone regions (Business New Brunswick 2009, 37-8). However, it is still early to have a good idea of the new dynamic behind these actions. Francophone immigration continues to be a challenge, as only one francophone out of every 50 in New Brunswick is an immigrant (Fraser 2009).

This chapter provides an overview of current immigration issues in New Brunswick. Numerous studies on the realities and specific characteristics of immigration to smaller provinces – the urban-rural divide, the anglophone-francophone dimension, the economic and socio-cultural issues of integrating into areas unaccustomed to diversity – reveal an even larger number of studies, as well as a wide range of initiatives and action on the ground. New Brunswick might appear to be a province left out of the development of the major migration dynamics of Canadian society, one with little interest in immigration. Some national columnists have portrayed the Atlantic region as unable to attract new immigrants because of a culture of "have nots" (Ibbitson 2004).[1] We believe that it is important to bear in mind three new dynamics at play. First, the growing diversity of the Canadian population is tending to trigger discussion of a new pan-Canadian identity that is spreading beyond the major urban centres (Anderssen et al. 2004) to small and medium-sized centres, such as those in the Atlantic provinces. Second, sustained growth in eastern Canada in recent years, along with the diversification of its economy toward high-tech fields, is making it more attractive to skilled workers arriving from other countries. Cities such as Charlottetown, Moncton, Halifax, and St John's are taking advantage of the new economy and starting to develop their reception capacity. Budding diversity is necessitating that public policy at provincial and municipal levels develop innovative strategies to bring together all local actors, both public and private, involved in economic and social development. Finally, Canada's declared interest in promoting immigration not only to major urban centres but also to rural areas and smaller communities may over time have an impact on immigration to New Brunswick and other "smaller communities" across the country.

Our approach in this chapter is a somewhat descriptive one. We begin with a brief sketch of the province's immigration history, stressing such things as the lack of interest in immigration demonstrated by the provincial government. We then describe in broad strokes recent government action in the area of immigration, including the new framework for the Population Growth Strategy. Next, we look at some of the realities of immigration to New Brunswick that may be pointing to a new migration dynamic: francophone immigration, the growth of the Korean community, and the recruitment of foreign students. We conclude with a few general observations and recommendations.

A BRIEF IMMIGRATION HISTORY

At the Rendez-vous Immigration conference held in St Andrews in June 2004, historian Margaret Conrad and student Heather Steel concluded their presentation with the following observation: "In 2004, nearly 97 percent of New Brunswick's population is native-born compared to 73 percent in Ontario and 74 percent in British Columbia. In short New Brunswickers seem content to be frozen in their pre-Confederation population patterns, unwilling to embrace the deep level of change that a successful immigration policy might entail ... To seek immigrants only as a quick fix to long-standing economic difficulties is unfair to immigrants and, if past experience is any indication, it is a policy that is unlikely to succeed" (Conrad and Steel 2005, 67-8).

The conference, which meshed with the activities marking the 400th anniversary of the founding of the first French settlement in North America, more or less served to announce the commitment of the New Brunswick government to have immigration play a more defining role in the economic and social development of the province. Interestingly, another major event revolving around immigration had been organized in a different era, a century before: "The high point of New Brunswick's immigration fever occurred in March 1912 when the Saint John and Fredericton Boards of Trade hosted an Immigration Congress at the Opera House in Fredericton" (ibid., 59). Discussions at that event revolved around questions similar to those raised at the 2004 conference in St Andrews: "Attended by over 400 people (in 1912), the event was designed to show that New Brunswick was firmly set on a new progressive track" (ibid.). The province was urged to do a better job of promoting itself abroad, to provide reception services that were better adapted to the newcomers and, finally, to structure its action by creating a government mechanism in this regard (ibid., 97).

Another interesting aspect of the 1912 congress was the prominence of parallel or concurrent discourse against recruiting immigrants at the expense of the local population. This kind of attitude reflected a traditional, rural political culture that did not care to make too many waves, preferring to focus on accommodating the province's two linguistic communities (Aunger 1981). It also revealed the government's caution or hesitation to state matters more clearly when it came to truly committing to immigration. The Graham government's Speech from the Throne in 2008 contained a brief reference to the exodus of young people, without ever suggesting immigration as a solution to the declining population:

"New Brunswickers across the province are saddened when their sons and daughters, their friends and neighbours have to leave New Brunswick to seek out opportunities elsewhere. In two consecutive budgets, your government demonstrated its commitment to bringing New Brunswickers home by doubling funding for the Population Growth Secretariat last year and increasing it by a further 63 per cent in the current year. New Brunswick's population has increased for six straight quarters and your government is on track to achieving its goal of boosting the province's population by 6,000 by the end of 2009" (Speech from the Throne, 25 November 2008).

The exodus of young people is being felt most keenly by New Brunswick's francophone and Acadian community, which recently introduced an initiative under its Enterprise Peninsula program aimed at "making it easier for young people with a college or university diploma to return to the Acadian Peninsula to live by providing them with a number of tools to help them look for work, start a business and network. Participants must be between 18 and 35 years of age and originally from the Acadian Peninsula" (Entreprise péninsule 2009; our translation). Like immigration, getting "our own young people" to "come home" to help meet the province's development needs has tended to be a challenge. "Over the past few years, assimilation, demographic instability, rural exodus, and the need for new skill sets have created a need for us to receive and integrate other francophones into Acadian society, to ensure its growth and survival. We need these other francophones to strengthen our language and expand our community; we also need them to help us look outward, to the world at large and to other cultures that share our language" (SANB 2009a; our translation).

As Conrad and Steel have pointed out (2005), looking at the past can help identify some of the distinctive features of migration in a small province in eastern Canada. Immigration is woven into the history of New Brunswick, some will say starting with French colonization in 1604. Prior to Confederation, New Brunswick received several waves of immigrants. As indicated by Peter Toner (1985, 4), "Almost all of the immigrants to the Maritimes who arrived during the latter part of the eighteenth century and throughout most of the nineteenth century were 'British' in origin." Some were merely passing through, while others settled on a more permanent basis. These included Loyalists fleeing the American Revolution, about 10 percent of them free or enslaved African Americans. Some time later, large numbers of immigrants arrived from Great Britain: Scots, Welsh, but primarily Irish immigrants. In the nineteenth century (1815–67) Irish immigration was the foremost policy issue in the province, sparking religious tensions and occasionally violent confrontation between Protestants and Catholics (Aunger 1981; See 1993).

White, Anglo-Saxon, Protestant immigrants, mostly from Great Britain and the United States (Toner 1985; Conrad and Steel 2005; See 1993), were assimilated fairly quickly, as they did not seriously disturb the province's ethnic landscape. However, Irish Catholics had more difficulty integrating and many ended up leaving the province for the United States. The image of New Brunswick as a province through which such immigrants transited is fairly strong: "For many years, there was no immigrant tax such as was imposed in the ports of the United States. The roads from Saint John and Fredericton to Saint Andrews, and the trails over the portage between Miramichi and St. John valleys, became avenues for unnumbered Irish" (Macnutt 163).

In the twentieth century, imigrants from other European ethnic groups such as Germans, Dutch and Scandinavians also arrived. "New Brunswick, for example, welcomed relatively high numbers of Dutch immigrants in the postwar period. New Brunswickers who claimed Dutch ethnicity rose from 5,920 in 1951 to 7,882 in 1961, but ... fell to 5,360 in 1971. Similarly, those of Scandinavian descent rose from 3,367 in 1951 to 4,901 in 1961 and declined to 3,600 in 1971" (Steel 2004, 31). The village of New Denmark in northwestern New Brunswick, founded by Danish immigrants in 1872, is an example of how these European immigrants quickly assimilated into the region's rural environment while maintaining some of their cultural traditions. Later, in the early 1970s, young Americans arrived in New Brunswick during the Vietnam War to avoid the draft (Conrad and Steel 2005, 104).

From 1970 to the present day, immigration in New Brunswick has averaged 700 to 800 immigrants per year – a very low number when compared with provinces such as Ontario and Quebec and with western Canada. The province did receive some Indochinese refugees and Vietnamese "boat people" over a period of a few years. Since 2005, however, the number of immigrants has been growing steadily as a result of a provincial strategy to attract immigrants and the development of a Provincial Nominee Program to attract economic immigrants.

Immigration was an issue not often raised by the government: "Government officials in New Brunswick believed that immigration was a divisive issue and worried that the local population would accuse the government of showing preferential treatment to immigrants over native-born New Brunswickers" (Steel 2004, 139). In the first half of the twentieth century (1900–45), the provincial government showed little interest in immigration other than to address certain issues affecting rural and farming communities, in particular the loss of farms because of the exodus toward industrial centres in central Canada and New England. In the 1960s and '70s, the national climate became more favourable for immigration. The culture of the 1960s, the modernization of the government machinery, and the passing of major national legislation – the *Official Languages Act* in 1969, the *Multiculturalism Act* in 1971, the *Immigration Act* in 1976 (Vineberg 1987) – resulted in major changes in Canada's political and social landscape. The province was undergoing its own kind of

TABLE 1
Permanent Residents Admitted into Canada and New Brunswick, 1970–2008

Year	Canada	New Brunswick (n)	New Brunswick (%)
1970	148,292	1,077	0.7
1971	120,967	1,033	0.8
1972	124,019	1,326	1.1
1973	185,309	1,741	0.9
1974	217,699	2,197	1.0
1975	189,597	2,155	1.1
1976	145,779	1,670	1.2
1977	114,049	1,162	1.0
1978	85,624	646	0.8
1979	112,117	1,145	1.0
1980	143,127	1,214	0.9
1981	128,624	988	0.8
1982	121,147	751	0.6
1983	89,181	554	0.6
1984	88,249	601	0.7
1985	84,311	612	0.7
1986	99,186	643	0.7
1987	152,069	642	0.4
1988	161,574	679	0.4
1989	191,450	905	0.5
1990	216,445	842	0.4
1991	232,803	684	0.3
1992	254,818	754	0.3
1993	256,703	701	0.3
1994	224,397	627	0.3
1995	212,872	639	0.3
1996	226,073	714	0.3
1997	216,038		
1998	174,197	724	0.4
1999	189,955	660	0.3
2000	227,458	758	0.3
2001	250,638	798	0.3
2002	229,049	705	0.3
2003	221,349	656	0.3
2004	235,823	795	0.3
2005	262,240	1,091	0.4
2006	251,643	1,646	0.7
2007	236,758	1,643	0.7
2008		1,859	

Source: Doiron (1990); Employment and Immigration Canada annual reports (1987–97)

"silent revolution" (Wilbur 1989). New Brunswick was recognized across the country for its Program of Equal Opportunity, the modernization of its government machinery, and its *Official Languages Act*. These reforms strengthened the state-building process begun under John Flemming's government (1952–60), broadly supported by the Diefenbaker government's regional development policy. The reforms led to greatly heightened awareness of identity, with the election of Louis Joseph Robichaud as New Brunswick's first Acadian premier and the consolidation of a francophone hub in Fredericton.

Government and bureaucratic capacity building led to changes to the immigration file, with responsibility for it shifting from the Department of Agriculture to Labour. As pointed out by Micheline Doiron, although the province was not very active, "it abided by the broad principles of Canada's immigration policy and each year received immigrants from each of the three immigration classes: family, refugees and economic immigrants" (Doiron 1990, 78; our translation). Yet despite the interest of some senior officials in attracting economic and skilled immigrants, the climate remained unfavourable for immigration, given the rather low immigration levels and the province's economic performance. It was not easy to promote immigration when there was not enough work for its own young people, who had to leave to seek opportunities elsewhere. Addressing this gap between the exodus of young people, particularly from rural areas, and the intensification of immigration, particularly in urban areas, was an ongoing consideration in defining policies promoting immigration in New Brunswick.

MORE RECENT NEW BRUNSWICK IMMIGRATION POLICY DEVELOPMENTS: ECONOMIC IMPETUS

Immigration is an area of jurisdiction shared by the federal and provincial governments pursuant to the *Constitution Act, 1867*. The interest of this chapter, however, resides in the issue of the heightened role of Canada's provinces in certain social policy issues such as health care, education, and immigration. Two considerations seem to point to a greater role for the provinces in the management of immigration. First, federalism in Canada is evolving toward decentralization/devolution of powers, which can only benefit the federated units as they gain more autonomy in given fields. Immigration no longer fits the classic image of a national issue of population growth and the affirmation of Canadian sovereignty. Rather, it has become a governance issue that provides sub-state actors with an opportunity to participate in the political process (Cardinal and Brown 2007). In addition, globalization has resulted in the internationalization of the roles of the provinces as stakeholders in their own right on the international stage (Nossal 1996). It is in this context that we are seeing a major shift in the way jurisdiction is shared by the central government and the provinces – what policy experts have defined as "High-Hard Politics" and "Low-Soft Politics" (Duchacek 1990). The provinces are increasingly developing their own separate foreign relations in specific areas such as trade, the environment, and culture, making it necessary for them to jockey for position in a clearly more competitive environment.

The process has had a particularly marked effect on New Brunswick, which, as the only bilingual province in Canada, has developed a tradition of involvement on the international scene, especially in institutions of La Francophonie since the late 1960s. In the 1980s, the province began to emphasize the importance of immigration for its economic and demographic development. Under Frank McKenna's Liberal government, the province pursued a strategy aimed at making greater inroads into national and global markets (Savoie 2001). The McKenna years (1985–95) were marked by intense government activity aimed at opening the province to the world and, in particular, the global francophone community (Belkhodja and Ouellette 2001). One interesting aspect of the McKenna government's action was the stress placed on the economic dimension at the expense of references to national unity. Promotion in the francophone world became a means of building ties abroad, especially by touting higher education and the contribution of international students to the academic life of the province's universities as well as the possibility of such students eventually settling in the province as skilled immigrants (Clews 2005).

In the 1990s there was a major shift in the way that immigration was promoted as an answer to the population decline and lack of skilled labour in sensitive sectors of the provincial economy. The province was facing the new reality of globalization and needed to develop new tools to promote itself and attract skilled immigrants. The challenge was a sizeable one in a province with a low attraction factor and a population that continued to hover around 750,000. A 2007 study by the Atlantic Metropolis Centre made the following observation: "New Brunswick is an immigrant-scarce province with a share of Canada's immigrant population that falls well short of its share of the national population. As of 2001, immigrants made up 3.1 percent of the total New Brunswick population compared to over 18 percent of the Canadian population. New Brunswick attracts less than 1 percent of total immigrant inflows, a figure that has trended down since the mid-1980s" (Akbari et. al 2007, v).

In recent years, a number of factors have led to changes in the province's situation. Like most Canadian provinces, New Brunswick has negotiated an agreement with the federal government for a Provincial Nominee Program (PNP). This agreement, signed in 1999 and renewed in 2004, allows the provincial government to "play an active role in selecting immigrants to meet specific economic and labour market needs" (CIC 2005). The PNP has led to significant changes in the number of newcomers to New Brunswick. Since its creation in 1999, the provincial government has accepted 2,104 principal applicants.

FIGURE 1
New Brunswick Provincial Nominee Program, 1999–2009

Number of Nominees* Admitted into New Brunswick

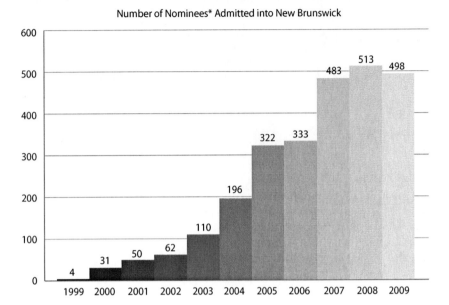

* Principal applicants.
Source: Business New Brunswick annual reports.

The number of permanent residents and temporary workers in New Brunswick has increased significantly since 2004. The impetus of the PNP and specific needs in seasonal industries such as the fishery and agriculture may explain the growth in immigration (Tables 2 and 3).

TABLE 2
Permanent Residents Admitted into New Brunswick, 2004–08

	2004	2005	2006	2007	2008
Moncton	204	187	262	343	363
Saint John	186	310	547	518	560
Fredericton	195	312	440	393	514
Other New Brunswick	210	282	397	389	422
New Brunswick	795	1,091	1,646	1,643	1,859

Source: Citizenship and Immigration Canada, RDM, Facts and Figures 2008 (http://www.cic.gc.ca/english/resources/statistics/facts2008/index.asp).

TABLE 3
Total Entries of Temporary Foreign Workers by Urban Area, New Brunswick, 2004–08

	2004	2005	2006	2007	2008
Saint John	130	193	204	283	375
Fredericton	162	164	149	139	200
Moncton	152	190	157	188	234
Other New Brunswick	305	388	533	682	905
New Brunswick	**749**	**935**	**1,043**	**1,292**	**1,714**

Source: Citizenship and Immigration Canada, RDM, Facts and Figures 2008 (http://www.cic.
gc.ca/english/resources/statistics/facts2008/index.asp).

Various Players Involved in Immigration

In this new context of regionalization of immigration, it is important to consider the role of stakeholders concerned with the issues of attraction and integration of immigrants. The purpose of this research is not to produce an exhaustive inventory of every initiative taken by all those involved; rather, it is intended to provide an overview of the dynamics that have evolved over the past few years around immigration and to look at how the involvement of a whole set of different players reflects recent developments, with an emphasis on regionalization.

Provincial Level

Initially, immigration in New Brunswick fell within the jurisdiction of the Department of Agriculture. In 1973 it was transferred to the Department of Labour, illustrating the economic rationale behind the new national system for selecting skilled immigrants. Responsibility for immigration was to be shared by two departments, Business New Brunswick and the Department of Intergovernmental and International Affairs. Immigration is addressed in a number of the latter department's publications, including its annual reports and the document entitled *Prospering in a Global Community: New Brunswick's International Strategy.* Launched in 2003, the Strategy was and is intended to articulate more clearly what New Brunswick does in the global arena, with La Francophonie internationally, for instance, and in its economic relations with the New England states. The province presents itself as a destination of choice for potential immigrants. In order to foster immigration, the Strategy sets out a number of initiatives, including developing the Provincial Nominee Program, raising New Brunswick's profile abroad, focusing more on attracting foreign students, and raising local awareness about the benefits of immigration (New Brunswick 2003). In January 2006, a progress report indicated the Lord government's intention to develop a provincial immigration policy: "To succeed in a global community, we must position New Brunswick as a place where immigrants want to live, work and raise their families. This requires a holistic approach to addressing New Brunswick's demographic challenges in dealing with a broad range of issues such as promotion, attraction, integration, retention, health, education and accreditation" (New Brunswick 2006, 9).

In 2006, the decision to create a government structure responsible for the immigration portfolio gave more substance to the provincial strategy. This structure, the Population Growth Secretariat, finally began operating in April 2007 and continues to report to the minister for Business New Brunswick. Immigration, settlement support services, and communications are the secretariat's three main areas of focus (Figure 2). The Immigration Division has 17 employees, while Population Support employs 16 people in three different sectors.

FIGURE 2
Population Growth Secretariat Organization Chart

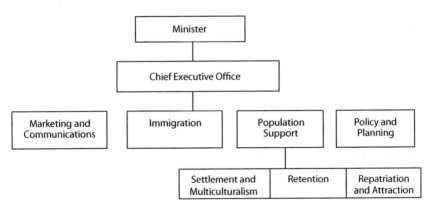

Source: Population Growth Secretariat, Government of New Brunswick.

In the summer of 2007, the province organized public consultations on the population growth strategy (New Brunswick 2007c). Briefs from approximately 40 organizations and comments from about 100 individuals provide valuable insight into the new provincial context in terms of repopulation issues. There seems to be public support for the provincial government's taking measures to counteract the population decline. Several interesting themes emerge from the comments gathered in the course of the consultations. Few of the letters submitted mention immigration as a means of revitalizing the province; instead, they address other components of the provincial strategy such as repatriating "locals" from provinces like Ontario and Alberta and implementing a family policy to encourage people in New Brunswick to have more children. Individual comments also refer to a recurring political issue in New Brunswick: the perception by some anglophones that official bilingualism is one of the reasons that skilled, but unilingual, youth leave New Brunswick to find work in other provinces:

- "The number one problem that I've seen and people that I've spoken to appears to be the bilingual issue. If you are not bilingual in the province you are going to have a difficult time landing a good paying position in this province" (7 July 2008).
- "While I think the bilingualism gives us some benefit, I think it hurts us too. It's almost impossible to get a decent job without being bilingual and that is just going to get more and more difficult" (2 August 2007).
- "It seems the federal and provincial governments do not welcome nor do anything to promote helping the English-speaking residents of New Brunswick. No wonder that we want to leave" (3 August 2007).

In November 2007 the Government of New Brunswick unveiled its provincial population growth strategy, entitled Be Our Future / Soyer notre avenir. This policy, which endeavour to address both the challenges of repatriating young New Brunswickers and of supporting dynamic, sustainable immigration, sets out four objectives: to increase and target immigration; to improve supports for settlement and promote multiculturalism; to retain youth and repatriate former New Brunswickers; and to adopt family-friendly policies (New Brunswick 2008). Where these objectives are concerned, the policy highlights include:

- By 2015 the province intends to attract at least 5,000 immigrants, primarily under the Provincial Nominee Program (PNP). Above and beyond this target, an important element in the strategy consists of developing a collaborative relationship among the various players: "One of the central elements in the Population Growth Strategy is to increase immigration . . . New Brunswick will work with the Government of Canada, employers and settlement and multicultural associations to expedite and streamline the immigration process. There will be increased attention paid to the skill requirements of New Brunswick employers" (ibid., 5).
- The province undertakes to improve supports for settlement services: "Communities can play a crucial role in helping integrate newcomers into the economic and social fabric of New Brunswick. Work will

begin with the federal government to ensure infrastructure and funding are available for settlement services for rural New Brunswick"
(ibid.). Some communities in New Brunswick have had structures
in place to support the integration and settlement of newcomers for
a long time. They have virtually single-handedly taken on the job
of integration with fairly limited resources. These structures are not
well known and work primarily with refugees. The new context of
economic immigration means, however, that the types of services that
are essential to immigrants have changed and require some major
investment.

- Another aspect of the provincial policy is the emphasis on raising
  awareness of cultural and ethnocultural diversity, which includes
  francophones, Aboriginal peoples, and immigrants. In 1986 the province adopted a policy on multiculturalism promoting equal treatment
  for all citizens of all cultures. The policy also represents a commitment
  to equality in matters of human rights, in matters of cultural expression, and in access to and participation in New Brunswick society.
  The Ministerial Advisory Committee on Multiculturalism is piloting
  the implementation of this policy in accordance with the recommendations of non-governmental organizations that have a particular
  interest in the multicultural nature of New Brunswick society.

As part of this strategy, the province undertakes to promote diversity and multiculturalism more effectively to "conduct a review of the
multiculturalism policy and ... focus on the promotion of diversity and
multiculturalism in the province. Further emphasis will be placed on the
importance of living in an inclusive society by ensuring educational material is available in schools across the province" (ibid.). New Brunswick
is basically a bicultural province and, even though it is home to an
Aboriginal community, the language of cultural diversity is less commonly
used. The issue of identity is quite often perceived as secondary when it
comes to immigration – the exception being the Acadian movement and
efforts to reconcile the concept of integration of "other" francophones
with the idea of contemporary Acadian identity (Violette and Traisnel,
forthcoming). Discussions around immigration, in both government and
community circles, tend to focus primarily on the economic aspect of the
phenomenon, on skill requirements rather than culture.

Urban and Rural Areas

One component of the provincial strategy is to work more closely with
local communities. Immigration cannot be confined to the province's
main urban centres; initiatives must also be taken to attract and retain
immigrants in various places, particularly in smaller communities. There

is research to support the involvement of municipalities in immigration, particularly in developing a strategy of attraction, integration, and retention (Gallant, Roy, and Belkhodja 2007; Bruce and Zwicker 2007). The economic dimension is of interest to many community stakeholders: municipalities, and particularly economic players such as the Business New Brunswick network, chambers of commerce, and the Conseil économique du Nouveau-Brunswick are all providing input on immigration. The province's three largest cities, Saint John, Fredericton, and Moncton, have created new structures to provide better coordination among the various stakeholders in this regard. In rural New Brunswick two very different experiences serve to illustrate the realities of this type of immigration.

The Carrefour d'immigration rurale in Saint-Léonard. In Saint-Léonard, a small French-speaking village in northwestern New Brunswick, the Carrefour d'immigration rurale (CIR) launched a community initiative in which all three levels of government have played a major role, both in financial terms and in the form of local commitment. The CIR's intent was to act as a model for attracting, welcoming, and integrating immigrants in rural areas using a collective approach involving all community players. Jacques LaPointe, a Franciscan priest originally from Saint-Léonard, now living in the Washington, DC, area, initiated this project. Father LaPointe convinced municipal authorities of the importance of using immigration to offset the population drain from the region. A successful visit by a West African delegation in 2001 spurred interest in the possibility of creating a reception centre for immigrants. With the opening of the CIR in 2005, Saint-Léonard gave itself a means of managing cultural diversity within the community. The CIR experiment has not actually been conclusive in terms of the ability of a small community to attract francophone immigrants. Isolation and the lack of immigrant communities in the region might explain the challenges involved in retaining immigrants. The project has served mainly to raise awareness in a rural community unused to diversity.

The case of Florenceville. In contrast to Saint-Léonard, the village of Florenceville in the northwest part of the province dealt with immigration not through a citizen-based initiative but rather through private sector involvement in recruiting foreign workers to meet labour requirements. The multinational McCain Foods has played a lead role in expanding Florenceville's population and in establishing an ethnocultural community outside the province's major urban centres. The McCain plant in Florenceville – nicknamed the "French Fry Capital of the World" – has approximately 260 employees. Many of these workers come from abroad. As a result, about 30 different nationalities are represented among residents of the municipality. Despite its small size, this municipality has the highest immigrant population per capita in New Brunswick. According to the 2006 Census, over the space of five years the population of the village of Florenceville grew from 808 to 860, an increase of 6.4 percent, while the province as a whole saw its population decrease by 0.1 percent. The Multicultural Association of Carleton County, created in 2001, tries to reflect the diversity of the inhabitants of Florenceville. The association's numerous objectives include facilitating communication and interaction among people from different cultures, building relations between the various cultural communities that coexist in Florenceville, raising local awareness around the issues of multiculturalism, and encouraging newcomers to become engaged in the host community (Multicultural Association of Carleton County 2009). After a brief lull, the association recently resumed its activities. In addition to organizing information or cultural activities, the association offers various services to newcomers through the work of volunteers and others. These services include information and assistance of various kinds, help in finding accommodation or schools, advice for buying household appliances or motor vehicles, and language courses.

The new provincial strategy is to encourage collaboration among those who play a role in immigration and to create settlement structures and services for newcomers in various regions of the province. Recently, the province invested in projects designed to attract and integrate immigrants in major urban areas and in communities that are less active in terms of immigration. Nine communities now have newcomer centres.[2] Funding is part of the logic of the provincial strategy, to support reception structures, language training, and projects designed to ensure better integration of economic immigrants.

Three Case Studies

From a practical standpoint, three examples serve to illustrate the province's immigration strategy.

Francophone Immigration

The issue of francophone immigration is of great importance in New Brunswick, given that approximately one-third of the population is of Acadian or francophone origin and that the province is officially bilingual. While the need to encourage francophone immigration is acknowledged, the statistics remain low. In 2006, out of a total of 1,646 new immigrants, only 58 permanent residents reported French as their first language and 110 indicated that they knew both English and French. In contrast, the majority of immigrants, 1,014 individuals, reported English as their first language, and a significant number (464) reported that they did not speak either English or French. These demographic and language issues are of great concern to New Brunswick's Acadian community.

Consequently, for a number of years now, the Société acadienne du Nouveau Brunswick (SANB, Acadian society of New Brunswick) has been working on the issue of immigration and, in particular, on the reception and integration of francophone newcomers in the province, setting up a Table de concertation sur l'immigration francophone (Panel on franco-phone immigration issues). Within this context, the SANB remains vigilant to ensure linguistic balance in the area of immigration. According to the SANB, "The members of the Table de concertation believe that maintain-ing the demographic balance of the Acadian and francophone community, raising awareness within the receiving community, and strengthening existing francophone reception and integration structures must remain the Secretariat's main objectives [for demographic growth]" (SANB 2009b, our translation). The SANB wants to open a dialogue between the receiving community and newcomers. In a document entitled *Plan de développement global de l'Acadie du Nouveau-Brunswick* (Global development plan for New Brunswick's Acadian community), the integration of newcomers is described as a big challenge for the Acadian community, which is faced with the ongoing assimilation of its population and at the same time a significant out-migration of francophone youth to urban centres. As a result, the SANB wants to develop an immigration strategy to "promote the integration of newcomers into the French language and the Acadian culture [and] … the integration of newcomers into the community and social life of New Brunswick's Acadian community" (SANB 2009b). An initial study laid out the main issues of francophone immigration in New Brunswick (Baccouche and Okana 2002). The study emphasized that the immigration debate tends to focus on two main concerns of New Brunswick's Acadian community. First, the demographic aspect largely dominates the debate. As a result of the low birth rate in the Acadian population, the high rate of assimilation, the out-migration of francophone youth to other regions, and the low rate of retention of francophone im-migrants, immigration is often viewed as a solution to the demographic issues of the francophone population. In fact, census data from 2001 and 2006 are of concern: New Brunswick's population continues to decrease while the national population is increasing. Second, the economic aspect of the debate limits the contribution of immigration to the issue of meet-ing resource needs in very specific areas of economic activity. Too often the contribution of immigration is reduced to the issue of employment and economic development.

In 2002 the SANB started the process of bringing together the vari-ous stakeholders from Acadian society and cultural associations with the creation of the Table de concertation provinciale sur l'immigration (Provincial panel on immigration issues) consisting of approximately

30 stakeholders from both levels of government, universities, and the concerned communities. While dialogue between the stakeholders has not always been easy, it has allowed a discussion to take place on the definition of a pluralist Acadian identity and has broadened the debate of the political, economic, and social stakeholders.

The federal government felt an urgent need to take action on the issue of francophone immigration following the 2008 *Report on the Government of Canada's Consultations on Linguistic Duality and Official Languages*, submitted by Bernard Lord as part of the renewal of the Action Plan on Official Languages. In setting out its new action plan, the federal government acknowledged that immigration is an important issue for official language minority communities:

> By welcoming a greater number of Frenchspeaking immigrants, Francophone minority communities help to maintain their gains while providing immigrants with opportunities to contribute to the community. To this end, the Roadmap will intensify current efforts to facilitate recruiting and integration, particularly by supporting Francophone immigration in New Brunswick, the only officially bilingual province in Canada.

> To facilitate the recruitment and integration of Frenchspeaking immigrants, Citizenship and Immigration Canada will strengthen partnerships among communities, provinces and territories, employers, educational institutions, and organizations that recruit abroad. In September 2006, Citizenship and Immigration Canada's Francophone Minority Communities Steering Committee launched the *Strategic Plan to Foster Immigration to Francophone Minority Communities*. The main objective of this plan is to increase the number of Frenchspeaking immigrants in Francophone minority communities and to facilitate their reception and integration within the communities (Canadian Heritage 2009).

Moreover, the federal government announced that it would provide $10 million to support the recruitment and reception of francophone immigrants in New Brunswick.

Korean Immigration

For a number of years, South Korea has ranked first among the top three sources of immigrants for the cities of Saint John, Moncton, and Fredericton. This dynamic represents a major shift in the source of immigrants to New Brunswick, especially in the significant portion of New Brunswick's total immigration population arriving from the United States. Most Korean immigrants arrive in large urban centres through the Provincial Nominee Program (PNP).

TABLE 4
Korean Immigration to New Brunswick

Table A. Number of Korean Immigrants to NB, 2002–07

Source Country	2002	2003	2004	2005	2006	2007
Korea, Republic of	/	/	10	193	540	384
Total Immigrants	706	665	795	1,091	1,646	1,643

Table B. Estimated Number of Korean Families in NB Cities (Provided by Korean Associations)

	# of Korean Families May 2009
Fredericton	250
Moncton	106
Saint John	250

Table C. Number of Landed Korean Immigrants through NBPNP, 2002–08

	2002	2003	2004	2005	2006	2007	2008
Korea, Republic of	4	7	14	148	416	274	330

Source: New Brunswick Population Growth Secretariat.

A study funded by the Population Growth Secretariat attempts to analyze the impact of the PNP both on Korean immigrants and on the receiving communities (Kim and Belkhodja, forthcoming). The study examines the settlement process for this new ethnic group and the strategies developed by the Korean community. It makes a number of interesting observations on the role of the receiving community in the integration process. First, Korean immigration to New Brunswick is an example of the new migration mobility of certain individuals who are able to enter Canada through a particular province's PNP. This climate of mobility shows a certain logic, where each party seeks some type of advantage: the province wants to attract economic immigrants who are able to quickly invest capital; the immigrants want to leave their country of origin to take advantage of new economic and family opportunities. The case of Korean immigration is a good example of the new spatial representation of the flow of migration between the global and local environments. Second, this immigration substantially changes the urban landscape of cities that are mostly homogenous, since Korean immigrants are present in urban spaces and in workplaces such as corner stores, motels, gas stations, and laundromats. Their presence is also felt in schools, neighbourhoods, and churches. The study also shows the extent to which this population has structured itself through social networks, in particular in the religious sphere by creating small religious denominations and churches, and in the virtual world of new communication technologies. Lastly, the study emphasizes that good economic integration is crucial in order to increase the rate of retention. The fact that most respondents stated that they chose New Brunswick because they wanted to give their children a quality education leads us to believe that these families may relocate to better performing provinces once their children are done school.

International Students

The contribution of international students is taking on increasing importance in the immigration debate in regions with limited diversity. Universities are increasingly called upon to play a more active role in the area of regional immigration (Walton-Roberts 2008; Suter and Jandl 2008). At least three factors may explain this new way of looking at the relationship between international students and immigration policies. First, as potential immigrants, international students are a solution to the problems of low birth rates and an ageing population, especially in communities outside large urban centres. Second, they become qualified workers and may improve the economic competitiveness of their receiving community. Third, international students who obtain a diploma in the receiving country can more easily access the labour market. As a result, universities have become important stakeholders in the immigration debate (Ziguras and Law 2006).

Since 2004, the international student population has been on the rise in New Brunswick, especially in university cities. The case of Université de Moncton stands out because it recruits international students from countries that are members of the international francophonie (Wade and Belkhodja 2010).

TABLE 5
Total Entries of Foreign Students by Urban Area, New Brunswick 2004-08

	2004	2005	2006	2007	2008
Saint John	156	155	171	186	186
Fredericton	334	317	337	328	355
Moncton	144	184	263	348	427
Other New Brunswick	324	280	273	322	360
New Brunswick	**958**	**936**	**1,044**	**1,184**	**1,328**

Source: Citizenship and Immigration Canada, RDM, Facts and Figures 2008 (http://www.cic.gc.ca/english/resources/statistics/facts2008/index.asp).

Post-secondary institutions place a great deal of importance on attracting international students and must develop specific strategies to recruit and integrate them into university life. One aspect that is taking on considerable importance is the economic integration of these students once they have completed their studies. In 2004, the province allowed international students to work off campus in order to "enhance the global competitiveness of Canada's academic institutions while giving international students opportunities to deepen their understanding and appreciation of Canadian society" (CIC 2004).

CONCLUSION: CHALLENGES AND ISSUES

In a small province, immigration remains a significant challenge, given the low number of immigrants, the low appeal of the location, the competition with other provinces, and the local population's lack of knowhow when faced with a cultural diversity that is, relatively speaking, a new phenomenon. Immigration in New Brunswick has always been thought of in terms of a population that tends to quickly assimilate into the local fabric, with no investment from the local community in the integration process. In a 1991 study on the Dutch population of New Brunswick, the sociologist Van den Hoonaard used the concept of "silent ethnicity" and observed that certain immigrant communities integrate well into the New Brunswick population. Silent ethnicity means that the community does not call attention to itself, nor does it necessarily want to be identified, but it does retain certain distinct cultural characteristics (Van den Hoonaard 1991).

However, immigration paradigms have changed. Governments and local communities are now realizing that it is essential to create a support system for the integration process for newcomers, and to ensure that this system leads the receiving community to place greater importance on a cultural diversity now recognized to be the foundation of the Canadian identity. Helping newcomers assimilate is no longer the issue; instead, the issue has become providing support for integration, organizing the reception of newcomers, and contributing to the recruitment of potential candidates for immigration. We have seen how even small provinces like New Brunswick have become more active in promoting their province abroad. They have developed policies and programs based on their assets and needs and also on their capacity to attract newcomers and their knowhow in terms of recruiting and retaining diverse immigrant populations. New Brunswick in particular has developed a functional relationship to immigration by considering it, first and foremost, as a means of meeting the labour force needs of local businesses and by designing its strategies around this objective. However, the Government of New Brunswick is not, as we have seen, the only stakeholder in immigration.

Other stakeholders include rural communities that are faced with youth out-migration and depopulation, and communities with a long history of immigration. Acadian institutions have also expressed a need not only in terms of having newcomers settle in their communities but also in terms of increasing their capacity to receive and retain these newcomers to New Brunswick. These local community issues contribute to the development of a greater cooperation between the different levels of government and communities. Little by little, and primarily as a result of the different programs mentioned above, a true culture of welcome is being built in New Brunswick.

NOTES

A French version of this chapter will be available in the Working Papers Series of the Atlantic Metropolis Centre.

1. Often articles in the country's major newspapers stress this dichotomy between a New Canada and an Old Canada, depicting the regionalist culture of Atlantic Canada as community centred and folksy in nature. One article in particular, "Why Atlantic Canada Remains White and Poor," by columnist John Ibbitson, which appeared in the *Globe and Mail* on 20 August 2004, stirred passions in the region and ignited a great deal of debate around immigration.
2. These immigrant resource centres offer settlement services, employment counselling, and second language training in both official languages to immigrants in the region.

REFERENCES

Akbari, A., S. Lynch, J.T. McDonald, and W. Rankaduwa. 2007. *Socioeconomic and Demographic Profiles of Immigrants in New Brunswick.* Atlantic Metropolis Centre.
Anderssen, E., M. Valpy, and others. 2004. *The New Canada.* Toronto: McClelland & Stewart.
Aunger, E.A. 1981. *In Search of Political Stability. A Comparative Study of New Brunswick and Northern Ireland.* Montreal: McGill-Queen's University Press.
Baccouche, N. and C. Okana. 2002. *L'accueil et l'intégration des immigrants francophones au Nouveau-Brunswick.* Société des acadiens et acadiennes du Nouveau-Brunswick.
Belkhodja, C. and R. Ouellette. 2001. "Louis J. Robichaud and Frank McKenna: Deux axes de l'action du Nouveau-Brunswick au sein de la francophonie." In *L'ère Louis J. Robichaud*, 115-26. Actes du colloque, Institut canadien de recherche sur le développement régional.
Bruce, D. and G. Zwicker. 2007. *Towards New Brunswick's Population Growth Strategy.* Submission to the Population Growth Secretariat, Rural and Small Town Programme.
Business New Brunswick. 2009. Annual Report, 2008–2009. At http://www.gnb.ca/0398/menu/paf/ar/AR2008-2009.pdf

Canadian Heritage. 2009. *Roadmap for Canadas's Linguistic Duality, 2008–2013*. Official Languages Secretariat. At http://www.pch.gc.ca/pgm/slo-ols/pubs/08-13-LDL/index-eng.cfm

Cardinal, L. and N. Brown, eds. 2007. *Managing Diversity: Practices of Citizenship*. Ottawa: University of Ottawa Press.

Citizenship and Immigration Canada (CIC). 2004. "Canada–New Brunswick Off-Campus Work Agreement for International Students." At http://www.cic.gc.ca/english/department/media/backgrounders/2004/2004-03-18.asp

—2005. *Annual Report to Parliament on Immigration*. At http://www.cic.gc.ca/english/resources/publications/annual-report2005/section

Clews, R. 2005. "Exploring and Overcoming Barriers to Immigration in New Brunswick." In *Rendez-vous Immigration 2004*, ed. H. Destrempes and J. Ruggeri, 263-92. Policy Studies Centre-Centre Métropolis atlantique.

Conrad, M. and H. Steel. 2005. "They Come and Go: Four Centuries of Immigration to New Brunswick. *Rendez-vous Immigration 2004*, ed. H. Destrempes and J. Ruggeri, 43-78. Policy Studies Centre-Centre Métropolis atlantique.

Doiron, M. 1990. "L'immigration internationale au Nouveau-Brunswick de 1970 à 1988." *Égalité* 28:57-82.

Duchacek, I.D. 1990. "Perforated Sovereignties: Towards a Typology of New Actors in International Relations." In *Federalism and International Relations: The Role of Subnational Units*, ed. H.J. Michelmaann and P. Soldatos, 1-33. Oxford: Clarendon Press.

Entreprise péninsule. 2009. *Initiative Jeunesse*. At http://www.ent-peninsule.ca/jeunesse.cfm

Fraser, G. 2009. *La diversité culturelle et son rôle dans l'évolution de l'identité acadienne*. Notes pour une allocution à la Conférence culture et identité de Caraquet, 27 March 2009. At http://www.ocol-clo.gc.ca/html/speech_discours_27032009_f.php

Gallant, N., J.-O. Roy, and C. Belkhodja. 2007."L'immigration francophone en milieu minoritaire: Portrait de quatre municipalités rurales." *Revue des cantons de l'Est* no. 29-39:79-98.

Ibbitson, J. 2004. "Why Atlantic Canada Remains White and Poor." *Globe and Mail*, 20 August.

Kim, A. and C. Belkhodja. Forthcoming. "Emerging Gateways in the Atlantic: The Institutional and Family Context of Korean Migration to New Brunswick." In *Korean Immigrants in Canada*, edited by S. Noh, A. Kim, and M. Noh. Toronto: Toronto University Press.

MacNutt, W.S. 1963. *New Brunswick: A History, 1784–1867*. Toronto: Macmillan.

Multicultural Association of Carleton County. 2009. At http://www.maccnb.ca/Enter.html

New Brunswick. 2003. *Prospérer à l'heure de la mondialisation: Stratégie internationale du Nouveau-Brunswick*. Ministère des affaires intergouvernementales et internationales.

—2006. *Prospérer à l'heure de la mondialisation: Stratégie internationale du Nouveau-Brunswick*. Ministère des affaires intergouvernementales et internationales.

—2007a. *C'est le temps d'agir: Élaborer la stratégie de croissance démographique du Nouveau-Brunswick*. Secrétariat de la croissance démographique.

—2007b. "Our Action Plan to Be Self-Sufficient in New Brunswick." Fredericton: Population Growth Secretariat.

—2007c. *Soyer notre avenir: Stratégie de croissance démographique du Nouveau-Brunswick.* Secrétariat de la croissance démographique.

—2008. "Be Our Future." Fredericton: Population Growth Secretariat. At www2. gnb.ca/content/dam/gnb/Departments/petl-epft/.../Strategy-e.pdf

Nossal, K.R. 1996. "Anything but Provincial: The Provinces and Foreign Affairs. In *Provinces: Canadian Provincial Politics,* ed. C. Dunn, 503-18. Peterborough: Broadview Press.

SANB (Acadian Society of New Brunswick). 2009a. "Immigration." At http:// www.sanb.ca

— 2009b. *Plan de développement global de l'Acadie du Nouveau-Brunswick (2009–2014).* Acadian Society of New Brunswick.

Savoie, D.J. 2001. *Pulling against Gravity: Economic Development in New Brunswick during the McKenna Years.* Montreal: Institute for Research on Public Policy.

See, S.W. 1993. *Riots in New Brunswick: Orange Nativism and Social Violence in the 1840s.* Toronto: University of Toronto Press.

Steel, H. 2004. "Immigration to New Brunswick, 1945–1971: A Study in Provincial Policy." Master's thesis, University of New Brunswick.

Suter, B. and M. Jandl. 2008. "Train and Retain: National and Regional Policies to Promote the Settlement of Foreign Graduates in Knowledge Economies." *Journal of International Migration and Integration* 9:401-18.

Toner, P. 1985. "Ethnicity and Regionalism in the Maritimes. In *Ethnicity in Atlantic Canada,* ed. Robert Garland, 1-18. Social Science Monograph Series, vol. 5. Fredericton: University of New Brunswick.

Van den Hoonaard, W.C. 1991. *Silent Ethnicity: The Dutch in New Brunswick.* Fredericton: New Ireland Press.

Violette, I. and C. Traisnel. In press. "L'Acadie de la diversité chez le militant acadien 'd'ici' et l'immigrant francophone 'venu d'ailleurs': Contradictions et convergences dans les représentations d'une identité commune."*Francophonies d'Amérique.*

Vineberg, R.A. 1987. "Federal-Provincial Relations in Canadian Immigration." *Canadian Public Administration* 30(2):299-317.

Wade, M. and C. Belkhodja. 2010. Gestion d'une nouvelle diversité sur un petit campus canadien: Le cas de l'Université de Moncton. Working paper No. 27, Atlantic Metropolis Center. At http://atlantic.metropolis.net/WorkingPapers/Wade_Belkhodja_WP27.pdf

Walton-Roberts, M. 2008. "Immigration, the University, and the Tolerant Second-Tier City." CERIS Working Paper no. 69.

Wilbur, R. 1989. *The Rise of French New Brunswick.* Halifax: Formac.

Ziguras, C. and S.-F. Law. 2006. "Recruiting International Students as Skilled Migrants: The Global 'Skills Race' as Viewed from Australia and Malaysia." *Globalisation, Societies and Education* 4(1):59-76.

CHAPTER 10

IMMIGRATION, SETTLEMENT, AND INTEGRATION IN NOVA SCOTIA: PROVINCIAL PERSPECTIVES

A. MARGUERITE CASSIN

In January 2005, at the Canadian Museum of Immigration at Pier 21 in Halifax, Premier John Hamm announced an immigration strategy for Nova Scotia, launched the Office of Immigration and the Nova Scotia Immigration website, and held a swearing-in ceremony for the first minister of immigration, Rodney MacDonald. Present at the ceremony were immigrant advocacy and service providers including the Metro Immigrant Settlement Association (MISA), community organizations, and business groups including chambers of commerce and immigrants who offered testaments to the opportunities Nova Scotia offered.

The event mirrored the immigration strategy, the product of an extensive public consultation and communications process that began in August 2004 with the discussion paper "A Framework for Immigration." The paper invited Nova Scotians to participate in a dialogue on immigration. The framework set the tone and identified four topics for discussion: ensuring that immigrants would find a welcoming community, attracting more immigrants to the province, helping immigrants integrate into Nova Scotia society, and retaining those immigrants over the long term. In the consultation that followed, the Immigration Taskforce received 41 written submissions, conducted 45 consultation meetings, and received hundreds of emails. It engaged a wide range of organizations and individuals to think about and discuss immigration and its importance to Nova Scotia.

The development of the immigration strategy followed the 2002 Canada-Nova Scotia agreement on a Provincial Nominee Program and was driven by recognition of implications of the labour force demographic

Integration and Inclusion of Newcomers and Minorities across Canada, ed. J. Biles, M. Burstein, J. Frideres, E. Tolley, and R. Vineberg. Montreal and Kingston: Queen's Policy Studies Series, McGill-Queen's University Press.

and the province's poor record of immigrant retention. The 2005 strategy announced by Premier Hamm was collaborative and inclusive. It stressed the importance of making immigration – in particular, settling immigrants – the job of everyone in Nova Scotia. Both the announcement and the strategy were directed towards fostering the engagement of business, community, and government in making Nova Scotia a desirable immigrant destination. The tone of the strategy's launch is reflected in *Update*, the newsletter of the Pictou Chamber of Commerce: the February 2005 issue is devoted to the premier's immigration framework and emphasizes the importance of members taking initiative around immigration.

The sponsorship and leadership offered by the premier was central to giving immigration a profile in Nova Scotia. The strategy represents a shift in the focus and interest in immigration and accelerates a project of culture change in the way Nova Scotia is experienced and known.

LOOKING BACK

Nova Scotia's more recent history is one of colonial settlement. When the first French colonists arrived and set up a permanent base in 1604 at Port Royal, the area was home to several regions of the Mi'kmaq nation of Mi'gma'gi. Later, the British gained control of the region and established a new capital in Halifax, which today is the most populous city in the province. Over half of present-day Nova Scotians can trace their ancestry to the population shifts that occurred after the expulsion of the Acadians in the mid-1700s. During this time, a large number of United Empire Loyalists, including black Loyalists, migrated to the province. The late eighteenth and early twentieth century also saw the arrival of Gaelic-speaking Highland Scots. These earlier migrations were very influential in Nova Scotia's development and remain a strong part of the province's cultural composition.

In the mid-twentieth century, Nova Scotia, and particularly Halifax, was part of the experience of many newcomers to Canada. For more than a million immigrants between 1928 and 1971, Halifax was the port of entry, commemorated today by the Canadian Immigration Museum at Pier 21 (Pier 21 2010).

Historically, then, Nova Scotia had a diverse population: Mi'kmaq, Acadians, English, Highland Scots, United Empire Loyalists, including Loyalists of African origin, Dutch, German, and Irish. All have influenced the province, yet until recently, that diversity has not been reflected in depictions of the culture of province or in public policy. Nova Scotia has been characterized in literature and public policy largely as a province of British traditions and values (Marshall 2009). Halifax's history as a British garrison has been preserved and is reflected in current urban planning policy that recently has been a matter of contentious political and policy debate (Barber 2006). These homogenous characterizations of the "traditional" culture of the province have been broadly held and reinforced in public images, particularly tourism-oriented ones. This view of the province, held by Nova Scotians as well as in outside characterizations, is an ideological barrier to more contemporary immigration, including the attraction and settlement of immigrants and integration into communities. Nova Scotians need ways of seeing and knowing ourselves that are more accurate, equality oriented, and inclusive and allow us to see the diversity and difference among us. These ways of seeing and knowing are developing through the contribution of social and local history and cultural heritage projects, community groups, advocacy, and public policy at all levels of government. Immigration policy and programs are contributing in significant ways to this project of culture change.

Demographics

Nova Scotia is the most populous of the Atlantic provinces and is Canada's seventh most populous province, with a population of 913,462 in 2006, placing it ahead of New Brunswick and behind Saskatchewan. Halifax is Canada's 13th most populous census metropolitan area, with a population of 372,858 in 2006. It is by far the dominant urban centre for the province; in 2006, Halifax Regional Municipality accounted for over 40 percent of the province's population, while Cape Breton Regional Municipality accounted for just over 11 percent, and Regional Municipality of Queen's and the Town of Truro accounted for just over 1 percent.

Nova Scotia has the largest foreign born population in the Atlantic provinces; in 2006, 5 percent of its population was foreign born. Over the last census period (2001–06), the Atlantic region saw a slightly larger share of Canada's total recent immigrants (1.2 percent) than over the previous period (1 percent in 1991–96) (Statistics Canada 2006). Following trends in the rest of the country, recent immigrants to Nova Scotia largely settle in major urban areas (Akbari 2005). The 2006 Census also showed that Halifax had the largest foreign-born population of any centre in the Atlantic provinces. It received 0.5 percent of all newcomers to Canada in 2006, which constituted 18.4 percent of the foreign born population in the census metropolitan area. A little over half of the newcomers to Halifax were born in Asia or the Middle East. To break this figure down further, the People's Republic of China was the leading source country of newcomers to the city (10.7 percent), followed by the United States (7.6 percent), the United Kingdom (7.5 percent), Egypt (7.3 percent), and India (4.9 percent). A study by Kazemipur and Halli (2001) found Halifax to have among the lowest poverty rates for immigrants in Canada. The study found that the highest poverty rates for immigrants were in Montreal (31.4 percent) and Quebec City (29.4 percent), while the lowest rates were in Victoria (13.1 percent) and Halifax (12.6 percent) (ibid., 1142). This result for Halifax could be due to a number of factors, including the socio-economic status and existing network of recent immigrants to the city (Akbari et al. 2007).

Nova Scotia's aboriginal identity population from the 2006 Census is 24,175; of that, 7,680 identify as Métis. These figures represent a large increase from the previous census period (2001), when the aboriginal identity population for the province was 17,010.

The major ethnic origins in the province are representative of long-standing immigration groups. In the 2001 Census, almost half the province (47 percent) self-identified in a count of total responses. Following from this, major ethnic origins by total count included Scottish (29 percent out of total population), English (28 percent), Irish (19 percent), French (16 percent), German (10 percent), Dutch (4 percent), North American Indian (3 percent), and Welsh (1 percent). The ethnic makeup of the Halifax CMA corresponds closely to that of the province as a whole, except for a slightly greater English than Scottish presence.

The visible minority population of Nova Scotia as a whole was approximately 4 percent in 2001 (2001 Census), while that of Halifax was 7 percent. The 2001 Census shows those under the grouping "black" as making up the proportionally largest visible minority group, constituting 57 percent of the total visible minority population in the province and 52 percent of the visible minority population in the Halifax CMA. "Chinese" was the second largest visible minority group in the province (9 percent of the total visible minority population), followed by "South Asian" (8 percent).

Nova Scotia is a predominantly an English-speaking province, much more so than Canada as a whole. For example, 92 percent of Nova Scotians count English as their mother tongue, as opposed to 57 percent nationally. Proportionally fewer Nova Scotians count French at their mother tongue as compared to the population of Canada as a whole: 3 percent in Nova Scotia versus 22 percent nationally.

In terms of religious affiliation, Nova Scotia is predominantly Protestant (49 percent as reported in the 2011 Census); the second proportionally largest religious group are Catholics (36 percent). This is reversal of national trends, where Canada as a whole is predominantly Catholic (44 percent) followed by Protestant (29 percent) (see Table 1).

Nova Scotia's changing demographics will be a major factor in shaping the province in the years to come (see Figure 1). A 2006 demographic analysis of the province to 2026 projected that virtually all of those who will be in the labour force of 2026 have been born (McNiven and Foster 2009). The report projects a decrease in Nova Scotia's total population from 932,389 in 2001 to 894,777 in 2026 (ibid.). Nova Scotia is expected to be a province with a labour force shortage. Concurrently, it can expect a continuing push for inter-provincial and international migration to help with projected labour shortages and a declining provincial tax base upon which to meet the needs of an aging population.

TABLE 1
Population by Religion, Province of Nova Scotia and Canada, 2011

Religion	Nova Scotia, Percent Religious Affiliation out of Total Population	Canada, Percent Religious Affiliation out of Total Population
Catholic	36.62	43.65
Protestant	48.82	29.20
Christian Orthodox	0.40	1.62
Christian not included elsewhere	1.13	2.63
Muslim	0.39	1.96
Jewish	0.24	1.11
Buddhist	0.19	1.01
Hindu	0.14	1.00
Sikh	0.03	0.94
Eastern religions	0.06	0.13
Other religions	0.13	0.22
No religious affiliation	11.85	16.53

Source: Statistics Canada (2011).

FIGURE 1
Nova Scotia's Population by Age and Gender, 2006

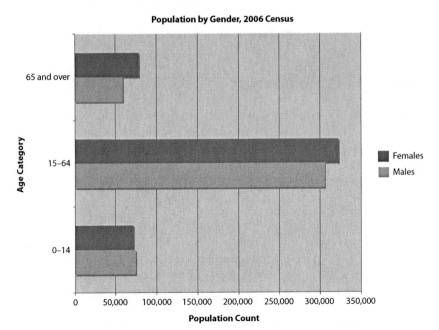

Source: Statistics Canada (2006).

Nova Scotia and Canada Immigration Agreement

All immigration to Canada is organized under the legal framework of the federal *Immigration and Refugee Protection Act* (IRPA). Provinces have the ability to negotiate federal-provincial agreements, which provides them with some flexibility in place-based immigration strategies. While Citizenship and Immigration Canada (CIC) is the main federal department responsible for immigration issues, other federal departments and agencies collaborate on certain initiatives – for example, in Nova Scotia, the Atlantic Canada Opportunities Agency (ACOA), Enterprise Cape Breton Corporation (ECBC), Human Resources Skills Development (HRSD), and Canadian Heritage.

Immigration policy determined in the centre has not served Nova Scotia well (or indeed most provinces, and in particular less populous cities and rural areas). The characterization of Canada as a multicultural country with coherent immigrant communities has attracted immigrants to large centres (Toronto, Montreal, and Vancouver) but has not been a faithful characterization of the diversity and culture in communities and provinces outside these centres. In 1995 the Government of Canada offered provinces the opportunity to share immigration policy through federal-provincial agreements that defined a provincial nominee program (PNP). Manitoba was an early participant in this arrangement, and its success offered encouragement and models for other provinces including Nova Scotia.

In 2002 the governments of Canada and Nova Scotia entered into an agreement to jointly administer the Provincial Nominee Program (CIC 2007a). This locally oriented immigration program is described in the agreement as intending, first, to expediently encourage skilled immigration based on local labour market demand, and second, to encourage the development of the francophone community (ibid). Under this agreement, the Nova Scotia Department of Economic Development created the first program, which was designed to attract business immigrants.

Nova Scotia has had comparatively low immigrant retention rates. The province's Office of Immigration stated that it wished to achieve a retention rate of 70 percent over the 2006–11 period and was seeking to achieve this goal in large part through an increase in levels of immigration (NSOI 2007). It should be noted that such rates are difficult to track due to inter-provincial mobility. A Statistics Canada longitudinal survey of immigrants to Canada reveals a discrepancy between the expectations and experiences of recent immigrants (Schellenberg 2007). Factors such as quality of life and perceived opportunities both now and in the future are thought to be important components of retention.

The greater involvement of the provincial government with new immigration prerogatives offers the province the ability to create place-based and locally oriented policies to attract and retain immigrants. Policies are now being created and implemented in the provincial socio-cultural context as opposed to federally developed and administered ones (Chundry 2008). Earlier manifestations of Nova Scotia-specific immigration policy were couched largely in terms of the economic benefits of targeting immigration with special provisions to encourage the development of the francophone community (CIC 2007b). Recent agreements take a broader, more integrated approach.

Government of Nova Scotia

While immigration, settlement, and integration of "newcomers" is the mandate of the Office of Immigration in Nova Scotia, immigrants, like the rest of us, live in communities, work, send their children to school, and need and use government services. In this respect the provision of services for immigrants is a horizontal issue; that is, it affects all government departments and mandates. One way to consider the capacity of a community to integrate and retain immigrants is to look at how government services provide for and assist newcomers. The following discussion of initiatives and programs, while not exhaustive, does show the increasing emphasis on immigration and emerging patterns of attracting, settling, and integrating immigrants.

Nova Scotia Office of Immigration (NSOI)

The Nova Scotia Office of Immigration, established in 2006, brings a policy and organization focus to immigration to the province. The NSOI manages the Nova Scotia Nominee Program (NSNP) with the Nova Scotia office of Citizenship and Immigration Canada and promotes immigration to and settlement in the province through a variety of programs.

The NSNP "offers a quicker entry into Canada for qualified workers and experienced entrepreneurs who wish to settle in Nova Scotia and become permanent residents of Canada. It allows Nova Scotia to recruit and select immigrants who can contribute to meeting the labour market and economic needs of the province. Individuals nominated by Nova Scotia, together with their spouse/partner and dependent children, are eligible to apply for a permanent resident visa from Citizenship and Immigration Canada visa under the federal Economic Class known as the Provincial Nominee Class" (NSOI 2010c). Successful applicants to the NSNP receive a Certificate of Nomination to a CIC visa office. CIC reviews the application and retains final approval. Upon approval, nominees are granted permanent resident status in Canada.

NSNP program streams include:

Skilled Worker Stream: Fast-tracks applicants who have the needed skills and permanent full-time job offers in specific sectors that have opportunities for skilled immigrants.

Family Business Worker Stream: Helps family-owned businesses hire close relatives who have skills that cannot be found in Canadian citizens or permanent residents.

Community Identified Stream: Aimed at individuals who are employable, have strong established connections to a Nova Scotia community, and can contribute to the labour market and economy of that specific community.

International Graduate Stream: Helps employers hire and retain recent international graduates whose skills may be in limited supply in the province. This stream targets international graduates who have established strong ties to Nova Scotia and intend to live, work, and establish their careers in this province. (NSOI 2010c)

Progress on Attracting Immigrants

The number of NSNP nominees between 2003 and 2008 has been steadily growing (with a slight decline in 2008 over 2007) for a total of 1,554 nominations. More generally, Nova Scotia is increasingly a destination for immigrants. In 2006, 2,585 immigrants were granted permanent residence status in Nova Scotia, up over 1,929 for 2005. Immigrants are distributed among both Canada and Nova Scotia immigrant streams (CIC 2007a).

The face of immigration to Nova Scotia is also changing. In 2005 and 2006, the most frequent immigration regions and countries were South Asia (China, Korea, and Taiwan), the Middle East (Egypt, Jordan, Lebanon, and Iran), North America (United States), and Europe (United Kingdom). The most frequent countries of origin of refugees coming to Nova Scotia were Afghanistan, Sudan, and Liberia. The age composition of immigration to Nova Scotia was 48 percent under 24; 59 percent, 25–64; and 3 percent over 64, thus contributing to the increase in youth and labour force age workers, a critical overall goal for Nova Scotia (ibid.).

Settling, Integrating, and Retraining Immigrants

Judging from the recent past, the challenge for Nova Scotia is to settle, integrate, and retain immigrants. The process includes making the community more welcoming by shifting the "culture" of Nova Scotians with respect to the treatment of newcomers. Such a shift is a challenge for a province where even Canadians from other parts of the country can have trouble settling and fitting in. The NSOI is active in both assisting newcomers and conditioning the welcome offered by communities, business, and institutions.

Nova Scotia Immigration Branding and Attracting Immigrants

The NSOI sees the Internet as an important source of information for prospective immigrants and puts a great deal of effort into its website. The NSOI has branded Nova Scotia Immigration "Come to Live, Build Your Dream." This works well with current provincial rebranding: "Nova Scotia: Come to Life." Both brands and the images attached to them show Nova Scotia as culturally, economically, and socially diverse, offering opportunities to contribute and shape the province. The images emphasize lifestyle, opportunity, diversity, and community. These brands and themes are projected on the NSOI website (http://novascotiaimmigration. ca) and in print and commercials. The brands and themes are also being taken up by organizations and communities as part of their expression of welcome. They contrast favourably with earlier images presenting Nova Scotia as more homogeneous in culture and people. The website presents Nova Scotia as an attractive destination differentiated from the larger Canadian centres.

Programs

The NSOI has taken a broad approach to settlement and integration. The office is using its resources to engage communities, organizations, Nova Scotia government departments, and municipalities in immigration. Using a combination of direct information, policy and analysis activities, and grants and contribution programs, it is investing in communities and organizations to foster a successful immigration strategy. This approach is directed toward building community, organization, and institutional capacity to integrate newcomers in Nova Scotia as well as to provide services to immigrants.

In addition to the NSNP, the NSOI has two additional program areas (NSOI 2010d). Settlement program funding is directed to funding settlement services to support projects or organizations. Labour Market Agreement (LMA) Funding for Immigrant Programs is directed to employers seeking to establish employment programs for immigrants. These grants and contributions for programs are awarded on a competitive basis by an annual call for proposals. The Settlement and LMA programs for 2010–11 invited submissions along four priorities: labour market and employment, language training for adults, orientation and integration, and community capacity building programs (NSOI 2010b).

Immigrant Settlement Program Funding (ISPF) pays for programs directed to helping NGO immigrant support groups with their programming. Since its inception in 2005, the program has provided annual grants of between $2,500 and $107,000 for organizations engaged in a broad range of supports for immigrants. The activities funded include language training, labour market orientation, supports for employers, cultural orientation, and communication skills. The program supports ten to 13 projects each year to a number of NGOs, which include business (Greater Halifax Partnership), culture, and language (Fédération Acadienne de la Nouvelle-Ecosse), immigrant oriented organizations (Metro Immigrant Settlement Association or MISA, now Immigrant Support and Integration Services), and rural local economic development (Regional Development Authorities). Expenditures in 2005–06 were reported at approximately $870,000 and in 2007–08 at $1.54 million. In addition $250,000 was granted to the Department of Education for ESL in public schools. These grants represent a substantial contribution from the province. They are well distributed across Nova Scotia and address many dimensions of settlement and integration.

The NSOI has also interested itself in communication. Website development grants (NSOI 2010a) were provided in 2008 to 11 settlement-related organizations. The grants allowed organizations engaged in settlement activity to announce and provide access to services and information to immigrants, other immigrant organizations, community groups, and government bodies.

Francophone Immigration

There are provisions for strategies for attracting francophone immigration to Nova Scotia and programs for their support and integration (Fontaine 2008). The NSOI website describes the services and initiatives in the French language (NSOI 2010e). The Acadian community is actively engaged in promoting Nova Scotia (Gallant 2007a, b, c; Gallant and Belkhoja 2005; Gallant, Belkhodja, and Dugas 2005). Early research on the municipality of Clare suggests that immigration is revitalizing and strengthening this Acadian municipality (Dugas and Roy 2007).

Transparency and Increasing Awareness, Knowledge, and Skills of Nova Scotians

The NSOI is fostering integration both through the support it is giving immigrant settlement work and the work it is doing with employers. There is ongoing engagement with business and government to make employers more aware of immigration and the opportunities that immigrants offer the province. The NSOI's Nova Scotia Business Mentorship program is associated with the economic stream of immigrants. In addition, it is actively supporting projects that seek to develop foreign credential recognition. The office is also building capacity in government through the development of employees who are skilled and knowledgeable in immigration and in the promotion of employee interchange with the Government of Canada, particularly Citizenship and Immigration Canada (CIC), to deepen the experience of public servants and foster intergovernmental capacity. This investment in young public servants is likely to produce talent and innovation in future immigration work and will contribute to culture change in institutions and departments.

The NSOI is working in a consultative and collegial style and practising and promoting transparency in its work. Its grants and contributions are reported in a timely fashion and adjudicated through a collaborative process. This is a welcome contrast to the first Provincial Nominee Program; the Economic Immigrant Stream (2002), initiated by the Department of Economic Development and transferred to the NSOI, was the subject of two very critical reports by the Office of the Auditor General of Nova Scotia (2008).

Nova Scotia Department of Health (NSDH)

Health is an important area for services to immigrants and for immigrant employment. In partnership with Prince Edward Island, Nova Scotia has been participating in a five-year (2005–10) Health Canada-funded initiative to increase the capacity of internationally educated health professionals (Nova Scotia Department of Labour and Workforce Development 2007). The Internationally Educated Health-Care Professionals Initiative (IEHPI) is working on strategies to integrate immigrants into a number of practice areas including pharmacy, occupational therapy, physiotherapy, medical laboratory technology, and medical radiation technology.

NSDH has also fostered the Cultural Competence Guidelines for the Delivery of Primary Health Care in Nova Scotia (Health Team Nova Scotia 2008). The guidelines aim to increase multicultural awareness, knowledge, and skills of staff and health practitioners in the province. This awareness is recognized as an important dimension of "decreas[ing] disparities in health services, address[ing] inequitable access to primary health care and respectfully respond[ing] to the diversity of Nova Scotians (race, ethnicity, language, sex, sexual orientation, gender identity, (dis)ability, spirituality, age, geography, literacy, education and income, etc." (ibid.).

Department of Labour and Workforce Development (LWD)

LWD programs focus on training, employees, employers, and development. Generally they are inclusive and direct attention to immigrants, generally referred to as "newcomers." The services are delivered by the department and with partners. In this respect the strategy differs from the NSOI approach.

Pathways to trade certification for new Nova Scotians are part of the Skills Nova Scotia framework (Nova Scotia LWD 2007). The International Credential Recognition allows for review of experience and offshore qualifications related to one of the designated trades in Nova Scotia. (The full list of designated trades can be found at www.nsapprenticeship.ca.) New residents in Nova Scotia who wish to work in one of the designated trades are offered three paths: credential recognition, trade qualification, and apprenticeship qualification.

The programs in the department are part of the Canada-Nova Scotia Agreement on Labour Market Development (LMDA) (Human Resources and Skills Development Canada 2010) and the Nova Scotia Labour Market Agreement (LMA) (Nova Scotia LWD 2010a). The LMDA provides for the delivery of EI and related services by LWD. The LMA is a six-year economic and social framework focusing on labour force development, skills, and labour force attachment. It provides annual funding to Nova Scotia to address labour market inequality. In negotiating the agreement, policy was reviewed, and government objectives were an important framework for the discussions. As a result, the LMA objectives are congruent with provincial priorities. Nova Scotia Labour Market Agreement Annual Plan 2008–09 and 2009–10 (Nova Scotia LWD 2009, 2010b) priority areas include immigration.

The NSOI receives and administers a portion of the LMA monies allocated to immigration. As discussed above, it has a call for proposals and a grants and contributions plan. Within its business plans for 2008–09, immigration was allocated $120,000 for business skills, $775,000 for occupational skills training, $646,000 for language training for labour market participation, and $1.89 million for transferable skills (Nova Scotia LWD 2009).

Opportunities Nova Scotia, initiated in the Department of Education and moved to the LWD, is a "retention and recruitment initiative to better connect, inform and support Nova Scotia employers and job seekers (Nova Scotia DoE 2010a). The initiative is focused on population retention (helping Nova Scotians stay home), persuading former Nova Scotians to "come back home," and attracting newcomers including immigrants. Employers are encouraged to learn and meet the recruitment and retention challenges of the Nova Scotia labour market. Job seekers and current employees are encouraged to learn about opportunities and engage in lifelong learning. Phase 1 included a series of networking events across the province. Phase 2 took Nova Scotia's largest employers to major Canadian cities to showcase the many opportunities the province has to offer. Opportunities Nova Scotia is a forum that highlights and popularizes knowledge about the changing Nova Scotia economy. Following the series of in-province and national networking events, participating employers can continue to post available positions, and job seekers can continue to submit their resumés online. Opportunities Nova Scotia sets a popular context in which to see business and labour market initiatives. It is described as an "important information resource component of Nova Scotia's labour market strategy, within the Department of Labour & Workforce Development's Skills and Learning Division" (Nova Scotia DoE 2010b).

Other programs initiated under the LMA include Business Development and Entrepreneurship Counselling for Immigrants, which provides counselling for immigrants considering self-employment. The current immigration agreement with the federal government removes restrictions on the number of people the province is able to nominate for residency, making it easier and faster for temporary foreign workers to enter. The agricultural sector of the province's economy is making increasing use of foreign worker provisions. At the same time the LWD is actively working with other jurisdictions to develop information in several languages for temporary foreign workers on their basic rights.

It is also worthwhile noting that immigration and labour force initiatives, as well as the coordination and leadership of the NSOI and the Treasury and Policy Board Policy Division (until 2009), have increased coordination and horizontality within government. The Labour and Workforce Development Business Plan, 2008–2009, is guided by the province's economic plan, Opportunities for Sustainable Prosperity, and its social plan, the Social Prosperity Framework. The plan outlines five immediate priorities intended to lead the province to economic and social security (Nova Scotia LWD 2009).

Department of Economic and Rural Development (DERD)

The DERD, under various names, has for the past 15 years been engaged in supporting local development and community economic development as part of the overall economic strategy for Nova Scotia. It has also been increasingly involved in planning and seeking the engagement of communities and business in economic futures. Engagement across governments (particularly Atlantic Canada Opportunities Agency, ACOA) has made economic development more coherent, and the creation of policy frameworks including Opportunities for Sustainable Prosperity establishes directions that can be used to coordinate initiatives (including the LMA, already discussed) (Nova Scotia DERD

2010a). The department has had field offices and officers engaged with communities and municipalities and has supported the development of 13 Regional Development Authorities (RDAs). The experience and work with communities and policy and planning has given the DERD expertise in working with communities and organizations related to immigration (Flint 2007, 2008).

The department has several immigration related programs. There is research evidence that recognition of credit history is an ongoing issue for immigrants (Rebelo 2005). The Immigrant Small Loans Program (Nova Scotia Department of Economic and Rural Development 2010b), underwritten by the DERD and administered through the Nova Scotia Cooperative Council by credit unions, is thus an important initiative. The RDAs have been encouraged to work with municipalities to investigate immigration for their communities. The DERD initiatives involve partnerships and emphasize business development, expansion of expertise, and economic spinoffs. The Progress Media Group (2010) provides communication vehicles, *Open to the World* and *Progress Magazine,* for the department to profile Nova Scotia business; among their stories, they report on immigration (Nova Scotia Co-operative Council 2010).

Department of Education

In its role of setting curriculum for primary and secondary education, the Department of Education (DoE), along with the Nova Scotia Teachers' Union (NSTU) and boards of education in the province, has been working to produce inclusive programs directed towards immigrant children and their parents.

The Skills Nova Scotia Framework highlights provincial programs, services, and initiatives that are helping to improve Nova Scotia's competitive edge in attracting and retaining skilled international workers, and promotes equity, fairness, and diversity throughout labour market programs and services offered in Nova Scotia. Based on the collaborative efforts of partners in government, business, industry, training, and educational institutions, the DoE through its Skills and Learning Branch provides leadership and support for Skills Nova Scotia Framework initiatives of all government departments. The program has recently been moved to LWD.

The Department of Education is also central to the implementation of multiculturalism, racial equity, and diversity in the schools (Nova Scotia DoE 2010a). These interrelated responsibilities mean that the department creates conditions for the social contexts for formal and informal learning. While these issues are not immigration specific, they are important for newcomer children and parents.

Department of Tourism, Culture, and Heritage

In 2005 the Department of Tourism, Culture, and Heritage initiated the Interdepartmental Forum for external stakeholders working on an approval process for multiculturalism policy, and the work is ongoing in view of the *Nova Scotia Multiculturalism Act*. The forum facilitates the development and implementation of strategy in support of multiculturalism in partnership with stakeholders. It focuses on sharing information, identifying community needs and priorities with respect to policies, programs, and services. The department has been active in building consensus on actions that government can take in support of multiculturalism and has identified resources and implementation implications, forming this into a report. The department has participated in networks and shared information with the community stakeholders on the progress of policy development.

The department is also working to (re)define cultural and heritage sites and activities in view of the multicultural and diverse character of Nova Scotia (www.gov.ns.ca/tch/). This is an important part of culture change, offering many opportunities for development and shifting the focus to profile the social history of Nova Scotia more broadly.

Nova Scotia Advisory Council on the Status of Women (NSACSW)

The NSACSW has been active on behalf of immigrant women. It initiated the Diversity Round Table, which brings together immigrant and youth settlement associations, and the Atlantic Metropolis Gender Domain (NSACSW 2004). The council participated in the Valuing Diversity Action Plan, led by the Nova Scotia Public Service Commission. The summary report of the Round Table has now been incorporated into the sector of their website devoted to immigrant women (NSACSW 2011).

Nova Scotia Human Rights Commission (NSHRC)

The NSHRC has responsibility for the *Nova Scotia Human Rights Act* (NSHRC 2010a), for receiving, investigating, and resolving complaints under the act, and for public education on human rights. The NSHRC's active employment equity initiative works to inform and foster positive community relations. The complaints process offers an important window on immigrant settlement and integration, because all complaints begin with inquiries from the public; while not all inquiries become complaints, they offer an overview of what is happening to immigrants. The NSHRC has for some time seen an increase in inquiries from immigrants seeking their rights (NSHRC 2010b).

Department of Community Services (DCS)

The DCS is active in providing social supports for Nova Scotian children, youth, and families and for persons with disabilities, including income assistance and social housing. Immigrants are among those served by the department, and attention is paid to this fact in programs and program delivery. The DCS has also been active in anti-domestic violence initiatives, including a recent task force that has made recommendations on immigrant services (Nova Scotia DCS 2010).

Nova Scotia Public Service Commission (PSC)

The PSC has programs and policy on diversity, including a summer program for students aimed at attracting young people of diverse backgrounds to public service (Nova Scotia PSC 2010a). There is also a Diversity Accommodation Fund (Nova Scotia PSC 2010b), and a Diversity Talent Pool (Nova Scotia PSC 2010c). The NSOI is the leader in employing immigrants and developing best practices in its office and with employers, and it is hoped that this leadership will in time influence the larger public service.

Local Government and Education

Boards of Education

Boards of education are key institutions for immigrants who come to Nova Scotia seeking a better life. The school experience of their children is a key factor in settlement and integration. The discussion of boards of education below is not exhaustive but gives some examples of programs and initiatives.

Halifax Regional School Board (HRSB). The HRSB's Student Identification Survey provides valuable contextual information on students. If the survey achieves high response rates, its schools use the information to support the diverse cultural needs of all students. The survey provides a demographic profile that indicates where schools need to respond. The survey is an important planning tool and rationale for resource allocation (HRSB 2006).

The Race Relations, Cross Cultural Understanding and Human Rights in Learning Policy (RCH) was approved by HRSB on 23 May 2007. HRSB support for teachers and students includes the identification, development, and implementation of programs, learning supports, and strategies to enhance academic achievement and address systemic inequities and barriers affecting racial and ethno-cultural groups (ibid. 2010).

Annapolis Valley Regional School Board (AVRSB). The AVRSB's Korean Elementary Program is designed for Korean elementary students between the ages of seven and 12. The program provides for supported integration into school and can be from eight to 20 weeks in length. It is associated with 30 elementary schools within the school district. The Annapolis Valley is approximately two hours from Halifax, and the program can arrange for host families for children living in other parts of the province.

AVRSB's Community Education service promotes lifelong learning and enrichment for the well-being of citizens within the communities in the school district. The program is focused upon active citizenship and community education.

Chignecto-Central Regional School Board. Education services in this board include the International Student Program, the development and implementation of Race Relations, Cross-Cultural Understanding, and Human Right initiatives and support services, and the coordination of technology acquisition, allocation, integration, and maintenance. All of these services support newcomer students.

Regional Development Authorities (RDAs)

The province has 13 RDAs, which focus on helping new businesses succeed and on encouraging new business ideas. These community-based organizations have partners in municipalities, Nova Scotia DERD, and ACOA. The RDAs are encouraged to be open to immigration and to develop immigration strategies in view of local needs and aspirations and in partnership with municipalities and boards of education and non-government organizations. There is evidence that RDAs and municipalities are working together to develop immigration strategies (Flint 2007, Nova Scotia Association of Regional Development Authorities 2010).

Municipalities

The Nova Scotia Immigration Strategy and the work of the NSOI and DERD have sought to engage municipalities and RDAs.

Halifax Regional Municipality (HRM) and Partners. The HRM has argu- ably the most to gain from immigration. The HRM, the Greater Halifax Partnership (GHP), Immigration Leadership Council, and the Chamber of Commerce have a strong working relationship focused upon immigra- tion. Among the initiatives is a communication plan in which the HRM is presented as open to the world (Halifax Regional Municipality 2010a). For example, the GHP has placed advertisements at the airport welcom- ing immigrants (Greater Halifax Partnerships 2010). This initiative is as much about conditioning the community as welcoming newcomers. The Immigration Action Plan (ibid.) brought together a wide range of partners and focused upon what people, communities, and organizations can do to foster immigration. The *Halifax Newcomers' Guide* is a directory of municipal services organized to help newcomers including immigrants (Halifax Regional Municipality 2010b).

HRM has subscribed to the UNESCO initiative Cities against Racism (UNESCO 2010) and has equity initiatives within its administration. The HRM Police have community programs and engagement with groups including immigration initiatives, as does the Halifax Port Authority. The Immigration Leadership Council, led by the CHP, is focused on implementing the Immigration Strategy. Projects funded by the United Way are active in immigration (United Way 2008).

Immigrant Service Provider Organizations

Immigrant Settlement and Integration Services (ISIS)

ISIS, the main settlement services organization in HRM, is a recent amalgamation of the Halifax Immigrant Learning Centre and the Metro Immigrant Settlement Association (MISA was a key participant in form- ing the Nova Scotia Immigration Strategy). This community inspired and based organization provides services to newcomers and works to increase the welcome of employers and communities to immigrants. ISIS offers a full range of programs and services that include the Government Refugee Program. It is proactive and centrally involved with community groups and with city and government initiatives in immigration. Funding includes NSOI, CIC, ACOA, and related initiatives. ISIS is a leader in identifying policy issues and making agencies aware of emergent topics of interest. It has a research office and is working with other groups to inform its work (ISIS 2010).

YMCA Immigrant Services

The YMCA immigrant services, focused on youth and women, include a YMCA Host program, Youth Outreach, Student Services, and an active living program. There are international services as well as an employment and education program.

The women's program offers companionship and orientation to women immigrants and provides a forum for exchange. The Y has been innovative in its programming. There is a long-standing program to help schools and students in practical ways with issues of racism. The program is reliant on searching for and finding government grants and contributions programs. (YMCA Halifax/Dartmouth 2010).

Multicultural and Issue-Based Non-Governmental Organizations

The Multicultural Association of Nova Scotia (MANS 2010), a registered non-profit organization supported by the Department of Tourism, Culture and Heritage, is a long-standing (since 1975) group that represents cultural organizations and conducts programming. It includes outreach programming and engagement in presenting Nova Scotia's cultures. MANS is highly involved with government, immigrant service providers, and the community. It includes numerous ethnicity and nationally affiliated multicultural organizations with various levels of activity. The groups create a broad basis for consultation, and the views of people in these organizations are regularly sought. The association's normal activities include festivals, social events, and, at times, political mobilization.

The Halifax Refugee Clinic, founded in 2000 and funded by the Law Foundation of Nova Scotia, offers legal services to refugees. The issues (poverty, housing, women's shelters, youth initiatives) addressed by the multicultural organizations, and the legal services offered by the Halifax Refugee Clinic, together form the basis of the services used by immigrants and of the knowledge that these organizations offer to government and settlement organizations (Tastoglou and Peruvemba 2009). Many of these organizations are funded under the umbrella of the United Way (2008).

Universities

The universities in Nova Scotia all have international student offices and services. In the current climate, most Nova Scotia universities are working to attract international students, both for increased enrolment and for the differential fees paid by international enrolments. Services for international students include advance information for registering students, website information for prospective students, and services during their time as students. The provision of services to students is dynamic and responsive to issues or problems that arise. The services include cultural acclimation, counselling, social activities, and study supports. Related to but not the same as student services are the university student unions, under whose umbrella services and affiliations for international students are offered. Student unions provide avenues for engagement in student politics and advice and services related to student and academic life.

International students are an immigration attraction priority in Nova Scotia. Completing a post-secondary education in the province is itself an integrating experience from a variety of perspectives. International students learn about Nova Scotia and form friendships with Nova Scotia students while pursuing their education. If they are in programs with work terms, they gain further Nova Scotia experience and engagement with employees and at least one employer. The NSOI is giving attention to this group and has altered regulations as it has learned about post-graduation timelines for labour force entry.

Atlantic Metropolis Centre (AMC)

The AMC, one of the centres in the Metropolis network, is a research program on immigration, diversity, and integration. Developed with a great deal of engagement with the NGO and immigrant communities, it provides both networking and research opportunities for NGOs. An AMC research grants program engages professors and their students in the Atlantic region in immigration topics (AMC 2011a). The research grants requirements favour proposals that have the engagement of NGOs working in immigration and that involve students in the research. There are also knowledge transfer activities that engage affiliates to the AMC and the communities more generally in exploring research results. The AMC website provides a bibliography of research papers (AMC 2011b). The AMC has been important in giving immigration a profile as a research topic and in offering opportunities for researchers and organizations to work together.

Immigration in Nova Scotia

Driven by demographic analysis and a projection of labour shortages, Nova Scotia is placing increasing emphasis on immigration. In contrast to the first Provincial Nominee Program in 2002, current priorities emphasize four streams for provincial nomination. The inclusive approach taken by the NSOI, the engagement of government at all levels, the strength and innovative character of the immigrant services, related NGOs (including ISIS and the YMCA Newcomers Program), MANS, and the network of multicultural organizations are all increasing Nova Scotia's capacity to attract and settle immigrants. The methods of funding and supporting programs have engaged large networks to increase their capacity to work with immigrants. For example, the Immigrant Small Loans Program builds capacity in the credit unions as well as providing a service to immigrants. Strong links with many organizations make the NSOI nimble in terms of accepting feedback and making changes in regulations and programs.

The approach now being taken to immigration in Nova Scotia is clearly positive in terms of government, community, and NGO capacity. Will this translate into integration and retention of immigrants? This is the challenge. People make decisions to stay or leave partly on the basis of what they experience in daily life, and it is not clear that the immigration strategy is affecting how Nova Scotians accept newcomers. Culture change remains the province's greatest challenge.

NOTE

Acknowledgements go to Tamara Krawchenko for her work on the demographic section and more generally for her contribution to our ongoing discussion of futures in Nova Scotia; to Reama Khayat for research assistance and enthusiasm for this project; and to Lina Cheruiyot and Jon McDonald for editing and research.

REFERENCES

Abdul-RazAkbari, A.H. 2005. "Comings and Goings of Immigrants in Atlantic Canada." *Workplace Review* (April).

Akbari, A.H., S. Lynch, J.T. MacDonald, and W. Rankaduwa. 2007. "Socioeconomic and Demographic Profiles of Immigrants in Atlantic Canada." Atlantic Metropolis Centre.

Atlantic Metropolis Centre. 2011a. "Research Grants." At http://www.atlantic.metropolis.net/research_policy_e.html (accessed 26 August 2011).

—2011b. "Working Papers." At http://www.atlantic.metropolis.net/working_papers_e.html (accessed 26 August 2011).

Barber, L. 2006. "Heritage Landscape Aesthetics and Downtown Revival in Halifax, Nova Scotia." MA thesis, Department of Geography, University of British Columbia.

Chundry, D. 2008. "Nominee Program Boosts Atlantic Immigration." *APEC* (July).

Citizenship and Immigration Canada (CIC). 2007a. "Nova Scotia Nominee Program; Canada-Nova Scotia Agreement on Provincial Nominees." *CIC News*. At http://www.cicnews.com/2007/09/nova-scotia-nominee-program-0927.html

—"Canada-Nova Scotia Co-operation on Immigration." 2007b. At http://www.cic.gc.ca/english//department/laws-policy/agreements/ns/ns-2007-agree.asp#cont%20idcont

Dugas, P. and J.-O. Roy. 2007. "Rural Immigration in a Minority French Speaking Area: Clare." Working Paper Series No. 10, Nova Scotia Atlantic Metropolis Centre, Halifax.

Flint, J.D. 2007."Rural Immigrants Who Came to Stay: A Case Study of Recent Immigrants to Colchester County, Nova Scotia." Working Paper No. 07-2007. Atlantic Metropolis Centre, Halifax.

—2008. "Recent Immigrants in a Rural Nova Scotia County: A Tentative Typology." *Our Diverse Cities* 5 (Spring).

Fontaine, L. 2008. "L'immigration rurale et francophone en Nouvelle Écosse." *Canadian Issues* (Spring):73-5.

Gallant, N. 2007a. "La francophonie minoritaire et l'immigration: Enjeux symboliques." Colloque de l'Observatoire de l'immigration hors metropoles, immigration en dehours des metropoles et territoire(s). ACFAS, UQTR (May).

—2007b."Ouverture et inclusion identitaire en milier francophone minoritaire: Quand les immigrants sont la minorite dans une minorite." *Nos diverses cites* 4:93-7.

—2007c. "Representations de l'acadianite et du territoire de l'Acadie chez des jeunes francophones des Maritimes." In *Acadies, francophonies, sous la direction,* ed. M. Paquet and S. Savard, 323-47. Quebec: Presses de l'Universite Laval.

Gallant, N., and C. Belkhodja. 2005. "Productions d'un discours sur l'immigration et la diversite par les organisames francophones et acadiens au Canada." *Études ethniques canadiennes* 37(3).

Gallant, N., C. Belkhodja, and P. Dugas. 2005. "L'intergration des immigrants dans les communities francophones rurales minoritaires." Symposium dur la repopulation rural, Secretariate rural, Moncton, November 2005.

Greater Halifax Partnerships. 2010. "Immigration Leadership Council." At http://www.greaterhalifax.com//home/about_the_partnership/Projectsinitiatives/immigration/leadership_council.aspx (accessed 2 May 2010).

Halifax Regional Municipality. 2010a. "HRM Immigration Action Plan." At http://www.halifax.ca/communications/ImmigrationActionPlan.html (accessed 2 May 2010).

Halifax Regional Municipality. 2010b. "Newcomers." At http://www.halifax.ca/newcomers/index.html (accessed 2 May 2010).

Halifax Regional School Board. 2006. "Student Identification Survey Update and Employee Identification Survey." At http://www.hrsb.ns.ca/files/Downloads/pdf/reports/2005-2006/January/06-01-918.pdf

—2010. At http://www.hrsb.ns.ca (accessed 2 May 2010).

Health Team Nova Scotia. 2008. "Cultural Competence Guidelines for the Delivery of Primary Health Care in Nova Scotia." At http://www.healthteamnovascotia.ca/cultural_competence/CulturalCompetenceGuidelines_Summer08.pdf

Human Resources Skills and Development Canada. 2010. "Canada-Nova Scotia Agreement on Labour Market Development." At http://www.rhdcc-hrsdc.gc.ca/eng/employment/partnerships/labour_market_development/ns/index.shtml (accessed 2 May 2010).

Immigrant Settlement and Integration Services (ISIS). 2010. At http://www.isisns.ca (accessed 2 May 2010).

Kazemipur, A. and S.S. Halli. 2001. "Immigrants and 'New Poverty': The Case of Canada." *International Migration Review* 35:1129-56.

Marshall, S. 2009. "We Are Most Ourselves When We Are Changing": Michael Winter, Lynn Coady, Lisa Moore, and the Literary Reconfiguration of Atlantic Canadian Regionalism." PhD thesis, Department of English, Dalhousie.

McNiven, J. and M. Foster. 2009. "The Developing Workforce Problem: Confronting Canadian Labour Shortages in the Coming Decades." At http://www.aims.ca/site/media/aims/WorkforceProblem.pdf

Multicultural Association of Nova Scotia (MANS). 2010. At http://www.mans.ns.ca (accessed 2 May 2010).

Nova Scotia Advisory Council on the Status of Women. 2004. "Immigrant Women and a Framework for Immigration to Nova Scotia." At http://women.gov.ns.ca/pubs2004_05/immigration%20brief%20oct%2019-04.pdf

—2011. "A Guide for Immigrant Women." At http://women.gov.ns.ca/immigrant-women.html (accessed 8 September 2011).

Nova Scotia Association of Regional Development Authorities. 2010. At http://www.nsarda.ca (accessed 2 May 2010).

Nova Scotia Co-operative Council. 2010. "Immigrant Small Business Program." At http://www.nsco-opcouncil.ca/serv_microcredit.php (accessed 2 May 2010).

Nova Scotia Department of Community Services (DCS). 2010. At http://www.gov.ns.ca/coms/department/documents/DVPC_recommendations.pdf/econ/ofsp (accessed 2 May 2010).

Nova Scotia Department of Economic and Rural Development. 2010a. "Business Information." At http://www.gov.ns.ca/econ (accessed 2 May 2010).

—2010b. "Opportunities for Sustainable Prosperity." At http://www.gov.ns.ca (accessed 2 May 2010).

Nova Scotia Department of Education (DoE). 2010a. "Diversity, Multiculturalism and Racial Equity." At http://www.ednet.ns.ca/index.php?t=sub_pages&cat=1009 (accessed 2 May 2010).

—2010b. "Skills and Learning Branch Moving." At http://www.ednet.ns.ca/lwd.shtml (accessed 2 May 2010).

Nova Scotia Department of Labour and Workforce Development (LWD). 2007. "Skills Nova Scotia Action Plan, 2006–2007." At http://skillsnovascotia.ednet.ns.ca/documents/SkillsActionPlan06-07_web.pdf

—2009. "Nova Scotia Annual Plan, 2008–2009." At http://www.gov.ns.ca/lwd/lmda/docs/LMAAnnualPlan0809.pdf

—2010a. "Canada-Nova Scotia Labour Market Agreement Annual Implementation Plan, 2009–2010." At http://www.gov.ns.ca/employmentnovascotia/lma-information/documents/LabourMarketAgreement2009-2010Implementation Plan.pdf

—2010b. Nova Scotia Department of Labour and Workforce Development. "Labour Market Agreements." At http://www.gov.ns.ca/lwd/lmda (accessed 2 May 2010).

Nova Scotia Human Rights Commission. 2010a. "Human Rights Act." At http://www.gov.ns.ca/legislature/legc/statutes/humanrt.htm (accessed 2 May 2010).

—2010b. "Initiatives." At http://www.gov.ns.ca/humanrights/initiatives.asp (accessed 2 May 2010).

Nova Scotia Office of Immigration. 2007. "Annual Accountability Report for the Fiscal Year 2006-07." At http://novascotiaimmigration.ca/sites/all/files/documents/publications/corporate-documents/FINAL_2006-07_accountability_report.pdf

—2010a. "Immigration Web Development Funding." At http://novascotiaimmigration.ca/sites/all/files/documents/publications/Immigration_Web_Development_Funding_Projects.pdf (accessed 2 May 2010).

—2010b. "Labour Market Agreement for Immigrant Programs." At http://novascotiaimmigration.ca/node/110 (accessed 2 May 2010).

—2010c. "Nova Scotia Nominee Program." At http://novascotiaimmigration.ca/nova-scotia-nominee-program (accessed 2 May 2010).

—2010d. "Programs." At http://novascotiaimmigration.ca/programs (accessed 10 April 2010).

—2010e. "Services en français." At http://novascotiaimmigration.ca/services-en-francais (accessed 2 May 2010).

Nova Scotia Public Service Commission. 2010a. "Summer Diversity Program." At http://www.gov.ns.ca/psc/v2/jobCentre/careerStarts/hiring/summerDiversity.asp (accessed 2 May 2010).

—2010b. "Diversity Accommodation Fund." At http://www.gov.ns.ca/psc/v2/employeeCentre/diverseWorkforce/accommodationFund.asp (accessed 2 May 2010).

—2010c. "Diversity Talent Pool." At http://www.gov.ns.ca/psc/v2/employeeCentre/diverseWorkforce/talentPool (accessed 2 May 2010).

Office of the Auditor General Nova Scotia. 2010. "Chapters from the Reports of 2008 Relating to Office of Immigration." At http://www.oag-ns.ca/imm.html (accessed 2 May 2010).

Pictou Chamber of Commerce. 2005. *Update.* At http://www.pictouchamber.com/updates/update0205.pdf

Pier 21. 2010. "About Canada's Immigration Museum Pier 21." At http://www.pier21.ca/about (accessed 26 August 2011).

Port of Halifax. 2010. At http://www.portofhalifax.ca (accessed 2 May 2010).

Progress Media. 2010. *Nova Scotia Open to the World Magazine.* At http://www.progressmedia.ca/content/subscribe/open-to-the-world (accessed 2 May 2010).

Rebelo, S. 2005. "Recognition of the Credit History of New Immigrants." Atlantic Canada Economics Association Meeting, Halifax.

Schellenberg, G. 2007. "Canadian Social Trends: Immigrant Perspectives on Their First Four Years in Canada." Statistics Canada (April). At http://www.statcan.gc.ca/bsolc/olc-cel/olc-cel?catno=11-008-X20070009627&lang=eng

Statistics Canada. 2006. "Immigration in Canada: A Portrait of the Foreign-Born Population. Census: Immigrants in the Provinces and Territories." At http://www12.statcan.ca/census-recensement/2006/as-sa/97-557/p8-eng.cfm

—2011. "Major Religious Denominations, Nova Scotia, 1991–2011." At http://www12.statcan.ca/english/census01/Products/Analytic/companion/rel/tables/provs/nsmajor.cfm

Tastsoglou, E. and J. Peruvemba. 2009. *Immigrant Women in Atlantic Canada: Feminist Perspectives.* Toronto: Women's Press.

UNESCO. 2010. "International Coalition of Cities Against Racism." At http://www.unesco.org/shs/citiesagainstracism (accessed 2 May 2010).

United Way of Halifax Region. 2008. "2008 Annual Report." At http://www.unitedwayhalifax.ca/about/annual-reports

YMCA Halifax/Dartmouth. 2010. "Immigrant Services." At http://www.ymcahrm.ns.ca/search (accessed 2 May 2010).

CHAPTER 11

NEWFOUNDLAND AND LABRADOR: CREATING CHANGE IN THE TWENTY-FIRST CENTURY

REETA CHOWDHARI TREMBLAY AND AMANDA BITTNER

In 2008, Statistics Canada reported that the population of Newfoundland and Labrador was 507,895 as of 1 July. That number was 1,436 more residents than at the same point a year prior, reversing a trend of decline that had characterized the previous 16 years. The historic decline had resulted largely from out-migration in search of employment, due to the 1992 closure of the northern cod fishery, as more than 20,000 fishermen and fish plant workers were put out of work by the fisheries moratorium. Two other factors played a major role in population decline in the province: a drop in the birth rate, from once among the highest in the country to among the lowest, and a high death-to-birth ratio. Indeed, while recent population statistics suggest some growth, Newfoundland and Labrador has some distance to go before reaching its 1991 all-time population high of 568,474. Whether the recent steady state in population figures can even be sustained is to yet to be seen. This will largely depend upon in-migration of workers and the aggressive implementation of the province's two-year-old immigration strategy.

In June 2005 the discussion paper "An Immigration Strategy for Newfoundland and Labrador: Opportunities for Growth" was released, announcing the province's intention to develop an immigration strategy. The document became the basis for the government's consultations with several provincial stakeholders, including the business community, labour organizations, the education sector, and women's groups. In 2007 the government officially launched its immigration strategy, Diversity – Opportunity and Growth. An official provincial proactive approach has

Integration and Inclusion of Newcomers and Minorities across Canada, ed. J. Biles, M. Burstein, J. Frideres, E. Tolley, and R. Vineberg. Montreal and Kingston: Queen's Policy Studies Series, McGill-Queen's University Press.

been essential in light of two facts. First, while Atlantic Canada in general has received a small proportion of Canadian immigrants, Newfoundland and Labrador's share was the smallest amongst the four Atlantic provinces for the period 2001–06. Moreover, the province fared the worst in terms of the retention of its newly arrived immigrant population. Table 1 depicts trends over the five year period.

TABLE 1
Annual Arrivals of Immigrants to Atlantic Canada

	2001	2002	2003	2004	2005	2006	Total Arrivals	Resident in 2006	Retention Rate (2001–06)	Retention Rate (1996–2001)
NS	1,700	1,418	1,474	1,770	1,929	2,585	10,876	6,900	63	48
PEI	134	106	153	310	330	565	1,598	855	54	60
NL	393	407	359	579	496	511	2,745	1,440	52	48
NB	798	706	665	795	1,091	1,646	5,701	4,295	75	67
Total	3,025	2,637	2,651	3,454	3,846	5,307	20,920	13,490	64	52

Sources: Akbari (2008); CIC website, "Facts and Figures."

In their 2007 study of socio-economic and demographic profiles of immigrants in Newfoundland and Labrador, Akbari et al. label the province "immigrant scarce" in contrast to "immigrant abundant" regions such as Ontario, Quebec, and British Columbia. They note that "from the 2001 Census, immigrants represent a very small proportion of the population of Newfoundland and Labrador. For example, as of 2001, immigrants account for 1.5 percent of its total population of Newfoundland and Labrador. In comparison with the 1986, 1991, and 1996 census data, this proportion has been remarkably constant at approximately 1.5 percent" (Akbari et al. 2007, v).

While recognizing that immigration has the potential to address the demographic challenges facing the province and that it can contribute to economic development by fostering innovation as well as addressing the skill shortage in the labour market, the provincial immigration strategy has broader objectives, as its title suggests – the building of an inclusive and diverse community. The goals of building awareness of the benefits of immigration among the population, while simultaneously trying to create and foster supportive communities to welcome immigrants from "new cultures," are accompanied by specific strategies for their integration and retention. With the understanding that immigration helps enhance the economic, social, and cultural growth of the province through both diversity and innovation, the government of Newfoundland and Labrador announced both the launch of its immigration strategy and the establishment of an Office of Immigration and Multiculturalism. The office has been mandated to promote active and inclusive citizenship, to encourage the province's population to welcome newcomers, and to promote cross-cultural dialogue and understanding. In June 2008, the office launched the government's policy on multiculturalism – an integrated policy where the goals of creating an inclusive citizenry cut cross all sectors of the society, such as education, health, law, youth, and business. The province is making substantial efforts to rectify past practice in order to increase the number of immigrants and to ensure that they will find a welcoming environment that will help them to decide to stay.

A Brief History of the Province: Immigration and Diversity

Newfoundland and Labrador has an exceptionally complex and variegated history of settlement and migration. From early scattered fishing communities and through colonization to well into the late nineteenth century, the British, mostly English and Irish, came to settle in Newfoundland. The colonial government saw the economic advantages of immigration. For example, Sir John Glover, governor of Newfoundland in 1876–81 and 1884, noted "the great disadvantage under which this country suffered was that it was so entirely undermanned. A country one-sixth larger than Ireland with a population of 210,000 has a good deal of room to spare. We want our solitudes filled up and our resources developed" (Bassler 1994, 166). With its attempts to diversify its economy beyond the fishery through the development of railways, mining, and forestry, the colonial government hoped to compensate for the loss of its emigrating unskilled and underemployed rural population through the immigration of skilled workers from Europe. Sean Cadigan observes, "From the mid-nineteenth century, there had been a trickle of German, Norwegian, Dutch, and Danish immigrants, who came to work as merchants, ships' captains, medical professionals, engineers, and entrepreneurs, particularly in mining and forestry. The colony became a home to a smaller number of Chinese immigrants and refugees from among the persecuted minorities of Eastern Europe, such as Polish Jews, or of the Ottoman Empire, such as Maronites, Druze, or Christian Syrians. These immigrants became an important, if not particularly welcome, part of Newfoundland society and economy" (2009, 66). However, these numbers were very small, and the island saw virtually no net in-migration. Repeated efforts to attract British settlers, Finnish farmers, and Swedish lumbermen in the early twentieth century all proved to be largely unsuccessful. The last major influx, thus, remained confined to English and Irish immigration to Newfoundland in the nineteenth century.

Bassler attributes the attitude of the local elite, labelled "the fishocracy" (in 1900, the traditional fish merchants controlled 15 firms in Newfoundland and through these firms dominated the export of fish and other consumer-oriented trade activities), for blocking the promotion of a proactive public policy encouraging immigration. Instead, through their influence on the members of the Legislative Council, they encouraged the restriction of the so-called "undesirable immigrants" (1994, 155). Following the Canadian trend of anti-Asian sentiment (as illustrated by the *Chinese Immigration Act* of 1885 requiring that Chinese Immigrants pay a $50 head tax, the *Coal Mines Regulation Act* of 1890 limiting the use of Chinese labour in certain industries such as mining, and the subsequent increase of head tax in 1903 to $500), in 1904 Newfoundland's House of Assembly passed legislation preventing the entry of Chinese and Japanese immigrants. The Legislative Council defeated the bill, although the reasons were fundamentally economic rather than due to "progressive thinking" – they feared retaliation by the Chinese against British and Newfoundland goods. Nevertheless, in 1906, Newfoundland's open door immigration policy officially ended with the passage of *An Act to Regulate the Law with Regard to Aliens* modelled on the British *Alien's Act* and *An Act Respecting the Immigration of Chinese Persons* modelled on the Canadian *Chinese Immigration Act*. The latter imposed a $300 head tax on Chinese immigrants. The Chinese were also required to register. The Chinese community was to be restricted to a maximum of 200 persons and only to male members. Moreover, the passage of these two acts allowed the Newfoundland government to declare undesirable anyone suffering from a financial, physical, mental, or criminal debility and anyone likely to become a charge on the public purse (ibid.).

Treatment of the new immigrant population was to undergo further deterioration during the First World War. In 1914 Newfoundland passed the *War Measures Act*, giving unprecedented powers to the government to detain, arrest, or deport anyone perceived to be the enemy of the state. Cadigan records that the government "detained almost everyone from Germany or the Austro-Hungarian Empire as enemy aliens, including Moravian missionaries in Labrador, although most of the people who came to St John's were Jews leaving Eastern Europe. The war proved to be an uneasy time for most immigrants, except Syrian Christians, who openly supported the British effort because of the persecution of their communities in Ottoman Empire" (Cadigan 2009, 190).

The *1926 Immigration Act* further restricted immigration to Newfoundland by providing a more efficient way of handling unwanted immigrants by authorizing the exclusion of certain races, ethnicities, nationalities, and occupations. Additionally, it gave the government the power to prescribe the minimum amount of money, depending on race, occupation, and destination, that an immigrant must possess on landing (ibid.). Moreover, the act authorized the deportation of immigrants belonging to any race deemed unsuited to the climate or the requirements of the colony or immigrants of any specified class, occupation, or character. As a consequence, the few immigrants who were allowed to settle in Newfoundland were quite homogeneous. In 1932, exacerbated by the Depression, the 1926 act was replaced by a proclamation disallowing immigration for two years from all Central and East European countries, of all races from Asia and Africa, and non-natives from the labour class. Although the 1932 proclamation lapsed after two years, the practice of prohibiting immigrants from the non-British category continued (ibid.).

When Newfoundland joined Canada in 1949, laws restricting access to Newfoundland were no longer determined by Newfoundland but rather by Canadian immigration policy. As such, previous immigration policies that were restrictive in nature were replaced by Canada's comparatively more open policies that did not discriminate by nationality, race, ethnicity, social class, or occupation. As a result, Newfoundland experienced a small net in-migration of new Canadians and mainland personnel who had been excluded prior to 1949.

Demographics

The current demographic picture of the province reflects the historic legacy of immigration policies. Based on numbers from the 2006 Census, approximately 48.5 percent of the population is male, and 84 percent of the population is over the age of 15, with over two in five of this age category above the age of 50. The median age is almost 42. These numbers are indicative of a population that is aging fairly quickly, particularly given the halving of the birthrate over the last 20 years.[1]

The population distribution within the province is concentrated in a few areas. The bulk of residents (nearly 36 percent of the total population) are located in the metropolitan area of the provincial capital, St John's, which includes most of the province's largest cities and suburbs. The next largest Census Metropolitan Areas (CMAs) include Corner Brook on the west coast of the island with 5.3 percent of the population, Grand Falls-Windsor with 2.7 percent, and Bay Roberts with 2.1 percent.

While the remaining 46 percent of the population is dispersed throughout the province, the overall linguistic and cultural makeup is fairly uniform. Figure 1 compares linguistic makeup of the province as a whole in comparison with that of St John's (Census Metropolitan Area), Atlantic Canada, and Canada overall.

Nearly 98 percent of the population claims English as its mother tongue, while French is the mother tongue for less than 0.4 percent of the population. The other 1.5 percent claim a non-official language as their original language, including a number of different Aboriginal languages and European languages, as well as some from Africa, the Middle East, South America, and South and East Asia.

FIGURE 1

Language Spoken at Home and Mother Tongue: Newfoundland in Comparison with Other Parts of Canada, 2006

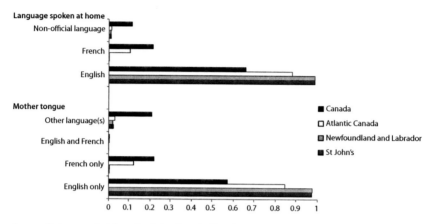

Source: Data compiled from Statistics Canada (2006).

The lack of linguistic diversity in the province is mirrored in the pattern of ethnic origins, according to 2006 counts. Nearly 48 percent of the population claims a "Canadian" ethnicity, whether through single or multiple mentions. Further, the other major ethnic origins claimed are largely from the United Kingdom, particularly when we examine multiple mentions: 43 percent claim English heritage, 21 percent claim Irish heritage, 7 percent identify as Scottish, 6 percent are French, and 7.7 percent claim Aboriginal, Inuit, or Métis ethnicity. Single mentions of these ethnic backgrounds are substantially smaller. The major ethnic groups thus reflect an older, historic picture of immigration and settlement rather than the more contemporary pattern that we see in other provinces across Canada. Figure 2 looks at the proportion of those claiming visible minority status.

As these numbers suggest, the total visible minority population in the province is relatively small at just over 1 percent of the population. Of these, 28 percent include those of South Asian descent; 23 percent are Chinese, 16 percent are black, 5 percent are Filipino, 8 percent are Latin American, and 2 percent are Southeast Asians. The proportion of visible minorities in St John's nearly reaches the proportion found in Atlantic Canada as a whole. Among visible minorities in the province, most are of Chinese or South Asian descent, with a substantially smaller black population in comparison to Atlantic Canada as a whole.[2]

Indeed, the total number of non-citizens constitutes less than 1 percent of the population, and the number of immigrants residing in

Newfoundland in 2006 was 8,385, or less than 1.5 percent of the total provincial population. Of these, 64 percent had immigrated prior to 1991. The remaining immigrants arrived in gradually increasing numbers from 1991 to 2006 (695 between 1991 and 1995, 855 between 1996 and 2000, and 1,440 between 2001 and 2006). Figure 3 compares the number of immigrants in Newfoundland with those in the rest of the country.

FIGURE 2
Visible Minority Status: Newfoundland in Comparison with Other Parts of Canada, 2006

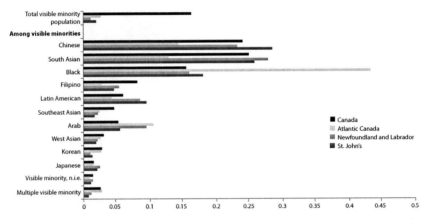

Source: Data compiled from Statistics Canada (2006).

FIGURE 3
Patterns of Immigration: Newfoundland in Comparison with Other Parts of Canada, 2006

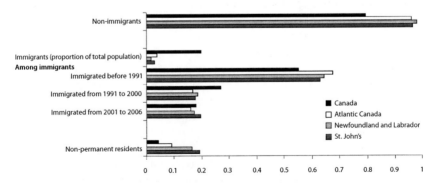

Source: Data compiled from Statistics Canada (2006).

The pattern around temporary residents in the province tells a part of the story surrounding the demographic breakdown in Newfoundland and Labrador. Table 2 lists the number of temporary residents in the main categories for which temporary residents are admitted to the province. The data suggest that the total number of temporary residents has not changed substantially over time, but the distribution of residents within each of the categories has changed slightly.

TABLE 2
Temporary Residents, 1998–2007, by Category

	1998	1999	2000	2001	2002	2003	2004	2005	2006	2007
Foreign Workers	1,065	1,597	2,092	2,145	2,226	2,298	2,271	2,355	1,935	2,263
Foreign Students	821	906	923	916	1,018	1,039	1,104	1,264	1,451	1,738
Humanitarian	101	177	185	194	182	182	164	149	128	96
Other[a]	845	827	877	1,055	902	1,240	1,015	1,024	766	663

[a]"Other" includes those not fitting into the other categories but for whom a temporary visitor's permit or visitor record was issued.

Source: Data obtained from CIC (2007).

As Table 2 suggests, the number of foreign students has increased gradually in the last ten years, more than doubling since 1998, with half of that growth having occurred in the last two years. The number of foreign workers has also doubled since 1998, but most of this growth occurred by 2000, and numbers have slowed since that time. Similarly, the number of temporary residents in the "humanitarian" category peaked in 2001 and has since decreased, with 2007 reflecting numbers even lower than in 1998.

Examining trends among permanent residents provides some additional insight into the nature of immigration to Newfoundland and Labrador. Figure 4 compares recent immigration trends in Prince Edward Island and Newfoundland and Labrador to trends in Atlantic Canada as a whole.[3]

The data suggest that in Atlantic Canada as a whole, the largest group of immigrants arrive as economic immigrants, followed by refugees, followed by those in the family class. The region has made substantial gains in immigrants in the last decade, nearly doubling the total number of permanent residents. PEI and NL combined have made proportionately larger gains, nearly tripling the total number of immigrants in that same period. Figure 5 illustrates these trends.

The majority of immigrants in the province arrived from Europe (48 percent) or the United States (17 percent), with 12 percent immigrating from the Middle East, Central, and South Asia, 9.3 percent from Eastern and South East Asia, 6.7 percent from Africa, and 6.4 percent from South

FIGURE 4
Immigrant Trends: Number of Permanent Residents by Category, 2008

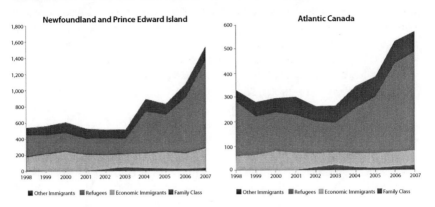

Source: Data obtained from CIC (2008).

FIGURE 5
Immigrant Trends: Total Number of Immigrants,
Newfoundland and Prince Edward Island Compared to Atlantic Canada, 2008

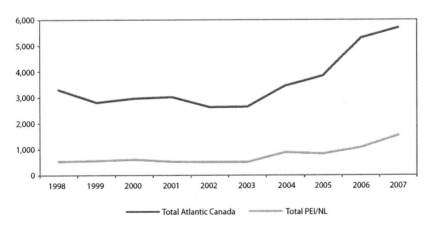

Source: Data obtained from CIC (2008).

and Central America. The more recent immigrants (those arriving between 2001 and 2006) came primarily from the latter regions mentioned above, suggesting that contemporary immigration patterns do mirror those of the rest of Canada, with increased immigration from Africa, Asia, and South America, although 34 percent of recent immigrants arrived from either the United States or Europe.

Religious diversity is also relatively minimal, with most claiming affiliation with some form of Christianity. Historically, the two main religious groups in the province were Catholics and Protestants, and with the secularization of the school systems in the province in 1997, the role of religion appears to be gradually decreasing. According to the 2001 Census, 37 percent of the province's population was Catholic, 26 percent was Anglican, 17 percent United Church, 8 percent Salvation Army, and nearly 7 percent Pentecostal. Approximately 2.5 percent claim no religious affiliation. The remainder of the population is divided among numerous other religions, including Jews, Buddhists, Sikhs, Muslims, Hindus, and others. None of these groups constitutes more than 0.1 percent of the province's population.

A total of 23,455 residents identify themselves as Aboriginal. Of these, 33 percent are North American Indian, 28 percent are Métis, and 20 percent are Inuit.[4] The Aboriginal population of Newfoundland and Labrador is younger in comparison to the rest of the province's population, with 77 percent of Aboriginal people over the age of 15. Of these, only one in five is over the age of 50, compared with two in five in the population as a whole. The median age is 32.

This relatively young Aboriginal population has a lower high school completion rate than that of the provincial population as a whole. Of Aboriginal people aged 15 or older, 58 percent have at least a high school certificate. Of those who have a high school certificate or more, 67 percent have continued with their education and achieved a diploma, degree, or trade. Within the population as a whole, 66 percent of Newfoundlanders and Labradorians have completed high school or more, and of those in this category, 67 percent have continued with their education and achieved a diploma, degree, or trade. Thus amongst those who continue their studies beyond high school, both Aboriginal and non-Aboriginal populations achieve success in higher education at similar rates.

Only 14 percent of the adult population (aged 25–64) in Newfoundland and Labrador were university graduates in 2006, below the national average of 23 percent. Moreover, 26 percent in this age category had not finished high school, a much larger proportion than the national average of 15 percent. About 22 percent of the province's adults had a college diploma, while 20 percent had a high school diploma. Some 15 percent had a trades certificate as their highest level of educational attainment, a proportion second highest among the provinces, behind Quebec. Similarly, the vast majority (86 percent) of post-secondary graduates obtained their certificate, diploma, or degree in the province. This proportion of students "studying local" is second only to Quebec. Overall, education levels in the province are increasing. The proportion of the total population with a high school diploma increased by 4 percentage points between 2001 and 2006, suggesting that the education gap is decreasing. In comparing the immigrant population with the population as a whole, it becomes clear that immigrants tend to be more educated overall: 37.4 percent hold a bachelor's degree or higher.

There were 113,970 full-time, full-year earners in Newfoundland and Labrador in 2005. The median earnings for these workers in 2005 were $37,429, up from $36,079 in 2000. The median earnings were lower among the women in this group, however. The median earnings for women working full time in 2005 were $31,130, up from $30,292 in 2000. The number of workers increases when we incorporate part-time or seasonal workers. The total number of individuals receiving some earnings in 2005 was 271,250. Of these, the median income was $18,086, down from $19,746 in 2000. Focusing on women only paints a different picture again, as the median income for all women earners was $14,346 in 2005, up from $13,922 in 2000. Median income for all of these groups was lower than the national average, which may reflect the lower levels of education in the province compared with the national average.

The picture painted by the census and the CIC data suggests a province of relative cultural homogeneity compared with the rest of the country, including few linguistic, religious, or ethnic differences. The level of immigration has traditionally been low, although recent numbers suggest a gradual increase, particularly in the last five years. The population is aging, the level of education is increasing, and income levels, while lower than the national average, are increasing, especially among those who work full time.

FEDERAL-PROVINCIAL COLLABORATION

Prior to recently embarking upon its own strategy for immigration, after Confederation Newfoundland and Labrador tended to let the national government provide policy direction in the area of immigration. Vineberg points out that while initially the postwar Canadian national government "perceived immigration as a national program and, therefore, assumed full responsibility for recruitment, selection and admission of immigrants" (2009, 14), by 1966 some provincial governments had created their own immigration units. Several Canadian provinces were beginning to realize the significance of immigration and its link to economic and socio-cultural development, but Newfoundland and Labrador was not amongst those creating their own immigration initiatives. With the introduction of the 1976 Canadian *Immigration Act*, which authorized the minister of immigration to enter into immigration agreements with the provinces, a new era of federal-provincial cooperation and consultation was ushered in:

> In the spirit of the new *Immigration Act*, the federal government had invited all provinces to enter into agreements even prior to proclamation of the act and it persuaded two other provinces to sign on along with Quebec. On 20

February 1978 Bud Cullen, the Minister of Employment and Immigration, and Marc Lalonde, the Minister of State for Federal-Provincial Relations, signed the Canada-Nova Scotia Immigration Agreement, and three days later they signed the Canada-Saskatchewan Immigration Agreement. Over the next year, the provinces saw that the agreements might help to meet growing needs and immigration agreements were also concluded with Newfoundland, New Brunswick and Prince Edward Island. Each agreement was different and was negotiated to meet both federal and provincial needs while establishing mechanisms for ongoing consultation and cooperation. The agreements spawned different procedures, directives and sub-agreements in each province, but in every case they brought about improved communications and understanding on the part of both levels of government. (Vineberg 2009, 38)

Later, with continued efforts on the part of the federal government to devolve certain responsibilities with regards to immigration, as well as the growing demands from the Atlantic and Prairie provinces to regionalize immigration policy, the Provincial Nominee Program (PNP) was developed in 1995 to meet specific local and regional economic immigration objectives. This program would allow each province to identify economic immigrants to meet specific regional needs.

Newfoundland and Labrador and the Provincial Nominee Program (PNP)

The Canada-Newfoundland and Labrador Agreement on Provincial Nominees was first signed in 1999 and then re-signed in 2006. The agreement sets the framework for "the province to determine the specific needs of the province vis-à-vis immigration"; for Canada and Newfoundland and Labrador to "share all pertinent information related to prospective and actual immigrants' applications for nomination in the provincial nominee class"; for "tracking of provincial nominees to Newfoundland and Labrador for a minimum of three years from their date of entry, as a basis for assessing the effectiveness of targeted recruitment and integration and retention activities"; for Newfoundland and Labrador to "undertake targeted active recruitment initiatives designed to implement its Nomination Plan"; and for the federal government "to assist Newfoundland and Labrador to identify prospective immigrants to fulfill Newfoundland and Labrador's targets in its immigration strategy." Most significantly, this agreement gave Newfoundland and Labrador "the sole and non-transferable responsibility to assess and nominate candidates who, in Newfoundland and Labrador's determination, will be of benefit to the economic development of Newfoundland and Labrador and have a strong likelihood of becoming economically established in Newfoundland and Labrador" (CIC 2006).

The main focus of the Newfoundland and Labrador Provincial Nominee Program is addressing skill shortages and labour market requirements. In a recent Harris Centre workshop on immigration and settlement, Nellie Burke, executive director with the Newfoundland and Labrador Office of Immigration and Multiculturalism, summarized the objectives of the PNP as threefold: "to enhance the provincial economy; to address particular skills shortages and gaps in identified sectors and regions of the province; and to increase the population base and enhance social and cultural development" (Harris Centre 2008). In addition to its initial categories of occupation/skilled workers and immigrant entrepreneurs, in 2008 the PNP broadened its priorities to include family connections and international graduates. The latter category allows international students who have graduated from a recognized Newfoundland and Labrador post-secondary educational institution to be considered for nomination for permanent residence in Canada. The family connections category allows sponsorship of family members by eligible permanent residents or Canadian citizens who reside in Newfoundland and Labrador (Government of NL 2009).

It is estimated that since the program's inception, 530 individuals have been nominated to immigrate to Canada. In January 2009, John Noseworthy, Newfoundland and Labrador's auditor general, severely criticized the program in his annual report. He argued that "the province does not know how many of the 530 individuals it nominated moved to Newfoundland and Labrador ... As a result, it is not possible for the province to make any conclusion about whether the PNP achieved its goals of attracting and retaining immigrants to the province" (Auditor General of NL 2009, 321). He also pointed to the absence of follow-up and the lack of monitoring, particularly of the nominees under the entrepreneurial category. In response to his criticisms, Susan Sullivan, the provincial human resources minister, pointed out that the report covers an eight-year period. Initially the Department of Innovation, Trade and Rural Development administered the PNP program. In April 2007 it was brought under the jurisdiction of the Department of Human Resources, Labour and Employment (HRLE). This sectoral shift also implied a shift in the program's focus – from attracting investment to focusing more on people and the labour needs of the province. Sullivan referred as well to the program's emphasis on attracting skilled workers and international graduates in the scientific and medical fields. These developments suggest an increased focus on behalf of the province in appealing to and retaining immigrants who would assist in the province's development in terms of innovation and research and development. In its response to the auditor general, HRLE stated that the report did not reflect "current practice":

For most of the period covered by the report, the PNP was administered by the Department of Innovation, Trade and Rural Development (INTRD). The report covers an eight-year period of which HRLE has administered the program for 19 months (April 2007-November 2008). Therefore, much of the information is dated and does not reflect current practices. The mandate of INTRD included economic development through business and investment attraction. As a result, the PNP was utilized to fulfill that mandate. Since the program has been in HRLE, the focus has shifted to the attraction and retention of skilled workers, international graduates and their families. The area of immigration in general and specifically the Provincial Nominee Program are quite complex. There are instances throughout the report which reference the process whereby an individual may immigrate to the province through the Provincial Nominee Program, but in order to clearly and adequately understand this process, further clarification is required. For example, all nominations do not necessarily result in a permanent resident visa being issued by the federal government which has the sole jurisdiction for deciding who enters Canada. In some cases nominees are refused a visa. Also, of the 530 nominations, approximately one third are still in the federal processing system at embassies abroad and would not be expected to officially settle in the province until some time in the future. Therefore, until they are issued a permanent resident visa, they will not show up on a "landing" report. Furthermore, sometimes individuals are recorded as "landed" in another province, usually Ontario or British Columbia, because they entered Canada though either the Toronto or Vancouver airport. (Department's Response," in Auditor General of NL 2009, 337-8)

The department's response also pointed out that since its inception, the Provincial Nominee program has undergone three different iterations that the auditor general's report does not take into account in its assessment. For example, HRLE said, "during the early years of the PNP, the investment transaction was deemed to be a private matter between the local business and the prospective immigrant. As the program evolved, tighter regulations were put in place including a Performance Contract and a Good Faith Deposit. Furthermore, the Partner category, through which most of applications were previously processed, was discontinued in August 2008" ("Department's Response," in Auditor General of NL 2009, 339)

INTEGRATION, SETTLEMENT, AND INCLUSION OF NEWCOMERS AND MINORITIES

Newfoundland and Labrador's 2007 launch of its provincial immigration strategy, Diversity – Opportunity and Growth, was combined with a government commitment of over $6 million over three years (Government of NL 2007, 8-12). The integration, retention, and inclusion of newcomers into Newfoundland society feature prominently in this strategy. While the HRLE has the primary responsibility for this initiative, the provincial immigration strategy is intended to be integrated or holistic, cutting across functional and sectoral boundaries. The provincial government departments and agencies (aside from HRLE) that share in responsibility for the integration/settlement of newcomers and the inclusion of minorities include the Departments of Education, Health and Community Services, Innovation, Trade, and Rural Development, and the Rural Secretariat.

The Office of Immigration and Multiculturalism: Coordinating Immigration and Multiculturalism

HRLE established the Office of Immigration and Multiculturalism in 2007. At a cost of $4.1 million over three years, the office is responsible for promoting the province to prospective immigrants, implementing retention measures, and enhancing settlement and integration services. The remaining $1.9 million of the government's $6 million commitment goes to support immigration initiatives within the departments of Education, Health, and Community Services and the Women's Policy Office. One of the major tasks of the Office of Immigration and Multiculturalism was to formulate the government's multiculturalism policy. This was accomplished in June 2008. In introducing the policy, the HRLE minister underlined the goals of this initiative to create an inclusive and welcoming society:

> The Office of Immigration and Multiculturalism will partner with community groups and agencies and other government departments to promote active and inclusive citizenship that respects the rights and responsibilities of all. The new policy encourages residents of the province to welcome newcomers into our communities. It serves to support people from diverse cultural backgrounds who make Newfoundland and Labrador their new permanent home. It celebrates the cultural mosaic of Newfoundland and Labrador and recognizes the collective contribution being made to grow the province. It also promotes cross-cultural understanding and highlights the importance of public awareness and education regarding the benefits of a diverse and vibrant population. (Government of NL 2008b)

To assist the office in implementing its mandate, two major initiatives were undertaken by the provincial government. First, a new interdepartmental ADM Committee on the Provincial Immigration Strategy was established to assist the office. The role of this ADM Committee is to ensure that government policies and programs support the provincial immigration strategy by coordinating immigration and multicultural initiatives in their respective departments and reporting annually on the progress of their departmental commitments to deputy ministers and ministers. Second, a Multiculturalism Working Group was established to assist executive staff, including ministers, deputy ministers, and assistant deputy ministers, in identifying and managing specific activities/initiatives related to implementation of the policy on multiculturalism within government departments and at the local, regional, and community level.

Since the launch of the policy, the Office of Immigration and Multiculturalism has held a series of provincial focus groups at the municipal level, and committee meetings were held with various stakeholders and government departments to obtain input into the implementation process. During September and October 2008, a total of 13 focus groups were held in ten locations: Happy Valley-Goose Bay, St Anthony, Corner Brook, Stephenville, Clarenville, Marystown/Burin, Carbonear, Gander, Grand Falls-Windsor, and St John's. In addition, three sessions were held in St John's, to which specific participants such as francophone stakeholders, women's groups, and education stakeholders were invited. The ultimate goal of these groups has been to establish effective partnerships to leverage funding and promote multicultural activities at the regional and community level. All participants expressed widespread support for the policy of multiculturalism and acknowledged the economic and cultural contributions of the diverse immigrant community. There was also a general consensus that municipalities and their leaders are key partners in ensuring the successful implementation of the provincial goals. Some of the specific suggestions made by the participants included:

- Promoting awareness of policy at all levels of government;
- Establishing a linkage between the multiculturalism policy and the provincial strategic cultural plan;
- Enhancing awareness within curriculum in the formal educational system;
- Establishing settlement services outside the city of St John's; and
- Increasing the province's capacity to provide services in rural areas (Government of NL 2009).

Sharing the Responsibility: Role of Provincial Departments and Agencies

The Department of Education's mandate is to increase awareness within the education system of the benefits of immigration. This task is to be accomplished by distributing information to the Newfoundland and Labrador Teachers' Association, school boards, and other education stakeholders, as well as by updating the multicultural education policy.

The Department of Health and Community Services will play an important role in the province's immigration strategy, particularly in regard to the recruitment and retention of immigrant physicians and other health care professionals. The province has historically relied on physicians from other countries to provide medical services for its residents, and while the province has been successful in recruiting immigrant physicians and health care professionals, the same success does not exist in regards to retention. This department will thus focus on developing retention strategies to provide incentives for physicians to remain in the province.

Women and women's issues hold a key position in the immigration strategy, as they are viewed as central to the retention of newcomers. Accordingly, the Women's Policy Office is to implement and support the development and distribution of information and resource material to assist immigrant women during pre-arrival, arrival, and settlement. As a result of this policy emphasis, HRLE, in collaboration with the federal government's Status of Women's Partnership Program, sponsored the Multicultural Women's Organization of Newfoundland and Labrador to deliver five workshops for immigrant women in Newfoundland and Labrador on such issues as legal aid, child care, and poverty (Government of NL2008a).

Although it has been shifted out of INTRD to HRLE, the Provincial Nominee Program figures prominently in the provincial immigration strategy to attract new immigrants. The department has set out a plan to increase the province's capacity for innovation to be competitive and prosperous in the changing global marketplace. Increased immigration has been shown to cultivate new ideas, new ways of thinking, new expertise, access to capital, and access to global markets. INTRD has been given responsibility for guiding the economic development of the nine key regions of the province. Economic development strategies have been identified for each region based on its particular strengths. Short, medium, and long term strategies will be continually identified for each region to generate new industry, small business, and employment opportunities. The department's mandate also includes the creation of a climate conducive to innovation in business through the facilitation of research and development, technology transfer, and technology commercialization within provincial industries and individual business enterprises. Increased immigration, particularly of international graduates and recruitment of skilled workers, investment capital, skill transfer, and access to foreign markets, are some of the elements that are perceived to be essential to grow and diversify regional economies.

The Rural Secretariat will play an important role in the province's immigration strategy as it seeks to build awareness of the benefits of immigration and diversity. This will be accomplished by promoting the benefits of increased immigration to the members of the regional council, supporting the delivery of cultural awareness workshops for regional communities, providing promotional materials to council members, and encouraging participation by immigrants in civil society through, for example, municipal councils, zone boards, school boards, and non-governmental organizations.

Role of Municipalities

To date, municipalities within the province have not played a prominent role in the integration and retention of immigrants. Other than focus group discussions conducted by the Office of Immigration and Multiculturalism in 14 city locations, there has been little activity at the municipal level. The province launched a Newfoundland and Labrador Immigration Portal in March 2009 and has engaged 20 municipalities in developing their own community portals. Municipal governments will, however, have to take on a greater role in the province's immigration strategy. The province intends to partner with the Newfoundland and Labrador Federation of Municipalities to build awareness of the potential for immigration to address community development needs. Workshops for municipalities interested in attracting and retaining immigrants will also be held, and municipalities will be encouraged to promote their communities through websites, which will also be linked to the provincial immigration website.

Universal Service Providers

At present the Association for New Canadians is the only universal service provider to newcomers, and it is doing a commendable job. It is widely acknowledged that the province needs a broader network of such organizations, which could play a significant role in the integration and retention of immigrants. While universal service providers have not been explicitly included in the province's immigration strategy, there is a general recognition that the availability of services must be increased. In addition, there are only a few non-governmental organizations that have undertaken the responsibility to address the needs of new immigrants, and their role is quite peripheral. A welcoming community has been identified as being key to the successful retention of immigrants (Government of NL 2005a). As such, there is the potential for universal service providers to extend their current activities to create welcoming communities for immigrants.

The Association for New Canadians (ANC)[5]

The ANC, the only federally funded immigrant service agency in the province, has been in operation for the past 26 years and has a staff of 50, of which approximately 25 percent are immigrants. Nearly 100 volunteers assist the association in program delivery (Government of NL 2005b). Since its inception, the organization has grown significantly and is now a full service immigrant settlement agency offering a comprehensive array of programs and services to the newcomer community throughout the province. Over the years the ANC has grown substantially and the infrastructure now includes a head office, an ESL and employment training centre with child-minding and licensed daycare facilities, a reception house, and several housing units.

The ANC's mandate is to empower immigrants with the skills, knowledge, and information necessary to become independent contributing members of their communities (ANC 2007). It aims to provide settlement services to immigrants and refugees, to facilitate their successful integration into Canadian life, and to foster understanding and awareness in Newfoundland and Labrador society through a comprehensive array of community education and volunteer programs. In order to fulfill its mandate, it provides a variety of services including public education activities, life skills training, interpreters and translators, cultural awareness/sensitivity activities, and refugee complainant services. It also offers programs including a Host Program, Language Instruction for Newcomers to Canada Program (LINC), Resettlement Assistance Program (RAP), Linguistic Eligibility Determination (LED), AXIS Employment Program, Settlement Workers in the Schools (SWIS), Integration Support Programs (Special Initiatives), targeted programming for women, men, children, and youth, and research/development projects.

The Resettlement Assistance Program (RAP) was created to ensure that newcomers would receive the information and services necessary to become settled in their new communities and to become independent and self-sufficient. These support services are available to pre-approved Government Assisted Refugees upon arrival in Canada. The program gives newcomers a basic orientation and information about Canada and the variety of federal and provincial programs available to them, including language instruction and employment resources. The Immigrant Settlement Adaptation Program (ISAP) is designed to supplement the RAP and includes any support services that are offered to newcomers to assist them in integrating into their new community. These services include interpretation and translation services as well as referrals to community resources and government programs and services. The RAP and ISAP programs are traditionally provided for one year but can be extended to a maximum of three years. The duration of the individual's participation in a program is decided overseas when he or she first applies for resettlement in Canada.

The association has wide-ranging English language programs. The Language Instruction for Newcomers to Canada (LINC) Program, a federally funded English as a Second Language program assists adult learners in acquiring the language skills necessary to settle and integrate into Canadian society. Some of the ESL programs offered include the Enhanced Language Training Program (to provide newcomers with occupationally specific language training coupled with career bridging services), the Test of English as a Foreign Language (TOEFL) and Test of English for International Communication (TOEIC) Preparation Course, and Precise Pronunciation – Clear Speech Concepts for Newcomers Program (for immigrants and refugees who currently have a reasonable level of fluency but who require assistance with pronunciation and accent reduction). In addition, the association offers several volunteer programs for newcomers to improve their linguistic abilities. Volunteer tutors are matched with newcomers requiring one-on-one assistance in learning English. Throughout the school year, volunteer tutors provide homework assistance, reinforce language and literacy skills, and provide support for exam preparation.

The Acquiring Experience, Integrating Skills (AXIS) Program provides a wide variety of employment services to internationally educated professionals and tradespersons. Career Essentials (providing current information on Canadian labour market conditions plus comprehensive employment assistance services), Strategic Transitions and Employment Partnerships (a career placement service), Career Connections Workshops, Occupation-Specific Language Training, and Portfolio Preparation Seminars are some of the services and programs. In 2006–07, with funding from Human Resources and Social Development Canada (HRSDC) and in collaboration with the provincial government, the Department of Education, and HRLE, the association undertook the Foreign Credential Recognition (FCR) Project. The first phase of the project identified potential employment barriers and suggested actions required to break down these barriers and effective incentives for hiring immigrants. Phase 2 of the project is currently underway.

Other association programs are aimed towards children and youth. The Settlement Workers in the Schools Program (SWIS) assists children and youth with their transition into the Canadian school system and the community. The program currently assists approximately 150 immigrant children and youth throughout the elementary, junior, and senior high school system. Through this program, association staff work closely with ESL teachers to facilitate immigrant children's transition to the regular school system. In 2008, with funding from the Department of Education, the association offered a three-week summer enrichment program, targeting immigrant students aged 13–21, with the goal of addressing learning gaps. It aimed to help students retain knowledge gained throughout the school year and to provide skills and information that would assist them in the upcoming school year. The program was again approved and delivered in 2009. On the heels of the success of SWIS, the association developed an after-school enrichment program. Offered twice weekly, it provides assistance to immigrant and refugee students to strengthen their English language and math skills and offers directed instruction one day per week along with one day of supervised homework support. This initiative is administered with support from the Department of Education, the Eastern School District, and ESL teachers. Since 2006, the ANC has been also been delivering a program designed to improve the literacy rate among refugee children. The sessions are designed to engage both child and parent, focusing on diversity, promoting the value of reading while supporting improved language, literacy, and numeracy skills development. In addition to all the above-mentioned programs, each year the association coordinates a summer program for immigrant children.

The ANC is also actively promoting services in the area of health for both the immigrant and refugee populations through three specific programs. Since 2007, the association has partnered with Eastern Health to provide a public health nurse to deliver basic health services to newcomers for one to two days per week. In addition to basic services, this program provides vision and hearing screenings, preschool health assessments, Healthy Beginnings and Long Term Healthy Beginnings follow-ups, and liaison with communicable disease nursing staff as well as the Department of Health and Community Services. Through the Public Health Nurse Partnership program, the association also provides health information on a variety of issues such as infection control and communicable diseases, nutrition, healthy eating, sexuality, feminine hygiene, menstruation, cervical screening, and birth control. In addition to hosting a public health nurse, the association has also retained a settlement health worker whose main role is to educate the immigrant and refugee population on preventive health care practices and to promote a healthier lifestyle among an at-risk population. In partnership with Memorial University's medical faculty, first and second year medical students take medical histories and match the client or clients (if a family) with a physician. Interpreters are used when required.

The association is also aware of the need for creating support structures for immigrant individuals and families. The ANC's Family Reunification Support Group provides support and assistance to those awaiting reunification. In addition to promoting recreational activities such as sporting events, social nights, movies, summer barbecues, and holiday celebrations, the association has dedicated a common room where volunteers and newcomers can meet and socialize.

A number of documents developed by the ANC assist newcomer integration and promote their inclusion into Canadian society. These include the *Newcomers' Guide to Services and Resources, Immigrant Parents' Guide to the Newfoundland and Labrador School System, An Anthology of Immigrant Entrepreneurs,* and *Peace and Harmony: A Society of Respect* (a component of Diversity Training Project). The association also offers a toll-free helpline to provide information on settlement and language supports, community, health, employment, and recreation services as well as general information and referral to a variety of federal, provincial, and municipal government programs.

To promote cross-cultural awareness and understanding, under the rubric of the Diversity Training Initiative the ANC has offered targeted training modules that address themes and topics related to cultures, stereotypes, prejudice, discrimination, respect, inclusion, human rights, and accommodation. In March 2009 the association hosted a diversity symposium for business. The issues addressed related to current employment practices and explored different methods that would lead towards the creation of a welcoming and inclusive working environment.

The association actively collaborates with its external partners – municipal, provincial, federal and NGOs – to fulfill its mandate of welcoming, including and integrating the newcomers into the province of Newfoundland and Labrador. The organizational mechanism for this multi-leveled collaboration is the Coordinating Committee on Newcomer Integration (CCNI). Formed ten years ago, the CCNI is a partnership between the ANC, municipal, provincial, federal departments, and the Harris Centre of Memorial University. The committee actively participates in activities such as forums and workshops sponsored by different government departments/agencies and organizations, to respond to emerging immigration and citizenship issues.

Non-Governmental Organizations

The provision of services for immigrants by NGOs is still in its infancy in the province. Some organizations exist, but unlike the ANC, they have minimal levels of funding and are run largely on volunteer input. They include the Refugee and Immigrant Advisory Council, the Multicultural Women's Organization of Newfoundland and Labrador, and the Coalition on Richer Diversity. It is widely acknowledged by the community as well as government that more effort is required to ensure the success of these organizations, and efforts to increase their resources are gradually being made, although they are still in their early stages.

The Refugee and Immigrant Advisory Council Inc (RIAC) is a nonprofit organization that provides advice, support, and settlement services to immigrants and refugees within the province (RIAC 2008). Its many services include orientation in the community, counselling and assisting with crises, conversational and language classes, and the provision of translators. The council employs no full time staff and depends strictly on volunteers, approximately 20 working within the office and an additional 15 volunteers for the provision of the above services. RIAC receives no government assistance and relies exclusively on donations from individuals and religious groups.

The Multicultural Women's Organization of Newfoundland and Labrador (MWONL), a provincial voluntary non-profit organization, comprises seven non-salaried executives as well as one volunteer who organizes workshops and various programs. The organization has no funding from the provincial government but occasionally receives money from Status of Women Canada to complete research projects on issues related to immigrant women. The organization recently received a $13,000 investment from the Atlantic Canadian Opportunities Agency, through its Women in Business Initiative, to expand MWONL's annual food and craft show (MWONL 2010). The show is designed to promote entrepreneurship among immigrant women by giving them an opportunity to sell products representative of their homelands.

The Coalition on Richer Diversity (CORD) is an umbrella organization that reaches out to organizations, groups of immigrants, and those who provide social services, offering networking opportunities, encouraging them to collaborate and helping them to become sensitive to diversity (Coalition on Richer Diversity 2007). CORD's aim is to create more opportunities, assess needs, further develop services, and ease the pressures on social support systems. Its organizational structure is volunteer based, with a core group of individuals and organizations working with others and promoting solutions and new approaches. Funding comes exclusively from fundraisers and donations in kind.

Universities and Colleges

The provincial government's immigration strategy indicates that Memorial University, the College of the North Atlantic and private training institutions will play key roles. As the Provincial Nominee Program aims to attract larger numbers of international students with the objective of bringing more potential immigrants to the province, the government hopes to work with universities to increase post-secondary international student enrolments. By providing a quality educational experience and assisting in the successful integration of international students into the province's society and culture, it is hoped that an increased number may opt to make Newfoundland and Labrador their permanent home. And since educational institutions offer employment opportunities to newcomers, that aspect will also play a key role in the retention of immigrants within the province.

There is a great deal of convergence between the provincial government's goal to pursue an immigration strategy for the province, and Memorial's recently developed strategic plan. The five pillars of its strategic plan include 1) students, 2) research and scholarship, 3) the needs of the province, 4) conditions for success, and 5) institutional responsibility.

The plan makes a clear commitment to playing a major role in the province's cultural, social, and economic development. The university can bring its expertise out into the communities of Newfoundland and Labrador, actively engaging in a dialogue to learn more about the issues facing these areas. As well, the university can implement models to enable better knowledge and research transfer throughout the province. In addition to these actions, Memorial is undertaking efforts to grow international student enrolment and expand the international focus and opportunities to students.

At present, students from 80 countries are enrolled at Memorial. The university is working to diversify its student body even more, intensifying its international recruitment activities. Two significant steps have been taken by the province to help in this area. First, the province and the Government of Canada signed a memorandum of understanding in 2005 allowing international students to work in the province for up to two years after graduation. Second, in 2008, the provincial government extended health insurance privileges to international students, making international recruitment easier for the university.

Research on immigration issues, another prominent responsibility of post-secondary educational institutions within the province, will also play an important role in the successful implementation of the province's immigration strategy. At present there is a negligible research capacity on immigration-related issues at Memorial.[6] The Leslie Harris Centre for Regional Policy and Development of Memorial University undertook a major initiative, organizing an Immigration and Settlement Workshop in March 2008 (funded by the Newfoundland and Labrador Office of Citizenship and Immigration Canada). The workshop brought together decision-makers, practitioners, and academic researchers to discuss the current state ofknowledge about immigration issues and to identify key research questions relevant to immigration in the province. The workshop addressed questions such as current trends in attracting, integrating and retaining immigrants, the knowledge gaps experienced by provincial, federal and non-governmental stakeholders, and opportunities for collaboration between governments, NGOs, immigrants, and university researchers (Harris Centre 2008).

Following this workshop, the university undertook two major initiatives. The Harris Centre established a fund for research projects dealing with two broad themes: first, how to increase the number of immigrants to Newfoundland and Labrador; and second, how to retain those immigrants who already reside in the province. As well, the Faculty of Arts at Memorial has created a research cluster bringing together faculty and students interested in immigration issues. This network shares knowledge, engages in research projects, and generally builds Memorial's capacity to undertake work in the field of immigration.

CHALLENGES

While substantial changes have taken place over the last five years to increase immigration to Newfoundland and Labrador, a number of key challenges remain. These challenges are related to recruitment and retention, the provincial labour market, and the dearth of information and research on immigration in the province.

Recruitment of Immigrants

Attracting immigrants is a key factor in ensuring that immigration numbers increase in the long term. Attraction is a common problem for all of Atlantic Canada, as noted in this chapter's introduction. Simply put, Atlantic Canada is considered "immigrant scarce," and the draw for immigrants to this region is not the same as for other parts of the country. The challenge for Newfoundland and Labrador is to identify, recognize, and promote a competitive edge in the region. A number of factors have the potential to appeal to prospective immigrants, and provided these are widely promoted, the province may be able to ensure greater immigration numbers in the future.

The province is at an advantage economically compared to the rest of the region. While other Atlantic Canadian provincial economies are shrinking, Newfoundland and Labrador has a growing economy and has recently moved from "have not" to "have" status within the Canadian federation. Strong economies generally mean more jobs, more entrepreneurial opportunities, and more resources for economic development (including increased investment in innovation and the "creative class"), and the potential is there for success and financial security for prospective immigrants.

The central position of Memorial University in the province is also a key advantage to potential immigrants. As the largest university in Atlantic Canada, it has strong provincial support to recruit international students and faculty. Increasing excellence in research and development as well as making greater efforts to promote and develop international linkages provide a welcoming environment for potential immigrants that will lead to improvements in both recruitment and retention.

Retention of Immigrants

While Newfoundland and Labrador increases its appeal to potential immigrants, a number of challenges still exist in ensuring that they do not leave. In particular, the province will need to make efforts to support and promote organizations such as the ANC. With additional funding and

resources for existing groups, as well as the creation of an environment
that allows for the introduction of new organizations, newcomers to the
province will be better able to avail themselves of services, resulting in
greater likelihood of integration, job satisfaction, and a sense of community belonging. All these are integral to retention. NGOs do not necessarily
emerge from the grassroots level (particularly with few resources), and
thus there is room for the provincial government to step in and support
the creation of key organizations to promote community development.

The role of municipalities is currently underdeveloped, and is essential
to a successful long-term immigration strategy. Immigration cannot be
concentrated only in urban communities, and as such municipalities will
need to take on a leadership role in developing and fostering welcoming
environments, ensuring that resources exist for newcomers outside St
John's. Welcoming communities are necessary for families to be made
to feel at home, particularly when it comes to spouses accompanying
primary wage-earners, in order to ensure that the isolation that may set
in does not become a problem.

Labour Market Issues

According to the Canadian census, the number of full time earners has
risen in the province between 2000 and 2005, and the percent change in
median earnings has grown by a higher rate than in the rest of Atlantic
Canada, suggesting that the labour market is one of increasing opportunities. The legacy of the province, however, is one of "have not" status,
out-migration, and limited economic growth. As a result, there is room
for promoting a new provincial image, one of a growing and shifting
economy. As efforts are made to develop knowledge-based industries to
complement existing strengths in resource-based industries, the potential
for increasing immigration increases, alongside with greater innovation
and encouragement of the "creative class."

Research on and Information about Immigration

A key mechanism to improving the immigration status of the province
from "immigrant scarce" to "immigrant rich" is linked to increasing information about immigration in general – to Canada, to Atlantic Canada,
and to Newfoundland and Labrador specifically, as well as to other
jurisdictions world-wide with similarities to the province. In general,
the state of information and knowledge on the issues of immigration to
the province is one of scarcity, and the dearth of information prevents
a solid understanding of the issues present, and the potential strategies
for moving forward. Needed is evidence-based research into the issues

surrounding immigration to Newfoundland and Labrador, and at present there is no systematic structure of information available.

The university has begun to play a key role in this arena, acting as a broker between researchers and political actors both outside and inside of the province, and providing an academic environment fostering further research in this area. By developing an inventory of current and existing research from all sources, and working with immigration specialists on an international level, the province has the potential to determine needs, challenges, and strategies to ensuring both recruitment and retention of newcomers, as well as cultivating an environment that is welcoming of diversity and multiculturalism.

Conclusions

Newfoundland and Labrador has undergone substantial change over the past decade, given the history of the province. The provincial government has recognized the need to counteract the effects of out-migration and an aging population, and combined with increased attention to the importance of education, economic diversity, research and development, and innovation, it has directed its efforts towards issues surrounding immigration.

The province is poised for change, and the circumstances are ideal. A growing economy and recently developed resource wealth have provided the provincial government with tools to widen its focus and expand its efforts towards economic diversity and provincial growth. These circumstances have led to the creation of the provincial immigration strategy Diversity – Opportunity and Growth, as well as a new Office of Immigration and Multiculturalism. Both developments suggest that provincial resources and support are being allocated in order to increase the focus on immigration in Newfoundland and Labrador, with efforts being made to ensure that the province assists in developing a welcoming community, open and encouraging of greater diversity. Provided that efforts are made to extend evidence-based research into the issues surrounding immigration to regions with circumstances similar to that of the province, and provided that the state assists in the creation of political culture and the civil society necessary to facilitate long-term growth in diversity, the future looks promising.

Notes

The authors would like to thank Dr Smita Joshi, director, Multiculturalism, Office of Immigration and Multiculturalism, Department of Human Resources, Labour and Employment, Government of Newfoundland and Labrador, for her helpful and insightful comments on an earlier draft of this paper. We would also like to thank Scott Hagell and Garikai Chaora for their research assistance in this project.

1. Recent data from the Centre for Health Information of Newfoundland and Labrador suggest that the birth rate in the province is on the rise. A total of 4,905 babies were born in the province in 2008, an increase of 7 percent since 2007. The province's birth rate rose from 9.0 per 1,000 in 2007 to 9.6 per 1,000 in 2008.

2. The high number in Atlantic Canada compared to both the rest of Canada and Newfoundland and Labrador reflects the proportionately large black population in Nova Scotia.

3. Unfortunately the CIC records that provided these data do not separate Newfoundland and Labrador from PEI in presenting this information. Thus we display the combined results for the two provinces, while noting that the number of total permanent residents arriving in NL was 512 in 2006 and 550 in 2007. This number represents approximately half of all permanent residents to the two provinces in 2006 and approximately one-third in 2007.

4. These numbers do not add up to 100 percent. The remaining individuals either claimed multiple Aboriginal identities, or else did not specify one of the three.

5. The authors would like to think Bridget Foster, executive director of the Association for New Canadians, for providing information about the association's mandate and activities.

6. In total there are four studies, two of them sponsored by the Harris Centre. Harris Centre supported studies include "A Survey of the Attitudes of Employers in Newfoundland and Labrador toward the Recruitment and Employment of New Canadians and International Workers," W. Locke and S. Lynch (2005); and "The Role of International Medical Graduates in the Provision of Physician Services in Atlantic Canada," R. Audas, A. Ross, and D. Vardy (2004). The other two studies are S. Reitmanova and D.L. Gustafson's "Mental Health Needs of Visible Minority Immigrants in a Small Urban Center: Recommendations for Policy Makers and Service Providers," *Journal of Immigrant and Minority Health* (2008) and their "'They Can't Understand It': Maternity Health and Care Needs of St. John's Immigrant Muslim Women," *Maternal and Child Health Journal* (2008).

References

Akbari, A. 2008. "Immigrant Inflows and Their Retention Rise in Atlantic Canada." Working paper series, Atlantic Metropolis.

Akbari, A., S. Lynch, J.T. McDonald, and W. Rankaduwa. 2007. "Socioeconomic and Demographic Profiles of Immigrants in Newfoundland and Labrador." Working paper series, Atlantic Metropolis.

Association for New Canadians (ANC). 2007. "History of ANC." At http://www.anc-nf.cc/history_of_anc.html

Auditor General of Newfoundland and Labrador. 2009. "Report of the Auditor General to the House of Assembly on Reviews of the Departments and Crown Agencies, for the Year Ended 31 March 2008." At http://www.ag.gov.nla.ca/ag/annualReports/2008Annualreport/AR2008.pdf

Bassler, G.P. 1994. "Deemed Undesirable: Newfoundland's Immigration Policy, 1900–1949." In *Twentieth Century Newfoundland: Explorations*, ed. J. Hiller and P. Neary. Newfoundland History Series 7. St John's: Breakwater Books.

Cadigan, S.T. 2009. *Newfoundland and Labrador: A History*. Toronto: University of Toronto Press.

Citizenship and Immigration Canada (CIC). 2006. "Canada-Newfoundland and Labrador Agreement on Provincial Nominees, 2006." At http://www.cic.gc.ca/English/department/laws-policy/agreements/nfld/can-nfld-2006.asp#1_0

— 2007. "Immigration Overview: Permanent and Temporary Residents." *Facts and Figures 2007*. At http://www.cic.gc.ca/english/resources/statistics/facts2007/permanent/17.asp

— 2008. *Facts and Figures 2008 – Immigration Overview: Permanent and Temporary Residents*. At http://www.cic.gc.ca/english/resources/statistics/facts2008/permanent/11.asp

Coalition on Richer Diversity (CORD). 2007. "CORD: What Is It About?" At www.cancord.org/about.html

Government of Newfoundland and Labrador. 2005a. "An Immigration Strategy for Newfoundland and Labrador: Opportunity for Growth." Discussion paper. At http://www.hrle.gov.nl.ca/hrle/publications/immigration/ImmigrationStrategy.pdf

— 2005b. "Retention and Integration of Immigrants in Newfoundland and Labrador – Are We Ready?" At http://www.nlimmigration.ca/media/2854/immigrationstudyfinal.pdf

— 2007. "Diversity: Opportunity and Growth." At http://www.nlimmigration.ca/media/2842/strategydoc-mar07.pdf

— 2008a. "Annual Report of the Women's Policy Office." At http://www.exec.gov.nl.ca/exec/wpo/publications/wpoannrep200708.pdf

— 2008b. "Policy on Multiculturalism." At http://www.hrle.gov.nl.ca/hrle/department/branches/labourmarket/pdf/MultiPolicy.pdf

— 2009. "Policy on Multiculturalism: Report on the Focus Group Session." Department of Human Resources, Labour and Employment. At http://www.nlimmigration.ca/media/10347/final percent20focus percent20group percent20consultations percent20of percent20multiculturalism.indd percent20with percent20communication percent20edits percent208.5 percent20x percent2011.pdf

Harris Centre (Memorial University). 2008. "Report of the Immigration and Settlement Workshop." At http://www.mun.ca/harriscentre/reports/research/2008/Immigration_Workshop_Report.pdf

Multicultural Women's Organization of Newfoundland and Labrador (MWONL). 2010. At http://mwonl.info/

Refugee and Immigrant Advisory Council (RIAC). 2008. "Vision, Mission, Values." At http://www.riac.ca/index.php?option=com_content&task=view&id=16&Itemid=33

Statistics Canada. 2006. "2006 Census Community Profiles." At http://www12.statcan.gc.ca/census-recensement/2006/dp-pd/prof/92-591/index.cfm?Lang=E

Vineberg, R. 2009. "History of Federal-Provincial Relations in Immigration and Integration." Metropolis Seminar, Canada West Foundation, February 2009.

CHAPTER 12

PERSPECTIVES ON INTEGRATION AND INCLUSION IN PRINCE EDWARD ISLAND

PART 1 – BREAKING INTO A CLANNISH SOCIETY: THE SETTLEMENT AND INTEGRATION EXPERIENCE OF IMMIGRANTS ON PRINCE EDWARD ISLAND

GODFREY BALDACCHINO[1]

While Canada earns high marks as a country that looks kindly on immigration, not all parts of Canada qualify. A closer and more discerning approach reveals that those locales where immigrants move to stay continue to remain concentrated in large cities. Rural areas, the sparsely populated northern latitudes, and also Atlantic Canada, all of which lack large cities – find it difficult to attract *and retain* immigrant settlers. Yet the four Atlantic provinces – unlike most of the rural or remote regions of the country – have of late actually been the destination of much larger inflows of immigrants. Despite the influx, the evidence so far suggests that few of these newcomers choose to stay in the region. While "hyper-diversity" (Biles, Burnstein, and Frideres 2008, 3) may be what brands Canada, mono-culturalism still largely rules in Atlantic Canada.

As well as the author's own familiarity with the immigrant story on "the Island" and in the region, based on both primary and secondary research (especially Baldacchino 2006, 2008; Baldacchino and Hood 2008; Baldacchino and McAndrew Fall 2008; Fall 2008), this chapter reflects the author's personal observations and experience since immigrating to Charlottetown, Prince Edward Island, with his wife and son from Malta in July 2003.

Integration and Inclusion of Newcomers and Minorities across Canada, ed. J. Biles, M. Burstein, J. Frideres, E. Tolley, and R. Vineberg. Montreal and Kingston: Queen's Policy Studies Series, McGill-Queen's University Press.

The Regional Picture

The Atlantic region suffers from a series of vicious cycles that contour the migration experience, with no end in sight. Stagnant or slow population growth, or even population decline, is a function of a recent history without significant migration. While the country as a whole absorbs a whooping 250,000 or so newcomers every year, Atlantic Canada attracts only around 2.6 percent of these, even though the region comprises some 7 percent of the national population (Fall 2008, 55). Although visible minorities now represent some 75 percent of immigrants to Canada, the proportion of visible minorities in the Atlantic provinces remains abysmally low, ranging from 0.8 percent (NL 2001) to 3.9 percent (NS 2001), with a mean of 2.2 percent of the total resident population (2001 Census). (The latest 2006 census registers a change in this range from 1.1 percent (NL 2006) to 4.2 percent (NS 2006), with a mean of around 2.6 percent, but a commentary on this follows below.)

Moreover, the retention rate of those immigrants who *do* come to the region is equally poor when compared to the rest of the country. Along with Saskatchewan, the four Atlantic provinces have consistently had the lowest retention rates of immigrants by province in the country, ranging from 36 percent (NL) to 62 percent (NB). Such a record of immigrant attraction and retention makes the region less attractive to would-be immigrants, perpetrating the cycle (see Tables 1 and 2).

TABLE 1
Relationship between Population Change and Proportion of Visible Minorities in the Local Population, 2001–2006

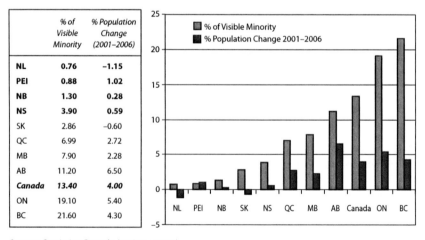

	% of Visible Minority	% Population Change (2001–2006)
NL	0.76	–1.15
PEI	0.88	1.02
NB	1.30	0.28
NS	3.90	0.59
SK	2.86	–0.60
QC	6.99	2.72
MB	7.90	2.28
AB	11.20	6.50
Canada	*13.40*	*4.00*
ON	19.10	5.40
BC	21.60	4.30

Source: Statistics Canada (various years).

TABLE 2
Relationship between Immigration Retention Rates and Proportion of
Visible Minorities in the Local Population, 2001–2006

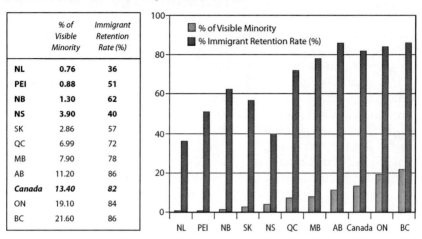

	% of Visible Minority	Immigrant Retention Rate (%)
NL	**0.76**	**36**
PEI	**0.88**	**51**
NB	**1.30**	**62**
NS	**3.90**	**40**
SK	2.86	57
QC	6.99	72
MB	7.90	78
AB	11.20	86
Canada	*13.40*	*82*
ON	19.10	84
BC	21.60	86

Source: Statistics Canada (various years).

The outcome of these dynamics is that the Atlantic provinces linger on as locales that seem impervious or immune to the waves of immigrants that are impacting and changing other parts of the country. In its booklet *Welcome to Canada* (2004 edition), Citizenship and Immigration Canada (CIC) can only list seven "key immigrant serving organizations" located in the four Atlantic Provinces.[2]

ENTER PRINCE EDWARD ISLAND

With a surface area of just over 5,500 square kilometres, and a population of 140,000, Prince Edward Island is the smallest of Canada's ten provinces. An island on the Atlantic seaboard of North America, the territory has been inhabited by the Mik'maq First Nations people "since creation." It became, as Île St Jean, a part of New France; most of its Acadian community was expelled by the British in 1758. Thereafter, the new colony was settled by immigrants mainly of Scottish Presbyterian or Irish Catholic background. These waves of new settlement slowed significantly in the 1840s, allowing the existing population and its descendants to craft an Island identity around a strong sense of rooted pride, robust communities, ownership, and proprietary rights. The PEI Population Strategy Panel (1999, 56) explained that such a legacy fostered, and celebrated, "a strong cultural norm of sameness." Given the small size of this community, and the intertwined roles and relationships, this Island identity is bolstered by pervasive and cross-cutting family, kin, party political and Christian church networks.[3] These socio-political networks provide a whole range of commendable supports and services that explain much of the Island's cultural vibrancy, its cohesiveness in relation to external "threats," the resilience of its voluntary sector, and the high level of voter participation in the polls.[4] It is this complex set of connected homogeneity and rich social capital – supported by a very accessible provincial government – that constitutes the Island community and society. This is what recent immigrants – largely excluded from this nexus – have explained as finding bewildering, exasperating, clique-like, clannish, small-minded, even racist, and invariably difficult to plug into. No wonder immigrants find themselves befriending and confiding in other immigrants. The Islander versus the "come from away" category is an important contemporary social divide on PEI (just like the red-blue partisan one) and contributes to a reservoir of mutual misunderstanding (Baldacchino 2006, 74).

On the occupational front, PEI is a small economy with a labour force of just 76,800 (Service Canada 2011). With this labour force, it has to run a comprehensive provincial infrastructure, contribute to the federal effort, maintain traditional economic industries which are primarily seasonal (farming, fishing, forestry, tourism), and still launch itself into the beckoning future (aerospace, bio-science, knowledge industries, clean energy). This is a very tough undertaking, and some of the consequences, even when things go well, include significant seasonal employment, wages and salaries remaining below the national average, and workers expected and obliged to be multi-functional and polyvalent rather than too finely specialized.[5] Immigrants express frustration about lack of suitable job openings, lack of full-time positions, and the inability to specialize (Baldacchino 2006, 49-51).

Prince Edward Island exhibits the same vicious cycle of immigrant attraction and retention that bedevils the whole Maritime region. While Ontario has hundreds of immigrants attending citizenship ceremonies at the rate of *three a day*, PEI typically has three citizenship ceremonies *a year*, with the highest number of those invested with Canadian citizenship in any particular ceremony being around 75 (CIC official, Charlottetown, personal communication, June 2008). The 2006 Census reports a total visible minority population[6] of 815 in the provincial capital of Charlottetown (2.6 percent of its total resident population), followed by 185 in Summerside (1.3 percent), 130 in Stratford (1.8 percent), 40 in Montague (2.3 percent) and 25 in Cornwall (0.5 percent) (Canadian Press 2008a). According to census data, the proportion of visible minorities in PEI's population has gone up marginally from 0.9 percent in 2001, to 1.3 percent in 2006.

"Migration" to and from PEI is mainly inter-provincial, with 2,000 to 3,000 annual movements registered in and out of the province from the rest of Canada, a flow that is 10 to 20 times higher than the comparable, in-and-out-movement of non-Canadians. The source of most immigrants to PEI remains Ontario. No wonder, then, that only three CIC officials – recently up from a complement of two – staff the Charlottetown office that services the province. The PEI Provincial Government's Population Secretariat, set up in 2004 with just one person, was staffed in the interim by a complement of three (Biles 2008, 160-1, Table 1) but boasted a staff of 10 in 2009.

The province has seen various institutional and semi-formal measures developing of late, meant largely to attract and retain immigrants specifically on its territory. Notable amongst these measures are:

1. *The Provincial Nominee Program.* In April 2001, PEI embarked on a pilot partnership agreement with the federal government for a five-year term, which has since been extended. Through this agreement, a Provincial Nominee Program (PNP) was created, administered locally by Island Investment Development Inc., a crown corporation, with Citizenship and Immigration Canada (CIC) acting as overseers (PEI-PNP 2008).

2. *The Population Secretariat.* In 2004, the Government of PEI created the Population Secretariat in order to develop promotional strategies for potential immigrants to PEI, to consider population challenges, and to assist in addressing related inadequacies (as in the labour market) by proposing demographic solutions. The Population Secretariat has also supported research regarding the challenges being faced by immigrants in coming and settling on PEI. Since 2010, the Population Secretariat is officially recognized as the lead agency in supporting the province's first-ever settlement strategy (Government of Prince Edward Island 2010).

3. *The PEI Population Network* (PEI PopNet). The network was formed in December 2006 by some 20 of the participants at an Atlantic Forum on Rural Repopulation in Moncton, NB, along with members of the PEI Rural Team. It is now the standing provincial clearing house for disseminating information about initiatives that deal with immigration, repatriation, and retention in the province, with an overall view to support population growth (Prince Edward Island Population Network 2007).

4. *The PEI Association for Newcomers to Canada (PEI ANC).* Incorporated in 1993, the association is mandated to aid with short-term settlement services and long-term social inclusion and community integration programs for immigrants. As the only support and settlement agency for immigrants on PEI, it rightfully prioritizes cross-cultural awareness and public education programs. Its immigrant client base has been expanding fast and reached 842 in November 2007, of which 569 were beneficiaries of the PNP.

5. *The Islander by Choice Alliance (IBCA).* A "friendly group of people who love PEI," this self-help initiative by civil society is meant to facilitate social and cultural integration by newcomers. The IBCA "is a non-profit organization (soon to be incorporated) that works to create information, resources, and networking opportunities for all who are interested in the issues related to being a Prince Edward Islander, an Islander by Choice or Circumstance, a Part-Time Islander by Choice, a CFA ('Comes from Away'), or an Honourary Islander."[7]

PEI also receives refugees, another category of immigrant administered directly through the federal government with the cooperation of the province. In the past decade, PEI has received a yearly average of 60 to 70 refugees, who would be registered with the PEI ANC. Freedom of mobility within Canada inhibits an accurate figure of how many refugees remain on PEI in the medium to long term. However, the PEI ANC staff has estimated that 75 percent of all refugees coming to PEI leave before their second year in the province (Baldacchino 2006, 16).

The Provincial Nominee Program has been responsible for the majority of immigrant landings on PEI since 2006. Applicants are able to apply directly to the PNP and, if the reviewed application and accompanying documents are endorsed, the province submits the paperwork to the federal government for final approval. The waiting period for this process is around eight months, whereas an application for immigration through the conventional channels may take much longer.

Besides examining applications for fraudulent documentation and the financial requirements, the provincial criteria for immigration via the PNP focus on four main initiatives: increased business and economic development; the supply of skilled workers; increased population; and achievement of provincial demographic, social, and cultural objectives (see www.gov.pe.ca). The PEI PNP presently has four categories: Professional and Skilled Worker; Immigrant Entrepreneur; Immigrant Partner (or Investor); and Immigrant Connections. The large majority of immigrants to PEI have been provincial nominees in recent years (see Table 3).

TABLE 3
Immigrants to PEI, 1991–2010

Period	1991–96	1996–01	2001–06	2007	2008	2009	2010
Immigrants to PEI	792	765	1,391	992	1,483	1,725	2,581*
Of which are provincial nominees (PN)				690	813	1,560	2,200*

Sources: Statistics Canada (2007b); *PEI Annual Statistical Review*, various years; Government of PEI (2010). * = author's estimates.

The PNP "expedites immigration to Canada for individuals and their families who meet provincial criteria in support of the following initiatives: (1) increased business and economic development; (2) increased supply of skilled workers; (3) increased population, and (4) the achievement of provincial demographic, social and cultural objectives" (PEI PNP 2008). The regulatory process to create the Provincial Nominee Category was concluded for Prince Edward Island in 2001. Like the other original agreements, the agreement was a pilot project with a fixed period and low numerical limits; but, as with all the other agreements concluded since 2002, it was renewed indefinitely and without numerical limits until a federal review and policy change in 2008.[8] With the line-ups to enter the country getting longer for "conventional" immigrants – typically, from five to seven years – the PNP allows a fast-track approach to those potential immigrants who match the identified market needs and can provide a $200,000 investment or more, if applying under the "immigrant investor" or "immigrant entrepreneur" category. A deposit of $100,000 is required, to be repaid to applicants only if they are still in the province of entry 12 months after landing in Canada.[9] The policy is meant to encourage retention in the province of landing; however, the evidence that is building up suggests that, while the program is very attractive, around half of these immigrants actually settle in PEI or the Maritime region.

It is still too early to pronounce definitive judgment on the impact of the PNP. Certainly, it is ensuring that a more affluent immigrant is being given precedence to enter the country. It has also led to larger waves of immigrants being landed in the four Atlantic provinces, possibly the largest in many decades. In the period 2001–06, the annual immigrant inflow in the region rose by 75 percent (from 3,025 registered landings in 2001 to 5,307 in 2006).[10] However, with no social, occupational, or cultural commitment to the province of landing, these droves of PNP-enabled immigrants to PEI have had precious little to keep them there. Having secured the all-important entry ticket into Canada, they often, and quickly, follow the path of so many other immigrants and settle in more populous cities, closer to family, friends and similar language, ethic, religious or cultural groupings, and where they perceive business and employment opportunities to be stronger.[11] Some are even willing to forfeit their PNP deposit while doing so.

Akbari (2008) provides some insights into this flow of newcomers broken down by province. Ironically, while PEI was the province in the region with the *largest* percentage increase in the number of landed immigrants during the inter-census period (from 134 landings in 2001 to 585 landings in 2006, a staggering 437 percent increase),[12] it was the only province in Atlantic Canada that saw its retention rate of landed immigrants actually *fall* from 60 percent to 53 percent in the same period (NB, NL, and NS registered modest increases of 8 percent, 4 percent, and 15 percent, respectively; see Table 4).

TABLE 4
Immigrant Arrival and Retention Rates in Atlantic Canada (by year and province)

	Year						Total Arrivals (2001–06)	Still Resident in Province in 2006	Retention Rate (1996–2001) (%)	Retention Rate (2001–06) (%)
	2001	2002	2003	2004	2005	2006				
NS	1,700	1,418	1,474	1,770	1,929	2,585	10,876	6,900	48	63.4
PEI	134	106	153	310	330	565	1,598	855	60	53.5
NL	393	407	359	579	496	511	2,745	1440	48	52.5
NB	798	706	665	795	1,091	1,646	5,701	4295	67	75.3
Atlantic	3,025	2,637	2,651	3,454	3,846	5,307	20,920	13,490	52	64.5

Number of Permanent Residents – PEI (1998–2008)

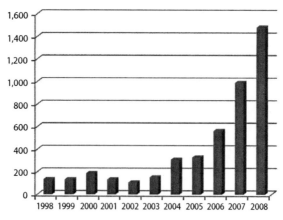

Source: CIC website: "Facts and Figures."

The data need to be complemented and further substantiated by longitudinal data. The *Longitudinal Survey of Immigrants to Canada* (LSIC) created a template and a methodology for tracking and studying the internal migration of immigrants within the country (Houlé 2007; Statistics Canada 2007a). However, the number of respondents from the Atlantic provinces in this research frame was far too small to permit any valid observations for these individual provinces, and only barely large enough to do so for the region as a whole. In any case, the LSIC has now been discontinued.

Socio-Cultural Barriers to Successful Integration

Meanwhile, policy analysts have identified two main barriers to successful immigrant integration: the inability of migrants to adapt to the host society, and systematic discrimination in the host society (Wang and Lo

2007). Both barriers are at work on the Island. PEI's singular cultural mould – already described above as "a strong cultural norm of sameness" (PEI Population Strategy Panel 1999, 56) – is a powerful source of the bonding social capital and resourcefulness that have benefited this small society handsomely in the face of rampant globalization. Growing up in an ascribed network of relatives and friends, most Islanders walk through life in regular company of the same social cohort, with whom they connect and thus reinforce relationships. It is this same intensive social interaction – a "communal togetherness" (Weale 1992, 10) that doubles as a "straitjacket of community surveillance" (ibid., 9) – that can induce Islanders to seek escape and solace via self-imposed exile. For better or for worse, immigrants to Prince Edward Island automatically do not belong to this network. Nor can they ever fully belong, though their children might, if they persevere: one has to be *born* on PEI to be an Islander. Otherwise, immigrants will forever remain "CFAs" – "come from aways." Thus, what is a source of support for self-professed Islanders acts to thwart diversity and can even be perceived as a subtle (but unintentional) form of racism.

Islanders are badly equipped in the skills that would enable them to reach out to newcomers to help them integrate better into the host society: they lack "bridging social capital" (Woolcock and Narayan 2000). The practice becomes effectively, though not intentionally, exclusionary and discriminatory. Newspaper columnist John Ibbitson fails to appreciate the value of social solidarity and is thus harsh in his commentary on the outcome of this, yet another, vicious cycle: "The racial homogeneity is pronounced ... Immigrants shun these communities ... These communities, in turn, display little zeal to attract immigrants, reveling instead in their so-called cultural heritage, which is really a desiccated remnant of Canada's colonial past" (2005, 34). It is not always clear how this tight social webbing acts to exclude newcomers. The dynamics are subtle and not self-evident, and so an example is appropriate.

A National Physician Survey in 2008 reported that only 2 percent of physicians on PEI said that "their doors were open to all new patients": the "most dire" proportion in Canada by province (Canadian Press 2008b). Intending to allay any concerns that this media release may have raised, Dr Alfred Morais, head of the PEI chapter of the College of Family Physicians of Canada, said in an interview to a local newspaper reporter: "What I am seeing in a lot of practices is that they will end up taking new patients, but it is usually in a different way. Maybe it's a family member, or a relative, or a connection of someone they're currently looking after" (Tobin 2008).

That arrangement would work just fine *if* one had a family member, a relative, or some connection already enrolled with a family doctor. Islanders would be relieved by such a comment. But most immigrants would not, since they tend to arrive to settle on the Island without any of these connections. Accordingly, and with all other things being equal, immigrants are therefore more likely to be denied access to a family doctor. This dynamic may work in similar ways with other public goods, effectively cheating at least some immigrants of access or equal treatment.

And so these observable trends continue to bear out two sets of important characteristics. First, no large cities, no immigrant clusters, no perceived economic opportunities, lower wages, and a shortage of health human resources and services all conspire to make the Atlantic region less attractive to immigrants. Second, a tightly webbed "WACS" (White, Anglophone, Christian and Straight/heterosexual) monoculture acts as a rather understated socio-cultural barrier to successful immigrant integration (Baldacchino 2006, 74).

RECENT IMMIGRANTS SPEAK

These characteristics are borne out in responses to a qualitative survey of recent settlers to Prince Edward Island in the autumn of 2005 ("recent" meaning those who had moved to the province with a view to settling there since 1998 and before 2003). The survey's main objective was to move beyond faceless statistics, identifying the real-life stories and narratives behind why people had chosen to move to PEI, had chosen to stay, or else were planning to leave. Within three months, a snowballing strategy had identified 320 respondents who agreed to complete a questionnaire (either web-based or in hard copy) or else consented to being interviewed by trained graduate students (Baldacchino 2006).

Disapproving of a Clannish Society ...

It may come as a surprise that, while a variety of economic reasons are the most often cited inducers towards likely out-migration, the alleged close-mindedness of Islanders is given as the most common explanation for the desire to relocate by the 35 respondents in this study who claimed to be preparing to leave PEI. The Island is seen to be occupied by a clannish, patronage driven, conservative society where "who's your father" is more important than objective and certifiable skill and merit, where privacy is eroded and gossip is rife. By virtue of not being part of this intricately webbed community, immigrants – which, for the purposes of this study, include "other Canadians" – cannot fit in or are not allowed to do so. (Is this also one of the reasons why these immigrants are forced to consider self-employment?) They feel that they are distrusted and discriminated against, and that they are welcome only as long as they are seen as "temps" – temporarily servicing the local labour market. Here are some of their actual commentaries.

Respondent #019: "PEI is too 'closed' a society: fundamentalist ideologies and a distrust of people from away."

Respondent #100: "I feel that, unless one is from PEI, he or she is looked down on. I have felt this while trying to gain and maintain employment. I have had employers tell me that they have received calls complaining about the hiring of someone 'from away' in positions."

Respondent #134: "PEI doesn't treat people as persons who have potential or ability; they treat people as 'sub-categories' such as a daughter of this politician or important member of this party, etc. ... So, people who came from outside have no possibility to get jobs, benefits or social trust."

Respondent #166: "Social life here is nearly non-existent; people are casually friendly, but most don't want you to 'invade their space.' I have made one friend from amongst Islanders; all the others are from away."

Respondent #215: "Islanders seem to welcome people who come to visit for a short time and then leave with open arms, but are very guarded about people who come to stay."

Respondent #269: "I have also found that Islanders are superficially friendly and welcoming. There is great prejudice to people from away that grows increasingly wearing as time goes on."

... But Discovering How to Break into It

More importantly for the purpose of this chapter, and with a view to identifying patterns of successful integration and settlement in the host society, some survey respondents do comment on and identify the critical role played by certain institutions – such as local churches, sport associations, local employers, or local friendship and neighbourhood groups – which can allow newcomers a social space where they may feel sufficiently welcome and at ease. These spaces tend to be non-threatening environments where immigrants (and other newcomers) play a more significant role, are active or involved in greater numbers, and interact with hosts in a manner that does not reinforce or showcase their difference.

Breaking into PEI society, therefore, may be tough but not impossible: various survey respondents narrate personal episodes of some success. These usually include the involvement of one of four kinds of brokers: (a) the *community broker* such as a neighbour, local employer, local school, Welcome Wagon program, Newcomers Club, local sports club, the federally sponsored Host Program run by the PEI Association for Newcomers to Canada, or Island relatives of one's spouse; (b) a local *church*: (c) an *"alternative" forum* such as the (already fairly liberal) arts community, farmers' market, or the Island Cricket Club; and (d) an *employer* in the private or public sector obliged to recruit from beyond the Island's restrained labour market, such as the University of PEI, Holland College, Genzyme Diagnostics (formerly Diagnostic Chemicals), Biovectra; the firms in the aerospace sector; and the Federal Departments of Veterans Affairs in Charlottetown, the Tax Office in Summerside, and the RCMP.

Respondent #028: "When I first returned to PEI, I was working in isolation. I felt the need to connect with people, so I contacted Avonlea Village and offered to work for free as a 'village weaver' on Sundays. [I was] readily accepted. The welcome I received at Avonlea Village was phenomenal. I enjoyed the work and the camaraderie so much."

Respondent #081: A couple of months after I arrived, the Welcome Wagon Lady came to visit. She was wonderful. She introduced me to another woman … whose husband was with the RCMP here. They had moved from Ottawa. My foster-father was a Mountie. The three of us formed the Welcomers' Club (now called the Friendship Club). We now have 30 or 40 members. They are all from away, except three of us who were born here and returned to live here. I am enjoying living here. I do volunteer work for CNIB and the library and my church. I have one sister living here and my foster-mother as well as all my new friends."

Respondent #089: "My expertise was not sought out by Islanders during the first couple of years; however, my wife and I had formed a consulting company, and I did some pro bono work for Diagnostic Chemicals & Biovectra. Meanwhile, my name was placed in nomination for the board of the PEI Food Technology Centre early in 2003. That opening and visibility to the business development community and to a lesser extent the UPEI community has led to enjoyable service."

Respondent #122: "I have met and married an Islander and, we have developed a small business that is doing fairly well. We continue to access the medical and community supports we need and have developed friendships and become involved in various community activities on the Island. We love the music culture here and have become actively involved in promoting and supporting fiddle music in PEI."

Respondent #185: "Another major reason [why we have decided to stay] is that there is so very, very much to do in the way of activities, community involvement, festivals, plays, dinner theatre, restaurants, farmers markets, farm days, studio tours, community school, provincial parks, beaches, museums, socials, family picnics, family histories so, so, so, much that I cannot name them all here. Many things are at an affordable price."

Respondent #227: "Probably the biggest reason for my feeling more settled here and knowing I will stay for good is that we found a church that we feel very much part of the spiritual family there. We are able to be very active members there and their vision is our vision. My work is going very well here, and I work out of my home, which is very convenient for me and comfortable, yet professional for my clients. This is now almost three years of living here and I am just now feeling at home. Last year was rough as it still didn't feel like home; but that has now changed dramatically, primarily because we found a church we can call home."

A REAL CHALLENGE OF BELONGINGNESS

The most common challenge to attracting new immigrants to PEI, according to the 2005 survey respondents, relates to the difficulty of landing a good job (or any job at all) and the associated challenge of foreign credential recognition. Just over half of the respondents (172, or 55 percent) identified this as the key problem for immigrant attraction and retention. But the second most commonly identified set of challenges (with 59 respondents, or 18 percent, commenting) deal variously with the Island society as being racist, bigoted, discriminatory, conservative, exclusivist, and/or clique-ist with regards to those branded for life as CFAs. Some respondent comments about this are barbed and even cruel in their criticism: they manifest pain and frustration. Other comments are more guarded and clinical, attributing this phenomenon (I would add, correctly) to a cultural condition of which Islanders – especially those ones who have never lived away – are as much victims as perpetrators. It seems that a *close society* cannot help being a *closed society*. What follows are two judicious and rather dispassionate assessments of the situation:

> *Respondent #040*: "The 'come from away' problem is one that probably results in settlers not staying settled for very long. This should not be seen as a 'fault' of native Islanders; it's a condition. They've grown from childhood with friends and family around them and therefore have had no need to develop whatever skills are required to seek out and make welcome new people with a view to forming friendships. That simply hasn't been necessary. It's also true that those settlers who have traveled the world a little have experiences and knowledge to which the majority of Islanders can't relate. Again, it is not a criticism, but it is a condition."

> *Respondent #217*: "Conservative social attitudes and what seems to be a 'closed' society to newcomers may make it difficult for settlers to feel that they fit in. If there were not some existing family ties to PEI, I think it would be quite challenging to make social contacts. Most people want to know how you may be related to them or their neighbour or someone they know, to figure out how you fit into the overall picture of PEI society – your place or role or standing, somehow."

The CFA descriptor is applied widely and casually. It may appear cute, but it can be bitterly resented and, in some circumstances, it portrays what could be an implicit racist naïveté, arguably more prevalent in the rural areas of the province. The Island simply takes care of its own, and by extension, no one else. Being "from here" seems to be a fundamental criterion for social division, in both Island-based organizations as well as Island wide generally – perhaps as important as social class, political party affiliation, or ideology. Some respondents claimed that being a CFA was equivalent to being a member of a visible minority. The following two comments describe this burning issue quite candidly:

> *Respondent #031*: "It became fairly obvious that *who* you were (family name), *who* you knew, etc., are factors as to how successfully you can conduct life in general on PEI. This has not affected me to date (that I'm aware of), but I've seen it in operation. It is hard to miss since it is prevalent and blatant. The funny thing is, it is much the same everywhere since people are people wherever they are, but in a 'PEItri' dish, it's more noticeable" (emphasis in original).

> *Respondent #165*: "PEI is a closed society. Despite trying to be friendly and make personal connections, establish rapport with people, I often feel shut out – something I did not experience on such a regular basis in other places. I now believe (although I am trying to keep an open mind) that many Islanders are polite but *not* friendly. My closest friend here, born in Ontario but a PEI resident for 30 plus years, says there is a pervasive passive aggressiveness. The idea is kind of funny, but I'm not sure he is wrong" (emphasis in original).

The situation from the host society perspective is complementary. In spite of a healthy dose of politically correct rhetoric from government, business organizations and civil society groups – championing diversity, the need to grow the local population, and the importance of attracting skill and talent – most Prince Edward Islanders have no appetite for immigration. When Stephen Stewart, a PEI mussel grower, hired 11 workers from Sri Lanka in 2006, only to see them disappear to Ottawa after two weeks on the Island, he reported, "People in the community criticized us for bringing in foreign workers and said we got what we deserved" (Duplain 2006). Islanders remain suspicious of newcomers, especially those who do not have the Irish-Scottish background that most Islanders (other than the First Nations Mi'kmaq and the descendants of French Acadians) claim as their own. At best, immigrants are *curiosa*, the objects of voyeurism, exotic specimens that one encounters formally and rarely, in such cultural extravaganzas as the International Tea House (or Culturama) and annual DiverCity events, in the company of strange music, song, food, and clothing.[13] When the provincial government set up its Population Secretariat in 2003, its mandate seemed predicated more on local Islander retention and repatriation than on immigration proper.[14]

One should thus not be surprised by the outcome of a May 2008 national poll on attitudes to immigration commissioned for the journal *Policy*

Options (Nanos 2008). Atlantic Canadians emerged as the least convinced that immigration is important to the future of the country; the least convinced that immigration is the most important response to the country's workforce skill requirements; but the most convinced that immigration is important for family reunification. Immigration strikes a chord with Atlantic Canadians if it means bringing back home one's own.[15]

CONCLUSION

Already back in 1999, the Population Strategy Panel had advised (1999, Recommendation 22, vii) that "established host communities are an attraction for newcomers and contribute to successful integration; accordingly, PEI should place particular emphasis on working with established host communities in PEI to attract new immigrants."

Host communities constitute micro-societies that can welcome and help in the process of integration and eventual settlement. Churches, friendship clubs, Welcome Wagon, and sport teams are all structures that already exist and operate at the local level. The farmers' market, the hybrid arts community, and specific workplaces act effectively as magnets for suitable employment and social integration. People deciding to come and stay on PEI must be helped to connect. Friendliness would then eventually develop into friendship; close communities eventually would become less closed, or perhaps more open.

In more recent years, the dynamics of the host-settler encounter on Prince Edward Island have been changing dramatically. PEI welcomed around 4,000 newcomers in 2007–09, with some 3,000 of these being provincial nominees under the investor program, hailing from the People's Republic of China and Taiwan (Government of Prince Edward Island 2010, 13). This sudden and major influx of Chinese residents, especially in Charlottetown, has created for the first time in PEI's history a specific immigrant community large enough to provide services for itself (including, as from June 2011, a Mandarin language provincial newspaper[16]), and perhaps reducing the necessity for these newcomers to engage deeply with traditional island residents (Carlson 2011).

Diversity is not a threat; nor is it just a means of demographic or economic revival. If PEI, its political and economic establishment, and (above all) its people really believe in immigration, then immigrants should be deliberately drawn in to participate in Island life, facilitating their eventual settling in and settling down. Such a task involves all levels of government, especially the local/municipal level, but also civil society. Perhaps immigrants too can come to call this place "home"; perhaps immigrants too can come to call themselves "Islanders by choice."

NOTES

1. Godfrey Baldacchino is a professor of sociology and Canada Research Chair (Island Studies) at the University of Prince Edward Island, Canada; visiting professor of sociology at the University of Malta, Malta; executive editor of *Island Studies Journal*; member of the PEI Population Network and former board member and vice-president of the Prince Edward Island Association for Newcomers to Canada (2007–10). The contents of this article represent his own views and not necessarily those of the PEI ANC or of any other association.
2. Saskatchewan is the next represented in this booklet with four entries, followed by Manitoba (8); British Columbia (10); Quebec (11); Alberta (22); and Ontario (75).
3. Church attendance amongst Catholics in Canada is highest in rural PEI (46 percent), and lowest in Quebec (15 percent) according to a 2002 study. See http://www.ccri.ca/rcn11-18.pdf.
4. In the 2 May 2011 federal election, 74.0 percent of eligible Islanders turned out to vote: again, the highest turnout by province in Canada. National average turnout was 61.4 percent. See http://transpedia.ca/index.php?title=2011_Canadian_Federal_Election_Stats_%E2%80%93_Voter_Turnout.
5. Around 10 percent of the labour force is also a recipient of employment insurance, partly a function of the structural seasonality of labour demand.
6. In this case, "visible minority" includes Arab and Latin American, some of whom would be "white."
7. http://islandersbychoice.ning.com/page/who-are-we.
8. Current Federal-Provincial-Territorial Agreements on Immigration can be found on the CIC website at http://www.cic.gc.ca/english/department/laws-policy/agree.asp.
9. More details available at http://www.canadavisa.com/pnp-business-immigration.html.
10. The actual figures are even higher than those reported here. Census data for 2006 is only until May. Moreover, "the Atlantic Provinces Economic Council calculates that immigration in the region reached 5,583 in 2007, a jump of 1,197 from the previous year" (Tutton, 2008). Also, Statistics Canada (2007) suggests that in the third quarter of 2007, "immigrants entered the province [of PEI] at an annualized rate of 12.1 for every 1,000 population" (around 1,700 persons), significantly above the national mean of 8.7.
11. "The attraction of major immigrant gateways, with their corresponding large immigrant and ethnic communities, along with access to ethnic, social, cultural, or religious opportunities, is a powerful attraction for new arrivals and aids in their adaptation to Canada. Conversely, smaller centres have few inducements to [immigrants to] settle or stay" (Newbold 2006, 20).
12. The number has continued to rise: in January 2008, the executive director of the PEI Association for Newcomers to Canada reported 951 new clients for the Association during 2007. See http://childcarecanada.org/documents/child-care-news/08/01/something-talk-about-ca-pe.
13. For two examples, visit http://www.buzzon.com/whats-going-on/community/8641-international-tea-house; and http://madankgiri.blogspot.com/2011/06/urmila-khanal-performing-during.html.

14. "The Population Secretariat's mandate is to retain youth, repatriate former Islanders and attract and retain immigrants" (Government of Prince Edward Island 2008).
15. These differences are significant at 95 percent confidence level. National Sample Size = 1,002. Poll was conducted in May 2008. Margin of error is ± 3.1%. Atlantic Canadians in sample = 97.
16 For further information, see http://www.wireservice.ca/index.php?module=News&func=display&sid=5684.

REFERENCES

Akbari, A.H. 2008. *Immigrant Inflows and Their Retention Rise in Atlantic Canada,* Moncton/Halifax, Atlantic Metropolis. At http://atlantic.metropolis.net/ResearchPolicy/Akbari_-_Immigration_Trends_(2001-2006).doc

Baldacchino, G. 2006. *Recent Settlers to Prince Edward Island: Stories and Voices.* Charlottetown: University of Prince Edward Island for the Provincial Government of PEI.

—2008. "Population Dynamics from Peripheral Regions: A North Atlantic Perspective." *European Journal of Spatial Development* No. 27. At http://www.nordregio.se/EJSD/refereed27.pdf

Baldacchino, G. and M. Hood. 2008. *Challenges of Internationally Educated Health Professionals on Prince Edward Island.* Charlottetown: University of Prince Edward Island for Atlantic Health Connection.

Baldacchino, G. and C. McAndrew Fall. 2008. *Immigrant Entrepreneurs on Prince Edward Island.* Charlottetown: Population Secretariat, Provincial Government of Prince Edward Island.

Biles, J. 2008. "Integration Policies in English Speaking Canada." In *Immigration and Integration in Canada in the Twenty-First Century,* ed. J. Biles, M. Burnstein, and J. Frideres, 139-86. Montreal and Kingston: McGill-Queen's University Press/Metropolis.

Biles, J., M. Burnstein, and J. Frideres. 2008. Introduction to *Immigration and Integration in Canada in the Twenty-First Century,* ed. J. Biles, M. Burnstein, and J. Frideres, 3-18. Montreal and Kingston: McGill-Queen's University Press/Metropolis.

Canadian Press 2008a. "Census: One-Third of Charlottetown Residents List Canadian as Ethnic Background." *Charlottetown Guardian,* 3 April, A4.

—2008b. "Saskatchewan Doctors Most Open to New Patients: Report," 19 March. At www.ctv.ca/servlet/ArticleNews/story/CTVNews/20080319/doc_survey_080319?s_name=&no_ads='

Carlson, K.B. 2011. "Goodbye Green Gables: Chinese Immigrants transforming P.E.I.'s cultural landscape." *National Post,* 3 July. At http://news.nationalpost.com/2011/07/03/goodbye-green-gables-chinese-immigrants-transforming-p-e-i-%E2%80%99s-cultural-landscape/

Citizenship and Immigration Canada (CIC). 2004. *Welcome to Canada: Finding Help in Your Community.* Catalogue No. Ci51-87/3-2004. Ottawa: Minister of Public Works and Government Services Canada.

Duplain, R. 2006. "PEI Mussel Grower Burned for over $50,000 by Foreign Workers." *The Guardian,* 4 November 2006.

Fall, C. 2008. "Immigration, Repatriation and Retention: Population Strategies on Prince Edward Island and Comparable Jurisdictions." In *Pulling Strings: Policy Insights for Prince Edward Island from Other Sub-National Island Jurisdictions*, ed. G. Baldacchino and K. Stuart, 55-73. Charlottetown: Island Studies Press.

Government of Prince Edward Island. 2008. *Population Secretariat*. At http://www.gov.pe.ca/popsec/

—2010. "Prince Edward Island Settlement Strategy." Charlottetown, November. Summary at http://www.gov.pe.ca/photos/original/settlement_bro.pdf.

Houlé, R. 2007. "Secondary Migration of New Immigrants to Canada." *Our Diverse Cities*, No. 3. Metropolis Project, 16-24.

Ibbitson, J. 2005. *The Polite Revolution: Perfecting the Canadian Dream*. Toronto: McClelland and Stewart.

Nanos, N. 2008. "Nation Building through Immigration: Workforce Skills Comes Out on Top." *Policy Options* (June): 30-2.

Newbold, B. 2006. *Secondary Migration of Immigrants to Canada: An Analysis of LSIC Wave 1 Data*. Research Report. Hamilton, ON: Statistics Canada, Research Data Centre at McMaster University. At http://socserv.mcmaster.ca/rdc/RDCwp10.pdf

PEI Population Strategy Panel. 1999. *A Place to Stay?* Charlottetown: Prince Edward Island Population Strategy 1999 Panel.

Prince Edward Island Provincial Nominee Program (PEI-PNP). 2008. "Immigration: Prince Edward Island Provincial Nominee Program." At http://www.gov.pe.ca/immigration/index.php3?number=1014385

Prince Edward Island Population Network. 2007. *Strategic Direction 2007 and Beyond*. Facilitated by Robert Maddix and Erin Docherty. Charlottetown: PEI-PN.

Service Canada. 2011. "Labour Market Update, December 2005, Prince Edward Island Labour Market Information." At http://www.servicecanada.gc.ca/eng/pe/lmi/update/lmu-december05.shtml

Statistics Canada. 2007a. Longitudinal Survey of Immigrants to Canada (LSIC). At: http://www.statcan.gc.ca/cgi-bin/imdb/p2SV.pl?Function=getSurvey&SDDS=4422&lang=en&db=imdb&adm=8&dis=2

—2007b. Canada's Population Estimates." *The Daily*, 19 December. At http://www.statcan.ca/Daily/English/071219/d071219b.htm

Tobin, A.-M. 2008. "Most PEI Physicians Not Taking 'All New Patients,' Survey Reveals." *Charlottetown Guardian*, 22 March, A12.

Tutton, M. 2008. "Atlantic Canada Seeks Immigrants to Stem Out-Migration, but with Mixed Results." *Charlottetown Guardian*, 28 June, A11.

Wang S. and L. Lo. 2007. "What Does It Take to Achieve Full Integration? Economic (Under) Performance of Chinese Immigrants to Canada." In *Interrogating Race and Racism*, ed. V. Agnew, 172-205. Toronto: University of Toronto Press.

Weale, D. 1992. *Them Times*. Charlottetown: Institute of Island Studies, University of Prince Edward Island.

Woolcock, M. and D. Narayan. 2000. "Social Capital: Implications for Development Theory, Research and Policy." *World Bank Observer* 15(1):225-49.

PART 2 – PRINCE EDWARD ISLAND SETTLEMENT STRATEGY: A SUMMARY

PAULA M. BROCHU

This summary of Prince Edward Island's settlement strategy focuses on three main themes. First, it describes Prince Edward Island's present involvement in settlement, detailing the ministries involved and their current actions. Second, it outlines the province's settlement strategy as well as the initiatives proposed going forward. Finally, it highlights the stakeholders involved in the strategy's implementation. The source of information summarized in this report is the November 2010 document "A Prince Edward Island Settlement Strategy."

BACKGROUND

Historically, Prince Edward Island's population has always been comprised of immigrants. Its original settlers from France, Ireland, and Scotland joined the Mi'kmaq; settlers from Lebanon, Holland, China, and many other countries later followed. The Island today is home to newcomers from over 60 countries.

The recent wave of newcomers to Prince Edward Island is strategic and steady in order to meet the challenges of an aging population. From 1995 to 2005, the number of immigrants annually receiving permanent residency in Prince Edward Island doubled from fewer than 200 to nearly 400; from 2005 to 2009, the numbers more than quadrupled to approximately 1,700. Most permanent residents are recruited from the economic class, which in 2008 represented 78 percent of total immigration to the province. The majority of newcomers are recruited through the Provincial Nominee Program; they are from Asia and the Middle East, are highly educated, want to be employed in their chosen fields, regard education very highly, and are of working age. The province seeks to take advantage of opportunities for population growth through recruitment, repatriation, settlement, and retention strategies because it recognizes newcomers as valuable economic and social resources.

PRINCE EDWARD ISLAND'S PRESENT INVOLVEMENT IN SETTLEMENT

Spending on settlement services in Prince Edward Island has increased along with growth in the immigrant population, totalling over $4.2 million in 2009, a 48 percent increase over spending in 2008. Over and above this, newcomers access many of the same services as all Islanders. All departments of the provincial government supply some level of information or service to the public, and as such, interact with newcomers as well.

The Department of Innovation and Advanced Learning is responsible for settlement services in the province. The department contributes funding and support to a variety of settlement services regarding language skills, settlement information, and employment opportunities through the Population Secretariat, Island Investment Development Inc., Skills PEI, and the Post Secondary and Continuing Education division. The Population Secretariat, developed in 2004 to retain youth, repatriate former Islanders, and attract and retain newcomers, oversees the funding of language training for newcomers and administers settlement tools such as the online immigration and employment portal (www.OpportunitiesPEI. ca) and the *Newcomer Guide.* In 2008–09, the Population Secretariat took on additional staff to identify settlement issues and improve settlement services. Island Investment Development Inc., established in 1993, oversees the provincial nomination program. Part of this responsibility involves administering the skilled worker category for newcomers, which saw an 82 percent retention rate of applicants in 2008–09. Skills PEI was founded in 2009 and is the lead provincial body on foreign qualifications assessment and recognition. In addition, a division of Skills PEI has an immigrant work experience program that provides newcomers with work exposure opportunities. The Post Secondary and Continuing Education division also helps newcomers with equivalency recognition for learning completed in other countries.

The Department of Education and Early Childhood Development seeks to provide all newcomer children with a comfortable transition to the province's education system. The department established a section on English / French as an Additional Language in the school curriculum, and manages an intake centre for students in kindergarten through grade 12 that assesses language proficiency and provides additional support to learners in the school system as needed, such as interpretative services and tutoring. The section has been roundly successful, growing in three years from a staff of six to 29 and currently working with over 640 international students in 41 schools.

The Department of Health and Wellness grants immediate access to all provincial health programs to newcomers and meets all their immunization needs. In 2009, over 300 newcomers were immunized at clinics that had translation and interpretation services on site. The Internationally Educated Health Professionals initiative navigates the recognition of foreign qualifications process and seeks to provide greater access to relevant employment opportunities. The program has experienced steady growth and currently supports over 90 individuals with services in employment counselling, language classes, and orientation to the health care systems in Canada and Prince Edward Island. The department also hires international medical graduates to work as family physicians or specialists and provides them with support in progressing through the immigration and licensure processes. Currently, 28 percent of family physicians and 20 percent of physician specialists in Prince Edward Island are international medical graduates.

The Department of Community Services, Seniors, and Labour provides newcomers with social services including those offered under the *Child Protection Act* and *Social Assistance Act* and the Child Care Subsidy Program, which are the primary sources of assistance available to newcomers in Prince Edward Island after the one year subsidy from the federal government's Resettlement Assistance Program. The department is responsible for international adoptions, and it is also currently working to establish new protocols for the fair treatment of temporary foreign workers in the province.

The Department of Transportation and Infrastructure Renewal has taken a number of steps to make the process of obtaining a driver's licence easier for newcomers by translating the licensing exam into other languages (e.g., simplified Chinese) and training more driver examiners to meet greater demand. Since 2006, approximately 1,950 Island newcomers have taken the licensing exam.

The Department of Tourism and Culture is the lead department for multicultural issues and contributes to the settlement experience of newcomers through the Culture, Heritage, and Libraries division by funding and hosting multicultural activities. The public library employs multicultural front line staff and provides a range of products and services to newcomers, including a volunteer-based English as a Second Language tutoring program that trains tutors and matches them with an immigrant. Since its inception in 2006–07, the public library has supported 50 to 60 tutor-immigrant pairs. The public library is also currently developing additional services to help landed immigrants become citizens and navigate the citizenship process.

The Department of Finance and Municipal Affairs (Public Service Commission) is often the first point of contact for newcomers seeking employment within the provincial government. It is involved in determining what an individual's qualifications are relative to Prince Edward Island requirements and assessing eligibility for particular occupations. The department also has a diversity consultant and is directly involved in diversity training within government.

The Department of Justice and Public Safety in 2009 published an H1N1 vaccination information sheet and victim services information sheet in five languages and is currently assessing how culture, ethnicity, and religion can best be considered in public safety alerts and other emergency planning.

The Department of Agriculture offers the Future Farmer Program, which assists interested newcomers to enter the farming community by providing each applicant with a staff member and business mentor to provide information and discuss challenges. Currently, five newcomers are enrolled in the program or are in the process of enrolling.

The Department of Fisheries, Aquaculture, and Rural Development provides a range of services to newcomers through Access PEI, a division of the department that serves as a gateway for newcomers looking for a variety of government services. Newcomers' needs range from exchanging foreign drivers' licences to information about taxation and permits. Efforts are ongoing within the department for all front line staff to take cultural diversity training.

The Department of Environment, Energy, and Forestry is currently involved in a cooperative project with the Chinese Association that offers customized firearm and hunter safety training, in which over 50 people have taken part. A newcomer fluent in Mandarin has been certified to deliver both the firearm and hunting safety programs and is a registered hunting guide. The department also offers presentations on wildlife laws that include translation and live interpreters.

This detailing of Prince Edward Island's present involvement in settlement initiatives highlights how broad the government's involvement in settlement already is.

Prince Edward Island's Settlement Strategy Initiatives Going Forward

The vision of Prince Edward Island's settlement strategy is "a welcoming One Island Community whose service and support to newcomers is contributing to a culturally diverse and prosperous province." Five principles underlie the settlement strategy: that it be equitable, accountable, respectful and ethical, inclusive, and community based. In this way, the settlement strategy makes use of a balanced approach through the efficient deployment of settlement resources while maintaining a respectful relationship with all residents, working collaboratively with partners, and building community throughout the province. The province seeks to retain as many newcomers as possible and provides services to ensure their social and economic integration.

To support the settlement strategy, a number of government initiatives are being implemented. First and foremost, the Population Secretariat is to be responsible for implementation of the settlement strategy and for conducting an annual review of its effectiveness. In order to measure retention and to assess the success of the settlement strategy, the Population Secretariat will implement new protocols for interdepartmental information sharing. Communication and working relationships between the province, its departments, non-government organizations involved in settlement, and the Government of Canada will be fostered to ensure a comprehensive approach to service delivery and the provision of settlement information. As well, gaps identified in the labour force will inform newcomer recruitment and retention efforts to ensure maximum benefit for both newcomers and the province.

Based on feedback from newcomer communities and the experiences of other provinces, Prince Edward Island's settlement strategy will focus on three priority areas: language skills, business and employment opportunities, and quality of life. English language skills are necessary for newcomers to become integrated in the community. Initiatives in this area will focus on language training for adults and students in kindergarten through grade 12. For adults, language training is provided through the Language Instruction for Newcomers to Canada (LINC) program and follows Canadian language benchmarks. Newcomers have indicated, however, that English language training could be accelerated and that language skills and training for the workplace are needed. Going forward, the province seeks to develop a comprehensive language training framework to provide newcomers with more appropriate training. To this end, the province will work with service providers to offer accelerated, evening, weekend, or summer scheduling opportunities as well as conversational language training sessions, in English and other languages, for those wishing to learn an additional language. For students, the English/ French as an Additional Language section of the Department of Education and Early Childhood Development provides language training. Going forward, the province plans to build on current success by monitoring the demands and needs of newcomer children and of educators who are working with international students.

Business and employment opportunities are essential for both newcomers and the province to gain maximum benefit from immigration. Initiatives have been put forth by the province in three areas: job search and employment, entrepreneurship and business investment, and post-secondary students. To improve job search and employment opportunities for newcomers, the settlement strategy seeks to link existing employment support programs to bridge work experience and employment opportunities. This strategy involves working with service providers to supply more information to newcomers about employment, business, and current events through an online information source and other programming, and working with businesses to provide diversity training. Other initiatives involve using employer needs to inform the recruitment of temporary foreign workers. To develop entrepreneurship and business investment opportunities, the province plans to deliver business workshops and seminars for newcomers on Canadian and Prince Edward Island business environments. A business mentorship program will connect newcomers with key business and government contacts, and an immigration forum series will be designed to educate local businesses about the importance and benefits of immigration. To improve retention of post-secondary students in the province, plans are in place to assess the number of international post-secondary students in the job market, as well as to provide international students with information on employment opportunities. An International Student Strategy will be established to identify markets in the province in which there are labour gaps and to inform students of these opportunities.

The settlement strategy seeks to improve newcomers' quality of life by improving settlement information and access to health care and forming community networks. Because newcomers arrive with a host of information needs, the province seeks to revise, translate, and distribute the *Newcomer Orientation Handbook* both in print and online versions, and to create a translation and interpretation policy that includes qualification criteria for interpreters and translators, service standards, and guidelines for translation of departmental and agency materials. In order to provide some newcomers with more intensive orientation services as needed, additional settlement case worker positions will be created.

The province also ensures that newcomers have access to health care services upon arrival and sees to it that their health needs are addressed fully. Other health initiatives involve providing newcomers with access to interpreters when filling prescriptions to allow for effective and accurate communication of dosage and safety precautions.

In order to further develop community networks, the province seeks to promote an education and awareness campaign informing Islanders on how to welcome newcomers, highlighting the social and economic benefits of immigration, and profiling newcomer success stories. Other initiatives include working with the Rural Action Plan to help communities develop local approaches for sustainable and inclusive settlement outcomes and working with the Department of Tourism and Culture to launch a pilot initiative to develop new special events (i.e., cultural, sport, culinary, and business) intended to strengthen both settlement and tourism in the province.

Prince Edward Island's Settlement Strategy Stakeholders

Prince Edward Island's settlement strategy requires the involvement of a wide range of stakeholders so that a comprehensive suite of programs and services focusing on language skills, business and employment opportunities, and quality of life are available to newcomers. The list of stakeholders that can make a positive contribution to settlement includes all Islanders in general, the government of Prince Edward Island, the Prince Edward Island Association for Newcomers (PEI ANC), the business community, municipalities and local communities, religious organizations, academic institutions, service groups, and the Government of Canada. The engagement of a wide range of stakeholders increases the likelihood that distinct, individual needs will be addressed.

Under the Settlement Strategy, the people and institutions of Prince Edward Island are called upon to make the province a more welcoming place for newcomers. In this regard, the PEI ANC has an important role to play through the services it delivers. With a staff of 26, it offers a large complement of programs in the areas of information and awareness, language, community connections, and employment. The business community in the province is also called upon to help. The business sector benefits from newcomers' skills and perspectives and can help welcome newcomer employees and entrepreneurs into the workplace, into community institutions, and into business associations. Service groups and the voluntary sector can also assist newcomers to build stronger ties to the community through inclusion in the many men's and women's groups, ethnic associations, church groups, and charitable organizations that operate in the province. Good working relationships among agencies, departments, and organizations will ensure the social and economic integration of newcomers in Prince Edward Island.

REFERENCE

Government of Prince Edward Island. 2010. "Prince Edward Island Settlement Strategy." Charlottetown (November). At http://www.gov.pe.ca/photos/original/settlement_eng.pdf

Part 3 – Reaction to the Prince Edward Island Government's Settlement Strategy

Craig Mackie

These notes provide reaction from the perspective of the PEI Association for Newcomers to Canada (PEI ANC) to the Settlement Strategy delivered by the Government of Prince Edward Island to the Legislature on 1 December 2010.

The PEI ANC was established in 1993 to deliver short-term settlement assistance and longer-term integration services to immigrants and refugees arriving on Prince Edward Island. The association currently offers a wide range of programs and services including settlement services for Government Assisted Refugees and many other classes of immigrants; immigrant youth programs; language assessments and referrals to LINC (Language Instruction for New Canadians) classes; employment and self-employment assistance services; community connections programs; and multicultural education. The PEI ANC is funded primarily through the federal Department of Citizenship and Immigration and the Population Secretariat of the Government of Prince Edward Island. The overall budget for the PEI ANC in 2010-11 was approximately $1.8 million, of which about half was provided by the province.

The PEI ANC has grown rapidly in the past half decade, reflecting the dramatic rise in the number of immigrants needing services through the association. In 2005, the PEI ANC took in about 400 newcomers. By 2009 that number had risen to just over 1,200, and in 2010 the association recorded an intake of 1,840 cases. About 80 of these newcomers were refugees; the rest had mostly entered via the Provincial Nominee Program.

The PEI Settlement Strategy had been a work-in-progress for at least a couple of years before its release in late 2010. PEI's Liberal government of the day had been stung by criticism of its handling of the Provincial Nominee Program and, as a consequence, proceeded slowly and with a great of deal consultation before releasing the strategy. During its development, the government consulted with PEI ANC on several occasions.

The Settlement Strategy is a balanced and inclusive document. It builds on work currently being done by almost every provincial government department along with the services provided by various associations and agencies that receive government funding for immigrants and newcomers. The strategy continues the three-pronged efforts by the PEI government to attract people from other parts of Canada, to encourage and promote immigration, and to repatriate Islanders who had moved away.

The document also recognizes that much work remains to be done for PEI to become more effective in the area of settlement. Naming the Population Secretariat as the key agency in this area is viewed by the PEI ANC as an important and positive step for advancing the larger strategy. In this regard, the Population Secretariat has several important roles. First, it is required to measure the effectiveness and success of programs and services. Second, it is required to implement new protocols for inter-departmental information sharing, which is widely seen as essential for increasing the effectiveness of government services and supports. This said, implementation of protocols will not be easy, especially for departments that have traditionally guarded information about their clients.

The Settlement Strategy's focus on the three priority areas of language, employment and self-employment, and quality of life fits well with the objectives of the PEI ANC. The association sees language as the key to both short-term settlement and long-term integration. Having a job or opening a business is an equally important element of retention. Social inclusion is the final piece that will keep newcomers in PEI.

Currently, a large number of immigrants are arriving in PEI from Asia. Most of these arrivals are entrepreneurs with low levels of English. If the province wants to retain more of them, the approaches described in the Settlement Strategy are moving in the right directions. The strategy places significant emphasis on language instruction alongside other approaches, including volunteering to support tutoring, conversation circles, etc. Without being able to quickly improve their English, the current group of newcomers will not be able to engage in entrepreneurial activities which they wish to do and which the province needs. Furthermore, they will need significant assistance if they are to open new businesses, buy existing firms, or partner with Island businesses. The strategy speaks to a variety of initiatives that, if implemented, should provide the necessary help and significantly increase retention rates and business success in PEI.

The Settlement Strategy also recognizes the increased demands on the PEI ANC for programs and services. In light of this, the government has offered to fund two more positions, which will go a considerable way to making PEI ANC a more effective and efficient service provider. The government also recognizes the need for new facilities with greater accessibility and visibility, although funding for that purpose has not yet been confirmed.

Prince Edward Island is undergoing unprecedented social, cultural, and economic changes as a result of the sizeable and sudden influx of immigrants. Overall, the Settlement Strategy strikes the right tone. It recognizes where the key challenges are and offers useful solutions and directions for change. The proof will be in what is implemented and achieved in the next twelve months.

CHAPTER 13

IMMIGRATION AND INTEGRATION OF IMMIGRANTS IN CANADA'S TERRITORIES

ROBERT VINEBERG

This chapter provides an overview of immigration to Canada's three northern territories, Yukon, the Northwest Territories, and Nunavut, reviewing the history of immigration to the region, examining the current situation, and suggesting future directions for their immigration policies.

BEFORE CANADA

The story of post-Aboriginal migration in the territories is founded on resources – first furs, then gold and other base metals, and, now diamonds as well as base metals and, potentially, oil and gas. The small but increasing numbers of immigrants to the three territories have the potential to increase the prosperity of the North. But the North is the homeland of many Aboriginal peoples, and therefore overseas migration must be managed not only in terms of immigration policy but also in terms of urban planning, so that the cities and communities of the North will not only be welcoming communities for newcomers but will continue to maintain their distinct character and culture.

Immigration has had a huge impact on parts of the original Northwest Territories, a jurisdiction that was much bigger than the territory that bears the same name today. All of what is now Alberta, Saskatchewan, Manitoba, Yukon, Nunavut, and the Northwest Territories as well as the northern parts of Ontario and Quebec was once the domain of the Hudson Bay Company (HBC). Granted to the company by the English king in

Integration and Inclusion of Newcomers and Minorities across Canada, ed. J. Biles, M. Burstein, J. Frideres, E. Tolley, and R. Vineberg. Montreal and Kingston: Queen's Policy Studies Series, McGill-Queen's University Press.
© 2011 The School of Policy Studies, Queen's University at Kingston. All rights reserved.

1670, this huge region consisted of Rupert's Land – the hydrographic basin of Hudson Bay (what is today northern Quebec and Ontario, the entire province of Manitoba, most of Saskatchewan, and part of southern Alberta) – as well as the North-Western Territory, consisting of the areas to the north and west of Rupert's Land. In this territory the HBC had not only a trade monopoly but also served as the colonial authority.

This vast empire was easy for a company to administer – so long as there were few people to manage. At first this was the case. In addition to the original inhabitants of Inuit, Dene, Cree, Assiniboines, Arthapaskans, and many other groups of First Nations, there were only a handful of Hudson Bay Company traders at posts on the shore of Hudson Bay. When the Canadien and Scottish fur traders of the Northwest Company reached the Prairies in the late 1700s, the HBC traders were forced inland to compete. The only immigrants at this time were the Scottish settlers at the small Red River Colony sponsored by Lord Selkirk, as well as Métis – mostly the offspring of Canadiens or Europeans who married First Nations women and settled on the Red or Assiniboine Rivers near the current site of Winnipeg.

The two competing fur companies eventually merged in the early 1800s – really a takeover by the HBC – and the new headquarters of the company was established at Lower Fort Garry, about 20 miles north of the future site of Winnipeg. Why there? Lower Fort Garry was just north of the Grand Rapids on the Red River, which flowed north to Lake Winnipeg with access from there to Hudson Bay as well as to the rivers flowing across the Prairies from the west. It was also accessible from the east via the Great Lakes and the Winnipeg River system. So from this key transportation point, the Hudson Bay Company and its vast territory were administered.

However, the company was not good at managing settlers as well as the fur trade, and by the mid-nineteenth century, the HBC knew that when its Royal Charter came up for review, it was likely to lose exclusive control of the vast territory. Indeed, the ownership of the HBC had changed and was now equally if not more interested in land development. In 1868 the HBC, the British government, and the new Dominion of Canada began a three-way negotiation that led to the 1869 agreement for the purchase of the North-Western Territory and Rupert's Land by Canada for £300,000 in 1870 (LAC 2006, Order-in-Council PC1869-0591, 17 August 1869). With this agreement the HBC also received title to enormous landholdings. More importantly, Canada became one of the largest nations in the world, and its dream of spanning the continent and convincing the western colony of British Columbia to join Confederation became a definite probability rather than a mere dream.

Canada now had to administer the new territory and manage the flow of people into it, mostly from Ontario but in small numbers from abroad. Therefore, Canada created the Northwest Territory (NWT) on 15 July 1870 and designated Winnipeg as its capital (Canada 1870). The dominion government also established the Northwest Mounted Police (NWMP) to bring law and order to the territory. Furthermore, the province of Manitoba was carved out of the territory, though the Manitoba of 1870 was much smaller in area then than now, covering essentially the area within 150 kilometres of Winnipeg. The NWT's capital was not even in the territory; this expedient was so that the lieutenant governor of Manitoba could also be lieutenant governor of the NWT (Canada 1870b; LAC 2006, Order-in-Council PC1870-0040, 23 July 1870). He would be responsible for an enormous territory and an as yet tiny province. The 1872 *Canada Year Book* estimated the population of the territory to be 28,700 and the population of Manitoba to be about 12,000 (*Statistical Canada Year Book* 1872, 234).

EARLY MIGRATION MOVEMENTS

With the promise of a transcontinental railway, British Columbia with its roughly 50,000 people joined Confederation in 1871. The railway, finally completed in 1885, brought large numbers of eastern Canadians and immigrants who began to settle in the southern reaches of the NWT, which soon after sought provincial status. By 1901, the population of the Canadian Prairies and North would reach almost half a million – 255,000 in Manitoba and 212,000 in the territories (*Year Book* 1872, 80).

However, it was the discovery of gold in the Klondike in 1895 that resulted in the first mass movement of people into the areas north of the 60th parallel. While some came overland from Canada, the fastest way to the Yukon was via Skagway, Alaska, on the Pacific coast. Thousands of men, many of them veterans of the California and Caribou (British Columbia) gold rushes, headed for the Klondike. The trek from Skagway over the mountains was arduous. Many did not make it, and those who did often did not have the means to survive in the Arctic regions. The NWMP soon established a post on the border, mostly to ensure that those who sought gold could survive. Only those with sufficient supplies and food for six months were admitted. This meant that each man had to transport close to a tonne of goods over the Chilkoot Pass or the White Pass into the territory. The Canadian government recognized that the huge population explosion could not be properly managed from distant Winnipeg, and so a second portion of the NWT was split off in 1898 to create the Yukon Territory (Canada 1898). This decision also allowed the dominion government to focus on how to govern the Klondike in the longer term.

The population of the territory exploded from a few thousand, and Dawson City grew, almost overnight it seemed, to over 40,000 inhabitants. The *Canada Year Book* for 1901 conservatively gave the population of Yukon as 27,219. However, once the gold rush ended, Dawson City declined to a hamlet of less than a thousand souls; by 1911 the population of Yukon was only 8,512. Notwithstanding this precipitous drop in population, its separate territorial status remained.

In 1905 the provinces of Alberta and Saskatchewan were carved out of the NWT with their northern borders set at the 60th parallel (Canada 1905). In 1912, the provincial boundaries of Ontario, Quebec, and Manitoba were extended north as well, leaving the territories with the land mass they currently occupy. Finally, in 1999 the NWT was again partitioned to create Canada's third territory, Nunavut.

The next major migration to the territories had to wait for a new form of transportation to open up wider exploration and geological surveys. This was the airplane. Many veteran airmen of the First World War took their skills north. Once gold was discovered near Yellowknife, that hamlet started to grow quickly. Gold, silver, lead, and copper were found elsewhere as well, and people, largely from "south of 60," headed north to make their fortune. Immigrants among this number were generally those who had settled first in the South before moving to the North; there was no real direct immigrant movement to speak of. It was only in the 1970s and '80s, with the establishment of territorial governments in Whitehorse and Yellowknife, that immigrants, along with Canadians from "south of 60," were sought, usually for professional positions in the public service, teaching, and health services.

IMMIGRATION AND THE TERRITORIES TODAY

While immigration has not yet taken on the importance in the North that it has in the South, all three territories are today more aware of the importance of immigration to their futures. However, unlike the provinces to their south, the territories need to take account of their large Aboriginal populations – 25 percent in Yukon, 50 percent in the NWT, and 85 percent in Nunavut – and ensure that immigration complements the development of opportunities for Aboriginal peoples. By contrast, the immigrant populations are much smaller: 10 percent in Yukon, 7 percent in the NWT, and less than 2 percent in Nunavut (Table 1).

The bulk of permanent migration has traditionally gone to the three capital cities (Table 2). These communities dominate the demography of their jurisdictions. According to the 2006 Census, Whitehorse, with over 20,000 people, accounts for two-thirds of Yukon's population; the next largest community, Dawson, has only 1,300. In the NWT, Yellowknife with 18,500 people accounts for almost half the territory's population, and the next largest communities, Hay River and Inuvik, each have about 3,500 people. While Iqaluit with a population of just over 6,000 has only 20 percent of Nunavut's population, it is the only major centre. The next largest communities, Rankin Inlet, Arviat, and Baker Lake, are all in the 2,000 range.

TABLE 1
Canada's Territories: Population Overview, 2006

Territory	Total Population	Aboriginal Population	% Aboriginal	Immigrant Population	% Immigrant	Visible Minority	% VM
Yukon	30,190	7,580	25	3,005	10.0	1,220	4.0
NWT	41,060	20,635	50	2,815	6.9	2,270	5.5
Nunavut	29,325	24,915	85	455	1.6	420	1.4
Total	100,575	53,130	53	6,275	6.2	3,910	3.9

Note: Statistics Canada's estimates of population of the territories, as of 1 January 2011, are Yukon, 34,306; NWT, 43,554; and Nunavut, 33,303 (Statistics Canada 2011).

Source: Statistics Canada (2006).

TABLE 2
Canada's Territories: Population Overview by City, 2006

City	Total Population	Aboriginal Population	% Aboriginal	Immigrant Population	% Immigrant	Visible Minority	% VM
Whitehorse	20,290	4,100	20	2,295	11.3	1,220	6.0
Yellowknife	18,510	4,105	22	2,140	11.6	2,270	12.3
Iqaluit	6,085	3,650	60	235	3.9	195	3.2

Source: Statistics Canada (2006).

Primary immigration to the three territories combined was in the 160–200 range for each of the five years prior to 2008, but in 2008 the total jumped to 288, and by 2010 it had reached 506. In the past two years Yukon and the NWT together have received over 95 percent of the immigrants destined for the North (Table 3). Nunavut uses immigration principally to fill key professional positions, mostly in health care and education, whereas the movements are more generalized in the other territories.

However, primary immigration is only part of the story. The primary immigration figures are not sufficient to account for the numbers of immigrants in the northern population. The immigrant population of 6,275 in 2006 would suggest perhaps 300 immigrants arriving per year over the past 20 years. Therefore, relatively large numbers of immigrants originally destined to cities in the southern parts of Canada have been drawn to the North by the same factors that draw Canadians: the lure of the frontier, the space, the jobs, the money, and the opportunity to make a new start. This pattern reflects an opportunity for the territories, as they can thus recruit immigrants much more cheaply from Toronto and Calgary than from New Delhi or Manila.

TABLE 3
Canada's Territories: Immigration, 1999–2008

Year	Yukon	NWT	Nunavut	Total
1999	76	58	14	148
2000	59	83	13	155
2001	65	95	13	173
2002	50	60	12	122
2003	59	94	11	164
2004	62	89	8	159
2005	65	84	12	161
2006	65	98	12	175
2007	83	88	19	190
2008	110	127	50	287
2009	174	107	10	291
2010*	350	137	19	506

*Preliminary data

Sources: 1999–2005, CIC (2009b, 64); 2006–10, CIC (2011).

The other significant element of the migrant population is that of Temporary Foreign Workers. Though totalling only 742 in 2010 (Table 4), the numbers have been growing substantially in the last several years, driven by the northern economy in general but also by specialized needs such as the diamond industry. Several dozen foreign cutters and polishers work in the diamond factories in Yellowknife. These factories are there rather than in Antwerp or New York because the Government of the Northwest Territories requires that 10 percent of the output of its diamond mines be cut and polished in the territory. While Aurora College offers a cutting and polishing course, the core of skilled cutters and polishers have come to Canada as Temporary Foreign Workers.

Given the major projects planned for the North, including several new diamond mines, a mammoth iron ore mine in Nunavut, the Mackenzie pipeline, and the Alaska Highway pipeline, as well as the growth in the tourism and hospitality industry, it can only be expected that the demand for jobs will outstrip the local population's capacity and that further recourse to foreign workers will be a necessity.

FEDERAL-TERRITORIAL RELATIONS IN IMMIGRATION

All three territories have close working relationships with the federal government through Citizenship and Immigration Canada (CIC). However, each is at a different stage of formalizing its relationship with the federal

TABLE 4
Canada's Territories: Stock of Temporary Workers (as of December 1), 1999–2010

Year	Yukon	NWT	Nunavut	Total
1999	69	149	16	234
2000	56	196	16	268
2001	49	237	14	300
2002	54	199	25	278
2003	76	248	33	357
2004	97	269	33	399
2005	95	284	44	423
2006	106	270	50	426
2007	157	306	68	531
2008	245	302	32	579
2009	349	278	43	670
2010	409	280	53	742

Sources: 1999–2005, CIC (2009b, 64); 2006–10, CIC (2011).

government in respect to immigration. Each has been offered the opportunity to conclude formal federal-territorial agreements on immigration, but to date only Yukon and the Northwest Territories have chosen to do so.

The minister of citizenship and immigration and the Yukon minister of education signed their first framework agreement and territorial nominee agreement on 2 April 2001. The original agreement and territorial nominee annex were for a five-year period. On expiry, the agreements were extended year by year until the latest agreements were signed on 21 May 2008 in Whitehorse by Diane Finley, minister of citizenship and immigration, and Patrick Rouble, minister of education for Yukon (CIC 2008c). Both the framework agreement and the territorial nominee annex follow much the same pattern as similar agreements signed with other jurisdictions. In particular, these agreements have no expiry date but are to be jointly reviewed by the two governments every five years (section 10.7). Canada and Yukon, after exploring the possibility of devolving settlement services to the territory, decided not to pursue it but committed to ongoing cooperation in settlement delivery, and the agreement provides for the possibility of "settlement realignment" in the future (section 6.6). Furthermore, Yukon will provide CIC with an annual immigration plan including its projected number of territorial nominees (section 4.5.a) (CIC 2008a).

Once Yukon concluded its agreement, CIC met with senior officials of both the Northwest Territories and Nunavut to encourage their jurisdictions to enter into similar agreements (CIC 2008b, 19). In 2008 the premier of the Northwest Territories indicated that the Government of the NWT (GNWT) had become seriously interested in concluding an agreement. On 28 May 2008, the *Yellowknifer* newspaper reported: "The GNWT will look into launching an immigration nominee program similar to one in Yukon in order to battle the territory's chronic labour shortage, said Premier Floyd Roland last week. 'We're starting to have discussions with the federal government to see how we can make it work in the NWT.'" Negotiations between the GNWT and Canada in late 2008 and early 2009 resulted in the signing of a nominee agreement on 5 August 2009, as opposed to a full framework agreement as is in place in Yukon. The agreement is similar in scope to Yukon's nominee annex, and once it is fully implemented, it should have an important impact on immigration to the territory (CIC 2009c).

Federal Immigration Presence and Settlement Activities

CIC does not have a strong presence in the North. There are CIC offices in both Whitehorse and Yellowknife, but each is staffed by only one person, with support provided from larger offices in the South. Nunavut has no resident CIC officers; CIC Winnipeg provides services to that territory, assisted by the officer in Yellowknife.

The normal range of settlement services is provided in both Whitehorse and Yellowknife but on a relatively small scale. While funding is earmarked for Nunavut, to date the nature of the small immigrant movement (either professional or family class) has not required orientation or language training.

In fiscal years 2008–09 and 2009–10 in Yukon, CIC concluded two-year contracts with the Association Franco-Yukonaise (AFY) to deliver a range of settlement programming. Pursuant to their agreement, Yukon was involved in the decision to contract with the AFY. Three separate contracts were in place. A contract for $131,520 provided orientation, counselling, needs assessment, and referrals to community services as required. A contract for $214,860 provided basic language training to adult newcomers. Finally, a contract for $68,982 undertook to to ease newcomers' adaptation to Canada by matching them and their families with a trained volunteer and his or her family. As well, a two-year contract for $111,274 was in place with Yukon College for training aimed at improving language and employability skills, formerly known as Enhanced Language Training (CIC 2009d).

In the Northwest Territories, CIC contracted with Aurora College for similar programming over a two year period. The basic language training contract was for $66,384, the orientation and counselling contract was for $58,919, the contract to match newcomers and their families with a trained volunteer and his or her family was for $31,419, and the contract for training aimed at improving language and employability skills was for $57,621 (CIC 2009e).

Aurora College has been the traditional settlement service provider in the NWT. However, CIC also recently concluded an orientation, counselling, and referral services agreement with the NWT's francophone organization, the Féderation Franco-TéNoise, for approximately $105,000 (CIC 2010b).

TERRITORIAL ORGANIZATION TO FACILITATE IMMIGRATION

The capacity of the three territories to provide mainline services to immigrants is consistent with their capacity to deliver services such as education, employment, health, and social services to all their residents. Specific territorial programs for immigrants are essentially non-existent, with the exception of Yukon's and the NWT's Territorial Nominee Programs.

In Yukon, the responsibility for immigration lies with the Department of Education; in the NWT, it is with the Department of Education, Culture and Employment; and in Nunavut, it is with the Department of Executive and Intergovernmental Affairs. Each territory is a member of CIC's Federal-Provincial-Territorial Planning Table, and the Economic Working Group and senior officials (assistant deputy minister, deputy minister) meet once or twice a year on average to discuss big picture issues. In addition, in recent years, the minister of citizenship and immigration has held meetings with his/her provincial and territorial colleagues on a roughly annual basis.

The only territory to aggressively encourage immigration is Yukon, through its Nominee Program. The territory's main website has a link to "Immigrate to Yukon" under "Popular Topics." The immigration pages offer background material on Yukon, general information on the immigration process, links to CIC, and, of course, information on and application forms for the Yukon Nominee Program (Yukon 2008). The program remained quite small until 2008. The introduction of the Critical Impact Worker category in November 2007 has attracted much attention from the Yukon business community, particularly in the retail and hospitality sectors. By December 2008 the program had attracted 299 principal applicants, 201 of them in the Critical Impact Worker category. The result is that Yukon has surpassed the NWT as the major destination for immigrants in Canada's North, at least until the NWT gets its new nominee program up and running. In addition, Yukon is planning to propose a Temporary Foreign Worker annex to its immigration agreement in order to help address the need for seasonal workers in the mineral exploration and hospitality industries.[1]

The Northwest Territories has concluded a portal agreement as well, and the GNWT intends to enhance its "Jobs North" website to include information for immigrants.

While several cities in the South have developed specific services for immigrants, this level of activity has not yet taken place in the North, presumably because of the relatively small number of immigrants and the relatively small size of even the largest communities, Whitehorse and Yellowknife.

Non-Governmental Organizations

Apart from the Association Franco-Yukonaise, the settlement service provider in Yukon, and the Féderation Franco-TéNoise, which provides services to francophone immigrants in the NWT, there is only one NGO with a specific mandate to assist immigrants. The GNWT provides funding to the Newcomers Ethno-Cultural Centre, an NGO in Yellowknife that has started a program to assist immigrants to that city. The programs focus on life skills, personal development, English literacy, and other assistance for immigrants. In 2008-09, the contract was for $30,000, with an increase expected for 2009–10.[2]

In Whitehorse and Yellowknife, the United Way agencies can offer services to immigrants and, throughout the North, church congregations are often involved in welcoming immigrants. The Islamic Centre of Yellowknife serves this function for Moslems in that city.

All three capital cities have a chamber of commerce but, again, none seem to have specific activities for immigrants or immigrant entrepreneurs. However, the chambers of commerce in both Yukon and the NWT are supportive of their governments' efforts to attract immigrants.

Some Thoughts for Policy Planners in the North

Nunavut is the only jurisdiction in Canada that does not have the means of selecting its own immigrants. Quebec has a unique agreement, and every other province and territory has a nominees agreement with the federal government. While Yukon only made modest use of its nominee program in the past, it is now growing faster than anticipated. Both the NWT and Nunavut were concerned about the potential cost of operating a nominees program, but the NWT has nonetheless gone ahead with a provincial nominee agreement, recognizing that the potential costs of *not* having a program are likely higher. Already, diamond cutters and polishers in Yellowknife have been applying to immigrate, but many, with little formal education, would not meet the federal skilled worker criteria; the Canadian Experience Class, which is only open to skilled workers, will not help them (CIC 2010a). However, as territorial nominees, they and other workers in demand in the North could qualify as immigrants.

A cost-effective way for Nunavut to operate a nominees program could be to contract with another jurisdiction. Nunavut has traditional ties with Manitoba, which operates the largest provincial nominees program. However, there is a risk that the relatively small numbers in that territory might be lost among the thousands of cases processed annually by Manitoba. A better solution might be for Nunavut to contract with Yukon or the NWT, which could grow its own nominee capacity at the same time as providing service at much lower cost to Nunavut than establishing its own stand-alone program. Yukon previously offered its expertise to the NWT and Nunavut to assist them in establishing nominee programs.

In addition, the NWT and Nunavut need to promote themselves as immigrant destinations, as Yukon does already. CIC is making approximately $200,000 per year available to each territory (CIC 2007) to develop an immigration web portal, and this will be a key promotional tool for each territory, as it already is for Yukon. The NWT is in the process of establishing its web portal, but Nunavut has yet to start the process. All three territories should also consider launching aggressive advertising campaigns in major southern cities to attract immigrants in those cities to move to the North. The Government of Quebec, recognizing that most immigrants to the province will initially move to Montreal, has organized information sessions on various regions in Quebec. At these sessions, offered in Montreal, new arrivals can meet representatives from these regions to obtain information on available jobs and business opportunities, as well as services offered in those areas (Quebec 2006). This is a model that the three territories might find attractive and cost effective.

Yukon and the NWT also need to ensure that the settlement funding allocated to their jurisdictions by CIC is utilized both to respond to current needs and to develop capacity. This capacity to welcome newcomers should be available in both English and French. In recent years, CIC has increased the available settlement funding from $150,000 or less in each territory to $633,000 in the NWT and $598,000 in Yukon in fiscal year 2010–11, including funding for enhanced language training, anti-racism initiatives, and web portal development. As immigration increases, so will the CIC funding for settlement. The two territories need to ensure that the funds are not only spent but well spent. Should the numbers of migrants to Nunavut increase, the government in Iqaluit will need to push CIC to provide settlement services there as well. The money is available, as $460,000 was allocated for Nunavut in 2010–11 (CIC 2009a).

Part of this effort will need to be the development of local capacity, not only in the capital cities but in other centres that will see immigrant movements. The National Working Group on Small Centre Strategies, with the assistance of CIC, has developed a useful resource to assist smaller communities to attract immigrants and support their settlement and integration. This publication, *Attracting and Retaining Immigrants: A*

Tool Box of Ideas for Smaller Centres, is required reading for any community wishing to mobilize its resources to get and keep immigrants (National Working Group on Small Centre Strategies 2007).

Finally, immigration must be regarded as a "whole of government" issue. Immigrant workers are not just so many more minds and hands for the economy. They are human beings with needs and ambitions, and they come with families with their own set of needs. While the planning issues around immigration to the North may seem unimportant in comparison to the huge issues surrounding rapid growth of both the Aboriginal and the domestic non-Aboriginal populations, there are still factors that must be taken into consideration. First and foremost is that immigration is increasing the overall pace of growth, and infrastructure, especially schools, housing, and medical facilities, need to keep pace. Also, as with Aboriginal families, first generation immigrant families are often larger than the Canadian average, and so appropriate housing needs to be available. Accessible locations and adequate space for parking at new churches, temples, and mosques need to be planned. For example, devout Muslims often visit mosques several times a day, which can create significant traffic problems around the mosque. "At Dhuhr, the Muslim midday prayer, white taxicabs swarm around the little mosque, and the parking lot erupts with kufi caps and robes of all colours," reported the *Globe and Mail* of the Islamic Centre of Yellowknife (White 2007). Planning needs to make allowances for such practices. Finally, immigrants often depend more on public transit than do other residents, and adequate public transit on all days of the week is an essential element of a community seeking to welcome immigrants.

CONCLUSION

The increasing number of immigrants and migrant workers to Canada's northern territories is and will be a key element of northern development. At the same time, the territories must balance their need for foreign workers with the requirement to develop their indigenous workforce and provide welcoming environments for all in the increasingly diverse cities and communities of the North. This work is not the responsibility of one level of government, nor is it the responsibility of government alone. Federal, territorial, and municipal governments working together with all people across the North is the essential formula for success.

NOTES

1.   Email to author, 2 December 2008, from Brent Slobodian, assistant deputy minister, Advanced Education, Yukon Department of Education 2008.

2.   Emails to author, 11 and 13 January 2009, from Gloria Iatridis, assistant deputy minister, Advanced Education and Careers, Northwest Territories Department of Education, Culture and Employment 2009.

REFERENCES

Canada. 1870a. *An Act for the Temporary Government of Rupert's Land and the North-Western Territory When United with Canada,* 32-33 Victoria, c. 3.
—1870b. *An Act to Amend and Continue the Act 32 and 33 Victoria, Chapter 3; and to Establish and Provide for the Government of the Province of Manitoba, Statutes of Canada 1870,* c.3, 20-27.
—1898. *The Yukon Territory Act, Statutes of Canada 1898* (v. I-II), c.6, 55-61.
—1905. *Alberta Act, Statutes of Canada 1905,* c. 3, p. 77 and *The Saskatchewan Act, Statutes of Canada 1905,* c.42, 201.
Citizenship and Immigration Canada (CIC) 2007. "Improving Online Information for Newcomers." Backgrounder, 24 May 2007. At http://www.cic.gc.ca/english/department/media/backgrounders/2007/2007-05-24b.asp (accessed 1 September 2008).
—2008a. *Agreement for Canada-Yukon Co-operation on Immigration.* At http://www.cic.gc.ca/english/department/laws-policy/agreements/yukon/can-yukon-agree-2008.asp (accessed 2 April 2011).
—2008b. *Departmental Performance Report for the Period Ending March 31, 2006.* At http://www.tbs-sct.gc.ca/dpr-rmr/0506/CI-CI/ci-ci-eng.pdf (accessed 8 October 2008).
—2008c. "Canada and Yukon Announce New Agreement on Immigration; Launch New Web Portal Aimed at Attracting Newcomers." News release, 21 May 2008. At http://www.cic.gc.ca/english/department/media/releases/2008/2008-05-21a.asp (accessed 2 April 2011).
—2009a. "Settlement Funding Allocations for 2010–11." Backgrounder, 22 December 2009. At http://www.cic.gc.ca/english/department/media/backgrounders/2009/2009-12-22.asp (accessed 2 April 2011).
—2009b. *Facts and Figures 2008.* Ottawa: Public Works and Government Services Canada.
—2009c. "Government of Canada Signs First-Ever Immigration Agreement with Northwest Territories." News release, 5 August 2008. At http://www.cic.gc.ca/english/department/media/releases/2009/2009-08-05.asp (accessed 24 November 2009).
—2009d. "Agencies in Yukon." Proactive Disclosure Section. At http://www.cic.gc.ca/english/disclosure/grants/2009-Q2/g-009.asp; http://www.cic.gc.ca/english/disclosure/grants/2009-Q2/g-010.asp; http://www.cic.gc.ca/english/disclosure/grants/2009-Q2/g-008.asp; http://www.cic.gc.ca/english/disclosure/grants/2008-Q4/g-008.asp (accessed 24 November 2009).
—2009e. "Agencies in NWT." Proactive Disclosure Section. At http://www.cic.gc.ca/english/disclosure/grants/2008-Q4/g-022.asp; http://www.cic.gc.ca/english/disclosure/grants/2008-Q4/g-024.asp; http://www.cic.gc.ca/english/disclosure/grants/2008-Q4/g-025.asp; http://www.cic.gc.ca/english/disclosure/grants/2008-Q4/g-023.asp (accessed 24 November 2009).

—2010a. *Canadian Experience Class: Who Can Apply.* At http://www.cic.gc.ca/english/immigrate/cec/apply-who.asp (assessed 2 April 2011).

—2010b. Proactive Disclosure Section. At http://www.cic.gc.ca/english/disclosure/grants/2010-Q1/g-287.asp (accessed 2 April 2011).

—2011. *Facts and Figures 2010.* At http://www.cic.gc.ca/english/resources/statistics/menu-fact.asphttp://www.cic.gc.ca/english/resources/statistics/menu-fact.asp (accessed 2 April 2011).

Library and Archives Canada (LAC). 2006. Orders-in Council, RG2, Privy Council Office, Series A-1-a. At http://www.collectionscanada.gc.ca/databases/orders/index-e.html (accessed 2 April 2011).

National Working Group on Small Centre Strategies. 2007. *Attracting and Retaining Immigrants: A Tool Box of Ideas for Smaller Centres.* 2nd ed. Victoria: Inter-Cultural Association of Greater Victoria.

Quebec. Ministère d'Immigration et Communautés culturelles. 2006. "Information Sessions on Life and Employment in the Regions." At http://www.immigration-quebec.gouv.qc.ca/en/settle/regions-sessions/index.htmlhttp://www.immigration-quebec.gouv.qc.ca/en/settle/regions-sessions/index.html (accessed 1 September 2008).

Statistical Year Book of Canada for 1901. 1902. Ministry of Agriculture. Ottawa: Government Printing Bureau.

Statistics Canada. 2006. *2006 Census of Canada.* At http://www12.statcan.gc.ca/census-recensement/index-eng.cfm (accessed 2 April 2011).

—2011. *The Daily.* 24 March 2011. At http://www.statcan.gc.ca/daily-quotidien/110324/dq110324b-eng.htm (accessed 4 April 2011).

Year Book and Almanac of Canada for 1872. 1872. Ministry of Agriculture. Ottawa: James Bailiff.

Yukon. 2008. *Immigration* web page. At http://www.immigration.gov.yk.ca (accessed 2 April 2011).

White, P. 2007. "Little Mosque on the Tundra." *Globe and Mail,* 6 December 2007.

CONCLUSION

JOHN BILES, MEYER BURSTEIN, JAMES FRIDERES,
ERIN TOLLEY, AND ROBERT VINEBERG

This volume brings together much information about immigration, integration, and inclusion across Canada, illuminating the range of actors, resources, and models deployed across the country to assist in fostering an integrated society. Although poor public reporting in many jurisdictions, the divergent interests of contributing authors, and the sheer number of actors and programmatic and policy solutions that exist often make comparisons between provinces difficult, we provide here a brief summary of common challenges, findings, and observations. These will be instructive for readers interested in integration and inclusion, intergovernmental relations, multi-level governance, and the role of non-governmental organizations and communities in policy formation and service delivery.

Some common challenges discussed in the chapters include strategic direction setting, accountability, coordination, and inclusion of numerous actors, the need for a stronger focus on "host communities," the regionalization of immigration, and issues related to trust and collaboration. A number of chapters speak to further challenges, such as how to tackle the integration of increasing numbers of temporary foreign workers (Alberta, British Columbia, Quebec), how to ease tensions between newcomers and Aboriginal peoples (Manitoba), the appropriate level of funding needed to ensure satisfactory integration and inclusion outcomes (Alberta, Quebec, Saskatchewan), and – the perennial favourite of researchers – the need for more research (Newfoundland and Labrador). Leaving these specific challenges to individual chapters, we briefly discuss the crosscutting themes and summarize the more promising innovations and practices that the authors have highlighted. We conclude with some thoughts about the future of settlement in Canada.

Integration and Inclusion of Newcomers and Minorities across Canada, ed. J. Biles, M. Burstein, J. Frideres, E. Tolley, and R. Vineberg. Montreal and Kingston: Queen's Policy Studies Series, McGill-Queen's University Press.

Common Challenges

Strategic Direction Setting

Despite increasing provincial interest in immigration, integration, and inclusion, it is striking that two of the largest recipient provinces do not have a public strategy that outlines how they intend to attract and retain the newcomers they profess to need. This deficiency is most obvious in Ontario, where, throughout the life of the Canada-Ontario Immigration Agreement, the province has focused more on the allocation of federal settlement funding and less on developing its own contribution to integration and inclusion.[1] Curiously, British Columbia has also not released a unified public plan that sets out what the province wishes to achieve, although components can be found in Welcome BC, its work force strategy.[2] By contrast, other provincial governments have emulated Quebec's approach of publishing an immigration and settlement strategy (Ministry of Immigration and Cultural Communities 2008). Plans were released by Alberta and Nova Scotia in 2005, Manitoba and Newfoundland and Labrador in 2007, New Brunswick in 2008, Saskatchewan in 2009, and Prince Edward Island in 2010. At the federal level, after a hiatus, Citizenship and Immigration Canada (CIC) has once again prepared a five-year strategic plan that complements the annual immigration plan tabled in the House of Commons as required by the *Immigration and Refugee Protection Act* (CIC 2010a).

Accountability

While the federal government publicly discloses information on grants and contributions over $25,000, as well as details about contracts over $10,000, this level of financial detail is not consistently made public by provinces or by non-governmental and community organizations. Not even the annual reports that British Columbia and Manitoba provide, pursuant to their realignment agreements with Citizenship and Immigration Canada,[3] are placed in the public realm (Seidle 2010a, 2010b). Not surprisingly, authors in this volume have had difficulty ascertaining the allocation of resources to immigration, integration, and inclusion activities. A further complication is the repackaging of federal funding into a variety of provincial programs, including labour market development activities, support for immigration portals, initiatives related to welcoming communities, and programs for attracting and retaining francophone newcomers.[4]

A second weakness in accountability concerns the evaluation framework used to assess investments in integration and inclusion. While both federal and provincial governments conduct program evaluations, only the federal assessments are easily accessible to the public.[5] Moreover, none of the evaluations includes baseline needs assessments for newcomers against which to measure the efficacy of program investments. That being said, the federal, provincial, and territorial working group on settlement has recently agreed in principle to a number of macro-societal indicators that can be used to assess settlement and integration. Eventually these data will provide a useful starting point for comparisons, but we were not able to take advantage of them in our analysis (CIC 2010b).

A third concern relates to what others have referred to as the swinging pendulum of grants and contributions management – between the Scylla of providing resources rapidly to communities with few strings attached, and the Charybdis of tight control and oversight. In the former case, there may be inadequate attention paid to accountability, while in the latter, more attention may be given to efficiency and cost-effectiveness at the expense of delivering optimal outcomes (Good 2003).

Coordination and Inclusion of Various Actors

The chapters chronicle an increased provincial interest in immigration, integration, and inclusion as well as the emergence of bureaucratic struc- tures with dedicated resources – both financial and human – addressing these areas. Quebec, Manitoba, and British Columbia are by far the most ambitious in this regard, although other provinces are moving to close the gap. Encouragingly, just as CIC has sought to engage a wide range of federal departments and agencies,[6] a number of provinces have also shown progress in implementing a horizontal, whole-of-government approach. Newfoundland and Labrador, Nova Scotia, Prince Edward Island, Quebec, and, to some extent, British Columbia all have models that other provinces might wish to explore.

It is not only provincial governments that have begun to express a more active interest in immigration: so too have municipal governments and a wide range of other actors. Indeed, all of the chapters (with the apparent exceptions of those on PEI and Newfoundland and Labrador) provide fascinating examples of how municipal and local governments have become more actively engaged – a finding in common with much recent literature (Andrew et al. forthcoming; Burr 2011; Good 2008; Tolley and Young 2011). The same phenomena can be detected among so-called universal service providers such as the United Way and YMCA/YWCA, as well as local foundations, post-secondary institutions, and a wide swath of civil society organizations, whether immigrant serving, multicultural or ethno-specific, issue-based, or other. At the same time, it is notable that very few chapters, with the exception of Ontario, Quebec, and Nova

Scotia, draw attention to chambers of commerce. This suggests that these organizations are not overly active in integration matters, in spite of increased employer attention to immigration.

"Host" Communities

Interestingly, many chapters highlight the need to actively engage "host" populations if immigration, integration, and inclusion are to be successful in fostering an integrated society. As Garcea and Hibbert (this volume) note, a fairly robust policy framework exists, although resources for engaging host communities are in short supply. For example, over the same period that federal resources for settlement programs tripled to almost $960 million per year, resources for federal multiculturalism programming remained fixed at around $26 million annually (Government of Canada 2011). Similarly, in some provincial jurisdictions like Ontario, there is currently no specific programming for multiculturalism; although Ontario has a modest "Community Builders" fund, the multiculturalism infrastructure was dismantled by the previous government and has yet to be restored.

In comparison to most other immigrant-receiving countries, Canadians tend to be exceptionally supportive of immigration, integration, and inclusion (German Marshall Fund Survey 2010). There are, however, vulnerabilities. Across the country, support for high levels of immigration is somewhat fragile (Greenaway 2010), while in Quebec, perceived challenges to the French language and to secularism have led to concerns about social and cultural diversity (Adams 2007; Bouchard 2011).

Regionalization

Concerns about community receptivity to immigration have increased as newcomers have settled in a wider range of communities, many of them with little recent experience of immigration-fuelled diversity (Wulff et al. 2008). This has program and policy ramifications, given that the program and policy responses available to metropolitan areas with large numbers of newcomers are not only quantitatively but also often qualitatively different from those available in smaller communities with few newcomers.

Interestingly, the wider distribution of newcomers across the country has generated a need for more local involvement and for institutions and strategies able to support cross-regional exchanges of knowledge and advice. This development undermines an oft-cited argument for devolution of settlement to the provinces – that the provinces are better able to adjust to local circumstances and context (Mendelsohn 2010). In fact, it would appear that the federal government is better positioned to work across provinces and better resourced to promote cross-regional comparisons. The Metropolis Project and successor networks are strong examples of this capacity. Moreover, scale matters. Rural areas arguably can learn more from each other than they can from the major urban centres in their own provinces. In the same way, mid-size urban centres are finding that models developed in Montreal, Toronto, and Vancouver not suited to their contexts.

Trust

As is clear in the preceding chapters, there is a level of distrust among players involved in immigration, integration, and inclusion. Negotiations between Canada and Ontario on a new immigration agreement have been played out in the media, resulting in hard feelings (Keung 2011). Meanwhile, Manitoba and British Columbia have come under pressure for not living up to the obligations contained in their realignment agreements; the result has been stronger accountability provisions in their new agreements. Concern has also mounted regarding British Columbia and Quebec's consistent redirection of settlement resources to general revenues (Smith 2009). Recent pressure from settlement agencies in Quebec has highlighted how little financial support actually flows to community agencies (Reichold 2010).

Other areas of tension can be found in the relations between the federal government and service providers, between provinces and municipalities, and among the various organizations involved in service delivery. At the federal level, CIC has drawn fire for the short notice it provided to agencies whose contribution agreements were not going to be renewed by the federal government (Standing Committee on Citizenship and Immigration 2011a, 2011b). Meanwhile, municipalities in many jurisdictions yearn to be more actively engaged in newcomer recruitment and integration, but find their provincial governments keeping them from the table. Only the Canada-Ontario Agreement includes direct engagement of municipalities and an agreement with the City of Toronto. There is also growing competition between immigrant service organizations and other organizations eager to enter the settlement "market" and rapidly developing the capacity to do so. Finally, eligibility requirements that restrict access to particular services have diminished trust between newcomer communities and immigrant settlement agencies (Burstein 2010).

Despite these tensions, there is room for optimism. There are more federal-provincial-territorial interactions in settlement and integration than at any time in the past. There are also many encouraging examples of measures to engage a wide range of stakeholders at multilateral tables. These measures include the Local Immigration Partnerships (LIPs) that have been piloted in Ontario and will soon extend to other jurisdictions

(WCI 2011). The LIPs have the potential to build on path-breaking work in Quebec and Manitoba and to break down the stifling clientalist mentality that has characterized the relationship between funders and settlement agencies across the country.

In addition, given the finality with which Minister of Citizenship and Immigration Jason Kenney has dismissed full devolution of settlement services to the provinces, attention has shifted to the potential of a generalized co-management approach (Kenney 2010).[7] Co-management appears to be the preference of the settlement sector itself, as it affords protection against settlement resources being redirected to general revenues, brings both the federal and provincial governments to the table, promotes harmonization of eligibility requirements, thus maximizing coverage for newcomers, and holds the promise of minimizing duplication and overlap (OCASI 2009).

INNOVATION, PROMISING INITIATIVES, AND BEST PRACTICES

Among the encouraging signs to emerge from the preceding chapters is the extent of innovation that exists across the country. Some of the high notes include the co-management of settlement in Alberta that has developed gradually over the past 30 years (KPMG 2009). Similarly, the flow of resources into Ontario through the Canada Ontario Immigration Agreement has allowed for experimentation such as the development of welcome centres, newcomer information centres, and LIPs. Saskatchewan's gateways and British Columbia's Welcome BC initiatives have encouraged high levels of community involvement. Meanwhile, Newfoundland and Labrador, Prince Edward Island, and Quebec have experimented with different strategies to engage a wide range of provincial ministries; New Brunswick and Manitoba have developed a variety of initiatives to increase francophone immigration; Alberta has experimented with providing limited settlement services to temporary foreign workers; and Manitoba has passed legislation to protect migrant workers from unscrupulous recruiters and consultants.

Growing interest and attention to best practices and rigorous performance measures that have been widely accepted should in future help policy-makers and practitioners separate the best practice wheat from the merely promising chaff (Burstein 2010; Turegun 2011; WCI 2010), accelerating the exchanges already taking place. For example, Ontario's introduction of a fairness commissioner to facilitate foreign credential recognition was quickly emulated by Manitoba. Similarly, Alberta's immigrant access fund, which offers loans to newcomers to assist them through credentialing exams, is now being funded by CIC's Foreign Credential Referral Office to expand into Saskatchewan and Manitoba and may soon be implemented nation-wide. The importance of such knowledge exchanges was recognized by the Standing Committee on Citizenship and Immigration, which stressed the evaluation and sharing of best practices with a view to replacing inefficient and ineffective practices with those proven to work (Standing Committee on Citizenship and Immigration 2010). If the present support for improved outcomes for newcomers proves durable, the settlement sector could be on the cusp of renewal.

THE FUTURE: FROM SETTLEMENT SECTOR TO SETTLEMENT SYSTEM

In this final section, we would like to build on the practices and themes appearing throughout the volume to offer a number of suggestions for how the settlement system could be tweaked to realize some modest near-term improvements. Several observations are in order, however. First, the stand-alone era of settlement is clearly over. All three orders of government must be involved in settlement if outcomes are to improve; no one level of government holds a monopoly over the full range of essential services. Similarly, immigrant serving agencies must clarify their competitive advantages and equip themselves to more effectively and productively engage with each other and with a range of institutions that also aid in the settlement of newcomers. Second, there is a clear imperative to engage a wider cross-section of ministries at each level of government. Specialized settlement services should not be the first choice or a replacement for appropriate adjustments to mainstream institutions. Rather, immigrant-specific arrangements should only be pursued when mainstream services cannot effectively meet the needs of newcomers. Third, the linkages between selection and settlement must be strengthened. It is counterproductive to engage in a multi-year immigration levels plan on the selection side without adopting a similar strategy on the settlement side. Fourth, in a time where settlement resources have plateaued and are likely to decline in the foreseeable future, a robust commitment to transparent performance measurement is an essential strategy for defending expenditures, which currently exceed $1 billion per year. Transparent performance measures would also reward efficiency and effectiveness and reduce the scope for capricious and arbitrary decisions. Finally, settlement programming must be accompanied by a more coherent settlement-integration continuum that spans the time from initial information gathering by potential immigrants to when newcomers have adapted and feel that they truly belong in Canada. We take up this point more fully below.

Before proceeding, however, we would like to advance three broad ideas. First is a set of principles consistent with the mantra "settlement if necessary, but not necessarily settlement." In other words, where possible, newcomers' needs should be addressed by mainstream institutions and programs. This means that immigrants will deal with the same institutions as other Canadians, which serves an integrative purpose. The only fiscally viable option in smaller municipalities and communities, this mainstreaming approach is also the only logical option in Montreal, Toronto, and Vancouver, where newcomers will soon comprise the majority of the population. It is also the case for the provision of francophone immigration services outside of Quebec, where dedicated single-language settlement-specific organizations are often impractical. Where possible, settlement organizations should deliver services in both languages.[8]

The second idea concerns the machinery of settlement production. Notwithstanding a recent significant injection of resources, the settlement sector feels under threat. Funder expectations have risen, organizations are delivering a more complex array of services and interacting with a wider range of ministries, and new competitors have emerged in the quasi-public and even commercial sectors. To address these challenges, settlement agencies will need to focus on areas where they enjoy a comparative advantage over other organizations; they will need to partner with immigrant and ethno-cultural organizations as well as mainstream agencies. Governments must also recognize that they have a shared interest in facilitating and assisting this transition and should pursue action rather than additional consultation and discussion (Burstein 2010).

The third idea concerns the role of the private sector and employer engagement. To date, success in terms of recruitment, hiring, training, and modifying job requirements to take advantage of immigrants' skills has largely been confined to big employers.[9] We should look to models that might even see these employers covering some of the settlement costs of the immigrant workers they employ. On the other hand, the small and medium sized employers (SMEs), who are the major source of employment growth, have been reluctant to hire immigrants and to work with settlement service providers. Renewed efforts are needed to engage SMEs and to convincingly make the case for hiring immigrants, although it is unlikely that these employers would be able to provide settlement assistance to the few newcomers they employ.

Based on these points and the observations made in the preceding chapters, we now briefly articulate some of the components that should be included along the settlement-integration continuum. These components include an overseas strategy, orientation, and needs assessment, a coherent network of services for newcomers, a revitalized citizenship program, a more robust stance on welcoming communities, and a greater emphasis on integration and inclusion strategies. Attention needs also to be paid to governance, performance measurement, and best practices and innovation. We outline each of these points below.

Overseas Strategy

Prior to arrival, newcomers struggle to get a realistic picture of what settlement and integration in Canada requires. To assist in this process, an improved settlement strategy would have two overseas components. First, it would provide potential immigrants with information on outcomes and prospects so that they can make informed choices prior to applying. The importance of official language fluency would be emphasized, as would requirements for licensing and credential recognition. Second, immigrants should have opportunities to prepare themselves prior to arrival through some mix of online and personal coaching related to settlement planning, adapted to their specific education and language abilities. An improved overseas strategy would require an expansion of the information made available through the immigration portals and the *Welcome to Canada* publication produced by CIC.[10] Pending the evaluation of overseas in-person counselling, a modest expansion of services may be feasible.[11]

Orientation and Needs Assessment

There is close to unanimous agreement in the settlement strategies developed by the LIPs that a common "front door" to settlement services would improve accessibility and efficiency.[12] The exact construction of this front door is less important than ensuring that a common needs assessment is undertaken early on. Such an assessment would eliminate concerns related to self-referrals and would diminish the "institutional hoarding" to which particular funding incentives give rise.[13] Universally administered needs assessments at mandatory orientation sessions would also resolve lingering concerns about the uptake of settlement services[14] and would protect the most vulnerable entrants by educating them about their rights and the resources available to them. Moreover, various pilots across the country suggest that common front door systems can be introduced efficiently and effectively.

Coherent Network of Services

This common front door would need to be supported by a coherent network of service providers to whom newcomers could be referred for specialized services. Some of these services would need to be coordinated much more effectively. This is particularly the case with language and labour market programs but also applies to networking and mentoring, referrals, and settlement counselling, as we outline below. Nonetheless, various mechanisms could be employed to improve service coherence; these would include making better use of the existing settlement sector umbrella organizations than is presently the case[15] and relying on the LIPs to drive program integration and rationalization (Burr 2011).[16] The LIPs are a critical means for drawing in a wider range of stakeholders and identifying common concerns to guide settlement and integration policy development. To maximize the potential contribution of the LIPs, federal and provincial ministries will need to invest both in the LIPs and in their own internal capacity to understand and respond to local plans.

Language

A common assessment process could be used to place newcomers in federally and provincially funded language courses. Assessment could be modelled on systems used in Alberta's language centres and centres presently under development in Ontario.[17] In all mid-size communities, a suite of language training programs should be available; in smaller communities, a somewhat smaller range of options with alternative delivery models could be provided. In addition, funding should be made to available to employers and others looking to diversify language training options with innovative approaches. Promising practices exist across the country; these are being examined by the Welcoming Communities Initiative, and many will be captured in a joint federal-provincial-territorial repository of language best practices presently in development. [18]

Bilingual regions such as Moncton, Ottawa, and Winnipeg should be designated so that newcomers destined for the labour market would be eligible for both English and French language training up to a modest maximum level.[19] At the same time, enhanced language training to support job-specific language development and bridge-to-work opportunities would be pursued for all eligible newcomers where numbers warrant. Standardized testing would ensure quality, comparability, and cost-effectiveness across service providers.[20] Emphasis should be placed on aiding all newcomers to attain the required language standards necessary for the acquisition of citizenship and participation in the labour market.[21] Literacy classes should also be made available where necessary.

Labour Market Preparation and Programming

A range of newcomer-specific labour market preparation services should be offered where numbers warrant. These services would complement the broader labour market preparation initiatives that already target the general population.[22] The services offered to newcomers would include resumé preparation, soft skills and job search training, and interview preparation. Moreover, when Human Resources and Skills Development Canada renegotiates labour market agreements and labour market development agreements with the provinces, immigrants should be identified as a key client population requiring specialized programming, dedicated funding, and transparent reporting on outcomes.

Credential recognition initiatives, including loans to support newcomers taking credentialing exams, could also be offered, as is already the case in Alberta. That being said, foreign credential recognition remains one of the truly confounding settlement problems in Canada. Responsibility for credential recognition generally lies with professional associations that are provincially regulated, but the federal government has a role to play in terms of easing inter-provincial mobility for all Canadians, whether born and trained in this country or abroad. To that end, CIC's Foreign Credential Referral Office has worked with its provincial and territorial partners to establish a Pan-Canadian Framework for the Assessment and Recognition of Foreign Qualifications.[23] More work is needed here, however. In addition, other jurisdictions might want to consider the introduction of a fairness commissioner to oversee licensing and credentialing issues, as has been done in Ontario and Manitoba.

Networking and Mentoring

The loss of social capital is one of the near certainties of migration, but research suggests that the sooner that immigrants are able to (re)forge their networks – particularly with individuals from different backgrounds – the more rapidly their social and economic outcomes will improve (Young 1998; Xue 2007). Most settlement programming contributes directly or indirectly to building social capital, but mentoring and networking are the only components that directly target newcomers' connections to the broader community. More emphasis should thus be placed on mentoring and bridge-to-work programs for labour market destined newcomers. These programs could build on the innovative work of the Maytree Foundation's ALLIES project, an initiative that created networks of employers in eight locations across the country. The networks facilitated the mentoring of highly skilled newcomers by Canadians in similar fields, with the intention of identifying and securing eventual employment. Similar programs could bring together immigrant seniors, while newcomers with preschool-age children could be connected to early childhood development programs, women could be connected to women's networks, and youth could be connected to youth programs. Support for programs and for institutional change would be needed, although the LIPs are ideally suited to forge some of the needed connections.

Referrals

Almost as frequently as they request a common front door, newcomers indicate frustration with a referrals process that does not always connect them to appropriate programs. Overcoming this frustration is a major challenge for most communities where the ubiquity of "pilot projects" means that many different programs are initiated and terminated each year. Regular community-based program asset mapping needs to be undertaken and the results shared with those working in settlement provision to ensure that knowledge of the ever-changing programscape remains current. Here, the LIPs could assist. For example, LIP strategies could be analyzed annually to identify service provision gaps or insufficient institutional capacity to address newcomers' needs.

Settlement Counselling

Newcomers seek at least three types of settlement counselling, and in all three areas improvements could be made. In the first type of counselling, we see a combination of information provision and issue management. Here, a newcomer seeks the assistance of a service provider, generally through a referral or to resolve a specific issue. The interaction is typically one time, and these services tend to be low cost. If co-funded with the provinces, such counselling could be available to all immigrants, regardless of permanent resident status, which would resolve one of the most difficult eligibility concerns facing service providers. In some situations, such as document translation, service could be provided on a cost-recovery basis. The second kind of counselling, para-counselling, typically involves high-needs or multiply disadvantaged clients. These clients generally seek advice in their mother tongue and often return many times. In this context, a case management approach is most logical. Here, the settlement counsellor could accompany the client to visits with mainstream service providers to handle interpretation and ensure equitable treatment. This type of arrangement entails an explicit policy trade-off between mainstream institutional change where numbers warrant, and an ongoing investment in counsellors who act as an interface with mainstream institutions. A third kind of counselling sought by newcomers involves steering through immigration paperwork. This type of support is particularly sought by privately sponsored refugees and newcomers in the family reunification stream.[24] Ethno-cultural and religious organizations are generally called upon for assistance, suggesting that a more organized (and possibly funded) approach might fill an important gap.

Citizenship

Citizenship acquisition is a key milestone on the settlement-integration continuum, marking the end of settlement and beginning of integration. Settlement programming should include a two-day citizenship preparation course focusing on both citizenship and integration issues. Exemptions similar to those already in place for naturalization requirements could be granted. In addition, acquiring citizenship should open doors, not close them; as such, there is a need to revisit the restriction of settlement services to permanent residents. This is a policy decision that often affects women who have stayed home to raise children and thus delayed their integration; their acquisition of citizenship and resulting ineligibility for settlement services only exacerbates the problem.[25]

Welcoming Communities

Welcoming communities initiatives are at the intersection between settlement and integration and between newcomers and hosts. Settlement service provider organizations can play a critical role by, for example, sitting on police boards and advisory committees and bridging with other mainstream institutions. In addition to this more informal linking, two formal approaches merit examination. These are the LIPs and an initiative that places settlement workers in institutions typically accessed by newcomers.

LIPs bring a community's major private and public players together to map assets, identify gaps, and develop innovative approaches to enhance the welcome for newcomers and minorities. Importantly, the partnerships extend beyond the capacity of the immigrant-serving sector, engaging the entire community and the full range of local institutions as well as applicable provincial and federal agencies. By design, many of the remedial strategies and actions developed by the LIPs thus far invoke systemic responses that affect not only newcomers but the entire community. LIPs should thus be established in all communities with significant newcomer populations. In addition, the LIPs should work closely with francophone networks to ensure that issues specific to francophone immigrants are addressed more broadly than is currently the case.[26]

The strategy of locating settlement workers in institutions where immigrants are concentrated has also been extremely valuable. Such programs have seen settlement workers placed in schools and libraries. In addition to enhancing service delivery, this practice also encourages institutional change such as adjustments to curriculum and programming, as well as changes in the composition of staff and management. Placing and supporting settlement workers in mainstream institutions would appear to provide fruitful terrain for co-management between CIC and its provincial partners. Consideration should thus be given to co-management and co-funding, extending the model to other logical sites (health centres, for example) and should include other federal and provincial ministries.

Integration and Inclusion

In contrast with settlement, which tends to focus specifically on immigrants, integration seeks to engage individual Canadians, communities, and existing institutions in the longer-term process of welcoming and including newcomers in Canadian society. In this way, integration is a two-way street. With this in mind, integration programs work to accelerate the convergence of outcomes between newcomers and the Canadian born, to tackle institutional and attitudinal obstacles, and to ensure that the public is aware of the challenges that newcomers face and the contributions that they make to Canada. The rationale for such programs is twofold: considerations related to equity and fairness, on the one hand, and on the other, a mix of self-interest with newcomers using their skills for the benefit of all Canadians.

Nonetheless, more could be done. A public education campaign should be initiated to emphasize Canada's success in building a society in which diverse cultures are able to live together peacefully, at the same time stressing – to newcomers and the Canadian born – the rights and responsibilities of citizenship. The campaign's aim would be to encourage inclusion in everyday actions and to promote activities such as volunteering and political participation that build community and encourage forging connections with a range of organizations. Indeed, there is a need to connect new Canadians to one another and to build on the work, started during settlement, linking immigrants to citizens and the Canadian born. Action in this area could include funding festivals in smaller communities, supporting inter-faith dialogue and exchange, or capitalizing on federal initiatives such as Exchanges Canada and Explore, the official language summer bursary program. We must look also at the outcomes of second-generation Canadians, the Canadian born children of immigrants, to ensure that they are achieving the same outcomes as other Canadians.[27]

Of course, integration requires not only individual strategies but institutional ones. Key institutions such as schools, religious institutions, municipal agencies, and voluntary sector organizations must be identified, sensitized, and sometimes transformed. At present, there is no systematic government approach to institutional reform or adaptation. The result is piecemeal programming and the introduction of costly interventions that do not necessarily produce "newcomer friendly" reforms within the implicated organizations. Integration and inclusion programming must include an institutional strategy that engages, persuades, and supports institutional reform.

Structure and Governance

Throughout this volume, we have seen that federal and provincial collaboration is viewed as essential to effective newcomer integration. Such collaboration must extend beyond ministries of immigration and integration to the full range of relevant departments. It could take the form of co-management or co-funding in some areas, or having one order of government deliver services on behalf of both. Bringing municipalities to the table in a meaningful capacity is also critical. In a similar vein, attention needs to be paid to the capacity of the settlement sector, including strengthening its analytic capacity to initiate change, plan effectively, and develop timely and thoughtful reactions to federal and provincial initiatives.

In order to realize the full potential of the broader partnerships and heightened level of engagement that are being advocated, some kind of supra-governance structure is required. This structure must be broader than the present federal, provincial, and territorial forum, which includes only governments, and broader than the Settlement and Integration Joint Policy and Program Council, which brings together government officials and umbrella organizations from the settlement sector but not from the wider community. Such a structure should be capable of setting strategic directions, endorsing best practices, promoting innovation, and initiating work to address common challenges. A means to include the francophone networks in this expanded discussion is also needed.[28]

Performance Measurement, Best Practices, and Innovation

We must look, in addition, at developing and adopting outcome measures to assess settlement and integration interventions. At the project level, assessment measures are needed to guide expenditure, and at the national and provincial/territorial level, to support overall system design. They are a critical step towards improving the effectiveness, efficiency, and overall management of the settlement and integration continuum. Moreover, results must be made *publicly* available so as to support decision-making and comparative analysis and to reassure the public that interventions are producing value.

Institutional reform within the settlement sector – the major "producer" of settlement services – requires at least two changes. First, individual agencies must be equipped with the tools to analyze their own practices and identify innovative features. Second, this analysis must extend throughout the settlement "industry" so that agency practices can be compared and disseminated and their relative strengths identified. To be effective and viewed as legitimate, the assessment process should be co-managed with funders and involve the academic community. These changes would endow the settlement sector with the machinery to drive innovation and improvement; with appropriate funding, that machinery could form the basis of changes in policy and practice.

FINAL THOUGHTS

If the golden age of multiculturalism in Canada came in the late 1980s with the introduction of the *Canadian Multiculturalism Act*, the *Employment Equity Act*, and the creation of the Department of Multiculturalism and Citizenship, the next decade may well represent the golden age for settlement and integration. An aging population will continue to drive immigration and underpin the need for successful integration. Most of the key players are now interested and engaged, and present resources far exceed the wildest dreams of those who worked in the settlement field even as recently as 30 years ago. Nonetheless, we cannot lose sight of the prize, namely, better outcomes for newcomers, minorities, and all Canadians. With a focus on this end and a spirit of open cooperation, the impact can be truly profound.

NOTES

The opinions expressed in this conclusion are those of the authors and do not necessarily reflect those of Citizenship and Immigration Canada or the Government of Canada.

1. There is a strategic plan to guide expenditures under the Canada-Ontario Immigration Agreement, but it is a plan for federal settlement resources and does not encompass provincial expenditures in the same manner as the other provinces do (CIC 2007).
2. While British Columbia does not publish a comprehensive immigration strategy, the major elements of its strategy can be found in two public documents, "Skills for Growth, BC's Workforce Strategy" and "WelcomeBC." See http://www.aved.gov.bc.ca/skills_for_growth/docs/Skills_for_Growth_Strategy.pdf and http://www.welcomebc.ca/local/wbc/docs/wbc_annual_report.pdf (p. 5).
3. The Canada British Columbia Immigration Agreement was recently renegotiated. Full details can be found at http://www.cic.gc.ca/english/department/laws-policy/agreements/bc/index-bc.asp. For our purposes, what is noteworthy is that the specificity of instructions related to the service plan and annual report has been significantly enhanced. The Canada Manitoba Immigration Agreement is presently under negotiation. Specifics

on the existing agreement, with its less stringent reporting requirements, can be found at http://www.cic.gc.ca/english/department/laws-policy/agreements/manitoba/can-man-2003.asp#integration.

4. In addition to the funding envelope for settlement programming, CIC also annually administers approximately $55.4 million for enhanced language training, $5.6 million for the immigration portal, and $3.2 million for the Welcoming Communities Initiative. As well, under the Road Map for Canada's Linguistic Duality, the department spends $4.5 million to support attraction and retention efforts to boost the number of francophone immigrants settling in francophone minority communities. Much of this funding is transferred to provinces under various arrangements and is then frequently counted as part of "provincial expenditures" on settlement. Many of the authors in this volume struggled with similar accounting issues in drafting their chapters. To further complicate matters, Human Resources and Skills Development Canada has signed Labour Market Agreements (LMAs) with provincial and territorial governments. These commit a total $3 billion over six years (see http://www.hrsdc.gc.ca/eng/employment/partnerships/lma/index.shtml). In addition, Canada has entered into bilateral Labour Market Development Agreements (LMDAs) with provinces and territories. Expenditures for these programs amount to $1.95 billion annually (see http://www.hrsdc.gc.ca/eng/employment/partnerships/labour_market_development/index.shtml). Many of these resources are then promoted by the provinces as their contribution to labour market initiatives.

5. Evaluations must be posted online. See http://www.cic.gc.ca/english/resources/evaluation/index.asp.

6. At least 14 federal departments and agencies are involved in the settlement and integration of newcomers. Over the last 15 years, they have all been active participants in the Metropolis Project (Biles 2008, n4). Integration Branch at CIC also co-chairs a Directors-General Forum with officials from CIC, HRSDC, and other federal departments, which meets biannually. In addition, many integration files are horizontal in nature and require partnerships between federal ministries. For example, the official language minority community work is shared by CIC, Canadian Heritage, and many other ministries, while the immigration portal is shared by CIC and HRSDC.

7. Co-management in settlement services is an approach that has been piloted by CIC and the Government of Alberta. It is premised on reciprocity and close collaboration along the entire continuum of settlement programming. It includes information sharing and joint priority setting as well as shared monitoring, evaluation, and reporting.

8. Experience suggests that, in the absence of francophone agencies, francophone newcomers will often integrate into the English-speaking community instead of the francophone minority community. This is not, however, a reason to cease trying to build bridges between settlement agencies in the two official language communities.

9. Among the most successful strategies for engaging larger employers have been the immigrant employment networks like Hire Immigrants Ottawa (Adey and Gagnon 2007), the Waterloo Region Immigrant Employment Network (McFadden and Janzen 2007), and the ubiquitous Toronto Region Immigrant Employment Council (TRIEC, n.d.). Based on these early models,

the Maytree Foundation launched its ALLIES Project, which seeks to connect newcomers to the labour market effectively (see http://maytree.com/integration/allies). With respect to the funding of settlement services by employers, some already provide some services to their workers. Examples include Maple Leaf in Manitoba, All Weather Windows in Alberta, and Essar Steel in Ontario.

10. The Going to Canada Immigration Portal is a key component of the Internationally Trained Workers Initiative. The 2005 federal budget provided funding for the development of an integrated, comprehensive, national immigration portal. The portal has been developed in collaboration with the provinces and territories through the enhancement of the existing Going to Canada website. It is jointly managed by CIC and HRSDC (see http://www.hrsdc.gc.ca/eng/cs/comm/hrsd/news/2005/050425be.shtml).

11. The three elements of the nascent overseas strategy are Canadian Orientation Abroad (COA), the Canadian Immigration Integration Project (CIIP), and the Active Engagement and Integration Project (AEIP). The COA initiative, implemented in 1998, provides orientation sessions abroad to assist refugees and others who have been accepted for immigration to Canada in preparing for their move to Canada and to facilitate their integration into Canadian society. For more information, see http://www.iom.int/jahia/Jahia/canadian-orientation-abroad.

   The Canadian Immigration Integration Project (CIIP) was created to improve employment prospects for new immigrants to Canada. It is currently a pilot project in Manila, Delhi, Hong Kong, Beijing, Gujarat, and Punjab that consists of a day-long workshop at the overseas offices. Prospective immigrants are grouped by profession or by destination in Canada and then receive one-on-one counselling from Canadian representatives to create their own Canadian Settlement Plan. For more information, see http://www.newcomersuccess.ca/index.php/en/about-ciip.

   The Active Engagement and Integration Project (AEIP) delivers pre-departure services in South Korea (Seoul) and Taiwan (Taipei) to skilled workers, members of the family class, and live-in caregivers. It comprises group orientation, specific workshops tailor-made to meet immigrants' needs, and one-on-one Active Engagement Case Management. For more information, see http://aeip.successbc.ca/index.php?option=com_content&view=category&layout=blog&id=3&Itemid=27.

12. Almost all of the settlement strategies developed by the LIPs call for a similar "common front-door" approach. See http://www.welcomingcommunities.ca/index.php?option=com_content&view=article&id=42&Itemid=4.

13. Critics contend that competition among settlement agencies could entice some providers to refer newcomer clients to their own programs, regardless of fit, as a means of meeting targets established in their contribution agreements with funders. Whether or not this claim is accurate, the appearance of a conflict of interest is often damaging enough. For this reason, in areas like language training, assessment centres are funded with the requirement that they themselves not deliver the programs.

14. It is difficult to calculate service uptake. However, based on evaluations of federal settlement programs between 2009 and 2011, as well as reports from the Longitudinal Survey of Immigrants to Canada, it is widely suggested that

approximately 25–30 percent of newcomers to Canada avail themselves of formal settlement services. Some have suggested that even when factoring out school age children, fewer newcomers are availing themselves of services than anecdotal evidence of need would suggest. However, in the absence of universal needs assessments, it is difficult to ascertain whether and to what extent uptake is in fact a problem.

15. In most jurisdictions, an active and visible umbrella organization of immigrant serving organizations has been established. The notable exception appears to be Manitoba where there is an organization, but it does not have a web presence (Manitoba Immigrant and Refugee Settlement Sector Association, MIRSSA). In British Columbia, the umbrella organization is the Affiliation of Multicultural Societies and Service Agencies of BC (http://www.amssa.org/ links.html); in Alberta, the Alberta Association of Immigrant Serving Agencies (http://www.aaisa.ca/); in Saskatchewan, the Saskatchewan Association of Immigrant Settlement and Integration Agencies (http://saisia.ca/); in Ontario, the Ontario Council of Agencies Serving Immigrants (http://www.ocasi.org/ index.php); in Quebec, La table de concertation des organismes au service des personnes réfugiées et immigrantes (http://www.tcri.qc.ca/). In the Atlantic provinces, there is a regional organization, the Atlantic Region Association of Immigrant Serving Agencies (http://www.peianc.com/content/lang/en/ page/community_araisa/).

16. The LIPs have been piloted in Ontario and will soon be extended to the Prairies and the Atlantic Region (see www.welcomingcommunities.ca).

17. Two major language assessment centres have been established in Alberta, one in Calgary for southern Alberta and one in Edmonton for northern Alberta. In Ontario, the Common Language Assessment and Referral System (CLARS) is part of the work plan for the Canada-Ontario Immigration Agreement. When implemented, it should connect newcomers to all language training options available to them, whether federally or provincially funded. Interestingly, CIC and the Province of Saskatchewan have also begun to utilize the same language assessors.

18. A good example is LINC Home Study, a program to help newcomers improve their listening, speaking, reading, and writing skills in English (see http:// www.tcet.com/linc_homestudy/).

19. At present, newcomers are only eligible for training in one official language. In bilingual environments where some facility in both languages is required, this rule can be a barrier to labour market attachment.

20. No standardized language testing is currently required to determine whether language training programs have been successful, although two kinds of tests are being developed. One targets the development of language skills required for naturalization; the other will build on Manitoba's portfolio model, which will be useful as a pedagogical tool and will also aid students in their language learning.

21. The Canadian Language Benchmarks (CLB) are the national standard used in Canada for describing, measuring, and recognizing the English language proficiency of adult immigrants and prospective immigrants in Canada. The Centre for Canadian Language Benchmarks promotes the CLB as a practical, fair, and reliable national standard for second language proficiency in educational, training, community, and workplace settings. Generally, CLB 4 or 5

is thought to be necessary for comfortable social interaction while CLB 7 to 9 is necessary for most workplaces. For more information, see http://www.language.ca/.

22. This was the case when labour market training was with the federal government. However, with their transfer to the provinces, the Labour Market Development Agreements did not specify that there ought to be specific programs for newcomers who cannot qualify on the basis of employment insurance eligibility as they have no Canadian work experience.

23. More information can be found at http://www.hrsdc.gc.ca/eng/workplaceskills/publications/fcr/pcf.shtml.

24. The complexity of the paperwork and the stakes are far higher in the immigration domains than in most policy domains. Much of CIC's handling of these materials is done through a call centre. Newcomers often turn to alternative options, particularly those that allow them to interact with someone in person. The result is increased work for settlement agencies, MPs' constituency offices, consultants, and lawyers.

25. To some degree, this difficult eligibility question is well tackled through co-management where the terms and conditions of federal and provincial programs differ so that wider coverage is possible. This is equally true of alternative funding sources such as the United Way.

26. As part of its work on the Road Map for Canada's Linguistic Duality, CIC has funded a series of francophone networks in many regions of the country that need to be engaged in the work undertaken by the LIPs (http://www.pch.gc.ca/pgm/slo-ols/strat-eng.cfm).

27. While in the aggregate the outcomes for second-generation Canadian youth are quite respectable (Corak 2008), it is clear that some second-generation Canadian youth fare less well (Boyd 2008).

28. The Council of Ministers of Education and the Council of Ministers of the Environment, which are supported by a joint federal-provincial secretariat, may provide a useful model in this regard.

References

Adams, M. 2007. *Unlikely Utopia: The Surprising Triumph of Canadian Multiculturalism.* Toronto: Penguin.

Adey, G. and C. Gagnon. 2007. Engaging Employers: Strategies for the Integration of Internationally Trained Workers in Ottawa. *Our Diverse Cities: Ontario* (4):54-8.

Andrew, C., J. Biles, M. Burstein, V. Esses, and E. Tolley, eds. Forthcoming. *Integration and Inclusion in Ontario Cities.* Montreal and Kingston: McGill-Queen's University Press.

Biles, J. 2008. Integration Policies in English-Speaking Canada. In *Immigration and Integration in Canada in the Twenty-first Century*, ed. John Biles, Meyer Burstein and James Frideres, 139-86. Montreal and Kingston: McGill-Queen's University Press.

Bouchard, G. 2011. "Quebec Headed toward 'Radical Option' on Religious Minorities, Sociologist Fears." *Globe and Mail*, 2 March. At http://www.theglobeandmail.com/news/national/quebec/quebec-headed-toward-radical-option-in-dealing-with-religious-minorities-sociologist-fears/article1927736/ (accessed 14 March 2011).

Boyd, M. 2008. "Variations in Socioeconomic Outcomes of Second Generation Young Adults." *Canadian Diversity* (Spring). At http://canada.metropolis.net/pdfs/socioeconomic_e.pdf (accessed 31 March 2011).

Burr, K. 2011. "Local Immigration Partnerships: Building Welcoming and Inclusive Communities through Multi-Level Governance." *Horizons.* At http://www.policyresearch.gc.ca/doclib/2011_0061_Burr_e.pdf (accessed 14 March 2011).

Burstein, M. 2010. *Reconfiguring Settlement and Integration: A Service Provider Strategy for Innovation and Results.* Report prepared for CISSA-ACSEI. At http://welcomingcommunities.ca/images/docs/eng%20final.pdf (accessed 5 March 2011).

Citizenship and Immigration Canada (CIC). 2007. "Strategic Plan for Settlement and Language Training: Canada-Ontario Immigration Agreement." At http://www.cic.gc.ca/english/resources/publications/settlement/coia-plan.asp (accessed 11 March 2011).

—2010a. *Report on Plans and Priorities 2010–2011.* Ottawa: Minister of Citizenship, Immigration and Multiculturalism. At http://www.tbs-sct.gc.ca/rpp/2010-2011/inst/imc/imc01-eng.asp (accessed 11 March 2011).

—2010b. "Federal, Provincial and Territorial Governments Agree to Improve Canada's Immigration System." News release, 15 June. At http://www.cic.gc.ca/english/department/media/releases/2010/2010-06-15.asp (accessed 11 March 2011).

Corak, M. 2008. "Immigration in the Long Run: The Education and Earnings Mobility of Second Generation Canadians." http://www.irpp.org/choices/archive/vol14no13.pdf (accessed 31 March 2011).

German Marshall Fund. 2010. "Transatlantic Trends: Immigration 2010." At http://www.gmfus.org/galleries/ct_publication_attachments/TTImmigration_2010_final.pdf;jsessionid=aiCFHc_Am3yd4ywci6 (accessed 5 March 2011).

Good, D.A. 2003. *The Politics of Public Management: The HRSDC Audit of Grants and Contributions.* Toronto: University of Toronto Press.

—2008. *Municipalities and Multiculturalism: The Politics of Immigration in Toronto and Vancouver.* Toronto: University of Toronto Press.

Government of Alberta. 2005. "Supporting Immigrants and Immigration to Alberta." At http://www.employment.alberta.ca/documents/WIA/WIA-IM_policy_framework.pdf (accessed 10 March 2011).

Government of Canada. 2011. "Main Estimates, 2011–12." At http://www.tbs-sct.gc.ca/est-pre/20112012/me-bpd/docs/me-bpd-eng.pdf (accessed 14 March 2011).

Government of Manitoba. 2007. "For Communities: Manitoba Settlement Strategy." At http://www2.immigratemanitoba.com/browse/regionalcommunities/print,settlement_strategy.html (accessed 10 March 2011).

Government of New Brunswick. 2008. "Be Our Future: New Brunswick's Population Growth Strategy." At http://www2.gnb.ca/content/dam/gnb/Departments/petl-epft/PDF/PopGrowth/Strategy-e.pdf (accessed 11 March 2011).

Government of Prince Edward Island. 2010. "Prince Edward Island Settlement Strategy." http://www.gov.pe.ca/photos/original/settlement_bro.pdf (accessed 11 March 2011).

Government of Saskatchewan. 2010. "Saskatchewan's Immigration Strategy: Strengthening Our Communities and Economy." At http://www.aeei.gov.sk.ca/sk-immigration-strategy-brochure (accessed 11 March 2011).

Greenaway, N. 2010. "Support for Immigration Has Limits, Government Research Shows." *Ottawa Citizen,* 12 November. At http://www.ottawacitizen.com/opinion/Support+immigration+limits+government+research+shows/3815604/story.html (accessed 7 March 2011).

Kenney, J. 2010. "The Future of Immigration to Canada." Address to the Economic Club of Canada, June 9. At http://www.cic.gc.ca/english/department/media/speeches/2010/2010-06-09.asp (accessed 14 March 2011).

Keung, N. 2011. "Feds Playing Politics with Immigrants, Says Ontario." *Toronto Star,* 24 February, A3.

KPMG. 2009. "Alberta Employment and Immigration and Citizenship and Immigration Canada: Canada-Alberta Integrated Service Program Review." Unpublished report.

McFadden, P. and R. Janzen. 2007. "The Importance of Immigrants to Waterloo Region's Prosperity: A Dynamic Collaborative Community Response." *Our Diverse Cities: Ontario* 4:104-7.

Mendelsohn, M. 2010. "Getting the Feds out of Immigrant Settlement Services." At http://www.mowatcentre.ca/opinions.php?opinionID=36 (accessed 14 March 2011).

Ministry of Immigration and Cultural Communities. 2008. *Plan Stratégique, 2008–2012.* Quebec: Government of Quebec. At http://www.micc.gouv.qc.ca/publications/fr/planification/PlanStrategique2008.pdf (accessed 11 March 2011).

Newfoundland and Labrador Department of Human Resources, Labour and Employment. 2007. *Diversity, Opportunity and Growth: An Immigration Strategy for Newfoundland and Labrador.* St John's: Department of Human Resources, Labour and Employment. At http://www.nlimmigration.ca/media/2842/strategydoc-mar07.pdf (accessed 11 March 2011).

Nova Scotia Office of Immigration. 2005. *Nova Scotia's Immigration Strategy.* Halifax: Communications Nova Scotia. At http://novascotiaimmigration.com/sites/all/files/documents/Immigration_Eng_web.pdf (accessed 11 March 2011).

Ontario Council of Agencies Serving Immigrants (OCASI). 2009. *Canada-Ontario Immigration Agreement (COIA): Crafting the Vision for the Sector.* OCASI discussion paper. At http://www.ocasi.org/index.php?qid=1005 (accessed 14 March 2011).

Reichold, S. 2010. "Do Community-Based Organizations Serve the People or the State?" *Our Diverse Cities* 7:37-41.

Seidle, F.L. 2010a. "Intergovernmental Immigration Agreements and Public Accountability." *Policy Options* (July-August):49-53.

—2010b. *The Canada-Ontario Immigration Agreement: Assessment and Options for Renewal.* Toronto: Mowat Centre. At http://www.mowatcentre.ca/research-topic-mowat.php?mowatResearchID=12 (accessed March 2011).

Smith, C.C. 2009. "Speech to OCASE Executive Directors' Forum, November 3." At http://www.charlescsmithconsulting.ca/images/Modernizing%20Settlement.doc (accessed 14 March 2011).

Standing Committee on Citizenship and Immigration. 2010. *Report on Best Practices in Settlement Services* (March). At http://www2.parl.gc.ca/HousePublications/Publication.aspx?DocId=4388396&Language=E&Mode=1&Parl=40&Ses=3 (accessed 15 March 2011).

—2011a. "Evidence No. 41." At http://www2.parl.gc.ca/HousePublications/Publication.aspx?DocId=4937615&Language=E&Mode=1&Parl=40&Ses=3 (accessed 14 March 2011).

—2011b. "Evidence No. 42." At http://www2.parl.gc.ca/HousePublications/ Publication.aspx?DocId=4949136&Language=E&Mode=1&Parl=40&Ses=3 (accessed 14 March 2011).

—Tolley, E. and R. Young. 2011. *Immigrant Settlement Policy in Canadian Municipalities.* Montreal and Kingston: McGill-Queen's University Press.

Toronto Regional Immigrant Employment Council. n.d. "About Us." At http://www.triec.ca/about (accessed 15 March 2011).

Turegun, A. 2011. "Developing Criteria for Best Practices in Settlement Services." Unpublished report commissioned by Integration Branch, Citizenship and Immigration Canada.

Welcoming Communities Initiative (WCI). 2010. "New Projects Commissioned by CIC, Ontario Region: LIP Best Practices, Assessment, and Outcome Measures." *eBulletin* (December). At http://welcomingcommunities.ca/images/docs/ ebulletin9.pdf (accessed 15 March 2011).

—2011. "A New Framework for Multi-Level Governance: Working Together to Improve Outcomes for Newcomers in Communities across Canada – An Important Message from the Community Connections Team in the Integration Branch of Citizenship and Immigration Canada" (January). At http:// welcomingcommunities.ca/images/docs/ebulletin10.pdf (accessed 15 March 2011).

Wulff, M.A., T. Carter, R. Vineberg, and S. Ward, eds. 2008. "Attracting New Arrivals to Smaller Cities and Rural Communities: Findings from Australia, Canada and New Zealand." Special issue, *Journal of International Migration and Integration* 9 (2).

Xue, L. 2007. "Social Capital and Employment Entry of Recent Immigrants to Canada: Evidence from the Longitudinal Survey of Immigrants to Canada." Unpublished paper prepared for Citizenship and Immigration Canada.

Young, J. 1998. "Getting a Job in Canada: Social Networks and Chinese Immigrant Integration." Master's thesis, University of Manitoba.

CONTRIBUTORS

BENJAMIN AMOYAW is currently a senior policy analyst with the Immigration Division, Manitoba Labour and Immigration.

CAROLINE ANDREW is the director of the Centre on Governance at the University of Ottawa; her research interests are in the area of urban governance and the role of municipal governments in the integration of immigrants.

GODFREY BALDACCHINO is a professor of sociology and Canada Research Chair (Island Studies) at the University of Prince Edward Island, Canada. He immigrated to Charlottetown, PEI, with his wife and younger son from Malta in 2003.

CHEDLY BELKHODJA is a professor of political science at the Université de Moncton and one of the directors of the Atlantic Metropolis Centre. His research interests are in policies of regionalization on imigration.

JOHN BILES is a special advisor to the director general of the Integration Branch at Citizenship and Immigration Canada.

AMANDA BITTNER, assistant professor in the Department of Political Science at Memorial University, studies public opinion and voting in both Canadian and comparative contexts, focusing more recently on attitudes towards immigration.

PAULA M. BROCHU is a postdoctoral fellow in the Department of Psychology at Yale University, with research interests in social inequality, prejudice, stereotyping, and discrimination.

MEYER BURSTEIN is an international consultant in the area of social and economic policy and a senior policy fellow with the Welcoming Communities Initiative. He is the former director general responsible for strategic planning and research at Citizenship and Immigration Canada and co-founder of the Metropolis Project.

TOM CARTER is Canada Research Chair in Urban Change and Adaptation and a professor of geography at the University of Winnipeg.

A. MARGUERITE CASSIN teaches public policy on equality at the School of Public Administration, Dalhousie University and is Dalhousie director of the Atlantic Metropolis Centre.

VICTORIA ESSES is a professor of psychology and director of the Centre for Research on Migration and Ethnic Relations at the University of Western Ontario; she is co-chair of the Ontario-wide Welcoming Communities Initiative.

JAMES FRIDERES is a professor of sociology at the University of Calgary. He also holds the chair of Ethnic Studies and is the program coordinator for the International Indigenous Studies program.

JOSEPH GARCEA is an associate professor in the Department of Political Studies at the University of Saskatchewan, with research and teaching interests in federalism, multi-level governance, local governance, immigration, and multiculturalism.

ANNICK GERMAIN is a professor at INRS University-Centre Urbanisation Culture Société and director of the Quebec Metropolis Centre–Immigration et métropoles.

NEIL HIBBERT is an assistant professor in the Department of Political Studies at the University of Saskatchewan, specializing in citizenship and social justice in diverse societies.

DANIEL HIEBERT is a professor of geography at the University of British Columbia and co-director of Metropolis British Columbia. In the latter role he has worked closely with officials who administer settlement and integration services in the province.

CRAIG MACKIE is the executive director of the Prince Edward Island Association for Newcomers to Canada.

KATHY SHERRELL is a doctoral candidate in geography at the University of British Columbia, and division manager of Settlement Services, Immigrant Services Society of British Columbia.

ERIN TOLLEY is a Trudeau Scholar and doctoral candidate in political studies at Queen's University.

CHRISTOPHE TRAISNEL is professor of political science at the Université de Moncton. His work is concentrated primarily in the areas of the political construction of collective identities, French-speaking communities in Canada and internationally, and immigration.

REETA CHOWDHARI TREMBLAY is vice-president academic and provost and professor of political science at the University of Victoria.

TUYET TRINH is coordinator of the Quebec Metropolis Centre–Immigration et métropoles. She has a PhD in Administration of Education.

ROBERT VINEBERG studied history at University of Toronto and at Carleton University prior to a 35-year career with the Canadian government and is now researching and writing Canadian history.

Queen's Policy Studies
Recent Publications

The Queen's Policy Studies Series is dedicated to the exploration of major public policy issues that confront governments and society in Canada and other nations.

Manuscript submission. We are pleased to consider new book proposals and manuscripts. Preliminary enquiries are welcome. A subvention is normally required for the publication of an academic book. Please direct questions or proposals to the Publications Unit by email at spspress@queensu.ca, or visit our website at: www.queensu.ca/sps/books, or contact us by phone at (613) 533-2192.

Our books are available from good bookstores everywhere, including the Queen's University bookstore (http://www.campusbookstore.com/). McGill-Queen's University Press is the exclusive world representative and distributor of books in the series. A full catalogue and ordering information may be found on their web site (http://mqup.mcgill.ca/).

School of Policy Studies

A New Synthesis of Public Administration: Serving in the 21ˢᵗ Century, Jocelyne Bourgon, 2011. Paper ISBN 978-1-55339-312-2 Cloth ISBN 978-1-55339-313-9

Recreating Canada: Essays in Honour of Paul Weiler, Randall Morck (ed.), 2011. Paper ISBN 978-1-55339-273-6

Data Data Everywhere: Access and Accountability? Colleen M. Flood (ed.), 2011. Paper ISBN 978-1-55339-236-1

Making the Case: Using Case Studies for Teaching and Knowledge Management in Public Administration, Andrew Graham, 2011. Paper ISBN 978-1-55339-302-3

Canada's Isotope Crisis: What Next? Jatin Nathwani and Donald Wallace (eds.), 2010. Paper ISBN 978-1-55339-283-5 Cloth ISBN 978-1-55339-284-2

Pursuing Higher Education in Canada: Economic, Social, and Policy Dimensions, Ross Finnie, Marc Frenette, Richard E. Mueller, and Arthur Sweetman (eds.), 2010. Paper ISBN 978-1-55339-277-4 Cloth ISBN 978-1-55339-278-1

Canadian Immigration: Economic Evidence for a Dynamic Policy Environment, Ted McDonald, Elizabeth Ruddick, Arthur Sweetman, and Christopher Worswick (eds.), 2010. Paper ISBN 978-1-55339-281-1 Cloth ISBN 978-1-55339-282-8

Taking Stock: Research on Teaching and Learning in Higher Education, Julia Christensen Hughes and Joy Mighty (eds.), 2010. Paper ISBN 978-1-55339-271-2 Cloth ISBN 978-1-55339-272-9

Architects and Innovators: Building the Department of Foreign Affairs and International Trade, 1909–2009/Architectes et innovateurs : le développement du ministère des Affaires étrangères et du Commerce international,de 1909 à 2009, Greg Donaghy and Kim Richard Nossal (eds.), 2009. Paper ISBN 978-1-55339-269-9 Cloth ISBN 978-1-55339-270-5

Academic Transformation: The Forces Reshaping Higher Education in Ontario, Ian D. Clark, Greg Moran, Michael L. Skolnik, and David Trick, 2009. Paper ISBN 978-1-55339-238-5 Cloth ISBN 978-1-55339-265-1

The New Federal Policy Agenda and the Voluntary Sector: On the Cutting Edge, Rachel Laforest (ed.), 2009. Paper ISBN 978-1-55339-132-6

Measuring What Matters in Peace Operations and Crisis Management, Sarah Jane Meharg, 2009. Paper ISBN 978-1-55339-228-6 Cloth ISBN 978-1-55339-229-3

International Migration and the Governance of Religious Diversity, Paul Bramadat and Matthias Koenig (eds.), 2009. Paper ISBN 978-1-55339-266-8 Cloth ISBN 978-1-55339-267-5

Who Goes? Who Stays? What Matters? Accessing and Persisting in Post-Secondary Education in Canada, Ross Finnie, Richard E. Mueller, Arthur Sweetman, and Alex Usher (eds.), 2008. Paper ISBN 978-1-55339-221-7 Cloth ISBN 978-1-55339-222-4

Economic Transitions with Chinese Characteristics: Thirty Years of Reform and Opening Up, Arthur Sweetman and Jun Zhang (eds.), 2009. Paper ISBN 978-1-55339-225-5 Cloth ISBN 978-1-55339-226-2

Economic Transitions with Chinese Characteristics: Social Change During Thirty Years of Reform, Arthur Sweetman and Jun Zhang (eds.), 2009. Paper ISBN 978-1-55339-234-7 Cloth ISBN 978-1-55339-235-4

Dear Gladys: Letters from Over There, Gladys Osmond (Gilbert Penney ed.), 2009. Paper ISBN 978-1-55339-223-1

Immigration and Integration in Canada in the Twenty-first Century, John Biles, Meyer Burstein, and James Frideres (eds.), 2008. Paper ISBN 978-1-55339-216-3 Cloth ISBN 978-1-55339-217-0

Robert Stanfield's Canada, Richard Clippingdale, 2008. Cloth ISBN 978-1-55339-218-7

Exploring Social Insurance: Can a Dose of Europe Cure Canadian Health Care Finance? Colleen Flood, Mark Stabile, and Carolyn Tuohy (eds.), 2008. Paper ISBN 978-1-55339-136-4 Cloth ISBN 978-1-55339-213-2

Canada in NORAD, 1957–2007: A History, Joseph T. Jockel, 2007. Paper ISBN 978-1-55339-134-0 Cloth ISBN 978-1-55339-135-7

Canadian Public-Sector Financial Management, Andrew Graham, 2007. Paper ISBN 978-1-55339-120-3 Cloth ISBN 978-1-55339-121-0

Emerging Approaches to Chronic Disease Management in Primary Health Care, John Dorland and Mary Ann McColl (eds.), 2007. Paper ISBN 978-1-55339-130-2 Cloth ISBN 978-1-55339-131-9

Fulfilling Potential, Creating Success: Perspectives on Human Capital Development, Garnett Picot, Ron Saunders and Arthur Sweetman (eds.), 2007. Paper ISBN 978-1-55339-127-2 Cloth ISBN 978-1-55339-128-9

Reinventing Canadian Defence Procurement: A View from the Inside, Alan S. Williams, 2006. Paper ISBN 0-9781693-0-1 (Published in association with Breakout Educational Network)

SARS in Context: Memory, History, Policy, Jacalyn Duffin and Arthur Sweetman (eds.), 2006. Paper ISBN 978-0-7735-3194-9 Cloth ISBN 978-0-7735-3193-2 (Published in association with McGill-Queen's University Press)

Dreamland: How Canada's Pretend Foreign Policy has Undermined Sovereignty, Roy Rempel, 2006. Paper ISBN 1-55339-118-7 Cloth ISBN 1-55339-119-5 (Published in association with Breakout Educational Network)

Canadian and Mexican Security in the New North America: Challenges and Prospects, Jordi Díez (ed.), 2006. Paper ISBN 978-1-55339-123-4 Cloth ISBN 978-1-55339-122-7

Global Networks and Local Linkages: The Paradox of Cluster Development in an Open Economy, David A. Wolfe and Matthew Lucas (eds.), 2005. Paper ISBN 1-55339-047-4 Cloth ISBN 1-55339-048-2

Choice of Force: Special Operations for Canada, David Last and Bernd Horn (eds.), 2005. Paper ISBN 1-55339-044-X Cloth ISBN 1-55339-045-8

Centre for the Study of Democracy

Jimmy and Rosalynn Carter: A Canadian Tribute, Arthur Milnes (ed.), 2011.
Paper ISBN 978-1-55339-300-9 Cloth ISBN 978-1-55339-301-6

Unrevised and Unrepented II: Debating Speeches and Others By the Right Honourable Arthur Meighen, Arthur Milnes (ed.), 2011. Paper ISBN 978-1-55339-296-5
Cloth ISBN 978-1-55339-297-2

The Authentic Voice of Canada: R.B. Bennett's Speeches in the House of Lords, 1941-1947,
Christopher McCreery and Arthur Milnes (eds.), 2009.
Paper ISBN 978-1-55339-275-0 Cloth ISBN 978-1-55339-276-7

Age of the Offered Hand: The Cross-Border Partnership Between President George H.W. Bush and Prime-Minister Brian Mulroney, A Documentary History, James McGrath and Arthur Milnes (eds.), 2009. Paper ISBN 978-1-55339-232-3
Cloth ISBN 978-1-55339-233-0

In Roosevelt's Bright Shadow: Presidential Addresses About Canada from Taft to Obama in Honour of FDR's 1938 Speech at Queen's University, Christopher McCreery and Arthur Milnes (eds.), 2009. Paper ISBN 978-1-55339-230-9 Cloth ISBN 978-1-55339-231-6

Politics of Purpose, 40th Anniversary Edition, The Right Honourable John N. Turner 17th Prime Minister of Canada, Elizabeth McIninch and Arthur Milnes (eds.), 2009.
Paper ISBN 978-1-55339-227-9 Cloth ISBN 978-1-55339-224-8

Bridging the Divide: Religious Dialogue and Universal Ethics, Papers for The InterAction Council, Thomas S. Axworthy (ed.), 2008. Paper ISBN 978-1-55339-219-4
Cloth ISBN 978-1-55339-220-0

Institute of Intergovernmental Relations

Canada: The State of the Federation 2009, vol. 22, *Carbon Pricing and Environmental Federalism*, Thomas J. Courchene and John R. Allan (eds.), 2010.
Paper ISBN 978-1-55339-196-8 Cloth ISBN 978-1-55339-197-5

Canada: The State of the Federation 2008, vol. 21, *Open Federalism and the Spending Power*, Thomas J. Courchene, John R. Allan, and Hoi Kong (eds.), forthcoming.
Paper ISBN 978-1-55339-194-4

The Democratic Dilemma: Reforming the Canadian Senate, Jennifer Smith (ed.), 2009.
Paper ISBN 978-1-55339-190-6

Canada: The State of the Federation 2006/07, vol. 20, *Transitions – Fiscal and Political Federalism in an Era of Change*, John R. Allan, Thomas J. Courchene, and Christian Leuprecht (eds.), 2009. Paper ISBN 978-1-55339-189-0 Cloth ISBN 978-1-55339-191-3

Comparing Federal Systems, Third Edition, Ronald L. Watts, 2008.
Paper ISBN 978-1-55339-188-3

Canada: The State of the Federation 2005, vol. 19, *Quebec and Canada in the New Century – New Dynamics, New Opportunities*, Michael Murphy (ed.), 2007.
Paper ISBN 978-1-55339-018-3 Cloth ISBN 978-1-55339-017-6

Spheres of Governance: Comparative Studies of Cities in Multilevel Governance Systems,
Harvey Lazar and Christian Leuprecht (eds.), 2007. Paper ISBN 978-1-55339-019-0
Cloth ISBN 978-1-55339-129-6

Canada: The State of the Federation 2004, vol. 18, *Municipal-Federal-Provincial Relations in Canada*, Robert Young and Christian Leuprecht (eds.), 2006.
Paper ISBN 1-55339-015-6 Cloth ISBN 1-55339-016-4

Canadian Fiscal Arrangements: What Works, What Might Work Better, Harvey Lazar (ed.),
2005. Paper ISBN 1-55339-012-1 Cloth ISBN 1-55339-013-X

Canada: The State of the Federation 2003, vol. 17, Reconfiguring Aboriginal-State Relations, Michael Murphy (ed.), 2005. Paper ISBN 1-55339-010-5 Cloth ISBN 1-55339-011-3

Centre for International and Defence Policy

Security Operations in the 21st Century: Canadian Perspectives on the Comprehensive Approach, Michael Rostek and Peter Gizewski (eds.), 2011. Paper ISBN 978-1-55339-351-1

Europe Without Soldiers? Recruitment and Retention across the Armed Forces of Europe, Tibor Szvircsev Tresch and Christian Leuprecht (eds.), 2010. Paper ISBN 978-1-55339-246-0 Cloth ISBN 978-1-55339-247-7

Mission Critical: Smaller Democracies' Role in Global Stability Operations, Christian Leuprecht, Jodok Troy, and David Last (eds.), 2010. Paper ISBN 978-1-55339-244-6

The Afghanistan Challenge: Hard Realities and Strategic Choices, Hans-Georg Ehrhart and Charles Pentland (eds.), 2009. Paper ISBN 978-1-55339-241-5

John Deutsch Institute for the Study of Economic Policy

The 2009 Federal Budget: Challenge, Response and Retrospect, Charles M. Beach, Bev Dahlby and Paul A.R. Hobson (eds.), 2010. Paper ISBN 978-1-55339-165-4 Cloth ISBN 978-1-55339-166-1

Discount Rates for the Evaluation of Public Private Partnerships, David F. Burgess and Glenn P. Jenkins (eds.), 2010. Paper ISBN 978-1-55339-163-0 Cloth ISBN 978-1-55339-164-7

Retirement Policy Issues in Canada, Michael G. Abbott, Charles M. Beach, Robin W. Boadway, and James G. MacKinnon (eds.), 2009. Paper ISBN 978-1-55339-161-6 Cloth ISBN 978-1-55339-162-3

The 2006 Federal Budget: Rethinking Fiscal Priorities, Charles M. Beach, Michael Smart, and Thomas A. Wilson (eds.), 2007. Paper ISBN 978-1-55339-125-8 Cloth ISBN 978-1-55339-126-6

Health Services Restructuring in Canada: New Evidence and New Directions, Charles M. Beach, Richard P. Chaykowksi, Sam Shortt, France St-Hilaire, and Arthur Sweetman (eds.), 2006. Paper ISBN 978-1-55339-076-3 Cloth ISBN 978-1-55339-075-6

A Challenge for Higher Education in Ontario, Charles M. Beach (ed.), 2005. Paper ISBN 1-55339-074-1 Cloth ISBN 1-55339-073-3

Current Directions in Financial Regulation, Frank Milne and Edwin H. Neave (eds.), Policy Forum Series no. 40, 2005. Paper ISBN 1-55339-072-5 Cloth ISBN 1-55339-071-7

Higher Education in Canada, Charles M. Beach, Robin W. Boadway, and R. Marvin McInnis (eds.), 2005. Paper ISBN 1-55339-070-9 Cloth ISBN 1-55339-069-5

Our publications may be purchased at leading bookstores, including the Queen's University Bookstore (http://www.campusbookstore.com/) or can be ordered online from: McGill-Queen's University Press, at **http://mqup.mcgill.ca/ordering.php**

For more information about new and backlist titles from Queen's Policy Studies, visit http://www.queensu.ca/sps/books or visit the McGill-Queen's University Press web site at: **http://mqup.mcgill.ca/**